MODERN JAPAN
The American Nexus

by

John Hunter Boyle

D1566644

Harcourt Brace Jovanovich College Publishers

Fort Worth   Philadelphia   San Diego   New York   Orlando   Austin   San Antonio
Toronto   Montreal   London   Sydney   Tokyo

> *For*
> *Dennis and Mary*

PUBLISHER: Ted Buchholz
ACQUISITIONS EDITOR: Drake Bush
PROJECT EDITOR: Steve Norder
PRODUCTION MANAGER: Jane Tyndall Ponceti
BOOK DESIGNER: Bill Brammer

Illustration credits appear on p. 411.

Library of Congress Catalog Card Number: 92-072355

Copyright © 1993 by Harcourt Brace Jovanovich, Inc.

Address for Editorial Correspondence: Harcourt Brace Jovanovich, Inc., 301 Commerce Street, Suite 3700, Fort Worth, TX 76102

Address for Orders: Harcourt Brace Jovanovich, Inc., 6277 Sea Harbor Drive, Orlando, FL 32887. 1-800-782-4479, or 1-800-433-0001 (in Florida).

ISBN 0-15-500324-0

PRINTED IN THE UNITED STATES OF AMERICA
2 3 4 5 6 7 8 9 0 1   0 9 0   9 8 7 6 5 4 3 2 1

MODERN JAPAN
The American Nexus

by

John Hunter Boyle

CONTENTS

PREFACE

In writing this book, I have tried to keep in mind the harshly self-critical Professor Dixon in Kingsley Amis' *Lucky Jim*. Ever mindful that his study of the English shipbuilding industry, 1450 to 1485, represented something less than a historiographical milestone, professor Dixon reflected that,

> . . . it was the prospect of reciting the title of the article he'd written. It was a perfect title, in that it crystallised the article's niggling mindlessness, its funereal parade of yawn-enforcing facts, the pseudo-light it threw upon non-problems. Dixon had read, or begun to read, dozens like it, but his own seemed worse in its air of being convinced of its own usefulness and significance.

Chastened by Dixon's experience and by twenty-five years of teaching undergraduates, I have done my best to shun "yawn-enforcing facts" and to write a history textbook which, at a minimum, will be engaging. To that end, I have not tried to achieve an encyclopedic breadth in this treatment of modern Japan. Many topics of consequence—the development of party politics in pre-World War II Japan, for example—have been omitted or adumbrated in order that a select list of issues might be dissected in fuller detail. These issues all met two criteria for their inclusion: they are central to understanding the evolution of modern Japanese history and they all involve an American nexus.

I will be pleased if *Modern Japan: The American Nexus* succeeds in enlisting the minds of undergraduates similar to those I face over the lectern each semester. For the most part these are not men and women who will go on to become professional historians or authorities on Japan. Rather, most are college students whose impressions of Japan and its people are going to be shaped by one teacher and one textbook during a single course crammed into a four-year academic stew whose main ingredients are likely to be marketing, computer science, physical education, and something called communication studies. Precious few of them share the natural affinity for history of the William Faulkner character who said, "The past is never dead. It is not even past." Many more identify with Henry Ford's arch assertion that "history is bunk." None have much patience with a textbook or an instructor straining to cast "pseudo-light" on "non-problems." Most students do respond, however, to exercises which engage the mind as a problem-solving tool and the century-and-a-half of the Japan-U.S. nexus over-flows with issues which perplex and challenge and stretch students' imaginations beyond their own time and place—to what Senator Bill Bradley's Commission on History in the Schools has called the exploration over space and time of a sense of "shared humanity." By examining the successes and failures of the very real "problems" of the Japanese–American nexus, by seeing where we resemble and where we differ as peoples, by questioning stereotypes, facile analogies, and simple answers to complex predicaments, history becomes both alive and instructive. By enticing us with an occasional irony—the preeminence of Japan in the world so soon after its abject defeat in war is a striking one—history helps us appreciate the irrational and the unpredictable and bestows skepticism without cynicism.

Unlike the fictional Dixon, I am blessed with a topic that needs little defense of its "usefulness and significance." During much of the past hundred and forty years since an American commodore compelled an intentionally secluded Japan to open its doors to the world, the destinies of the United States and Japan have been closely intertwined. In the broad sweep of Japan's long national record, only China has been more pivotal to the shaping of Japan's history and culture. In the half century since Pearl Harbor, the nexus between Japan and the United States, sometimes corrosive, sometimes benign, has evolved into arguably—as former U.S. Ambassador Mike Mansfield insisted—the most important bilateral relationship in the world. There is much evidence that that relationship has veered toward distrust in recent years, that mutual admiration has turned into mutual disillusionment. If that unwelcome evidence foreshadows anything like a wave of the future, it only underscores the need to plumb all that history has to offer as a guide toward understanding. And if the Japanese–American nexus is to remain strained in the years to come, we may at least ponder Alexis de Tocqueville's dictum that many of the most vexing problems of democracies do not have neat and definitive resolutions.

Scores of able scholars on both sides of the Pacific have explored in fine detail and in broad stroke the modern interaction between Japan and the United States. I have tried to express my debt to them either in the text itself or in the bibliographic notes appended to each chapter. I regret that, inevitably, some deserving entries were overlooked. In addition to the sources of information, I am pleased to acknowledge my gratitude to the following good people for their encouragement and critical reading of one or more chapters of the book in manuscript.

The list begins with Joe Conlin because he was the first to read and encourage and because his own textbooks are models of this genre, blends of erudition, style, and wit. Others who generously offered help include Lancelot Farrar, Betty Heycke, Robert James, Chalmers Johnson, Jeff Livingston, Henrietta Lo, Kimihiko Nomura, Yoshihiko and Yoshiko Ohki, Michael Perelman, and Hugh and Reiko Young. They have saved me from countless sins of omission and commission but must be excused from the flaws which remain.

The Asia Foundation's Translation Service Center was the source of several translations from the Japanese press used in Chapters 10 and 11.

From my initial contact with them, all the editors and staff at Harcourt Brace Jovanovich have been models of friendly, helpful, and professional collaboration. Every writer should be so fortunate!

The dedication acknowledges a lifetime of favors (the Japanese *on* says it nicely) which I have received from a cherished brother and sister.

Finally, I owe much to Barbara for always being there. She patiently and cheerfully prodded me into acquiring a measure of computer literacy and then patiently and cheerfully endured as I occasionally self-destructed in front of the machine. Without her continuing enthusiasm for my projects, large and small, they would not be nearly as rewarding.

A NOTE ON PROPER NAMES AND ROMANIZATION

Japanese and Chinese personal names usually appear here in the conventional East Asian order, with the surname first and the given name(s) second. Western-style order, with surname last, is used for Japanese–Americans and others who have lived or published in the West and have adopted the Western custom. I have romanized Japanese words according to the Hepburn method. Instead of Pinyin, I have employed the older Wade-Giles system for most Chinese names. In transcribing both Chinese and Japanese, I have omitted diacritical marks.

1

LAND AND PEOPLE

To describe Japan as a "poor" country, as Japanese occasionally do, begs an explanation. For more than twenty years, Japan has been recognized as the vanguard of the most rapidly developing part of the world, the Pacific basin. The high income levels and the proliferation of expensive consumer goods among its people, the global power of the yen, and the nation's consistently favorable trade balances all suggest a country that is abundantly rich. By the late 1980s, the biggest banks in the world were in Japan, and they had amassed the largest pool of surplus capital available for export in world history. Yet, in an important sense, the Japanese perception of themselves as poor is accurate: The Japanese are resource poor. This has not always been so evident. In pre-modern times, when the population was small and economic life was centered on farming and handicrafts, well-being was possible. However, with a rapidly expanding population and the advent of modern industry in the 1870s, the scarcity of resources became increasingly evident. With Japan's defeat in World War II and the loss of its overseas empire, the problem became especially severe.

A PAUCITY OF RESOURCES

The automobile industry which has earned Japan international respect and enormous earnings is a case in point. It depends primarily on two resources which the Japanese home islands do not provide: iron ore and petroleum. As much as two-thirds of the total iron ore exports of major exporting nations like Australia and India are required to supply the near inexhaustible demands of Japanese industry. The steady procession of supertankers arriving in Japanese ports after a 6,500-mile journey from the Persian Gulf underscores the fact that

Japan is dependent upon imports for 99.8 percent of its petroleum needs. Japan also must import 90 percent of the natural gas it uses. Coal has been mined extensively in Japan in modern times, but the remaining deposits, located in thin seams far below the surface, can no longer be profitably removed. As a result, it is now more cost-effective to import West Virginia coal to satisfy domestic energy needs. The closing of the coal mines in Japan has created severe problems of unemployment in that industry, comparable to those suffered in the American auto and steel industry in recent decades.

The scarcity of other minerals vital to modern industry further illustrates Japan's have-not status. Though the nation has some usable reserves of copper, lead, and zinc, it still must import far more than half of its needs of those minerals. Aluminum, bauxite, tin, and nickel are in even less supply or totally lacking. Mention of the word *nuclear* produces among Japanese people a mixture of fear and loathing borne of remembrances of Hiroshima and Nagasaki—Japanese refer to the dread as their "nuclear allergy" *(kaku arerugi)*. Still, while the "allergy" has caused Japan to renounce the development of atomic weaponry, the need for alternate energy sources is so great that well over a quarter of Japanese energy needs are met by the more than thirty atomic power plants scattered over the country. All of the costly materials needed to fuel these plants must be imported.

Japan's resource-poor circumstances help to explain perhaps the most fundamental fact of Japanese national life: a sense of insecurity and vulnerability. These features are part of the modern Japanese mentality and are never far from the surface even in the midst of apparent affluence and are related to other character traits of the Japanese which have contributed to their economic success in modern times: discipline, frugality, and a commitment to hard work.

The scarcity of natural resources has profoundly affected the historical development of Japan and continues to influence national policies and attitudes. Japan's drive for overseas empire early in this century rested in part on the nation's determination to secure access to vital resources. When the United States, an important supplier of petroleum, tried to thwart Japan's expansion by placing an embargo on all oil exports to Japan in the summer of the crisis year of 1941, a downward spiral of events was set into motion. As the clock ticked and oil reserves gradually drained away, Japan's leaders were faced with backing away from the nation's overseas empire. That would satisfy American demands, but it would result in the loss of economic assets acquired over the preceding half century. The alternative was to persist in the empire and face ever tighter economic strangulation. Since neither alternative was acceptable, a desperate substitute—the attack on Pearl Harbor—followed on December 7.

More recently, in 1973, in the midst of a period of unprecedented economic growth, Japan's resource vulnerability was again demonstrated. When oil-producing Arab nations, angry at Western nations' support of Israel in its conflict with Arab neighbors that year, suspended the flow of oil to some countries and raised prices elsewhere, the entire world felt the blow. But the *oiru shokku* (oil shock), as the Japanese called it, hit Japan with especially stunning force. One

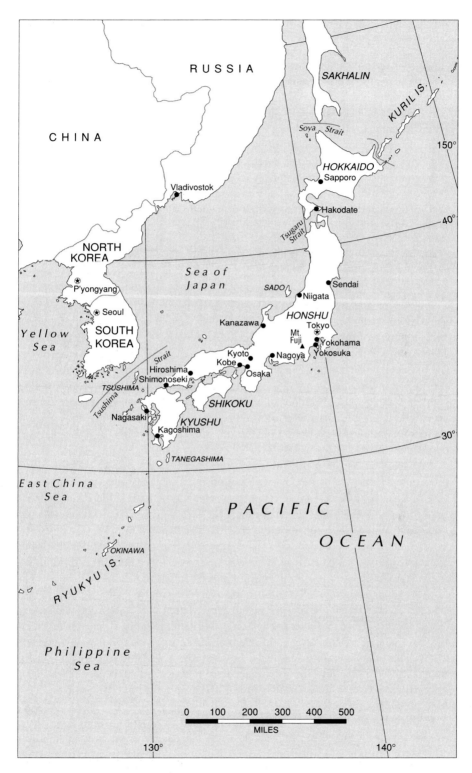

The Japanese Home Islands

major condition of the "economic miracle" which the country had been experiencing for the previous eighteen years was its ability to import cheap and abundant energy, especially oil. Japan rode out the oil shock of 1973—and another one a few years later—but the sense of vulnerability remains acute. A recent Japanese novel depicted the consequences for Japan of a long curtailment of petroleum imports from the Gulf region. If oil imports were cut by 70 percent for two hundred days, three million Japanese people would die, and 70 percent of all property would be severely damaged or completely lost. Most Japanese would probably concede that the novelist's predictions are alarmist and exaggerated, but still, the writer was speaking to a widespread insecurity among Japanese that is not grounded in fiction.

CONGESTION

The resource in shortest supply is land. Though the country is about the size of Montana, more than 125 million people are crowded into Japan, making it one of the most densely packed nations in the world. Aggravating the population density is the fact that Japan is a country without any extensive plains areas. The mountains that dominate the topography of all four main islands are one of the scenic glories of Japan, but they are largely uninhabitable. Calculated as a ratio of people to habitable land area, Japan is *the* most densely crowded nation on earth. A three-hour train ride down the industrial corridor that stretches southwest from Tokyo to the Osaka–Kyoto area traverses a nearly continuous belt of cities where fully fifty million people live and work.

As a result of this congestion, land which has always been a precious commodity in Japan, has in recent years soared in value to astonishing heights. By the mid-1980s, it was estimated that the nation's total land value was more than double the U.S.'s value—this in spite of the fact that Japan is only about three percent as big as the United States. With prime urban land costing as much as $50,000 for a parcel the size of a newspaper page, it is little wonder that open space is a luxury few can afford. The sidewalks and lawns that are commonplace in middle-class residential areas in the United States are rare in Japanese neighborhoods, where homes often abut narrow, noisy streets. Tokyoites enjoy only ten square feet of park space per person (less than a twelfth of that available to New Yorkers). For the average citizen, this land scarcity translates into the highest housing costs in the world and makes the purchase of even a small suburban home increasingly difficult for newlyweds. According to government figures, slightly more than half of Japanese live below an "average standard" of only 818 square feet for a family of four; and 11 percent live in homes that are less than 473 square feet.

When a European official publication referred to Japanese homes as "rabbit hutches" some years ago, the remark struck a sensitive nerve among Japanese who were offended by the foreigner's mockery. Nonetheless, the description stuck and the prominent place given to discussion of costly, cramped housing in the Japanese press testifies to the national distress over this seemingly unsolvable problem. Hard work, thrift, and ingenuity have enabled the Japanese to create just about everything needed for the good life—except space. The phrase *tomeru Nihon, mazushii Nihonjin* (rich Japan, poor Japanese) captures the contradiction between the nation's productive economy and the relatively low standard of living.

The Spartan housing conditions Japanese endure makes privacy an experience so remote that a foreign word has been imported to express the concept. A recent movie portrays a vexed couple retreating from their tiny apartment to the building's subterranean garage, where they manage to find a few moments of *puraibashii* (privacy) in their parked car. Businessmen returning from overseas assignments frequently cite their spacious housing as the most enjoyable feature of their posting abroad. Foreign visitors to Japan, often disappointed that they are not invited to the homes of Japanese friends, need to be reminded that social life, certainly the night-life of business entertainment, is centered in restaurants and bars rather than at home. Americans seeing the thousands—literally thousands—of *rabu hoteru* (love hotels) which dot the Tokyo landscape are likely to assume that they provide venues for illicit affairs but in fact they are just as often places to which married couples retreat to escape crowded apartments and children.

Crowded living conditions mean long commute times on trains and subways. Even with superb public transportation facilities which operate with split-second efficiency and with trains running every two minutes during *rashuawa* (rush hour), ninety-minute commutes each way are commonplace for urbanites. The trains are so jammed with passengers that "pushers" (*shiri-oshi*, literally bottom pushers) have to be employed at rush hour to lean on the last boarders, courteously, so as to pack them into the cars before the automatic door closes "like a zipper sealing an overstuffed suitcase." Sports and recreation facilities are equally overtaxed. Approximately ten million Japanese have taken up golf, but fees at the thousand or so golf courses are so high that, unless company expense accounts can be charged, most golfers must remain content with night-time visits to floodlit practice ranges. Found throughout the country, often located on the roofs of buildings and sometimes stacked two or three stories high, these ranges are a good symbol of Japan's relentless need to accommodate maximum numbers of people in minimum amounts of space.

DO NOT ATTEMPT THIS AT HOME

According to a Japanese life insurance company's study of the Tokyo rail system at rush hour, almost all parts of the system had at least five people crowded into each square meter. (A square meter adds up to a floor space with 39 inches on each side.) Some parts of the system are jammed with up to seven people per square meter; none had fewer than three.

A TENSE SOCIETY

Japanese employ a play on words to describe their predicament. Formerly, according to an old saying, Japanese referred to themselves as a "divinely chosen people" (*tenson minzoku*). More recently, however, they have been transformed into a "tense people" (*tenshon minzoku*) according to a pun which became popular in the 1960s as the nation became more prosperous and at the same time more harried. The increasingly compressed and frantic life-style made necessary by crowded conditions takes its toll on the mental well-being of the people. A medical specialist comments on a craving for solitude and its consequences: "Many hypertensive persons are calmer after they buy an automobile," Professor Hayakawa Kazuo writes. "They need a private space of their own. This also partly explains why so many of the elderly seek outpatient care they really don't require, and why adolescents spend a lot of time in Japan's ubiquitous coffee shops or get into trouble on the streets. They want to escape their tiny rooms."

Population pressures, severe as they are, would be much greater except for a demographic revolution which took place after the war. As families were reunited after long years of wartime separation and as millions returned from the destroyed overseas empire, birth rates soared. With rapidly improving health care and an enlightened, voluntary population control program, growth rates declined in the 1950s and are now among the lowest in the world. Still, the crowding of the main cities is so severe that grandiose schemes have been proposed in recent years to alleviate the pressures. Projects to build skyscraper cities up to one mile in height are under serious consideration. Another proposal calls for building a multilevel population center a hundred miles off shore. "It would be ironic," one writer comments, "if the Japanese, who still consider themselves closer to Nature than any of the Western peoples, were to be the first to create a wholly artificial habitat."

In the countryside, less than one-fifth of the land is considered to be arable—and this after centuries of painstaking efforts at terracing crops up and down the sides of steep terrain. Rainfall is plentiful, but the quality of the arable land which is available is poor. Japan has more than two hundred volcanoes, ten percent of the world's total. Some, like the legendary Mount Fuji, are breathtakingly beautiful, but the thin, highly acidic ash and debris they have spewed over much of the country is inherently infertile and requires extensive treatment with fertilizer and compost to ameliorate soil conditions. In addition, many of the nation's forty-five active volcanoes pose a continuing threat to the lives and livelihood of those living nearby. Earthquakes present even more of a hazard. Nearly ten percent of the energy released throughout the world by earthquakes is concentrated in and around Japan. The massive quake which struck the Tokyo–Yokohama area on September 1, 1923, resulted in the death of more than one hundred thousand people and is ranked among the worst natural disasters in human history. Floods and typhoons are so frequent and destructive that one expert writes of "a typhoon mentality"—the Japanese are accustomed to "expect natural catastrophes and to accept them with stoic resilience."

The Japanese are of course not the only people who must contend with adversity. However, the particularly unfavorable combination of circumstances in which they live, the paucity of natural resources, extreme dependence upon vital imports, poor land, and population pressures, serve as a reminder that Japan's stunning record of economic achievement in this century cannot be viewed as a result of any bountiful advantage created by nature or geography. Japan's resource base is poor when compared not only to singularly blessed countries such as the United States but even when compared to underdeveloped nations like Burma. To fathom its success we must look first at the Japanese people—their character and institutions—rather than accidents of geography. Viewing the history of Japan as a sequence of *events* makes for an exercise that is both bland and one-dimensional. Understanding its history is inseparable from understanding its people.

THE SAMURAI CLASS

An effort to understand the historical roots of the modern Japanese character must consider the ancient warrior elite known as the *samurai*. This warrior caste monopolized power and political influence during Japan's feudal past. More than that, the samurai set the cultural tone for about eight centuries of Japan's history, and its martial values permeated the life of the whole nation. Numbering only about six or seven percent of the total population, samurai were sharply set apart from all other Japanese—the commoners. Status was determined by birth: You were born into a samurai family or you were born a commoner. Crossing class lines was forbidden. Only the samurai was allowed to wear the long sword with its gracefully curved blade and incomparable cutting edge, no less a work of art than a weapon and the outward sign of the warrior's honored place in society. The samurai could cut down with impunity any commoner who dared to offer insult. However, along with privilege and status came heavy responsibility, the obligation to live up to his calling which was service—the very word samurai derives from the word *saburau* meaning "to serve." The samurai was expected to devote his life to the service of his *daimyo*, or "lord"—there were about two hundred or so lords who controlled the principal estates into which feudal Japan was divided.

This single-minded dedication required the samurai to perfect his skills in such martial arts as archery and swordsmanship. It also called for the samurai to lead a life-style that was simple and unostentatious. A samurai who betrayed an attachment to luxury and comfort was deemed unworthy of his high station. The "samurai virtues" included frugality, and the ideal samurai was, in fact, one who was totally unfamiliar with money—the use of which was assumed to be a tainted, merchant activity. Warriors unfortunate enough to find themselves in a situation where money had to be handled might pass it from one person to another on an outstretched fan to avoid being contaminated by touching it. Merchants might well be wealthier than the proud—but often poor—samurai, but merchants were presumed to have different—and much lower—ethical standards, since they spent their days greedily searching for profit, while the samurai was motivated—in theory at least—by a pure sense of duty.

The gap between the ideals of the samurai and the merchant is illustrated by an anecdote recounted by the influential educator and modernizer Fukuzawa Yukichi (1835–1901). In his autobiography, Fukuzawa tells of how his samurai father had dispatched the young Yukichi and his brothers to a tutor to study calligraphy and ethics, subjects appropriate to the training of a samurai. To the father's horror, however, he discovered that the teacher, accustomed to having merchants' children among his pupils, had included mathematics in the curriculum. Fukuzawa recalled his father's horror at hearing that the teacher was exposing samurai children to the distasteful talents of the businessman:

> This today seems a very ordinary thing to teach, but when my father heard this, he took his children away in a fury. "It is abominable," he exclaimed, "that innocent children should be taught to use numbers—the tool of merchants. There is no telling what the teacher may do next."

Just as the feudal knight of Europe was guided by a code of honor, chivalry, so too was the samurai bound by *bushido*, the way of the warrior. In many respects they were similar—both emphasized courage and loyalty and a kind of gallantry that sometimes made warfare seem like a sports contest. Before an important military engagement, for example, the samurai rules of etiquette required that the two opposing warriors address each other by reciting their family pedigrees. Only after this formal exchange of credentials did the bloodletting begin.

But the contrasts between European and Japanese warrior ethics are perhaps more revealing. The European knight had a religious purpose—he was a "Christian soldier." He often had obligations to serve his bishop and took seriously his commitment to defend the faith. No such cause stirred the conscience of the more secular-minded warrior of Japan. The samurai often attached themselves to Zen monasteries for spiritual training, but this had nothing to do with concerns that were at the heart of Christianity—God, salvation, and the afterlife. Zen Buddhists believe that the Buddha nature resides within each person and can be recognized through meditation. Samurai appreciated the value of Zen meditation techniques, not so much for this transcendental purpose but for more practical ends: Through meditation, the samurai might develop an iron control over his emotions.

In Europe, idealization of women was a major feature of chivalry, and storytellers would "sing of Knights and Ladies gentle deeds." Even in this century, chivalric poetry had its appeal. "My soul to God/My life to the king/My heart to the ladies/And honor for me," were the parting words of an English gentleman leaving for the war in France in 1914. "My heart to the ladies"? Such a grandiloquent statement would strike Japanese men—whether sixteenth-century samurai or twentieth-century soldiers—as unworthy of a military calling if not downright comic.

A similar tradition of warrior literature exists in Japan, but the tales rarely devolve around the fair sex or the rescue of damsels in distress. Samurai were married and had families, but the notion of romance and courtly love, a central cultural concern in Europe, was virtually absent from warrior society. A samurai who allowed personal emotions to control his behavior and lead him into romantic entanglements was obviously one who had forgotten the meaning of duty. Marriages were entered into with the same sense of duty and obedience to higher authority that governed other decisions of the samurai.

Another feature of bushido which distinguished it from chivalry was the importance assigned to the manner of death. "Bushido is a way of dying," the samurai classic *Hagakure* declares. "One's way of dying can validate one's entire life," another states. Few heroes in the Western world have ended their lives in voluntary suicide, a option made unacceptable by Christianity. The dominant samurai ethos in Japan, however, has meant that self-destruction has been not only tolerated but extolled. Death was always viewed as preferable to compromising one's duty *(giri)* to one's lord. Life is full of occasions when *giri* clashes with *ninjo* (human feelings), but no matter how agonizing the conflicts might be, duty must come first. The kabuki theater in Japan would hardly exist were it not for plays in which the leading characters are obliged to take their own lives (or the lives of their loved ones) in order to fulfill *giri*. Of course, Japanese have human feelings—notwithstanding Arthur Koestler's modern observation (after a few weeks in Japan) that they are "robots." The toughest samurai had feelings of pity, despair, fear, and had worldly attachments. Presumably, many yielded to the pull of "selfish" attractions. The ideal, however, remained unshakable: Do not *display* emotion and do not give in. While the samurai class was officially abolished as a step toward modernization in the early 1870s, the samurai value system—duty, discipline, self-sacrifice—has been inherited by the contemporary descendants of the samurai and the Japanese people as a whole.

GIRI-NINJO IN THE THEATER

The "archetypal *giri-ninjo* play" was *The Tale of the Forty-Seven Ronin*.[1] "Rarely," writes critic Ian Buruma, "has one story captured the imagination of an entire nation to this degree; certainly no single story has caught as many aspects, as succinctly, of Japanese life, as this one." It is still performed—to standing-room-only audiences—on the stage, and several movie versions have been made of this classic. It dramatizes historical events which occurred from the years 1701 to 1703. This is a brief synopsis of the dramatic events:

A lord, Asano, has been goaded into violating some palace rules by a rival lord, Kira. The exact historical details are clouded—but in any case unimportant to

---

[1] The play, which dates back to 1748, is known in Japanese as *Chushingura*. A *ronin* is a "wandering samurai," a samurai left masterless by the death of his daimyo. If a daimyo died without a successor to inherit his estate and his samurai retainers, it would not be easy for samurai to redirect their loyalties to a new lord. They were thus set adrift, to "wander."

the play. Asano was in some fashion insulted and responded to the affront by drawing his sword and wounding the evil lord Kira. Since Asano's actions were a breach of the shogun's rules, Asano was forced to commit ritual suicide. His lands were confiscated and his samurai retainers—forty-seven of them—became ronin. As good warriors, they were obliged to avenge the unjust death of Lord Asano. However, the evil Kira was alert to the danger of an attack, and his mansion was heavily fortified. The forty-seven ronin therefore devised a plot. They would distract attention from themselves by pretending to have abandoned their sense of duty. They feign a life of dissolution, becoming drunkards, frequenting the brothels of Kyoto. They suffer this humiliation—and most keenly the disgrace that it brings to their families—for two years in order to make certain that none of Kira's allies will suspect their plan. Finally, after their opponents have lost track of this worthless band of samurai, on a late winter's night in 1703, the forty-seven spring into action, attacking the headquarters of Kira—by that time only lightly guarded—and assassinate the evil lord. Victory, revenge.

But there is no happy ending. For now, the forty-seven brave ronin have also committed a capital crime, and there is no recourse for them but to commit harakiri. In the last scene of the most recent movie version, the camera focuses on some falling cherry blossoms. The cherry blossom, *sakura*, as every Japanese in every theater knows, is a symbol of the samurai: It falls only a few days after its full beautiful blooming just as the samurai goes to his end in the fullness of his manhood. The blood of the dying warriors mingles in the white snow with the pink petals. By this time, the theater crowd is openly weeping—the theater is one public place where Japanese *do* permit themselves displays of emotion—as engrossed in the giri-ninjo dilemma as the original victims had been. What has moved audiences for two-and-a-half centuries is the endurance, the sincerity of the ronin. Buruma explains the word "sincerity" *(makoto)*:

> *Makoto* is written with a graph composed of two parts. The left-hand side means word or speech, and the right-hand side means becoming. Taken together, they convey the notion that sincere equals speech turned into action, that the sincere person is someone who carries out what he says.
>
>
>
> MAKOTO   word or speech   becoming

The usual translation of makoto is "sincere," but that is not exactly what it means. Sincerity in English means being honest, frank, open, meaning what one says. Makoto is more like "purity of heart," believing in the rightness of one's cause, irrespective of logic and reason. No matter if the position one has adopted is wrong or untenable: it is the purity of motive that counts.

THE GROUP

Most Japanese know the medieval tale of the Mori family patriarch who assembled his three samurai warrior sons together for a death-bed lesson. Taking an arrow out of its quiver, the old man snapped it in half. Then, after binding three arrows together, the senior Mori invited his sons to break the bundle. They could not. The message about the importance of family unity was so obvious that it did not need to be elaborated. The Mori parable underscores perhaps the most striking feature of Japanese society—the importance of the group. In all societies, of course, people attach themselves to groups, but in Japan the group seems to play an especially large role in the life of the people. Extraordinary levels of loyalty and dedication are summoned by the group—the family, school, the military unit, sports team, and especially, in modern Japan, the company. It is no exaggeration to say that Japanese find their identity far more in the group than Americans do. Americans admire the individual who "thinks for himself," "stands on his own two feet," "does his own thing." The Japanese language does not validate the merits of this kind of behavior with so many positive-sounding expressions. "The squeaky wheel gets the grease," Americans say, to applaud the person who speaks out even at the risk of annoying or alienating those around him or her. That kind of behavior, far from being frowned upon, will be rewarded, the "squeaky wheel" maxim suggests. The Japanese, by contrast, speak of the "protruding nail that gets hammered down" to caution against standing out from the group. In a heterogeneous society like America, where scores of ethnic groups and nationalities mingle and go their separate ways, it is easier to stand out, to be a maverick, than it is in Japan, which is essentially a homogeneous society.

Where did the homogeneity of Japanese society originate? Archeology and geography offer important clues. Like other major groups of peoples in the world, the Japanese are the products of mixing. The earliest inhabitants of Japan are shown by archeology to have come to the islands from Korea and other places in continental northeast Asia. As late as the eighth century, a third of Japan's aristocratic register traced its origins to the continent. However, the mixing of peoples came to an end about that time. There has not been in Japan for the past twelve centuries the in-and-out drift of peoples that has characterized the history of most of the world during that time span. For most of recorded history, in other words, the Japanese have lived in isolation, becoming more and more culturally distinctive and unified, on islands well-removed from the Asian mainland—the hundred miles which separates Japan from Korea makes Japan five times more distant from its continental neighbors than Britain is from Europe. Among such a culturally and racially distinct people it is not surprising that they would come to think of themselves as a single "family" and develop strong bonds of group identity.

Even today in Japan, while the nearly total isolation of the past has ended, the Japanese people remain remarkably "pure." The largest single foreign commu-

The Marunouchi business district, Tokyo, 1992.

nity living in Japan, the Koreans, constitute far less than one percent of the total population. Yet, the Japanese treatment of this minority group is evidence of an extreme ethnocentrism. Though ethnic cousins of the Japanese and though many have resided in Japan for generations, the Koreans are denied the benefits of full citizenship and remain the subject of systematic discrimination in employment and education. Similarly, the Japanese response to the plight of another people who might be termed "ethnic cousins," the Vietnamese, amounted to what one writer calls "a massive indifference" to the Southeast Asian refugee problems of recent years and was evidence of Japan's "long-standing adherence to the concept of the monoethnic state." In the period from 1975 to 1987, at a time when other nations around the world were taking in tens of thousands of the 1.7 million Indochinese "boat-people," Japan accepted less than five thousand for resettlement—and those only with foot-dragging reluctance and after sharp criticism from the international community.

Confucius

Another factor which has contributed to the group-centered outlook of the Japanese is the influence of Confucianism, perhaps the single greatest achievement of Chinese culture and an influence of enormous magnitude throughout East Asia. Countries from Japan and China south to Vietnam and Singapore can be placed in the same cultural sphere because of their common Confucian heritage. In Japan and these other countries, Confucianism from very early times provided the philosophical underpinnings for their notions of morality and social behavior. Confucius, a fifth century B.C. Chinese philosopher, is sometimes spoken of as the founder of one of the great religious traditions in world history. However, since Confucius paid little heed to God or gods, the spirits, or afterlife, Confucianism is better described as a philosophical tradition or as a system of teachings in ethics. What mattered to Confucius was not man's relationship to God or a creator, but man's relationships to his fellow man. His indifference to the suprahuman realm was expressed by an answer he once gave to an inquiry concerning death: "Not yet understanding life, how can you understand death?" In that sense, Confucius was a "this-worldly" philosopher who emphasized the importance of social harmony here and now. "Human affairs are hardly worth considering when compared to service to the gods," Plato said. Confucius was preoccupied with "human affairs."

To some Westerners, the Master's teachings seem unexciting and commonplace, lacking the intellectual depth of, Plato or of Socrates, his contemporary half a world away. However, the principle articles of the Confucian tradition have displayed a lasting power in East Asia quite comparable to the teachings of Western Classical philosophers.

The key to social harmony is the gentleman, the man of refinement and cultivation, but above all the man who is virtuous. Within the body of literature known as the "Confucian Classics," treatises written by disciples of the "Master" (and their disciples) is the description of the ideal man: "The gentleman understands what is right; the inferior man understands what is profitable. The gentleman cherishes virtue; the inferior man cherishes possessions. The gentleman makes demands on himself; the inferior man makes demands on others." From the Confucian injunctions regarding possessions and profit can be seen an enduring suspicion of the merchant throughout the Confucian cultural zone. To be sure, China and Japan have never wanted for profit-oriented businessmen, but it is equally true that they have not enjoyed prestige and honor within traditional society. How those traditional ways of thinking have changed in the last century will be considered later.

To achieve social harmony, Confucius taught, requires moderation and balance in all things, the Golden Mean. Emotions of joy, sorrow, anger are proper enough but must be kept under control, in proper balance. "If you do not want to spill the wine, do not fill the glass to the brim," a Confucian maxim advises. Emotional control is thus an important Confucian virtue. It has nothing to do with God or salvation. The proper Confucian gentleman, whether in China or Japan, might spend hours practicing calligraphy not so much to produce an artistic masterpiece, still less to please his Creator or fulfill a religious commandment. The purpose has more to do with achieving an inner equilibrium. In a documentary movie showing a modern housewife writing out a poem with brush and ink, the narrator comments that she is "practicing her characters to refine her character."

The principle virtue of the Confucian system is filial piety—respect for one's parents—and more generally for one's elders. "Ancestor worship," an important ingredient in the ritual life of East Asian family, is an expression of filial piety. Westerners confuse themselves regarding the nature of these customs by employing the word "worship" which suggests something akin to the obligation Judeo-Christian believers owe to God. Ancestor "worship" is better thought of as veneration or respect directed toward one's parents (and grandparents, and so on) even after they have died, a continuing expression of gratitude for favors received.

Confucius is not remembered as a great defender of democratic principles. It is not surprising that notions of individualism, equality, and human rights failed to develop from Confucian wellsprings. A rigid, authoritarian social hierarchy was basic to the Master's teachings in which the family was the fundamental social unit. Children owed obligations and respect to their parents; younger brothers to their elder brothers; wives to husbands. Ranks are far more meticulously defined and heeded in the Confucian social order than in Western society. In the Japanese (and Chinese) languages, there are no commonly used words to generically express the English nouns for brother or sister. Instead, the words which are used are "elder brother," "younger brother," "elder sister," and "younger sister." The same distinctions apply to uncles and aunts and other relatives; it matters whether the person in question is the elder brother of your father or the younger brother. Similarly, in the larger society outside of the family, the delineation of junior and senior relationships is always important.

From this brief digression into Confucian teachings, it should be clear that the precepts of the ancient Chinese Master fit in very well with the samurai ethos of Japan. What better principles than these to forge warrior relationships—duty, discipline, respect for authority and rank, self-denial, and total commitment to the demands of the group. Whether we think of these traits as "Confucian virtues" or "samurai virtues," we should keep them in mind as we trace the persisting influence of these moral values on Japanese history and the conduct of the Japanese people.

RICE CULTURE

Another historic factor which may help to account for the group-centered outlook of Japanese is to be found in the rice culture, which is almost synonymous with Japanese civilization. During all of its recorded history, the vast majority of the Japanese people lived in the countryside and were engaged in producing the staple crop, rice. It is not surprising then that Japan's traditional social values, values still alive today in spite of the wrenching impact of the modern urban West, were formed among these rural people. The single most striking feature of that early society was the premium placed on group endeavors. Water is the principal necessity in rice cultivation, but in order to build and maintain the complex network of irrigation canals, dikes, ditches, and reservoirs, community effort was needed. In addition, adjusting the flow of water and the rate of flow were decisions which required villager consensus. As Ike Nobutaka writes, "A noncomforming individual who insisted on doing things his own way could wreck the whole enterprise." Thomas C. Smith expands on this theme in a description of the transplanting of rice shoots:

> Since enormous quantities of water were required to work the soil to the consistency of a thick paste preparatory to receiving the young plants, and since few fields could be given the necessary amount of water simultaneously, it was necessary to flood and plant fields one after another in rotation. This reduced the period allowed for planting any one field to a matter of a few hours. To accomplish the planting in the allotted time required a labor force far larger than the individual family could muster. And the various lineages in the village—main family, branches, and pseudo-branches—proved stable groupings for performing this critical work. Mobilizing all its adult members for the planting, the group moved with the water from field to field, without regard for individual ownership; not only did this permit fields to be planted in the extremely short time water was available to each, but it added to the sociability of this exhausting and otherwise wholly disagreeable task. Needless to say, the power to refuse a family this help and sign of solidarity gave the group enormous power over its members.

The contrast between the Western emphasis on the individual and Japanese identification with the group is apparent in many daily-life situations. Upon meeting a stranger, a Japanese will invariably identify himself by saying that he is with such-and-such a firm rather than by stating his own occupation or profession. "The listener," writes sociologist Nakane Chie, "would rather hear first about the connection with B Publishing Group or S Company; that he is a journalist or printer, engineer or office worker is of secondary importance."

Western anthropologists are struck by the way Japanese groups—whether college faculty, company employees, labor unions, artistic schools, even gangsters—model themselves on *the* basic social group, the family. Japanese use kinship terms when speaking of their place of work, for example. The word *uchi* is commonly used to refer to one's company, even though the word means "we" and has connotations of "our family circle." Factory workers—or underworld hoodlums—refer to their boss as *oyaji* (my old man). Also within the group—whether corporate, academic, artistic, or underworld—a spirit of family loyalty and obligation prevails. The Japanese *sarariman* does not simply put in his eight hours a day, punch the clock at 5:00 P.M., collect his pay, and move on to a separate world called "private life." Just as family loyalties go beyond such coldly contractual considerations, so do loyalties to the "pseudo-kinship groups" in the work place, the university, the mob, and so on. In return for devotion and duty, the company (and the other pseudo-kinship groups) are expected to offer paternalistic concern to its rank-and-file.

Consider the following question submitted to Japanese employees by sociologists: Which of these two bosses would you prefer? "One demands extra work all the time in spite of the fact that there are rules against it and in spite of the fact that you get no extra pay for it . . . but he looks after his employees in personal matters not connected with work." The other boss "sticks to rules, is never unreasonable, but does not go out of his way to help his employees after hours." Which would you prefer? Which do you think most American employees would choose? How do you think Japanese workers responded? (The answer to the last question is seven to one in favor of the first boss—who would be branded by most self-respecting labor union leaders in America as "paternalistic.")

LONGING TO BELONG

Robert Ozaki speaks of this group identification as a "longing for belonging." Submerging one's identity in the group is seen as a mark of a healthy and mature person. In contrast to the Western outlook, which prizes independence, Japanese like to be dependent. To the Japanese, Ozaki declares, the word stranger *(tanin)*, carries a "chilling connotation." The *tanin* is someone who has disconnected himself from the human community and toward whom you experience no feeling. "This is the feeling the Japanese dread. They tremble at the thought of being ostracized by their group and of becoming tanin about whom no one cares. . . ." In traditional Japan, in fact, the penalty of *murahachibu* (expulsion from the village, ostracism) was reserved for the worst crimes; it was almost worse than death itself. For the Japanese, then, the prescription is (in Ozaki's words):

> Find your group and belong to it. You and the group will rise or sink together. Without belonging, you will be lost in the wilderness. Apart from dependence, there is no human happiness. Contentment through independence is a delusion."

Psychiatrist Doi Takeo raises this sense of dependency to the level of *the* fundamental principle in Japanese social dynamics. The need to be loved, for ongoing group reassurance, is summed up, Doi says, in the Japanese notion of *amae*, which means sweetness and in its verb form means to depend upon another's benevolence or the need to be pampered. Doi relates amae to the obvious physical and psychic dependence of the infant on its mother. In Japan, this natural yearning for gratification and indulgence is prolonged by certain child-rearing practices such as feeding when hungry (rather than on schedule) and late weaning. Studies have shown that Japanese children are rarely left alone, and are in physical contact with their mother much more than American children. Japanese youngsters often sleep with their parents until their early teens, a practice dictated by necessity—the scarcity of space in the Japanese home—as well as preference. All of this encourages passive dependency while

THE *AMAE* RELATIONSHIP AND JAPAN–U.S. TRADE TENSIONS
"The Japanese long found it hard to understand why the United States, pressed by real economic difficulties, insisted on at least equal treatment with Japanese business (that is, if a Japanese firm could do unrestricted business in the United States, an American firm should get the same clearance to do business in Japan). For this is not the way an *amae* relationship works. It is the elder, the parent, the teacher, the rich uncle who must give. It is the child, the pupil who must be indulged."

—Frank Gibney, *Japan: The Fragile Superpower*

at the same time fostering security. Anthropologists invariably comment on the polar opposite attitudes which prevail among Japanese and Westerners concerning child-rearing philosophies. In the West, the prevailing belief is that an infant begins life as a totally dependent creature, and every effort is made to move the child along the road to independence and individuality. In Japan, on the other hand, the belief is that the infant is born as a separate individual who must, through nurturing and example, be drawn into the group. "The meaning of being an adult," observes one scholar, "is to realize one's connectedness to others and to learn how to maintain those links." By the time of adulthood, the *amae* syndrome is diffused to the point where *amae* shapes the Japanese "whole attitude to other people and to 'reality,'" Doi writes.

Just how different these attitudes might be from the American persuasion is illustrated by an incident Professor Doi recalls. He was a young scholar on his first visit to America and was being entertained by an American family when he was apparently invited to "help yourself." The phrase, he writes, had a "rather unpleasant ring in my ears before I became used to English conversation." Doi explains:

> The meaning, of course, is simply "please take what you want without hesitation," but literally translated it has somehow a flavor of "nobody else will help you," and I could not see how it came to be an expression of good will. The Japanese sensibility would demand that, in entertaining, a host should show sensitivity in detecting what was required and should himself "help" his guests. To leave a guest unfamiliar with the house to "help himself" would seem excessively lacking in consideration.

The ideal among Japanese adults, comments a Western observer, is to know people so well "that you trust and confide in each other unstintingly, fully secure in knowing that your trust will not be taken advantage of, that you will never be laughed at or spurned and that you can always presume upon the other's indulgence in a totally accepting reciprocal relationship."

There is no need to explore more deeply the psychological nuances of *amae*. Nor should a judgment be made about how healthy or unhealthy *amae* might be. To Westerners the desire to be taken care of unconditionally will doubtless seem somewhat childish and self-indulgent. On the other hand, the assurance of gratification and unconditional love can be thought of as a "source of high human motivation." Oh Sadamaru, Japan's Babe Ruth, writes of the role of *amae*, of the way he was cared for, indulged, and nurtured, to achieve his legendary accomplishments on the baseball diamond in Japan. "*Amae* warms the heart but it also enables you to work twice as hard, to overcome the siren songs of laziness." The point here is that, as a personal value, *amae* permeates Japanese society. Further, it is an important indicator of the group-centeredness of the Japanese people. Finally, it highlights a significant departure from American notions of freedom. The word *jiyu* used to translate the English word "freedom" into Japanese does not have the same positive overtones as it does in the West. To Americans, freedom implies human dignity and is therefore seen as something good and desirable. It means electing on your own, with little concern for the choices others might prefer for you. To Japanese, however, this assertion of personal autonomy and isolation from the group is deeply troubling. To Japanese, the "freedom" of *jiyu* easily shades into the selfish *(wagamama)* behavior of someone who does only what they please, someone childishly immature and unwilling to accept the social constraints necessary to function harmoniously within the group. If there is a single stereotypical image which Japanese identify with Americans, this is probably it.

KNOWING ONE'S PLACE

Within the group, rank is all important. In all societies, there are established hierarchies; in Japan, social bracketing is much more widespread than in the United States. To "know your place" is a an expression which makes Americans vaguely uncomfortable in a way which is not true for Japanese. Americans like to believe that they are all equal and are quick to adopt informal habits in their personal relationships. It is not long before two strangers address each other on a first-name basis, even though they may be generations apart in age or several ranks apart in a corporate hierarchy. This kind of casual disregard for one's place almost never occurs in Japan. Japanese would find it impossible to imagine a teacher or college professor inviting students to "Just call me Takeo." Teachers are always addressed as *sensei*, an honorific indicating a professional or expert status. First names are appropriate only in very long-established friendships among people with approximately the same social standing. In addressing people of superior rank, the suffix -*san* is added to the person's family name as in "Tanaka-san" or "Watanabe-san." In addressing people of lower rank, the suffix -*kun* replaces -*san*. In the workplace, occupational titles are the preferred mode of address. Rather than addressing your boss by his surname, in other words, it is likely you would refer to him as "Mr. Section Chief," "Mr. Deputy

The custom of bowing, common throughout East Asia, provides an exact measure of social distance and respect. Although shaking hands has become an acceptable method of greeting, certainly where foreigners are involved, the bow is necessary etiquette in most ordinary occasions when Japanese meet or when special courtesy is required. Lessons on bowing are learned early in life. Infants, in Japan carried strapped to mothers' back and shoulders, bow when she bows. Specific relationships determine the frequency and depth of the bow—the rules are meticulously defined, and nothing is left to chance or individual style. If a grocery-store clerk receives a nod, a neighbor would deserve a shallow bow, an immediate superior at work a deeper bow, and grandparents a profound obeisance. If something has gone wrong or if the occasion calls for an expression of gratitude, every gentleman knows what is expected: hands rigidly pressed to the seam of the trousers, a 45-degree bow or perhaps several bows, and simultaneous recitation of formula courtesies. It is a habit so deeply ingrained that it is not unusual to see Japanese bowing to the voice on the other end of a telephone line.

Department Chief," and so on, because titles delineate the person's place in the hierarchy with precision. Often within the family, "titles" (elder son, younger daughter, and so on) are more commonly used than given names.

Americans recoil from such formal speech in their own land. In Japan, even those Americans who have reached a high level of competence in spoken Japanese usually find it impossible to master the many levels of politeness in *keigo* (formal speech) which is essential to refined communication in Japan. Even among Japanese—well-educated Japanese—one sometimes hears that they are more at ease speaking an acquired second language such as English rather than struggling with some of the more demanding reaches of *keigo*. This is especially true among Japanese who have lived abroad for some time and have grown accustomed to the relatively uncomplicated structure of spoken English.

Aside from titles, the Japanese language itself reflects this stress on hierarchy. In Western languages, there is a single "I" used to refer to the first person, singular, all of the words (*je* in French, *ich* in German, and so on) deriving from the Latin *ego*. The Japanese speaker is not permitted such a simple way of identifying him/herself. There is a choice of at least a dozen different commonly used words for "I," and it makes a difference which one is used. The correct choice depends on the status of the speaker and the status of the person addressed. Unless they were striving for comic effect, the wife would *never* refer to herself as *boku* or *ore*, and the husband would likewise never say *watashi* in addressing his wife (though he might employ it in addressing colleagues); still less would he use the cloyingly feminine *atashi*; and neither husband nor wife would presume to use *chin* which is reserved for the emperor. Yet, all those words and many more translate as "I" in English.

THE CALLING CARD

Business cards are an ubiquitous feature of modern corporate life, but they serve different functions in Japan and the United States. For Americans, exchanging cards is a convenience, a helpful way to recall a telephone number, address, or proper spelling of a name. For Japanese, however, the business card (*meishi*) serves a much more important function, one closely connected to the hierarchical ways we have been discussing. Japanese cannot properly relate to someone until he knows with some precision the rank and position of the person he is addressing. The most important data on the card, then, is not the telephone number or address but the title and position of the card-bearer. Until that is learned, neither party in the exchange can be quite certain of how deferential he should be in his bowing, choice of polite and humble speech, and general demeanor. Accordingly, the card is carefully read when it is presented. Americans who casually distribute *meishi* as if dealing a hand of poker reveal their boorishness.

The ritual is an important social moment and, as with all courtesies in Japan, is meticulously codified. In a "Do's and Don'ts" of *meishi* etiquette, a Japanese writer tells his readers that a businessman receiving a visitor without a *meishi* "is like a samurai going off to battle without his sword." After advising on the correct place for carrying the *meishi* (breast pocket is best but *never* in a hip pocket because they will have a "disagreeable trace of body heat"), posture (*always* standing up), language ("state your name quietly but forcefully"), the calling card instructor allows that there are several techniques for actually presenting the *meishi*. While the writer adopts a somewhat jocular style in discussing the various techniques, it would be a mistake to miss the serious purpose of the sermon:

Crab style: held out between the index and middle fingers.

Pincer: clamped between thumb and index finger.

Pointer: offered with the index finger pressed along the edge.

Platter fashion: served in the palm of the hand.

Dedicatory style: served with both hands.

Elevator: waved up and down a few times while holding it out.

Parabolic trajectory: the hand makes an arc like a falling projectile.

Friction format: slid across the surface of the table.

WOMEN'S PLACE

From the American point of view, the most put-upon victim of Japan's hierarchic value system is the woman. To meet the expectations of potential suitors and parents-in-law, young Japanese women develop personalities which can be summarized with adjectives like "submissive," "passive," "obedient," and "docile." To girls, few adjectives can be more uncomplimentary than *namaiki* (cheeky, strong-willed). Bright girls learn to "act a little stupid because they knew that boys couldn't stand intelligent girls," a Japanese woman states. Women employed in offices routinely accept the role of *shokuba no hana*—flowers of the workplace—a tag which defines their auxiliary status. They are expected to prettify the office, pour the tea, tend to clerical matters, and generally to assist men in their more demanding tasks. There are exceptions, of course, but they are few in number, and the path to independence and career is strewn with the most formidable of all obstacles: the general expectations of the public, both men and women. These expectations reflect the traditional Confucian belief that woman's place is in the home. Nowadays, young women may work for a few years after high school or college, but everyone—young men, parents, employers, and the young women themselves—knows that there is a "proper age" *(tekireiki)* to settle down, get married, and raise a family. In Japan, what is "proper" is not left to guesswork or comfortably wide options: *tekireiki* for women is between the ages of twenty-three and twenty-five.

It has not always been so. In the beginning, Japan seems to have been a matriarchal society. In legends of Japanese origin, the central figure was the Sun Goddess. In the seventh to eighth centuries, as Japan emerged from its mythic era into recorded history, the occupants of the throne were often empresses. After that, in the glorious "classical" flowering of Japanese arts and literature during the Heian period around the year A.D. 1000, while women were no longer politically powerful, the preeminent cultural leaders of the day were talented ladies of the court. With the rise of the samurai class in the late twelfth century, however, women's position declined. For a period of several centuries, Japan was torn by civil strife. This "medieval" era of Japanese history (to borrow European periodization), from approximately the twelfth to sixteenth centuries, was a time when might made right, when martial skills and feudal alliances determined whether families and clans prospered or declined. Women, obviously less capable at wielding swords that men, were pushed into a role of complete subordination. Entrusting ownership of family assets and estates to a woman—a daughter or wife—was seen as a certain way of endangering the future security of the family. Accordingly, the right of inheritance which women had enjoyed in earlier centuries was gradually denied to the women of medieval times. Contact with men outside of the family was seen as potentially subversive to the interests of the family. As a result, most warrior clans had strict prohibitions about women going out-of-doors, receiving male visitors, or even attending religious services alone. (We speak here of the women of the families of the elite warrior class. Peasant families were different—they had no estates, no property, no recorded lineages; for the most part, they quite literally had no names to safeguard.)

Ideal womanhood was firmly established in the minds of this strongly male-dominated society: Women were important for their role in perpetuating the family, for child bearing and raising. Sexual attraction and romance were at most incidental to the family order. Conjugal love might or might not develop, but that was not important. To serve the lower needs of the man—not the woman of course—sexual companions, concubines, could be introduced into the family.

CHRISTMAS CAKES

Japanese have wonderfully humorous ways of viewing their own social arrangements—and predicaments. For example, a young woman who remains a spinster beyond the *tekireiki*, anyone, that is, who turns 26 unmarried, is said to have become a *Kurisumasu keeki* (a Christmas cake) in the jargon of young women. The explanation is that in the period leading up to Christmas Day (widely celebrated in non-Christian Japan), the Japanese enjoy a frothy strawberry confection decorated with Santas and known as a "Christmas cake." Since nobody wants one after the 26th, the expression "Christmas cake" came into vogue as a grim metaphor for ladies who have delayed tying the knot. Only recently, the eligible age has moved up to thirty and, accordingly, a new metaphor has gained some currency. *Shime-kazari* are the straw decorations placed above doorways at New Year's. Since they must be acquired by the thirtieth, they stand for the upper limits of *tekireiki* in youthful banter.

Once married, according to a current adage, the wife may expect to hear *"Meshi, Furo, Neru!"* (Food, Bath, Bed!), barked by her husband when the tired businessman returns home in the evening after a long work-day and a long commute. The written language reinforces her status as housekeeper: The character *tsuma* (wife) depicts a woman holding a broom. While the woman is addressed as *kanai* or *okusan* (both convey the idea of the "person who spends her time inside"), husbands deserve respectful terms like *danna-san* or *go-shujin*—both have the flavor of the English expression "lord and master."

In less-formal discourse, however, husbands do not fare so well. An indication of the domestic financial power of women is the 1960s nickname wives gave to their spouses: *hyaku-en teishu*, one-hundred yen husbands. The lords and masters routinely hand over their wage packets to their wives intact. The wives then allocate a hundred yen per diem pocket money for cigarettes and other incidentals. A distraught wife may nowadays call her mate *gokiburi teishu* (cockroach) for invading her kitchen domain and making a nuisance of himself *or* for *not* lending a hand in the kitchen, especially in recent years when shared housework has become a matter of contention in some families. With equal irreverence, a retired man might be designated *raberu no nai kanzume* (unlabeled canned goods), a moniker which calls attention to his loss of identity. Also humorously employed is the term *sodai gomi* (bulk garbage). It literally denotes hard-to-dispose-of junk (used refrigerators, couches, and so on), but in recent parlance it stands as a synonym for superannuated husbands who mope aimlessly around the house and are always getting in the way.

While the custom is not widespread—it is obviously an expensive luxury—it still exists. Modern-day auxiliary wives (*ni-go-san*, Mrs. Number Two) are not the source of scandal in Japan that they would be in American public life. Several post-World War II prime ministers survived unscathed media revelations of their second wives.

WOMEN'S LIBERATION. The model woman (*ryosai kenbo,* good wife and wise mother) was single-mindedly devoted to serving the needs of her husband's family under the demanding supervision of her mother-in-law. The *ryosai kenbo* ideal of womanhood, like samurai ideals generally, was underwritten by the supremely male-chauvinist principles of Confucianism in which women had no identity in themselves but only in relationship to their fathers, brothers, and husbands. While modified and diluted by the modern incursion of Western individualism and to a slight degree by the feminist movement (*uman-ribu,* women's lib), the *ryosai kenbo* ideals remain vigorously supported by most Japanese men and women. Americans might expect that the sexist discrimination which prevails in the male-club atmosphere of the business world would lead to rage and frustration of the kind that exploded into American-style women's liberation movements. A woman's liberation movement exists in Japan, but it enjoys little popular support. The concept of feminist (*fueminisuto*) is so feeble, one American observer writes, that the word in Japanese "refers not to women but to men who say, 'Ladies first.'"

In answer to American critics, Japanese women respond in a variety of ways. "My husband stamps papers all day. Is that important? Knowing this and enjoying my own pastimes thoroughly, it hardly seems worthwhile to struggle for something that might not be very desirable if you did achieve it." Another housewife declares:

> I don't know which is better, working or being close to home, but in my family, our grandmother played a central role, influenced our values, our education and therefore our lives, and was deeply respected by all of us. I wonder if she did not leave a more profound legacy than our grandfather, who worked hard all his life, but never really got to know us.
>
> I don't think that Americans, even American women, should lecture us on how we should be liberated. Japanese women are not as weak as you think. We don't compete needlessly with men, as you seem to. We have many strengths you can't see, and we also have different values than you.

Another Japanese woman discusses those values and the question of women's power:

> American women are powerful—but when a Japanese says that you have power, it isn't necessarily a compliment. Japanese women have inner strength. To have this inner strength and know when and how to use it is the mark of what I would call a truly mature person. To have just power, by our standards, means to be insensitive and overaggressive.

And, finally, the comments of a woman anthropologist, Professor Hara Hiroko, one of the very few to have been admitted to the ranks of the faculty at Tokyo University:

There is a great inequality in work conditions, salary, and in important legal areas. Many of us are resigned to prejudice. More of us are working to change things, but to infer from all this that we are weak, or dominated by men, is far from the truth. The problem with this stereotype is that if you judge Japanese—men or women—only by their *public* social status, you miss the vital other half, perhaps the most important half of Japanese life. Japanese men look down on women in many categorical ways but they do not look down on the woman's role. She is not simply the one to cook, bear children and keep house. For generations, most Japanese women have been the key person to handle not only the family finances but all the delicate and extremely important personal relationships involving the family, the community, and often the business or profession. In these important areas, and others, men depend on *us*.

ACHIEVING CONSENSUS

When Americans think of hierarchy and rank, military institutions come to mind. It would be wrong to imagine, however, that because Japanese society is hierarchical, Japanese behave toward each other in a coldly authoritarian way, passing orders down from top to bottom as in an army. Doubtless there are such arbitrary dictators in Japan—the phrase "*tsuru no hitoke*" (screech of the crane) alludes to the way in which people perceive them. While it would be folly to imagine that all groups in Japan operate in a certain fashion, it is possible to state what the ideal social dynamic is. Robert Ozaki describes the traits of the ideal leader in a corporate setting by noting that the leader's task is not to impose his will on those below but to cultivate a "we-feeling" within the company. "The most important quality of a leader is the capacity to harmonize his group and arouse collective enthusiasm among his men." Accordingly, the men at the top need not be the "best and the brightest" in Japan, Ozaki says, and indeed it might be preferable that the leader is not too bright or sharp-witted lest that weaken the motivation of his subordinates. "Thus, group dynamics depends not so much upon the superb ability of the leader himself as upon his capacity to pull the best and the most out of everyone in the group," Ozaki concludes.

It follows from this that consensus—the collective opinion of the group—is critical to the functioning of Japanese organizations. Japanese are not happy in decision-making situations when a single person imposes his will on the group *or* in situations when conflicts are settled by majority vote. The search for consensus, then, is not necessarily a democratic process. Indeed, the pressure to avoid "rocking the boat," the pressure to "get in step" with the group's evolving consensus may become so great that potentially recalcitrant voices are likely to be muffled—or, more correctly, to muffle themselves. Recall here what happens to the protruding nail of the Japanese adage. In any case, Japanese groups strive to reach decisions through a process of consultation and conciliation that Americans would usually find tedious and roundabout. Since the goal is to find a compromise solution which everyone in the group can accept, it is necessary that each member of the group avoid not only open confrontation but even unpleasantly jarring exchanges. "Telling it like it is" is not a conversational skill that is much prized among Japanese. Rather, Japanese admire the person who proceeds cautiously, sensing what others feel and sparing them any embarrassment. This is the essence of the Japanese—and Asian—virtue known as "saving face" (where "face" equates with honor). In an honor-conscious society, one suffers from any slight received in public and, accordingly, the decent man will not wish to cause others to lose face. As anthropologist Kunihiro Masao writes, "English is intended strictly for communication. Japanese is primarily interested in feeling out the other person's mood."

INDIRECTION. Read the following description of a process known as *ringi* for the insights it gives concerning sensitivity to the group and the roundabout search for consensus (which is approximately what *ringi* means). While not all decision-making in Japan proceeds in such exemplary fashion, this passage does suggest a chain of command in which decisions and opinions travel up rather than percolate down.

A typical decision-making meeting opens with a statement of the problem by the group's senior member. Each member then exposes a slight portion of his thinking, never coming out with a full-blown, thoroughly persuasive presentation. After this, he sits back to listen to the same sort of exposition from the others. The Japanese, who has a tremendously sensitive ego, does not wish to put himself in a position where he is holding a minority or, worse, an isolated view. Nor does he wish to risk offending an associate by coming out bluntly with a proposal that might run contrary to his colleague's thoughts. The discussion goes on at great length, each person slowly and carefully presenting his opinion, gradually sensing out the feelings of other people, making a pitch subtly, following it without pressing if he finds it acceptable, quietly backing off and adjusting his views to those of the others if he finds himself not in tune with the evolving consensus. When the leader of the group believes that all are in basic agreement with a minimally acceptable decision, he sums up the thinking of the group, asks whether all are agreed, and looks around to receive their consenting nods. Nothing is crammed down anyone's throat. If, by chance, a consensus does not emerge and a deadlock seems likely, the group leader does not press for a decision, does not ask for a vote, does not rule that no consensus seems possible and thus embarrass people. Instead, he suggests that perhaps more time is needed to think about the problem, and sets a date for another meeting. . . . In all of this, the most important principle is not to stand on principle but to reach agreement. All else is subordinate to this point.

As the *ringi* passage indicates, Japanese excel at "indirection" in their communications. Indirection means avoiding a harsh "No!" This does not mean that conversational paralysis sets in when a disagreement surfaces. A whole host of

The hazards of "indirection" in conversation are illustrated in an incident which occurred during talks between President Nixon and Prime Minister Sato in 1971. The subject was Japanese textile exports to the United States, and when Nixon asked for Japanese cooperation in restraining the volume of those exports, Sato responded (through his interpreter): *Zensho itashimasu*, which on its face means something like "I will take appropriate measures." Nixon took the prime minister's remark as a commitment—"I'll take care of it"—and was subsequently angered by Sato's failure to deliver on his "promise." Whatever the literal meaning of *zensho itashimasu* is, Japanese understood that in the context in which it was made, the remark signified something closer to "I'll try but I can't promise" and really represented Sato's effort to change the subject on an awkward matter.

indirect methods of saying "no" are available to the Japanese, and they come to the Japanese speaker naturally and easily: *"Saa, do desho," "doomo," "kangaete-okimasu,"* or *"ichiyo yatte-mimasho"* ("I wonder," "somehow or other," "I'll think about it," or "I'll try," respectively). The last two phrases do not connote what they literally state: Both speaker and listener know that they really mean that some matter is to be dropped. Similarly, when a Japanese responds *"Chotto muzukashi"* (That's a little difficult) to a request, the listener knows that the respondent is really *not* saying that something is "difficult" but that it is absolutely out of the question. In a Japanese group setting it will invariably be so understood. How many Americans have been confused by hearing Japanese respond to a proposal by saying, *"Sore mo ii desu, ne"*? A *gaijin* (foreigner) with a few weeks of language study would recognize that as an affirmative, "That's fine." But more often than not, it is liable to signal a polite brush-off as in "Thanks, but no thanks." To an American, all this seems evasive, misleading, or downright deceitful and cross-cultural misunderstandings are always a hazard.

CONFORMITY

Even Americans, prone to extolling the "loner" and the "rugged individualist," can easily see the worth of cooperative effort and appreciate how Japan's group-centered values might explain some of the extraordinary economic achievements of this country in recent decades. A highly motivated work force thinking of themselves as something akin to a family is likely to generate tremendous group energy. Another facet of group mentality, conformity, however, strikes most Americans as an undesirable trait. Groups exist and are strong only when members share common values and commit themselves wholeheartedly to group efforts—even at the expense of personal ambition and need. Viewed positively, the result is *wa*, social harmony, important in any country, especially important in a country where 125 million people are crowded together in an area the size of Montana. But, although Americans will have no trouble thinking of examples of the herd instinct at work in their own country, it is safe to say that conformity is a more pervasive feature of Japanese society. At the superficial level, the conformity is seen in the dress of the Japanese *sarariman* (salary man, that is, a businessman) whose attire (black shoes, conservative tie, and dark-blue suit) matches the attire of most armies in uniformity. Abruptly, when the male college student takes the company employment examination, his garb shifts to the dark blue suit. In college, as one Japanese commentator puts its, the students' clothing varied from "outright scruffy to passably neat" but upon entrance into the real world, "young people spontaneously homogenize themselves into look-alikes." "This says much about Japan today," a Japanese critic writes. "No company dress code is needed when they embrace conformity so enthusiastically."

Americans are hardly immune to the herd instinct in fashion and clothing styles. The 1955 novel, *The Man in the Gray Flannel Suit*, was after all an American commentary on the phenomenon. At other levels, however, the conformity patterns in Japan run deep and are troubling to many Japanese thinkers. This is especially true in matters of the mind. "The very meaning of 'to think' is not well understood in our culture," educational psychologist Azuma Hiroshi writes in a stern critique of Japanese schools. "To us it means something like: to find out an answer which can be shared by others."

LEARNING IN JAPAN

Classrooms in Japanese secondary schools are rarely the scene of lively or searching discussion. Reasoning and analysis all too often give way to rote learning. At least two factors play a role here. First, much of the learning process is devoted to learning how to read and write. American youngsters have only to learn twenty-six letters of the alphabet; most other alphabets around the world have only a few more or less phonetic symbols. The Japanese writing system, however, makes use of semantic symbols—graphs (called *kanji*) which stand for *meanings* rather than *sounds*. Accordingly, there are many more to be learned. At present 1,945 of these *kanji* "characters" are taught in the nine years of Japan's compulsory schooling system; many hundreds more are required for true mastery of the language. Obviously, the long road to literacy is one in which rote learning is imperative. There is no room for debate or discussion as students try to reproduce the complex characters, some of which require upwards of twenty strokes to draw. The student simply follows the example provided by the teacher. Exactly how much this extended learning experience affects a child's disposition to conform and accept authority is difficult to measure, but it seems likely that it is a factor of some significance.

Another factor which fosters conformity and stifles individuality in the classroom is the deeply ingrained practice of "teaching to the examinations." The

TODAI
    "At the top of the system is mighty Todai, Tokyo University, an institution with the power, prestige and all-around intimidation value of the entire Ivy League, plus Stanford, Berkeley, West Point and the next dozen most famous American universities thrown in, too. . . . Between our two most recent Ivy League presidents, John F. Kennedy and George Bush, America's presidents were graduates of Southwest Texas State, Whittier, the University of Michigan, the Naval Academy and Eureka College. Only two of Japan's postwar prime ministers have not been from Todai. In the upper reaches of the U.S. civil service, something like one senior bureaucrat in twelve has a connection to Harvard, including going there for summer school. In Japan's most powerful ministries, notably the Ministry of Finance, almost ninety percent of the senior bureaucrats come from this one university."

—James Fallows, "The Best Years of Their Lives," *Rolling Stone*, 1990.

educational world in Japan is competitive to a degree difficult for Americans to appreciate. Upward mobility in Japan, whether in the world of business, the professions, or prestigious service within the government, is determined almost exclusively by academic performance. The elite levels of corporate or bureaucratic hierarchies are drafted from the graduates of a very few universities—preeminently from the graduates of Tokyo University (abbreviated as "Todai"). The course of study at superior schools like Todai is *not* rigorous and, in fact, university life for Japanese students is a singularly *un*challenging time. A Todai student's chances for a degree will not be jeopardized by skipping a third of his or her classes to hang around coffee shops or the ski slopes. Grades are *not* important, few students fail courses, and even fewer are dropped from the rolls. What matters is getting *in*; thus, the quintessential experience of Japanese youth known as "examination hell" (*juken jigoku*).

The culmination of this ordeal usually occurs in late February when the destiny of nearly a million college-bound, high-school seniors is settled all across Japan during a few hours of standardized test-taking. Only the test scores influence the admissions directors at prestigious universities: athletic skills, well-rounded extracurricular development, creative why-I-want-to-attend-Todai essays, and rave letters of recommendation all count for naught. Twelve years of rigorous schooling calling for the iron-willed discipline of the samurai and the full-time dedication of "education moms" (*kyoiku mama*) climax at this crucial turning point in the Japanese life cycle. While the process reaches the crisis stage in high school, it begins much earlier. Getting started as early as possible is important because there are also entrance examinations which govern admission to the best high schools, which can significantly improve chances of passing the college entrance exams. Some especially ambitious parents seek to have their youngsters get into the very best preschool establishments, which also have strict admissions policies. In any case, it is important to get on the *esukareta* (escalator) as early as possible. Japanese youngsters take home serious homework assignments on a daily basis as early as the first grade.

As the time of the entrance examination approaches, something close to a national fixation occurs. Some education moms go over the edge, developing *Todai-byo* (Todai sickness, a feverish condition brought on by an obsession to have your child admitted to that school). Hotels offer special "examination plans," where the anxious high-school seniors check in (with their education moms) for last-minute preparations and cramming. Special meals, designed for easy digestion, are served. Doctors and dentists are on call lest a health crisis occur at this most inopportune moment. The more thoughtful hotels provide graffiti wallboards where students can relieve tension—perhaps by scribbling peppy inspirational messages to themselves along the line of "endure, hang in there" *(Gambare!)*. A midnight snack service is a necessity. Sleep is a luxury which well-motivated aspirants eschew. *Go-raku shi-to* is the only slightly facetious maxim which students recite to indicate their chances of passing exams: It means that you can hope to pass if you limit yourself to four hours of sleep but can expect to fail if you indulge yourself in five hours. How close the adage matches reality is not clear, but one researcher discovered that superior students—the approximate half who attend after-hours cram schools *(juku)* in their teen years—had in fact averaged about five hours a day of homework for at least the three years prior to examination hell. That is five hours *after* a long school day *and* perhaps two or three hours of cram school.

The general predisposition of Japanese to conform, added to the weight placed on easily graded written exams, has led to great distortions in the educational process. Analytical skills have to give way to an emphasis on mastery of facts and control over details, with the result that pupils are virtually turned into "information junkies." Even practical knowledge is slighted as Japan specialist Thomas Rohlen points out in his analysis of examination questions. Who, except the most dogged memorizer of detail, is likely to be able to fill in the proper words in this question on European geography (taken from a recent university entrance exam):

> The Rhine turns north from Basel and the view suddenly opens up before it. This indicates that the Rhine has entered (1)_____, a long and narrow plain 30 km. wide and 300 km. long bounded by (2)_____ on the east and the Vosges mountain range on the west. (The correct answers are (1) the Rhine Trough or Graben; and (2) the Black Forest.)

The English language—most students study English as a foreign language—is taught, as one critic writes, "from passages so stupefyingly vacuous that the students are lucky they can't really understand them." In order to satisfy the examiners, Japanese youngsters memorize obscure grammatical distinctions which would confound all but the most skilled English teachers in America. Yet, it is sad

BASEBALL AND THE *GAMAN* SPIRIT

"Baseball is more than just a game. It has eternal value. Through it, one learns the beautiful and noble spirit of Japan."

Of Japan? Tobita Suishu, pioneer baseball player and manager, known as the "god of Japanese baseball" until his death in 1965, made this assertion in the course of linking the game to *gaman* and other virtues most Japanese normally associate with Zen and Bushido. *Gaman*, which translates as the ability to endure hardships patiently, is practically what it means to be Japanese. (Japanese are likely to tell each other in times of difficulty to *"Gambare!"*—the imperative form of *gaman.*)

Gaman is a good place to start if you want to understand such diverse puzzles as why Japanese high school students score higher on math exams than American college students, how American Nisei recovered and prospered after wartime detention, and why Japanese computer-chip makers have a defect rate 90 percent lower than American chip manufacturers.

Tobita's version of *gaman* involved what the San Francisco Giants might call infield practice. He called it "death training." Players would shag balls, Tobita prescribed, "until they were half dead." More precisely, until "froth was coming out of their mouths."

"If the players do not try so hard as to vomit blood in practice, then they cannot hope to win games. One must suffer to be good." Now, *that* is *gaman.*

to report that most pupils complete years of language training with little or no speaking fluency. University exams, Rohlen concludes, seem "like nothing more than a giant trivia contest compiled by scholars. . . ." "The youthful energy spent in developing this skill is appallingly great," Rohlen states.

A POSITIVE ASSESSMENT . . .

There are two ways of viewing this intensity of purpose. As will be emphasized from time to time in this book, Japanese K–12 youngsters absorb far more formal education than Americans, and probably more than any other children in the world, although the students in neighboring Korea and the Republic of China on Taiwan have similar approaches to education. This commitment to classroom demands shows up in the stunning performance of Japanese (and other East Asian) pupils on competitive examinations given worldwide. Studying for the exams means that elective subjects are largely absent from the Japanese curriculum; all students are engaged in hard-core study almost all the time. Does the variety of electives in American high schools—ceramics, shop, driver education, cooking, auto repair, photography, and so on—enrich the academic experience of

American students? Or trivialize it? Are Japanese students impoverished when they are denied these options and are forced to spend extra years in science, math, and foreign language classes? The question bears reflection as the United States struggles to understand the decline of its competitive position in the world. (This subject will be discussed in greater detail in the final chapter.)

Nor are the achievements of the Japanese schools entirely in the realm of statistical accomplishments in math and science tests. The cooperative group-oriented activities teach important lessons in social cohesion and respect for work. The point of all that numbing memory work is that *effort* is being judged. Two Western writers comment on this notion, with insight and wit, from slightly different perspectives. James Fallows writes:

> The tests aren't really about their stated subjects anyway—they're about your determination to try. Americans boast about walking into tests unprepared and acing them on raw brains. Japanese students would not brag about it even if they could do it, because the years of buildup are the point. Effort is what the country values, and it can select for it through the exams. . . . Effort is also what employers value, which is which they hire so strictly according to entrance-exam scores. Companies don't even pretend that there is a connection between university education and business skills—they actively look for generalists . . . [*T*]hey value students who survived the exams, because they've proved their iron will.

British sociologist Ronald Dore writes that, while Japan's conservative leaders might shake their heads over the educational system, they are "secretly well satisfied."

> The examination hell sorts the sheep from the goats; a man who can't take the psychological strain would be of no use anyway. If you need convincing of the virtues of meritocracy—of getting top brains in top places— look, they would say, at our economic growth record. And as long as you can keep adolescents, in those crucial years when they might otherwise be learning to enjoy themselves, glued to their textbooks from 7 in the morning to 11 at night, the society should manage to stave off for quite a long while yet that hedonism which, as everybody knows, destroyed the Roman empire, knocked the stuffing out of Britain, and is currently spreading venereal disease through the body politic of the United States.

Even allowing for occasional excesses, the dedication of the education mothers amounts to a national treasure—as will be appreciated by anyone who has seen mothers dutifully attending classes which an ill son or daughter has been forced to miss. The typical primary school does not usually have a maintenance staff. The children dust the desks, clean the windows, wet-mop the floors of halls and classrooms, and take their turns serving at lunch counters. Witnessing a monthly *o-soji* ("a grand cleaning") when brigades of ten-year-olds, wearing smocks, dust-scarves and plastic boots, tackle serious maintenance chores is enough to bring tears of admiration to a visiting American teacher.

. . . AND A NEGATIVE ASSESSMENT

The Japanese seem to have taken to heart Thomas Edison's dictum that genius is "ninety-nine percent perspiration and one percent inspiration." Still, Americans who observe the school scene in Japan are likely to be dismayed by the many ways in which the inspiration factor is stifled by the pressure to conform, by the ways in which teachers discourage speculation and controversy. Japanese scholars echo these concerns. "Children are trained on how to give an answer as correctly as teachers expect," says an Japanese education journalist. "Those who come up with a unique and interesting idea are turned down." A high-school principal adds: "We have a problem in that students don't try to improve their own abilities from within. They are very tame. If homework is given, they do it very well, but they won't do more than that." While many American high-school principals would probably be deliriously happy to settle for students who did their homework "very well," there is no doubt that American classrooms produce a kind of excitement and spontaneity that is largely absent in Japan.

Consider this comparison of Japanese and American classrooms by a Japanese educator returning from a stay in the United States:

> I would not hesitate to tell anyone who asked that American college campuses have far more vitality than their Japanese counterparts and in general offer a more congenial environment. The lively, direct response of my American university students puts to shame anything one could expect in Japan. Questions, comments, arguments, and counter-arguments fly. In Japanese universities even considerable effort on the teacher's part usually fails to elicit any response or reaction. When the teacher solicits the students' opinions, they sit in stony silence, many of them casting their eyes downward lest they be called on.

The same phenomenon frequently causes a form of culture shock for Japanese youngsters returning to Japan after a year or two of study in American schools. In recent years, as more and more children accompany parents on business transfers to an American location the phenomenon has found a name: the returnee problem *(kikoku shijo mondai)*. "Japan is so homogeneous and intolerant of deviation," writes Agnes Niyekawa, a University of Hawaii professor who has studied returnees. "Even after 10 years back in Japan, returnees may be criticized because their way of thinking is too direct." Being too "direct," abrasive, outspoken is a common description of returnees by elders who expect teenagers to be deferential. This is an especially severe problem for young female returnees who are often seen as having lost the docility expected of them while under the contaminating influence of Western cultural modes. Some fear that these *han-japa* (half-Japanese) young women will have strayed so far from the norm that they will not be marriageable. Nor is the stigma of overseas living limited to children. In her study of the problem, sociologist Merry White finds that it is the workplace that "most adamantly resists the returnee's

DON'T LOSE YOUR CURLY HAIR CARD
   The penchant for uniform behavior and appearance is reinforced by rules which call for a school uniform (typically black sailor-style suits for girls and black Nehru-like jackets for boys). This is a practice in many countries of course and is seen as a useful income-leveling tactic: Children of poor and rich alike dress the same. In addition, however, administrators commonly go on to prescribe the exact width of pants legs (with allowances made for overweight students), as well as the number of buttons and tucks in pants and skirts and the number of eyelets in shoes. One high-school rule book states that boys' hair may not touch their eyebrows, any part of their ears, or their collars. Girls may not wear ribbons, accessories, or permanent waves, and they must wear modest-colored gloves. Girls' hair must not touch the shoulders. If it does it must be tied back with a ribbon—a brown ribbon. Girls with naturally curly hair are issued a "curly hair card" to carry as proof that they did not break rules by getting a permanent.

reentry." This "stems primarily from his breaking of ties—his absence from the group," White says. "This absence, coupled with the exposure to alternative work settings, is perceived as threatening to the highly structured predictable Japanese work setting."

CRIME

   Crime, especially violent crime, is not the serious problem in Japan that it is in the United States. In a typical year, the homicide rate in the United States is about seven times higher than Japan; the robbery rate is an astonishing two hundred times higher; rape occurs thirty times more frequently. Crime has not corroded urban lifestyles: Parks are safe after dark, children ride subways to and from school, young girls can walk without fear through darkened neighborhoods in Tokyo in a way quite unimaginable in New York—or most other major cities in the world. In neighborhood shopping districts, scarcity of space obliges merchants to place vending machines on the sidewalks. They are not broken into or vandalized, and underage youngsters don't buy beer or other alcoholic beverages that are available in the unsupervised machines. Japanese newspapers in recent years have commented on an increase in the incidence of crime, especially among youth, and warned against the dangers of this "American disease" *(Amerika-byo)*.
   While there is evidence of an increase in juvenile delinquency, it tends to take forms which American law-enforcement officials would regard as almost benign. Bullying *(ijime)* for example is a nasty fact of life in many school yards. Characteristic of the group orientation of Japanese, the bullying usually involves teasing,

ostracizing, or physically abusing youngsters who dress or wear their hair differently, bring a different sort of lunch to school, or speak differently. The often cruel pressure to conform exerted on such youngsters should not be dismissed lightly. It can be traumatic and, in a few well-publicized cases, has led to suicides. Still, withal, there is an enormous difference between *ijime* and similar examples of Japanese misconduct and the epidemic of shootings, stabbings, rapes, muggings, and robberies that bring terror and fear to millions of American school children—and their teachers. In a single semester of a recent year, the number of student assaults on teachers in New York City alone exceeded by a factor of three the number of assaults throughout all of Japan during an entire school year.

Much of the violent crime which does exist in Japan is confined to organized gangs which inflict violence on each other in turf wars and vendettas. Organized crime in Japan goes under the name *yakuza*, a Japanese version of the Mafia. Like mafiosi, the hundred thousand or so yakuza mobsters thrive on extortion, the protection rackets, and giving the public what it wants but is not supposed to have—gambling, prostitution, pornography, and drugs. The yakuza see themselves—and thanks to romanticized treatment in the cinema are widely viewed by the general public—as preservers of traditional virtues and customs which the straight people in the mainstream have discarded. There are no other groups in Japanese society, for example, where duty is more firmly entrenched than in a yakuza mob where self-amputation of a finger is considered proper atonement for a blunder or lapse of dedication. It is estimated that more than a third of professional gangsters are missing at least part of one digit.

Yakuza–police relations reflect the Japanese fondness for order, predictability and doing things according to the rules. The police, of course, monitor yakuza activities with great efficiency and occasionally crack down in force, especially on occasions when gang wars have spilled over onto the streets. Still, there are group ties and a prevailing cordiality between police and yakuza which baffles foreign observers. Yakuza regularly call press conferences to polish their public image and travel to police headquarters to extend traditional New Year's greetings to the authorities. Authors of a recent study of the yakuza write that police actions "often seem tailored toward dealing not with a menacing underworld but more with a somewhat guided loyal opposition." Foreigners immediately suspect bribery and collusion—but they are only part of the answer. A more important explanation is that the police have come to see organized crime as preferable to random crime. Through the kind of patient conciliatory give-and-take at which Japanese excel, police liaison teams endeavor to place limits on criminal activity which would not be possible if they were dealing with large numbers of unorganized gangsters. Drug trafficking is a good example. Hard drugs and marijuana are rigidly controlled. Throughout the post-World War II era, no drug or alcohol subculture has existed among Japanese youth except for the tiny band of ne'er-do-wells who sniff airplane glue and paint thinner. On the other hand, methamphetamines are widely available and there are even fairly large numbers of "speed" abusers among salary men—Japanese do not use drugs to escape but to find the energy to cope.

YAKUZA

Some say the name derives from a legend which places the yakuza gangster in the tradition of dispossessed samurai of earlier times. Glorified in popular literature, these Japanese Robin Hoods supposedly roamed the countryside and undertook daring deeds on behalf of defenseless shopkeepers and peasants. These adventurers played a card game in which the worst possible hand in the deck was the sequence 8–9–3 which can be pronounced "ya-ku-za." They adopted this unflattering name—it might be translated as "worthless"—on the grounds that they were society's rejects.

The comparison to the Mafia can be misleading. It is difficult to imagine, for example, "Bugsy" Siegel trumpeting the news of his organization in something called, let us say, the *La Cosa Nostra Gazette*. Leading yakuza syndicates, however, regularly publish their own magazines. The *Yamaguchi-gumi Jiho* (Yamaguchi Syndicate News), house organ of the Yamaguchi mob, is delivered monthly to the 10,000 bookies, swindlers, loan-sharks, pimps, drug-pushers, and assorted thugs who belong to the nation's best-known and most-powerful gang. A typical issue contains a message from the godfather, greetings from important consiglieri, a section on legal advice, photos and announcements of initiation rites, jailings, prison releases, funerals, and patriotic undertakings of the syndicate—there are few Japanese who exceed the yakuza in their devotion to the emperor. Of course, no Japanese magazine is complete without a *haiku* corner devoted to traditional-style poetry.

The yakuza probably deserve some grudging credit for cooperating with police to minimize crime among the young and to keep the country free of the most dangerous drugs. A yakuza spokesman explained the public and official tolerance of professional crime by saying that it helps to ensure a low crime rate generally: "We have to remember that the Japanese yakuza are very open about their activities. Japanese public security is very high. The crimes to be tolerated are a basic choice of the Japanese people." (The yakuza of course feel no obligation to restrain themselves when it comes to narcotics trafficking overseas, and ominously, police in the United States have learned in recent years of growing yakuza involvement in this new enterprise.)

LAW AND LAWYERS

According to a recent reckoning of the American Bar Association, there are now almost 800,000 licensed lawyers in the United States. That works out to one lawyer for every three hundred Americans. The rising number of attorneys in the United States—in 1950 the ratio was only 1:1100—has prompted frequent attacks on the legal profession. Some years back, Chief Justice Warren Burger spoke of the danger that America was becoming a "society overrun by hordes of lawyers, hungry as locusts." In 1991, Vice President Dan Quayle, an attorney, asked "Does America really need seventy percent of the world's lawyers?"

Conventional wisdom suggests that modernization and urbanization are factors which generate litigation and lawyers. Great Britain and Canada have large numbers of lawyers—though far less than the United States. However, Japan belies the assumption. As critics of the American legal system point out, Japan gets along with only one-twentieth of the lawyers (per capita) that the United States has.[2] Also while the American numbers expand rapidly, the Japanese do not. Whereas, about thirty-five thousand new lawyers are being turned out of American law schools each year, only about 450, hardly enough to compensate for attrition, are graduated in Japan. Humorist Russell Baker once suggested that the U.S.–Japan trade imbalance could be corrected by "exporting one lawyer to Japan for every car Japan exports to the United States."

As with all the social phenomenon we have been analyzing in Japan, there are varied and even contradictory ways of assessing Japan's apparently utopian freedom from lawyers.

The positive assessment argues that there are fundamental differences between the United States (and the West in general) and Japan concerning interpersonal relationships. The Japanese, according to this view, prefer that disputes should be settled on the basis of compromise and negotiation. By creating winners and losers, litigation works against the traditional ideal of *wa*, social harmony. Japanese therefore prefer compromise to the open-and-shut kind of decisions, guilty or not-guilty, that emerge in the courtroom. In addition to this preference for shades of gray over black and white, another factor may be face. In a society in which the first rule of social interaction is to be sensitive to the other person's face, to avoid shaming an adversary, it stands to reason that Japanese prefer to resolve disputes privately and informally.

Whether this is the reason or not, it is a fact that disputes are far more often handled through informal third-party mediation or arbitration than through lawyers reaching settlements in courts of law. Most Japanese probably go through their entire lives without ever consulting a lawyer. Of divorce cases in Japan, only two percent are handled by lawyers; 90 percent are settled by mutual consent. Those who do practice law are often engaged in technical matters such as taxes, patent law, and international law. Even in big business, corporate leaders rely on legal counsel far less often than their counterparts in the United States. Contracts do not carry the almost sacred weight to Japanese that they do to Westerners. Japanese do not take a cynical attitude that contracts are made to be broken, but if you are really concerned about harmonious relations, you must

---

[2] Cross-national statistical comparisons can be misleading. The figure 15,000 is frequently given as the total number of lawyers *(bengoshi)* in Japan. However, since many licensed nonlawyer legal specialists such as tax agents *(zeirishi)* perform work generally done by lawyers in the United States, Japan's professional legal work force should be numbered much higher, perhaps many times higher, than the 15,000 figure. Still, even using the broadest definition of lawyer, Japan is served by far fewer lawyers than the United States.

recognize that conditions change, and you must be prepared to make concessions. Faced with an unforeseen contingency, a businessman will ask another to "Please take my situation into account" *(Watakushi no tachiba o gokoryo itadaite).* A treatise on Japanese law written by Japanese scholars puts it this way:

> . . . we [*Japanese*] are certainly not very serious about honoring contracts. One might say that a breach of contract is not often accompanied by a sense of guilt. In fact, we view contracts in such a light-hearted manner that a contract is often regarded as a sort of tentative agreement (which may be revised as the circumstances change). If a party to a contract is subsequently urged by the other party to perform his contractual obligations to the letter, he considers such a demand to be an inhumane act.

When representatives of American companies get together to discuss a controversy or if there is a dispute between a government agency and a company, the contending parties will routinely bring their attorneys with them. In Japan, such a move would be a serious breach of good taste, tantamount to an insulting statement which calls into question the good faith of the other party. Frank Gibney, an American businessman with years of experience in Japan, writes:

> When an American calls his lawyer, he is confident and happy to rely on the strength of his social system—including the rule of law. When a Japanese calls his lawyer, he is sadly admitting that his social system has broken down. The system of interpersonal relationships and commitments has failed.

THE UNPROTECTED CITIZEN

A less sunny appraisal of Japan's legal system stresses what one writer calls the "unprotected citizen." Traditionally, law in Japan was seen as harsh, penal, "little more than lists of commands to be blindly obeyed by commoners." While modern, Western-inspired legal codes have theoretically extended to all citizens Western notions of justice, including civil rights protection, due process, and so on, traditional attitudes remain strong. The idea that laws exist to protect people against arbitrary powers is not firmly rooted in the consciousness of either the government or the citizenry. It is a "myth" to imagine that Japanese people are less litigious than others, argues law scholar John Haley. Rather, the authorities have systematically closed the options to its citizenry by a variety of measures. The government, for example, prohibits the overwhelming majority of would-be lawyers from practicing law by refusing admission to all but a tiny number to the government-run Legal Training and Research Institute (LTRI) through which all attorneys (as well as judges and other court officials) must pass. The LTRI therefore functions like the state bar examinations in the United States. On a per capita basis, approximately the same number of Japanese apply for entrance to the LTRI as take the bar exams in America. However, while about

75 percent of those taking the bar examinations pass, the success rates for appli-cants to the LTRI has consistently been in the one to four percent range over the past thirty years.

Further reducing the chance for judicial relief are long court delays and the high cost of litigation. Since lawyers are scarce (one lawyer per 9300 people in a recent study), they are expensive. Parties who are injured avoid litigation not out of some commitment to group harmony but because they cannot afford to litigate. Bringing a civil damage suit requires high, nonrefundable filing fees, payable in advance. American-style contingency agreements, under which losers pay no fee, are regarded as unethical in Japan. If claimants do file suits, it is argued, they are unlikely to receive fair compensation for injuries and so they often end up accepting apologies and only nominal amounts of compensation. The case of a disastrous hotel fire in Tokyo a few years ago seems to support this line of analysis. The owner, one of the wealthiest men in Japan, failed to install a sprinkler system which probably would have prevented the thirty-three deaths that resulted from the fire. He settled with many of the victims' families for approximately $100,000 per claim. An American attorney accepting such a "petty sum" probably would have been disbarred, one American lawyer com-mented in a letter to the *New York Times*. After acknowledging that Japanese tra-ditionally valued harmony over individual rights, he goes on:

> I suspect Americans would be far less comfortable about forcing victims to suffer silently, however. America has long recognized the principle that a member of society who injures another must compensate the victim. . . . In a society without meaningful access to the court system . . . violations of individual freedom could simply be ignored. As the Japanese experience demonstrates, if lawyers were scarce and expensive, the wronged party would have to suffer without adequate recourse.

A UNIQUE PEOPLE?

There can be few other peoples quite as introspective as the Japanese, few other peoples who speculate so widely on their identity. "Are we Asian or are we really closer to the West, or perhaps a bridge between the two worlds?" Japanese have been asking themselves these questions for more than a century. In the early 1970s, the search for identity reached the level of a *bumu* (boom). (Japanese frequently employ the English word "boom" to describe periods of rapid economic growth, commercial fads and social and intellectual trends.) In one of the early years of the "introspection boom," no fewer than forty books were published with titles like *Nihon to wa nanika?* (What Are We Japanese?). One of the pivotal questions of these books, and the ongoing introspection boom, hinges on debates about whether the Japanese are a "unique" people. Another related question centers on whether Japan is or should be more inter-nationalized. Both of these debates promise to be matters of concern to Japanese for many years to come.

THE JAPANESE NOSE

In another introspective volume which would seem surely to be farce (but is not), an author analyzes *Nihonjin no hana* (The Japanese Nose). Are there other nationalities blessed with their own nasal studies—The Danish Nose, The Peruvian Nose, and so on? Jared Taylor reminds us that this book may not be as silly as it first appears. Nose size is one of the physical differences between Orientals and Westerners that the Japanese find most striking, he comments. Both Chinese and Japanese have, from their earliest contacts with Westerners, remarked on the over-size noses of the foreigners.

There is no doubt that Japanese character, customs, aesthetic sense, likes and dislikes, are different. Japanese often express surprise to learn that foreigners have acquired a taste for raw fish, seaweed, soybeans, and other staples of the Japanese diet. Many assume that their language is not only maddeningly difficult to write but that there are many words so purely Japanese in nuance that foreigners cannot be expected to grasp their meanings. Many of these words, like *wabi* (the fondness for pottery and other objets d'art which are weathered and imperfect), are in the realm of aesthetics. However, do they express unfathomable ideas, or are they simply words for which there are no single-word equivalents in English? Edward Seidensticker, a respected translator of Japanese literature, writes of encounters with Japanese: "'But how do you manage the nuances of Japanese?' the Japanese are fond of asking, as if other languages did not have nuances, and as if there were no significance in the fact that the word 'nuance' (*nyuansu*) had to be borrowed from French."

Are the Japanese so attuned in their conversational style to unexpressed thoughts, communicating through silence, that they are a different species? Is it something in the genes that moves Japanese to submerge their individual selves, gravitate into groups, and conform to discipline so naturally and spontaneously. Or, as critics of these notions say, isn't it more likely that indoctrination and social pressure should be seen as formative factors of Japanese behavior? Do Japanese reason differently, and does the Japanese brain process information differently from the brains of *gaijin*? Dr. Tsunoda Tadanobu advanced that theory in a widely acclaimed book *Nihonjin no no* (The Japanese Brain). Western critics have generally responded to Tsunoda's theories with derision, but they were reviewed quite positively in the English journal *Science*.

Are, then, the Japanese incomparably different to what the rest of the world offers? Are the Japanese truly unique? The true believers, those who answer an unqualified "yes" to those questions, are at the far end of the spectrum of Japanese thinking on *Nihonjin-ron*.[3] Many Japanese would probably settle for an adjective like "distinctive" rather than unique. Still, the issue is almost

---

[3] *Nihonjin-ron* does not translate smoothly into English. Literally, it means "theorizing about the Japanese." A looser translation might be the "introspection" that I have adopted.

omnipresent. Karel van Wolferen argues that "very little serious writing by Japanese on anything relating to their society is entirely free of Nihonjin-ron influence." In recent years, the *Nihonjin-ron* notions have spilled over into the Japanese-American trade controversy. In 1983, Prime Minister Nakasone made clear in plain language that he felt that "The Japanese have been doing well for as long as 2,000 years because there are no foreign races." Japanese pleaded that they were slow in importing American-made skis because they were deemed unsuitable for Japanese snow and American beef because it was not suitable for the Japanese digestive system. "Everyone knows that Japanese intestines are about one meter longer than those of foreigners," said a spokesmen for an association of agricultural cooperatives.

KOKUSAI-KA

Internationalization *(kokusai-ka)* became something of a national buzz-word in Japan in the late 1980s. It is not precisely defined but refers to many things: opening up, narrowing the gap between "we" and "they," and accepting international responsibilities befitting the nation's economic power.

In many respects, the Japanese are already extremely internationalized. Examples are numerous. Some are superficial, others more consequential. Like baseball, for example, coffee shops have become an imported national institution and are found in the smallest, remotest towns, an assertion of urban cosmopolitan taste and life-style. Other examples of *kokusai-ka* at the level of popular culture include: the astonishing popularity of foreign entertainers, musicians, artists; the eclectic reading habits of Japanese; the foreign travel boom, the fondness for Christian wedding ceremonies in non-Christian Japanese households; the incorporation of alien holidays like Christmas and Valentine's Day into the national calendar; and the elevation of baseball—arguably to the rank of *the* national sport—can we imagine the American analog of this trend? Americans being joined in wedlock wearing kimono and blessed in Shinto rites? Americans scattering roasted beans around the house on the winter feast of Setsubun while shouting "Devils Go Away, Fortune Stay Home"? Monday-night sumo?

There are very few years when books by Western authors in translation do not make Japan's ten best-sellers list—Paul Kennedy's *The Rise and Fall of the Great Powers* was number six in 1988 and Stephen Hawking's *A Brief History of Time* was number five the following year. When was the last year a Japanese author enjoyed such a distinction in the United States? National reading habits can be important, not just as a mark of sophistication, but as a way of keeping attuned. When Herman Kahn, Peter Drucker, and Daniel Bell have written on the implications of post-industrial societies, their most attentive audiences have been Japanese businessmen. Drucker's *The Age of Discontinuity* made Japan's ten-best list in 1967. Although American businessmen have taken a more focused interest in Japan in recent years, too many of them, if tempted to learn about Japan, have settled for facile answers. Wall Street executives in the early 1980s eagerly studied the homilies of Miyamoto Musashi, a seventeenth-century samurai-turned philosopher: "If you fail to take advantage of your enemies' collapse, they may recover. . . . You must understand now to utterly cut down the enemy." Japanese entrepreneurs, similarly inclined, might have borrowed maxims from Wyatt Earp and other pop heroes of the Wild West.

For all the bungled language training that goes on in Japanese schools, Japanese are infinitely more skilled in English than Americans are in Japanese. An American looking lost while standing on a street corner in a remote city in Japan will almost certainly be rescued within minutes by a courteous Japanese with at least some command of English. How likely is it that a Japanese would enjoy reciprocal treatment while stranded in, say, Sioux Falls or Peoria?

Yet, while Japanese seem very internationalized, many foreigners and Japanese alike retain suspicions that *kokusai-ka* does not run deep, that it is not what it ought to be. Centuries of isolation on islands populated almost exclusively by a single ethnic group have worked to create what Japanese concede is a *shimaguni konjo*, an island or insular mentality. A Japanese cliche *Ware-ware Nihonjin* (We Japanese) begins many sentences, almost always designed to distinguish the way Japan's 125 million people think or behave from the way *gaijin* do. Shuttered for so long from the rest of the world, it is easy for Japanese to regard their own ethnic homogeneity as strength and the diversity of America as a fatal flaw. Mistreatment and prejudice against the Korean minority within Japan suggests that Japan has far to go before it is "internationalized." Crude depiction of blacks, portrayed with gross features, simpleton expressions, and carrying spears, have been used in advertising to sell toothpaste, soft drinks and other consumer items. More than once in recent years, racially insensitive remarks by leading political figures (including the prime minister) have sparked international outcries. When in 1990 Kajiyama Seiroku, a former Justice minister, compared prostitutes with American blacks (both ruin the neighborhood), an Asahi newspaper writer apologized for Japanese "narrow-minded chauvinism" and conceded that "the sad truth is that Kajiyama simply said publicly what many think privately."

William J. Holstein suggests that many Japanese who enjoy exotic cuisines or travel extensively "may seem internationalized, but in reality, they regard this foreign exposure as a mere life-style enhancement that has little impact on their commitment to think and act in Japanese ways." An internationalist in Japan, Holstein suggests, is not someone who has thoroughly studied and absorbed Western values and attitudes but is, perhaps, someone who is sophisticated enough to manage foreigners. Japanese spokesmen frequently criticize themselves for the failure to take responsibility in world affairs commensurate with their national economic power. Why, for example, was business disinvestment from South Africa not even the subject for serious discussion in Japanese boardrooms, some ask. "Does Japan have the soul of a merchant or a samurai?" one government official remarked. "It's time to decide if we are a nation of salesmen or statesmen. There's no glory in an abacus, so I vote for grandeur."

Finally, as Edwin Reischauer notes, while foreigners in Japan are usually treated so generously as to make them embarrassed when it comes to reciprocating, it remains almost impossible for a Westerner to be accepted as "one of the group." Reischauer goes on:

> As an external adornment he or she may be lionized, but no one wants him as a full member. A Westerner who becomes very well informed about Japan may even be resented. To the extent that he becomes accustomed to Japanese habits of thought and ways of life he may come to be considered a *hen na gaijin*, a "foreigner with a screw loose," who makes the Japanese feel ill at ease. True fluency in Japanese may raise feelings bordering on hostility, though a few outrageously mispronounced phrases will produce enthusiastic praise. The Japanese feel that foreigners should never forget that they are foreigners.

MORE LIKE THEM . . .

In 1979, Ezra Vogel wrote *Japan as Number 1*. The book chided Americans for their complacency and provincialism at a time when their country seemed to be going the way of England as a declining power and at a time when Japan was becoming the world's dynamic center. Long-held assumptions about the superiority of Western civilization and invincible Yankee know-how made it difficult for Americans to acknowledge that we might have things to learn from Asians, Vogel noted. But perhaps we could take a page from Japan's historical experience. "Other countries were devastated by foreign influence, but Japan was invigorated," he suggested.

There is much to impress—and even dazzle—the foreign observer of Japan. First-time visitors there consistently comment that Japan is a country in which everything works, the trains and buses are always punctual, taxis are sparkling clean and the white-gloved taxi drivers are unfailingly courteous even if they are not tipped. (Only foreigners tip in Japan; a Japanese worker would likely feel uncomfortable if tipped by a fellow Japanese, as if he were being bribed.) Delivery men and service vehicles arrive at the appointed moment rather than "between nine and five." Public telephones and telephone books are where they should be. Vandalism and graffiti are conspicuously absent. The frayed nerves which come with high population density is supposed to increase violent behavior, but crime rates in Japan's crowded cities peaked more than thirty-five years ago.

How can an outsider not be impressed with a nation which recovered from one of the worst military defeats in history and built arguably the most dynamic and productive economic machine in the world? Here is a nation of nearly 130 million people crammed into one-tenth of one percent of the world's inhabitable space producing 11 percent of world economic value! Japanese lived close to starvation and epidemic disease forty-five years ago. Today, they enjoy the longest life expectancy and the lowest infant mortality rates of any in the world. From being a nation with great extremes of poverty and wealth only two generations ago, Japan was recently ranked with Sweden and Australia as one of the

> The following treatment cannot be guaranteed to every foreigner experiencing car trouble in Tokyo. But most foreigners would agree that the example rings true:
>
> "When our beat-up Nissan Bluebird blows a tire near the prime minister's house, a half-dozen riot policemen jog over, suspicion melting into sympathy as they notice our children in the back. They take charge, change our tire and send us on the way with salutes far snappier than our jalopy."
>
> —Fred Hiatt and Margaret Shapiro, *Washington Post*, 1990.

three industrialized democracies with the least spread in income between rich and poor. There are slums in Japanese cities but they do not bear comparison to the desolate urban wastelands of America. Sanya, Tokyo's largest skid-row district, can be traversed on foot in less than thirty minutes. Vagrants and panhandlers are not often seen on city streets—the occasional one you encounter might well be a displaced American.

How much of Japan's success story can be transplanted to American soil? Is there some magic ingredient we can borrow so that our teenagers can get the same high scores that Japanese youngsters do on math and science exams? To do that, do we have to adopt an educational regimen that even many Japanese agree is frightfully distorted? Must we goad youngsters into study habits that seriously hinder the development of adolescent social skills and satisfactions? Japan's low crime rates cause justifiable envy abroad. However, the Japanese police presence in the community is far more intrusive than Americans would tolerate. The kind of snooping done by Mr. Walkabout *(o-mawari-san*, the policeman) on his daily neighborhood rounds and his semi-annual residential "surveys" would be quickly challenged in the United States as unconstitutional invasions of privacy.

. . . OR MORE LIKE US

Maybe, then, the answer is to stick to our own ways? They can't be too bad. For all the criticism of the *Amerika-byo*, the American disease, our ways have had a seductive influence on people everywhere. It would be nice if pupils here had some of the respect for their teachers that Japanese children express with a polite bow in the morning; it would be nice at least if American pupils did not address their mentors as "Hey, teach!"[4] However, there is something to be said

---

[4] Nothing said here should suggest that Japanese are frozen in their ways. The older Japanese generation deplores the gradual disapearance of the polite morning classroom rituals. Moreover, the irreverent greeting "Senko!" has exactly the same disrespectful overtones as "Hey, teach!"

for American informality. Kometani Fumiko, a celebrated novelist in Japan, writes of a meeting she had with the U.S. Ambassador to Japan, Mike Mansfield. Mansfield, well-liked and respected by the Japanese, was eighty-three when Kometani met him in 1986. Kometani recalls that she was concerned about linguistic faux pas until she decided to speak in English, where a simple "you" was sufficient regardless of a person's rank. "What a relief," she writes. (In Japanese, there would be several levels of the honorific "you" to consider.) The author noticed that water was boiling in an anteroom. To her bewilderment, it was not an aide who prepared and served the coffee but the distinguished ambassador himself who served the coffee to the novelist, her husband, her son, and the ambassador's aide. I was "astonished," Kometani writes.

> It was as though he was back in Montana, relaxing with his shirt sleeves rolled up, and a neighbor had dropped in. "The wife's out, so have some coffee and tell me what you're up to," he would have said, and brought out a pot of coffee from the kitchen. It was completely natural and unpretentious. As I sipped my coffee I wondered if ambassadors from countries like France, Great Britain or Japan would ever be so informal.

Would that Americans were more disciplined, more like Japanese workers—and baseball players. Perhaps not. Maybe Japanese are too disciplined, too conformist—the suggestion comes from novelist Yamagawa Junji, reflecting on an incident involving the American expatriate ballplayer Mark McGwire. McGwire skipped the final game of the 1987 season and skipped a chance to extend the new record he had set for rookie home runs. The reason was that he wished to be with his new wife who was having their first baby. He was generally assailed for his poor team spirit. As strong as family ties are in Japan, duty to the team had to come first. *Giri* over *ninjo*. Novelist Yamagawa came to McGwire's defense in an article that reached the nine million readers of *Yomiuri*, the world's largest newspaper. "The incident," he wrote, "reminded me that despite the United States' social problems, such as juvenile delinquency and a high divorce rate, traditional values are still strong." Yamagawa found it refreshing that American players "march to their own drummer, unlike Japanese players who try to conform."

"They [the Japanese] have excelled in production. They have excelled, in other words, in the realm in which their more perdurable moral fiber stands them in best stead. So we should obviously look to our own fiber," writes literary scholar Edward Seidensticker. James Fallows—as an editor of *The Atlantic* he lived and reported from Tokyo and other Asian capitals for three years—develops that same theme. The true American genius, he writes in his recent book *More Like Us*, is "a talent for *dis*order." He goes on: "Japan gets the most out of ordinary people by *organizing* them to adapt and succeed. America, by getting out of their way so that they can adjust individually, *allows* them to succeed."

ADDITIONAL READING

    The writings of four authors stand out above all the others in sharpening Western thinking about modern Japanese society. The dean and one of the founding fathers of modern Japanese studies, Edwin O. Reischauer, has written extensively on Japan with an approach that is challenging to scholars and yet accessible to general readers. For the most recent and best introduction to his views, see *The Japanese Today* (1988). I have discussed in the text Ezra Vogel's important contribution, *Japan as Number 1* (1979). In the same way that Vogel's book became a touchstone for thinking about Japan in the 1980s, journalist Karel van Wolferen's, *The Enigma of Japanese Power: People and Politics in a Stateless Nation* (1990), is on its way to becoming a touchstone for the 1990s. Finally, no one seems to capture the contemporary issues and dilemmas concerning the Japan–U.S. nexus with quite the penetrating and succinct style of James Fallows. His recent *More Like Us: Making America Great Again* (1989) is recommended, but his best writing on Japan—which deserves to be collected in an anthology—has to be searched out in issues from the past twelve years of his own magazine, *The Atlantic*, as well as *Rolling Stone, New Republic, New York Review of Books*, and others. Though somewhat less accessible, the writings of Australian journalist Murray Sayle (for example in the *Far Eastern Economic Review* and *New Republic*) are always informed and interesting.

    Most of the following general studies of Japanese history and culture include chapters or sections on the topics I have discussed. I have relied heavily on the interpretations of these authors: Mikiso Hane, *Modern Japan* (1986); Frank Gibney, *Japan: The Fragile Superpower* (1979); Dick Wilson, *The Sun at Noon: An Anatomy of Modern Japan* (1986); Peter Tasker, *The Japanese: A Major Exploration of Modern Japan* (1987); Jared Taylor, *Shadows of the Rising Sun: A Critical View of the 'Japanese Miracle'* (1983); Robert S. Ozaki, *The Japanese: A Cultural Portrait* (1978); Yoshio Sugimoto and Ross Mouer, *Images of Japanese Society* (1986); Ellen L. Frost, *For Richer, For Poorer: The New U.S.–Japan Relationship* (1987); and Harumi Befu, *Japan: An Anthropological Introduction* (1971). Though dated and the subject of dispute, Ruth F. Benedict's *The Chrysanthemum and the Sword: Patterns of Japanese Culture* (1946) remains a classical source. The lengthy introductory chapter by John Dower in his *Origins of the Modern Japanese State: Selected Writings of E. H. Norman* (1975) is full of challenging and original ideas.

    On education, consult: Thomas Rohlen, *Japan's High Schools* (1983); Merry White, *The Japanese Educational Challenge* (1987); William Cummings, *Education and Equality in Japan* (1980); Ronald Dore, *The Diploma Disease* (1965); and Herbert Passin, *Society and Education in Japan* (1965).

    On women, see: Joyce Lebra, et al, eds., *Women in Changing Japan* (1976); Jane Condon, *A Half Step Behind: Japanese Women of the '80s* (1985); Dorothy Robins-Mowry, *The Hidden Sun Women of Modern Japan* (1983); Nicholas Bornoff, *Pink Samurai: Love, Marriage and Sex in Contemporary Japan* (1991); Liza Dalby, *Geisha* (1983); and a very witty sociolinguistic study by Kittredge Cherry, *Womansword: What Japanese Words Say About Women* (1987).

    On law and crime, consult: David H. Bayley, *Forces of Order: Police Behavior in Japan and the United States* (1976); Walter L. Ames, *Police and Community in Japan* (1981); David E. Kaplan and Alec Dubro, *Yakuza* (1986); Frank K. Upham, *Law and Social Change in Postwar Japan* (1987). See also the provocative and influential article by John O. Haley, "The Myth of the Reluctant Litigant," *Journal of Japanese Studies* (Winter 1978).

    Literature, especially stories written by Japanese authors, offers fine opportunities for delving into Japanese society and the Japanese character. Three places to start are the translated anthologies compiled by Donald Keene, *Modern Japanese Literature* (1956); Ivan Morris, *Modern Japanese Stories* (1962); and Howard Hibbett, *Contemporary Japanese Literature* (1977).

Students are warned that the subject of the Japanese language and its relationship to Japanese culture is remarkably controversial—not to say acrimonious at times. Good sources include Roy Andrew Miller, *The Japanese Language* (1967) and Peter N. Dale, *The Myth of Japanese Uniqueness* (1986). Uninitiated readers interested in avoiding some of the minefields in this perilous territory would do well to read reviews of some of these authors' books in, for example, *Journal of Asian Studies* (November 1988) and *Monumenta Nipponica* (Autumn 1983). Reviews by and about the most controversial of the Japan language experts, Roy Andrew Miller, can be found in various issues of the *Journal of Japanese Studies* (for example, Summer 1987 and Winter 1989).

Other specialized insights into modern Japanese society are found in Ian Buruma, *Behind the Mask: On Sexual Demons, Sacred Mothers, Transvestites, Gangsters, and Other Japanese Cultural Heroes* (1984); Merry White, *The Japanese Overseas: Can They Go Home Again?* (1988); H. Byron Earhart, *Japanese Religion: Unity and Diversity* (1982); Takeo Doi, *The Anatomy of Dependence* (1973); Donald Richie, *The Japanese Cinema* (1971); Walter Edwards, *Modern Japan Through Its Weddings: Gender, Person, and Society in Ritual Portrayal* (1989); Brian Moeran, *Okubo Diary: Portrait of a Japanese Valley* (1985); Samuel Coleman, *Family Planning in Japanese Society* (1983); and Thomas Rohlen, *For Harmony and Strength: Japanese White-Collar Organization in Anthropological Perspective* (1974). Concerning baseball—but plunging into Japanese mores at many levels—is Robert Whiting's well informed and funny *You Gotta' Have Wa* (1989).

Finally, many of the books recommended at the end of Chapter 10 can also be usefully consulted here.

2

A DOUBLE-BOLTED LAND

The earliest Japanese and Americans to reach each other's shores have been all but forgotten by history. They were not famous explorers. Their voyages and experiences, however, illuminate the most noteworthy feature of Japanese history in the period before 1853—her isolation from the rest of the world.

George Washington had been in office only two years when John Kendrick, a sea captain sailing out of Wareham, Massachusetts, arrived in Japan. In those days, commerce with Japan did not interest Kendrick or the other intrepid sailors who were crossing the Pacific in sloops no larger than modern yachts. Instead, it was the lucrative "China trade," selling furs and buying much prized Chinese teas and porcelains at Canton on the South China coast that intrigued them. However, in May 1791, Kendrick, unable to find Chinese customers for a cargo of sea otter pelts, was returning to North America when, apparently, he decided to search for buyers for his goods in Japan. The venture failed. He had scarcely landed in the small port of Kashinoura when Japanese authorities ordered him to leave. For nearly two centuries, Japan's rulers, shoguns of the Tokugawa family, had rigorously enforced a policy of excluding foreigners from their land.

Kendrick was fortunate in being allowed to leave Japan unharmed. Others who challenged the shogun's rules were often imprisoned or otherwise mistreated. Tokugawa isolationism also forbade Japanese to leave their homeland under penalty of death. The first Japanese visitor to North America—at least the first to leave a documented record—was a certain cargo-ship captain named Jukichi. He was not foolhardy enough to defy the shogun's rules about overseas voyages but was a hapless shipwreck victim, a "drifter." When his small coastal

NAKAHAMA REMEMBERED

You may not know that I am the grandson of Mr. Warren Delano of Fairhaven, who was part owner of the ship of Captain Whitefield which brought your father to Fairhaven. Your father lived, as I remember it, at the house of Mr. Tripp, which was directly across the street from my grandfather's house, and when I was a boy I well remember my grandfather telling me about the little Japanese boy who went to school in Fairhaven and who went to church from time to time with the Delano family.

—Letter from President Franklin D. Roosevelt to
Nakahama Toichiro, June 8, 1933.

vessel lost its rudder in a storm in 1813, Jukichi and a crew of fourteen floated out across the Pacific. Sustained by a cargo of soya beans and their own fishing and water distillation skills, they drifted for an incredible eighteen months until Jukichi and two surviving crew members were rescued off the California coast near Santa Barbara in March 1815.

Thanks to a hospitable Anglo-American ship captain who befriended them, the Japanese drifters were introduced to Spanish California, Russian Alaska, and Siberia before being returned to their homeland, where they were promptly arrested for having ventured abroad. Jukichi was eventually released. He had fantastic stories to tell of survival at sea and of his adventures among the blue-eyed, pork-eating barbarians of many nationalities. His tales, however, reached only a limited audience of his countrymen via an illegal clandestine publication. The authorities not only forbade overseas travel but strictly monitored the distribution of "dangerous thoughts"—that is, any information about the outside world carried by returnees tainted by foreign travel.

Until 1850, only one of these returnees actually lived in the United States. In 1841, a castaway waif of fourteen, Nakahama Manjiro, was picked up by a whaleboat captain and taken to Fairhaven, Massachusetts, where he was enrolled in school. The lad eventually mastered surveying and navigation before he returned to his homeland in 1851, where he was subjected to a year of imprisonment and interrogation during which he presumably imparted his impressions of America. It is not known what use the authorities made of his accounts of American lore (including the cherry tree incident in George Washington's youth), but authorities clearly gleaned from him a picture of a classless society quite different from their own. "Officials are hard to distinguish as they never display the authority of their office. They do not demand courtesies from citizens along the road," Nakahama related to listeners who were always conscious of rank and never tolerated the slightest evidence of discourtesy from citizens "along the road." While Nakahama's reports described the character of Americans in generally flattering terms ("very generous and honest and they do little wrong"), he had one reservation: "They are lewd by nature, but otherwise well-behaved." Evidence of this single moral flaw was the penchant Americans had for kissing in public, still offensive to proper Japanese who regard public displays of affection as tasteless. Americans visiting Japan in later years, as we will see, professed shock at the innocent Japanese custom of mixed bathing and were quick to draw the conclusions about the "gross debauchery" of the "natives."

In this enforced isolation of Japan, it is hardly surprising that rumor and superstitious dread of foreigners combined to produce bizarre images of Westerners in the Japanese mind. It was easy to think of them as being crafty and fox-like, constantly seeking ways to violate Japan's space. Westerners were commonly referred to as "barbarians" *(banjin)* or "red hairs" *(komojin)* not because they were all thought to be red headed but because the devil was often portrayed in Buddhist iconography as having red hair. In the popular mind, rumor had it that the foreigners' trousers concealed a bushy tail and that men would lift their legs like dogs to urinate. Everything about them was different and baffling. One scholar was reduced to metaphoric overkill as he ridiculed the Westerners' writing for being,

> confused and irregular, wriggling like snakes or larvae of mosquitos. The straight [letters] are like dog's teeth, the round ones are like worms. The crooked ones are like the forelegs of a mantis, the stretched ones are like the slime lines left by snails. They resemble dried bones or decaying skulls, rotten bellies of dead snakes or parched vipers.

China's Cultural Daughter

Japan had not always been so paranoid about contact with foreigners. Indeed, Japan emerged in history as a fully civilized nation only after extensive and fruitful contact with her large mainland neighbor, China, which throughout history knew itself as the magisterial *Chung-kuo,* the Middle Kingdom, the center of the civilized world.

As late as A.D. 550, Japan was still best described as a primitive society. The art of early Japan displayed charm and promise but little sophistication. The early architecture, seen in Shinto shrine construction, was severely simple. For the most part, Japanese had no way to express themselves in writing; only a few Japanese had been introduced to the mysteries of the Chinese script by visitors from Korea. There were no Japanese books, much less philosophical and literary traditions. Social and political life centered on loosely organized clans, one of which had only recently emerged to claim paramount status, but its authority hardly extended beyond the Yamato valley on the main island; most of what we now know as Japan was at that time frontier dominated by outlaw bands and a racially distinct group of people known as the *Ainu.* One could hardly speak of inventions or discoveries native to Japan. What technology existed was crude and limited to agriculture. There was no commerce. There were no cities. The earliest written descriptions of Japan, recorded in Chinese dynastic histories,

AN EARLY CHINESE DESCRIPTION OF THE *WA* PEOPLE OF JAPAN
  "When they travel across the sea to come to China, they always select a man who does not comb his hair, does not rid himself of fleas, keeps his clothes soiled with dirt, does not eat meat, and does not lie with women. He behaves like a mourner, and is called a 'keeper of the taboos.' If the voyage is concluded with good fortune, every one lavishes on him slaves and treasures. If someone gets ill, or if there is a mishap, they kill him immediately, saying that he was not conscientious in observing the taboos."

—From *Wei chih* (History of the Wei), compiled about A.D. 297.

speak of inhabitants of the Japanese home islands as the *Wa* people, a pejorative signifying "dwarfs." These early accounts bristle with condescending remarks about the unrefined Japanese.

Japan's primitive stage of development stands in sharp contrast to China. By A.D. 550, the "Middle Kingdom" was already a mature civilization with artistic and cultural traditions which had been maturing for more than a thousand years. Measured by its inventions and discoveries, China was surely the most technically advanced nation on earth. During the first thousand years of the Christian era, while Europe was stagnating in the Dark Ages, China was experiencing an explosion of technological growth. The list of Chinese firsts include paper, printing, the clock, the compass, gunpowder, sericulture, porcelain, the rotary fan, matches, kites, the foot stirrup, the rudder, the paddle-wheeled boat, tuned bells and drums, the wheelbarrow, and the crossbow. China's dazzling achievements in astronomy, medicine, mathematics, and engineering would not be replicated in the West until the Renaissance.

Given the enormous discrepancy between the two cultures, Japanese and Chinese, it is not surprising that the Japanese would stand in awe of the Middle Kingdom and welcome all the civilizing influences the Chinese had to offer. Some awareness of Chinese culture had already filtered into Japan from Korea, but with the introduction of Buddhism to Japan in the mid-sixth century — A.D. 552 is the date customarily assigned—these sporadic contacts turned into a floodtide of influence. Far from being too proud to borrow from China, the Japanese were quick to acknowledge the superiority of Chinese culture. In what one writer describes as "the world's first program of organized study abroad," Japanese priests, scholars, and artists were drawn like magnets to the magnificent T'ang dynasty capital at Ch'ang-an, the largest and most cosmopolitan city in the world during its heyday. As they returned to Japan, these travelers transformed their homeland into a cultural daughter of China.

Japan's first city, the capital at Nara, was consciously constructed on the model of Ch'ang-an although the Japanese version was tiny by comparison. Japanese scholars, Buddhist priests at first and then others, set about mastering the complicated Chinese writing system composed of thousands of characters, a task rendered all the more difficult because the spoken languages of China and Japan were not even faintly similar. Nevertheless, familiarity with the Chinese writing system became the essential mark of the educated man and one of the most important civilizing influences Japan was to import from abroad. To this day, Japanese write "Chinese characters" *(kanji)*.

Later, when Japanese studied the "Classics," it was the Confucian Classics, the teachings of the ancient Chinese sage, Confucius, which absorbed them; there were no "Japanese classics." Poetry was written in the Chinese style on Chinese themes with allusions to Chinese places most Japanese poets had never seen. Buddhist pagodas and temples were erected using techniques learned in China. Paradoxically, Japan today possesses the only surviving examples of the magnificent architecture of the T'ang dynasty; the Chinese originals have all been destroyed by fire or earthquake. Even minor arts which we often think of as uniquely Japanese, such as *ikebana* (flower arranging), *cha-no-yu* (tea ceremony), *bonsai* (dwarf-plant cultivation), and the game of *go* all trace their origins to China. Making this cultural borrowing all the more enduring was the Japanese genius for not *merely* borrowing but for adapting, innovating, and improving on the imports, a talent which would serve Japan well later on in history. This means that, for all of their cultural indebtedness to China, and more recently to the West, Japanese have never stopped thinking of themselves as a distinct and indeed unique people. Borrowing from abroad while maintaining a strong sense of their own national identity has been one of the persistent hallmarks of Japanese history.

JAPAN'S "CHRISTIAN CENTURY"

The reason for Japan's seclusion from the outside world at the time of Captain Kendrick's attempted visit must be found in Japan's initial contacts with Europeans in the sixteenth century. Spanish and Portuguese adventurers arrived in the Far East at that time, drawn there by a variety of motives—including plunder, commerce, and saving souls. As the earliest missionaries, priests from the Society of Jesus, better known as Jesuits, made their appearance in Japan in 1549. First impressions on both sides were largely positive. The Japanese admired the Jesuits for their dignified bearing, their learning, and their eager determination to plunge into the difficult task of mastering the Japanese spoken and written languages. At the same time, the Jesuit priests were writing back to Europe of the sterling qualities of the Japanese they met, traits that would impress visitors to Japan for centuries to come: their courtesy, cleanliness, frugality, courage, and, as Father Francis Xavier noted in a letter to Rome, "their honor which they prize above everything else." The well-traveled Xavier, founder of the missionary movement in Japan, described the Japanese to be the "best race yet discovered" and went on to develop a high optimism for the prospects of converting Japan to Christianity.

Xavier's optimism must have seemed warranted, for Christianity spread more rapidly in Japan than in any other Asian country, and by 1600 the number of Christian converts reached more than two percent of the population. As it turned out, however, that was the high-water mark for Christianity in Japan— and about double the percentage today. After some promising beginnings for cultural understanding and tolerance, Japanese authorities started promulgating a series of edicts in 1587 which eventually resulted in the banning of Christianity, persecution of converts who refused to recant and the expulsion of foreigners.

The policy of national seclusion and the outlawing of Christianity were, in spite of appearances, only indirectly related to religion. Japanese history records moments of bigotry and sectarian violence, but in general the nation's life has been marked by religious tolerance. Shinto, a native religion emphasizing reverence for nature and fertility, has existed since the dawn of Japanese history and has been closely associated with myths regarding the sacred origins of the Japanese people and the imperial line. Traditionally, emperors were regarded as having descended from Shinto deities. Despite the close identification of state and Shinto which might have been expected to produce hostility to alien religious competition, the Japanese enthusiastically absorbed the doctrines of Buddhism which came from India via China and Korea. From the sixth century onward, this foreign religion deeply affected Japanese with its message that self-cultivation could lead to enlightenment. In addition, it became, as we have mentioned, the vehicle for the transmission of great Chinese traditions in art, sculpture, architecture, and music.

At a later time in history, Japanese embraced the ethical teachings of the great Chinese philosopher Confucius, who stressed such this-worldly virtues as duty, loyalty, respect for authority, and strict observance of proper social ritual and etiquette. The impact of Confucianism on Japan can be seen in the importance attached to education and the faith in hard work that have survived from traditional times to the present. These ethical and social values, imported as a philosophical system, have permeated Japanese thinking for centuries. As Japan historian Edwin O. Reischauer has written, "Confucianism probably has more influence on [the Japanese] than does any other of the traditional religions or philosophies."

Prevailing attitudes of most peoples in the West make religion an *exclusive* concern—one is either Baptist or Catholic, either Orthodox Jew or Reformed Jew, either Sunni or Shiite Moslem, and so on. By contrast, attitudes in Japan historically tended to be more *inclusive*, permitting people to accept teachings, customs, and rituals of various religious traditions, native and alien, without a sense of contradiction or heresy. Foreign observers are often surprised to find that religious preference statistics from Japan reveal that most adult Japanese regard themselves as *both* Shintoist and Buddhist and many homes contain shrines of both those faiths. From birth to death, Japanese alternate between patronizing Shinto shrines and Buddhist temples. Japanese do not consider themselves married until they have been blessed by a Shinto priest at a Shinto shrine in ceremonies almost as old as Japan itself. On the other hand, however, it is invariably the Buddhist priest who is summoned to officiate at funerals.

EXPULSION OF THE EUROPEANS

It was not therefore any objection to Christianity on theological grounds that impelled Japan to crack down on the foreign presence and usher in the long period of national seclusion. It was rather a fear that, with Christianity, might come attempts by the Catholic colonial powers of Europe to extend their conquests to Japan. The Japanese authorities were well aware of the competition for empire that was bringing European powers to Asian waters, and they knew about the speed with which flag had followed cross in the Spanish conquest of the Philippines in the late sixteenth century. And thanks to the arrival in Japan about 1600 of some English and Dutch seafarers, the ruling shoguns became acquainted with a Protestant slant concerning the frightful wars of religious persecution which were engulfing Europe. In the conversations around this time between the English sea-dog Will Adams and the shogun, the Jesuit padres and the Catholic powers in general emerged as a distinctly menacing force. (Adams, who arrived in Japan in 1600 and became a trusted adviser to the shogun Tokugawa Ieyasu, was the model for "Blackthorne" in James Clavell's epic novel and movie *Shogun*.)

In addition, the shogun was concerned that native converts might develop conflicting political loyalties which in turn would threaten the authority of powerful warlords like Oda Nobunaga (1534–1582), Hideyoshi Toyotomi (1536–1598), and Tokugawa Ieyasu (1542–1616). These military giants were engaged in a historic struggle to eliminate rivals and pacify a nation just emerging from more than a century of civil warfare. They at first tolerated and indeed benefited from contact with the foreigners—they learned to forge cannons and were trained in advanced gunnery techniques by the priests, and their military headquarters incorporated the most up-to-date European styles of fortified castle construction. As these three national unifiers gradually expanded their power bases in the latter years of the sixteenth century, however, they increasingly came to see the foreign presence in Japan as more threat than asset. There was ample evidence that their concerns were justified.

Among the nation's powerful regional lords (*daimyo*) were converts to Christianity, two of whom had dispatched a mission to visit the pope as a mark of their zeal and devotion. To win favor from the foreign priests, one of the "Christian daimyo" had gone so far to permit the Jesuits to act as overlords at Nagasaki, the leading point of contact with the outside world and by 1580 virtually a Portuguese settlement. An occasional samurai might even go into battle carrying rosaries or wearing a crucifix. Some daimyo compelled their vassals and the peasants in their fief to adopt the foreign religion. In order to prevent Christianity from spreading and becoming the basis for potentially subversive alliances among the ranks of the daimyo, Hideyoshi and Tokugawa Ieyasu and their successors implemented an isolation policy and the ban on Christianity, in a series of edicts beginning as early as 1587 but promulgated in earnest from 1616. Japanese Christians who refused to defile images of Christ or the Madonna in a gesture of apostasy were subjected to cruel persecution—the church recognizes some 3400 martyrs from this period. In 1637, at a dilapidated old castle on the Shimabara peninsula, not far from Nagasaki where the church had sunk its deepest roots in Japan, some thirty-seven thousand Christians attempted a final resistance to the authorities. Exhausted from a year-long siege and dying of starvation, the mostly peasant army of rebels was finally crushed in April 1638, marking the death knell of Christianity in Japan for the next two-and-a-half centuries.

Significantly, the Shimabara Rebellion was also the last occasion until modern times when guns would be used by Japanese. Japanese had become thoroughly adept in the manufacture and use of the Western-style weaponry introduced at the beginning of the Christian century. Still, the impersonal long-range warfare that musketry promoted was at odds with the man-to-man fighting traditions of the samurai and the cult of the sword which was seen as not merely a weapon but the "soul of the samurai." Moreover, it made very good sense for the shogun, interested as he was in establishing firm control over the political order, to forbid the use of guns which were associated with hastily thrown-together outlaw armies rather than professional samurai warriors. The ban on guns worked, and Japan became perhaps history's only example of a nation voluntarily discarding a superior modern technology which it had mastered. While this contributed to the long period of peace and political stability that the Tokugawa government brought Japan in the wake of the Shimabara Rebellion, it also left Japan in a seriously weakened military state in the nineteenth century, when a new wave of foreign pressure would challenge Japan's isolation policy.

The isolation policy did not bring about the total seclusion of Japan. Some closely regulated trade with Korea and China was permitted. In addition, because Holland managed to convince the Japanese that it had no territorial or religious ambitions in Japan, the Dutch were allowed to maintain a small trading post under conditions of virtual imprisonment on the island of Deshima, off the southern port of Nagasaki. For two-and-a-half centuries, beginning in the early 1600s, the enclave at Deshima and the annual ship that called there constituted the only authorized window to the Western world. Accompanying the expulsion edicts were prohibitions in 1635 on foreign voyaging by Japanese and laws outlawing the construction of ships capable of sailing the high seas. In short order, a lively Japanese trade with Southeast Asia dried up and Japanese resident communities from Manila to Bangkok vanished from history. Japan entered the longest period of national isolation ever undertaken by a major nation. The *shimaguni konjo*, the insular mentality which is discussed in the first chapter, was to be greatly reinforced by this self-imposed seclusion.

The few foreigners like Captain Kendrick who tried to enter Japan during the next two hundred years did not succeed in breaking the shogun's seclusionist position but seemed rather to reinforce a sense of vigilance. Ships of several

REAL SAMURAI DIDN'T USE GUNS

While the Japanese warrior took pride in owning and wearing his swords and regarded separation from them a matter of grave dishonor, he was also quick to recognize the tactical merits of muskets which appeared in Japan with the first Westerners in 1543. When the local daimyo saw one of the Portuguese take aim and shoot a duck, "the gun enters Japanese history," one historian wrote. The bravest samurai, armed with only his sword and bow, could not hope to stand up against a rival armed with one of the new imports. Before long, Japanese gunsmiths were manufacturing high-quality imitations of the Portuguese weapons in mass quantity. Their use spread in Japan more rapidly than in Europe and the skillful gunnery tactics employed by the Japanese warriors helped make these weapons a decisive factor in the battles for national unification being fought in the latter half of the sixteenth century. Once the Tokugawa shogunate had been established, however, the samurai reverted to the use of the sword, guns fell into disuse, and the manufacturing of firearms came to a complete halt. It was a rare example, perhaps the only one in history, as Noel Perrin, author of *Giving Up the Gun*, states, of a "civilized country that encountered a new piece of technology, tried it for several generations, then dropped it." It seems that the gun found favor in Japan during the late 1500s, a dog-eat-dog era of treachery and civil war when might made right, but was discarded as the Tokugawa shoguns brought order to the nation in the early 1600s. As traditional attitudes and modes of conduct were re-established, the sword regained its cult-like status as a weapon of honor, and the gun was dismissed as the weapon of a coward. Although Western-style weaponry was reintroduced into Japan and widely used in the nineteenth century, the "samurai sword" retained its mystique as a visible reminder of Japan's glorious history and the warrior's duty and was regularly carried into battle by officers in World War II.

nations were firmly, sometimes cruelly, turned away. By the nineteenth century, foreign policy wavered between a hard-line resolve to drive all foreign ships from Japanese waters by force to a moderately conciliatory approach, adopted in 1842. This allowed for providing food, water, and fuel *under certain circumstances* to ships *accidentally* arriving in Japanese ports. A true opening up of Japan was deemed out of the question by the shogun's advisers. In 1846, when Commodore James Biddle sailed into Edo Bay with a request for friendly trade, he and his two warships were ordered to "Depart as quick as possible, and not come any more in Japan." By this time, however, there were signs that various nations, notably Britain and Russia, were growing impatient with the Japanese. From different directions, the drive for empire was bringing these two countries ever closer to Japan.

SECLUSION CHALLENGED

The British Empire, the dominant force in the age of sea power, had expanded from India to Burma and Malaya in Southeast Asia and in 1842 had forced a stunning defeat on China in the notorious Opium War. That war, fought to preserve England's right to expand its narcotics exports to China in defiance of Chinese laws, exposed both the driving force of imperialist greed at its worst and the inability of the Chinese Empire to respond vigorously to the challenge posed by the British Navy. The Opium War ushered in a century-long descent into defeat and humiliation for China. As China's weakness was revealed, other European powers were encouraged to take advantage of the situation, and Russia, which until this time had faced westward, now began to see its destiny in an expansion eastward toward the Pacific. Both Britain and Russia were pressing Japan to open its doors to diplomatic and commercial contacts, and at mid-century an observer might well have predicted that it would be one of those two powers which would compel Japan to break its seclusion policy. That was not to be. The challenge to Japan would come from a wholly unexpected quarter, the United States of America.

THE LURE OF THE CHINA MARKET

America from the earliest time had faced toward Europe, where its cultural, linguistic, and religious roots were to be found. However, at mid-century, the country was also exploring in new directions. The New England whaling industry was just then reaching its zenith—home lighting and machinery lubricants depended on the oil brought in by scores of whalers which pursued their game in the North Pacific and Japanese coastal waters. Shipwrecks were inevitable and the reception castaways received in Japan was inhospitable at best. The typical case involved a period of rough treatment, imprisonment, release through the good offices of the Dutch, and eventual repatriation to America, where their plight aroused indignant protest. Concern about shipwreck victims prompted Herman Melville to write into *Moby Dick* his prediction that, "If that double-bolted land, Japan, is ever to become hospitable, it is the whaleship alone to whom the credit will be due; for already she is on the threshold."

The acquisition of Oregon and California further made the United States a Pacific power, gave the nation harbors thousands of miles closer to the Orient, and heightened interest in trade with the East. When prospects for the construction of a transcontinental railway were debated in 1847, it was seen as not simply a link between the Atlantic seaboard and California but as a link to Asia. "This, sir, is the road to India!" one early enthusiast declared. For all the glamor and riches associated with the "passage to India," however, it was the lure of a fabulous commerce with China that beckoned Yankee merchants. "The European merchant, as well as the American, will fly across our continent on a straight line to China," Senator Thomas Hart Benton declared. Japan then enters the picture as a mere way station on the Great Circle Route to China.

At mid-century, the total value of the China trade carried under the American flag was still only a small percentage of the total foreign trade of the United States, but it was creating the first American millionaires among an influential group of families, including the Delano family. (President Franklin Delano Roosevelt was linked to that era through his mother, Sara Delano.) Competition in Asian waters with Britain and the other established maritime powers stimulated feelings of achievement and confidence in young America. Symbol of that confidence was the long, sleek, white-winged clipper ship which made its appearance just before the California gold rush of 1849. Clippers, the swiftest and perhaps the most beautiful sailing vessels ever designed for ocean commerce, competed with each other to break records for speed and to give the United States a larger share of the world's peacetime carrying trade than ever before. In 1850, the clipper *Oriental* ran home to New York from the south China coast with a cargo of tea in a breathtaking eighty-one days, almost slicing in half the average time for conventional sailing ships. Making the China trade all the more attractive was the British decision of that same year to throw open the British tea market to American clippers—a testimony to England's commitment to free trade. It needs to be stressed that, while China ventures brought huge fortunes to a few, the appeal of an immensely profitable China trade turned out to be more myth than reality. It is now a century and a half after the Opium War opened China to extensive contact with the West, and the China market has yet to materialize. Nonetheless, the myth exercised a powerful effect on the American imagination.

STEAMSHIPS AND COAL

The era of the clipper ship was brief. By the early 1850s, advances in technology caused the clipper to be replaced by the more dependable ironclad steamship which made up in cargo-carrying capacity what it lost in design beauty and speed. Now one of the new merchantmen propelled by steam could raise China from Oregon in under three weeks. By contrast, it took the fastest British overland mail almost ten weeks to reach Canton from London. The United States had within its grasp the commercial domination of the Pacific. On the Pacific ocean voyages, however, an especially nettlesome problem plagued the investor with his eye on profit margins. The earliest marine boilers were notoriously inefficient. Steamships would burn so much coal over the great distance from Canton to San Francisco that there was scarcely room for tea, silk, peppers, and porcelains in the cargo hold. The obvious answer of course was a coaling station to permit refueling in the mid-Pacific. The Sandwich Islands, as the Hawaiian Islands were then called, were considered, but nature bestowed no coal on Hawaii.

Nature did however bestow coal on Japan, in abundance. While American knowledge of the isolated Japan was scanty, rumors about the coal deposits did surface in the 1840s. Some statesmen could scarcely contain their satisfaction. Secretary of State Daniel Webster, in the kind of rhetorical flight for which he was famous, exclaimed that the coal deposits in Japan were a "gift of Providence, deposited by the Creator of all things in the depths of the Japanese Islands, for the benefit of the human family." It can be left to the reader's imagination how Webster might have responded to a similar pronouncement by Japanese concerning the deposits of gold in the hills of California. As impatience with Japan mounted, missionary groups added their support for an expedition, and Secretary of the Navy John P. Kennedy served notice on Japan that it must recognize "its Christian obligation to join the family of Christendom." Newspapers joined the call with one New Orleans journal declaring that "The world cannot stand still to accommodate a nation in night caps." By 1851, President Millard Fillmore had become convinced of the need for a naval mission to bring pressure on Japan to abandon its seclusion policy. In asking for Congressional support, the president emphasized humanitarian concern for the stranded seamen, but a Washington newspaper editor argued that the seamen issue was only a "flimsy cloak" to conceal the real objective: coal.

If the statements of Webster and Kennedy now seem truculent they were at the time entirely consistent with the spirit of "manifest destiny" then prevailing in America. The westward expansion across the North American continent which was taking place at the time was viewed as a rightful—even divinely blessed—course of events, a working out of the inevitable progress of mankind. If the murky notion of destiny could be summoned to rationalize the drive to the west coast, it could also justify the domination of northern Pacific waters and the Orient trade as a legitimate extension of American boundaries.

Not all Americans agreed with the latter proposition. Many felt that the competition for overseas empire was fraught with risk and improper for a nation founded on principles of freedom and independence. Indeed, for most of the nineteenth century, until the Spanish–American War in 1898, America did hold back. As imperialist rivalry grew and most of the world outside of Europe and the Americas was absorbed, either formally or informally, into one of the great empires of the day, the United States remained amply occupied filling out its own continental frontiers. Nevertheless, while the outright annexation of overseas territory remained exceptional, the United States was always interested in expanding its overseas economic influence, and the Perry mission to Japan offered evidence that it would not rule out the use of force if force were necessary.

THE PERRY MISSION

The man entrusted with the task of opening up Japan was Commodore Matthew C. Perry, a veteran of forty years of service, a hero of the recent war with Mexico, and a fervent disciple of manifest destiny. Absolutely convinced of the righteousness of his cause, Perry believed it "self-evident" that the United States would have to "extend its jurisdiction beyond the limits of the western continent." He wrote in 1852, "Our people must naturally be drawn into the contest for empire." Of the Japanese, Perry knew all that the scanty American archives could provide and on the basis of that information concluded that they were a "weak and semi-barbarous people," a people "vindictive in character" and so "deceitful" that customary standards of diplomacy were meaningless.

Perry, a skilled negotiator who had frequently been entrusted with diplomatic missions, was granted the unusual privilege of writing his own orders. He used the opportunity to instruct himself to seek a treaty in which Japan would agree to provide decent treatment to castaways and allow American vessels to obtain provisions and coal. In addition, he would seek to draw Japan into a trade agreement by pointing out that the Pacific "will soon be covered with our vessels" and that even limited Japanese–American trade would be mutually profitable. Should means of friendly persuasion fail, Perry authorized himself to change his tone and inform the Japanese that they would be "severely chastised" if Americans were harmed in the future. Finally, Perry provided himself with an escape clause that would allow him the broadest possible latitude in carrying out his mission. The commodore should feel assured, the instructions read, "that any departure from usage, or any error of judgment he may commit will be viewed with indulgence."

With these instructions and commanding a squadron of four ships, two of them driven by steam, backed by a force of just under a thousand and equipped with sixty-six guns, Perry entered Tokyo Bay (then called Edo Bay), in defiance of the shogun's laws, on July 8, 1853 and cast anchor a mile off the town of Uraga. The landmarks Perry encountered all had perfectly good Japanese names but more out of ignorance than arrogance, they were assigned American names on Navy's charts: Negishi Bay was transformed into Mississippi Bay; the commodore's first anchorage was comfortably nearby to "Plymouth Rock," "Point Fillmore," and "Saratoga Spit." On the hills surrounding the bay, beacon flares were lit to warn of the approach of barbarian ships, Shinto priests offered prayers of deliverance, defensive earthworks were hastily thrown up, and gunners manned their antiquated, rusting coastal batteries. In some cases, the cannon were dummies made of wood. Perry, studying them through his telescope, pronounced them "a false show."

In the confusion of the day, hearsay circulated unchecked in Edo (Tokyo) thirty miles away. Japanese on shore, bewildered by the sight of black smoke belching from the smokestacks of the steamships, were convinced that half of Perry's squadron was on fire. Some consoled themselves with the rumor that the Americans were no match for samurai because of their peculiar feet. It had been observed that, unlike Japanese footwear, American shoes were fitted with leather heels. That prompted the conclusion that the luckless foreigners had no heels on their feet and could with a deft shove be easily toppled onto their backs.

The Tokugawa shogun was not, however, caught by surprise. Both the American and European press were reporting the progress of the Perry expedi-

THE BLACK SHIPS

Japanese were struck with the black-painted hulls of Perry's ships, probably because the wood on Japanese ships was left in a natural appearance. The phrase "Black Ships" *(kurofune)* took subtle hold on the Japanese mind and in the Japanese language as a metaphor of crisis—and of Yankee aggressiveness. Even today the phrase "Black Ships" frequently appears in the remarks of politicians or editorial writers who wish to call attention to an American action deemed offensive.

tion—it had sailed east from Norfolk seven months earlier—and the Dutch had transmitted the news to the shogun. Among the first to move within sight of Perry's squadron were some small sampans bobbing up and down in the harbor while quick-sketch artists recorded for the perusal of the shogun's officers details of the rigging of the "Black Ships." Although a passing attempt was made to intercept Perry's ships, Japanese guard boats failed to secure their lines on the American vessels and the shogun's representatives resigned themselves to the necessity of a correct, if distinctly cool, reception for the foreigners. When Perry and his aides were escorted to a reception hall on the appointed day, July 14, scowls on the faces of the samurai reception committee signalled their displeasure with the proceedings, but no hostile acts were taken. Americans took great satisfaction that they had met with Japanese officials and "remained erect," that is, avoided the "disgraceful humiliations" of deep bowing and other rituals commonplace on ceremonial occasions in Japan. Commodore Perry was not aware that ten two-sworded samurai were concealed beneath the floor with orders to emerge and slay the Commodore and his aides should the visitors attempt any violence. As naval historian Samuel Eliot Morison writes in his biography of Perry, "Excellent discipline on each side prevented an explosion which might have touched off a war instead of a treaty."

Perry's initial task was to transmit to the emperor of Japan President Fillmore's letter containing the requests for a treaty. The letter, signed "Your good friend, Millard Fillmore," must have mystified the Japanese who are not given to such casual expressions of instant friendship. More than that, however, the message revealed Perry's confusion regarding the Japanese polity. There was indeed an emperor of Japan, though he resided not in Edo as some believed but in Kyoto. Although emperors were accorded ceremonial respect, they had not ruled Japan for centuries. While powerful men occasionally gravitated *around* the imperial institution, the emperors themselves were figureheads who, far from making political decisions, were barely even consulted. It was the military aristocracy, headed by the shogun, which controlled the government and, as we have seen, established and enforced the policy of national isolation.

Perry knew of the existence of the shogun—he called him the "tycoon"—but seems to have regarded him as a co-emperor. Another officer on board later wrote in explanation, "The Tycoon is their king. There is another chap somewhere to the west. The Mikado. We think he is a spiritual ruler. A pope perhaps."[1] In any case, Perry always thought that he was dealing with representatives of the emperor. The Japanese were content to leave the Americans confused on this matter. They insisted that it would be impossible for the commodore to travel to Kyoto for an audience with the emperor but did promise to transmit a copy of Fillmore's letter, a compromise which Perry accepted. Perry also was flexible enough to realize that the Japanese were not prepared to provide a quick reply to the sweeping proposals he was making. "As this is no place to negotiate with foreigners, so too we can offer you no entertainment nor hold any conference with you," Perry was told. "The letter has been received, therefore you are able to depart."Alternately conciliatory and firm, Perry had made a strong point by maneuvering his ships closer to the shogun's headquarters at Edo than any other had dared and had surveyed the bay in preparation for any future contingency. He could now afford to pull back. He would sail for China and return the following spring for the Japanese response. "Would he return with all four vessels?" he was asked. "Probably more," Perry replied. With drums obbligato provided by Marine musicians, "Yankee Doodle" rang out on Japanese soil for the first time, and the commodore made his way back to his flagship. After only nine days in Japanese waters, Perry sailed away.

> The Japanese have enthusiastically borrowed foreign words, chiefly English, so much so that dictionaries of "borrowed words" (*gairaigo*) cannot keep up with the process. Much rarer has been the reverse process, of Japanese words entering the English language. "Tycoon" (more properly *taikun*), literally a "great prince," was sometimes used to refer to the shogun in his dealings with foreigners. In English, it has taken on overtones of great business wealth.

DEBATING THE AMERICAN DEMANDS

The Perry Expedition placed the Tokugawa shogunate in the most perilous position it had known and posed hard alternatives.[2] Japan's hallmark policy, isolation, was being openly challenged. While tactful, the American commodore had made it clear that the only reply which would be acceptable to the

---

[1] The word *mikado*—it refers to the "exalted gate" of the imperial palace—added to the air of "oriental inscrutability." Though seldom used by Japanese, early Japan experts in the West adopted it as a synonym for the emperor. In 1885, it gained international currency when Gilbert and Sullivan's operetta *Mikado* acquainted audiences with the "gentlemen of Japan."
[2] The shogun in power at time of Perry's first visit (Tokugawa Ieyoshi) died shortly after Perry's departure. Typical of the confusion surrounding who-was-who in the political hierarchy, Perry and his officers believed that it was the emperor who had died. Because the shogun's successor (Tokugawa Iesada) was young and incompetent, power devolved into the hands of advisers, notably Abe Masahiro.

United States was one which would effectively end national seclusion. Resistance would be all but useless. The shogun knew, perhaps even better than Perry, just how imperiled his defenses were. It was not just the superiority of the foreigner's ships and weapons but the vulnerability of the shogunal capital. Edo was one of the world's largest cities and its population of more than a million survived on seaborne supplies of rice. The configuration of Edo Bay, less than five miles wide at the entrance channel, would permit a hostile fleet to blockade Edo and impose starvation on its inhabitants. And yet, bowing to the demands of the foreigner would be a humiliating move that would enable rival daimyo, some of whom had been nursing grudges against the Tokugawa for 250 years, to muster support for his overthrow.

In his consternation, the shogun took the unprecedented step of consulting all the daimyo in the hopes of generating some kind of a consensus which might diminish the political damage that would accompany a treaty settlement with the United States. Though more than two hundred daimyo responded, there was little consensus. Some few advocated outright rejection of the foreigner's demands. The views of this stalwart minority are revealing. Most harbored no illusions concerning the nation's material weakness compared to the West but stressed that it was moral decay that had sapped the nation's will to resist. They knew that their rallying cry of *joi* (expel the barbarian) and rejection of Perry's demands might well lead to defeat in the short run. However, they were confident that such a defeat would have a shock effect on the nation which would bring about a rejuvenation of the warrior spirit that had been eroding during the long period of peace that had accompanied national isolation. They argued passionately that spiritual power, based on the samurai traits of courage and discipline, constituted the true "national essence" of Japan, and once the nation was unified in recognizing this spiritual power, Japan would prevail.

This emphasis on the importance of national unity and determination, a potent ingredient in modern Japanese nationalism, was strikingly articulated by the samurai scholar Aizawa Seishisai whose *Shinron* (New Proposals), though written some years earlier, was widely read during the crisis year of 1853 and appealed to many Japanese, even those who suggested more-moderate tactics in coping with the Perry demands. Aizawa underscored the link between Christianity and conquest:

> Now we must cope with the foreigners of the West, where every country upholds the law of Jesus and attempts therewith to subdue other countries. Everywhere they go they set fire to shrines and temples, deceive and delude the people, and then invade and seize the country. Their purpose is not realized until the ruler of the land is made a subject and the people of the land subservient.

In arguing for vigorous antiforeignism to protect the "divine realm" (*shinkoku*), Aizawa cited an ancient adage which stressed the value of bold action even when it seemed futile. "Put a man in a position of inevitable death, and he will emerge unharmed," went the old saying. "The ancients also said that the nation would be blessed if all in the land lived as if the enemy were right on the border. So, I say, let a policy for war or peace be decided upon first of all, thus putting the entire nation into the position of inevitable death," Aizawa insisted in his uncompromising call to "smash the barbarians whenever they come in sight."

For the most part, however, the replies which the shogun received counselled the impossible: peace and procrastination. It was easy enough for scores of daimyo, distant from the center and with no need to confront the foreigners, to advise the shogun to avoid conflict *and* stall for time. The shogun gave lip-service to this impractical advice but knew that it was not a realistic option. Moreover, the shogun was well aware that Britain, France, and Russia were all poised to challenge Japan, and there was fear, well justified, that the Europeans would impose even harsher demands than the Americans. To foreclose that possibility the shogun decided on a "realistic" foreign policy which involved concessions to Perry followed by efforts to strengthen Japan. The shogun's realism was confirmed by the early re-appearance of Perry's squadron, now expanded to eight ships, nearly, a quarter of the U.S. Navy, in February 1854.

TREATY RELATIONS

After a month of negotiations and compromises on both sides, Japanese negotiators bowed to the inevitable, and a historic treaty ending Japanese isolation was signed at the port of Kanagawa on Edo Bay near what was then the small fishing village of Yokohama. Befitting the solemn occasion, champagne toasts were offered. ("It seemed to be their favorite drink," one officer noted.) The American national anthem was played (national anthems were not an Asian custom), salutes were fired (also not an Asian custom and seen as a typical example of the belligerent manners of Westerners), banquets were held, and gifts exchanged. These ceremonial niceties measure some of the cultural distance that existed between East and West. At one particularly tense junction in the negotiations, the Americans sought to break the ice by asking Japanese delegates to bring their wives to a dance. The puzzled Japanese could scarcely contain their mirth at a suggestion so much at odds with Japanese custom which dictated that state affairs, even at the ceremonial level, were the exclusive domain of men.

The presents given by the Japanese at the treaty-signing ceremonies, fine porcelain cups, gold-sprinkled lacquerware boxes, rich brocades and silks, all exquisitely wrapped, reflected artistic and decorative skills and subtle nuances in gift-giving that went unappreciated by the American envoys. By contrast, the official gifts presented by the United States ran to the practical and utilitarian: various mechanical devices heretofore unseen by the Japanese including a telegraph and a working, quarter-sized model railroad complete with rails, ties, nuts and bolts. Firearms manufacturer Samuel Colt, hearing that Japan was populated by large armies of warriors none of whom carried sidearms, sent along a pair of six-shooters with the hope of developing a new market. Illustrated vol-

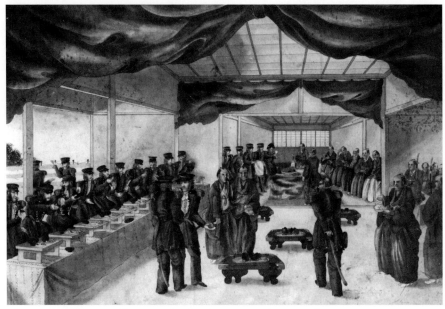

From a Japanese scroll, 1854, showing banquet for Perry's officers.

umes of the *War with Mexico* were presented to the Japanese dignitaries, perhaps with the intention of impressing them with the might of America. Greeting cards were exchanged; one of the American officers was so impressed with the fine quality of one he received that he later had it printed—upside down—with his memoirs. "Ethiopian minstrels," sailors in black-face presented a song-and-dance ensemble and some thirty Japanese sumo wrestlers put on a demonstration of their skills. Although highly ritualized, entirely bloodless and without mayhem, sumo wrestling was found to be "brutal" by the American guests who, as Morison wryly notes, were accustomed to "bareknuckled boxing matches of a hundred or more rounds."

And for the first time, American sailors were given shore leave to explore the Japanese locale, sample Japanese cuisine, experiment with chopsticks, and imbibe the native rice-wine called *sake*. A visit to the public baths seems to have been a popular diversion. Dr. James Morrow, the expedition's botanical expert, was unstrung by what he saw there and reeled—we imagine—back to his ship to report on the "licentiousness and degradation of these cultivated heathen." His official journal included this expression of indignation:. "A scene at the public baths, where the sexes mingle indiscriminately, unconscious of their nudity, was not calculated to impress the Americans with a very favorable opinion of the inhabitants." This was, of course, the age of Victorian prudery when, as one writer reminds us, proper Bostonians "draped the nude statues in their museums and on occasion even put little trousers on the legs of their pianos."

U.S. Marines "testing the flesh" of a Sumo wrestler, 1854.

Japanese artists were endlessly fascinated by the Americans and entertained by their antics. A lively retail market sprung up among Edo townspeople hungry for eyewitness pictures of the *ketojin* ("hairy foreigners")—the prevalence of bearded faces earned Caucasians that epithet. The captions accompanying the pictures on one scroll reveal the easy-going informality of these first encounters. "This picture shows how, entering a hair oil shop, [a sailor] mistook hair oil for something edible and, tasting it, was greatly dumbfounded." "Picture of an American in a Shimoda inn dallying fondly with harlots." "Picture of American sailors dancing about under the influence of strong drink." "This picture shows how at Daian-ji, a temple in Shimoda, [two sailor-photographers] took great pains to record the appearance of a courtesan to show the American king." Perry, who is invariably described in contemporary American accounts as "stern" and "unsmiling," is captured in a thoroughly demonic caricature by the scroll's anonymous painter. Though Perry was in real life cleanshaven, the artist provided him with a beard to fulfil the *ketojin* stereotype.

The Treaty of Kanagawa was a compromise. It provided assurances of good treatment for the shipwrecked and the opening of two ports, Shimoda and Hakodate[3] to ships seeking provisions. The Japanese had preferred to open but one port, the commodore had asked for six. Japanese authorities were not willing to discuss trade relations, and Perry relented on this important point. Instead, it was

---

[3]One of the enduring snags in the Japan–U.S. nexus is pronunciation. Thus, sailors in the first American squadron arriving at Hakodate called it "Hakky" or "Hack yr. daddy."

ENTREPRENEURIAL SPIRIT

William Heine, the official artist of the Perry expedition and a keen observer of Japanese ways, writes in his journal of his ship's two visits to Hakodate:

"Two large trader junks, arriving from Edo while we lay in the harbor, delivered many items for sale, including a great lot of superbly handsome lacquerware. Shops had nearly doubled in number in the interval; shopkeepers' profits from us had obviously quickened the entrepreneurial spirit. Prices at the same time had dropped as competition increased. Only let enough American ships visit the ports we have opened, and the Japanese get used to trade with us, and both sides I feel sure will enjoy a brisk trade. . . . I met universally a deep desire to learn the English word for every last thing. As a result many people besides the interpreters have grown notably more fluent in our language. Already most shopkeepers make themselves understood quite well."

agreed that an American consul could be dispatched in Japan to negotiate a commercial treaty. The man chosen for the task was a New York merchant with business experience and several years of residence in the Far East, Townsend Harris.

Harris was posted to Japan in 1856 but found the Japanese far from hospitable. For fourteen months, the patient and resourceful Harris remained

The caption to this depiction of the Perry mission at play reads, "American soldiers dancing under the influence of strong drink."

Commodore Matthew Calbraith Perry, daguerreotype by Mathew Brady.

largely cut off from the world in the first American consulate in Japan—an abandoned temple in the port of Shimoda near Edo. Harris endured his rat- and spider-infested dwelling, the lack of companionship, and an unfamiliar diet which may have contributed to his chronic "St. Anthony's Fire" (indigestion). The samurai guards assigned to protect the American consul were more appropriate for a prisoner than a diplomat and yet, in the end, did not prevent a fatal assault on Harris's only assistant, the Dutch interpreter Heusken. For more than a year, Harris was restricted to contact with only minor officials. By 1858, however, shogunal authorities were ready to accept the principle negotiating premises of Harris, that the steamship was destined to make the whole world "like one family" and that no nation could hope to stand aloof from others in this family. Further resistance from Japan would likely prompt military intervention by the obdurate British, who were anxious to impose on Japan the same harsh treaty conditions which it was obtaining by force at that very time from China. Rather than imperil its own national honor and independence in a violent clash with Britain, it behooved Japan to abandon for good its national isolation and join the family of nations by accepting the trade treaty America offered.

In 1858, the shogun relented. The Harris Commercial Treaty marked the true opening of Japan to trade and foreign residence. It opened up other "treaty ports" and granted extraterritorial rights to American residents in Japan. Extraterritoriality, already a well-entrenched feature of Sino–Western treaty rela-

"A true portrait of Perry, envoy of the Republic of North America," reads the caption to this caricature by an unknown Japanese artist.

tions, granted the foreigner exemption from native law and allowed him to be tried in his own courts by his own judges. In addition, the Harris treaty compelled the Japanese to place limitations on their import and export duties to the advantage of U. S. trading interests. The treaty set the pattern for relationships between the other Western powers and Japan in the years ahead.

As treaty relations between the United States and Japan were normalized, living conditions for the hard-pressed Townsend Harris also improved. Harris was afforded a change in diet, for example, when the government permitted him to purchase beef. A placard in Tokyo marks the spot where the first cow was slaughtered to provide meat "for human consumption." Of more interest to future generations of Japanese was a young woman assigned by Japanese authorities to duties at the American consulate. Historians dispute whether Okichi was a prostitute or a washerwoman performing mundane household chores, but popular literature has made a legend of Okichi as a beautiful courtesan engaged in a distasteful but patriotic spy mission at the expense of the churchly, decorous American diplomat. The journals of Harris do not refer to liaisons, romantic or otherwise, with Okichi. Hollywood, casting John Wayne as Harris, perpetuated the romantic legend in the 1958 movie, *The Barbarian and the Geisha*.

From the standpoint of the United States, commercial relations with Japan were now on a solid footing. Within two years, the little fishing village of Yokohama was transformed into a bustling international port with a rapidly growing foreign settlement boasting banks, warehouses, great mansions, hotels, and its own English-language newspaper. Christian missionaries began to arrive in 1859 even though it would be several more years before the seventeenth-century ban on Christianity would be formally lifted. Elegantly dressed foreign merchants and their wives out for a "Sunday parade" on the harbor embankment, known as the bund, gave Yokohama an air of cosmopolitan prosperity.

However, the foreigners' prosperity was won at the expense of Japan's dignity. The treaties forced on Japan by the United States were only the opening wedge. In rapid succession, the Dutch, Russians, British, and French took advantage of the obvious weakness of Japan to dictate their own treaties, each of which further escalated the inequities of Japan's relationship with the West. Furthermore, by virtue of the "most-favored-nation" clauses inserted in each of the treaties, each Western power automatically received any privilege or concession that was granted to the *most* favored power. The result was that Japan became the victim of an interlocking network of unequal treaties, backed up with the implied use of force. Until Japan could extract itself from this treaty relationship with the Western powers, it was unlikely that it could regain its pride and sovereignty. To appreciate from a Japanese perspective how

---

POINT–COUNTERPOINT: TWO VIEWS ON PERRY'S VISIT TO JAPAN

"Perry opened Japan. He did it with tact and forbearance. He came not as a conqueror but as a peaceful envoy to invite Japan into the society of nations. . . . Japan was fortunate that her first relations were with the United States. We were not building an Empire and were not a militaristic nation. Trade with the Orient was becoming important, however, and it was natural that we should trade with Japan."

—John K. Emmerson, U. S. State Department, memo, 1942.

"Haven't you ever heard of Perry? Don't you know anything about your own country's history? . . . Tokugawa Japan believed in isolation; it didn't want to have anything to do with other countries, and had its doors locked tightly. Then along came Perry from your country in his black ships to open those doors; he aimed his big guns at Japan and warned that 'If you don't deal with us, look out for these; open your doors, and negotiate with other countries too.' And when Japan did open its doors and tried dealing with other countries, it learned that all those countries were a fearfully aggressive lot. And so for its own defense it took your own country as its teacher and set about learning how to be aggressive. You might say we became your disciples. Why don't you subpoena Perry from the other world and try *him* as a war criminal?"

—General Ishiwara Kanji, in testimony to the International Military Tribunal for the Far East, 1947.

inequitable the new treaties were, imagine that Japanese envoys had come to America, dictated import–export tariffs to Washington, dispatched Japanese judges to try Japanese residents of San Francisco in Japanese courts and sent Buddhist missionaries to New Orleans, where their rights would be protected by gunboats of the Imperial Navy. Renegotiation of these humiliating "unequal treaties" would become a principal object of Japanese statesmen for the remainder of the nineteenth century and a principal motivating force impelling a new generation of Japanese patriots to modernize their nation so that it would stand as an equal to the mighty nations of the West.

SAMURAI AT THE WHITE HOUSE

As required by the Harris Commercial Treaty, the shogun despatched an embassy to the United States in the spring of 1860, the ambassador and a retinue of more than 170 samurai and other retainers arriving in Washington less than a year before the U.S. Civil War would break out. It was the first official mission sent abroad by the government of Japan since seclusion began, the first to carry the rising sun emblem of Japan across the Pacific. The political significance of the mission is slight—there was a formal exchange of ratification instruments of the Harris Treaty—but the mission provides an almost laboratory condition for examining the earliest responses of Japanese and Americans to each other.

Fortunately, many of the Japanese delegates kept diaries and notebooks in which they recorded their impressions of their journey. The sights and encounters which caught the attention of the often bewildered Japanese serve as a measure of cultural and social distances between East and West in 1860. After more than a century of contacts, some of the gap remains to be bridged.

Americans live by informality, enjoy casual first-name basis relationships and like to dispense with ceremony as quickly as possible. The Japanese, by contrast, as inheritors of the Confucian tradition, associate good manners with formal etiquette, rite, and rituals. The social codes of the Japanese spell these observances out with meticulous detail, leaving few situations where the Japanese feels comfortable acting "on his own." "Sticking to the rules," then, is a major virtue for Japanese and reflects their commitment to the teachings of Confucius, who taught that man's highest aim should be the achievement of social harmony.

It is not surprising, then, that Japanese records abound in perplexed commentaries on their hosts' manners. They were astonished to discover the president (James Buchanan) walking from the White House to a hotel reception without any entourage—this was long before the Secret Service—and wearing an ordinary business suit. They were somewhat offended at their initial reception at the State Department. They were treated cordially enough, indeed as though they had been old friends, one envoy wrote, but "without the slightest etiquette." The Americans, for their part, were dumbfounded by the barrage of questions they received from the Japanese concerning official protocol: Should the Japanese take off their shoes in the White House (as is the custom when entering a residence in Japan), where and how often should they exchange bows (which in Japan are not only the equivalent of a handshake but a means of paying respect), and which salutations were appropriate in addressing men of high rank. Although the Americans had little of the Japanese appreciation for the symbolic language of politics, they did caution the visitors against addressing Buchanan as "Your Majesty, the President of the United States" in a short sermon on the American Revolution.

The Japanese were endlessly intrigued by the high respect paid to women—men tip their hats to women on the street, one noted, but they don't show the same courtesy to their own parents! Another commented, "Whenever there aren't enough chairs, men stand by and women sit down. When a wife is thirsty, she makes her husband bring her a glass." Vice-Ambassador Muragaki was not entirely pleased to find himself seated at a White House banquet next to the president's niece who tried to pry from him his opinion on such weighty topics as the complexion of American versus Japanese women. "So typically feminine," the ambassador sighed to his diary.

Ballroom dancing evoked wonderment as this passage reveals:

> Music started, and to my amazement I saw an officer in uniform put his arm around a lady's waist and they began to jump around the room on their toes. Others were soon doing the same. We were extremely curious, and when we enquired what we were seeing, we discovered that this was a dance. . . . We witnessed this spectacle of men and bare-shouldered women hopping about arm-in-arm with one another with such wonder, I began to doubt whether we were on earth or some other planet.

It seemed so strange, the diarist wrote, because in Japan dancing is not for men—certainly not for dignified military men—but is performed only by "professional girls and women."

The visitors knew something of American history and knew the honored place that George Washington had in the United States. Coming from a country in which pedigree and heritage counted for much, they constantly inquired about the descendants of the Father of the Republic. They were astonished to find that none seemed to be around and taken aback at the total indifference on the part of the Americans to their questions. Similarly, they were puzzled that Buchanan "should be childless and still a bachelor, although he is over seventy, with no one to continue his line." "This would be unthinkable in Japan," the ambassador wrote.

An inspection of the Smithsonian museum brought shock to the ambassadors when they found mummies displayed alongside birds and beasts. Such a crude disregard for the remains of someone's ancestors offended Japanese standards of filial piety and prompted one to write, "These foreigners are not nicknamed barbarians for nothing." A visit to the halls of Congress provided still more of a culture shock. In Japan, political dialogue was (and is) expected to conform to prescribed rules of etiquette. Expressions of personal opinion and even strong disagreement are perfectly proper, but they must be made, in the words of a Japanese writer, "tentatively and unobtrusively so that they will subtly harmonize with the consensus that all are expected to do their utmost to bring about." Imagine, then, the confusion as the Japanese envoys are escorted to the visitors' gallery to observe the highest lawmaking body of America at work. Ambassador Muragaki describes the scene:

> One of the members was on his feet, screaming at the top of his voice and gesticulating wildly like a madman. When he sat down, his example was followed by another, and yet another. Upon our inquiring what it was all about, we were informed that all the affairs of state were thus publicly discussed, and that the Vice-President made his decision after he heard the opinion of every member. . . . The way they behaved, with the Vice-President presiding on the elevated platform, the whole scene reminded us, we whispered among ourselves, of our fishmarket at Nihonbashi.

The Japanese were observers, and they were also the observed. The reporting of the Japanese mission found in American newspapers and magazines of the day abound in condescension. A few to be sure voiced self-criticism or attempted to understand the visitors' culture. "Etiquette which almost stands as a State religion with the Japanese had to be studied carefully," commented a San Francisco newspaper after reporting on the arrival of the group in that city. One east-coast magazine, after a particularly difficult day in which the embassy had been jostled and taunted by unruly crowds at a parade, contrasted the unfailing courtesy of the visitors with the vulgar curiosity of the crowds, allowed that the Japanese were men of character and refinement to whom the New World could teach nothing in "propriety of demeanor."

For the most part, though, the smugness and the racism of the news accounts make chilling reading even today. A New York newspaper reporter covering a White House reception commented at length on the difficulty he had controlling laughter at the envoys as they arrived: "To speak honestly, they looked a comical group," he wrote. Descriptions of the visitors are frequently laced with words like "monkeys" and "Niggers" and cartoon caricatures invariably depict the Japanese in a degrading, sometimes subhuman fashion. The distinguished *Harper's Weekly* ran a cartoon in which a samurai-robed man with apelike facial features is approaching a self-satisfied Yankee reading a copy of what else— *Harper's Weekly*—under a chandelier of illumination which provides "Art," "Literature" and "Commerce." "If you please, I would like to borrow a little of your light," the uncivilized visitor pleads.

In balance, the effort to understand seems to have come more from the Japanese side than the American. Puzzled at hearing that high-ranking military officers sometimes attended the funeral of ordinary soldiers, Ambassador Muragaki wrote, "My countrymen suspect that the Americans, having no sense of either ceremony or true hierarchic distinction, are ruled by the expression of sincerity." A thoughtful analysis and, because of the importance given to sincerity in Japan, a high compliment.

The ambassador, in a touchingly naive, yet admirable, attempt to grasp democracy, a concept totally alien to Japanese in 1860, writes of his initial impressions of the White House. When shown "that enormous house," the political center of the nation, empty save for the bachelor president, and exhibited then as now to thousands of touring citizens, "I felt as though I had been bewitched by a badger," he wrote. The ambassador continued:

> . . . I believe I understand. This is the United States, where there is no king at the head of affairs. The people elect the president, so naturally he has to be nice to them. In reality, the entire American nation is entertaining us. How extraordinary!

THE IMPACT OF ISOLATION

The long period of national isolation did not mean cultural disaster for Japan. On the contrary, it is as if the Japanese, cut off from foreign influences, turned inward and developed their own native artistic and literary traditions to perfection.

The theater enjoyed a particularly dazzling and varied place on the cultural scene. Japan's classical theater, *No* drama, associated with the aristocracy from the time of its origins in the fourteenth century, is stately and slow moving. The best *No* performances, combining poetic chant, mime, and a solemn posture-dance, achieve an otherworldly sense of mystery that is heightened by the use of exquisitely carved masks and fantastic costumes. The *kabuki* theater developed in the seventeenth century in response to the growth of a lively urban merchant class which demanded more plebeian amusements, less mystery, and more action and excitement on stage. While kabuki reigned supreme in Edo, the puppet theater *(bunraku)* gained its biggest following in the Kansai region (Osaka–Kobe) to the southwest. It was brought to its fullest development by the dramatist Chikamatsu Monzaemon (1653–1724) who transformed popular entertainment into enduring theater in plays whose plots frequently centered on irreconcilable conflicts between human emotion *(ninjo)* and moral duty *(giri)*. These theatrical forms all survive today—flourish may be too strong a word—in spite of the inroads made by Western theater and the cinema.

Haiku poetry reached perfection with writers like Matsuo Basho (1644–1694), master of the art of miniaturization that is the hallmark format of this seventeen-syllable poetic style, and even today, Japan's most often quoted poet. In the graphic arts, the Tokugawa period saw the appearance of multicolored woodblock prints which were reproduced in large numbers and thus brought art to the masses. This vibrant art form, which was later to excite critics and inspire artists in the West—among them Degas, Gauguin, and Tolouse-Lautrec—

"Pray what can I do for you?" the American gentleman asks "our visitor" from Japan. From Harper's Weekly, *June 2, 1860, on the occasion of the first Japanese embassy to the United States.*

reached a dazzling culmination with the master landscapists Hokusai and Hiroshige who were at their peak in the first half of the nineteenth century.

Nor did isolation bring economic stagnation. The long years of peace and stability permitted Japan to prosper. Cities flourished and expanded in size— Edo, with its million people, may have been the world's largest metropolis by about 1750. In the countryside, cultivated acreage doubled and diligent attention to better seed strains, improved fertilizers, and multiple cropping all raised output. In addition, there was a shift from subsistence farming to the growing of commercial crops, and increasingly large numbers of farmers were engaged in cottage handicrafts, food processing, sake brewing, and the silk industry. While there were wide gradations of wealth and power and some violent unrest, notably in the countryside, the standard of living in Japan was high. Comparative data are hard to verify, but Japan was quite likely the most affluent nation in Asia by the time of the Perry visit. And the high standard of living in turn permitted a wide diffusion of basic education, with the result that Japan had literacy rates that were comparable to European nations at the time and far higher than the rates of many third-world countries, even today.

After all that is said, however, one overshadowing effect of isolation remained. Japan had been bypassed by the scientific revolution going on in Europe. There was, it is true, a precious flow of information filtering in through Japan's one window to the West, the Dutch outpost at Deshima. So-called "Dutch Scholars," samurai permitted by the authorities to study the Dutch language in order to be able to read Dutch tracts on such topics as medicine, astronomy, and botany, knew something of the scientific breakthroughs occurring in Europe. Pioneer surgeons like Sugita Gempaku (1733–1817), working with a scalpel in one hand and a Dutch dictionary in the other, came to appreciate how much more accurate European knowledge of human anatomy was compared to the Chinese sources upon which Japanese had relied for centuries. These Dutch Scholars became an important source of agitation for change, but they were few in number, were widely regarded as eccentrics, and were always subject to harsh crackdowns by shoguns suspicious of any contact with Westerners. Save for these exceptional men, Japanese knew nothing of the explosion of scientific inventions and insights that were radically altering the world's knowledge of physics, chemistry, medicine, geology, and mathematics and creating armies and navies of surpassing might.

Still less did they know of the more-recent changes, that had begun in Britain in the late 1700s, known as the Industrial Revolution. These changes, which had spread to other parts of Europe and to North America, permitted a quantum leap in the production of goods through the introduction of power-driven machinery and the development of new methods of factory organization. The wealth acquired from the new industrial enterprises and the drive for empire had produced an expansion of Western military technology that now, with Perry's

A DUTCH SCHOLAR DESCRIBES HIS PARTICIPATION IN THE DISSECTION OF A HUMAN CADAVER

"The Chinese *Book of Medicine (I Ching)* says that the lungs are like the eight petals of the lotus flower, with three petals hanging in front, three in back, and two petals forming like two ears and that the liver has three petals to the left and four petals to the right. There were no such divisions, and the positions and shapes of intestines and gastric organs were all different from those taught by the old theories. . . . That day, after the dissection was over, we decided that we also should examine the shape of the skeletons left exposed on the execution ground. We collected the bones, and examined a number of them. Again, we were struck by the fact that they all differed from the old theories while conforming to the Dutch charts. . . . At that time I did not know the twenty-five letters of the Dutch alphabet. I decided to study the language with firm determination, but I had to acquaint myself with letters and words gradually."

—Sugita Gempaku, The Beginning of the Dutch Studies, (1815).

arrival, threatened Japan with the same fate China was suffering—defeat and the humiliation of being on the receiving end of "gunboat diplomacy."

The result was a sense of alarm that was to govern Japan's response to the West and much of its history after 1853. When Perry arrived in that year, Japan had no transportation faster than a horse, no telegraphy, no ocean-going vessels, no modern factories, no universities, no steam engines, and no forges capable of casting cannon. Traditional wisdom said that the Westerners were barbarians from whom nothing of worth could be learned. However, the scraps of Western scientific lore assembled by the Dutch Scholars, the awareness of China's deepening tragedy, and the contacts with America all added up to a single message: Japan was faced with a terrible crisis that demanded radical change at home and a new and more open attitude toward the outside world.

PERRY PREDICTS

First-hand contact with the Japanese would cause Perry to alter his initial unflattering view of the Japanese. Soon after completion of his historic mission, in 1856, he was providing to a New York society of geographers a sympathetic interpretation of the Japanese isolation policy which he said stemmed from the "abominable wrongs" committed by the Christian missionaries of an earlier time. He went on to speak of the Japanese as a refined and rational people and allowed that he had "never met in any part of the world, even in Europe, with a people of more unaffected grace and dignity." Noting the great dexterity of the Japanese in the practical and mechanical arts, the commodore concluded with a stunningly accurate prediction (albeit one implying that the "civilized world" did not include Japan).

> Their curiosity to learn the results of the material progress of other peoples, and their readiness in adapting them to their own uses, would soon, under a less exclusive policy of government which isolates them from national communion, raise them to a level with the most favored countries. Once possessed of the acquisition of the past and present of the civilized world, the Japanese would enter as powerful competitors in the race for mechanical success in the future.

It is evident from other remarks made by the admiral on that same occasion that he was keenly aware of the geopolitical significance of his mission for the future. It seemed clear, he said, that the people of America would "extend their dominion and their power, until they shall have brought within their mighty embrace the Islands of the great Pacific, and placed the Saxon race upon the eastern shores of Asia." In doing so, however, the Americans would inevitably collide with a Russia intent upon stretching its domains eastward and southward. "And thus," Perry foresaw, "the Saxon and the Cossack will meet once more, in strife or in friendship, on another field. Will it be friendship: I fear not!"

ADDITIONAL READING

Interesting anecdotal accounts of the early contacts between Japan and the United States are found in Katherine Plummer, *The Shogun's Reluctant Ambassadors: Sea Drifters* (1984); Pat Barr, *The Coming of the Barbarians: The Opening of Japan to the West* (1967); Foster Rhea Dulles, *Yankees and Samurai: America's Role in the Emergence of Modern Japan, 1791–1900* (1965); Lewis Bush, *77 Samurai: Japan's First Embassy to America* (1968); and Harold S. Williams, *Foreigners in Mikadoland* (1963).

The most comprehensive account of the Perry expedition is *Yankees in the Land of the Gods: Commodore Perry and the Opening of Japan* (1990) by Peter Booth Wiley. The distinguished naval historian Admiral Samuel Eliot Morison has written the definitive biography of Perry: *"Old Bruin": Commodore Matthew C. Perry, 1794–1858* (1967). Also useful are *Black Ships off Japan: The Story of Commodore Perry's Expedition* by Arthur Walworth (1946) and *With Perry to Japan: A Memoir by William Heine* (translated, with an introduction and annotations by Frederic Trautmann, 1990). *The Black Ship Scroll* by Oliver Statler (1960) is a lively account of the Perry Expedition, based on color plates of a painted handscroll by a Japanese eyewitness to the events of 1853–1854.

As We Saw Them: The First Japanese Embassy to the United States (1860) by Masao Miyoshi (1979) is a richly documented account of events from the perspective of the Japanese participants. *Before the Dawn* (1987), a translation by William E. Naff of Meiji-era novelist Shimasaki Toson's *Yoake*, is an effort to link together fiction and the history of mid-nineteenth-century Japan.

Two books are helpful in establishing an American context for early Japanese–American relations: Richard Hofstadter, *Social Darwinism in American Thought* (rev. ed., 1955); and Frederick Merk, *Manifest Destiny and Mission in American History: A Reinterpretation* (1963).

Books similarly useful in constructing a Japanese context for these early relations include: W. G. Beasley, *The Meiji Restoration* (1972); Donald Keene, *The Japanese Discovery of Europe, 1720–1830* (1969); and Marius Jansen, ed., *Changing Japanese Attitudes Toward Modernization* (1965). Chapters 4 and 5 of Marius B. Jansen, ed., *The Cambridge History of Japan*, Volume 5, The Nineteenth Century (1989), contain a highly useful synthesis of recent scholarship.

3

THE MEIJI REVOLUTION

Western assessments of the strength of modern Japan always stress the homogeneity of the Japanese people. Many developing countries in the modern world have had to overcome deep divisions based on language, race, religion, and political traditions before they could develop the strength which comes with unity. Japan was not frustrated by such divisions. All Japanese spoke the same language, and there was relatively little regional variation in dialects to mar communication—in sharp contrast to China, where there are a dozen major languages and hundreds of dialects. There was no significant racial variation among Japanese, nothing similar to the shading in skin color from north to south as in India, for example. Religious and moral traditions had taken root throughout Japan well over a thousand years earlier and prevailed there little disturbed by imported notions of Christianity.

Feudal Japan

Politics, however, presented a problem. True, the *ideal* of unified political rule under the authority of the emperor went back as far as the fifth century, when the Yamato clan began to extend imperial sway over the islands. Some Japanese have argued that Japan's unique place among the nations of the world derives from its imperial institution, the longest political lineage the world has ever known. The present emperor is 125th in a line which stretches back to the dawn of Japanese history, indeed into legendary times since historians now assume that the first several emperors of the traditional listing are mythical figures. The central place of these rulers in the nation's history can be seen in the fact that the emperors were regarded as *kami* in the Shinto religion which is native to Japan. *Kami* is not easily translated into English. While sometimes rendered as "God," *kami* does not refer to a single all-powerful being. There are many *kami*, some good and some bad, some exist in human form, and some inhabit striking natural objects such as waterfalls or mountains. Mount Fuji (known in Japanese as Fuji-san or less commonly Fujiyama) is an example. Emperors were thought of as *kami* because, though human, they stood above ordinary humans as awesome figures who trace their ancestry back to the Sun Goddess.

However, as we have seen, that ideal clashed with the realities of warrior maneuvering which bequeathed to Japan a legacy of political fragmentation which is typical of feudal societies. However awesome and respected Japanese emperors might be, actual political and military power slipped out of their hands early on in history, and from the twelfth to the nineteenth century real power in Japan was exercised by a hereditary military aristocracy governed by a shogun (generalissimo). Emperors continued to preside over elaborate court rituals in the ancient imperial and cultural capital of Kyoto. Among the ceremonies performed by the emperors was one in which they bestowed the title of shogun on one or another powerful warrior. The title thus was all the more imposing because it was conferred by the emperor, the lineal descendant of the Sun Goddess.

Still, though emperors might be viewed as the *source* of authority, they did not exercise authority. They might solemnize the appointment of a shogun but they did not decide who should be shogun. That was left to military councils or to the battlefield, often far away from Kyoto. Because the emperor stayed above politics, it meant that the court could not be faulted for losing wars or for other blunders. This doubtless helps explain why the imperial institution, though politically outdated, was never overthrown. A general hungry for power need not eliminate the imperial household in order to grasp power. Power came from military conquest and alliances which could be made legitimate with an emperor's endorsement. It also helps to explain why there are no dynasties such as the Hapsburgs or Romanovs rising and falling in Japanese history. Since there has been only a single imperial family, it needs no name; the emperor of Japan was simply *tenno* (heavenly sovereign).

It may be useful to compare Japanese titles and institutions to those found in France or England during Europe's feudal period. Who in Japan most closely corresponded to the King of France or the King of England? It should be clear from what we have said that it was not the Japanese emperor but the shogun, standing at the top of the pyramid of Japan's hereditary military aristocracy. Beneath the shogun were more than two hundred daimyo, regional lords who may be thought of as similar to the various noble dukes, counts, barons, and so on in the European system. The daimyo swore oaths of loyalty to the shogun and were rewarded with territory, called *han*; in Europe these domains were called *feudum* (from which comes the word *feudalism*) or more commonly *fiefs*. In their *han*, the daimyo enjoyed considerable local autonomy, including the power of taxation and the right to maintain private armies of vassals. Serving beneath the daimyo were his samurai vassals, called knights in Europe.

While the imperial court could be found in Kyoto, the shogun's headquarters moved from time to time. From 1603 until 1868, however, the Tokugawa family of shoguns dominated Japan from their castle in the center of Edo—later called Tokyo.

Japan, at the time of the Perry mission, was only a loosely organized union of largely independent feudal domains. No emperor had exercised sovereign control over these territories for more than a thousand years. And while the two hundred or so lords (daimyo) who controlled these domains had been compelled to accept the authority of the Tokugawa shoguns in 1600, many did so grudgingly. In some of the more recalcitrant domains, mothers encouraged their samurai sons to sleep with their feet pointed to the east—toward Edo—as a sign of disrespect for the shogun. Now, in the wake of the Perry mission, certain of these lords and their samurai retainers felt free to act in open defiance of the Tokugawa. The period when this defiance came to dominate the Japanese scene, 1853 to 1868, is known as the "end of the Tokugawa shogunate" *(bakumatsu).*

SATCHO DOMAINS

The concessions which the shoguns were forced to make to the foreigners in the 1850s and 1860s were seen as a "blemish on our Empire and a stain on our divine land" by rivals to the Tokugawa family. The Tokugawa had its allies, loyal retainers, and they tended to be crowded around the Tokugawa estates on the central island of Honshu. Rivals were concentrated in remoter parts of the country. Two of these rival domains, Satsuma in Kyushu and Choshu in southwestern Honshu, were particularly strong and spirited in their resistance to the shogunate. Clan loyalty was much stronger throughout Japan than any sense of national loyalty, even as foreign encroachment became more and more menacing. Samurai continued to think of themselves as "Satsuma men" or "Choshu men." The notion that they were all Japanese is a modern idea. In the *bakumatsu* era, "Japan" was just that, an idea in the minds of some farsighted ideologues rather than a reality. Though samurai from Satsuma and Choshu were frequently at each other's throats, after 1853, they managed to put aside their differences, act in occasional concert, and lead a loose coalition of other domains against the increasingly besieged Tokugawa. (The alliance between Satsuma and Choshu is signified in the term *Satcho* composed of the first syllables of the two names.)

The Satcho samurai employed antiforeign rhetoric to mobilize support for their cause. *Joi* (Expel the barbarian) was an incendiary slogan which was frequently backed up by violent acts against the foreigners—for example, Satsuma's murder of an English businessman in 1862 and Choshu's attempts to blow American, Dutch, and French ships out of the water in 1863. These reckless acts failed to achieve the desired goal of expulsion. The Westerners were not intimidated. Rather, they invariably responded with shows of strength which soon began to impress some of the most boldly antiforeign Satcho warriors with the power of the foreign barbarians and the futility of random acts of violence against them. In the meantime, however, the antiforeign incidents fur-

A print from the 1860s warns against interracial marriages with the hairy foreigners.

ther weakened the Tokugawa shogun who was ultimately held responsible by the British, Americans, French, and Dutch.

The *joi* slogan became an even more potent antishogunal rallying cry when it was yoked to another slogan, *Sonno* (Revere the emperor). Leaders of the Satcho clans had good contacts in Kyoto, not with the Emperor himself—he played no role in the events of the *bakumatsu*—but with able palace courtiers in the emperor's service, notably Iwakura Tomomi. Iwakura and the Satcho warriors came to see the merits of an "imperial restoration" as the means of shifting diffuse shogunal and clan loyalties to a new modern state, the symbol of which would be the emperor. By acting in the name of the emperor, the Satcho coalition could claim a higher legitimacy for its assault on the Tokugawa and its efforts to direct the establishment of a new government. The nation would see the Satcho as not merely serving its own selfish, partisan interests in its quarrel with the Tokugawa. Instead, the Satcho would be viewed as carrying out a noble imperial mission designed to reassert national prestige and rescue the nation from the perils brought about by Tokugawa misrule. Thus, in the final years of the *bakumatsu* era, Satcho samurai, aided by stalwarts from a few other clans, went into battle as "imperial armies." Strengthened by the moral fervor of their *Sonno-joi* convictions, these patriots seized the imperial castle in Kyoto and secured custody of the emperor in January 1868. In succeeding months, the forces of the Tokugawa and its allies were overwhelmed, and the last Tokugawa shogun was compelled to resign his titles and surrender his lands.

THE MEIJI EMPEROR

The emperor whose name is linked to these events was only fourteen when he succeeded to the throne in 1867. His personal name was Mutsuhito, but Japanese emperors are usually not referred to by their personal names. Instead, following a custom imported from China, an auspicious title was chosen not for the emperor himself but for the era during which he would rule. Mutsuhito's reign title was Meiji (Enlightened Rule). The Meiji Emperor's reign would last until his death in 1912. It was a momentous epoch which saw feudal Japan transformed from a divided and vulnerable nation into a powerful, unified Empire. By 1912, Japan was a world power, and the only nation outside of the Western world which could be considered a modern, industrialized society. The Meiji Emperor did not initiate or implement the strategies which brought about this transformation. He was therefore not comparable to the leaders of national unification movements occurring in Europe at exactly the same time. Giuseppe Garibaldi in Italy and Otto von Bismarck in Germany plotted and fought to bring unity to their divided countries and achieved final success in 1871. In Japan, the young Meiji emperor merely lent his name to the process.

The architects of the changes in Meiji Japan were by and large the same men who engineered the overthrow of the Tokugawa, local samurai, most of them from the old domains of Satsuma and Choshu. No one of these men completely dominated the Meiji era. Instead, after 1868, the dozen or so most important of them were collectively designated the "Meiji oligarchs." Just as they had skillfully used the name of the emperor to ennoble their struggle against the Tokugawa, they now launched a series of reforms to unify and strengthen Japan not in their own names—until recently they were, after all, only upstart middle-ranking warriors. Better instead to claim that the changes they were introducing reflected the imperial will. Edwin Reischauer has written that, as the Meiji emperor matured, "his views and preferences did come to have some weight, but his ministers simply took for granted that they would not only carry out the 'imperial will' but would also decide for him what it was."

In addition, the Meiji oligarchs would have to formulate new civic values in the population. These would center on a cult of respect—indeed a cult of worship—for the emperor. This presented a dilemma to the oligarchs, who were anxious to popularize the all-but-unknown emperor and at the same time create an aura of divinity around him. In order to increase the emotional bonds between subjects and sovereign, it was decided that the new emperor should undertake "imperial excursions" throughout the land. The Meiji emperor, accordingly, made no less that 102 of these tours during his forty-five-year reign, most of them in the first decade. By contrast, his thirteen predecessors during the 260 years of the Tokugawa period had made only three such trips. The emperor's birthday was celebrated as a national holiday. It is clear from the scolding tone of a reminder in the *Yomiuri* newspaper in 1881 that, at that late date, not all the citizenry were fully aware of their sovereign. "Tomorrow, the third, is *Tencho setsu*," the paper advised. "*Tencho setsu* is the birthday of Japan's emperor. . . . Formerly the shogun ruled our country, but now it is different. . . . There are a good many people who do not know the name of *Tenchi Sama* [His Imperial Majesty]. But to be born in this country and not to know it is like not knowing your parents' age. This is unforgivable." At the same time, however, the emperor was being elevated by the oligarchs to such heights "above the clouds" that it became a crime for an ordinary citizen to gaze upon him or listen to to his voice. In the end, the Meiji leadership succeeded in making the emperor both well-known and augustly remote.

The schools became one of the chief training grounds in the new civics which aimed at "unifying the spirit of the people." In classrooms, students were taught as historical fact an imperial genealogy which linked the Meiji emperor to the Sun Goddess in a "line unbroken for ages eternal." Among impressionable

JAPAN'S NATIONAL FLAG AND ANTHEM

Every nation employs symbols to strengthen feelings of national belonging among the citizenry. However, not all nations attach the same importance or the same sacredness to the various symbols which are used, nor do all peoples respond with similar emotions to national symbols. Most Americans associate a strong emotional charge with the national anthem and flag; most Japanese do not. Use of the national flag, *hinomaru*, a red sun on a white field, has declined after World War II because many associate it with the militarism of the past. The national anthem is known as *Kimigayo*, from the beginning phrase, "My Lord's reign," which celebrates the eternity of the imperial line. The lyrics are from a tenth-century anthology of poems known as the *Kokinshu*. In 1870, William Fenton, a British military bandmaster, set the words to music and for several years, this version was the unofficial national anthem. Its appeal waned—it is almost unsingable from either a Western or Japanese point of view. In 1880, a Japanese composer wrote a new melody which was put into Western notation and arranged for band by a German musician hired to replace Fenton. The melody comes from traditional court music and sounds "ponderous" to modern ears, one Japanese critic writes. Although it has been little sung in recent years, it is always played at national sumo matches, leading children to call it the "sumo theme song."

> "The regal image of the emperor that was so widely projected in the late Meiji period owed a good deal of its persuasive detail to the curiosity of the public. Accounts of the emperor's equestrian and gastronomic interests—the ability of his palate to distinguished between a fish from the Katsura River in Kyoto and one from the Tama River in Tokyo—and other imperial anecdotes found wide circulation in the popular culture of the day. The press, the woodblock printers, the manufacturers of fans, scrolls, and mementos with imperial likenesses upon them, and the generally lucrative industry of royal purveyance were always ready to foster and assuage this curiosity with the full-blown exposure and half-baked paraphernalia that royalty is heir to. Although the *Kunaisho* [Imperial Household Ministry] tried in vain to control unofficial imperial renderings, in fact the Meiji emperor, though above the clouds once again, had become more fully public property than he had ever been before."
>
> —Carol Gluck, *Japan's Modern Myths.*

youth, mythology was thus mobilized by the Meiji oligarchs in the service of the cause of national unity. The most hallowed place in every school in the land was an altar where the imperial portrait was shrouded behind velvet curtains. In the event of fire, every student and teacher knew that the first priority was the rescue of the imperial likeness. So many lives were spent in the process that the altars were eventually made of fireproof material in order to discourage excessive heroism.

On solemn occasions such as the emperor's birthday, the veil would be ceremonially opened while the assembly sang the stately anthem *Kimigayo* (My Lord's Reign). The principal, in formal attire, would intone from a scroll held in white-gloved hands the emperor's words on the subject of education, more specifically on the obligation of the schools to foster love for the nation. These school convocations made an enormous impression on children, strengthening their devotion to the national cult in a way that was more religious than patriotic. Heightening the drama of the events was the meticulous attention to protocol. Everyone was aware that the slightest impropriety, a misreading of a single syllable of the imperial utterance, for example, brought disgrace. On more than one occasion, mortified officials committed suicide to atone for errors.

The military was another institution used by the Meiji oligarchs for disseminating ideology. By reintroducing to recruits the aura of divinity that had traditionally surrounded the throne, it became possible to indoctrinate soldiers with a spirit of unquestioning obedience and sacrifice. In 1882, the principles of military loyalty were codified in an imperial rescript or message. The Meiji emperor's "Rescript to Soldiers and Sailors" emphasized valor and obedience to authority and enjoined soldiers to avoid luxury and cultivate simplicity as a way of reinforcing courage and loyalty. The rescript was issued in such a way as to

The Meiji emperor, 1872.

suggest that the emperor had directly given instructions to his private army. The norms of conduct for soldiers and sailors were thus raised to the status of personal sacred obligations to the throne. Since universal conscription had already been adopted as the basis for Japan's new military, the 1882 rescript was destined to become not simply the moral basis of military training but one of the most important means for propagating the new imperial ideology among the general population. The 2500-word rescript was memorized by all military officers, read to units on designated occasions, and carried into battle much as the Bible was by Christians in the West. Just as lore accumulated in the West surrounding tales of Christian soldiers saved from bullets by a holy medal or a copy of the Bible carried over the breast, the Imperial Rescript was said to have saved the lives of Japanese soldiers. Upon release from service, reservists would transmit the message of the rescript to their home villages.

The task of inculcating loyalty was more easily accomplished because, as shown, the Japanese people already had a strong sense of loyalty. It had been developed over centuries as a feature of the family-centered ethics of Confucianism. Now in 1868, it merely became necessary to redefine the emperor as the "father" of the entire Japanese "family," a task made easier by the homogeneity of that family. The intense spirit of loyalty had been reinforced over the centuries in Japan by the martial traditions of the samurai. Now, in 1868, it was a simple matter to shift this loyalty from the daimyo to the emperor and the state. In this way, a national patriotic ideal was promoted, according to which all citizens should dedicate their lives to repaying the "favors" showered upon them by their father-emperor.

As historian Carol Gluck has observed, a whole new vocabulary, in fact, was popularized to underscore the patriarchal benevolence of the emperor. The emperor's every act was "graciously" *(kashikokumo)* performed. His every thought reflected his "deep concern" *(omikokoro)* for his people. The token gifts, sake or cigarettes, which he occasionally bestowed on his soldiers, invariably left them "overcome with gratitude." Change was in the wind in the Meiji era, and the oligarchs never missed an opportunity to invoke the throne and associate "the progress and advance of our country" *(wagakuni no shimpo hattatsu)* with the "will of the emperor."

The Meiji oligarchs referred to their designs as a "restoration" *(ishin)*. When they spoke of the Meiji Restoration, they did not foresee that the emperor would actually exercise the supreme authority which he possessed but rather that he was being restored to a central position of honor and prominence as symbol of a nation embarking on a new course. To further underscore the changes which would ensue, the emperor's residence was moved from his traditional quarters in Kyoto to the castle previously occupied by the shogun in Edo. At the same time, in 1868, the name of Edo was changed to Tokyo (the Eastern Capital). The oligarchs had no grand plan in mind as the Meiji era began, but the imperial edicts which poured forth from Tokyo produced changes so rapid and so sweeping that, with hindsight, the Meiji Restoration might better have been termed the Meiji Revolution. Although the Meiji era was born in violence, the political, social, and economic revolution which would ensue was accomplished with remarkably little bloodshed. The protracted internal warfare which was to be a hallmark feature of China's revolutionary entrance into the modern world was avoided in Japan. It seems likely that at least some of the credit for this fortunate development belongs to the Meiji oligarchs and their successful manipulation of the emperor as "father" of a harmonious and duty-bound Japanese family.

THE CHARTER OATH

The first indication of the radical new course the leadership was contemplating came in April 1868, even before the emperor's residence had been transferred to Tokyo. On April 6, an imperial proclamation of five short clauses was read to an assemblage of four hundred officials gathered in the palace enthronement hall. It was a statement of national policy written in the form of a pledge by the Meiji emperor to his imperial ancestors and thus has become known as the "Charter Oath." The statement pledged that the old political order of the Tokugawa shoguns would be dissolved. However, far more than political change was foreshadowed by the sweeping language of the last two articles, which read as follows:

(4) Evil practices of the past shall be abandoned, and actions shall be based on international usage.

(5) Knowledge shall be sought all over the world, so as to strengthen the foundations of imperial rule.

In the most traditional of countries, a leadership which had mobilized xenophobic hatred in its rise to power was now committing itself to radical change based on a new openness to the modern West. To be sure, the language of the Charter Oath was deliberately vague, and much of the new samurai leadership still remained hostile to change, but a core group of the newly empowered rulers was remarkable for their intellectual flexibility. Kido Koin, the principal author of the Charter Oath, is a good example of the rapid shift from xenophobia to xenophilia which marked the thinking of the Meiji oligarchs and brought about "the most remakable transformation ever undergone by any people in so short a time."

Kido started his career as a lower-rank Choshu samurai and a renowned swordsman. His swashbuckling deeds as an imperial loyalist (*sonno*), occasionally assisted by his geisha[1] lover, were celebrated on the stage during his own lifetime and even today are still depicted on the screen. To his father who was a "Dutch scholar" and one of the nation's earliest medical scientists, Kido owed an early interest in Western learning. As a twenty-year-old assigned to coastal defense at the time of the Perry intrusion, Kido was able to view the menacing "black ships" with his own eyes. His hostility for the West, however, was matched by determination to learn Western ways so that Japan might meet the foreigner's challenge. Still in his early twenties, he observed foreign shipbuilding methods in Nagasaki and designed the first Western-style schooner to be built in Choshu in 1856. To his skills as a swordsman, Kido added a modern expertise in artillery. In 1864, when a Western force bombarded Choshu's coastal defenses and landed troops to destroy fortifications and rout Choshu samurai bands, it became even more clear to Kido that the secrets of Western power had to be mastered. Samurai valor and boldness, even suicidal courage, could not bring about expulsion of the barbarians. While most samurai remained convinced that it was a dishonor to abandon their swords, Kido and a few others argued that it was necessary to adopt Western military techniques and arms. While most samurai still maintained a blind anti-Western stance, Kido began to urge his countrymen to broaden contacts with the outside world.

Adding their voices to Kido's were a small number of samurai who managed to travel abroad. One of these was a fellow Choshu clansman, Ito Hirobumi. Like Kido, Ito rose from the lowest ranks of the samurai order to become a dominant figure, first in clan politics and then in the Meiji restoration. Like Kido, Ito was a xenophobic extremist. In 1862, at the age of twenty-one, he was helping

---

[1] *Geisha* are female professional entertainers, skilled at traditional (and quite respectable) singing and dancing as well as the art of conversation. They were not considered to be prostitutes, although at a certain stage in their careers, they often took a lover rather than marry. The profession still exists and commands very high prestige and wages, but the numbers have declined sharply since the years of World War II. Although Americans tend to say "gee-sha," the word should be pronounced "gay-sha."

to burn down the British legation in Edo. The next year, however, we find him smuggled aboard a foreign ship bound for England—in defiance of shogunal rules which still forbade travel abroad. Like the handful of other Japanese who travelled abroad at this time, Ito was swept off his feet by the technical superiority of the West. On his return to Japan, he writes of the unsettling experience he had when his ship was docked in the Chinese port of Shanghai. The harbor was full of ships—but none of them was Chinese. By maintaining airs of complacent superiority over the Westerner, digging in its heels and refusing to change, the great empire of China was being swamped by the West. Ito returned to Japan ready to drop the impractical slogan calling for the expulsion of the foreigners. Instead, Ito, Kido, and others began to call for a *fukoku kyohei* (prosperous nation and a strong army). With the "restoration" of the emperor, the stage was set for Ito, Kido, and their allies to turn the slogan into reality.

A REVOLUTIONARY ARISTOCRACY

The first and most revolutionary act of Meiji leaders like Kido and Ito was to abolish the samurai class—their own class. "An aristocracy," Alexis de Tocqueville wrote, "seldom yields [its privileges] without a protracted struggle, in the course of which implacable animosities are kindled between the different classes of society." Yet, that is what Japan's warrior aristocracy did soon after engineering the Meiji restoration. While the samurai differed in some respects from the European aristocrats Tocqueville had in mind, the samurai were a privileged class of people, amounting to roughly six or seven percent of the population. Their privileges were based on heredity. While there were exceptions, the general rule was that you were either born a samurai or you were not. They alone could hold office in feudal Japan; they alone could bear arms. Historian Thomas Smith, in commenting on Tocqueville's observation, declares that Japan's warrior class "did not merely surrender its privileges. It abolished them. There was no democratic revolution in Japan because none was necessary: the aristocracy itself was revolutionary."

The process proceeded as follows. The samurai from Choshu and Satsuma took the lead in engineering the return of those domains to the central government in 1869. Satcho allies followed suit in the next year. Then, in 1871, the government in Tokyo felt sufficiently strong to order all remaining domains abolished in the name of national unity. With that act, the samurai lost their position as a hereditary elite. The daimyo who had supported them and been the focus of their loyalty no longer existed. With the abolition of tolls and other economic barriers, the once-fragmented nation moved toward centralization. The country was reorganized into seventy-five prefectures (later reduced to forty-five) with governors named by Tokyo. Generous financial allowances in the form of government bonds made the program palatable to daimyo who might have been tempted to resist. Instead of two hundred-some local armies, a new centralized army was created in 1872 under the direction of a Choshu samurai, Yamagata Aritomo. The new army, it was decreed, would be based on conscription. All young men, regardless of social origin, were liable to call-up for three years of active duty and four years in the reserves. Funnelling ordinary Japanese through the army was seen by the Meiji oligarchs as a way of educating the Japanese masses to patriotism few of them felt in 1872. A conscript army and an emperor-centered spirit of nationalism melded nicely. In addition, however, by eliminating the old distinctions between commoners and samurai, Yamagata cut to the heart of the feudal status system.

In the meantime, the samurai were being discouraged from wearing their swords. An 1871 law made the custom optional. An 1876 law strictly forbade the old privilege, a tremendous psychological blow to the once-proud class. Financially, the samurai were in trouble because of the loss of the stipends they had once received from their daiymo. The Meiji oligarchs, sympathetic of course to the problems of their samurai brethren, tried to ease their plight by continuing to pay them at least a portion of their previous salaries. This, however, created such a fiscal burden to the new regime that it was forced in 1876 to commute these payments into small lump-sum payments equal to about one year of their salaries. There was hardship and grumbling and, in time, these turned into local uprisings. "Restoration" leaders, notably Saigo Takamori from the old Satsuma domain, resigned from the government in sympathy with samurai discontent. This major split in the ranks of the new government turned into a full-scale rebellion led by Saigo in 1877. For six months, the Satsuma Rebellion threatened to bring the Meiji experiment to an end, but in September the better equipped, larger army of the central government, with modern telegraphy and steamships at its disposal, crushed the revolt. Saigo, then and now, a popular hero because of his allegiance to the traditional values of the samurai class, committed *seppuku* on the battlefield. With his death, the possibility of further armed challenge to the central government was foreclosed.

All of this, however, still leaves unanswered the question why. Why did the samurai leaders of the Meiji restoration preside over the destruction of their own class? Part of the answer is surely that, while many of the samurai would be dislocated by the reforms, the oligarchs ensured *themselves* positions of leadership in the new regime. Moreover, by the end of the Tokugawa period, much of samurai power and influence depended on bureaucratic skills. After centuries of peace, samurai swordsmanship was less in demand than administrative know-how. Many samurai, in other words, had become officeholders rather than fighters. For many years to come, in the new Meiji administration there would be no other class with the experience, education, or connections to challenge the old warrior class.

The new leadership, while revolutionary, should not be given credit for being democratic. The revolution they undertook was engineered from above. Had there been a revolution from below, from peasants discontented with their lot for example, the Meiji leadership would *not* have been revolutionary. As Thomas Smith writes, "Nothing unites an aristocracy so quickly and firmly in defense of its privileges as an attack from below by classes in which it can perceive neither distinction nor virtue."

The principal motivation of the Meiji oligarchs in abolishing the old class structure, however, was related to *fukoku kyohei* (prosperous nation, strong army)—as was every program they undertook. While unfamiliar with, and unappreciative of, democracy, they knew enough of history, including the French Revolution, to grasp what happened when governments remained tyrannical and restricted liberty too harshly. There was a growing appreciation of the fact that the strength of the West did not derive simply from its military and industrial might: Social organization and attitude had as much to do with *fukoku kyohei* as guns and factories.

FUKUZAWA YUKICHI

The most influential exponent of this notion was Fukuzawa Yukichi, a low-ranking samurai. Fukuzawa was one of the first to travel abroad to both Europe and America, twice before the Restoration. He was, one historian writes, "a virtual walking antenna, eager to absorb any and all information in these foreign lands." After returning to Japan, he wrote *Conditions in the West* in 1866. Japanese readers eagerly devoured its descriptions of Western life, institutions, values, and artifacts—everything from tax systems to the chamber pot. ("You always find this thing underneath the bed when you stay in a Westerner's house.") Its easy style—simple enough to be read by a household maid, it was said—turned it into an overnight best-seller with a first-year press run of 150,000 copies. Several more books followed in coming decades and the total output of this prolific writer resulted in an astonishing 7.5 million volumes sold. No other person was to have such an impact on the thinking of both the Meiji oligarchs and ordinary citizens as Fukuzawa. He is not regarded as one of the oligarchs because he never entered government service. Instead, he became the founder in 1882 of the *Jiji Press*, one of Japan's first modern newspapers, and in 1890 of Keio University, a distinguished private university. Both institutions served as vehicles to disseminate his ideas about the need for Japan to adopt not only Western technology but its values as well. In doing so, Fukuzawa became an "engineer of civilization," in his own words, and probably the most articulate spokesman of the *bunmei kaika* era, the first two decades of the Meiji period. *Bunmei kaika* means "civilization and enlightenment" and the key theme of writers like Fukuzawa was that civilization and enlightenment *as found in the West* were the gauge by which one measured progress along the road to civilization.

Fukuzawa observed that what made the West strong was not its upper class and not its poor but rather a dynamic, independent-minded middle class, precisely what Japan did not have. Japan could move into the modern world and compete with the West only if there was an explosion of energy and talent provided by a broad spectrum of the population. For Japan to develop a vital middle class, it was obvious that the samurai class first had to be discarded. Then, incentive to improve and work hard had to be given to all who could prove themselves in the new competitive environment. More than that, it was necessary to foster in Japan a spirit of personal independence and freedom.

POUNDING AN EGALITARIAN SPIRIT INTO BACKWARD FARMERS
"It was not only among the samurai and ruffians but even among the plain farmers and townsmen that I had to oppose the old tradition. Once when I was taking my children to Kamakura and Enoshima for a holiday, we met a farmer coming on horseback as we were passing along the seashore. As soon as he saw us, he jumped off the horse.

I caught hold of his bridle and said, 'What do you mean by this?'

"The farmer bowed as if in great fear and began to apologize in his voluble way.

'No, no,' I said. 'Don't be a fool! This is your horse, isn't it?'

'Yes, your honor.'

'Then why not ride on your own horse? Now, get back on it and ride on.'

The poor fellow was afraid to mount before me.

'Now, get back on your horse,' I repeated. 'If you don't, I'll beat you. According to the laws of the present government, any person, farmer or merchant, can ride freely on horseback without regard to whom he meets on the road. You are simply afraid of everybody without knowing why. That's what's the matter with you.'"

—Fukuzawa Yukichi, *The Autobiography of Fukuzawa Yukichi*.

These were not the kind of attitudes which were extolled in either the Confucian tradition or in *bushido*. Fukuzawa therefore came to a sweeping rejection of his own Eastern heritage, with its emphasis on paternalistic, hierarchic, and repressive values. Fukuzawa railed at the elitism of the samurai, which bequeathed to most Japanese a cringing, fawning behavior totally at odds with progress. The driving force in the new Japan was to be an ambitious citizenry able to think for itself. He ridiculed the dutiful son who doused himself with sake and slept naked by his parents' bed to attract mosquitoes which would otherwise annoy his parents. How much simpler, the pragmatic Fukuzawa wrote, if the respectful lad had bought mosquito netting.

While the obvious relevance of Fukuzawa's ideas to *fukoku kyohei* was appreciated by the Meiji oligarchs, not all were willing to accept Fukuzawa's broad assault on traditional values or his wholesale endorsement of Western liberalism. Fukuzawa's own life reveals incidents when his traditional samurai elitism clashed with his modern egalitarian ideals. (See box.)

IWAKURA MISSION

In 1871, at a time of political uncertainty while the Meiji leadership was still consolidating its power and dismantling the samurai class system, the oligarchs decided to send themselves abroad. This was not to be a ceremonial junket by one or two high-ranking officials. On the contrary, only a caretaker government would be left behind in Tokyo. A court noble, Iwakura Tomomi, virtually the only non-samurai in the new regime, was appointed as chief ambassador of the overseas delegation. More than fifty members, including Kido Koin, Ito Hirobumi, and at least half of the top ranks of government, joined the group. The planned length of the tour was nine months, but when that proved to be too brief, the junket was extended to 631 days, including seven months in the United States, four in England, and seven months on the European continent. No government in history has dispatched its top leadership overseas for such a long period of time and at such a critical juncture in its life. The mission failed to achieve its ostensible purpose—the renegotiation of the unequal treaties which had been forced upon Japan by the Western powers. That mattered little, however, for the real purpose of the travellers was to see the West for themselves and to carry out the spirit of the Charter Oath, to seek knowledge from abroad. The Iwakura Mission was an apt measure of the Meiji leadership's determination to institute a deliberate, rational program of reform in all spheres of national life.

Accordingly , nothing escaped the attention of the Mission. The delegates had audiences with a dozen heads of states and visited parliaments and courts everywhere. Following a whirlwind schedule, they toured cotton mills, iron foundries, shipyards, newspaper plants, breweries, prisons, banks, stock exchanges, cathedrals, telegraph offices, military fortifications, lunatic asylums, libraries, and art galleries. More out of a sense of duty than pleasure-seeking, the infinitely curious delegates—who had only recently given up wearing swords—visited zoos; attended the theater and opera; and took in endless concerts, ballets, and an occasional masked ball, circus performance, and fox hunt. "In this way," a scribe wrote, "strange sights and sounds filled our eyes and ears; our spirits sagged and our bodies were exhausted by all the invitations we received to this and that event." The official journal of the mission expresses an almost innocent wonderment of the travellers as they encountered for the first time things taken for granted in the West, everything from double-entry bookkeeping to the "social engineering" of factory managers who provided "fringe benefits" to employees to encourage their enterprise. Listen to a few of their reflections:

> On specialization: "Artists make the drawings, wheelwrights make the wheels. Dyers dye, painters paint. There is a fine division of labor, and the benefits are numerous. The various talents become increasingly specialized."
>
> On human energy-saving devices: "The people of Europe do not shoulder freight. . . . They use their splendidly maintained roads [and wheels] to carry their freight. The strength that would have been devoted to shouldering freight is used by European man in repairing the roads."
>
> On statistics: "The calculations of the credits and debits of trade are always carefully scrutinized by each country. These calculations are called statistics. Their essential feature is to call attention to the important products in the different regions of a country, and reference is made to such factors as population size, productive capacity, and the circulation of commodities. . . . These calculations are clear evidence upon which national profits can be assessed."

Even museums fascinated the travellers. Why would Japanese, with their sights fixed on the future, find repositories of old things such a clue to the dominant position of the West? Because, explains the journal, museums show that "by degrees there are advances." "We give this phenomenon a name and call it progress." There is nothing better than museums to illustrate the true nature of progress. It doesn't simply happen, the diarist writes. It is not random luck or mysterious process which explains why some countries are progressive and some are not. He explains:

> When one enters a museum and sees the old things, one senses the hard work and toil of times past. . . . As one sees the order of progress, one feels obliged to work harder thereafter. Inspiration moves the heart. Ideas for learning spring up, and one cannot control them. Thus books are collected and schools built for the purpose of acquainting people with the practical arts. . . . There has been [in Japan] no historical record-keeping of past and present progress to cause people to learn these things. No museums have stimulated the sight. No exhibitions have encouraged the acquiring of new knowledge.

THE "RATIONAL SHOPPER"

The travellers paid special attention to the signal achievements of the various countries they visited: centralized banking establishment in Belgium, naval engineering in Britain, the police system in France, public schools in Boston, silk-reeling technology in Switzerland, and military science in Bismarck's new German state. Upon returning to Japan, then, the new oligarchy carefully applied to Japan the national model, or elements from various national models, they felt best in each endeavor. In describing Japan's image as a borrower of Western culture and technology, some social scientists have used the phrase "rational shopper" to suggest that the Meiji leadership did not merely borrow but borrowed *selectively*. It examined numerous models from many "advanced" countries and after much "painstaking comparative shopping" selected what would best suit Japan. The "rational" emphasizes that the process was complex, involving extensive trial and error, shifting of models (in education, for example, from France at first, to the United States, and later to Germany). The word "rational" also emphasizes the fact that the borrowing also involved extensive adaptation to ensure that the transplanted model fit in with the special conditions or needs of Japan. For example, the early police in Meiji Japan, though modelled on the Parisian *gendarmerie*, took on judicial tasks such as imposing fines and prison sentences, though this was at variance with French practice. The modification was required because of the slow development of courts of justice in Japan.

In her study of the borrowing process, D. Eleanor Westney argues that this rational shopper designation is illustrated in the government's eclectic policy regarding the hiring of foreign advisors. In the early years of the Meiji era, some

2400 *oyatoi gaikokujin* (honored foreign help, *yatoi* for short), were brought to Japan. The figure refers to professional help, though it doubtless includes many *ikasama* (honorable frauds) who happened to be at the right place at the right time and were transformed into "instant professors." The salaries for the professional advisors inflicted a considerable burden on the government—the compensation necessary to induce foreigners to live in the little-known country was often higher than the salaries of their Japanese superiors in the top echelons of government. Evidence of the rational shopping can be seen in the fact that the foreign help came from twenty-three different nations, representing virtually every country in Europe and North America. The British, however, were the overwhelming favorites, providing about half of the manpower. French, Germans, and Americans were about equally represented though and, as we have noted, Yankees made an important contribution in the field of education.

EDUCATION

"Most prominent of American strands in the fabric of the new Japan was, without a doubt, the educational system which had to be created entirely new," writes the Japanese economist and critic Tsuru Shigeto.

In higher administration of their new schools, the Meiji leaders sought American guidance. While in the United States, the Iwakura Mission circulated among leaders in American education a letter in which the Japanese asked for opinions concerning their soon-to-be inaugurated reforms. Among the dozen or so prominent American educators to respond was Professor David Murray, a mathematician at Rutgers University in New Jersey. Intrigued by Murray's practical insights and perhaps flattered by his vision of Japan as "a boundless field for the applications of modern technological science," the Mission invited Murray to Japan as the senior foreign advisor in education with the title of Superintendent of Schools and Colleges, a position he held from 1873 until his return to America six years later. Some Japanese reformers were so excessively enthusiastic about the benefits of Western learning that it became necessary for Murray to argue his Japanese superiors out of a plan to introduce the English language as the language of instruction in the schools.

Many of the most prominent foreigners engaged in educational reforms in the early Meiji period were missionaries. While, as we have seen, Christian missionaries met with discouraging results in terms of the numbers of converts, their impact on education was prodigious. To put it another way, Christianity aroused little popular appeal but attracted much interest from intellectuals within the elite who saw in it the key to Western progress and strength and accepted it as an almost obvious wave of the future. J. C. Hepburn, a missionary of the American Presbyterian Church, was in Japan long before the ban on Christianity was lifted (in 1873) and, as a result, pursued his other career as a medical doctor. He opened a dispensary where he trained young Japanese in

Western medicine. He is credited with bestowing the first artificial limb in Japan—imported from America for a famous actor from the kabuki theater. A man of many talents, Hepburn also devised the standard method for romanizing Japanese; the Hepburn system, though modified, is still in use. In 1886, he helped found a school which eventually evolved into Meiji Gakuin University.

Doshisha University in Kyoto, though it has always been a Japanese university answering to its own board of trustees, has since its beginning enjoyed close ties with Amherst College in Massachusetts. Its founder and first president, Niijima Jo, had graduated from Amherst in 1870 and was an ordained Congregational minister. Doshisha became the first university in Japan to admit women.

In addition, Doshisha students included pioneers in the labor and socialist movements in Japan. Abe Isoo, one of the half-dozen founders of the first socialist political party in 1901 and widely regarded as the "grand old man of Japanese socialism," was a Christian and a graduate of Doshisha. Four of the other five initiators of this Social Democratic Party were also Christians. The party had a short life, however. The police suppressed it within three hours of its launching. Socialism, which stressed class conflict and, in the hands of radicals, class warfare, would never have an easy time sinking deep roots in Japan, though its notions of social justice gained it a following among intellectuals.

MORSE AND FENOLLOSA

Among the other Americans who took an important part in the early Meiji educational reforms was Edward Sylvester Morse, a Harvard scholar remembered as the father of modern zoology, archaeology, and anthropology. While spending two years (1877–1879) at the newly established Tokyo University, Japan's first and preeminent institution of higher learning, Morse helped introduce modern scientific methods to the study of biology, popularized Darwinian theories of evolution, and was instrumental in establishing the Japanese Imperial Museum.

A close observer of Japanese life, Morse wrote sympathetic accounts of the country upon his return to America. His *Japanese Houses and Their Surroundings* (1885) brought an informed and appreciative account of Japanese domestic architecture to Americans. In their methods of house-adornment, the Japanese showed greater refinement than the people of the West, Morse declared—long before the great architect Frank Lloyd Wright found Japan intriguing. For many Americans, Morse's daily journal, later published as *Japan Day By Day* (1917), was their first enlightened view of Japanese civilization—the tea ceremony, flower arranging, sumo, and the No theater. Morse was one of the first foreigners to take lessons in most of these Japanese arts. House-breaking and pocket-picking were unknown in this "pagan country," Morse advised his surprised readers. Japanese houses had no locks or bolts or keys, he said. A man was safer in the wilder regions of the country than he would be in the quiet streets of Salem, Massachusetts, Morse insisted. A century later, American expatriates in Japan would echo his remarks. Morse was probably during his time the most knowledgable foreign expert on Japanese pottery. A born collector, he donated his outstanding collection of five thousand ancient and modern ceramics to the Boston Museum of Fine Arts, where they are housed today.

Morse's Harvard colleague, Ernest Fenollosa, also taught at Tokyo University. During the years from 1878–1886, a great number of the distinguished men of the Meiji literary and academic world passed through Fenollosa's philosophy classes. More importantly, however, Fenollosa became one of the pioneer art historians of Japan. He deplored the way the Japanese were ignoring their own artistic traditions because of an almost indiscriminate fascination with Western art. He converted to Buddhism and helped to found a movement dedicated to saving and reviving Japan's past arts, meeting some of the expenses of the organization out of his own pocket in the beginning. (It eventually became known as the Tokyo University of Fine Arts and Music.) Like Morse, he accumulated an enormous collection of priceless paintings and other arts objects dating back seven centuries. Like Morse, Fenollosa turned his collection over to the Boston Museum of Fine Arts, where they became the basis of that museum's collection of Japanese paintings, regarded as the best anywhere in the world outside of Japan. Upon Fenollosa's return to Boston, the Meiji emperor awarded him the Order of the Sacred Mirror, the highest decoration ever given to any foreigner up to that time. The emperor thanked him, "You have taught my people to know their own art. In going back to your great country, I charge you, teach them also."

TSUDA AND MORI

The Iwakura Mission was accompanied by a group of students who were deposited in various countries for extended periods of study. The group included five girls, ranging in age from seven to fifteen. All of them returned to Japan to play prominent roles in public or professional life. One, trained as a piano teacher, helped to introduce Western musical education into Japan. She married Admiral Uryu Sotokichi, who studied naval science in America and became an important figure in the Russo-Japanese War in 1904. The youngest of the five, Tsuda Umeko, was carrying a doll when she was left with an American family in Washington, D. C. Tsuda eventually graduated from Bryn Mawr College in Pennsylvania and barely spoke her native language when she returned home. For a time, upon returning to Japan, she acted as an English-language tutor at the Ito Hirobumi household in Tokyo. Later, she was to play a major role in Meiji educational reforms by founding Japan's first school of higher education for women, now known as Tsuda College.

Of outstanding importance to Meiji educational developments was Mori Arinori. Born into a Satsuma samurai family, Mori studied physics in England and then spent a year at a New York religious colony run by a sexual mystic. At the time of the Iwakura Mission, Mori, only 25 years old, became Japan's first envoy to the United States. After several years of service as a diplomat, Mori returned to Japan to become the first Minister of Education when the cabinet system was formed in 1886. His personal life experiences contributed to his conviction that his country needed first-rate universities to prosper and that first-rate universities existed only where faculty and students were free to read and debate all the ideas of the world. His equating of scholarship with innovation dramatically challenged the accepted Confucian pedagogy which equated scholarship with the wisdom of the ancient sages.

Educators like Tsuda and Mori borrowed heavily from the West. French models were first tested and found wanting. Japanese came to adopt the regimentation, quasi-military drills, and heavy emphasis on training people to serve the state, which were hallmarks of the Prussian system. However, evidence of the American approach was seen in such Meiji adoptions as vocational, particularly agricultural, education.

CLARK AND CAPRON

William Clark, the president of the Massachusetts Agricultural College (later the University of Massachusetts), was engaged in 1876 to serve as the first president of a new agricultural college at Sapporo, on the northern island of Hokkaido, which was at the time a primitive frontierland. Modelled after Clark's own land-grant college, the new Japanese school eventually became the University of Hokkaido. The city of Sapporo itself was laid out in the rectangular plan of American cities, with American help. American mining engineers did the original mineralogical surveys of the island, and civil engineer Major A. G. Warfield, formerly of the Baltimore and Ohio Railroad, built a road from Sapporo to the coast—though his habit of brandishing firearms during his frequent drunken sprees caused Japanese officials to suspend his contract.

The hyper-energetic Clark had a major impact not only on the college but on the agriculture of the northern island, which is too cold for rice cultivation. Clark, along with another American educator and Civil War General, Horace Capron, introduced new crops, machinery, seeds, American-style large-scale farming techniques, and the dairy industry to the island. To this day, with their silos, barns, relatively large acreages and an occasional cowboy pounding leather, Hokkaido farms have more the look of South Dakota than Japan. The University of Hokkaido, with its grassy lawns and poplar-lined streets, has the look of an American campus. A legend known to schoolboys all over Japan has it that a score of his students accompanied him on the first stage of Clark's return home in 1877. When it was time to bid farewell, Clark turned in his saddle and said to his students, "Boys, be ambitious." This homespun advice, so close in harmony to the upward mobility credo of the Meiji oligarchs, was spread far and wide via textbooks and created an indelible impression on the minds of generations of students.

American influence was also manifest in the Japanese insistence that all children, of whatever birth, possessed the capacity for improvement. This was of signal importance in creating new attitudes toward social mobility, the kind of attitude casually expressed in Clark's parting salutation. The Meiji oligarchs

Japanese learn about Benjamin Franklin's electricity experiments in this print from about 1860.

were quickly becoming convinced that the goal of *fukoku kyohei*, prosperous nation and strong army, would be most likely achieved when the energies and talents of the entire population were mobilized. This required an open society in which a person's position and prestige were determined not by pedigree but by merit and achievement. Merit and achievement would be measured, above all, by performance in an open, competitive academic environment. Accordingly, the traditional class-based educational system was dismantled in the early years of the Meiji period, and Japan moved toward the adoption of an American-style coeducational common school as the basic unit. A system of free, compulsory, and universal education became a principal goal of the nation. It was not achieved overnight, but by the turn of the century, fully 98 percent of elementary-age youngsters attended school, approximately the same percentage prevailing today (although the number of years in school is much greater today). No other country in Asia could even approach that achievement in 1900. Even today, such an accomplishment remains an elusive goal for many countries.

The curriculum, with a heavy emphasis on practical subjects, "the three-R's," also reflected the American practice. Meiji officials became so enamored of the Boston public schools that a considerable sum of money was spent buying a complete set of classroom desks, blackboards, wall maps, and other teaching materials and shipping them to Japan. Before the decade of the 1870s was over, Japanese children were sitting at desks, rather than on the floor as tradition dictated, laboring over translations of McGuffey *Readers*, and memorizing New England place names from the McNally's *Geographies*. The stories of Benjamin Franklin and his kite experiment and Abe Lincoln and his log-cabin origins were almost as familiar to Meiji-era youngsters as to Americans. Western literary classics were translated into Japanese by the score, and Japanese high-school students were soon pondering the homilies of Benjamin Franklin as well as Shakespeare's "To be or not to be. . ." (*Yo ni aru, yo ni aranu, sore ga gimon ja. . .*). For at least four generations, and well after American schoolchildren had ceased to sing Stephen Foster songs, the refrains from "Jeannie with the Light Brown Hair" and "Camptown Races" could be heard in Japanese classrooms. The lyrics were not always kept the same as Foster wrote them. "My Old Kentucky Home," for example, was transformed into a more Japanese-sounding ode to fireflies.

BASEBALL

Baseball is not one of those recent American exports like break-dancing or Burger Kings. It goes back even further than the Ray Ban fad that swept Japan in the dark days after the war, when General Douglas MacArthur was American proconsul and a walking advertisement for the sunglasses; even further back than 1934, when Waseda, Keio, and Meiji universities formed a baseball league. It goes all the way back to 1873. In that year, only months after the Meiji government dropped a two-and-a-half-century ban on Christianity, a missionary teacher by the name of Horace Wilson arrived and instructed students on the campus of what is now Tokyo University in the rudiments of baseball.

The game caught on. Christianity never did.

According to the *Kodansha Encyclopedia of Japan*, however, baseball did not really become a popular sport until a team fielded by Tokyo's prestigious First Higher School (Ichiko) challenged the American Athletic Club in Yokohama to a contest. At first, according to Donald Roden's account in *Schooldays in Imperial Japan*, the Americans copped out with excuses about baseball being "our national game" and with warnings about the physical hazards posed by oversized Yankees playing smaller Ichiko lads.

After five years of temporizing, the Americans consented to a match on May 23, 1896, on the grounds of the Athletic Club, until then off limits to Japanese. In the best tradition of *gaman*, the Ichiko lads stoically endured the derision of the boorish *gaijin* (foreigner) spectators and then went on to trounce the blue-eyed barbarians, 29-4. When the Americans asked for a rematch two weeks later, the Japanese team agreed, vowing that they would play for the glory of the nation. Once again they triumphed by a huge margin. These victories were all the sweeter, Roden explains, because it was well known that the Yokohama Athletic Club cheated by recruiting players from the crews of American warships moored nearby.

SOAKING THE FARMERS

The Meiji government had ambitious plans for the development of Japan's industry but only very modest financial resources with which to accomplish its expensive goals. It was heavily burdened by an accumulation of Tokugawa debts which it had inherited from the old regime. The stipends to former daimyo and samurai, as we have seen, were a large drain on the government's revenues. In addition, in treaties with the foreign powers Japan had undertaken costly obligations including the improvement of ports and construction of lighthouses. It might have relied on foreign loans, but it rejected that option, convinced that foreign financial aid would inevitably bring foreign control. The few loans from the West were warily negotiated and quickly repaid, and it was not until 1900, by which time Japan was well on her feet, that she accepted significant amounts of foreign capital. This kind of fiscal self-reliance contrasted sharply with the extensive borrowing undertaken by Imperial China, most of whose important industrial projects were financed by Western capital. Even at the end of the Meiji period, by which time the modern urban sector of the economy was in high gear and might have been expected to pay a large share of taxes, the government continued the policy of soaking the countryside.

While the government had numerous sources of revenues, by far the most important was the land tax. In 1908, while merchants and industrialists paid 14 percent of their income in taxes, farmers paid 28 percent. This may not have been fair to the more than half the population who lived in rural Japan. It created hardships for the agrarian regions. Poor peasants, unable to pay the heavy taxes, were forced to sell their land and become tenants. Tenancy rates almost doubled in the countryside during the first two decades of the Meiji period, but the Meiji oligarchs knew that *fukoku kyohei* would be achieved only when Japan caught up with the West in industrial might.

What the Meiji tax policy did is succinctly summarized by historian Arthur E. Tiedemann: "The reforms assisted the transfer of capital and savings from the former Tokugawa aristocracy, which had tended to spend mainly on goods and services, to a government which channelled the wealth into investment and production. . . ." Thus, while the most dramatic and apparent breakthroughs occurred in the urban sector, the countryside was *the* important source of capital for those breakthroughs. Without the traditional skills and high productivity of the Japanese farmer, and his growing diversification into brewing, silk cultivation, pottery and other profit-generating cottage industries, it is difficult to see where Japan would have generated the income needed to fund the explosion of economic growth which took place in the Meiji era.

VITAL INDUSTRIES

Because funds were scarce, the oligarchs had to move a step at a time setting careful priorities. The first and highest priority was given to transport and communications because of their importance to security and administration. British technicians were hired to introduce the new technology of the telegraph, and in 1869 Tokyo was linked to its port of Yokohama by wire; ten years later a nationwide telegraph network was in place. Administratively, the telegraph was tied to the postal service, which also followed a British model.

Maejima Hisoka, a former samurai, spent a year in England, where he became enamored of the recent reforms introduced by Sir Rowland Hill, the "father of the modern post." Maejima returned to Japan in 1871 and introduced features of the British system including direct government operation of the system, postal savings, postage stamps, and unrestricted public access to postal routes. He was soon being referred to as the "father of the Japanese post." By the end of the decade, the people of the geographically diverse islands were joined together over seventy-six thousand kilometers of postal routes in a convenient, ably administered system that ran at a profit to the government. Before the postal system was established, letters were exchanged only through private postal couriers. In 1872, the new system carried only 2.5 million items, but the number passed 100 million in 1882 and a billion by the turn of the century. One thing led to another to bring about the centralization of the once-divided country and to link Japan to the Western world as well. The Postal Bureau needed standardized time to operate its route schedules. Accordingly, clocks were imported from the West (some, at least, from Seth Thomas of Connecticut). As D. Eleanor Westney informs us, Japanese set about reading the accompanying manuals and mastering the details of Western-style horology much as the rest of us did: "When the big hand is on one. . . ."

The new technology often baffled citizens encountering it for the first time. When the first post boxes were put in place, some citizens misconstrued the identifying characters with the word for "urinal," with results which are better left unimagined. The new trains were an endless source of fascination to woodblock artists who sold highly fanciful depictions of the trains, often on collision course "as if that should be no problem for something so wondrous." In the countryside, some took a quite compassionate attitude toward the great wheezing locomotive when it first appeared. "Thinking it must be hot, poor thing, they would douse it with water from embankments," one commentator writes. The telegraph lines became the center of a particularly wild set of rumors. Some people passed beneath the wires holding a fan on their heads when rumors spread that the wires could transmit people's thoughts. One man tied his letter to the wire in the mistaken notion that that was the way the wonderful new device carried messages.

In one case, the confusion became a matter of serious concern to the government. The lines appeared at the same time that the Meiji government announced the introduction of compulsory military service in 1873. The new conscription measure was described as a "blood tax" *(ketsuzei)*, countrymen being called upon to contribute their lifeblood for the sake of the country. All of this was quite alarming to simple commoners who had been denied access to the army or weapons for centuries. Compounding the confusion was the mysterious network of wires being strung from poles across the countryside. Along these wires it was said that messages could be transmitted. Peasants put two and two together and concluded that the army wanted inductees from whom they could draw blood—thus the "blood tax" everyone was talking about—which would be smeared on the telegraph wires so as to speed the messages along.

Another obvious priority of the oligarchs was the railway. In 1872, a nineteen-mile rail line was built from Tokyo to Yokohama; Kobe and Osaka were linked two years later. These efforts, launched with government funding and British technical services, acted as pilot projects to show the way. Once the feasibility and profitability of the industry was demonstrated, private entrepreneurs were quick to enter the market and by 1889, they owned somewhat more track than the government (671 miles versus the state's 551). Then the real boom began. By 1906, there was scarcely a village in Japan that was not within reach of rail service provided by nearly thirty-nine thousand miles of track. In the generation from 1888 to the end of the Meiji era, freight traffic grew from 848,000 tons to 40 million tons. Probably no feature of Japan's industrial revolution was more impressive than this "factor of movement," writes economic historian William W. Lockwood. Transportation in Japan in 1868, as he points out, had not even reached the "horse and buggy" stage. Even the lowly ricksha represented a significant innovation at that time. "Yet in a generation or two the Japanese were able to reorganize much of their life on an entirely new framework of mobility provided by a national network of railways and steam shipping."

A last example of the industries which received high-priority attention from the Meiji oligarchs was shipping. Tokyo's role in supporting the growth of a vigorous shipping industry is especially illustrative of the close relationship between government and big business.

After Japan was opened to trade, Western firms such as the American Pacific Mail Line and the British P. & O. Steamship Company immediately moved to capture the coastal trade between the treaty ports. The Meiji government deemed it necessary, for both commercial and security reasons, to eliminate the threat of a continued foreign domination of Japan's shipping. The growth of the shipping industry in the Meiji era is closely linked with the name of Iwasaki Yataro, a poor samurai from the Tosa domain in Shikoku. Most samurai found it impossible to make a successful transition to business life, but a few exceptional men, often using their government bond payments for investment capital, made outstanding contributions to economic growth in the Meiji era. Beginning with a few ships acquired from his domain after its dissolution, Iwasaki went on to found a firm which took the name Mitsubishi ("Three Diamonds," literally) in 1873 and which was destined to become the second largest of Japan's great commercial empires. (Mitsui has been larger.) Once the government came to see Iwasaki as a reliable businessman who could be trusted to put national interests ahead of private self-enriching goals, it did not hesitate to grant the firm subsidies, mail contracts and other forms of official aid. By the end of the decade Iwasaki had crushed the challenge from his principal American and British competitors and in 1879 his ships began to venture abroad.

The ricksha (more properly *jinrikisha*, man-powered vehicle) radically changed urban transportation in Japan. The device, a covered seat between two wheels pulled by a man in wooden shafts, did not exist in Japan prior to the Meiji Restoration. In earlier times, the elite were transported in palanquins, boxlike compartments suspended from poles carried on the shoulders of four or more men. Most authorities agree that the first ricksha appeared at the beginning of the Meiji era in the Yokohama foreign settlement. Historians, however, dispute the origins of the ricksha. A standard Japanese reference work attributes it to three Japanese inspired by the horse-drawn carriage recently introduced by the Westerners. An American account ascribes it to one Jonathan Goble from Hamilton, New York, described in contemporary records as "half-cobbler, half-missionary." Goble, a familiar figure in the foreign colony at Yokohama, is said to have constructed the first ricksha in 1867 for the convenience of his ailing wife.

In any case, the cheap fares made it a commonplace mode of travel. Among fashionable Western travellers in Japan, its exotic appeal made it a favorite photographic motif. "Globe-travelling ladies visit the Dieboots," picture post cards would be inscribed. "Dieboots," it turns out, is the "Daibutsu," the bronze statue of the "Great Buddha" at Kamakura. Government statistics show that the number of ricksha had grown to 137,000 by 1877. Pulling rickshas was always a despised and demeaning occupation. Though it lingered on much longer in other parts of Asia—even until today in some places—it rapidly disappeared in Japan with the appearance of bicycles around the turn of the century and automobiles somewhat later. By the time of the Great Kanto Earthquake of 1923, it was no more than a curiosity in Japan.

By the early 1880s, another giant steamship company, this one a subsidiary of the rival Mitsui empire, was rapidly gaining a share of the coastal trade. The Meiji oligarchs had no quarrel with healthy competition, and, in fact, they had encouraged the establishment of the Mitsui venture. However, an ominous trend began to appear. As the two firms competed, fares were slashed. Customers rejoiced as the price of passenger tickets between Yokohama and Kobe dropped from ¥5 to ¥.25, but the two companies nearly exhausted themselves in the process. With both of them deep in the red and on the verge of bankruptcy, government leaders feared the way would surely open for foreigners to make their move back into Japanese waters. At this juncture, Tokyo did not hesitate to intervene and insist that both parties set aside their rivalries. The result was a merger and the creation of a company known as *Nippon Yusen Kaisha* (Japan Steamship Company). This Mitsubishi-related firm went on to become one of the largest steamship companies in the world. The distinctive funnel NYK markings could be seen on its ships on regular service to Europe, the United States, and Australia by the 1890s. Statistics reveal the sharp rise of Japan as a shipping power. In 1893 only 14 percent of the ships entering Japanese ports were Japanese-owned; twenty years later, as the Meiji era came to an end, that percentage had risen to 51 percent. In 1893, only seven percent of the country's exports were carried in Japanese ships; that figure had risen to 52 percent by 1913.

TEXTILES

Modernization efforts, of course, could not be restricted to a few strategically important industries. For Japan to move into the ranks of the advanced nations, it had to develop profitable business endeavors across a broad spectrum of light and heavy industry. The shortage of capital and the high cost of importing foreign technology and expertise, however, dictated that Meiji oligarchs and entrepreneurs move cautiously. There could be no sudden leap into heavy industrialization for a country as poor as Japan. In addition, Japan was forced to develop consumer industries in order to correct balance-of-payment problems created by the unequal treaties which allowed foreigners to flood Japanese markets with cheap factory-made yarn and cloth. (Under the terms of its treaties with the West, Japan could not raise its import duties above five percent to protect its native industries.) This its resulted in large numbers of artisans in traditional trades losing their livelihood in the early Meiji years.

Textiles were seen as an area where relatively modest amounts of capital might produce maximum results in contrast to, say, the iron and steel industry where capital start-up costs would be prohibitively high. Japan's farm households had centuries of experience in cottage industries. Even the Chinese, who invented sericulture, conceded the superiority of the design and texture of Japanese silks. Rich in labor and poor in capital, it was natural for Japan to develop along the lines of its greatest economic advantage: labor-intensive industries. Operating on the excess labor supply in the countryside, largely teen-age peasant girls, textiles were to become Japan's earliest successful export. There were discouraging setbacks as the government established two pilot projects (1874–1875) using up-to-date Italian and French textile machinery—only to have them fail. However, the right lessons were learned; by 1885 more cotton cloth was being produced than imported, and an export trade began to develop thus easing the nation's balance-of-payment problems. A key player in the cotton industry was Shibusawa Eiichi, a wealthy peasant who had enjoyed a samurai education. Shibusawa, an enthusiastic promoter of the joint-stock company technique of industrial expansion, organized a highly successful cotton spinning mill in Osaka in 1880. This firm, the Osaka Spinning Company, was the first Japanese manufacturing firm of a large enough scale and using sufficiently modern machinery and techniques to become truly competitive in the world market. It in turn served as a model for other textile enterprises. Shibusawa himself went on to found the nation's first business school—it developed into the present-day Hitotsubashi University—and organize or become involved in the management of no less than three hundred other enterprises in fields as diverse as banking and paper manufacturing.

With rapid improvements in both cocoon raising and reeling processes, silk production grew and helped create a boom in worldwide demand. By the eve of World War I in 1913, Japan had passed China and European competitors in silk exports. The world's principal customer, the United States, was buying half of its silk from Japan. By that time, it was being turned out not only in cottages but in large mills employing hundreds of workers laboring around the clock under electric lights and operating electrically powered machinery. The consistently superior and uniform quality of the mechanically produced thread from Japan made it highly competitive abroad, allowing Japan to edge out competitors like China and Italy. By the end of the Meiji period, more than a third of the world's supply of silk came from Japan. In the long period from 1870 to 1930, raw silk exports alone provided at least 40 percent of the total net exchange earnings from commodity exports to foreign countries—much of that to her best customer, the United States. The earnings from the silk export trade were then applied to buying food, materials, and machinery from abroad.

As early as 1876, a young Japanese businessman by the name of Rioichiro Arai had set up a silk-importing establishment in New York City. The son of a locally prominent silk-weaving family in rural Japan, Arai had mastered English, acquired a second-hand Western-style suit and haircut, and at the age of twenty arrived in the United States to represent the family's hope for launching export sales to the West. One of Arai's first challenges was to dispel the bad reputation which some early Japanese exporters had won by shady business practices such as adding pieces of metal and other extraneous materials to their shipments in order to increase the weight. In his first major transaction with an American merchant in May 1876, Arai quoted a $6.50 per pound contract price for a shipment of raw silk to be delivered four months in the future. A long lag time was needed because of slow mail contact with Japan—a trans-Pacific cable would not be in place for another two years. Unfortunately for Arai, long before the silk had been shipped from Yokohama, the market price rose sharply as a result of a European silk blight. Although his business partner in Japan pleaded with Arai to renegotiate the contract, Arai refused on the grounds that his honor and the future success of his company were at stake. Although Arai had to pledge his entire family fortune to cover the loss, the contract was fulfilled and Arai went on to become an immensely successful entrepreneur, the "grand old man" of the silk industry in the United States and a pillar of the New York business community. His death at the age of 86 in 1939, brought on by pneumonia following his customary eighteen holes of golf, prompted the American Commodity Exchange to pay him the unusual tribute of silence while his funeral was in progress.

Japan was thus becoming an almost perfect example of a have-not nation successfully developing its industry: by paying for its needed imports of raw materials (such as iron ore, coal, raw cotton) with manufactured goods from light industry (cotton yarn, cotton and silk garments) and semi-manufactured goods (such as raw silk).

ENTREPRENEURSHIP

A key element in the successful economic development of Meiji Japan was the quality of the nation's entrepreneurial leadership. Dictionaries define "entrepreneur" as a person who organizes and manages a business. Modern usage also contains overtones of "dynamic," and "risk-taking." This was not the way of the merchant in pre-modern Japan, where the rule was to stay on the safe, well-marked path. Merchant houses of old always had family rules passed down from generation to generation, and the most typical injunction was to avoid innovations. To deviate from the practices of grandfather could easily be seen as casting doubt on the honor of the ancestors. Modern business endeavor calls for attitudes quite different from these, for a willingness to break loose from tradition. Japan was fortunate to have such a class of men willing to abandon traditionally safe channels of investments (such as land or moneylending) and risk fortunes and careers in the uncertain new world of steamships, railways, electrical machinery, and the like.

Many of the Meiji-era entrepreneurs, as we have seen, emerged from the ranks of the former samurai class. While the merchant had traditionally been despised as a parasite and the accumulation of wealth had been seen as unworthy, the entrepreneur of the Meiji Japan came to be viewed as a different breed of man. Capitalistic endeavor was seen by others as something noble and patriotic. Almost overnight, the Meiji entrepreneur was no longer scorned as the contemptible merchant in greedy pursuit of his own private well-being. Rather he saw himself and was seen as someone engaged in a cause, service to the nation, service to the Emperor. The Meiji businessmen often likened themselves to samurai, "rallying stockholders instead of vassals, and plunging into the fray armed with abacus and balance sheets instead of horse and sword." Shibusawa, the cotton magnate, was likened by business-school students to the great eleventh-century military hero, Minamoto Yoshiie. "Just as the samurai gathered behind Minamoto to follow him into the battle of war, so now the younger generation gathers around Shibusawa to follow him into the battle of enterprise, as merchants of a modern kind," wrote a student publication of the day.

Business directories of the time reveal the vogue for including the name *Teikoku* (Imperial) or *Kokueki* (Benefit the Nation) in the company names of banks and bean-curd makers alike. Even the sewerman operated an "Imperial Honey Bucket Service," comments one writer. This was at once similar and yet quite different from American contemporaries in the world of big business. The American corporate giants were raised in the spirit of the "Protestant ethic" to think of worldly success as outward evidence of inward moral and religious character, a divine stamp of approval on their profit-making activities. "Keep one eye on work, the other on heaven," said preachers. "God gave me my money," said John D. Rockefeller, oil baron and Sunday school teacher. The same sense of calling and righteousness is seen in the remarks of typical Meiji entrepreneurs, but the calling is to serve not God, but nation.

Here, for example is Suzuki Tosaburo, former samurai, a key figure in the development of the Japanese sugar-refining industry, summing up his own personal business philosophy around the turn of the century:

> I am a businessman. I have no interest in dabbling in books or paintings or in taking my ease in luxurious mansions. My calling *[honbun]* is to run businesses. Even if I lose capital, I have invested in a business and I do not regret it in the slightest, since business as a whole has gained. Even if my work should prove unsuccessful, the research will be inherited by those who come after me. . . . Once an enterprise has been launched, the nation ultimately benefits.

Or consider the reflections of Okano Kitaro, a banker, following the great earthquake of 1923:

> I lost my wife and daughter in the great quake. The two of them were on their way to a hotel in Yugawara for a rest when the quake struck and their train plunged into the sea. When the news of this misfortune reached me, my courage failed. But after a while my sense of responsibility returned sharply. I thought to myself: "You are the head of the Suruga Bank! You must discharge your duty as a banker in this time of trouble! Compared to that, your personal misfortune is a trifling matter." My whole body trembled.

There is no need to turn these entrepreneurial heroes into saints. Surely all, especially those who did not come from the samurai tradition, were motivated by a mixture of self-interest and patriotism. Many eventually became enormously wealthy. However, even those businessmen often had to forego easy, short-term profits in the interest of building a growth economy by making investments in long-range projects. This far sightedness was to become a characteristic trait of Japanese business which would arouse the admiration—and envy—of people throughout the world.

In 1919, after observing the success of Japan's modernization efforts, the American economist Thorstein Veblen commented that Japan's striking progress could be attributed to two factors. Japan had been able to join (1) industrial technology with (2) "a highly-wrought spirit of duty and chivalric honor," Veblen wrote. It was a stunningly perceptive analysis that even today commands attention. Veblen, however, went on to say that the second feature, the sense of duty, was only a relic of the past and could be expected to disappear as soon as Japanese society became more rationalized. In other words, one might expect to find such a quality among members of a feudalistic society, but it could hardly endure in a truly modern nation. From a more recent perspective, it will be useful to reconsider in later chapters whether this judgment of Veblen's has stood the test of time.

IMAGES OF JAPANESE

Only a relatively few Americans and Japanese came to know and experience each other's culture in the Meiji era. Accordingly, informed assessments accumulated very slowly. Filtered through a maze of prejudices and misunderstandings, a variety of impressions gradually emerged. Some reflected more or less accurate judgments, some were dead wrong. Most caught only the surface of things, but some were penetrating. Some of the impressions were hopelessly contradictory. Many have proved to be amazingly enduring. Perhaps the most enduring is the notion of Japan—as well as China—as a "Topsy-turvydom." That was the title of a section of a book on Japan by the West's foremost Japan scholar at the turn of the century, Basil Hall Chamberlain. They carry babies on their back rather than in their arms, politeness prompts them to remove their shoes rather than their hats, and after the bath, they dry themselves with a wet towel. In the West others are beckoned to come forward by motioning with palms up; the Japanese do it with palms down. All perfectly true but at the same time contributing to the notion that there was something inherently peculiar about those people. Other, far less-scholarly writers like the Englishman Douglas Sladen would practically make a career out of this kind of commentary as the titles of his oeuvres suggest: *The Japs at Home* (1904) and *Queer Things About Japan* (1906). Gilbert and Sullivan's *Mikado* (1885) made the point in plain language:

> Our attitude's queer and quaint—
> You're wrong if you think it ain't.

Westerners were, however, almost uniformly enthusiastic in their appreciation of Japanese artistic achievements. The enthusiasm for Japanese woodblock prints surged in France to the point where a phenomenon called *Japonisme*—a craze for Japanese things—was under way by the 1870s. Zola, Degas, Manet, and Monet as well as the American impressionist James McNeill Whistler competed with each other in collecting the works of Utamaro, Hokusai, and Hiroshige. The impressionists not only borrowed Japanese painting techniques but some, like Henri de Toulouse–Lautrec, truly captured the spirit of *ukiyo* in works like *"Divan Japonais"* (1892). (Lautrec's poster depicted a Montmartre cafe of that name, much patronized by the leading artists of the day.) Similarly, Japanese craftsmanship almost universally drew admiration from the West. Japan, both as a government and as individuals, participated in several American fairs and expositions, beginning with Philadelphia in 1876. Everything from ceramics and lacquerware to the patience and care of Japanese packing techniques were praised by the American visitors.

NUDITY IN ART AND DAILY LIFE

Nudity was a constant source of bewilderment and misunderstanding to Japanese and Westerners. There was a lively tradition of pornographic art in Japan, but the nude had no place in the repertory of legitimate artists at any time during that country's long history of art. Accordingly, Japanese were shocked to discover that Westerners displayed in their homes and in public places statues and paintings of completely unclothed bodies. The first nude painting by a proper Japanese painter was not shown until the 27th year of the Meiji era, when Kuroda Seiki, the undisputed leader of progressive Western painting, exhibited his "Morning Toilette" depicting an exotic French lady. Kuroda told the suspicious officials at the Kyoto gallery where the work was to be hung that the display was quite proper; the Westerners did it all the time. The officials remained puzzled; did not Christianity teach that the naked human body was shameful, they asked?

Westerners were in turn shocked to discover what seemed be an excessively casual attitude toward nudity in the public baths. Few plebeian homes in Japan at the beginning of the Meiji era had their own baths. Almost everyone went to a public bath, as much for companionship and gossiping as for bathing. Sometimes the sexes would be segregated; sometimes not. The Japanese, while not shameful of nudity, have always been exceedingly discreet. Towels can be manipulated with great dexterity to serve as fig leaves. In any case, to ogle nudity in the baths would be rude. Japanese learn to reflexively glance elsewhere as a courtesy when the occasion calls for it. The foreigner did not appreciate these cultural niceties and denounced the public baths as barbaric, causing the Meiji government, always sensitive to Western criticism, to ban public mixed bathing in the second year of the Meiji era. Neither that ban nor similar ones in 1870 or 1872 were vigorously enforced. As with prostitution and other practices the foreigners found offensive, the Japanese solution seems to have been to get them out of sight of the *gaijin*. In contemporary Japan, mixed public bathing is no longer common except in some hot-springs *(onsen)* resorts.

Tattooing, which the Japanese had developed to an exceptionally high level of artistic expression, was similarly banned in response to foreign objections. However, the foreigners did not know their own minds, Japanese complained. Because some *gaijin* became devotees of tattooing, special "export only" establishments were permitted to operate in Yokohama. Among the foreigners who were engraved there was a young midshipman, the future King George V of England, and the tsarevich of Russia, the future Nicholas II.

Excluding art, the more general accomplishments of Meiji Japan provoked contradictory estimates in the West. *The Edinburgh Review* could comment in 1872 that "The Japanese are the only nation in the history of the world that had ever taken five centuries at a stride." It was usually assumed that the continued progress of Japanese civilization meant that Japan must become without reservation a child of Western civilization and therefore divorce itself more and more totally from its Asian roots. If this sounds like Western arrogance, it needs to be emphasized that leading Meiji-era reformers also were adamant about the need to "break with Asia." In an 1885 editorial entitled *Datsu-A-ron* (Break with Asia), Fukuzawa Yukichi launched a national debate on the subject with his assertion that China and Korea were no longer of any help at all to Japan. "On the contrary, because the three countries are adjacent we are sometimes regarded as the same in the eyes of civilized Western peoples. . . . and indirectly this greatly impedes our foreign policy," Fukuzawa wrote. Without the West's science and its spirit of independence, the influential Fukuzawa told his countrymen, Japan could not hope to compete in the modern world.

Where Japan's economic ability would take it in the future provoked wildly contrary judgments from Western observers. From at least as early as the 1880s, when the first signs of Japan's modernizing abilities were evident, and increasingly in the 1890s as Japan launched its empire, there was a healthy respect for Japan's economic drive and the potential for dangerous competition. At the same time, however, there were numerous skeptics. Rudyard Kipling tells of hearing from a Western businessman in Kyoto in 1889 that, "The Japanese should have no concern with business. The Jap has no business savvy." It seems quite unbelievable in the light of contemporary Japanese successes in the world of commerce as well as the modern image of Japanese as "economic animals"—obsessed with business—that such an image would survive in the West. It did, however, and down through the years, at junctures in her history when the economic picture looked particularly bleak, writers far more seasoned than Kipling's informant have expressed grave doubts.

IMAGES OF JAPANESE WOMEN

Whatever Westerners thought of Japan in general, they were almost always swept off their feet by the charm and grace of Japanese women. One enterprising historian who chronicled in his Harvard PhD thesis the descriptions of American visitors to Japan during the Meiji period lists fully thirty pages of quotations eulogizing women. ". . . the most wonderful aesthetic products of Japan are not its ivories, nor its bronzes, nor its porcelain, nor its swords, nor any of its marvels in metal or lacquer—but its women," exclaimed Lafacadio Hearn, one of the chief interpreters of Japan to the West. Hearn, whose wife was Japanese, concludes his paean to Japanese women with this breathless toast: "Perhaps no such type of woman will appear again in the world for a hundred thousand years." Hearn and others were often quick to contrast the genders in Japan: "As a moral being, the Japanese woman does not seem to belong to the same race as the Japanese men!" Hearn wrote in language so overblown that it must be said that it helped trap Japanese women in the legend of their own perfection. In words which makes modern feminists wince, Hearn attributed the unique "moral charm" of Japanese women to the "extraordinary regulation and regimentation of Japanese society, a society in which all self-assertion was repressed, and self-sacrifice made a universal obligation." Hearn declared, "Her success in life was made to depend on her power to win affection by gentleness, obedience, kindliness." She was a creature "working only for others, thinking only for others, happy only in making pleasure for others."

The most exotic stereotypical images Westerners held of the Orient—as a dream setting for enchanted and forbidden pleasures—came together in an immensely popular novel *Madam Chrysanthemum* (1887) by Pierre Loti and the opera *Madama Butterfly* (1904) by the Italian maestro Giacomo Puccini. Puccini based his work on Loti's novel as well as a short story written for *Century Magazine* by a Philadelphia lawyer, John Luther Long. Puccini had never been to Japan. Long had never been to Japan. Loti had spent some time in Nagasaki brothels in 1885 while serving as a captain in the French navy. Not surprisingly, his mistresses were depicted as easily discarded pets—the book's namesake was described as a "quaint toy," *un jouet bizarre.* Similarly, Puccini has Lieutenant Pinkerton rhapsodize over Cho-cho San as she slips out of her weddding kimono into something more comfortable: "To think that this little toy is my wife." (Some writers could not resist the temptation to subsume all of Japan under the toy category. Japan, said the popular English novelist Clive Holland, was "tiny, toylike and ridiculous.")

There were occasional voices of dissent. Henry Adams, straying from Beacon Hill in 1886 to visit the East, commented on Japanese women in a dyspeptic letter to his friend, John Hay. They were, he wrote, "obviously wooden dolls, badly made, and can only cackle, clatter in patterns over asphalt pavements in railway stations, and hop or slide in heelless straw sandals across floors." Adams, who was not altogether charmed by Japanese men either, concluded that he had "Yet to see any women with any better mechanism than that of a five-dollar wax-doll."

Westerners anxious to read about Japanese women as people of flesh and blood with their own aspirations and struggles might well have turned to one of

David Henry Hwang, a young contemporary Chinese-American playwright, wrote an updated "deconstructed" version of Puccini's opera which includes an Asian point of view on *Madama Butterfly.* In Hwang's version, *M. Butterfly,* which reached the New York stage in 1988, one of the Asian characters comments on a Frenchman's sentimental response to Puccini's opera with this speech:

"Consider it this way. What would you say if a blonde homecoming queen fell in love with a short Japanese businessman? He treats her cruelly, then goes home for three years, during which time she prays to his picture and turns down marriage from a young Kennedy. Then, when she learns he has remarried, she kills herself. Now I believe you would consider this girl to be a deranged idiot, correct? But because it's an Oriental who kills herself for an American—ah—you find it beautiful."

several fine autobiographies written in English by Japanese women. (See bibliography.) Not enough did, however, and thus the prevailing image of Japanese women was the one transmitted by Loti's *mousmés*. The word which entered both French and English dictionaries about the time of Loti's book derives from the Japanese word for a young girl, *musume*. By the time American GI's got hold of it in the years after World War II, it had been abridged to "moose" and meant anything from girl friend to street-walker. From the petite eroticism of Pierre Loti's *mousmés* to Ian Fleming's James Bond and his lover "Kissy Suzuki," the Western depiction of Japanese women has either idealized or degraded but almost never fathomed Japan's womanhood.

THE SEARCH FOR WESTERN SPIRIT

While most Meiji reformers paid lip service to the shibboleth *wakon yosai*—Japanese spirit, Western techniques—enthusiasm for the West went well beyond techniques. At its height, during the "civilization and enlightenment" era, the craze for knowledge of the West knew almost no boundaries. "Let us change our empire into a European-style empire. Let us change our people into a European-style people," declared the foreign minister of Japan in 1887. The objects of Japanese interest during this era are nicely measured by literary trends of the day, particularly the popular appeal of books which translated or otherwise interpreted Western culture to inquiring minds. Two examples will illustrate a distinctive Japanese emphasis which helps isolate exactly what it was in Western ways that most interested Japanese:

SELF-HELP. When successful Japanese statesmen, generals, businessmen and educators were asked in a survey at the turn of the century what book it was that had been the greatest influence in their lives, half of them chose a single book. A book that had been as inspirational to them as the Bible was to their counterparts in the Western world, they agreed. The book they chose was not one by J. S. Mill, de Tocqueville, Herbert Spencer, or Benjamin Franklin though these names were familiar to the well-read young men of the Meiji period. Instead, the first choice was by a now all but unknown Scottish philosopher, Samuel Smiles. While Smiles enjoyed modest name-recognition in nineteenth-century England and America, it is no exaggeration to say that he was a household word in Japan where samurai quite literally camped out to be at the first of a line to buy the first printing. A million copies of *Self-Help* were eventually sold in Japan. (It was translated into Japanese by a samurai, Nakamura Masanao, in 1871.) Among those who professed to have been inspired by *Self-Help* was Toyoda Sakichi who produced the first Japanese-designed power loom in 1897. The next generation of his family branched out into automobiles and changed the English transliteration of the family name to "Toyota."

Smiles' book was one long elucidation of the title and its famous first line: "Heaven helps those who help themselves." It was an attack on hereditary wealth and power that was in keeping with the goals of the Meiji leadership which was busy abolishing the privileges of the samurai class the year when the translation went on sale in Japan. It fit the mood of the new schools where anything was possible to the ambitious, energetic young man who had the drive to succeed. Poverty was not a misfortune, Smiles counseled. Heeding the severe lift-yourself-up-by-your-own-bootstraps lessons of *Self-Help* would convert misfortune into a blessing. The "Horatio Alger" stories popular in America at the same time had no appeal to Meiji reformers. The rags-to-riches heroes of the "Horatio Alger" stories were forever being rescued by fairy godmothers or chancing to meet the daughters of rich industrialists. Nor was it simply the achievement of *personal* success that made Samuel Smiles' homilies so popular. "National progress is the sum of individual energy, industry, and uprightness, just as national decay is the sum of individual idleness, selfishness, and vice," Smiles wrote. The Scottish philosopher linked personal achievement to national destiny in a way that make good sense to Meiji-era nation builders.

The teachings of Smiles of course blended well with samurai virtues of discipline and duty, and both contributed mightily to the spread of the doctrine of "striving for success in the world" *(risshin shusse)*. So much that was done was said to have been done "for the progress and advance of our country" that the phrase could easily have degenerated into empty cliche. However, the strenuous rivalry in the schools that has characterized Japanese education since the Meiji era may be seen as just one example of Meiji "success fever" *(seiko-netsu)* at work. A turn-of-the-century magazine with the typical name "Success" *(Seiko)* promoted heartening examples of diligence. (The Japanese monthly was modeled on an American magazine of the same title. The first issue of the Japanese version featured a picture of Lincoln's log cabin, a popular Meiji-era symbol of diligence, and advertisements for Theodore Roosevelt's *Strenuous Life).* In one of the early issues, a student describes how he and his dormitory friends engaged in feverish reading competition:

> We really went all out that month. If one of us got a page ahead the others would turn pale. We hardly took time off to chew our food properly, and we drank as little water as possible in order that the others should not get ahead in the time wasted going to the lavatory so keen were we to get a line or two ahead of the others.

TOKAI SANSHI. A strong rival to Samuel Smiles was the Japanese writer Shiba Shiro who was better known by his pen name of Tokai Sanshi, "Wanderer of the Eastern Sea." Born into a samurai family, the Wanderer travelled to the United States for studies at Harvard and the University of Pennsylvania. He returned to Japan to pursue a career in politics, but it was his *Kajin no kigu* (Strange Encounters of Elegant Females, 1885) which made the Wanderer so well known to Meiji readers. For its literary merit, *Strange Encounters* enjoys almost no place at all in the dazzling history of Japanese literature. It was a "deplorably bad novel," wrote Sir George Sansom, the eminent British Japanologist. Nevertheless, in the exaggerated phrase of the day, "it raised the price of paper in Tokyo," that is, it was *very* popular. Of awesome length, *Strange Encounters* is essentially a guide to revolutionary movements around the world, as seen through the eyes and experiences of the two "elegant females" of the title. They are, implausibly, Yuran (Mysterious Orchid), daughter of a Spanish nobleman being pursued by assassins while he strives to make his native land a constitutional monarchy; and Koren (Crimson Lotus), a golden-haired daughter of an Irish patriot who has expired in prison.

In one episode, the hero—the author himself—is in Philadelphia, standing in front of the Liberty Bell when his musings upon the successful struggle of the colonies against the tyranny of England is interrupted by the arrival of the two European beauties, Yuran and Koren. Sansom summarizes the wild improbabilities and coincidences which follow:

> The Wanderer stands by the window eavesdropping in a refined way; and here, as throughout the book, his thoughts are recorded at length, frequently in Chinese verse or with difficult allusions to Chinese history. The ladies leave after a coy glance at him. A day or two later he takes a boat and rows up the Delaware River, where he encounters them both again. He is addressed by one, who explains that she and her companion have been impressed by his romantic character, for they first saw him brooding upon a historic scene and now find him enjoying the beauties of nature in a secluded spot where, it so happens, they are living in retreat. He is invited to join them, and with but little encouragement they tell him the stories of their lives. . . . Their several experiences are related at great length in high-flown discourse. . . . When Koren has told her story, the Chinese butler who has been filling their wineglasses discloses himself as a once distinguished rebel against the Manchus but now in indigent exile. He also tells a long tale of oppression and tyranny, by which the Wanderer is moved to anger and grief at the wickedness of men. . . . He is consoled by Yuran, who holds out bright prospects for Japan and encourages him to believe that he can render great service to the cause of freedom in his own country. At this he weeps copiously and his tears fall upon the dress of Yuran. . . . By this time it has grown late, the moon has risen. Yuran throws open the window and says: "Let us not spend this delicious night in melancholy. Let us be brave and cheerful. Let us dance and sing." Thereupon, to an accompaniment played on harps by the two ladies, they all sing the *Marseillaise*, in a Chinese version obligingly furnished by the butler.

While Yuran and Koren were clearly in love with the Wanderer, any hope his readers might have had for international romance as the trio moves about the world would have been dashed. As Sansom says, the Wanderer's "bosom is so filled with patriotic fervor, with hatred of tyrants and contempt of human folly, that it cannot give permanent lodging to more romantic emotions." What readers were rewarded with was a veritable encyclopedia of comparative history, a working knowledge of Western philosophy from Socrates to Macauley, and a completely intoxicating spirit of nationalism informed by the histories of America and Europe. Similarly, *Robinson Crusoe*, which inspired three translations into Japanese, was intended by its translators not as a book for children and not as an adventure story. Readers of the earlier editions were led to believe by the translators, in fact, that *Robinson Crusoe* was a true account of a castaway. The introduction to the 1883 translation makes it clear that, although written in a novel form, the book should teach its readers the importance of overcoming hardship. ". . . it shows how an island can be developed by stubborn determination." What could be more important for a people intent upon making their insular nation strong. Similarly, the optimistic belief in progress, given the right mix of ingenuity and determination, in Jules Verne's *Round the World in Eighty Days* accounted for its appeal to the adventurous spirit of Meiji readers.

Civilized Beef Stew

While life-style and attitudes were slow to change in the countryside, a revolution was taking place in the cities of Japan. Early Western visitors to Japan, in the 1850s, the decade of Perry's visit, invariably reported that Japanese observers were amused to the point of raucous laughter by their European garments. By the 1870s, however, the report was that the most prosperous tradesmen in Tokyo were tailors specializing in Western finery. Wearing frock coats, curly-brimmed London hats, and leather shoes was a mark of distinction. For officials on duty in government offices and in all state-sponsored schools, Western-style clothing was mandatory. Men showed off by dangling gold watches, carrying black Western-style "bat-shade" umbrellas (as opposed to the pretty bamboo-and-paper variety traditionally favored), growing beards, and interjecting English phrases into their conversation. The first Western-style barbershop opened on the Ginza in 1869 and soon "randomly cropped" *(zangiri)* heads outnumbered those with traditional haircuts. (The old style, for both samurai and commoner, called for shaving a part of the head and permitting the remainder of the hair to grow long so that it could be pulled into a topknot.)

With so much borrowing of Western ways going on, it is easy to appreciate that the borrowers were easy targets of parody. After many centuries of being denied beef by Buddhist injunction (as well as the shortage of grazing land for cows), the consumption of beef suddenly became acceptable. In 1871, the Emperor sat down to a beef dinner thus endorsing the foreigners' habit. (*Sukiyaki*, thinly sliced beef with vegetables and soy sauce, is not a traditional Japanese dish but appeared in the early Meiji era when beef consumption became fashionable.) Before long, partaking of beef was not only acceptable but was being transformed into an essential ingredient of "civilization and enlight-

BORROWED VOCABULARY

Meiji-era adoptions of Western—mostly English-language—words included many related to clothing. *Moningu* from the English "morning coat" is still the word for a man's formal attire. *Haikara* ("high collar") signified up-to-date, cosmopolitan but contains a nuance of affectation. *Sebiro* referred to a Western-style business suit and is still in common use; it derives from the Savile Row district of London, reputedly the center of world-class tailoring. (It must be recalled that there are no "v" or "l" sounds in Japanese; "b" and "r" are the closest approximations.) Later, *waishatsu*, from "white shirt," entered the language. It too remains in common use but it does not really mean "white shirt." It means a man's dress shirt. Thus, it is possible to have a *pinku waishatsu*, a dress shirt colored pink. Women's clothing styles changed much more slowly but the female dress lexicon is now almost entirely composed of borrowed words: *sueta* (sweater), *skatsu* (skirt), *wan-pisu* and *tsu-pisu* (one-piece and two-piece). Even measurements in dressmaking have become Anglicized. There is obviously a good word in Japanese for a hip measurement *(koshi-mawari)* and a bust measurement *(mune-mawari)* but *hippu* and *basuto* are now preferred.

enment." This is the message delivered by the central character in the comic essay *Aguranabe* (Beef Stew, 1871) by journalist Kanagaki Robun. Robun's foppish beef eater, with his calico undergarments, gingham-covered bat-shade umbrella, gilt watch, and a whiff of eau-de-Cologne in his hair, is thoroughly stylish and ridiculous as he transmits the wisdom of the great reformer Fukuzawa Yukichi: "Unless you eat beef stew, you cannot be civilized."

DISILLUSION AT THE ROKUMEIKAN

This kind of indiscriminate and unquestioning borrowing from the West could not go on forever. All along, conservatives had fumed over the disappearance of native values and traditions. It is easy to see how Japanese rankled at the proposal of educator Mori Arinori to abandon the use of the Japanese language or the suggestion of Meiji bureaucrats that foreign women be imported to mate with Japanese to invigorate the race. It is easy to imagine the general resentment toward the high-salaried foreign advisors and teachers and the prominence of missionaries whose very presence was seen by some as an affront to Buddhism and Shinto. It is also easy to imagine that conservatives were annoyed to find their children singing the "Civilization Ball Song," written to impress on young minds the advantages of Western culture. (Names of Western objects deemed most worthy of adoption—gas lamps, cameras, steam engines, and so on—were recited to the cadence of a bouncing ball.) Why, asked one critic, did Japanese have to have a "Sunday" just because the foreigners observed such a day? If it was spent in "excess and dissipation" a total of 1500 lost days would accumulate in thirty-years time, the critic insisted.

The controversy reached a symbolic turning point at a fancy costume ball—a *fuanshi boru*—at the Rokumeikan in Tokyo in 1887. The Rokumeikan (Hall of the Baying Stag) was a large Western-style building, partly a hotel for distinguished guests and partly a social hall. Erected by the government in 1883, the hall became the scene of regular Sunday night state-sponsored parties. The idea was that the Japanese government and business elite, mixing together with the foreign diplomatic community, would learn by practice the social graces required of modern civilized gentlemen: how to dine with knives and forks, play cards, shoot billiards, smoke cigars, drink champagne, organize charity bazaars, and above all, how to dance the waltz and the quadrille. Ladies and gentlemen were expected to wear Western dress. Foreign teachers were hired as consultants. The most talked of event of this gilded era was a grand masquerade ball held on April 20, 1887, attended by the leading dignitaries of the nation including the Prime Minister Ito Hirobumi and his "Dancing Cabinet." One notable came as a swan. The prime minister appeared as a Venetian nobleman while Foreign Minister Inoue Kaoru was dressed as a strolling musician. Inoue was among the most enthusiastic Westernizers, one of those proposing interracial breeding to improve the genetic strain. There was a serious political purpose behind the festive entertaining. As with much of the Westernization effort, Ito and the other reformers hoped not merely to strengthen Japan but to demonstrate to the foreigners how Westernized Japan was in order to further the treaty revision effort.

However harmless the Rokumeikan diversions were, the spring 1887 gala proved to be the last straw. It was quickly exploited by the conservative opposition. It was simple enough, and perhaps not entirely unfair, to portray the affair as ludicrous, a demeaning attempt to win the approval of foreigners no matter the cost to Japan's national dignity. The Japanese "regard whatever is their own as inferior to the others', i.e., the West, whether it is good or evil, beautiful or ugly, and do not in the least regret abandoning the traditions and teachings of their ancestors," wrote one irate critic of indiscriminate borrowing. The attacks on the headlong Westernization process of the early Meiji era produced a more sober reflection by all concerning the need for a balance between important national traditions and ideologies and borrowing essential features of Western civilization. Unquestioning acceptance of the West as superior disappeared. In 1890, an "Imperial Rescript on Education" proclaimed that "The Way here set forth has been bequeathed by our Imperial Ancestors. . . infallible for all ages and true in all places." How different in tone and substance from the "Charter Oath," issued by the same emperor twenty-two years earlier, which affirmed that the standards of civilization and learning were to be found abroad.

Western steamship technology, mathematics, and medicine were imperative; ballroom dancing could wait. In between was an enormous grey area, and the same cycle of dazzling captivation and enthusiastic borrowing followed by doubt and rejection would repeat itself again and again in the century ahead.

JAPAN AND CHINA CONTRASTED

It may be useful here to pause for a moment and contrast Japan's performance with China's, perhaps the single most important contrast which modern Asian history has to offer. Admittedly, a cursory digression raises more questions than it answers, particularly when looking for the complex answers to explain the contrasting performances of the two nations. Still, the exercise is worthwhile if for no other reason than that it throws into sharper relief the magnitude of the Japanese achievements already discussed.

Nations are not likely to achieve enduring benefits of modernization if they narrowly concentrate on economic change alone. The changes engineered by Japan's Meiji-era leadership affected nearly every aspect of the nation's cultural and social life. While the word *revolution* in recent usage has been associated with violence and left-wing causes, Japan's Meiji era deserves to be regarded as revolutionary if we think of that term as referring to sweeping changes brought about in a short period of time. Remarkably little domestic bloodshed accompanied the time of radical change in Japan—in sharp contrast to the century-long history of violence and civil warfare that engulfed China beginning in the mid-nineteenth century. A Japanese leadership, flexible and responsive, came to the fore in time to make the changes necessary to effect *from above* the *fukoku kyohei* goals it set for itself. The failure of a similar leadership to emerge in China doomed the Middle Kingdom to revolution, protracted and chaotic, *from below*.

CHINA AND THE WEST

The impact of the West was approximately the same for both China and Japan. In a word, it was devastating. Western imperialism exhausted and demoralized both countries. Both nations were overwhelmed by the superior power of Western navies and armed might. Both felt the impact of Western industrial societies with their superior technology and productivity. Both felt the sting of Western arrogance and racism. The sign at the entrance to the public park in the foreign section of Shanghai forbidding entrance to "Chinese and dogs" became a lasting emblem of Western audacity.

Yet, if the impact of the West was the same, the response of the two countries was quite different.

The very size of China impeded its response to the Western challenge. China was large and difficult to steer even in tranquil times. A more important liability, however, was China's inertia. China was a nation in the grip of its own dazzling past. It is quite simply the oldest continuous civilization in the world. It has survived for a span of four thousand years, while all the other great civilizations of the ancient past disappeared long ago. For so long, China had been *Chung-kuo*, the Central Kingdom, had thought of itself as *the* center of the civilized world, it was understandably difficult for its nineteenth century leaders to imagine that it had anything to learn from the West. If change was necessary to meet the challenge of the West, Chinese leaders insisted that the changes be made *within* the framework of traditional ways. The framework itself, the political, social, and educational institutions of old China, could not be violated. Thus, it was guaranteed that the changes China instituted would be superficial, as temporary and piecemeal as footdragging officials could make them. If there was an immediate, specific need for this or that project, an armory here or a shipyard there, the foreigners might be asked to help. The possibility of wholesale, radical change was, however, adamantly rejected.

When reformers in 1867 proposed to set up a school where foreigners would be invited to teach astronomy and mathematics on a very limited basis, the emperor's adviser Wo Jen objected vehemently, suggesting that the barbarians were so cunning and unreliable that they well might intentionally mislead their Chinese students. In addition, he said, I have "never heard of anyone from ancient down to modern times who could use mathematics to raise the nation from a state of decline or to strengthen it in time of weakness." The empire is very big, Wo Jen reminded the emperor, and if it was deemed absolutely necessary to teach modern mathematics, a search could be made for some Chinese citizen who has mastered the technique. "Why is it limited to barbarians, and why is it necessary to learn from barbarians?" he complained. In all similar debates on borrowing ideas from the West, there was a consistent strain of conservative thinking which insisted that Westerners were simply barbarians, people without principles, people who had stumbled on to some trifling inventions—steamships, and Gatling guns, for example—which had given them a momentary edge in world affairs. To the conservatives, it made no sense to risk China's glorious cultural legacy in exchange for a few barbarian "techniques." The Japanese were aware of the risks, were troubled by them, but in the end opted to try for the best of both worlds.

To take a specific example, consider the difference between the Japanese and Chinese attitudes toward travel abroad. Recall the Iwakura mission and the thousands of students and officials who were dispatched overseas in its wake. Nothing remotely similar occurred in China. Far from going abroad en masse, the Chinese were unwilling to even open an embassy in any foreign country. The first Chinese ambassador was appointed only in 1877, to London, and then only because the British had demanded an apology mission be sent to make amends for the murder of a British official on Chinese territory. Ambassador Kuo Sung-tao was a brilliant student of foreign affairs, with exactly the kind of inquiring, open mind China needed to acquaint itself with the Western world. The letters and advice he sent to Peking from his post in London were sorely needed and might have provided the government with much-needed grounds for reform. Instead, they were almost totally ignored, and the ambassador was attacked as an ignorant man who had fallen into the clutches of the barbarians. A reactionary court official, Liu Hsi-hung, sent along to keep an eye on Ambassador Kuo, did everything possible to undermine the authority of the ambassador. Some measure of Liu's sophistication as a judge of the modern world may be gained from his account of England.

England, he wrote, was the inverted image of China, and everything in England was abnormal; England's days were China's nights; Englishmen wrote from the left, Chinese from the right; England honored women, China honored men; England was governed by people's representatives, while China was ruled by a supreme emperor. For this inverted condition, Liu offered an explanation: "It is because their country is situated under the axis of the earth. Their heaven, which is above them, is actually under our ground. Hence their customs and institutions are all upside down." Japan had its share of narrow-minded xenophobes too, of course. It was Japan's good fortune, however, that their voices were drowned out by more openminded and farsighted reformers. It was China's tragedy that the voices of men of the caliber of Ambassador Kuo were muffled. When a diary record of Ambassador Kuo's mission to London was published in China, conservative literati saw to it that it was banned and the printing plates destroyed. They were aghast because Kuo had lauded Western nations for having supported a civilization of two thousand years' antiquity. These Western nations, Kuo declared, did not deserve to be equated with barbarian tribes that populated China's frontierlands as official Chinese teachings insisted.

A similar fate befell the first students to study abroad. After years of debate, a group of 120 long-gowned youngsters was sent to America in the 1870s for schooling. Though modest when compared to Japan's embrace of Western education, it was an ambitious project calling for a fifteen-year term of study abroad. In 1881, however, the project was terminated and the students recalled on the grounds that the young scholars were neglecting their Chinese studies and "indulging in foreign customs."

With reactionaries as strong as they were in places of influence, it is not surprising that their attitudes undermined even some of the modest beginnings at modernization in China. Unlike Japan, the initiative to build the first railway in China came from the foreigners. Built in 1876 with foreign capital, China's first railway, the Shanghai–Wusung line, aroused widespread opposition to the railway from conservative gentry. The gentry in turn fanned local fears by saying that the railway violated traditional *feng shui*, the natural flow of energy in the land, which would in turn lead to floods, famines, and other disasters. Within a year, the authorities forced the railway's owners to sell the line to the government. There would have been merit in this action—at least from a Chinese nationalistic point of view—if it had been a ruse to stifle foreign takeover of a vital national asset. Instead, the local Chinese governor had the track ripped out of the earth and transported to a swamp on the island of Taiwan where it could do no harm. Twenty years later, the total railway mileage on the China mainland was still only 240. By the time the Empire of China collapsed in 1911, China had about six thousand miles of track, almost all of it built, operated and financed, by foreigners. In much smaller Japan, the network of thirty-seven thousand miles of track laid down by 1906, almost entirely built, operated and financed at home, is essentially the same system that is in place today.

The striking difference between the Chinese and Japanese response to the West will be important to bear in mind in an examination of the rise of Japanese imperialism.

ADDITIONAL READING

For general overviews of the Meiji era, see Kenneth B. Pyle, *The New Generation in Meiji Japan: Problems in Cultural Identity, 1885–1895* (1969); Marius Jansen, "The Meiji State: 1868–1912," in James B. Crowley, ed., *Modern East Asia: Essays in Interpretation* (1970); Roger F. Hackett, "The Era of Fulfillment, 1877–1911," in Arthur E. Tiede-mann, ed., *An Introduction to Japanese Civilization* (1974); John W. Hall, "A Monarch for Modern Japan," in Robert E. Ward, ed., *Political Development in Modern Japan* (1973); Donald Shively, ed., *Tradition and Modernization in Japanese Culture* (1971); and Marius Jansen, ed., *Changing Japanese Attitudes Towards Modernization* (1965).

More specialized studies include Carol Gluck, *Japan's Modern Myths: Ideology in the Late Meiji Period* (1985); Donald J. Roden, *Schooldays in Imperial Japan: A Study in the Culture of A Student Elite* (1980); Edward Seidensticker, *Low City, High City: Tokyo from Edo to the Earthquake: How the Shogun's Ancient Capital Became a Great Modern City, 1867–1923* (1983); Robert A. Rosenstone, *Mirror in the Shrine: American Encounters with Meiji Japan* (1988); and Carmen Blacker, *The Japanese Enlightenment: A Study of the Writings of Fukuzawa Yukichi* (1964).

Studies focusing on economic growth during the Meiji era include Thomas C. Smith, *Political Change and Industrial Development in Japan: Governmental Enterprise, 1868–1880* (1955); Byron Marshall, *Capitalism and Nationalism in Prewar Japan: The Ideology of the Business Elite, 1868–1941* (1967); William Lockwood, *The Economic Development of Japan: Growth and Structural Change, 1868–1938* (1954); Kazushi Ohkawa and Henry Rosovsky, "A Century of Japanese Economic Growth," in William Lockwood, ed., *The State and Economic Enterprise in Japan* (1965); and Earl Kinmonth, *The Self-Made Man in Meiji Japanese Thought: From Samurai to Salary Man* (1981).

On the subject of educators and foreign employees in Meiji Japan, see Ardath W. Burks, ed., *The Modernizers: Overseas Students, Foreign Employees, and Meiji Japan* (1985); D. Eleanor Westney, *Imitation and Innovation: The Transfer of Western Organizational Patterns to Meiji Japan* (1987); Ernest Presseisen, *Before Aggression: Europeans Train the Japanese Army* (1965); F. G. Notehelfer, "On Idealism and Realism in the Thought of Okakura Tenshin," *Journal of Japanese Studies* 16/2 (Summer 1990); and F. G. Note-helfer, *American Samurai: Captain L. L. Janes and Japan* (1984).

The account of the experiences in America of Meiji businessman Arai Rioichiro is based on *Samurai and Silk: A Japanese and American Heritage* (1986), by Arai's grand-daughter, Haru Matsukata Reischauer.

4

IMPERIALISM

The last decades of the nineteenth century saw a dramatic intensification of international rivalry among European powers, joined at the end of the century by the United States, for overseas colonies. As a result, in an arc of ancient lands from India, through Burma, Cambodia, Laos, Vietnam, Malaya, and on to the islands of the East Indies, only Siam managed to escape being turned into a colony of one Western power or another. While the Chinese Empire maintained its formal independence, it was reduced to "semi-colonial" status in a succession of wars and incidents in the years after the Opium War (1840–1842). Emerging as the victor in each of these engagements, the foreigners gained extraordinary economic, military, and legal privileges on Chinese soil, especially along the coast in the great "treaty ports." These rights were legitimized in a network of interlocking treaties and backed by armed power, so-called "gunboat diplomacy," which left China prostrate and Japan an alarmed observer. Britain had led the imperialist drive into Asia, including China, but other nations, including France, the Netherlands, Germany, and Russia competed to gain position and advantage in that region.

THE EXPANSIONIST URGE

At the root of the expansionist urge was the need for markets, cheap labor, and raw materials to fuel economic growth at home. Japan felt especially insecure because of the paucity of industrial raw materials available at home. Once economic growth took off and generated profits too large to be invested in the mother country, there was an added need to find overseas opportunities for lucrative capital investment schemes. Military, especially naval, bases were then required to guarantee the security of the assets and properties and personnel sent from the homeland.

In addition to commercial gain which promoted imperial expansion, there were some less-tangible motivating and rationalizing factors at work. Social Darwinism, which sought to apply the biological theories of Charles Darwin to society, had a powerful appeal. The complex of doctrines which were included under this name included a survival of the fittest interpretation of economics. Competitive struggle weeded out the weak, incompetent, and unfit and selected the strong, able, and wise. This notion, whether applied to the domestic economy or to the competition among nations or races, provided the strongest players, whether they were millionaire bankers or the superpowers of the day, with the satisfying reassurance that they were products of an inevitable and entirely healthy process of natural selection.

To be sure, some stressed a corollary doctrine which reverberated with Christian charity, that the stewardship of wealth obliged the prosperous to try to ameliorate the condition of those less well off. Doubtless because of this, the very word *imperialism* had a positive ring to it. In the twentieth century, the label came to have pejorative overtones—it was associated with plunder and greed. However, in the heyday of imperialism, the late nineteenth century, the term was associated with progress and enlightenment. Frenchmen spoke proudly of the propagation of French language and law as their *mission civilisatrice*, "to bring into light and into liberty the races and peoples still enslaved by ignorance and despotism." England's responsibility for governing India had been placed by the "inscrutable decree of providence upon the shoulders of the British race," said Rudyard Kipling. It was the "white man's burden," said the great English poet and story writer who was fond of describing Eastern peoples as "lesser breeds."

THE MISSIONARY AND CULTURAL IMPERIALISM

Among the most keenly felt burdens of the white man was the obligation to spread the Gospel to the "unwashed bundles of original sin" in the Eastern world. Not long after the United States obtained the Philippine Islands as its first major imperialist acquisition, President McKinley revealed to a group of clergymen that God told him to do it. On his knees at his bedside in the White House praying for divine guidance, the president learned that God wished him to annex the islands and "do the best we could for them." More often, however, it was China that excited the religious ideals of Americans. "Planting the shining cross on every hill and in every valley" of China was the way Anson Burlingame, the American ambassador to China in the 1860s, expressed this impulse to export Western beliefs. The prospect of converting China, with nearly a quarter of the planet's population, represented the biggest opportunity to Christendom since the conversion of the Roman Empire, and by 1900 the China mission field attracted more Americans than any other. The urgency of their mission emerges in the writings and sermons of the mission-aries. The Reverend Hudson Taylor, the founder of the China Inland Mission, speaking to a church group in Detroit in 1894 of the "heathens" awaiting the ministry, said:

> The gospel must be preached to these people in a very short time; they are passing away. Every day, every day, oh how they sweep over. There is a great Niagara of souls passing into the dark in China. Every day, every week, every month, they are passing away. A million a month are dying without God.

There can be no disputing the noble intention of many Christian missionaries who travelled to Asia in ever-increasing numbers in the late 1800s and often endured lifetimes of hardship and privation. They were responsible for an abun-dance of good works, for the establishment of hospitals, clinics, and orphanages. Some were in the vanguard of assaults on the social evils of the day: prostitution, narcotics, and footbinding. Missionary-established schools, from kindergartens to universities, made a major contribution to modern China, and the graduates of these schools went on to become leaders in business, science, medicine, government and education.

Still, it is proper to discuss evangelism within the context of imperialism. It was the cultural arm of imperialism, many Chinese nationalists insisted. The missionaries constituted a "protected elite" in China. Their presence on Chinese soil, certainly in the era of the unequal treaties, always implied the presence behind them of their nation's flag, laws, and threat of arms in the pro-tection of their rights. "There is no group of foreigners who have done more harm to China than the modern missionaries. . .," wrote T'ang Leang-li, an ardent advocate of Western culture, who nevertheless faulted the missionary for his "subversive activities." Criticizing the bigotry and intolerance of the mis-sionary and their general ignorance of Chinese culture, T'ang wrote:

> By their teachings they have denationalised hundreds of thousands of Chinese converts, and have thus been instrumental, to a great extent, in dis-integrating not only the body but also the spirit of the nation. Indirectly, by their misrepresentations, they have made the civilization of China griev-ously misunderstood in the West, and are therefore largely responsible for the loss of prestige which China has suffered for nearly a century.

Making missionaries all the more important in East–West relations was the fact that, until well into the twentieth century, they were the chief source of information about the countries of the East for Americans and others in the Western world. While some few became sympathetic interpreters of these little-known worlds to Western audiences, the majority dwelled on the supposedly bizarre traits of Chinese (they eat with sticks, write from right to left, and the family name comes first). Or worse, and quite commonly, denigrated the Chi-nese as a morally and culturally inferior "species." "The needs of China will be met permanently, completely, only by Christian civilization," one prominent missionary wrote. Henry Ward Beecher, "the greatest preacher since Saint Paul," could say from his Brooklyn pulpit, "I don't know any way, except to <u>blow</u> them (the Chinese) up with nitroglycerine, if we are ever to get them to heaven." American Protestant missionary S. Wells Williams—author of an 1882 compendium, *The Middle Kingdom*, for many years the standard authority on China—could sum up the character of the Chinese as "vile and polluted in a shocking degree." After setting forth a litany of evil traits including the "alarming extent of the use of opium" (enthusiastically conveyed to China by British and American merchants, it might have been noted), Williams warms up to his condemnation of Chinese frailties in this remarkable epiphany of malice. Their faults, he wrote, "form a full unchecked torrent of human depravity, and prove the existence of a kind and degree of moral degradation of which an excessive statement can scarcely be made, or an adequate conception hardly be formed."

Little wonder that the novelist of China, Pearl Buck, herself a daughter of missionary parents, recalled the missionaries as "so scornful of any civilization except their own, so harsh in their judgments, so coarse and insensitive among a sensitive and cultivated people that my heart has fairly bled with shame."

The image fostered by the missionary blended well with a congruent set of attitudes which gained wide currency in the Western world in the late nineteenth century: the notion of an impending struggle between the forces of light, represented by the advanced countries of the Christian West, with the forces of darkness, represented by the backward nations of the pagan East. It was one thing to suggest that the West should bestow the blessings of superior civilization on China, that we should carry our "happiness and liberty" across the ocean to Asia, as poet Walt Whitman suggested. But what if the Chinese, with their well-known numbers (or hordes), rejected the offer? The highly regarded American historian, Charles Eliot Norton, noted near the end of the century how much American power and influence had grown in the 1800s. However, he pondered, "we are brought face to face with the grave problem which the next century is to solve—whether our civilization can maintain itself, and make advance, against the pressure of ignorant and barbaric multitudes." It was the destiny and the duty of the West to confront and control the rest of the world, many argued. John Fiske, a popular essayist and lecturer, saw the history of mankind as being one long struggle between the East (with its "barren and monotonous way of living and thinking") and the West ("making life as rich and fruitful as possible in varied material and spiritual achievement"). The dimensions of the United States, Fiske exulted, would one day reach from "pole to pole" and surpass "any empire that has yet existed."

ALFRED THAYER MAHAN

It was Alfred Thayer Mahan, however, more than any other American who became the most articulate and well-known spokesman for imperialist expansion, and more specifically the idea that it was not the meek, but the nations with the biggest navies who inherited the earth. Mahan, a teacher and ultimately president of the Naval War College, argued that it would be impossible for any nation in the modern world to stand still. Nations must either expand or stagnate. Not only were markets and raw materials at issues but the spiritual vitality of a nation hangs in the balance. Heroic values, moral discipline, and integrity all accompanied the acceptance of great challenges, he insisted. His monumentally important book, *The Influence of Sea Power on History* (1890), one of twenty he authored, won him an ardent following both at home and abroad. His close friend Theodore Roosevelt would take Mahan's professorial exhortation that command of the seas was the price of survival and translate it into blustery chauvinism: "Our people are neither cravens nor weaklings, and we face the future high of heart and confident of soul, eager to do the great work of a great power." In response to Mahan's arguments, naval construction grew rapidly. In 1880, the U. S. Navy ranked twelfth in the world. As late as 1891, when a sailors' fracas in a Chilean port city threatened to erupt into war, the United States backed off in part because the Chilean fleet was superior to the American. By 1900, however, the U.S. fleet, with seventeenth battleships, was third in size to that of Britain and France. During the Roosevelt presidency (1901–1909), the U.S. Navy continued its buildup.

Mahan's *Influence*, required reading for naval cadets in the United States as well as Britain, was soon translated into Japanese and, in 1897, was adopted as a textbook by both army and navy military academies and distributed by the government to the libraries of high schools throughout the nation. For the next four decades down, it would have nearly the same influence in shaping Japanese strategic thinking as it did in the West. The samurai of old had always possessed a strong sense of mission, but now, looking through the prism of Mahan's doctrines, the new Japanese leadership began to acquire a powerful sense of national mission which was no longer confined to the home islands of Japan.

It should not be imagined that the spokesmen for imperialists went unanswered in the United States. Anti-imperialist sentiments were widespread and deeply rooted in American traditions, the origins of the country in a revolution against overseas rule, as well as the national commitment to freedom and liberty. Even big business, usually regarded as the spearhead of imperialism, was unsure of the advantages of expansion into China. The Chinese, "poor as a rat," has nothing except "silk handkerchiefs and bamboo pipes" to pay for expensive American products, groused an executive of the Great Northern Railroad in 1893. Americans situated in a vast continent full of resources to explore and exploit did not feel the same imperative for overseas ventures as their European cousins and were more prone to contemplate the dire effect a vigorous imperial policy would have on American values and ideals.

Still, while America was not in the vanguard of the imperial drive, it did slowly, even reluctantly, participate. For example, while America did not join the British, French, and Russians in military assaults on China, she was quick to take advantage of the Middle Kingdom's weakness and vulnerability. Americans ended up claiming the same privileged status under the unequal treaties which the more overtly aggressive imperial powers dictated to the Empire of

China. This allowed the United States, as historian John K. Fairbank notes, to maintain a holier-than-thou attitude, "to enjoy the fruits of European aggression, without the moral burden of ourselves committing aggression." In the Pacific, America took some first tentative steps at empire building by occupying the Midway islands in 1867 and securing naval-station rights in Samoa in 1878. In 1887, the United States received exclusive rights from the still-independent Kingdom of Hawaii to build naval facilities on Oahu island, and a few years later American planters, bankers, and clergymen were conspiring to overthrow Queen Liliuokalani's government. American expansionists confidently began to claim the Pacific as an "Anglo-Saxon sea."

PRIORITIES IN JAPAN

The generation of reformers which dominated the scene in Japan after 1868 was, as seen, preoccupied with a myriad of tasks aimed at transforming the nation's political, economic, educational, and military institutions. From time to time, however, disgruntled samurai (or ex-samurai) proposed overseas military campaigns, usually against China, Korea, or Russia. Such campaigns would serve both emotional and practical purposes. They would help to assuage the wounded feelings of warriors troubled by the inability of samurai swords and *bushido* spirit to prevent the Western incursion into Japan and the unequal treaties. In addition, the proposers calculated that overseas adventures would require the government to reconsider its policy of dismantling the samurai class. Their skills and courage would be needed, it was argued, to ensure the success of any military undertakings. Particularly vehement demands to "chastise Korea" for supposed insults to Japan were considered in 1873, for example. Debate over the proposal to punish the Koreans seriously fragmented the Restoration leadership , resulting in assassinations and riots, and was in part the cause of the full-scale civil war of 1878, the Satsuma Rebellion.

NORMANTON INCIDENT

The sinking of the British freighter-passenger ship *Normanton* off the Wakayama coast in 1886 focused the attention of the Japanese public on the unequal treaties. The Japanese public was outraged to learn that Captain Drake and his English crew took to their lifeboats and escaped with no loss of life while all twenty-three of the abandoned Japanese passengers drowned. A consular court in Kobe heard the case, and the British judge exonerated the captain and his crew. Widespread indignation forced a re-hearing, but even then the captain received only a three-month sentence, and no compensation was awarded. More than any economic issue, the *Normanton* case underscored the highhandedness of the foreigner and the helplessness of the Japanese forced to endure the unequal treaties.

In the end, however, Meiji oligarchs stood firmly against this and similar proposals on the grounds that they would sidetrack the nation from its first priority, which was to concentrate all the nation's resources and energies on domestic rebuilding. Only then would Japan be able to achieve its most urgent foreign policy goal, the revision of the unequal treaty system in order to break the semicolonial ties forced on Japan by the Western powers in the years after the Perry visit. Early steps toward an equal treaty relationship with Japan were taken by the United States. As early as 1878, America signed an agreement returning tariff autonomy to Japan—but with the understanding that implementation would be delayed until the other powers similarly restored tariff rights to Japan. England was the key player in this game; other nations would follow the lead of the mighty British Empire. By 1894, England, aware of Japan's growing power and the commercial value of her good will, signed treaties which marked the beginning of the end of Japan's unequal legal and economic status in the world community. Less than three weeks later, Japan declared war on China. This First Sino–Japanese War (1894–1895)—there would be a Second Sino–Japanese War in the 1930s—was fought to determine who would control Korea.

KOREA

In 1894, Korea was an independent kingdom with a monarchy of its own. Parts of the small country had been ruled and settled by China in early times, but direct Chinese control came to an end in the early fourth century. Still, the Korean people, like the Japanese, remained deeply indebted to China for much of their culture. The higher civilization of China, its art and architecture, political and economic institutions, religion and philosophy, flowed across the Yalu River boundary and moved south down the Korean peninsula—and ultimately across the sea to Japan. When Korean scholars studied the Classics, it was the Confucian Classics which absorbed their attention. Korean kings justified their rule by claiming moral superiority and invoking the Confucian notion of the "mandate of heaven." Korean painters and sculptors took inspiration from Chinese masters.

And yet, Koreans have never considered themselves to be simply an offshoot of Chinese civilization. They are proud of their individuality. Like the Japanese, they have borrowed, but they have also modified and innovated. Buddhist temples in Korea share some features with Buddhist temples in China, but they also have distinctive Korean touches. Traditional Korean clothing does not look like Chinese or Japanese. Korean homes are different from their neighbors in China. Korean cuisine is different. The language is a good illustration of the difficulty of being too categorical about Chinese influence. The spoken language, first of all, belongs to a family of languages totally different from Chinese. When it came to writing, however, the Koreans early on borrowed the thousands of Chinese ideographs. In the fourteenth century, the scholar-king Sejong, irritated at the thought that his people had to rely on this cumbersome imported method of writing, commissioned experts to devise—on solid linguistic principles—an easily mastered alphabet of phonetic symbols. The result was *han'gul* (Korean writing), the most scientific system of writing in general use anywhere in the world. A glance at street signs or a printed page of a Seoul newspaper today reveals that both the native *han'gul* and the borrowed Chinese characters are still employed to write Korean.

While the Korean kingdom was not under the direct political control of China, it did defer to China in certain matters. In traditional Chinese terms, Korean rulers maintained a tributary relationship toward the Chinese emperor. In theory at least, the Son of Heaven ruled "all under heaven" (*t'ien hsia*), the Chinese expression for the entire known world. Of all the Asian nations which regularly sent tribute missions to pay their respects in Peking, Korea was the most loyal and dutiful. In modern Western terms, Korea was a protectorate of China. This meant that Korea was entitled to govern itself internally but would consult with China in matters related to royal succession, defense, and foreign relations. In turn, China was expected to act as defender of Korea. Such protection would be welcome, because nineteenth-century Korea was governed by a reactionary court and beset by internal rebellions. The nickname "Hermit Kingdom" suggested how isolated and technologically backward Korea was. By the latter half of the century, however, the Chinese Empire, weakened and humiliated by a string of defeats in wars with the Western imperialists, was clearly unable to defend its own frontiers, much less guarantee the security of clients like Korea and Vietnam. Accordingly, Korea became an international battleground for contending powers.

The United States was one of the first powers to attempt to force the Hermit Kingdom into contact with the West. In 1866, an American merchant ship, *General Sherman*, sought entry into Korean waters. A Korean crowd, enraged by the crew's cavalier resort to armed force, seized the ship, burned it to the waterline, and slayed the crew. It is little wonder that the Koreans remained firm in their seclusion policy and regarded the foreigners as "thieves and robbers"—one of the goals of the *General Sherman*, and a similar mission two years later, was to plunder treasure thought to be buried in Korean royal tombs. In 1871, in a move reminiscent of the Perry mission, President Ulysses Grant authorized the American minister to China, Frederick P. Low, to lead a naval squadron of five ships on a surveying expedition preparatory to opening it up for trade. When the American flag was insulted, the surveying expedition turned into a punitive expedition to teach a lesson to Koreans or, as Ambassador Low called them, that "semi-barbarous hostile race." The lesson was harsh: Korean fortifications were destroyed and several hundred Koreans were killed. Although the cost in American life and material was low, Washington decided that further efforts to open Korea were not worth the probable cost.

For Japan, however, it was a different story. Weak and isolated, Korea *by itself* represented no threat to Japan. But a Korea, only fifty miles distant at the closest point, so weak that it fell into the hands of another power—that was an alarming prospect. Such a Korea was "like a dagger pointed at the heart of Japan," warned Klemens Wilhelm Jakob Meckel, a Prussian officer, tactician, and adviser to the General Staff of the Japanese Army in the Meiji era. Meckel lectured Japanese cadets on European military history and led them into the field for their first staff exercises in 1885. He taught the importance of communication and transportation in the modern army and provided the high command with the structure that would endure until 1945. But Meckel's dagger metaphor may have been the most enduring contribution he made to military thinking. General MacArthur would borrow the metaphor to underscore the importance of a non-Communist Korea in 1950. The meaning then was the same. Korea as Korea was no menace, but Korea as part of an expanding Communist bloc was a "dagger."

It was Imperial Russia that worried Japan most. Russia, which had faced west toward Europe for so long, began to turn its attention to the East in the nineteenth century. From 1858 to 1860 she acquired 400,000 square miles of territory from China, a vast emptiness at the time. This "Russian Far East," however, and the schemes to populate it, and develop its timber and maritime resources and the military and naval bases that were built in the area, signalled the Czar's intention to make Russia an Asian power. Of greater concern to Japan was the growing interest of Russia in Korea, which could provide Russia with the kind of year-round ice-free "warm-water port" not available in the Russian Far East. Even the southern-most port of Vladivostok was ice-bound for several months each winter. When Russia began making agreements to provide military advisers to the Korean government in 1885, the British responded by occupying an island off the south coast of Korea in order to prevent "probable occupation by another power." This little phrase says worlds about imperialist rivalry. It encapsulates what American diplomat George Kennan calls "contingent necessity," a favorite device of expansionists, including the United States. It says that "we do not covet a certain territory or exclusive right, but we know that if we fail to act, some other country will surely do so." With five or six countries using the same rationale for expansion, it becomes difficult to isolate any one culprit as the predator.

JAPAN'S "LINE OF ADVANTAGE"

In 1890, in a speech before the first session of the newly created Diet, Yamagata Aritomo, the architect of Japan's modern army, made an important distinction between Japan's "line of sovereignty" and its "line of advantage." Following Western thinking of the time, Yamagata stated that the nation must first defend its line of sovereignty which ran along its frontiers. Beyond that, however, because Asia seemed destined to be an arena of fierce conflict between the Western powers, Japan must have a line of advantage which it had to defend against any unfriendly power. Yamagata did not define with precision the exact course of the line of advantage, but he did state that it included Korea. Japanese would henceforth argue that Yamagata's "line of advantage" should have been understandable to Americans who enunciated a similar line in their Monroe Doctrine. That position, however, became less easy to rationalize after Japan formally annexed Korea into its empire in 1910.

In 1891, the Russians announced the beginning of the construction of the 5,000-mile-long Trans-Siberian Railroad to link European Russia with the Far East via the frozen wastelands of Siberia. Work on this giant undertaking would not be completed until after the turn of the century, but the project increased Japan's concern about the likelihood of expanded Russian activity in the East. In the meantime, China was struggling to maintain its status as overseer in Korea. By 1894, China, at the invitation of pro-Chinese royalty in Seoul, was close to turning the peninsula into its own satellite. When a pro-Japanese Korean reformer was assassinated in March 1894, Japan linked the deed to Chinese machinations and characterized it as an insult. Relations between the two countries worsened a few months later when China sent troops to Korea to help put down internal disturbances. Japan did likewise and demanded that Korea declare an end to its special relationship to China. A declaration of war followed on August 1.

THE FIRST SINO–JAPANESE WAR (1894–1895)

Hostilities in the Sino–Japanese War lasted only a few months and were confined mainly to the coastal areas. Foreign observers, looking at the map and the sheer bulk of China and comparing the size of the two nations' navies, expected a victory by China. The war turned out to be a test case for the generation-long modernization efforts of the two countries. Although the Chinese navy had nearly twice the number of capital ships as Japan, the crucial naval battle off the mouth of the Yalu River in September 1894 proved that other factors were more important. China was a badly divided nation, in the grips of what would come to be known as "warlordism." The nation did not pull together; several naval squadrons remained "neutral" in the interest of their own self-preservation. The Chinese ships were older, slower, and maneuvered poorly. The Chinese officers were poorly trained in modern tactics—Admiral Ting brought his ships out in the formation of a cavalry charge, not altogether surprising since he had been a cavalry general. Too late, it was discovered that many of the shells for their Krupp guns were full of sand rather than gunpowder. The Navy had been systematically starved for funds by a corrupt dowager empress who diverted monies intended for modernization of her Navy into pet private projects, the most notorious of which was a luxurious marble barge for entertainment at her Summer Palace. It stands there still as a symbol of imperial extravagance and corruption. In the engagement at the Yalu River, one of the first modern naval battles in history, the Chinese fleet was decisively routed or sunk. One Chinese defeat followed another until a final fiasco at the Chinese port of Weihaiwei brought the war to an end. The Japanese captured the port from the rear and turned the Chinese guns in the forts on the Chinese ships in the harbor.

When one of the leading architects of the Meiji-era modernization drive, Ito Hirobumi, met with the Chinese statesman and modernizer Li Hung-chang to discuss peace terms in 1895, Ito recalled that the two leaders had met ten years earlier on Chinese soil. "Ten years ago I talked with you about reform. Why is it that up to now not a single thing has been changed or reformed?" Ito asked. Li's reply was the most succinct possible explanation for China's defeat: "Affairs in my country have been so confined by tradition that I could not accomplish what I desired."

SHIMONOSEKI

The peace talks were held at the port of Shimonoseki on Japanese soil, itself a galling symbolic affront for the Middle Kingdom, accustomed throughout its history to having its Eastern neighbors come to China in search of civilization and learning. In the Treaty of Shimonoseki (1895), the Chinese were forced to recognize the independence of Korea, thus terminating the age-old tributary relationship between the two countries. With Korea now independent—and as weak as ever—Japan could expand its influence on the peninsula without worrying about Chinese involvement. Russia, however, would remain a concern. Most importantly, the treaty provided for the cession of the island of Taiwan[1] and the Liaotung peninsula, southern gateway to Manchuria. In addition, China agreed to pay a large financial indemnity to Japan to cover war costs. The indemnity would have been much larger were it not for an incident in which Li Hung-chang was shot by a Japanese fanatic. The Japanese, mortified by this stain to their honor, lowered the indemnity figure by a third and dispatched the emperor's personal physician to treat the Chinese envoy.

The benefits to Japan were enormous. The indemnity from China, the equivalent to about 15 percent of Japan's gross national product in 1895, was channelled into launching a government-owned iron and steel industry at Yawata on the southern island of Kyushu. The Yawata Iron and Steel Works, after several organizational changes and mergers, was to become after World War II the Nippon Steel Corporation, the world's largest producer of steel. The Chinese withdrawal from Korea did not, of course, mark true independence for Korea in anything but name. The Hermit Kingdom, as weak as ever, became increasingly vulnerable to encroachment by both Japan and Russia, and the rivalry there would lead to another war for Japan a decade later. The cession of Taiwan to Japan marked the official beginning of *Dai Nihon* (Greater Japan, the Empire of Japan). Japan, only one year after the unequal treaties began to be lifted from its shoulders, went from being a victim of imperialism to becoming an imperialist power itself.

All the elements of imperialist advantage were enhanced by the stunning Japanese victory. The cardinal principle of Japanese military planning—preventing Korea from falling under the control of another power—was a step closer to realization. Liaotung would give Japan a foothold on the Asian main-

---

[1]Taiwan is both the Japanese and the Chinese pronuciation of the island. It has sometimes been referred to in the West as Formosa, a name bestowed on the island in the 16th century by would-be Portuguese colonizers who called it the "Beautiful Island" (Ilha Formosa)

TWO VIEWS OF CIVILIZATION AND NATIONAL DESTINY
"Does it not look as if God were not only preparing in our Anglo-Saxon civilization the die with which to stamp the peoples of the earth, but as if he were massing behind that die the mighty power with which to press it?"

—The Reverend Josiah Strong, *Our Country*, 1898.

"The Corean War is to decide whether Progress shall be the law in the East, as it has long been in the West, or whether Retrogression, fostered once by the Persian Empire, then by Carthage, and again by Spain, and now at last (last in world's history we hope) by the Manchurian Empire of China, shall possess the Orient forever."

—The Reverend Uchimura Kanzo, Japanese Christian leader, 1895.

land for the first time, in a zone ideal for military bases and the exploitation of mineral resources which were in abundant supply nearby. Taiwan gave Japan a strategic anchor that would allow Japan's "advance to the south" and an opportunity to develop the island's agricultural resources, especially rice and sugar, for the needs of the mother country. The indemnity, as we have seen, helped to catapult Japan toward the heavy industry stage of economic development.

GLORY

In addition, there was glory. The war had been immensely popular in Japan. Artists delighted in depicting scenes of bravery and daring on the battlefield. Every Japanese came to know, through poems, plays, books, and finally in the school curriculum, the (possibly fictitious) story of the brave bugler boy who went on bugling with his last breath long after bullets had felled him. "I blow my bugle with my soul; its voice is the voice of *Yamato damashii*," one poem read. The emphasis on the gallantry of unknown farm boys with humble ranks and no warrior pedigree may or may not have been intentional. It validated, however, the decision of the Meiji oligarchs to opt for a conscript army. As cultural historian Donald Keene writes, "The fact that humble soldiers could perform deeds of gallantry normally associated with the samurai proved that their virtues were shared by the entire Japanese people and not the property of professional soldiers."

Artists' war prints, issued with the announcement of each new engagement, were so popular as to require special warnings about the danger of pickpockets at the print stores where they were released to the public. Over three thousand of the brightly colored *nishikie* variety of colored woodblock prints (often in triptych form) were produced during the nine-month war, the most popular of them selling as many as one hundred thousand copies. Of the Chinese, only the luckless Admiral Ting was esteemed in the popular media in Japan. In contrast to most Chinese who were seen as cowardly, the admiral, "a lone crane among a flock of chickens," showed proper mettle by committing suicide after his surrender at Weihaiwei. Donald Keene has studied the phenomenon of the war prints and notes their racist content. It was not simply that the artists uniformly portrayed the Japanese soldiers as gallant and the Chinese as running pell-mell from combat. Even the physical appearance of the two peoples sets them sharply apart from each other:

> The Chinese are distinguishable from the Japanese not only by their costumes and grotesque grimaces of fear, but by their facial features. No two peoples ever seemed more strikingly dissimilar than the Japanese and Chinese of these prints. The Chinese have jutting cheekbones, broad noses, gaping mouths, slanting eyes and, of course, pigtails. The Japanese are dignified of mien and look distinctly European in their military moustaches and carefully trimmed haircuts. A print issued ten years later, at the time of the Russo–Japanese War, depicts the Japanese and Russians as virtually identical, except for the brownish tinge to the Russians' hair. Not only do the Japanese bear strong facial resemblances to the Europeans, but they stand as tall and maintain a similar dignity of demeanor, unlike the Chinese.

Japanese were no more immune to the feelings of martial achievement than the British who swelled with pride at maps showing a quarter of the surface of the earth in red—the color reserved for the British Empire—and boasted of domains on which the sun never set; or Americans, like the secretary of state, who would characterize the triumph over Spain in 1898 as that "splendid little war;" or Theodore Roosevelt who argued that "All the great masterful races have been fighting races." The more so for Japanese who, as a nation and a people, are keenly sensitive to the judgment of others. Perry's forced opening of Japan was seen as a humiliating blot on the nation's dignity, and the forty years of the unequal treaties had destroyed self-respect. Japan's desperate race to catch up with the advanced West had left its people feeling inferior and in awe of the West. How did the West regard the Japanese? Tokutomi Soho, social commentator and founding editor of *Kokumin no tomo* (The Nation's Friend), one of the Meiji era's most influential newspapers, expressed his irritation at Westerners who thought that Japan was a part of China. The better-informed Westerners, who know more of Japan's accomplishments, remained scornful because (as historian Kenneth Pyle translates Tokutomi's remarks):

> They regard the Japanese as a race close to monkeys, or as monkeys who are almost human. . . . They regard Japan's great reform of thirty years ago as a kind of sleight of hand. Regarding us as savages who have suddenly imitated civilization, they are impressed only by Japanese skill in imitating. . . . They overlook the fact that we have nurtured elements of civilization for three thousand years.

Tokutomi is a particularly apt example of the changing attitudes of what Kenneth Pyle calls "the new generation in Meiji Japan" in his book of that title.

Tokutomi was one of the new generation enamored of Western ways. For a time a convert to Christianity, he studied at Doshisha University, which opened in 1875 with close ties to the American Congregational church, and became convinced, as Pyle writes, "that the adoption of Western ethics and values was imperative for Japan's progress as a civilization." By the eve of the Sino–Japanese War, however, his Western reformist ideals were disappearing, and he was veering toward a militant nationalism. He favored a war to help establish a proud national identity which the world would have to recognize. Japan's rival, he reminded his readers, was not so much China as the Western world. Pyle quotes from an issue of *Kokumin no tomo* six weeks after the war began:

> We must remember that we are fighting before the whole world. Why do some Japanese say we fight in order to reform Korea, or to vanquish Peking, or to establish a huge indemnity? They should realize that we are fighting to determine once and for all Japan's position in the world. . . . If our country achieves a brilliant victory, all previous misconceptions will be dispelled. The true nature of our country and our national character will suddenly emerge like the sun breaking through a dense fog.

When the fighting was over, Tokutomi confided to his readers that the great lesson the war taught was that "the union of barbaric vigor and civilized learning is the greatest force in the world." Had they been able to read Tokutomi's newspaper, critics of Japan in the West would probably have joyfully seized on a Japanese using a word like barbaric (*yaban*) to describe themselves. What Tokutomi meant by the word, Pyle explains, is that Japanese had stunned the world not simply by their mastery of Prussian military tactics but by their "fearlessness, vigor, endurance, and daring as well." Tokutomi insisted that the higher standard of living enjoyed by Europeans had turned them soft, and only a shadow of their own barbarian vitality was preserved in such pastimes as mountain-climbing and horse racing.

THE WORLD REACTS

It was a theme that many Western writers would emphasize from this time on. Lafcadio Hearn, a writer and longtime resident of Japan, was one of the chief interpreters of Japan to America at the turn of the century, and his influential book, *Out of the East,* revealed his uncertainty about the fitness of Westerners to survive. They lacked the capacity of the Japanese to self-adapt to new conditions and the instant ability to face the unforeseen, he wrote in 1895. He goes on:

> For the Oriental has proved his ability to study and to master the results of our science upon a diet of rice, and on as simple a diet can learn to manufacture and to utilize our most complicated inventions. But the Occidental cannot even live except at a cost sufficient for the maintenance of twenty Oriental lives. . . . It may well be that the Western Races will perish—because of the cost of their existence.

Throughout the world there was mixed reaction to the Japanese victory. On the one hand, there was admiration for the Japanese success in building a modern nation in such a short period of time and, in some quarters, a shared pride that, after all, much of Japanese success derived from its adoption of Western models of modernization. In Britain, this positive response was carried a step further, to a growing awareness that Japan might be a useful ally. In 1902, the Anglo–Japanese Alliance was signed, linking in a military pact the largest navy of the Western world with the largest in the East, Great Britain with the "Britain of Asia" as some came to call Japan. It was the first such alliance, on equal terms, between an Eastern and a Western nation in modern times.

Feelings of admiration, however, were largely offset by another, contrary, reaction from the West. That is to say, most of the capitals of Europe greeted the Japanese victory as a catastrophe for the West. A terrifying image took shape in the minds of Europeans: a militarily aggressive Japan harnessing the vast resources and hordes of other Asian peoples under their domination, challenging an outnumbered and complacent West.

A new term playing upon racist forboding entered the lexicon of international relations: the "yellow peril." The term evoked the historical experience of Europeans—the havoc wreaked on the Roman Empire by the Huns and the later depradations of Mongol invaders. The term "yellow peril" was used earlier in the century, but it was Kaiser Wilhelm II who popularized it in 1895. Not long after the Japanese victory, the German Kaiser sent to his cousin, Czar Nicholas II of Russia, a drawing of a well-known German illustrator. The drawing, based on an allegorical sketch done by the Kaiser himself, revealed a nightmarish vision of a fiery storm sweeping toward Europe from the East. In the midst of the dark storm clouds was a seated Buddha. (It would have been hard to select a less apt symbol of Oriental militance—that of the Buddha, with his message of universal compassion and nonviolence.) In the foreground stands the Archangel Gabriel pointing out the approaching menace to armed women representing the nations of Europe. The drawing, entitled "Yellow Peril," was printed and circulated throughout the West, and in case anyone failed to understand the pictorial message, a caption was supplied: "Nations of Europe! Join in the defense of your faith and your home."

In the United States, sentiment against Japan was far less corrosive. In 1895, when the term "yellow peril" was used, Americans usually had Chinese immigrants in mind. The Chinese immigrants who, a generation earlier, had been welcomed as cheap labor to build the railroads, had now become targets for attack by those who saw them as competition to Caucasians in the workplace. Japanese immigrants did not become an important factor in domestic politics until after the turn of the century, when their numbers increased dramatically. As for Japan itself, Americans shared the British tendency to praise the Japanese as, in Mahan's words, "willing converts" to Western civilization. Charles Denby, American Minister to China, reported to the secretary of state that Japan "is now doing for China what the United States did for Japan. She has learnt Western civilization and she is forcing it on her unwieldy neighbor."

Of more immediate concern to Japan than yellow peril rhetoric was the swift diplomatic power-play response of Russia. Russia was alarmed by the foothold Japan gained on the continent, in Liaotung, the southern approach to Manchuria. Just six days after the signing of the Treaty of Shimonoseki, Russia instigated a move to force Japan to hand back, to retrocede, Liaotung "for the peace of Asia." Russia was joined in temporary alliance by Germany and France for this move which came to be known as the "Triple Intervention." Knowing that the intervention was backed by the threat of joint action by three hostile navies, Japan had no choice but to back down and agree to the return of Liaotung to China.

1898

Three years later, in 1898, the affront to Japan's dignity was compounded when it was learned that Russia had persuaded China to lease to her the Liaotung peninsula, including the naval base which the Russians christened "Port Arthur" (after the young Tsarevich). It was now clear, if there had been any doubt, that the Triple Intervention was unrelated to pious calls for peace in Asia. It was designed to allow Russia to seize what had been won by Japan. In addition, agreements were reached allowing Russia to build a network of railways across Manchuria to link up with the still-under-construction Trans-Siberian Railway. These were the 950-mile-long east–west "Chinese Eastern Railway" (CER) across Manchuria and a 650-mile-long north–south line known as the "South Manchurian Railway" (SMR).

At this stage in China's turbulent history, foreign-sponsored railroads were not simply railroads. They were the key elements by which countries gained exclusive control of parts of China. The Chinese Eastern Railway, for example, was financed by a new Russo-Chinese bank (Russian and French investments, despite the name). Russia was granted a belt of land along the railway where it would have exclusive administrative rights. This "leased territory" was so extensive that cities grew up within it; all the cities in this once sparsely populated section of China in fact stood on Russian soil. Harbin, at the junction of the CER and SMR, became the most famous of these Russianized cities. A small town in 1904, it grew to be the "Moscow of Asia," boasting a Russian university and several high schools, Russian courts, three Russian daily newspapers, Orthodox churches as well as administrative offices which were tantamount to being a Russian government. Russian "railway guards"—fifteen armed men per kilometer were permitted in the zone—became for all practical purposes an extension of the Tsar's army. Above all, exclusive mining and timbering rights were given to Russia. In this way, the CER and SMR became the framework for complete Russian domination of Manchuria. Japan, it seemed, would be effectively squeezed out of the rich treasurehouse.

Elsewhere in China, a similar scramble to "carve up the Chinese melon" was taking place. The Sino–Japanese War raised the fear in Europe that Japan's foothold on the mainland would menace the designs the European powers had of their own, and so the level of imperialist rivalry over China ascended to new heights as Britain, Germany, and France joined Russia in demanding and receiving leaseholds, naval bases, and economic concessions from a China too weak to resist. Most of this dismembering of China took place in 1898. Americans, fearful that U.S. businessmen might be squeezed out of China by Japanese and European efforts to establish exclusive "spheres of influence," responded with the famous "Open Door" policy. In a series of diplomatic notes circulated by Secretary of State John Hay in 1899, the United States asked the powers to keep the doors of China open and guarantee the "territorial integrity" of that beleaguered nation. In that way, all the powers would be able to exploit China on equal terms. Most of the powers, including Japan, responded to the notes by vaguely promising to observe the "open door"—as long as everyone else did.

Although the United States thus stayed out of the scramble for concessions on the China mainland, it formally became a colonial power in Asia in 1898 when an easy victory in the Spanish–American War caused the transfer of the Philippine Islands to American control. Hawaii also became an American territory in that year.

GAINING RESPECT

Speaking for many of his countrymen, journalist Tokutomi wrote that the Triple Intervention was to transform him psychologically and dominate the rest of his life. "Say what you will, it had happened because we weren't strong enough. What it came down to was that sincerity and justice didn't amount to a thing if you were not strong enough." Japan had learned to emulate the West. It had played by the rules. From the standpoint of the victim, they were not particularly fair rules, but they were the established rules of imperialism. Now, in Japan's moment of victory, it found that it was reviled by yellow-peril sloganeering and denied equal membership in the imperialist club. Japanese, even those who had been most enthusiastic about Western models, became convinced, as Marius Jansen writes, "that international law and institutional modernization alone would never bring full respect and equality from the West."

In the decade after the Triple Intervention, Japan became obsessed with expanding its power. Many ingredients went into the endeavor. The new Yawata iron and steel complex helped—Japan became much less reliant on imports of those expensive products than before. Industrial production soared— the number of factories employing more than ten workers quintupled between 1894 and 1902. The financial burden on the nation grew as the army sought a 300 percent expansion and the navy a 400 percent expansion. The country was told to "endure through hardship" *(gashin shotan)*. A new patriotic society, the "Amur River Society," was established to promote Japanese expansion onto the Asian mainland. (It became better known in the United States by the sinister-sounding "Black Dragon Society." The name is the English translation of the Chinese/Japanese name for the Amur river, which forms the boundary between

Manchuria and Russia. Japanese patriots chose the name to signify their determination to halt Russian expansion south of the river.)

Finally, the alliance with Britain was an important asset, for it gave Japan virtual assurance that it could go to war with Russia without concern that Germany or France would aid Russia (as in the Triple Intervention). The wording of the Anglo–Japanese Alliance was such that if another nation joined Russia in warring against Japan, Britain would join, on the side of Japan.

In 1904, two years after signing the pact with Britain, tensions between Japan and Russia reached the breaking point. In addition to ever-greater strength in Manchuria, Russia was increasing its pressure on Korea again. Japanese intelligence agents discovered that "lumberjacks" employed by a Russian timber firm in Korea were actually military personnel. It was well known that Russian generals favored military action against Japan. It was widely assumed in Russia and abroad that Russia would score an easy victory against the Japanese (privately referred to by the tsar as "monkeys"), and that would in turn ease domestic conditions in the country. "We need a small victorious war to stem the tide of revolution," the Tsar's Minister of Interior V. K. Plehve could say with astonishing candor. Cool heads in both Japan and Russia feared the risks and costs of war and sought a negotiated solution, but no compromise could be agreed upon. Time was on the side of Russia after the opening of the Trans-Siberian Railway to passenger traffic in late 1903. Japan, infuriated by procrastination by Russians who were eager to use the line for rapid delivery of its immense army to the Far East, broke off talks with St. Petersburg in January 1904.

RUSSO–JAPANESE WAR (1904–1905)

On the evening of February 8, without a declaration of war, a flotilla of Japanese torpedo boats commanded by officers from the old Satsuma clan, stole into the Russian base at Port Arthur. (The fleet commander, Uryu Sotokichi, had received his training at the U.S. Naval Academy at Annapolis.) The facilities were brightly illuminated to celebrate the name-day of the admiral's wife, and a reception was in full swing. In less than an hour, several Russian capital ships were damaged, and the port was nearly blocked by ships run aground. War was declared two days later, the first of the many great wars of the twentieth century and the first fought under conditions of developed industrialism. It was also the first war to be covered by modern media techniques, with correspondents (like the American writer Jack London) reporting their copy "from the front" by telegraph.

Critics would say, in years to come, that the opening events of this war constituted a "surprise attack" of the kind that occurred at Pearl Harbor in 1941. The case for surprise-attack charges against Japan in the 1904 war, however, are not so compelling. Russian troops had crossed into Korea two days earlier, and the Japanese had issued an ultimatum including a threat of war when negotiations collapsed in January. In any case, Japan quickly gained supremacy of the seas.

Unlike the war with China a decade earlier, however, the Russo–Japanese War included a severe test of Japanese military prowess on the land. One particularly grim campaign, for Port Arthur, was in fact a kind of trench-warfare rehearsal for World War I. General Nogi Maresuke, in command, watched through his field glasses as two of his own sons were cut down in battle. In December, he ordered a fight to the death; all officers were instructed to appoint their successors. The Russian base finally fell to Nogi's forces on New Year's Day, 1905, after a battle and siege lasting more than half a year and resulting in sixty thousand Japanese casualties. An even deadlier battle was fought later in the winter, on the snow-covered plains of Manchuria around the railroad city of Mukden, where 700,000 men from the two armies met in a ten-day struggle, the largest land battle in world history up until that time. Again, Japan won, but at a cost of seventy thousand casualties; the number of Russian dead and wounded was even higher. Field Marshall Oyama Iwao, in command of the Japanese armies at Mukden, had spent several years studying military science in France.

The war had been costly in lives and treasure, and there are indications that Japan was ready to negotiate a settlement. In the north of Manchuria, however, a large Russian army was still entrenched and ready to fight. Its chance for survival and for bolstering the Russian position in any peace talks depended upon the Russian Baltic Fleet, which the tsar hoped would save the day by denying Japanese control of the seas. The fleet set sail from the Baltic in October 1904. Denied help by Britain (use of the Suez Canal, for example), the forty-six ships lumbered half way around the world in an ill-starred eight-month voyage. On May 27, the column approached the narrow Straits of Tsushima, intending to make a beeline for the safety of Vladivostok. Admiral Togo Heihachiro accurately predicted the Russian route and was waiting in the fog. The two largest formations of warships since the Battle of Trafalgar, exactly one century earlier, were about to meet.

The engagement at Tsushima lasted for two days, but the fate of the Baltic fleet was determined in the first encounter by a series of Russian blunders and Japanese feats which have fascinated naval historians ever since. As the Russian battlewagons emerged from the fog in straight "line ahead" formation, Togo was in position to execute the dream maneuver of every naval strategist: He was able to cross Russian Admiral Z. P. Rozhestvensky's T, pouring all of his broadsides into the leading ships of the surprised Russian fleet. Within eighty minutes' time, all semblance of a Russian line of battle had been smashed. When the Russian flagship hoisted the surrender flag two days later, their losses stood at thirty-four warships, including all their battleships either sunk or captured. Of the 18,000 Russian sailors, 4,800 were killed and another 6,000, including Admiral Rozhestvensky, were taken prisoner. The Japanese lost three torpedo boats and 116 men killed.

Needless to say, Admiral Togo, who learned his naval skills as a midshipman at the Britannic Naval College at Dartmouth, became, along with General Nogi, one of the living legends of the war. Until the end of World War II, May 27 was celebrated as Navy Day. And the notion of a single, swift, decisive victory at sea, one which could change the destiny of a nation, took subtle hold on the mind of

---

GENERAL FLEET ORDERS AT THE BATTLE OF TSUSHIMA
"The Lord will strengthen our right hand, will help us carry out the task of our Emperor and with our blood wash away the bitter shame of Russia."

—Admiral Z. P. Rozhestvensky.

"On this one battle rests the fate of our Empire. Let every man do his utmost ."

—Admiral Togo's "Z" signal.

Japanese military planners. It is of more than symbolic importance that the Z-signal flag raised by Admiral Togo just before Tsushima to alert his command to do their utmost also fluttered above the strike force at Pearl Harbor. Its significance was immediately apprehended on December 7: a supreme confidence that Japanese spirit could change the odds just as it had earlier in the century.

AN ELECTRIFYING VICTORY

The news of the Japanese victory electrified the world. President Theodore Roosevelt pronounced it "bully" and cabled his congratulations to Tokyo: "No wonder you are happy! Neither Trafalgar nor the defeat of the Spanish Armada was as overwhelming." The United States, while officially neutral in the war, was sympathetic to Japan, viewing it as an underdog taking on the bullying Russian bear with pluck. New York banker Jacob Schiff of Kuhn, Loeb, and Company, angered by Tsarist repression of Jews in his Russian homeland, took the initiative to float the first Japanese war loans in both America and Europe. This aid significantly bolstered the buying power of the badly overextended Japanese economy. Schiff was awarded the "Order of the Rising Sun" by the Meiji Emperor in 1906, and decades later Japanese diplomats would remember Schiff's help with flowers at his grave on Long Island.

"MR. DOOLEY" ON JAPAN
"Mr. Dooley" was a fictional character created by the American humorist, Finley Peter Dunne. Mr. Dooley's comments on the affairs of the day, delivered in a thick Irish accent, were a popular syndicated feature in daily newspapers around the turn of the century. Responding to the Japanese victory over Russia, Mr. Dooley remarked:
"A few years ago I didn't think anny more about a Jap than about anny other man that'd been kept in th' oven too long. They were all alike to me. But today, whiniver I see wan I turn pale an' take off me hat an' make a low bow."

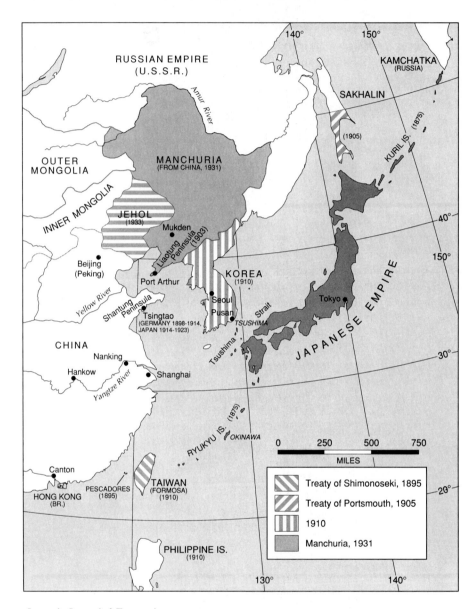

Japan's Imperial Expansion

In Russia, the war produced waves of unrest. The war had never been popular within Russia, and the disastrous defeats inflicted by Japan fortified revolutionaries intent on overthrowing the tsar. The Revolution of 1905 began only weeks after news of the fall of Port Arthur reached Russia. Though it was put down, it turned out to be the prelude to the great revolution of 1917. Elsewhere, echoes of the Japanese victory reverberated throughout the non-Western world as the realization sunk in. For the first time in modern history, an Asian nation had defeated a European nation in war. Colonial peoples everywhere overlooked the ominous fact that Japan itself was becoming an imperial power of great appetite and took heart that a non-Western people had pulled itself up from obscurity and weakness to reach the status of a world power. Stirred by events in the East, patriots launched anticolonial movements in India, French Indochina, the Philippines, and the Dutch East Indies. Nationalist reformers undertook major revolutions in Persia in 1905 and Turkey in 1908.

Chinese students were convinced as never before that the Japanese had unlocked the secrets of modernization. In a reversal of historic patterns, they flocked to Japanese universities and military academies to absorb what they could. In 1906, at the age of nineteen, Chiang Kai-shek, who would become the leader of the Chinese nationalist movement and, in time, an arch-foe of Japan, abandoned his studies in China in his determination to study in Japan. He was finally admitted to a military academy in Tokyo, studied there from 1908 to 1910 and received his field training while serving in the Japanese Army. Indian leader Jawaharlal Nehru later recalled his exhilaration at the news of the Japanese victory and how his own sense of nationalism was ignited—to the point where he immediately went out and purchased all the books about Japanese history he could find in order to learn the reasons for their success. Similarly, twenty years later, the Chinese nationalist leader Sun Yat-sen recalled being in the Middle East at the time the war ended:

> On my way home, in going through the Suez Canal, I met an Arab. Looking at my face, he said: 'Are you a Japanese?' I told him, no, I was a Chinese. He told me he had observed vast armies of Russian soldiers being shipped back to Russia from defeat in Asia, and the joy of this Arab, as a member of the great Asiatic race seemed to know no bounds.

TREATY OF PORTSMOUTH

President Roosevelt agreed to act as host and mediator for the peace talks between Russia and Japan. For his efforts he received the first Nobel Prize for Peace ever awarded to a head of state, a peculiar choice, some said, in view of the president's lusty glorification of war. Rather than face the heat and humidity of a Washington, D.C., summer, it was decided to move the talks north to Portsmouth, New Hampshire. Among the points covered by the Treaty of Portsmouth (1905) were the following:

KOREA. To a large extent, the war had been fought over the question of who would control Korea. At Portsmouth, Russia agreed to recognize the "paramount position" of Japan in Korea. Given the weakness of Korea, and Russia's withdrawal, it was only a matter of time until Japan made its move. Five years later, in 1910, Korean independence came to an end with its formal annexation by

Japan. From 1910 until the end of World War II, Korea was a part of the Empire of Japan.

LIAOTUNG. Russia was forced to transfer to Japan its rights and leases, including the South Manchurian Railway, in the Liaotung Peninsula. The territory, of course, was under China's sovereignty, and the powers agreed to recognize Chinese territorial integrity. Nevertheless, Japan soon began the economic exploitation of this gateway to Manchuria and began to station its own armed forces there. The Japanese soldiers deployed in the area were designated as the Kwantung Army (Kwantung being another name for Liaotung). The Kwantung Army became the spearhead for further expansion onto the Asian mainland.

INDEMNITIES. The Japanese had expected to receive a large financial settlement from Russia, but with the talks close to rupture over this issue, Roosevelt persuaded the Japanese delegates to drop their demand for indemnities. While the Japanese government was satisfied with the terms of the Portsmouth Treaty, the Japanese people harbored bitter resentment against both it and Roosevelt because of the indemnity issue. For the first time in Japanese history, anti-American demonstrations occurred in Japanese cities.

Roosevelt had consistently leaned toward Japan at the expense of its neighbors. "What nonsense it is," he told his friend, Secretary of State John Hay, "to speak of the Chinese and Japanese as of the same race." On another occasion he said, "a Russian triumph in the war would have been a blow to civilization." When the Korean nationalist leader Syngman Rhee came to Portsmouth to appeal for American help in sustaining Korean independence, Roosevelt politely but firmly rebuffed the pleas. America was not ready to go to war over Japanese expansion into Korea. High-principled statements about Korean rights to independence simply would not deter Japan from taking advantage of its weak neighbor and so why antagonize the powerful Japanese people? Instead, in the Taft–Katsura Agreement of 1905, the United States and Japan recognized each other's special positions in the Philippines and in Korea.

At the same time, however, the Japanese victory caused Roosevelt to see a menacing side to Japan. "Japan's motives and ways of thought" are not quite our own, he wrote. "No one can foretell her future attitude." He began thinking of Japan as a potential rival. The United States did have interests in China, after all, and looked forward to having more in the future—especially in the Manchurian north, where plans to build an American railway would soon be floated by the rail magnate E. H. Harriman. The United States was therefore anxious to have Japan observe its so-called "open-door" policy, and yet the territorial gains affirmed at Portsmouth suggested that Japan might well be closing some doors. Accordingly, Roosevelt aimed to see to it that Japan did not emerge from the war

YELLOW PERIL OR WHITE PERIL?

"What the Russians are paying for at this very moment in the seas of Japan and in the gorges of Manchuria is not just their avid and brutal policy in the Orient, it is the colonial policy of all the European powers. . . . It would not appear to be the case, however, that the yellow peril terrifying European economists is comparable to the white peril hanging over Asia. The Chinese do not send to Paris, Berlin or St. Petersburg missionaries to teach Christians feng-shui and cause general chaos in European affairs. . . . Admiral Togo did not come with a dozen battleships to bombard the roadstead of Brest in order to help Japanese commerce in France. . . . The armies of the Asiatic powers have not taken to Tokyo or Peking the paintings of the Louvre or the china of the Élysée."

—French novelist Anatole France, *Sur la Pierre Blanche.*

"We talk about the possibility of Japan's arming and leading the yellow race in a conflict with the white, and we shudder over the woes which might come to us, should she do this. But do we consider the actual woes which the white man is today inflicting on the yellow man by his presence and by his methods, by his armies and his commerce?"

—American missionary Sidney Gulick, *The White Peril in the Far East.*

"Win the war,

And Japan will be denounced as yellow peril.

Lose it,

And she will be branded a barbaric land."

—Japanese military-surgeon, novelist, poet Mori Ogai.

too strong. It was useful to keep a Russian "moderative influence" on Japan, he felt; thus, the denial of the indemnities. It also was useful from time to time to remind Japan of growing American might. Thus, in 1908, the U.S. Navy committed itself to a two-ocean navy and chose Hawaii as the site of its main Pacific base. Soon engineers began dredging a harbor at the mouth of the Pearl River on Oahu. Also, the president dispatched the "Great White Fleet" in 1907–08 on a round-the-world cruise to demonstrate U.S. naval strength, Roosevelt's "Big Stick." The battleships were received with champagne and other courtesies in Japan, but years later a Japanese Diet member reflected bitterly about the big stick and the ships that symbolized it:

America appears to think she is divinely appointed to rule the world with a big stick! What is the purpose of her colossal Navy if it is not to make her power supreme in every part of the Pacific? American statesmen profess an undying devotion to peace, and meanwhile they are building warships on a scale unparalleled in history. They preach the doctrine of racial equality and equal opportunity and yet refused to admit educated Japanese immigrants to American citizenship.

If Roosevelt's view of Japanese was equivocal, admiring their success while feeling concern about their growing power, the prevailing view in America was more one-sided. An intensification of yellow-peril fright followed in the wake of Japan's victory over Russia. Japan's defeat of China in 1895 had been one thing; her defeat of a European power in 1905 provoked new fears of a coming East-versus-West Armageddon. A San Francisco newspaper cartoon was typical. It depicted a Japanese soldier in caricature, with animal-like features, and a shadow lengthening across the Pacific until it reached American shores. Evidence of the heightened wave of yellow-peril antagonisms was most pronounced in American immigration policy.

THE JAPANESE IN AMERICA

The flow of immigrants from Japan to the United States increased markedly after 1900 and especially after the Russo–Japanese War, which created pockets of depressed activity and unemployment in areas of rural Japan. The result was that the number of Japanese in the United States tripled in the first decade of the century, from twenty-four thousand to seventy-two thousand, with a high percentage of these arrivees settling in the Pacific Coast states. To keep these numbers in perspective, however, it is useful to note that the percentage of Japanese living in the United States to the total population was only .08 percent; in other words, less than one in a thousand Americans either came from Japan or were children of Japanese immigrants. Even calculating the percentage living in the west-coast states yields only a 1.4 percent figure for the year 1910. More Italians entered the United States in a single year than Japanese entered in the entire period of their emigration through 1924, historian Roger Daniels observes.

The Japanese immigrant worked in a variety of mostly unskilled occupations: migrant laborers, gandy dancers, factory workers, and domestic servants. As early as 1900 in San Francisco, labor unions were lashing out against Japanese (as well as Chinese) competition to white workers with nearly unbelievable viciousness. The Chinese are bad enough, complained a union publication in that year,

> . . . but the snivelling Japanese, who swarms along the streets and cringingly offers his paltry services for a suit of clothes and a front seat in our public schools, is a far great danger to the laboring portion of California society than all the opium-soaked pigtails [that is, Chinese] who have ever blotted the fair name of this beautiful city.

Sample San Francisco newspaper headlines from a single month in the year 1905 convey the racial animosities which were fanned in the press:
"Crime and Poverty Go Hand in Hand with Asiatic Labor"
"Japanese a Menace to American Women"
"The Yellow Peril—How Japanese Crowd out the White Race"
"Brown Artisans Steal Brains of Whites"

It was, in fact, the issue of a "front seat in our public schools" that caused an especially severe eruption of anti-Japanese behavior in 1906. In that year, the San Francisco Board of Education ordered all Oriental children to attend a special school set aside for them, on the grounds that the public schools were overcrowded and that Oriental students were a corruptive element. "Our children should not be placed in any position where their youthful impressions may be affected by association with pupils of the Mongolian race," the Board said. Only ninety-three "Japanese" students, spread among twenty-three public schools in the system, were involved; a quarter of them were native-born American citizens. Still, the Board's move received widespread local public support. The *San Francisco Chronicle* said that it objected to Japanese children in the schools just as "we would to any other moral poison." Patriotic organizations, like the "Native Sons of the Golden West," asked the predictable question, "Would you like your daughter to marry a Japanese?"

The Board of Education case became an international issue. The White House was furious, called the segregation attempt a "wicked absurdity," and moved to force a compromise on the San Francisco officials. "Those infernal fools in California insult the Japanese recklessly," President Roosevelt said, "and in the event of war, it will be the nation as a whole that will have to pay the consequences." The *Chronicle* responded by asking the president if he was "afraid of the little brown men."

To the government of Japan, the events in San Francisco were a test case. Japan as a nation was now being accepted as one of the great powers of the world as a result of its wartime victories and alliances. Now, in San Francisco, was being decided whether or not Japanese as *individuals* would be allowed with dignity to enter into the sphere of worldwide activities. It comforted the Japanese little to be told that the doctrine of "separate but equal" facilities had been affirmed as the law of the land by the Supreme Court only ten years earlier (in the 1896 case, *Plessy* v. *Ferguson*).

The immediate tensions were reduced when the White House worked out a "gentlemen's agreement" with Japan in 1907. No treaty was signed, but the Japanese government promised that it would stop issuing passports to peasants and workers bound for America. Shortly thereafter, the San Francisco School

PICTURE BRIDES

"These imported Japanese brides must have been extraordinarily adaptable or extraordinarily dutiful. They had usually been brought up in a large family and were not accustomed to intimate interpersonal relationships with men. Probably most received the news that they were being sent to a bridegroom in America with very little notice, and often knew little more of their future spouses than a photograph would provide. Unhappily, the photographs were often retouched at that. Marriage meant leaving Japan, familiar tasks, relatives and friends, home. It meant the prospect of a strange land and a strange and intimate new relationship—with a stranger. . . .

"The bridegrooms were waiting on the docks, pictures in hand. The debarkation scene must have been remarkable for its total confusion. There were many joyful meetings and, undoubtedly, many disappointing ones. We have heard several stories of last-minute swaps and even refusals. But for the most part, the new brides, having found their bridegrooms, were bundled off to begin their new lives in the strange land."

—Harry Kitano, *Japanese Americans.*

Board withdrew its segregation order. The immigration problem did not, however, abate for long. Instead, "picture brides" emerged as a new source of tensions. Before 1907, there had been very few women among the Japanese immigrant population in this country. It seems quite possible that neither the State Department nor the government of Japan fully realized that in coming years large numbers of Japanese male immigrants would elect to stay on as residents and send home for brides—whose entry to the United States was not prohibited by the gentlemen's agreement. In any case, that is exactly what happened. The marriages were by proxy, arranged marriages which were legal and quite customary under Japanese law. As a result, the sex ratio among Japanese changed from one that was overwhelmingly male to one that approached a male–female balance by 1924.

Parallel with this growth in the *Issei*[2] population was a rapid expansion of farm acreage owned by Japanese. As the early Japanese farm workers saw the boundless miles of fertile California farmland, the worst of which was often of better quality than the tiny plots of volcanic soil they farmed in Japan, they concluded that a lot of land was being wasted or underused. They saved, rented land, often the very cheapest land, purchasing the marshy portions of the Sacramento delta, for example, from the railroads. After putting the whole family to work for several years of backbreaking labor, clearing, draining, and improving the land, they owned some choice farms. Issei who had owned a total of only 4500 acres of

---

[2]*Issei* (pronounced ee-say) means "first generation," that is, the generation of immigrants born in Japan. The *Nisei*, "second generation," were children of the *Issei* born in America.

farmland in 1900 in California found themselves in possession of a half-million acres by 1910. That was still a mere ten percent of the farm acreage in the state. However, because of the labor-intensive style of farming and the high-cost crops they tended to raise (like strawberries, asparagus, as well as flowers) the land owned by Issei produced more than ten percent of the dollar volume of California agriculture.

DISCRIMINATORY LEGISLATION

Therein—in their very success—lay their biggest problem. It might have been expected that they would be praised as model citizens—coming here with nothing, supporting themselves, and through their industry and acquired skills making an important contribution to California's prosperity. Instead, their Caucasian neighbors, hurt by the competition, raised the cry of "yellow peril" again. With the support of California political leaders like Senator James Phelan, who campaigned on the slogan "Keep California White," numerous discriminatory laws were put on the books to weaken the competitive position of Issei farmers. The Alien Land Law, enacted by overwhelming vote in the California legislature in 1913, hurt the most. It barred "aliens ineligible for citizenship" from owning land in the future and limited leases to just three years. Though the law did not specifically refer to Japanese, it was clearly aimed at them because legislation already existed making it impossible for Japanese to become naturalized American citizens.

The *Ozawa* case served to reinforce the intent of the Alien Land Law. An Issei, Ozawa Takao, had petitioned the courts to grant him citizenship. At every stage of the process, the courts agreed that Ozawa was by character and education "eminently qualified under the statutes" to become an American citizen. Nevertheless, the United States Supreme Court affirmed in its 1922 *Ozawa* decision that the petitioner was not qualified for naturalized citizenship because he was not Caucasian. The 1913 land law was not repealed, and the Ozawa case was not reversed until long after World War II when the McCarran Act of 1952 eliminated race as a barrier to the naturalization process.

In addition to the fears of economic competitors, near hysterical suspicion of the Japanese as a security menace mounted. Again, the popular press, newspapers, and weekly magazines like the *Saturday Evening Post* played a part in heightening anxiety about Japanese. The most prominent of the alarmists was Homer Lea, whose concern about Japan was grounded, somewhat paradoxically, in his admiration for the nation's bushido tradition, the fine points of which Lea explained to an American audience. While extolling the militant qualities of the Japanese people, Lea deplored the softness and decadence of Americans, whose Anglo–Saxon blood was being diluted by extensive immigration of inferior peoples from southern Europe. The imbalance between ever more virile Japan and increasingly feeble America doomed America in a future war for the control of the Pacific. Lea's 1909 best-seller, *The Valor of Ignorance*, was the most popular of a rising vogue of fictive future-war books. In it, Lea presented, complete with his own detailed charts, maps, and tidal surveys, the case for a Japanese landing on the American west coast. With too few native-born Americans to constitute a valiant fighting force, the United States would have to fall back to the Sierra barrier and yield control of the Pacific states to the Empire of Japan. Unless his warning was heeded, Lea admonished, the Japanese were on the verge of becoming the "samurai of the human race." "The remainder of man shall toil and trade for them. . . ," he wrote.

The Valor of Ignorance was a model of restraint and understatement compared to more-overtly racist stereotyping which appeared in the popular press and on the screen. For several decades, Americans who thought they knew anything about Orientals would likely concede that the Asian they knew best was Dr. Fu Manchu. The fictional character created by Sax Rohmer first appeared in novel form in 1913. Between then and 1941, ten Fu Manchu novels, frequent magazine serializations, and several film versions appeared. (Boris Karloff, best known for his screen portrayals of Dr. Frankenstein's monster, played Dr. Fu Manchu in the first Hollywood production in 1932.) It was not just the physical appearance of Fu Manchu—"terror in each split second of his slanted eyes"—which made him the embodiment of the "yellow peril" to a generation of Americans. It was the way Rohmer drew together in this character all the "strands of an otherwise inchoate fear," writes historian John Dower in his study of racial hatred, *War Without Mercy*: ". . . Asian mastery of Western knowledge and technique; access to mysterious powers and 'obscure and dreadful things'; and mobilization of the yellow horde ('shadowy,' in one episode, 'looking like great apes')." Fu Manchu of course was presented as a Chinese rather than Japanese villain, but that was a distinction which was lost on many Americans. In any case, the yellow peril was seen as frightful precisely because it was assumed that Japanese and Chinese would act together to engulf the Western world.

More specifically anti-Japanese was the motion picture *Patria*, a ten-part serial released by a film company associated with the Hearst press in 1917. It showed an attempt by Japan to conquer America with the aid of the government of Mexico as well as treacherous spies recruited from among the Issei population. As one writer notes, this was a neat pairing because it confirmed the racial prejudices of Californians against both Japanese and Mexicans. The chief villain, however, was a Japanese nobleman who was at the head of the Emperor's secret service in America. Japanese armies were shown invading America and committing atrocities including the violation of the heroine, popular screen star Irene Castle. President Woodrow Wilson saw the film and, to his credit, was incensed. The editors changed the script in response to pressure from the White House, with the result that many of the bad guys were turned from Japanese into Mexicans. *Shadows of the West*, distributed by the California branch of the American Legion, appeared about the same time as *Patria* and reinforced the image of a militaristic Japan aided by sneaky Issei agents.

It is hardly surprising, then, considering the numerous sources of yellow-peril sentiment, that pressure for further discriminatory legislation increased. In 1924, the culmination of the anti-Japanese trend was reached with the passage of a federal immigration law which expressly shut the door to Japanese immi-

"GENERAL" HOMER LEA

Depending on the source of one's information, Lea was either a "home-grown California eccentric" or a "visionary." A dropout at Stanford University, where he was a keen student of military history at the turn of the century, he yearned to serve in the U.S. Army but was rejected because of a hunchback deformity. After dreaming that he was the reincarnation of a famous Chinese warrior, the 24-year-old Lea went to China in 1900 to lend his services as a military tactician to patriots seeking to overthrow the Manchu dynasty. Little came of this visit except fame and a swagger stick engraved with a dragon and the words "To General Homer Lea," supposedly presented to him by Chinese comrades. Efforts to organize a California-based "reform army" to fight in China also accomplished little except to catapult Lea into notoriety and give him a ready-made audience for his second career as a writer and Asia expert. As with the writings of the more sober and scholarly Mahan, Lea's reached and influenced audiences in both the United States and Japan.

Two years after its appearance in America, Lea's *The Valor of Ignorance* was translated and published in Japan. It was quite favorably received. "Even Lea's dubious pretension to the rank of general was apparently accepted in Japan," writes a Japanese historian. Japanese readers were flattered to see themselves portrayed as a worthy and honorable—albeit enemy—people. At the same time, however, the book spawned a number of literary replies with names like *Nichi-Bei tatakawaba* (If Japan and America Fight). The Japanese writers, like Lea, stressed the strained relations between Japan and America and the urgent necessity for military and naval expansion to prepare for the worst.

The Valor of Ignorance was reissued in the United States after Pearl Harbor and hailed as prophetic in a new introduction written by Congresswoman Clare Boothe Luce. Generally overlooked by American readers in 1942, as in 1909, was Lea's argument that his fellow Americans would share responsibility for any future war by their treatment of Japanese immigrants as a "nation of lepers." True, Lea had aroused almost hysterical fear of the Japanese menace in his book. However, as historian Akira Iriye notes, "He tended to be hysterical about the presence of Japanese on the west coast not because he disparaged them racially but because he thought Americans were blind to the danger of mistreating them." Iriye cites one passage from *The Valor of Ignorance* as "remarkably prescient":

"To expect the Japanese to submit to indignities is to be pitifully incomprehensible of their national character. And the American people should realize that it is this cumulative memoranda of wrongs that they must, on some certain, sombre day, make answer to."

grants to America. The Immigration Act of 1924, which abrogated the earlier "gentlemen's agreement," was a monumental insult to Japan because other nations were allowed a quota under the law; only Japan was singled out for total exclusion. If the quota system had been applied to Japan, it would have meant that a mere 185 Japanese would have been allowed entrance into the United States each year. Even that figure, however, was unacceptable to the California congressional delegation in Washington and, as a result, total exclusion was written into law. The 1924 legislation provoked vehement protests from the Japanese government and outbursts in the Japanese press. The law "stamps Japanese as of an inferior race," one Tokyo newspaper complained.

In the lives of the Issei generation in America, the law was a major turning point, Ronald Takaki wrote. "They saw the handwriting on the wall: they had no future in their adopted land, except through their children—the Nisei. The Issei could see they had been doomed to be foreigners forever, their dreams destroyed and their sweat soaked up in an expanse called America." In answer to the frequently heard complaint of the anti-Japanese lobby that Japanese were incapable of assimilation into American life, one Issei conceded that Japanese were "clannish." However, he continued, "The process of assimilation can thrive only in a genial atmosphere of just and equitable treatment. . . . It seems hardly fair to complain of the failure of foreign elements to merge in a community, while the community chooses to keep them apart from the rest of its membership." Leading newspapers like the *New York Times* and the *Washington Post* deplored the congressional action as an "affront to Japan" and "a deliberate sabotage of our delicate international relations." The *Cincinnati Enquirer*, however, spoke for many in praising the new law: "The crux of this matter is that the United States, like Canada and Australia, must be kept a white man's country."

AN ERA ENDS

In Japan, the Meiji era came to an end with the death of the sixty-year-old ruler on July 30, 1912. In the popular mind, his death was hastened by exhaustion and anxiety brought on by his personal concern with the progress of the war with Russia seven years earlier. More prosaically, however, stomach cancer caused the passing of the Meiji emperor. General Nogi, hero of the Russo–Japanese War and for several years the personal tutor of the emperor's grandson Hirohito, watched from his residence near the palace as his sovereign's funeral cortege rolled across the palace moat and disappeared from view. Then, wearing his dress military uniform, the general knelt before an autographed picture of the Meiji Emperor and committed suicide in the agonizing manner of the ancient samurai. His wife, plunging a dagger above her heart, accompanied him in the "following one's lord in death" *(junshi)* ceremony. Some said that Nogi attempted to atone for the terrible death toll which occurred during his command of the battle for Port Arthur. Nogi left behind a testament in which he bewailed the growing moral decay of the times and called for a resurgence of "Japanese spirit." Nogi's death and his final testament became part of a phenomenon called "Nogi-ism" *(Nogishugi)* and were written into the schoolbooks of the post-Meiji generation as symbols of loyalty and self-sacrifice to the state. As with other sensational examples of twentieth-century *seppuku* (notably the 1970 death of novelist Mishima Yukio), voices of dissent were also heard. Thus, a minority saw Nogi's death as "theatrical bushido," an admirable act, perhaps, but largely irrelevant to modern Japan.

The Meiji emperor's successor is far less well remembered by his countrymen. The Taisho emperor reigned from 1912 to 1926 but, unlike his father, was little involved in state affairs. As a youngster, the emperor had suffered from meningitis. Proper treatment would have meant unthinkable (for the day) acts of *lèse-majesté*. As a result of medical neglect, the young man suffered from bouts of mental derangement throughout his life. According to one oft-repeated incident, the last imperial act of the emperor occurred at the opening of the Diet in 1915. The Taisho emperor was presiding over ceremonies when, after a long period of silence on the dais, puzzled legislators looked up from their normally respectful downward gaze to find the emperor peering at them through a telescope shaped by rolling up the proclamation he was supposed to read. After that, the emperor was excused from the performance of even ceremonial duties. The death of the Taisho emperor saw the throne pass to his son, the 124th of Japan's imperial lineage, the *Showa* ("Clarity and Harmony") emperor, better known in the West by his personal name, Hirohito.

WORLD WAR I

The Great War of 1914–1918, later to be known as World War I, was fought mainly in Europe to settle European squabbles. Within days of the outbreak of war, Britain called upon its Japanese allies to help defend British territories in Asia from attack by armed German merchant cruisers in Far Eastern waters. Japan promptly joined the war on the side of Britain and the Allies against Germany and the Central Powers. Japan, however, had its own agenda in mind. It viewed the war as an opportunity for almost uncontested territorial gain. With little opposition, Japan's "sunshine combatants" seized Germany's economic concessions and military bases on the Shantung peninsula in the north of China in 1914. At the same time, the Japanese Navy occupied Germany's South Pacific possessions in the Mariana, Caroline, and Marshall Islands, including places like Saipan and Tinian, which would become well-known battlegrounds in World War II. The international body known as the League of Nations, formed after the end of World War I, awarded Japan a "mandate" to administer these former German territories on the understanding that Japan refrain from fortifying them. Contrary to popularly held impressions in the West, Japan scrupulously observed this obligation—until the decade of the 1930s, when the entire mandate system and, eventually, the League of Nations itself began to collapse.

SHIDEHARA DIPLOMACY

While Japan's territorial reach grew in the Great War, so did its economy. Cut off from steel and other heavy-industry imports from Europe, Japanese industrial production soared, and the export trade boomed. As European businessmen withdrew from the markets in India, Indochina, and the Dutch East Indies, Japanese businessmen moved in to fill the void. The ship-building industry prospered, and Japan's own merchant fleet almost doubled in size during the war years. Japan's balance of payments shifted to a favorable position and, as a capital surplus nation for the first time, Japan found itself extending loans to a number of its allies, including Britain and France. At the same time, Japanese investors poured funds into textile factories in Shanghai and Tientsin to take advantage of cheap Chinese labor. The South Manchurian Railway, through its management of an ever-growing complex of coal mines, warehouses, banks, factories, electric power grids, and harbor facilities, expanded its economic domination over the Manchurian north of China.

This burst of economic prosperity led to a growing conviction on the part of Japanese political and business leaders that Japan's future lay in a peaceful economic expansion rather than in any further overseas military adventures. "It is not territory, but markets we seek," said Shidehara Kijuro, Japan's foreign minister during most of the period from 1924 to 1931 and the chief architect of the policy of restraint. The expression "Shidehara diplomacy" came to stand for the caution and conciliation which characterized international relationships in the twenties. Japanese big business interests, the *zaibatsu*, enthusiastically supported Shidehara diplomacy because it was convinced that Japan's prosperity was going to be closely tied to its ability to trade with the West. To America alone went 40 percent of Japan's exports in the decade of the 1920s. Such trade connections would obviously be endangered by reckless military expansion into areas where the Western powers had interests. Furthermore, the *zaibatsu* knew that the alternative to the Shidehara approach would entail a costly arms race which would send the budget and taxes spiraling upward. This attitude matched similar attitudes in the United States (and Britain) in the years after World War I. These were the Harding, Coolidge, and Hoover years in America when, as President Calvin Coolidge said, "The business of America is business." The war had been financially exhausting and businessmen grumbled at any hints of high taxes to support a continuation of military buildup.

Thus, in spite of irritations on the world scene, such as the American exclusionist policies towards immigrants, Shidehara diplomacy moved forward throughout the decade. Japan earned a good reputation in international circles, and the prospects for global harmony and reconciliation steadily improved. Milestones along the way included Japanese participation in the following organizations, conferences and treaties:

THE LEAGUE OF NATIONS, 1920. The League of Nations was a fulfillment of the dream—his critics called it an obsession—of President Woodrow Wilson, who labored mightily to persuade the victorious powers to support its creation. Wilson saw the League as a congress of nations which would replace the bellicose old system of alliances and secret treaties. It was not a superstate. The League's covenant obliged members to submit disputes to discussion or arbitration by a new Permanent Court of International Justice. But, the League would have no military enforcement powers; it could recommend, but not compel, the use of armed force to carry out its will. The League came into existence in Paris in 1920, but ironically, it was the United States which was the chief holdout. U.S. senators, some believing that the organization would be a threat to American sovereignty, others continuing to place their faith in armies and navies more than idealistic international organizations, refused to ratify participation in the League.

Japan agreed to join the League in spite of grave objections by some concerning the League's unwillingness to draft a resolution affirming the principle of racial equality. Several countries, including the United States, Canada, and Australia, objected to such a resolution, fearful that Japan might use it to defend the rights of its citizens emigrating abroad.

WASHINGTON CONFERENCE, 1921–1922. For three months beginning in November 1921, representatives of nine leading maritime powers met in Washington, D.C., to discuss the new postwar world order. Out of the talks came several agreements. In the "Four-Power Pacific Treaty," America, England, France, and Japan guaranteed to respect each other's rights and possessions in the Pacific and promised to consult if those rights were threatened. The same nations, with the addition of Italy, also signed the Five-Power Naval Limitation Treaty aimed at the establishment of military equilibrium in the Pacific. The treaty fixed the ratio of capital ships (battleships and aircraft carriers) for America, Britain, and Japan at 5:5:3; France and Italy would be allowed a 1.75 ratio. The reasoning for the larger ratios for the United States and Britain was that those nations supported two-ocean fleets whereas Japan possessed only a one-ocean navy. Still, the treaty required Japan's Imperial Navy to abandon its plans for a massive buildup. Other provisions of the treaty called for extensive scrapping of existing ships and abandoning the construction of ships in various stages of planning in order to reach the agreed-upon tonnage levels. In spite of misgivings about the inferior ratio it received—some Japanese likened the ratio to "Rolls Royce-Rolls Royce-Ford"—the government of Japan signed the treaty when Britain and the United States agreed to a freeze on insular fortifications between Singapore and Hawaii. Finally, in a "Nine-Power Treaty" dealing with China, the world powers including Japan agreed to respect China's territorial integrity and to abide by the open-door principle of equal opportunity in China. Japan agreed to return the German concessions in Shantung seized during World War I.

PACT OF PARIS, 1928. With the exception of the Soviet Union, all the great powers, including Japan, signed this agreement in which they renounced war "as an instrument of national policy in their relations with one another." Although the pact established no enforcement machinery—cynics sneered that the Paris pact was no more than an "international kiss"—it did signify Japan's continuing commitment to collective security during the 1920s. The unrestrained acclaim which greeted the signing of the pact in both parliamentary and popular circles in Japan suggested that Shidehara diplomacy had widespread approval there.

TAISHO DEMOCRACY

Parallel to this trend toward peaceful cooperation abroad was a hopeful internal trend toward political liberalization. The term "Taisho democracy" referred to a series of reforms instituted during the latter years of that emperor's reign. The liberal views of Minobe Tatsukichi, the nation's leading expert on constitutional law, became accepted throughout the academic world. For years, veteran parliamentarians like Ozaki Yukio challenged the government-by-clique style of the Meiji era. After the death in 1922 of Yamagata Aritomo, the last of the original Meiji oligarchs, the way was cleared for realization of some of the constitutional reforms Ozaki had advocated. Political party elites assumed a position of supremacy in government. As a feature of Taisho democracy, it became common for the prime ministership to be awarded to the president of one of the two main political parties which controlled the Diet in the twenties. Commoners gained political power, in other words, not because they were Meiji oligarchs, or their proteges, but because of experience they gained in the bureaucracy or in parties or, quite commonly, in both. The electorate was gradually extended until 1925, when all male subjects over the age of twenty-five received the vote. Female suffrage did not come until after World War II. The growth of mass media contributed to a better-informed electorate. During the Taisho era, nearly half the nation's households subscribed to a daily newspaper. The first experimental radio broadcasts began in 1925, and within three years over a half-million radio sets were in use. All of them were tuned to the nation's only broadcast network, the state-operated Japan Broadcasting Company (*Nippon Hoso Kyokai*), then as now identified by a crisp English pronunciation of its initials, NHK.

OZAKI YUKIO'S CHERRY TREES

It was Ozaki Yukio who was instrumental in sending the cherry trees to Washington, D. C. In 1912, at a time when Ozaki was mayor of Tokyo, he arranged to have 3000 cherry tree seedlings presented as a gesture of friendship from the people of Tokyo to the American people. The trees, eventually planted on the city's Tidal Basin, survived demands for their removal during World War II and remain today as one of the springtime delights of the nation's capital.

The Great Kanto Earthquake

At two minutes before noon on the first of September 1923, the seismographs at the Tokyo Imperial University began to register earth movement. That was nothing unusual in a country where earthquakes can be felt almost every day. However, in this case, the movements grew stronger with each passing second until the entire Kanto Plains area around Tokyo was billowing like the surface of the ocean. Most of the homes in Tokyo and Yokohama were built out of wood, and at noontime the cookstoves were being fired up with charcoal. The debris from the collapsed homes caught fire, and in no time the entire Tokyo–Yokohama area was in flames. Even the sea became part of the inferno as naval oil stockpiles spilled into Tokyo Bay and ignited. The magnitude of the 1923 Great Kanto Earthquake has been calculated to have been approximately the same as the 1906 San Francisco earthquake. While the loss of lives in the California tremor was about five hundred, well over 100,000 either died or disappeared in the Japan quake. Nearly three out of four of the residents of the Tokyo–Yokohama area were left homeless by the temblors, fires, and a 36-foot-high *tsunami* (tidal wave) which slammed into the coast.

As Edwin Reischauer has written, the earthquake cataclysm "cleared the ground, literally, for new cities and, figuratively for a new society." Downtown Tokyo, with its wide avenues and ferroconcrete buildings, its large movie houses, neon lights, banks, and department stores, and its first subway line (in 1927) took on the appearance of a Western metropolis. Former mayor Goto Shimpei, in charge of reconstruction, took note of the ruined trolley system and ordered one thousand American cars shipped over, most of them Model-T Fords which were rebuilt as buses. Their usefulness was quickly demonstrated, and two years later the Japan Ford Motor Company was established. General Motors came along the following year. By 1934, there were 120,000 automobiles operating in Japan, not many for a Western country but a large number by Asian standards. Most were Fords and Chevrolets. Although the Japanese automotive industry was turning

---

FRANK LLOYD WRIGHT IN TOKYO

As vindication of architect Frank Lloyd Wright's innovative methods, his recently opened Imperial Hotel survived the earthquake of 1923 without damage. Built on the principle of the "floating cantilever" which allowed it to give when the earth shook, the low building, with elements of East and West and a hint of the Mayans in its appearance, went on to become something of a wonder to Westerners and Japanese alike. True, the floors settled into the mud beneath in an irregular pattern causing rubbery corridors to dip and sway over the years, but the building lasted. After enduring the air raids of World War II, Wright's hotel was finally brought down in 1968, when land values and other financial considerations caused it to be replaced by a new high-rise Imperial Hotel.

BESUBORU II

Unlike American baseball, the Japanese game's heritage is grounded in amateurism. Professional teams did not appear until 1934. College baseball rivalries are the oldest in the nation. The one between Keio and Waseda universities is so well established that a special word had to be coined for it, sokei-sen. Student enthusiasm for the game was only partly behind the appeal. By the Taisho period, giant newspaper empires competed for circulation by concentrating on "third-page news" which consisted of social gossip, sensational crime stories—and sports. Papers like the *Asahi* and the *Mainichi* eagerly sponsored and promoted sports events and fostered the image of the Keio–Waseda game as one of the big three collegiate sports rivalries in the world. (The other two were the Cambridge–Oxford regatta and the Harvard–Yale gridiron classic.) Perhaps even more popular is the National High-School Baseball Summer Championship Tournament, an event which began in 1915 and rivals the Olympics in its pageantry and media coverage in contemporary Japan. For two weeks every August, nine hours of TV programming each day keep the nation's eyes fixed on the near-sacred Koshien stadium near Osaka, where the best forty-nine teams, pared down from almost four thousand participating schools, compete in the single-elimination event to select the best high-school baseball team in the nation.

It's only a game, of course, but commentators, Japanese and foreign, have read much into its significance. Tobita Suishu, the "god" of Japanese baseball, wrote: "If high-school baseball should become just a game, it would lose its essential meaning. High-school baseball should always remain an education of the heart; the ground a classroom of purity, a gymnasium of morality." The Dutch commentator Ian Buruma, noting the frequent TV comments on "sincerity of spirit," the identically shaven heads of the players, the solemn singing of school songs, and the austerity of the training (the winning team will probably have endured grueling practice sessions for about 350 days during the year), writes that the game has little to do with sport. "It is the cult of youthful purity," he maintains. American historian Donald Roden, on the other hand, associates the game with "the quest for national dignity." Similarly, William R. May relates baseball's appeal to the story of Japan's modernization. "Baseball was one of the most visible, most easily comprehended, and most successful applications of the Japanese spirit to a Western body of knowledge. . . . Japanese baseball invokes the spirits of the Meiji men who mastered Western civilization yet whose hearts remained quintessentially Japanese."

out *gatakura-gatakura* (chug-chug) models as far back as 1902, it was not until 1933 that total annual domestic production exceeded a thousand.

Student slang reflected and contributed to a sense of newness and cosmopolitanism. Once again, as in the early Meiji years, Western imports, superficial or not, had appeal—among urbanites. *Modan* became a synonym for stylish, as in *modan garu* or *moga* for short and *modan boi* or *mobo*, the modern girl and the modern boy. Fad-conscious young men and women liked to frequent Western-style restaurants and ballrooms and scandalize their parents by quoting Marx, smoking cigarettes, and dancing cheek to cheek. They professed to be interested in the *surii-esu*, the three s's: sex (*sekkusu* in the new jargon of the day), cinema (*shinema*), and sports. The sex was tame by New York or Parisian standards, but a Ginza dance hall chorus line performing the Charleston was light years distant from Meiji-era entertainment.

Movies produced in Japan were scorned as immature by Japanese intellectuals during much of the pre-World War II period, but a young generation of directors, many of them deeply influenced by Western—particularly American—films, pioneered the creation of Japanese film-making that would one day win international adulation. Mizoguchi Kenzo and Ozu Yasujiro, for example, were on the scene as early as the 1920s, and many more important directors, including Kurosawa Akira, appeared during the following decade. For much of the prewar period, however, films imported from the West led in popularity. Gary Cooper and Greta Garbo were popular in Japan and Charlie Chaplin was surely as well known to Japanese audiences as he was in America. From that time on, "sandwich men" on the Ginza, complete with cane, derby, and oversize shoes, invariably imitated Chaplin's wobbly gait.

Traditional sports did not disappear, but Western sports acquired a new and larger following than ever before. Baseball remained easily the most popular of the Western imports. The young also took up tennis, skiing, even bowling. Among the affluent, golf caught on and remains *the* prestige sport. Hirohito, recalling the pleasures of the game on his Grand Tour of Europe (in 1921), had a nine-hole course built on the palace grounds. It is said that he played there regularly, at least in the twenties, attired in a suit of plus fours with the same tweedy patterns favored by the Prince of Wales. Schools began to emphasize swimming, with the intention of making a good showing at the Olympics. In 1928, a Japanese swimmer became the first Oriental to win an Olympic event. Four years later, at Los Angeles, Japanese swimmers won five of the six events for men and topped the world record of Johnnie Weismuller, Hollywood's "Tarzan," in the men's 100-meter freestyle.

JAPAN'S UNDERSIDE

For all the optimism and promise the twenties held, hindsight enables us to identify unhealthy conditions. The Kanto earthquake was not only followed by reconstruction and progress but by ugly racial scapegoating. Soon after the temblor, rumors began to circulate that the Korean minority were responsible for the fires, as well as for poisoning wells and hatching a plot to kill the emperor. To some it seemed reasonable that Koreans would do these things to protest efforts by Japan to erase Korean nationalism in their homeland. For many Japanese there was always an eager willingness to believe the worst about Koreans who were (and often still are) stereotyped as crude, lazy, and dirty. Newspapers spread the rumors, some of which were intentionally planted to fan anti-Korean feelings. The result was a week-long wave of public hysteria during which time Koreans were hunted down by vigilante groups who administered linguistic tests to anyone suspected of being Korean. Those who spoke Japanese with a Korean accent were doomed to execution on the spot. An estimated two thousand Korean–Japanese were murdered. Communists, socialists, and other left-wing radicals also became targets of suspicion and were hunted down by ordinarily good-natured and polite city crowds who had been thrown off balance by the death and destruction of the quake.

In the political arena, the transition from government by oligarchs to government by popularly elected party leaders was only a modestly successful innovation. The public remained suspicious of the party elites in part because the parties' moral authority was frequently eroded by financial scandals and a soaring number of election law violations. In addition, public suspicion deepened because the parties were so enmeshed with the nation's two main economic interest groups from which both major parties drew their support: big business (*zaibatsu*) in the cities and landlords in the countryside. For their part, party leaders made little attempt to cultivate the appropriate skills to win mass public following. No Mussolini or Hitler emerged in Japan to harangue crowds with impassioned oratory. It was not the Japanese style, and it was irrelevant to winning the support party leaders *did* need—from the *zaibatsu*. In return for campaign funds, bribes, graft, and the extensive "gift-giving" that is a vital ingredient of all interpersonal relations in Japan, big business sought to control legislation favorable to itself. Rival party cabinets were routinely labelled as either a "Mitsui cabinet" or a "Mitsubishi cabinet."

A DUAL STRUCTURE

As a result, a dangerous "dual structure" divided Japan. While a new, generally well-educated middle class composed mostly of urban professionals and businessmen grew prosperous, the masses, especially the peasantry, lived and worked in appalling conditions. In desperation, farm families turned to infanticide. "To keep the children we already had, the others had to be sent back," one tormented mother said, adding that she knew that she would go to hell when she died. There was nothing idyllic or wholesome about farm work. "Long hours of painful, tortuous work reaped little in return," writes one authority. Factory work, grim as that was, was better when it was available, nearly everyone agreed. A young girl who made the move from farm to factory explained, "Think of weeding. . . in June in the rice field with the burning sun on your back and crawling on all fours in the boiling paddy-field water. Compared to that, indoor work is easy." Women were the special victims of rural poverty. The writer Yamashiro Tomoe recalls a family whose four young women, three daughters and a new bride, worked the loom every day from early in the morning until midnight:

> The young wife was more skilled in weaving than the three young daughters, and she came to be recognized as the best weaver in the village.

Her father-in-law and mother-in-law were pleased with her work. But because she was such an excellent weaver, they begrudged her taking any time away from the loom. They would complain, "Our young wife takes a lot of time in the toilet." Or, "She sure takes a long time feeding the baby." "She's so dumb. She's doing the washing again. It's better for the family if she lets the old woman do the washing, and does some weaving instead."

The provisions of laws regarded as progressive and humane serve to underscore the plight of the underclass. For example, the Factory Act which came into effect in 1916 did no more than prescribe an eleven-hour working day for women and children and a minimum work age of twelve. An amendment which became effective in 1926 raised the minimum age to fourteen and lowered the workday to ten hours, but it was far from rigorously enforced. In the mining industry, where safety and wage laws were notoriously lax and even then poorly enforced, the number of fatalities routinely topped a thousand a year. One out of twenty miners suffered serious major injuries each year; for an injury such as loss of eyesight, hearing, or limbs, the compensation to the surviving family was typically ¥100 (about $25, the cost of a draft animal). Again, the plight of women was invariably worse than men. In 1928, when employment of women in the mines was made illegal, women continued to work there because of lax enforcement of the law; they received, however, only half the pay the men got.

In the 1920s, there was great interest in radical ideologies imported from the revolution in Russia. Japanese intellectuals devoured books on the subject of communism and socialism—only the Soviet Union and Germany eclipsed Japan in the number of books on communism. Scholars debated the fine points of Marxism and how it should be applied to Japan but showed little inclination in leaving their studies to live among the proletariat or organize grass-roots support for radical causes (as Mao Tse-tung and other intellectuals were doing in China). Radical reform remained largely the property of idealogues from comfortable, urban, middle-class backgrounds. Still, in spite of this weak base of left-wing radicalism in Japan, conservatives in the government feared the spread of "dangerous thoughts." Accordingly, in 1925, the year which saw the liberalized suffrage law enacted, a harsh Peace Preservation Law was also passed by the Diet. It provided for severe penalties for anyone advocating change in Japan's political structure or for anyone who rejected the system of private property. "Thought police" under the control of the Home Ministry were assigned throughout the country to track down "thought offenses," and a special section within the Ministry of Education was created to watch and report on suspicious activities in the schools. In 1928, massive police roundups effectively crushed the pre-World War II Japan Communist Party.

DOUBTS OF A MODERATE

While Shidehara diplomacy remained the guiding principle of Japan, a strong feeling developed on the part of some Japanese that the entire peace settlement which ended World War I, including the League of Nations, was a

COMMUNISM IN PRE-WORLD WAR II JAPAN

A Communist party was founded in Japan in 1922, one year after the founding of the Chinese Communist Party. While the party itself was driven underground in Japan, communism still enjoyed a significant following in the universities and among intellectuals who found in the doctrines of Karl Marx and Vladimir Lenin "scientific" explanations of the historical tensions produced by capitalism and imperialism. Bookish economists debated the fine points of how these doctrines might be applied to Japan, but they were unsuccessful and largely uninterested in translating their ideas into a mass movement.

The few hundred "vanguard" members of the Japan Communist Party (JCP) called for violent class warfare, but their appeals fell on unsympathetic ears among a people long possessed of a highly homogeneous culture and increasingly well indoctrinated in the notion of *kokutai*, "national structure" or "national polity." According to this central principle of modern Japanese nationalism, the nation was a single family with the Emperor as its head. The JCP's demands for armed uprisings and the overthrow of the Imperial system were rejected not only because they challenged *kokutai* but because everyone knew that the party relied for guidance and help from the country's chief enemy, Soviet Russia. JCP slogans and tactics were invariably drafted in Moscow rather than in Tokyo.

Thus isolated from popular support, the small legion of radicals was an easy target for police dragnets. Nationwide roundups in the late 1920s left the party in the hands of a tiny band of ineffective desperadoes by the end of the decade. A few leaders, notably Nozaka Sanzo, slipped out of the country and agitated and recruited from foreign exile in Russia, China, and the United States. By the mid-1930s there were more active Communists in the Japanese section of the *American* Communist Party in California than there were in Japan. In China, a peasant-based Communist movement under Mao Tse-tung became the central force in shaping Chinese history. Their importance was underscored as Japanese armies invaded China in the 1930s. By mobilizing guerrilla resistance against the the Japanese enemy, the Chinese Communists effectively merged communism with nationalism, with defense of the motherland. By contrast, in Japan, the Communist Party remained marginal. The Japanese Communists, following Moscow's guidelines as well as the dictates of their own internationalist consciences, were persuaded to struggle against their nation's expansion into China. Unlike the Chinese Communists, the members of the JCP stood against the tide of Japanese nationalism which became ever stronger as the struggles in China expanded into a global war in which the survival of the nation seemed to hang in the balance.

self-serving formula devised to preserve a status quo favorable to the Anglo-American powers. A young prince, Konoe Fumimaro, who was to be his nation's prime minister during much of the crisis year of 1941, expressed this point of view best in a long and revealing article he wrote while serving as secretary to the chief of the Japanese delegation in the talks in Paris. Entitled "Reject the

Anglo-American-Centered Peace," Konoe's essay stands as a precursor of troubled times ahead, the more ominous because Konoe comes to be regarded as a voice of moderation. Konoe's reflections deserve to be quoted at length:

> The prewar European condition might have suited the Anglo–American powers best, but it never served justice and humanity. At an early stage, Britain and France colonized the "less civilized" regions of the world, and monopolized their exploitation. As a result, Germany, and all the late-coming nations also, were left with no land to acquire and no space to expand. Such actions violated the principle of equal opportunity among men and threatened to the equal right of existence for all nations. . . . The pacifism that the Anglo–American powers advocate is a peace-at-any-price, which only those who wish to maintain the status quo would uphold. It has nothing to do with justice and humanity. In actual fact, the present position of Japan in the world, like that of Germany before the war, demands the destruction of the status quo. . . .
>
> In the coming peace conference, should we decide to join the League of Nations, we must demand as the minimum *sine qua non* the eradication of economic imperialism and discriminatory treatment of Asian peoples by Caucasians. Economic imperialism, also, by enabling the most powerful to monopolize enormous amounts of capital and natural resources, prevents the free development of other nations and enriches the imperialists without requiring the use of force. Should the peace conference fail to suppress this rampant economic imperialism, the Anglo–American powers will become the economic masters of the world and, in the name of preserving the status quo, dominate it through the League of Nations and arms reduction, thus serving their own selfish interests.

TOWARD THE "DARK VALLEY"

Konoe's views, however, were thoughtful and decidedly moderate compared to the strident opinions of right-wing nationalists who found a small but dedicated audience for their impassioned ideas. Common to their thinking was a distrust of parliamentary democracy which they saw as an instrument of the privileged class. Similarly, they were contemptuous of the "weak-kneed" trade-oriented foreign policy of Shidehara which was viewed as a betrayal of Japan's destiny by greedy captains of industry and their political allies. Most talked in vague terms about the need for "national reconstruction" which would pave the way for the nation to assert itself more aggressively in Asian affairs. "Our seven hundred million brothers in China and India have no path to independence other than that offered by our guidance and protection," wrote the civilian rightist Kita Ikki. "It is my belief that Heaven has chosen Japan as the champion of the East," wrote Okawa Shumei who was convinced of the inevitability of a clash between East and West.

Many factors, then, were working against the tide of optimism and progress that was the hallmark of the 1920s in Japan. Two conditions gave Japan the final nudge toward the "dark valley" of the 1930s and a politics of national desperation. One was the resurgence of China under the leadership of Chiang Kai-shek and the Nationalists which threatened to end the special position Japan had built in that country. The second factor was the outbreak of the world depression in the fall of 1929. As the shock waves of economic collapse spread around the world, a drastic shrinkage of international trade ensued. Japan had become so tied into and dependent upon world trade—thanks in part to the success of Shidehara diplomacy—that its entire economic well-being was quickly placed in jeopardy. "When New York sneezed, Tokyo caught the flu," it was said. An almost hysterical fear of the "Made in Japan" label swept over American business and labor. In 1930, to protect American industry, President Herbert Hoover signed into law the Smoot–Hawley bill, the highest protective tariff in U.S. peacetime history. Duties on goods coming from Japan went up by as much as 200 percent. Other countries took similar steps to insulate their industries, and a disastrous ripple effect on world trade moved from nation to nation bringing a steep rise in factory closings and unemployment.

To take but one example, the United States was Japan's best customer for raw silk and silk fabrics in the 1920s. However, silk was a luxury product. In a depression, the demand for luxuries falls off rapidly. To put it simply, American women stopped wearing silk hosiery and did without or wore cheap, rayon substitutes. Overnight, Japan's silk export market collapsed. The whole country was hurt by the depression, but the peasant suffered most of all. Raising the silkworm cocoons and feeding them the leaves of specially cultivated mulberry trees was an important subsidiary occupation for millions of Japanese farmers, the difference between life and death for many. Now, the price brought by silk cocoons dropped by 65 percent in the first year of the depression. Overall rural cash income, never very high as we have seen, fell from an index figure of 100 in 1926 to 33 in 1931. In village after village, farmers, upon whose back and with whose labor and taxes much of Japan's prosperity had been built—were now starving or reduced to digging for the roots of wild plants or stripping the bark off of trees or begging for handouts on railroad platforms.

To those already predisposed to believe so, all of this confirmed that the international economic order was obviously unreliable. The responsibility for Japan's plight was placed squarely on the shoulders of the liberal reformers of the 1920s. Taisho democracy and Taisho internationalism, never very robust and possibly doomed anyway, were about to become two more victims of the world depression.

ADDITIONAL READING

For bibliographical guides to the roots of imperialism in East Asia, see the various essays ("Policies Toward the United States," "Policies Toward China," and so on) in James Morley, ed., *Japan's Foreign Policy* (1974); and Ernest R. May and James C. Thomson, Jr., eds., *American–East Asian Relations: A Survey* (1972).

W. G. Beasley, *Japanese Imperialism, 1894–1945* (1984) is a brief, comprehensive guide to the subject. Ramon H. Myers and Mark R. Peattie, eds., *The Japanese Colonial*

Empire, 1894–1945 (1984) is a more exhaustively documented study of the same subject. Equally thorough are Mark R. Peattie, *Nan'yo: The Rise and Fall of the Japanese in Micronesia, 1885–1945* (1988); and Peter Duus, Ramon H. Myers, and Mark R. Peattie, eds., *The Japanese Informal Empire in China, 1895–1937* (1989).

Akira Iriye has written widely on Japanese diplomatic history and Japanese–U.S. relations. Several of his works survey the period under consideration in this chapter: *Across the Pacific: An Inner History of American–East Asian Relations* (1867); *Pacific Estrangement: Japanese and American Expansion, 1897–1911* (1972); *After Imperialism: The Search for a New Order in the Far East, 1921–1931* (1965); and "Imperialism in East Asia" in James B. Crowley, ed., *Modern East Asia: Essays in Interpretation* (1970).

Other valuable works include: Marius B. Jansen, *Japan and China: From War to Peace, 1894–1972* (1975); and Richard R. Storry, *Japan and the Decline of the West in Asia, 1894–1912* (1979).

More specialized studies include: Shumpei Okamoto, *The Japanese Oligarchy and the Russo–Japanese War* (1971); James W. Morley, *The Japanese Thrust into Siberia, 1918* (1957); Ian Nish, *The Anglo–Japanese Alliance: The Diplomacy of Two Island Empires, 1894–1907* (2nd ed., 1985); Hilary Conroy, *The Japanese Seizure of Korea, 1868–1910* (1960); and Mikiso Hane, *Peasants, Rebels and Outcasts: The Underside of Modern Japan* (1982).

On the early history of Japanese in America, see the books by Roger Daniels including *The Politics of Prejudice: The Anti-Japanese Movement in California and the Struggle for Japanese Exclusion* (1968); and *Asian America: Chinese and Japanese in the United States Since 1850* (1988). The latter contains a fine up-to-date bibliography. *Strangers from a Different Shore: A History of Asian Americans* (1989) by Ronald Takaki is current, comprehensive, and highly engaging.

5

THE CHINA PROBLEM

In the bustling main railway station of Tokyo, commuters today take little notice as they walk past a small memorial plaque etched into the floor. It marks the spot where Prime Minister Hamaguchi Osachi was standing on the morning of November 14, 1930, about to board a train, when he was shot by a twenty-year-old patriotic hoodlum. The assassin, quickly arrested by the police, provided no explanation for his deed except that he resented the prime minister's role in bringing to pass a new naval limitations treaty which had received the emperor's seal only weeks earlier. The murder of Hamaguchi was to be the first of a series of violent assaults on the government hatched by right-wing nationalists and young army and navy officers in the 1930s. The shooting of Hamaguchi marked the end of a brief period of democratic ascendancy and the beginning of "government by assassination," as one foreign journalist dubbed the politics of Japan in the early 1930s.

THE TWENTIES AND THIRTIES CONTRASTED

Decades do not always delineate neat, reliable periods of historical trends. In international relations, however, the 1920s had in general been a hopeful decade marked by international conciliation and a growing network of treaty relationships aimed at accelerating disarmament and preserving peace. "Shidehara diplomacy" brought Japan squarely into the prevailing stream of international good will. The business and bureaucratic elites accepted Foreign Minister Shidehara's basic premise, that economic diplomacy and penetration of overseas markets in China and in the West offered brighter prospects to Japan than territorial expansion and a costly arms race with the Western powers. Japan's military elite permitted the trend to continue but never truly endorsed the spirit of Shidehara diplomacy.

The 1930 London Naval Conference conveniently marks the beginning of the end of the internationalism of the 1920s. Called as a follow-up to the Washington Conference agreement on naval limitations held in 1921–1922, the London meeting found the Japanese Navy in a far less conciliatory mood than it had been eight years earlier, when it had reluctantly accepted a 5:3 ratio, with Japan being allowed only three tons for every five tons of battleships permitted to the navies of Britain and the United States. At issue at the London meeting were light and heavy cruisers—among many other complex questions. The Western powers insisted that the old ratio of 5:3 be preserved; the Japanese naval general staff bridled at the inferior ratio and insisted on 10:7.[1] In the minds of Japanese naval strategists and patriots, the mathematical ratios were not empty abstractions. The two formulae would measure whether or not the West acknowledged Japanese naval supremacy in the Western Pacific. When Hamaguchi and his foreign minister Shidehara overrode the Navy's objections and forced the treaty, both were labeled as traitors by extremists, one of whom pulled the trigger on the prime minister.

AGRARIAN DEATHBANDS

Less than two years after the attack on Hamaguchi, another group of extremists conspired to murder Prime Minister Inukai Tsuyoshi, to blow up Tokyo's power plants, dynamite the Mitsubishi Bank, and attack the headquarters of Inukai's political party. Most of the plan failed, but the conspirators did succeed in killing the prime minister. They gained entrance to Inukai's official residence and shot him in cold blood on May 15, 1932. The assassins responsible for this "5-15 Incident" styled themselves the "Blood Pledge League" (*Ketsumeidan*). Known collectively as "deathbands" (*kesshitai*), such terrorists saw themselves in the samurai tradition, as selfless exemplars of vengeance, ready to face death to achieve their purpose. Through spectacular acts of daring they sought to focus public attention on the righteousness of their goals.

Exactly what the goals of the deathbands were, however, is not easy to define. The Blood Pledge League despised Inukai because they regarded as "weak-kneed" the prime minister's efforts to conciliate a settlement of disputes with China arising out of Japanese incursion into Manchuria (to be discussed later). Even more, Inukai earned their wrath because of his advocacy of constitutional

---

[1] The treaty ratios agreed upon at London have provoked much confusion. James Crowley explains: "Under the Reed–Matsudaira Compromise, Japan accepted the 'principle' of the 10:6 ratio, and the United States agreed that it would not build its full allotment of cruisers under this principle before 1936. This guaranteed Japan a de facto ratio of 10:7 until 1936, when the sea powers would meet again to reconsider the treaties negotiated at the Washington and London conferences." At the London Conference of 1936 (which began in December 1935 and is thus usually called the London Conference of 1935), Japanese delegates refused to participate after their proposal for full parity was rejected.

Tachibana Kosaburo, one of the agrarianist philosophers and a founder of a private patriotic academy to which radical youth gravitated, expressed his anti-urban sentiments in this comment on the Mitsukoshi department store. (The Ginza Mitsukoshi was—and is—the flagship department store of the Mitsui empire.)

"Even if grass were to grow on the roof of the Mitsukoshi Department Store, Japan would not fall, but if the rain leaked through the roofs of five million Japanese farmers' homes what would become of Japan?"

Ironists enjoy observing that after World War II grass did grow on the roof of Mitsukoshi—as part of a playland for youngsters.

democracy which the zealots associated with *zaibatsu* capitalism, party politics and the West. Political parties which had emerged as a powerful elite in the 1920s were seen, with ample good reason, as working hand in hand with big business in a way which left poor factory workers and peasant farmers weak and unrepresented. These elements in turn were held to be responsible for the economic hardships that the world depression was bringing to Japan.

Typically, the deathband members were themselves from the countryside and were especially enraged by the plight of the villages. For this reason, many of the radicals are identified as "agrarianists." Unsophisticated and with only meager educations, they longed for a return to the supposed solidarity and social harmony of the traditional village. Conversely, they were profoundly disturbed by the divisive, modern, urban drift of Japan which they associated with competition, greed, and materialism. They loathed the Ginza. Its neon lights, dance halls, foreign restaurants, and big business establishments were symbols of what the modern West was doing to Japan: stripping it of its identity.

At the same time, they were disturbed by morale problems within the army, most of whose recruits came from farmer conscripts. Notice how these various concerns blend together in the court testimony of one of the army defendants in the 5-15 Incident. After noting that it was the rural provinces of Japan's northeast that provided the army with its model soldiers, the accused declared,

It is extremely dangerous that such soldiers should be worried about their starving families when they are at the front exposing themselves to death. In utter disregard of poverty-stricken farmers the enormously rich zaibatsu pursue their private wealth. Meanwhile the young children of the impoverished farmers of the north-eastern provinces attend school without breakfast, and their families subsist on rotten potatoes. I thought that to let a day go by without doing anything was to endanger the army for one day longer.

A JAPANESE FASCISM?

Throughout the world, the deepening depression shook public confidence in capitalism and parliamentary democracy and invited radical solutions, from both left and right, to the world malaise. Japan, then, was no different. It is tempting—but misleading—to label Japan's radicals as fascists or communists; even labels like "left" and "right" oversimplify. As we have noted, they held leftist ideas about capitalism and saw Japan's *zaibatsu* class as the root of exploitation and injustice. At the same time, however the superpatriots of the deathbands uniformly feared the Soviet Union, and despised communism. They venerated the army and military virtues in a fashion which could be expected to earn them a rightist designation. Common to all of them was a "rightist" exaltation of the uniqueness of Japan, particularly its imperial institution.

Whatever similarities existed between the Japanese agrarian movement and the Italian fascist and German Nazi organizations are overshadowed by major differences. Strikingly, no equivalent to Der Führer or Il Duce emerged in Japan. Unlike Benito Mussolini and Adolf Hitler, the Japanese radicals demonstrated no interest in organizing the masses. They preferred to operate as blood brothers, in small groups of dedicated comrades who personally knew and trusted each other. Only about one percent of Japan's population belonged to the literally thousands of patriotic associations, right-wing study groups, chauvinist religious sects, antilabor organizations, and agrarian reform societies. None of the dozens of deathbands which carried out the terrorist plots could have boasted of memberships in the hundreds. The heart of the Blood Pledge League was a group of about twenty, assigned to kill twenty leading statesmen and business figures on a "one-man one-kill" (*ichinin issatsu*) basis.

Perhaps the single most common feature of the Japanese radicals was the very vagueness of their goals. They did not think things out systematically. "They were absorbed in fantasies and abstractions," one Japanese scholar has written. They certainly did not want to gain control of the National Diet—here again the contrast with European fascists is evident. There was no Japanese equivalent to Mussolini's "March on Rome." To the Japanese radicals, the Diet was the source of Japan's corruption. They wanted no part of it. "How could we fellow-patriots have been able to carry out our schemes if we had nourished

---

To most Japanese the blood oath—slicing the finger with a razor and sealing one's signature in blood on a membership roster—smacks of yakuza gangsterism. In 1973, however, when the conservative political club known as the *Seirankai* was inaugurated at the Okura Hotel in Tokyo, the ritual was observed by twenty-four junior Diet members including the prominent right-wing politician Ishihara Shintaro. The ceremony prompted this favorable comment:

"Those who ridicule the blood oath as a feudalistic atavism or a gamblers' ritual would probably be afraid to cut their own fingers anyway. In fact, it was the samurai who sealed their promises in blood, and it is fitting that present-day politicians, as statesmen and patriots, should follow their example. . . . A blood oath still symbolizes commitment to a course of action at the risk of one's life."

political ambitions or indulged in private fancies about the actual structure of government?" wrote the leader of a failed 1934 plot to kill yet another prime minister.

Most of the Japanese radicals were unwilling to even speculate on precise political goals or schemes and preferred to speak vaguely of "reconstruction," the "path of righteousness," "Japanese spirit" and the "Imperial Way." To have formulated a precise scenario for the future would have been tantamount to surmising the will of the emperor, an unthinkable presumption for humble farmboy-patriots. On only two occasions did plotters go so far as to plan military coups—both of which failed. These were not typical, and in any case senior military figures, while sometimes sympathetic to the radicals, turned a deaf ear to their talk of violent usurpation of power. Such plots might well throw the nation into chaos and impede the preparation for war, which was the abiding concern of the generals and admirals filling staff positions in Tokyo.

FACTIONAL RIVALRIES

High-ranking officers at the center were vastly different in outlook and training from the subordinate officers in the field. The lower-ranking officers' education had stopped at the level of an officer's training school, where they had been drilled in battle tactics; a "field-grade" command was the most they could expect. The senior officers had been selected to rise beyond that to the more sophisticated education offered at the Army War College. The lower-ranking officers, the ones who were sometimes attracted to the fanatical activities of the deathbands, tended to think of Japan's military strength in terms of traditional samurai values—spirit, courage, dedication. Senior officers, however, were obliged to concentrate more on military technology and planning, mechanization, strategic stockpiles, financial resources, and the like. This in turn required that they be in touch with the *zaibatsu* and make compromises with the politicians so despised by the junior officers.

Furthermore, there was little reason for the military to support the revolutionary destruction of the state system by junior fanatics when legitimate methods and evolutionary trends were working to the advantage of the generals and admirals anyway. These ranking military leaders emphasized tight control and discipline from the top down and, accordingly, came to be known as the "Control Faction" *(Tosei-ha)*. Their rivals, the young firebrands who supported assassination plots and more-militant overseas adventures, came to be known as the "Imperial Way Faction" *(Kodo-ha)*. The Control Faction might profit from the disorder created by the insubordination of Imperial Way hotheads—the Control Faction alone could promise nervous politicians that it had the ability to discipline unruly juniors and restore order. However, the army leaders had no intention to let the initiative slip from their hands.

The greatest challenge to the authority of the Control Faction—and to the government of Japan—came on February 26, 1936, when Imperial Way Faction officers staged an attempted takeover of the government. For the first and only time in the era of violent incidents, the extremists mobilized significant numbers of rank-and-file soldiers to help them. For three snowy days, some 1400 troops from the Tokyo garrison occupied the center of the capital, while leaders eliminated one after another of their political enemies. The prime minister escaped only because the rebels in confusion shot his brother-in-law who happened to resemble him. Control Faction leaders persuaded the emperor to issue a strong expression of his disapproval. Buttressed by this rare example of Imperial intervention in the affairs of the nation, the Control Faction moved with decisive force to crush the "2-26" incident.

This time, for the first time in the era of incidents, military courts dealt harsh penalties to the perpetrators; nineteen were condemned and executed by firing squads after secret trials designed to deny the rebels the rostrum from which they intended to present their cause to the public. Numerous officers who were linked to the Imperial Way Faction were then either removed from important posts or compelled to retire. With internal strife in the military diminished, the Control Faction more than ever became the driving force in the nation's political process. Among the important leaders of the Control Faction was General Tojo Hideki, who was to become Japan's leader on the eve of the Pacific War.

The radicals of the 1930s are perhaps best described as action-oriented visionaries. "I have no systematized ideas. I transcend reason and act completely on intuition," one of them professed in language that might have been used by a samurai inspired by a Zen distrust of intellect. The "dream-world optimism" of the radicals was always centered on the emperor. If noble-minded men of purpose like themselves somehow led the way, they felt, the course would become clear. "If only the dark clouds shrouding the emperor could be swept away, the imperial sun will naturally shine forth," one wrote. Their hazy ideals makes it difficult for us to assign success or failure to them. Like terrorist movements everywhere, they captured headlines and created a national, even international, sensation. Of course, they were not able to turn the clock back. There was no way of returning to the kind of agrarian utopia they idealized, and they never succeeded in bringing about a "restoration of the emperor"—whatever that undefined phrase meant.

CONTROL FACTION ASCENDANT

Yet, the deathbands had a profound effect on the history of Japan. With the murder of Inukai, the nation entered a "period of emergency" when party governments went out of existence. Political parties survived all through the decade of the 1930s, but after 1932 control of the premiership was no longer in the hands of party leaders. Demoralized party politicians steadily disappeared from the ranks of the key decision makers. Of the eleven men who led the government of Japan in the years between 1932 and 1945 only three were civilians, and they were all sufficiently conservative to be acceptable to the military. Increasingly after 1932, army and naval general staffs were awarded a larger voice in

BESUBORU III

While diplomatic relations with the United States worsened in the 1930s, American popular culture thrived in the large urban centers of Japan. Conservatives were scandalized by the "Takarazuka Girls Opera Company" which in the 1930s came to feature musical spectacles with bare-legged chorus lines patterned on New York's Radio City "Rockettes." Sports, however, were less problematic.

Interest in baseball was stimulated by a highly popular barnstorming tour of Japan by Babe Ruth, Lou Gehrig, and other American all-stars in 1934. The tour impresario, Shoriki Matsutaro, was also responsible for other American imports, including full-page color comic sections in his *Yomiuri* newspaper, Japan's most widely read daily. Stadium crowds appreciated that the Americans were willing to play in the rain rather than disappoint the throngs which had come to see them, and a photograph of one game shows Babe Ruth standing in the infield carrying an umbrella thoughtfully provided by a Japanese spectator. A bust of Ruth remains in a place of honor outside the main gate of Osaka's Koshien stadium, where he drew 75,000 fans in 1934.

In the wake of the Americans' visit, the first professional baseball team was launched, sponsored by Shoriki's *Yomiuri*. It was known as the *Dai Nippon Tokyo Yakyu Kurabu* (the Great Japan Tokyo Baseball Club) until Lefty O'Doul suggested "Giants," after O'Doul's New York Giants, as an alternative. The Giants, or Yomiuri Giants it became, were joined in 1936 by six other professional teams to make up Japan's first pro league. The sport flourished throughout the 1930s, but the drift toward war added an ominous flavor to the games. By the early 1940s spectators could count on watching not only the usual nine innings but grenade-throwing contests and exhibitions of sandbag carrying as well.

Among the "stars" who accompanied Ruth to Japan in 1934 was Moe Berg, an undistinguished second-string catcher for the Washington Senators. A graduate of Princeton and the Sorbonne, Berg made up in linguistic talent what he lacked as a player. "He spoke a dozen languages and couldn't hit in any of them," one coach complained. While in Tokyo, Berg managed to take some bird's-eye photographs of the city skyline from the roof of St. Luke's hospital, pictures which were used a decade later by U.S. flyers in their bomb runs over Tokyo. Berg gave up baseball and went on to perform wartime espionage work, posing as a U.S. businessman in Switzerland and spying on German nuclear research efforts.

determining the size of defense budgets and shaping Japan's international policies. Contributing to this newly won leverage was the ability of the army's Control Faction to present itself as the only authority able to rein in the extremists and save the country from more "government by assassination."

The decline of parliamentary democracy meant that the days of liberalism and internationalism of the 1920s were numbered. The case of the distinguished constitutional law scholar Minobe Tatsukichi is illustrative. Throughout the 1920s Minobe's theories of government had gained wide acceptance. Students hoping to pass civil service or university entrance examinations knew that they would be required to recite and explain Professor Minobe's scholarly underpinning of parliamentary democracy in Japan. In 1935, however, ultranationalists from within the Military Reservists Association accused Minobe of lèse majesté. For suggesting that the emperor was an "organ of the state" rather than identical to the state, Minobe was driven from his teaching post at Tokyo University and compelled to give up his appointive seat in the House of Peers. For added measure, his books were banned, and in 1936 an assassination attempt was made on his life.

In 1937, as if to set the record straight, the Ministry of Education issued a guidebook for teachers. The official *Cardinal Principles of the National Polity* (*Kokutai no hongi*) became a centerpiece in an intensive indoctrination effort to stimulate pride in the Imperial Throne "which is coeval with heaven and earth." "Japan is a divine country," the book intoned. "The heavenly ancestor it was who first laid its foundations, and the Sun Goddess left her descendants to reign over it forever and ever. This is true only of our country, and nothing similar may be found in foreign lands," teachers were instructed. As a corollary, *Principles* inveighed against Western vices including individualism, democracy, and communism. By the end of the 1930s, youngsters were pointing at Westerners and calling out "Spy!"

Perhaps, the ultranationalists' most baleful legacy was that they fostered within Japan an attitude of invincibility and arrogance toward the outside world. The main role of the ultranationalists, writes historian Peter Duus, "was anesthetizing public opinion to the dangers of a reckless foreign policy by constantly lauding the superiority of Japanese spirit [*and*] proclaiming the infallibility of the Imperial Way." Beginning in 1931, that "reckless foreign policy" brought Japanese imperialism to a new stage in Manchuria.

MANCHURIA

The Chinese call it simply *tung-pei*, the northeast. For centuries, the three northeastern provinces to the north of the Great Wall have been a part of China, and to call it *tung-pei* underscores the fact that the Empire of China extended well beyond the original centers of Chinese civilization which lay in the Yellow River basin to the south of the wall. To call the northeast anything else somehow suggested that it was another country, distinct from China.

Chinese sensitivities notwithstanding, the area to the north became widely known in the world as Manchuria. Indeed it *was* the homeland of a frontier people who called themselves Manchus. In the seventeenth century, these alien Manchus, though small in number, were able to capitalize on factional infighting and other failings in the great Chinese empire, penetrate the Great Wall, and overrun all of China. From 1644 until 1912, all the ruling emperors of

China were alien Manchus. By adapting themselves to Chinese culture and employing Chinese scholars to staff their political institutions, the Manchus led China into an era of remarkable growth and prosperity—for approximately a century and a half.

Beginning about 1800, however, China entered a period of decline marked by corrupt government, natural disasters, internal rebellion, and external aggression. The last century of the Manchu reign was a time of defeat and humiliation for China, with Japan joining the Western powers to take advantage of China's weakness. When a republican revolution associated with the name of Sun Yat-sen overthrew the Manchus in the final weeks of 1911, it was more than just another dynasty which came to an end. In its long history, China had seen more than a score of dynasties come and go, but this time the Empire itself was dissolved. When the last emperor of China, a Manchu youngster of five named P'u-yi, abdicated in February 1912, the longest surviving political tradition in the world, the twenty-one-century-old Empire of China, was swept into history.

The Republic of China which was established in its place did not measure up to the promise and hope that it seemed to offer in 1912. The tyranny of a corrupt and backward-looking Manchu monarchy was replaced by the tyranny of warlords. For well over a decade, the Republic of China was a government in name only. Real power in China was fragmented. No single authority, not even the respected Sun Yat-sen and his Nationalist Party, could claim authority throughout vast China. (The Nationalist Party also became well known throughout the world by its Chinese name, *Kuomintang.*) A dozen or so major warlord generals, with private armies loyal to them rather than to the nation, fought and divided up the land and parcelled out smaller domains to their lieutenants. China, which desperately needed national unity to meet the challenges of the modern world, check the inroads of the foreigners, and modernize itself, remained divided and vulnerable. The warlord era, at its peak from 1916 to 1928 (though it began earlier and ended later in some parts of China), was a time of almost total disorder, and it provided imperialist powers with an open invitation to further exploit the country. One country after another carved out its own "sphere of interest."

Japan's "sphere" was the area closest to home, closest to its Korean colony, the three northeastern provinces of China. Only sparsely inhabited, the huge northeast, four times larger than the Japanese home islands, offered the potential for absorbing some of Japan's rapidly expanding population. Rich in both agricultural and underground minerals, Manchuria seemed a treasurehouse to resource-poor Japan. Most important, Japanese military leaders saw Manchuria as a strategically vital buffer against the southward expansion of Russia. To these men, the Russian bear seemed all the more menacing after the 1917 Bolshevik revolution transformed tottering Imperial Russia into the Soviet Union, a world power of the first magnitude. Nineteenth-century Japanese dread of Russia deepened as Japanese came to view the Kremlin as the command post for the export of worldwide revolution. A Soviet advance into Manchuria, they argued, would turn that area into a giant base for the communization of all Asia.

Japan's Kwantung Army protected the nation's interests in Manchuria. (*Kwantung* is the Chinese name of the southern gateway peninsula to Manchuria; *Kanto* is the Japanese version.) During the warlord era, political officers of this overseas Kwantung Army adroitly cultivated close ties with a father and son warlord team, Chang Tso-lin (the "Old Marshal") and Chang Hsueh-liang (the "Young Marshal"), who dominated Manchuria. It was Japanese backing which allowed the Old Marshal to prevail in the constant give-and-take of warlord fighting in the north. In return, the Old Marshal had little choice but to allow his Japanese backers special economic and military privileges in Manchuria. Even so, in 1928, when the Old Marshal showed signs of defiance toward the Kwantung Army, a murderous plot by Japanese officers ended the life of the senior Chang.

When the Young Marshal succeeded to the leadership of his father's armies, he knew that he must make a choice. The patriotic thing to do was to cast his lot with the Chinese Nationalists under Chiang Kai-shek, who succeeded to the mantle of Sun Yat-sen upon Sun's death in 1925. By 1928, the armies of Generalissimo Chiang Kai-shek were fulfilling the longstanding dream of the Kuomintang. During a two-year campaign, they had crushed one warlord army after another. The Young Marshal, one of the last warlord holdouts, could now side with the Nationalists, or he could become a puppet of Japan. The Young Marshal chose the patriotic option. He would recognize Chinese nationalism as the wave of the future and ally his armies with Chiang Kai-shek's cause.

When Nationalist flags were hoisted over government buildings in the Manchurian city of Mukden in December 1928, it set off alarms in Japan. Chiang Kai-shek's armies were not yet strong enough to actually occupy the northern reaches of China, but the flags were a reminder to Japan that the rising tide of Chinese nationalism threatened Japan's "special position" in China's northeastern provinces. The response of the Japanese government was measured and conciliatory: Japan would rely on the peaceful principles of Shidehara diplomacy to maintain Japan's "special relationship" with China's northeast. For nearly three more years, until the crisis year of 1931, moderation prevailed. Meanwhile, however, a militant group of middle-ranking officers in the Kwantung Army, keenly aware of their vanguard responsibilities in an area increasingly hostile to Japan, explored more violent methods of response.

THE MANCHURIAN INCIDENT

Late on the evening of September 18, 1931, a dynamite explosion occurred on the tracks of the Japanese-owned South Manchurian Railway (SMR) just north of the northern Chinese city of Mukden. It was not much of an explosion. Minutes later, the southbound express from Changchun roared over a small gap in the tracks, heeled slightly to one side, recovered and sped on to a punctual 10:30 P.M. arrival at Mukden station. Passengers were unaware that anything untoward had happened.

Officers of Japan's Kwantung Army responded quickly to the commotion. Those at the scene proclaimed that the incident was the work of Chinese troublemakers intent on causing trouble. The army headquarters declared a "state of emergency" and issued orders to local garrisons to seize cities along the SMR as a measure of self-defense. Only by punishing the culprits could Japanese citizens and property in Manchuria be safeguarded, it was said. By dawn of the next morning, all the major cities along the 500-mile north-south railway were under the control of the Kwantung Army.

After World War II, as Japan's military archives were opened for the world to see, it became clear that the "Manchurian Incident" was not the work of Chinese saboteurs. What had been only surmised in 1931 was confirmed. The explosion on the tracks of the SMR had been a staged affair, a plot engineered by Colonel Ishiwara Kanji and other officers of the Kwantung Army. Initiative for the incident did not come from the civilian government in Tokyo which was still committed to "Shidehara diplomacy" and preferred to avoid overt military action on the China mainland. Impatient with their leadership's "weak-kneed" reliance on diplomacy and compromise, colonels on the scene in Manchuria manufactured an atmosphere of crisis which allowed them to undertake the kind of "direct action" which they knew would not have been authorized by the prime minister, nor indeed by the general staff. Even General Honjo, the commanding general of the Kwantung Army, learned of the incident and accepted responsibility for it only *after* the deed was completed.

The Manchurian Incident was therefore a textbook example of the fait accompli, an already accomplished fact. Faced with the insubordination of its military officers, what was the government of Japan to do? The operations along the SMR had been carried out with precision and skill and had resulted in only negligible casualties to the Japanese in spite of the fact that the ten thousand soldiers of the Kwantung Army were outnumbered by at least fifteen to one by Chinese troops in the areas affected. Efforts by Tokyo to disown the perpetrators, punish them, or disavow their deeds would surely be met with resistance from the Kwantung Army soldiers who thought of themselves as a patriotic

Japanese use the term *gekokujo* (those below overthrowing those above) to describe the way junior officers preempted authority in Manchuria. "A complex, highly Japanese and baneful phenomenon," historian Alvin Coox calls it. "In the modern manifestation of gekokujo," he writes, "junior officers—cocky and conceited because of their youth and supposed powers of execution, though still untested—reproached the prudence of older officers, mistaking deliberation for hesitation. Logic and persuasion yielded to the fait accompli; matters could always be worked out if only something were done. Important affairs were handled increasingly by young and forceful officers, for the seniors were often seen as lacking judgment, ability, and moral courage."

spearhead of the nation. Nobody in Tokyo wished to present to China and the world the picture of a Japanese military establishment veering out of control. In the months that followed the Manchurian Incident, the government therefore avoided a showdown struggle with its unruly officers and sought merely to moderate their behavior. Events in Manchuria, however, developed a momentum of their own as the Kwantung Army, emboldened by success, expanded its operations. By the beginning of 1932, all of Manchuria, from the modern ports of the south to the frozen Amur River boundary with the Soviet Union, had been effectively incorporated into the Empire of Japan.

THE LAST EMPEROR

The Kwantung Army shrouded its deeds in Manchuria with the illusion of respectability. The Kwantung Army, though unable because of opposition from Tokyo to formally annex Manchuria into the Empire of Japan, accomplished the next best thing. In Manchuria, in order to fabricate the "local character" of the Manchurian Incident, Japanese agents staged "popular" movements which "demanded" the creation of a state independent of the Republic of China. The Kwantung Army then graciously responded by engineering the creation of an "independent" Manchu state, Manchukuo, in 1932. The new nation had its own flag, currency, and postage stamps. To stand at the head of the new regime, Kwantung Army agents selected the last sovereign of China, the deposed child emperor of 1912, Hsuan Tung, better known to the world as Henry P'u-yi.

Only twenty-six in 1932 when Kwantung Army officers coaxed him from obscure retirement, P'u-yi was the ideal puppet. He led an "aimless existence," he later confessed. He was weak willed, given to outbursts of sadism, a hypochondriac debilitated by medicines and drugs. Stirred by dreams of reviving his family's imperial heritage, P'u-yi was not so much interested in power as in the trappings of power. These were freely bestowed on him by his Japanese handlers: lofty titles, the Imperial Dragon robes, palaces, and open cars. "I went wild with joy," he wrote of the ceremony in which he was enthroned as emperor in 1934. Kwantung Army officers observed polite formalities in his presence but made certain that P'u-yi bestowed on Japanese "advisers" a free rein in matters related to foreign relations, defense, transportation, and other concerns vital to Japan or, more precisely, to the Kwantung Army. No less than seventeen of the twenty-seven bureau chiefs in the new government were Japanese. Japanese were regularly named to the key post of vice-minister in one ministry after another.

Nationalist China's response to the Japanese incursion into its northeast was cautious. Chiang Kai-shek calculated that his nation's armies were no match for the Imperial Japanese Army. The Imperial Navy hopelessly outclassed the almost nonexistent Chinese Navy. However, Chiang's decision to avoid an armed clash with Japan was dictated even more by internal events in China. A

Communist movement, though still small and isolated in 1931, obsessed Chiang. He likened it to a "disease of the heart." The Japanese, in spite of their plunder, remained in Chiang's revealing metaphor a "disease of the skin." Diseases of the skin can be irritating, but they are not usually fatal; diseases of the heart, however, cannot be ignored. To be more precise, Chiang feared that if he turned his attention against the Japanese, his Communist rivals would take advantage of his weakness to attack him from the rear. Accordingly, it was necessary first to rid the nation of the menace from within, Chiang declared. At the time of the Manchurian Incident, the Nationalist armies were carrying out one of numerous "annihilation campaigns" directed at the Communists. Chiang refused to be distracted from that goal and looked instead for international support.

THE WORLD RESPONDS TO MANCHURIA

World response to the events in Manchuria fell far short of the kind of support Chiang hoped for. The United States was, of course, deeply disturbed by Japanese moves. They were a clear violation of China's territorial integrity, a challenge to the "Open Door" doctrine which America had espoused since the turn of the century. Now, however, America was forced to consider in concrete measures that which it had only discussed in generalities before: Were American vital interests truly threatened by events occurring in distant China? Was American security really jeopardized by Japan's apparent closing of the open door? In the wake of the Manchurian Incident, it became clear that American leaders were not persuaded that Japan's Manchurian adventure called for war, or the risk of war. In any case, given the woeful state of American military preparedness in 1931, it is doubtful that the United States could have controlled events by force. The Herbert Hoover administration (1929–1933) had the distinction—the "sad distinction," wrote naval historian Admiral Samuel Eliot Morison—of being the first one since the eighteenth century in which not a single keel of a naval combatant ship was laid down. There were only 132,000 Americans in uniform. The army of Greece was larger. Economic sanctions in the form of import-export restrictions were considered, but rejected, by Hoover. What good would it do to "stick pins in tigers," the president asked, mindful that neither the United States nor the nations of the West were ready or able to back trade embargoes with the ultimate sanction of military force.

With hindsight, it may seem obvious to later generations that the world's response to Japan's aggressive behavior was appeasement that only encouraged further aggression. At the time, however, alternative options seemed fraught with risk. Joseph Grew, the American ambassador in Tokyo from 1931 to 1941, from the beginning consistently warned of the danger in taking too strong a stand against Japan lest moderates opposed to territorial expansion lose ground to the hotheads.

Ambassadors, of course, are often accused of taking on the coloration of their assigned posts—becoming too sympathetic to the positions of their host country. Ambassador Nelson T. Johnson, the U. S. envoy to China, however, conceded that Japanese transgressions in China had not cost the United States anything. Furthermore, he added, "The development of this area under Japanese enterprise may mean an increased opportunity for American industrial plants to sell the kind of machinery and other manufactured goods that will be needed. . . ." Many Asian experts in Washington had grown so discouraged by China's long record of weakness that they were not ready to believe that Chiang Kai-shek's Nationalists represented any great new wave of the future. Accordingly, it was possible for erstwhile friends of China to believe, as historian Warren Cohen has shown, "that Japanese domination of China would be in the best interests of the United States—and of China, too!" In Washington, Stanley K. Hornbeck, Chief of the Far Eastern Division at the State Department throughout most of the 1930s and a key policymaker, brought an unmistakable bias against Japan to his job. Hornbeck was nonetheless a realist—of truly Machiavellian dimensions. U.S. purposes might best be served, he argued, if the Japanese were kept involved in an indecisive struggle in an area where the United States had no truly vital interests—such as Manchuria.

The official U.S. response to the Manchurian Incident was therefore a legally correct policy of "non-recognition." As enunciated by Secretary of State Henry L. Stimson in 1932, this notified Japan that the United States "cannot admit the legality nor does it intend to recognize" the gains made by Japan in Manchuria. Except for Japan, only a few nations extended diplomatic recognition to the new puppet state: Costa Rica and the Vatican were in the curious group.

In Geneva, the League of Nations took up China's charges against Japan. For the first time since its founding at the end of the world war, the collective will of the League would be tested by a major case of aggression. Geneva dispatched to Manchuria a commission under the Englishman Lord Lytton to investigate. Eventually, the League adopted the report of the Lytton Commission, censured Japan, and called for the withdrawal of the Kwantung Army from its newly gained territory. Shortly after the 42–1 vote of the League's Assembly was recorded, Japanese Ambassador Matsuoka Yosuke responded to the international condemnation by leading his delegation in a dramatic walkout from the League chamber. A month later, in March 1933, Japan announced its intention to withdraw from the League, a move which dramatically underscored the impotence of that world body. How effective could the League be when the most powerful nation in the Far East was no longer a member? Both Germany and Italy would feel safer with expansionist policies after Japan had demonstrated the League's insignificance.

For a short period in 1932, the conflict between Japan and China threatened to spread from Manchuria to other parts of China. Anti-Japanese boycotts in the great coastal city of Shanghai prompted the Japanese to deploy marines, supposedly to protect Japanese citizens. When the local Chinese commander resisted with unexpected determination, Japanese authorities ordered planes from nearby aircraft carriers into action. The air raid on the densely populated residential section of Shanghai known as Chapei on January 29, 1932, marked the beginning of a new era in modern warfare in which civilian populations would be subjected to terror strafing and bombing. The rain of bombs over Chapei, the thousands of casualties, and the stream of refugees caused by the attacks, intensified Chinese outrage and roused passionate world opinion against Japan.

Stimson and other world leaders hoped that the mobilization of international public opinion against Japan might strengthen the moderate voices of parliamentary parties in Japan and dampen expansionist ambitions of the military. More nearly the opposite happened. Matsuoka returned home to find himself a popular hero, and the nation's statesmen, *zaibatsu* leaders, and generals alike quickly grew at ease with the expanded empire which few of them had deliberately sought.

Strategists who engineered the seizure of Manchuria valued it as a buffer. It would shield Japan from expanding Soviet Communism and from growing Chinese nationalism. The problem with a buffer, Japan discovered, was that the buffer also needs a buffer. Once again, it was officers on the scene—Kwantung Army officers skilled at political intrigue—who took the initiative. For the next several years after the creation of Manchukuo, a trio of these men—using time-honored techniques of bribery, cajolery, and intimidation—worked to bring parts or all of several provinces in the new buffer area, the north of China and in the transition zone known as Inner Mongolia, under effective Japanese control.

Without belaboring geography too much, it may be said that the ultimate aim was to create an autonomous North China. Japanese hoped that they could make this scheme tolerable—if not palatable—to Chiang Kai-shek by permitting the Nationalist flag to fly in North China cities such as Peking. Technically, the area would not be considered as a separate state (like Manchukuo) but as a part of the Republic of China. In practice, however, when it came to matters related to defense and the economy, the area would be autonomous. This meant that it would be in the hands of Chinese collaborators friendly to Japan. They would permit Japan to forge an "especially close link" between autonomous North China and Manchuria. Chiang Kai-shek's Nationalists would have to abandon hope of establishing a firm presence in the north. Strictly speaking, then, North China would not be a part of the Empire of Japan, but it would be more closely tied to the "yen bloc" (Japan and Manchuria) than to Nationalist China, whose strategic heartland, like its capital, was in central China to the south. Chiang Kai-shek, still absorbed in annihilation campaigns directed against the Communists, allowed Japan to come close to achieving its autonomous North China objectives by default.

A KIDNAPING AT SIAN

In December 1936, that changed. Chiang travelled to the city of Sian in that month to spur his generals on to a sixth—and he hoped final—annihilation campaign. One of the generals whose cooperation he needed was Chang Hsueh-liang, the "Young Marshal," the last warlord general of Manchuria who had been chased out of his domain by the Japanese in 1931. Regrouped in the vicinity of Sian, the Young Marshal's armies would be decisive in any showdown against

Mao's Communist armies. This was the context in which a bizarre yet destiny-shaping incident occurred.

While staying in a villa on the outskirts of Sian, Chiang Kai-shek, the Generalissimo, the most powerful man in China, was kidnapped by troops of the insubordinate Young Marshal. The Young Marshal, like many other Chinese, was fed up with the civil war, with Chinese killing other Chinese, and pleaded with the Generalissimo to call off his extermination campaigns against the Communists and turn his attention to the Japanese. From Mao Tse-tung's mountain headquarters at nearby Yenan, the Communist negotiator Chou En-lai was dispatched to mediate the deliberations.

For two weeks, the attention of a stunned China and a curious world was focused on Sian as this mutiny unfolded. If Chiang had refused to yield to his captors' demands, he might well have been killed. All Chinese knew that the murder of the Generalissimo would have escalated disorder and civil war in China. That, in turn, would have played into the hands of Japanese who had always thrived on China's disunity. Many of the details of the "Sian Incident" remain murky, but on Christmas Day, 1936, the Young Marshal released his prisoner. Soon thereafter, Chiang Kai-shek, who must have tacitly agreed to the demands of the Young Marshal during his two weeks of captivity, announced to his people that he was ending the civil war. He would lead the country in a united front—Nationalists and Communists together—against any further aggression by Japan. As China entered the new year, it was more united in spirit and purpose than it had been in a century. With the advantage of hindsight, it seems almost inevitable that a clash was in the offing.

INCIDENT AT THE MARCO POLO BRIDGE

On the outskirts of Beijing is located a picturesque bridge which was already old when Marco Polo admired its graceful arches and marble lion carvings more than seven hundred years ago. An eighteenth-century poem by the Ch'ien-lung emperor calls attention to the beauty of the moon when viewed at break of dawn from the span. It has a Chinese name, *Lukouchiao*, but Westerners prefer to call it the "Marco Polo Bridge" in honor of the medieval Venetian traveller. In the twentieth century, its aesthetic legacy is little remembered, overshadowed now by an armed clash which occurred in its environs on a summer night in 1937 and a long, terrible war which followed.

Of itself, the bridge has no military importance, although a modern steel bridge at the junction of two rail lines commanding the southern approaches to the old capital city stands close by. It was here that a Japanese battalion, permitted there under treaty arrangements, was conducting maneuvers on the night of July 7, 1937. From the darkness, a volley of shots was heard by the Japanese soldiers at about 10:30 P.M. When their commander summoned his troops for a roll call, it was discovered that one of the soldiers was missing from the ranks. Accordingly, the officer asked permission of the Chinese commander of the nearby walled city of Wanp'ing to conduct a search. When permission was

"To My Brother Bob
The first American casualty in World War II
Shanghai, August 14, 1937"

> —From the dedication page of Edwin O. Reischauer's *Japan: The Story of a Nation*, in each of the four editions from 1946–1989.

Robert Reischauer, the elder brother of historian and diplomat Edwin Reischauer, was killed as he was standing in the lobby of a hotel on Shanghai's harbor embankment road, the Bund. At noon, on August 14, 1937, inexperienced Chinese fliers dropped bombs intended for the Japanese battleship *Izumo* tied up in the river nearby. The warship was never hit, but there were two thousand civilian casualties along the crowded Bund that day, including the promising young Princeton instructor of Japanese studies, Robert Reischauer.

refused, the town was shelled. Both Japanese and Chinese authorities then made efforts to resolve the incident locally. The military commander at Wanp'ing still refused to open the town gate, but in a scene out of the middle ages, negotiators were hoisted in wicker baskets up and down the city's thirty-foot walls in an attempt to end the hostilities. A cease-fire was arranged, but relations between the two countries, at a flash point because of decades of Japanese aggression, veered out of control before the month was over. In August, fighting spread to Shanghai, and all-out war ensued.

This eight–year-long Sino–Japanese War became the Asian phase of the Second World War four years later when Japan's attack on the U.S. naval base at Pearl Harbor drew America into global conflict. This chain of events was linked by cause and effect. It is no exaggeration, therefore, to describe the clash in the suburbs of Peking as the opening moments of World War II.

As an incident which triggered a chain of events wholly out of proportion to itself, the skirmish at the Marco Polo Bridge in 1937 is reminiscent of the assassination of Archduke Franz Ferdinand at Sarajevo in 1914 when the shooting of a minor Austrian nobleman put the match to all of Europe. However, whereas the facts surrounding the European incident are not in doubt, many crucial details of the 1937 clash remain disputed or unknown. If the assassin may be considered the central figure in the 1914 episode, he and his motives and movements are well known to history. In the case of the Marco Polo Bridge Incident, historians continue to debate where the initial shots came from. It is by no means clear that they came from Japanese guns—although that it is a possibility. More importantly, was the incident engineered by Japanese officers who were looking for a pretext to widen the Imperial Army's control over China? Although it was commonly assumed so at the time, careful study of Japanese archives available after Japan's defeat has led historians to the conclusion that the incident was spontaneous and unplanned. Who was the missing soldier, and why was he missing? The answer remains clouded, although a report by the Japanese

Japan did not officially declare a state of war until December 1941. The fighting in China before that time was referred to as simply the "China incident" although it became known in the West as the Sino–Japanese War (1937–1945). After December 12, 1941, Japanese referred to the four-year-old China incident and the new fighting in the Pacific and Southeast Asia as the "Greater East Asia War" *(Dai Toa senso).* Japanese historians now often speak of a "fifteen-year war," thinking of a single conflict beginning with the Manchurian Incident in 1931, continuing through the Sino–Japanese War, and turning into the Pacific phase of World War II after December 1941. (More accurately, that adds up to a little less than fourteen years of warfare, but in Japanese reckoning fighting went on during all or parts of fifteen years between 1931 and 1945.)

diplomat from Peking, one of the first to reach the scene, maintains that the soldier in question had gone off to relieve himself in the bushes and became lost. If the account is true, it offers an ironic comment on the folly and the unpredictability of history.

Whatever happened at the Marco Polo Bridge, it must be emphasized that the events of July 7 do not adequately explain the causes of the Sino–Japanese War which followed. To discover the roots of that war, recall the growth of Japanese imperialist designs on the Asian mainland. It was the accumulation of myriad incidents, encroachments, insults, and demands that led Chiang Kai-shek to cry out on behalf of his people a few days after the Marco Polo Bridge affair. The loss of even one more inch of Chinese territory was unacceptable, he said. To tolerate it would be an "unpardonable crime against our race." The American ambassador in Tokyo recorded in his diary a few months earlier that the Japanese seemed not to understand this new determination of China to yield no more. "It is strange but true," Ambassador Grew reflected, "that Japan appears to have been the last to appreciate the changed conditions in China."

ISHIWARA'S UNHEEDED VOICE OF CAUTION

Not all Japanese military planners were optimistic about Japan's success in China. The most influential of the voices of caution came from General Ishiwara Kanji. Ironically, it was Ishiwara who had masterminded the Manchurian Incident and helped create Manchukuo. By 1936, Ishiwara had been promoted to major general and a key planning post on the General Staff in Tokyo. By that time, his views had changed. For one thing, Ishiwara had come to regard the Soviet Union as the most immediate threat to Japan. War, in Ishiwara's mind, was not merely a possibility. In 1936, his calculations placed a showdown struggle with the Soviet Union as no more than five or six years in the future. Ishiwara was thoroughly convinced that Japanese military power on the Asian continent was

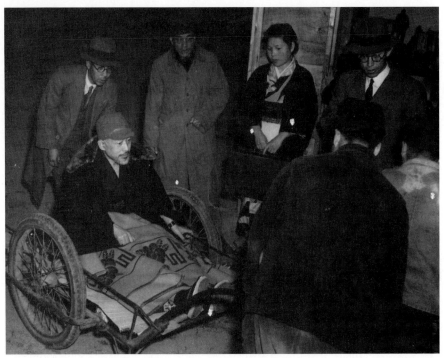

General Ishiwara Kanji, 1948, at the time of the Tokyo war crimes trials at which the general was a witness.

no match for the Red Army, the world's largest. In tanks and aircraft, the Soviets enjoyed even greater superiority, a calculation that was borne out by test encounters in 1938 and 1939 at Changkufeng and Nomonhan, where Japanese forces were overwhelmed by superior Soviet equipment and logistical support. Most ominously, Ishiwara noted, the Soviets had just introduced to the Far East a long-range bomber capable of hitting the Japanese home islands. When Ishiwara and his aides drew up a five-year defense plan for Japan in 1936, it was the inevitability of a second Russo–Japanese war that loomed uppermost in his mind. War with China had to be avoided; Japan simply could not generate enough war resources to prepare for the inevitable showdown with the Soviet Union and, at the same time, face a hostile China. The Japanese soldiers engaged in the skirmish at the Marco Polo Bridge on July 7, 1937, were *not* engaged in anti-Chinese maneuvers; the object of their training was the Soviet Army.

In addition, Ishiwara had developed an appreciation of the growing spirit of resistance and nationalism in China that was not evident a few years earlier. Again ironically, it was of course Ishiwara's own schemes in Manchuria as well as the move to create an autonomous North China (which Ishiwara came to oppose) which had promoted the growing spirit of nationalism in China. As Chinese resistance stiffened in the opening weeks of the all-out war in the summer of 1937, Ishiwara warned his more bellicose colleagues that their talk of a Blitzkrieg campaign (or as it was called in Japan, *sokusen-sokketsu*, rapid war-rapid settlement) displayed a shallow understanding of the character of the Chinese. To generals who promised that China would capitulate after Peking fell, then after Shanghai fell, then after the fall of Nanking, Ishiwara warned that even if Chiang Kai-shek himself surrendered, the 400 million people of China were not going to capitulate.

For decades, Japanese expansionists had grown accustomed to bribing and manipulating Chinese warlords and had developed a contemptuous disregard for China as being weak and vacillating. Those days were ending, Ishiwara warned, and failure to heed the changing mood of China would mean that Japan would be drawn into the endless quagmire of an unwinnable conflict—with the wrong enemy. Ishiwara, a student of European military history, was in the office of the War Minister General Sugiyama Gen two weeks after the Marco Polo Bridge Incident, predicting that unless Japanese troops were pulled back to Manchuria, the Imperial Army would be "bogged down in China just exactly as Napoleon had been in Spain." There is little reason to believe that General Sugiyama, known by a variety of nicknames indicating his dull wit, had any appreciation for Ishiwara's well-chosen historical analogy—which proved accurate. In any case, Sugiyama and the rest of the military leadership ignored the message and went on to speak of the need of "chastising" the Chinese. Ishiwara, never known for his agreeable disposition or a capacity for compromise, continued to belabor all who would listen to him with his vision of national calamity. Increasingly, however, he was regarded by his military colleagues as a troublesome eccentric, an alarmist. Accordingly, he was soon transferred from his staff position in Tokyo. By the time the Pacific War began, he had been involuntarily demoted to the ranks of the inactive reserves.

TWO GENERALS VIEW CHINA

"They [those looking forward to an easy victory in China] are guilty of a grave error in likening four hundred million Chinese to the savages of Ethiopia. There is no doubt that as long as the Chinese have an inch of land—even on some remote frontier—they are going to continue to resist us."

—Major General Ishiwara Kanji, ca. 1938. (Referring to the 1935–1936 Italian campaign in Ethiopia.)

"China is a society, but she is not a nation. Or rather, it would be fair to say that China is a society of bandits. . . . The Chinese people are bacteria infesting world civilization."

—Major General Sakai Ryu, Chief of Staff of the Japanese forces in North China, in 1938.

Saving face remains an important consideration in modern Japanese life. In a proud institution like the Imperial Army, to retreat from promised victory was unthinkable, all the more so after great loss of life had been sustained. Even those officers who shared Ishiwara's concerns could not contemplate a reversal of policy toward China, not without important concessions from Chiang Kai-shek, concessions which might allow the army to show that the nation's sacrifice had been justified. However, Chiang would not yield—at least not to Japan's continuing claim for special rights in an autonomous north China.

THE QUAGMIRE WAR

The quagmire Ishiwara predicted soon materialized. In the north, where Nationalist military presence was minimal, Peking fell to the Japanese with little resistance. In Shanghai, however, the Chinese fought heroically. Throughout the end of the summer and on into October, in bitter hand-to-hand street fighting, Chiang's best German-trained divisions held off the Japanese advance. The city and its 3.6 million people suffered greatly, however, from attacks by heavily armored Japanese marines, shelling by warships firing heavy guns at point-blank range, and air raids. At least 250,000 of China's finest forces were killed or wounded in the three-month siege. Many civilians were also casualties, as the picture of the crying, abandoned baby in the devastation of the North Railway Station testifies; it became one of the most widely published photographs of modern times.

Japan had no desire to rile the Western powers unnecessarily, so the International Settlement, a city within the city, was secure from attack. Except for a few errors which brought shells and bombs crashing into unintended targets like hotels, department stores, and theaters, the sixty-three thousand foreign residents (including four thousand Americans) went about their business. Western journalists could sit in penthouse lounges in hotels with names like Cathay, Astor, and Carlton, sip cocktails, watch the mayhem in the nearby Chinese districts, and then wire their eyewitness accounts back to their newspapers in New York or London. The world had a grandstand seat on the fighting in Shanghai. U.S. Embassy personnel argued that Chiang had sacrificed many of his best troops in Shanghai in a "ploy calculated to gain world support." The Generalissimo "gambled on the possibility that a serious incident involving foreigners in Shanghai would lead to intervention by the United States and Great Britain," wrote one. General Joseph W. Stilwell, the American military attaché in China, insists that Chiang finished an interview with him by screaming, "We are fighting the battle of the world. Intervene for Christ's sake!"

To be sure, Americans were overwhelmingly on the side of the Chinese underdog. To provide financial and material aid to China, prominent Americans like Pearl Buck and Henry R. Luce helped to organize and publicize private aid foundations to which Americans generously contributed. Nobody did more to

*Photograph by H. S. ("Newsreel") Wong of Chinese baby in bombed Shanghai railway,
August 1937.*

shape a sympathetic attitude toward the Chinese people than the writer and
Nobel Prize winner Pearl Buck, a "mishkid" raised by missionary parents in
China. In the 1930s, she was the most prolific and popular interpreter of Asia in
the Western world. *The Good Earth*—which appeared as a book in 1931, a
Broadway play two years later, and an immensely popular movie in 1937—was
the single most important source of most Americans' impression of what the
Chinese were like, and the uniform impression that emerged from *The Good
Earth* was that of a wonderfully attractive people. The Japanese had no similar
spokesperson who could reach American hearts and minds in those days. "Mr.
Moto," the fictional Japanese secret agent created by novelist John Marquand in
a popular series of detective stories (adapted by Hollywood for the screen with
Peter Lorre starring as the Japanese title character), was an altogether positive
hero—courageous, unassuming, and astute. However, after capturing the American imagination for only two years, "Mr. Moto" was dropped by Hollywood in
1938. American audiences were eager to embrace stereotypes of Japanese as
cruel and treacherous.

The American press treated China and China's plight with sympathy. Henry
R. Luce, another mishkid, was the founder and publisher of *Time* and *Life* and

perhaps the most influential force in American journalism in the first half of this century. His attitude toward Generalissimo and Madame Chiang Kai-shek, with whom he was personally well-acquainted, has been frequently described as "hero worship." He regarded them as the great hope of a democratic and Christian China, and his magazines virtually sponsored the Generalissimo as an Asian exemplar. The pictures of Chiang and his wife, always in gallant poses, often graced the cover of *Time*—in January 1938 as the "man and wife of the year." All of this positive publicity was made much easier by the glamorous figure of Madame Chiang. Americans were endlessly fascinated (FDR once playfully allowed that he had been "vamped," that is, seduced) by the Chinese woman who spoke eloquent English, sometimes with a soft Southern accent which she had acquired during her teen years as a student in a Macon, Georgia, academy. Again, no Japanese emerged to so charm the American public. However, sympathy and moral support and private donations did not translate into political intervention. At least not yet, not even after the war turned its ugliest at Nanking.

NANKING

In early November, the Japanese made amphibious landings to the south of Shanghai. The city was quickly outflanked, and the battle scene shifted two hundred miles upriver to the Republic of China's capital at Nanking. It is clear that somewhere between Shanghai and Nanking the Chinese will to resist had dissolved. Well over half of Nanking's one million people had fled the city in advance of the approaching Japanese. The commanding general in charge of the city's defenses had abandoned the city before the Japanese arrived—after solemn promises to defend it with his last breath. In a disorganized rout, thousands of Chinese soldiers also withdrew from the city, some of them killing to obtain civilian clothes needed as disguise. Accordingly, although there was fighting at the gates and walls of the ancient city, Japanese troops entering the city on December 13 encountered an essentially defenseless city of civilians and unarmed soldiers.

What followed was the rape of Nanking, one of the worst atrocities of the Second World War era. The city was systematically looted by organized bands of soldiers: arson and wanton destruction left a third of the city in ashes. The ordeal lasted for two and a half weeks at peak intensity, but the last of the incidents protested by an international commission, the rape of a twelve-year-old girl, occurred almost two months after the Japanese occupation of the city began. Estimates are that at least 20,000 women were raped during the first month of the Japanese presence in the city. Many were executed after being violated, others simply died after being manhandled by squads of soldiers. Pregnant women were bayonetted; even infants were reported impaled on bayonets. Soldiers and conscripted labor battalion workers, promised mercy in handbills distributed by the Imperial Army, surrendered by the thousands only to be doused with kerosene and burned to death. Others were buried alive or decapitated by officers giving demonstrations with their sabers. Men who did not surrender were searched out as deserters. Simple tests were devised to determine who had been a soldier: calluses on the hand or a ring around the head, evidence of wearing a cap, doomed the suspect. Some gruesome scenes, including victims tied up for bayonet practice, were recorded by soldiers on cameras as casually as tourists might snap scenes of local color. Copies of the souvenir photos were preserved as evidence by Chinese film shops to whom the film had been taken by the Japanese soldier-photographers.

Historians cannot agree on the exact statistical extent of the carnage, but so much of it took place in full view of neutral observers from many nations that the broad outlines are beyond doubt. The War Crimes Trials held in Tokyo after the end of the war accepted as minimum estimates that a total of forty-two thousand were killed in Nanking: thirty thousand fugitive soldiers and twelve thousand civilians. Chinese sources routinely use figures of 100,000 and up. One fact suggesting that the Chinese estimates are too high is that remarkably little notice of the incident was taken by either China or the Western powers *at the time*. Some of the confusion in numbers may stem from the fact that there were probably far more civilians killed in the area around Nanking than within the city itself.

Although some believe that the savagery at Nanking was part of a deliberate plan of terrorism to break the will of Chiang Kai-shek and the Chinese people, most historians believe otherwise. A near consensus holds that discipline within the Japanese Army simply broke down. Commanding officers clearly did not do what they should have done to restore order—and General Matsui Iwane, in charge of the armies at Nanking, was hanged in 1948 as a war criminal for his dereliction. Still, there is no evidence of a preordained, calculated plot to terrorize the Chinese population.

One Japanese historian attributes the savagery at Nanking to the high casualties taken by Japanese forces at Shanghai, as well as the "absence of any clearly stated war aim." Because of that, he writes, the military was encouraged "to regard the conflict as primarily a war of plunder." Some writers trace the savagery at Nanking to the brutal training received by recruits in the Imperial Army. All military training, by definition, must to some degree condition soldiers to violence. From the many accounts of Japanese army life, its training was particularly harsh. In the words of one Japanese psychologist, the army used brutality, violence, anger, and contempt as socializing agents to "program the soldier, to inhibit him from thinking or doing anything or even feeling anything of his own volition."

The result was what one former soldier called a "zone of emptiness" in which the soldier was prepared to accept death, discipline of any kind, and harsh treatment from superiors without question. Within the ranks, the oppression that one felt might be transferred down, from lieutenant to sergeant, sergeant to corporal and so on. The lowest ranks, of course, had nobody to oppress, no way of relieving their frustrations—until they found themselves in battle abroad. In this interpretation, Nanking represented a monstrous transfer of oppression by thousands of lowly recruits to any and all powerless Chinese they could find.

NANKING REMEMBERED—FIFTY YEARS LATER

More than a half-century later, the memory of the Nanking tragedy—and other wartime atrocities—remains alive and a barrier to reconciliation for many Chinese and Japanese. Especially aggravating to some Chinese is the belief that Japanese have never in postwar years expressed adequate remorse or even accepted responsibility for wartime excesses. They point to the fact that some Japanese have attempted to deny the existence of a Nanking incident—much as some Western writers have sought to prove that the Jews in Europe were not victims of a holocaust. Japanese books with titles like *Nankin gyakusatsu no maboroshi* (The Illusion of the Nanking Slaughter) might suggest that the Chinese criticism has at least some validity. While most informed Japanese would not accept the notion that atrocities in China were mere "illusion," there is a widespread ignorance of the war in China and the attack on Pearl Harbor, especially among the young. Somehow, the end of the semester always comes, it is often said, before Japanese history lessons reach the war years.

The most vexing example of this has been an ongoing "textbook controversy." For several years, so-called "revisionist" historians have attempted, sometimes successfully, to introduce textbooks into the schools which portray as favorably as possible the Japan-in-China experience. In the case of the Nanking incident, these books suggest that the massacre was provoked by Chinese actions, and in one book, the episode is relegated to a footnote which speaks simply of "numerous civilians" being killed. Typically, a choice of words softens nuances in Japan's favor. Texts might for example avoid the use of a harsh-sounding word like "invade" *(shinryaku)* and speak instead of Japan's "entering into" *(shinshutsu)* China. That particular choice of words caused a sensational flap in 1982 when it was widely reported in newspapers and resulted in anti-Japanese demonstrations in several Asian cities. The People's Republic of China officially protested.

Another well-publicized example was the censorship of Bernardo Bertolucci's epic film *The Last Emperor* in 1988. A half-minute sequence of authentic movie footage of the massacre of Chinese civilians in Nanking was snipped from the film before its first showings in Japan—evidently at the suggestion of distributors who feared it might reduce attendance and provoke right-wing attacks on the theaters exhibiting the film. Bertolucci's protest and a public clamor later forced the exhibitors to screen the uncut version.

Ronald P. Dore, a British expert on Japan, tried to put the Japanese textbook issue in a larger context by arguing that all countries tend to write slanted versions of their past. British history textbooks, he noted, hardly refer to the imperial era in India as an "invasion," preferring to describe how British soldiers "advanced" into India to establish the Raj.

Still another attempt to explain Nanking takes note of the fact that Japanese soldiers had been led by their superiors and the euphoric victory slogans of the day to believe that they would achieve an easy triumph. Instead, China was retreating but not surrendering. Japanese casualty losses, while only a small fraction of the Chinese, were frightfully high: Seventy thousand Japanese had been killed or wounded in the Shanghai–Nanking campaign. Adding to the sense of rage was an undeniable element of racist contempt for the Chinese in the thinking of many of the Japanese. A variety of ugly epithets was always close to the surface when Chinese were described: *tambo, chanchan,* and *chankoro* (the last has the same connotation as "Chinks" in English). A Japanese war correspondent wrote how surprised he was to find that the Chinese greeted with smiles and courtesy the Japanese units that marched through their town in the opening months of the war:

> Such a thing could never happen if any enemy occupied Japanese towns. Japanese men, women, and even children could never forget that they were enemies and would be hostile to the very end. Japanese would sooner die than be friendly with an enemy. We would be friendly with Chinese individuals and indeed came to love them. But how could we help despising them as a *nation* when they would show their smiles and flattery to an enemy for the price of their own skins at a time when the very destiny of their nation was in balance. To us Japanese, they were a pitiful, spineless people.

The Chinese, in other words, could not win. Resistance would surely lead to abuse. Mistreatment awaited those who were weak and servile as well.

STALEMATE

After the fall of Nanking, Chiang Kai-shek simply moved his government farther up the Yangtze River, first to Wuhan and then, after its fall, to Chungking in the mountains of Western China. These were heroic endeavors involving one of the largest human migrations in history—perhaps as many as 20 million people made the move, carrying with them all they could of factories, offices, and libraries and scorching a belt of wasteland behind them as they retreated. After that time, from the latter part of 1938, the character of the war changed from heavy fighting to something near a stalemate. Japan controlled most of north China, the coastline including many of the nation's biggest cities, and the lower Yangtze River Valley. In military terms, Japan controlled points and lines: the main population centers and the railways that linked them.

For the next six years, Japanese planes struck at the cities of the interior—Chungking alone was hit from the air 268 times between 1939 and 1941—but the battle lines on the ground remained frozen, with Japanese and Chinese armies often facing each other across a no-man's-land. To be sure, Chinese resistance continued, but it was largely in the form of hit-and-run guerrilla warfare conducted in the hills and mountains of the interior, where the superior Japanese mechanized forces had trouble operating. It was then and there that Mao's Communist bands perfected the tactic of "luring deep," drawing Japanese columns far into unfamiliar and inhospitable terrain where, isolated and cut off from supplies and reinforcements, they would be an even match for the Chinese.

Meanwhile, unknown to the Chinese public or the rest of the world, Japanese secret agents made approach after approach, to Chiang Kai-shek and other Nationalist leaders, with peace overtures and invitations to join Japan's "New Order in East Asia," proclaimed by Prime Minister Konoe in November 1938. That the Nationalists should pursue these contacts may strike us as unlikely, but we need to recall that Chiang Kai-shek and the Japanese, for all the mutual antipathy they projected to the public, shared an overarching fear: the expansion into the East of communism, whether it be the Chinese or Russian variety. (In the 1930s and for some time after that, few saw any distinction between Chinese and Russian brands of communism. It was widely assumed that the Chinese Communists took direction from the Kremlin.)

RESPONSE FROM WASHINGTON

In addition, Chiang knew that the peace feelers would give him leverage in asking for aid from the Western democracies. Without at least financial assistance from Britain or the United States, it was hinted that the Generalissimo just might decide that continued struggle with Japan was too burdensome for his war-weary nation. He might yield to the counsel he was receiving from some quarters within the Kuomintang that he settle the war and cooperate with Japan in achieving an "Asia for the Asians." How could the Generalissimo ever sell such an about-face to the Chinese people? Captain James M. McHugh, the U.S. Naval attaché and a palace intimate, asked Chiang that question after Chiang hinted that the Japanese would offer him "very easy peace terms." Before the Chinese leader could answer, Madame Chiang, often present as an interpreter, interrupted to say, "the people would accept peace with Japan if the Generalissimo told them that was the best thing for China." Was this kind of innuendo to be taken seriously, or was it bluff? Many American observers believed that the veiled threats were "mostly bluff"—surely Chiang could not realistically hope to survive if he made peace with the invader.

Nevertheless, the possibility of a Sino–Japanese rapprochement which would make Japan a nearly invincible power in the East could never be completely discounted by Washington. The remote chance that the Chiang regime might "make other arrangements" with Japan if Western aid fell short of its needs would remain a constant theme in Sino–American relations throughout the war years. To add another layer of complexity to the matter, Washington also had to worry that the Nationalists, if not more aggressively aided by the West, might fall more and more into the arms of the Soviet Union. The Soviets, far from sending assistance to its Communist brethren in China, took the world lead in sending both financial and military help to the Nationalist government under Chiang Kai-shek. The Nationalists, the Kremlin reasoned, had a better chance to check arch-enemy Japan than the tattered band of Communist irregulars in the hills at Yenan. (It was a judgment not verified by history.) By 1938, well before America made any such commitment, about a thousand Soviet "volunteer" aviators were flying for the Chinese Air Force.

THE NEW ORDER IN EAST ASIA

Konoe's "New Order" should resonate with students of European history, for it paralleled, at least superficially and at approximately the same time, Hitler's use of the phrase "New European Order" to signify the goal of a German-dominated Europe. Konoe, however, was light-years different from the German dictator in political outlook, style, and personality. Konoe, and most of his colleagues, never entertained the geopolitical fantasies of intercontinental wars, alliances, and national subjugation that preoccupied Hitler. As Prince Konoe, the Japanese prime minister was scion of one of the most illustrious family names in Japan's history. Unlike Hitler, neither Konoe nor his colleagues ever saw themselves as embarked on a scheme to guard the Holy Grail of pure blood, never dreamed of breeding a biologically preselected elite. Konoe's New Order, however it evolved, did not produce extermination squads, gas ovens, and death camps designed to eliminate nations and races of "inferior" peoples.

At a more personal level, Konoe sent his son to an American high school, followed by study at Princeton University. It is hard to imagine that Hitler, if blessed with children, would have sought a place for them in the Ivy League. Konoe, like Hitler, committed suicide rather than face the indignity of arrest and trial as a war criminal. Hitler's final message was the broadcast lie that the Führer had died fighting at the head of his troops. Found next to the body of Konoe after his death was an underlined passage from Oscar Wilde's prison memoir, *De Profundis:* "I must say to myself that I ruined myself, and that nobody great or small can be ruined except by his own hand."

Japan's proposal for a "New Order in East Asia" is best understood in light of the "old order." Japanese, and many Chinese as well, bitterly resented the old order, a system of international relations erected by Western imperialists during the century that had passed since the Opium War (1839–1842) in which Britain inflicted a humiliating defeat on the Empire of China. During that time, the Western powers had accumulated in China, as well as in other parts of Asia, a host of economic and political rights, guaranteed by a network of interlocking treaties that were sanctioned by international law and backed by the presence of foreign gunboats and marines stationed in privileged enclaves throughout China.

The expression "East Asia" *(Toa),* seldom used before this time, gradually replaced the "Far East" *(Kyokuto)* in Japanese parlance, since the latter term was seen as rooted in the English vanity that England was the center of the world. Japan saw itself as the unique example of an Asian nation that had been able to strengthen and modernize itself so as to repel the aggression of the Western imperialist bloc—and fend off Communism as well. In proclaiming the New Order in East Asia, Japan was offering to share with China its strength and successful experience in meeting the twin challenges of imperialism and Communism. What bothered the Chinese, however, was that Japan's own expansionist record in East Asia was no less self-aggrandizing than that of the Western imperialists.

THE LANGUAGE OF DIPLOMACY
Japanese Foreign Minister Hachiro Arita commented on the $25 million loan to China this way: "If, as the United States papers say, it is a political gesture of the United States towards Japan, I think there will be nothing more dangerous." Joseph C. Grew, the American ambassador in Japan, had already been instructed by the State Department how to respond to any assertions that the loan was an "unfriendly act." "You should state that you take decided exception to any such characterization of it. You should add that you regard with amazement any such characterization by a Japanese of an essentially commercial transaction consummated for the purpose of legitimately serving American industrial enterprises and American consumers."

It may be more than coincidence, then, that the first major American grant of credit to China was announced on December 16, 1938, a month after McHugh's conversation with the Generalissimo was reported to Washington. More significantly, the $25 million aid package came two days before a prominent Nationalist leader, Wang Ching-wei, defected from Chungking to create a rival Kuomintang government pledged to a peaceful resolution of problems with Japan and to joining Japan's newly proclaimed "New Order in East Asia." The loan was clearly political in purpose and clearly violated the spirit of the Neutrality Laws. (FDR, however, could say that the laws did apply in this case because China and Japan were technically not at war with each other.) The loan to China was not large, but it did strengthen Chiang's hand and weaken the impact of Wang Ching-wei's defection. Predictably, Japan lodged protests, the unstated gist of which was anger that the United States was interfering in Japan's dispute on the side of China. The Japanese army spoke of the aid as an "insult," the only thing that made possible China's continuing resistance. Japan feared, with good reason, that the loan contained the implicit promise of more aid in the future. China's Finance Minister H. H. Kung certainly saw it that way. "The $25 million was only the beginning," he stated, "further large sums can be expected . . . this is a political loan . . . America has definitely thrown in her lot and cannot withdraw."

AMERICAN ISOLATIONISM

Of all the factors influencing America's response to the crisis decade of the 1930s, the most critical was the prevailing mood of that era. In a word, that mood was isolationism.

Both Congress and the American public were strongly united in the belief that America had learned a lesson from its experience in World War I: Stay out of all foreign wars in the future. Because of American sympathy for Britain and the other allied powers in that war, we had allowed ourselves—against our better judgment, almost against our will—to be gradually dragged into the war. It is worth recalling that 116,000 Americans were killed during the brief period (1917–1918) in which the United States participated in that war. By comparison, in the eight years of the Vietnam War, the death toll was only half of the World War I figure. Since the population of the United States in 1917 was only about half of what it was during the Vietnam War era, it is easy to imagine the wide impact of the earlier war's casualties on American families.

And to what purpose? Americans had entered the war full of idealism—amid talk of a war to end all wars and a war to make the world safe for democracy. By the 1930s, whatever idealism remained evaporated rapidly as both European and Asian nations rearmed and gravitated toward war once again. Americans convinced themselves that those countries of the Old World were a predatory lot and could be expected to quarrel forever over their boundaries and empires. The United States, by contrast, was not threatened by its neighbors and was securely isolated from the Old World by two vast oceans. "I believe we can endure in this hemisphere, or on this continent, regardless of what happens abroad," the aviator-hero Charles Lindbergh said in a precise summary of the isolationist credo. Why, then, should the United States risk any actions which might cause itself to be drawn again into foreign wars?

Books and movies like *All Quiet on the Western Front* (the movie, one of the first "talkies," was released in 1930) had a powerful effect on the public imagination by its realistic portrayal of the grim horror of war. Isolationist members of Congress—and they included the most famous names in politics in the 1930s—kept the issue before the American public with sensational hearings and disclosures. The Senate's "Nye Committee" (headed by Gerald P. Nye of North Dakota), for example, shocked Americans with its revelations (1934–1936) that America had been dragged into World War I for one reason: to line the pockets of certain great industrial combines—the "merchants of death"—which made scandalously high profits out of the war. This is a vastly oversimplified explanation of America's entrance into that war, but the hearings set the stage for the passage of neutrality legislation. Without considering in detail the provisions of the three Neutrality Acts passed in the years 1935, 1936, and 1937, it may be said that the governing principal in all of them was that the best way of staying out of other people's wars was strict neutrality. The United States must not only refrain from committing its military forces in the aid of a friend, but it must also avoid the temptation of choosing sides and lending any help to any belligerent.

Isolationism, as well as the impoverished state of the depression economy, also led to restrictions on military budgets and on any buildup of the armed forces in the 1930s. When Germany invaded Poland in September of 1939, launching World War II, the U.S. Army was quite simply the smallest and worst-equipped army of any major power. With 188,000 men under arms, the all-volunteer U.S. Army stood between Portugal's and Bulgaria's in size. Worse still, proper equipment was available for less than half of the troops. Military field maneuvers (where trucks had "Tank" painted on their sides) were widely regarded as comic procedures. As late as 1940, the United States was equipped with only 350 tanks, most of them antiquated. The average infantryman was armed with a Springfield rifle dating from 1903; the standard artillery piece had been declared outdated at the end of World War I. As late as February 1941, the Air Corps possessed less than five hundred combat planes; of these, only fifty were the advanced long-range (two thousand miles) four-engine B-17 bomber which Boeing first brought into production in 1935. The Navy fared better but not without constant opposition from the isolationists who argued that the bigger the Navy the more likely it was that the United States would get into a fight with Japan or Germany. When Senator William E. Borah of Idaho took the floor of the Senate in 1938 to oppose President Franklin Roosevelt's naval appropriations bill, he spoke for the isolationists:

> Ever since I have been in the Senate, we have been building navies, allegedly to fight Japan, and now they are again citing Japan as a menace. However much we may disapprove of what is going on in the Orient, there is to my mind no probability of Japan attacking the United States. She would have to have a navy three times the size she now has if she were going, or coming, seven thousand miles to engage this country in war. In my opinion, it is sheer folly to talk about it.

Even when American interests were placed under direct attack, the isolationists held firm to their principles. In December 1937, for example, the American gunboat *Panay* was guarding Standard Oil Company tankers near Nanking on the Yangtze River, international waters by treaty. In bright sunlight, the ship was bombed by Japanese navy pilots. Two American lives were lost when the ship, with American markings clearly visible on the deck, went down in shallow water; other Americans were wounded in repeated strafing runs. Proper apologies and full restitution were promptly made by Tokyo, and in hindsight, it seems certain that the attack had not been ordered by the Japanese government. At the time, however, anti-Japanese emotions were inflamed. From Tokyo, Ambassador Joseph Grew recalled how the sinking of a ship ("Remember the *Maine*") had precipitated the Spanish–American War and wondered if this incident might also lead to war. For FDR, the lesson of the *Panay* incident was that the United States might sooner or later be brought into the Asian conflict against its will and that close consultation between the U.S. and British navies was advisable. He also considered applying economic sanctions but failed to gain the necessary support. The message for the isolationists, however, was that the United States should withdraw from the troubled waters of Asia. So long as neutrals remained in war zones, they "can be sure they will get injured or even killed!" said isolationist Senator Henrik Shipstead of Minnesota.

CONGRESSMAN LUDLOW'S PROPOSAL

An illustration of the strength of isolationist sentiment within the Congress was the legislation proposed by Indiana Congressman Louis M. Ludlow. The "Ludlow Amendment" was a proposed constitutional amendment that would have required that any declaration of war be approved by a direct vote of the American people. (An exception was provided if the United States, its territories, or the western hemisphere was directly subjected to an armed attack.) At different times in the 1930s, the proposal had varying degrees of support in both houses of Congress. Within a day after the *Panay* was sunk, however, Congressman Ludlow suddenly had the necessary votes to carry the House. The leadership of both houses, however, threw their weight against the measure—one of them arguing the measure was "little short of treason"—and managed to prevent the discharge of the proposed amendment from the committee. Therefore, neither house ever voted directly on the amendment.

Roosevelt, president from 1933 to 1945, did not share the sentiment of isolationists regarding the neutrality legislation. He criticized them for failing to make a distinction between criminal aggressors and innocent victims: According to the neutrality laws, everybody had to be treated alike. However, Roosevelt was above all a skilled politician and knew that in a democracy the president could never get very far ahead of public opinion—and public opinion was solidly isolationist. In 1935, a public-opinion poll revealed that 95 percent of those questioned believed that their country had no business involving itself in foreign squabbles. In January 1938, only weeks after the *Panay* incident, 70 percent of the American voters who were interviewed and had an opinion on the subject favored complete withdrawal from China—the Asiatic Fleet, marines, missionaries, medical teams, everything.

These astonishingly high percentages would decline in years to come, but the mood of isolationism remained very strong—especially in the American heartland. The American Midwest and Plains states had little or no stake in arms industries or in naval shipyards. Why, the argument ran, should South Dakota wheat farmers pay scarce depression tax dollars in order to build a powerful two-ocean navy in order to protect American interests in places like the Yangtze River and keep the Boston and San Diego employment rates high? Isolationist organizations evolved into peace organizations which rounded up millions of signatures opposing American involvement abroad (Europe, more than Asia, was on most people's mind in the beginning). Slogans like "Keep America out of war" and "the Yanks are *not* coming" gained currency. When Congress considered an extension of the Selective Service Act in August 1941, well after the peak of isolationist influence and less than four months before Pearl Harbor, the measure squeaked through the House of Representatives by a vote of 203 to 202. Except for the single-vote margin, there would have been no draft law in place at the time the Pacific war began. Charles Lindbergh added his voice to the "America First" organization committed to keeping the United States out of war. He had no favorite side in the European conflict, he was to tell a Congressional committee. The responsibility for the war there was about "evenly divided," he added. Little wonder that FDR said to a friend, "It's a terrible thing to look over your shoulder when you are trying to lead—and find no one there."

QUARANTINE JAPAN?

Nevertheless, Roosevelt sought to test the political climate from time to time. In a Chicago speech in October 1937, only a few months after the Marco Polo Bridge Incident, the president declared that "The epidemic of world lawlessness is spreading." When an epidemic of disease starts to spread, he said, the community joins together in a "quarantine." FDR's "Quarantine speech," a good example of the trial balloon technique, did not mention specific measures which the president had in mind, but it was widely assumed that he was calling for some kind of an international economic boycott of Japan or Germany or both. Perhaps a mild measure such as cutting off the shipment of scrap iron to Japan might be taken at first.

The "Quarantine speech" attracted the attention of the nation; to the president's dismay, however, it provoked not support but a wave of outrage. Isolationist congressmen led the attack. Senator Nye said that it was obvious that the president was "baiting" the American people, luring us toward war with the appealing idea that it was America's responsibility to police the world—a "world that was following insane leaders." That was typical isolationist rhetoric: The fact that the rest of the world was going mad should impel us to isolate ourselves all the more resolutely. Congressman Hamilton Fish went so far as to recommend that FDR be impeached. *Business Week* editorialized that any kind of a quarantine would only "inflame the Japanese people . . . drive them to military retribution." Describing Roosevelt's suggestion, the magazine said "kWARantine means war."

The business community in general, mindful that the United States had a considerable stake in close economic ties with Japan, did not want to jeopardize that trade with any hostile moves. Some citizens were outraged to discover that American-manufactured equipment had been used in the bombings of Chinese civilian targets and put pressure on the White House to declare a "moral embargo" on exports of aeronautical equipment and bombs to Japan. Public pressure compelled FDR to endorse the "moral embargo," but it never had the force of law and, in any case, did not extend to raw materials, such as scrap iron, which Japan used to make its bombs and bombers.

In spite of the age-old legend of the great "China market," and in defiance of Asian demographics (China's population was five times greater than Japan's), the fact was that America had far more important trade ties with Japan than with the giant Chinese republic. Total volume of exports and imports with Japan was roughly four times larger than that with China in the late 1930s. And the trend favored Japan. While U.S. trade with China remained stable or even declined a little throughout the 1930s, the Japan market was tripling. During the first half of 1938, for all of the bad press Japan earned as a result of the war in China, the *Panay* Incident, and Nanking, America remained Japan's best trading partner, providing nearly a third of all its imports. Detroit sold far more cars to Japan than to China. The volume of scrap iron sales became almost legendary, multiplying by a factor of forty between 1930 and 1939. More oil, both crude and refined, was sold to Japan than to China. Cotton growers in the South regarded Japan as their best customer for raw cotton. The American silk hose industry was big business, and as the effects of the depression eased American women again began buying silk stockings (until nylon hit the market in 1940). The silk came from Japan, and industry leaders pleaded that any boycott would hurt the United States just as much as Japan.

American business interests, then, remained exceptionally hostile to any moves to punish Japan. National City Bank, the largest U.S. bank in the Far East, with many operations in Japan, had from the beginning urged that Washington recognize Manchukuo. Some business leaders went so far as to say that perhaps it would be a good idea if Japan took over China (or parts of it). They could be expected to bring it up to date and make it more prosperous, *then* China would become a more lucrative customer for U.S. goods.

With such business-as-usual attitudes prevailing in America, it is little wonder that Japan felt comfortable in pushing into Asia, free of the risks of a confrontation with the United States. Before America's sense of isolation and near indifference to the expansion of Japan would change, the American people would have to be aroused out of their neutralist complacency.

ADDITIONAL READING

For a useful bibliographic guide, see Waldo H. Heinrichs, Jr., "1931–1937," in Ernest May and James Thomson, ed., *American–East Asian Relations* (1972).

Standard accounts of the "crisis decade" which began with Japan's move into Manchuria include Ienaga Saburo, *The Pacific War: World War II and the Japanese, 1931–1945* (1978); James B. Crowley, *Japan's Quest for Autonomy: National Security and Foreign Policy, 1930–1938* (1966); and Dorothy Borg, *The United States and the Far Eastern Crisis of 1933–1938* (1964). *Japan's Imperial Conspiracy* (1971) by David Bergamini is a richly detailed popular history which was widely criticized by scholars for its thesis that Emperor Hirohito was personally responsible for Japan's aggression in China.

On Sino–Japanese relations in general, see the following collections of essays: Akira Iriye, ed., *The Chinese and the Japanese: Essays in Political and Cultural Interactions* (1980); Paul K. T. Sih, *Nationalist China During the Sino–Japanese War, 1937–1945* (1977); James C. Hsiung and Steven I. Levine, eds., *China's Bitter Victory: The War with Japan, 1937–1945* (1992); Parks M. Coble, *Facing Japan: Chinese Politics and Japanese Imperialism, 1931–1937* (1992); and Alvin D. Coox and Hilary Conroy, eds., *China and Japan: A Search for Balance Since World War I* (1978). See also Allen S. Whiting, *China Eyes Japan* (1989), especially Chapter 3 ("The War As Historical Heritage").

Concerning the Manchurian Incident, see Mark Peattie, "Manchurian Incident," in *Kodansha Encyclopedia of Japan*, Vol. 5 (1983); Sadako N. Ogata, *Defiance in Manchuria: The Making of Japanese Foreign Policy, 1931–32* (1964); and Takehiko Yoshihashi, *Conspiracy at Mukden: The Rise of the Japanese Military* (1963). English-language versions of essays originally written in Japanese are found in James W. Morley, ed., *The China Quagmire: Japan's Expansion on the Asian Continent, 1933–1941* (1983).

On the second Sino–Japanese War, see Frank Dorn, *The Sino–Japanese War, 1937–1941* (1974); Dick Wilson, *When Tigers Fight: The Story of the Sino–Japanese War, 1937–1945* (1982); Chalmers A. Johnson, *Peasant Nationalism and Communist Power: The Emergence of Revolutionary China, 1937–1945* (1962); and John Hunter Boyle, *China and Japan at War: The Politics of Collaboration, 1937–1945* (1972). Though Barbara Tuchman's Pulitzer Prize-winning *Stilwell and the American Experience in China* (1970) focuses on General Stilwell, it still provides a highly literate account of the war in general. An admirably balanced essay on the Nanking massacre and other wartime atrocities is Lloyd E. Eastman's "Facets of an Ambivalent Relationship," in Iriye, *The Chinese and the Japanese* (1980). Concerning Ishiwara Kanji, see Mark Peattie's biography *Ishiwara Kanji and Japan's Confrontation with the West* (1975).

Domestic Japanese developments, including the rise of militarism and ultranationalist movements in the thirties, are treated in Richard Storry, *The Double Patriots: A Study of Japanese Nationalism* (1957); Maruyama Masao, *Thought and Behavior in Modern Japanese Politics* (1963); Robert Scalapino, *Democracy and the Party Movement in Prewar Japan* (1953); and Ben-Ami Shillony, *Revolt in Japan: The Young Officers and the February 26, 1936 Incident* (1973).

6

DOWNWARD SPIRAL

It was less events in Asia than those in Europe which gradually caused the neutralist mood of America to evaporate in favor of a more involved foreign policy. On the first of September 1939, German armies crossed the frontier into neighboring Poland. Two days later, Britain and France declared war on Germany, and World War II was under way. Hitler's timetable allowed a month for the defeat of Poland; many Western observers thought that Poland might last for two or three months. It was now that the German word *Blitzkrieg* (lightning war) was introduced to the West. Polish armed forces were essentially routed in only eleven days. When the Soviets invaded from the eastern front on September 17, the Polish fate was sealed.

After the fall of Poland, the war in Europe entered a lull. The western front remained quiet throughout the fall and winter of 1939–1940. Some, like isolationist Senator William E. Borah, spoke of a "phony war." A very real war erupted again in April 1940. In quick succession, Hitler's forces occupied Denmark and Norway and in six weeks' time overran Belgium, Holland, Luxembourg, and France. As France neared collapse, Hitler's ally, Mussolini, entered the war. In the summer of 1940, the Führer turned his attention toward England, the last remaining obstacle to victory in Europe. Hitler's generals made preparations for a cross-channel invasion, though the German leader convinced himself that the British would come to terms before that became necessary. Meanwhile, the Luftwaffe appeared over England to rain devastation on London. Abandoning all pretense of military justification, the air war aimed to destroy the will of the English people. This was high tide for Adolf Hitler, who had likened himself to Alexander, Caesar, and Napoleon. In America, War and Navy Department "realists" seemed to be persuaded by isolationist arguments. Two weeks after German armies entered Paris, the realists advised President

Franklin Roosevelt that, because Britain might not survive, America should concentrate on American defenses.

THE RETREAT FROM ISOLATIONISM

The president, however, decided to gamble on Britain. Public opinion polls revealed a significant shift in attitudes. In the wake of German victories, 69 percent of Americans felt that a German victory would imperil American security. It was a presidential election year in 1940 and FDR took his case to the American public. Answering charges that he was a warmonger for wanting to send aid to Britain, Roosevelt argued that the "realistic" way to keep America out of war was to keep Britain in the war. Only by stopping aggression in Europe could Americans hope to keep war from their shores. His Republican opponent, Wendell L. Willkie, polled 45 percent of the popular vote, but Roosevelt won his unprecedented third term by a large electoral-college majority.

Now, with growing popular and Congressional support, the president committed himself to work for an end to the neutrality laws. In his fireside chat of December 29, 1940, FDR told the American people that, "We must become the great arsenal of democracy." Only Britain and the British fleet, he declared, stood between Nazi aggression and the New World, but Britain was perilously close to being broke and, under the neutrality laws, it was impossible to extend credit to a belligerent nation. To give the words meaning, the president introduced legislation a few days later which would permit America to finance the purchase and supply of military equipment to any government "whose defense the president deems vital to the U.S." After months of debate, Congressional approval of this controversial "Lend-Lease" legislation came in the spring of 1941. Next came a series of moves which permitted American naval vessels to convoy British ships across the Atlantic—in spite of the inevitable exposure of Americans to the menace of German submarines. With the enactment of these measures, the biggest impediments of the neutrality laws was removed. Lend-Lease "meant nothing less than a full-scale U.S. commitment to the defeat of Germany, by aid to Britain, if possible, and by American military participation if that was necessary."

Compared to saving Britain, the rescue of China was almost an afterthought in the minds of decision-makers in Washington. America after all had been the chief economic supplier of the Japanese war machine for several years. Still, it was in America's interest to keep 850,000 Japanese soldiers tied down in fighting somewhere in China. So, in November 1940, as persistent rumors of impending collapse of Chinese resistance circulated everywhere, FDR approved a $100 million loan to Chiang Kai-shek, the most massive U.S. financial-aid package yet for China. In April 1941, China was formally linked to the Lend-Lease pipeline. Shipments of munitions, weapons, construction equipment, and other much-needed matériel began to arrive in Burma for transport into China on the 700-mile-long mountain lifeline known as the Burma Road. The road, hastily constructed in 1938 by hundreds of thousands of Chinese laborers working with hand tools, caught the attention of the world at this time as a symbol of Chinese will to fight. By the summer of 1941, an American Military Mission had arrived in China to oversee the distribution of Lend-Lease aid and to improve the Burma Road network.

Also by the summer of 1941, a hundred P-40 American fighter planes were on their way to revive the nearly defunct Chinese air force; while Japan had well over a thousand planes in China and Indochina at that time, the Chinese could muster a mere sixty-eight aircraft. An "American Volunteer Group" of aviators, quickly self-styled the "Flying Tigers," was sent to Burma and China to fly missions and train pilots for the Chinese air force. In an informal arrangement designed to satisfy the letter of the law, President Roosevelt in April 1941 authorized Army Air Corps and naval pilots to resign their commissions and join the AVG, commanded by Claire Chennault, a retired air corps officer who had developed close personal connections with the Generalissimo and Madame Chiang. The P-40s flown by the Americans were less maneuverable than the chief Japanese rival, the Zero, but the Americans compensated by avoiding one-on-one duels. The tactic succeeded. Even allowing for exaggeration, the 299 Japanese aircraft claimed to have been shot down by the Tigers in the seven months beginning in November 1941 is impressive, the more so because only four Tigers were lost. The exploits of this daredevil band of pilots, dressed in leather jackets and cowboy boots, plugging holes in their gas tanks with chewing gum and shooting down Japanese planes for a $750 bonus per plane, became an enduring part of American military lore and late-night cinema reruns. However, to Japan, they were mercenaries, a hostile provocation, and more unwelcome evidence that the United States was interfering in their war with China.

THE FLYING TIGERS AND VIETNAM

To sidestep legal complications and concerns about neutrality, a dummy corporation known as the Central Aircraft Manufacturing Company was created to "hire" the Flying Tigers in 1941. The technique foreshadowed the fabrication of the CIA-funded "Air America" during the Laotian phase of the Vietnam War in the 1960s. Indeed, there was a direct link between the two "corporations." The core of the Flying Tigers "employees" of the Central Aircraft Manufacturing Company stayed in China after World War II to fly support for Chiang Kai-shek during his civil war with the Communists. With defeat in that struggle, the group evacuated with him to Taiwan in 1949 where it became known as "Air Asia." Air Asia spawned two subsidiary companies. One of them was Civil Air Transport (CAT) which operated for a time as Nationalist China's commercial airline; the other offspring of Air Asia was Air America.

THE GREATER EAST ASIA CO-PROSPERITY SPHERE AND THE MONROE DOCTRINE

The message of an impending German victory had its impact on Japan as well as America. A bandwagon atmosphere swept over a Japan which had grown discouraged by its quagmire conflict in China and embraced any hope of salvation. Japanese leaders, dazzled by German successes, decided they would not await the final outcome of the European war but would pursue what Foreign Minister Matsuoka Yosuke called "blitzkrieg diplomacy."

In July 1940, the Cabinet unanimously approved a plan to mobilize the entire nation to a war footing by strengthening the nation's political structure, instituting a planned economy, and launching a huge military buildup. In order to break Japan's dependence on U.S. imports, a policy of national self-sufficiency would be sought through the promotion of an economic sphere in "greater East Asia." This would soon be formalized under the much-vaunted name of the "Greater East Asia Co-Prosperity Sphere" (GEACPS). The "co-prosperity" phrase suggested that although Japan would show the way, take the lead, it would do so for the mutual benefit of all the peoples of greater East Asia, who would live and prosper under the benevolent tutelage of Imperial Japan. It was a noble promise, but tutelage easily transforms into tyranny and exploitation.

"Greater East Asia" was emblematic of Japan's growing ambitions. In 1938, it will be recalled, Japan proclaimed a "New Order in East Asia" which embraced China, Manchuria, and Korea as well as the mother country of Japan. A "greater East Asia" envisioned a grander design of Japanese hegemony extending not only through East Asia but Southeast Asia and Pacific island territories as well, from the borders of India eastward all the way to Australia. Indeed, in more fervent proclamations to come after Pearl Harbor, the GEACPS boundaries sometimes widened to *include* India, Australia, and New Zealand. Similarly, after December 1941, the Hawaiian Islands were also included within the Co-Prosperity Sphere as its "eastern anchor." Japanese historians at that time produced documentation to prove that ancient Hawaiian legends of "dark people" on Maui referred to "suntanned" Japanese fishermen of the thirteenth century who had landed in Hawaii five hundred years before the time of Captain Cook.

Matsuoka, for all the bellicosity and recklessness that is usually assigned to him, insisted that he did not see that GEACPS should necessarily set Japan and the United States on a collision course. He earnestly pleaded with American officials to recognize world realities: The United States would have to learn to share power with Japan in the Pacific. It was pointed out over and over again that Japan had no intention of totally excluding the United States from greater East Asia. True, the United States and the Western imperialists could no longer expect to set the rules, but American investment and trade remained welcome. Japan's dominion over Manchuria had not led to an exclusion of America from Manchuria; in fact, total U.S. commerce with Manchuria increased after the Japanese takeover. Failure of America to recognize the new realities in Asia would mean that it was a "historical inevitability" that the two nations should collide, Matsuoka wrote in May 1940.

He and many other Japanese leaders professed to be puzzled as to why Americans could not see that GEACPS was entirely analogous to the Monroe Doctrine, which established the principle that the entire Western Hemisphere was under the care and protection of the United States, and that the United States would resort to war if necessary to ensure that European powers did not intrude into the hemisphere. President James Monroe's blunt warning of 1823 became an important cornerstone of American foreign policy. Japanese legal scholars asserted that there was international law, and there was law based upon the principle of "regionalism"—the latter being grounded in Monroe's doctrine. Japan was merely applying well-recognized American principles to the "region of greater East Asia."

Since as far back as 1916, Americans had been listening to arguments from Japanese intent upon justifying their moves in Asia. The response from Americans had always been the same: The Monroe Doctrine was defensive in purpose, a "self-denying statement" which reinforced the principle of nonintervention. We might have established the doctrine for our benefit, the State Department's Stanley Hornbeck once wrote, but we did not "endeavor in any way to restrain or coerce the other American states." Nor did the doctrine ask for any "special privilege for ourselves at the expense either of the smaller nations or of Europe." That rationale, which seemed so self-evident to Americans, rarely convinced skeptical Japanese.

THE AXIS POWERS

If Japan was to embark on a dangerous course of action, it would need allies. As early as 1936, Japan had signed a treaty with Germany, the "Anti-Comintern Pact," which provided for cooperation and exchange of information between the two powers in matters related to Communist subversion. Now, in the euphoria of September 1940, advocates of a full-scale military alliance with Germany and Italy prevailed over the voices of caution. At the heart of the Tripartite Pact signed in that month was an article which provided that if Japan, Germany, or Italy were attacked by any third power *not then engaged in the European War or the China Incident*, the other two Axis powers would aid the victim of the attack. The treaty, better known as the Axis Pact, was not to be kept secret: It was intended to serve as a warning. The United States, though not specifically mentioned, was put on notice that it could not hope to fight Germany alone in Europe or Japan alone in the Pacific. The Berlin–Rome–Tokyo Axis would stand together. Matsuoka insisted that the treaty was not meant to provoke war. He had launched a plan for world peace, he maintained. As the only high-ranking government official in Japan with long years of experience in America, Matsuoka felt that he knew Americans well. Only by taking a strong and clear stand might war with America be avoided, the Japanese Foreign Minister argued. "If you stand firm and start hitting back," he once told his son, "the American will know he's talking to a man, and you two can then talk man to man."

JAPAN'S "DELEGATE FROM OREGON"
Matsuoka Yosuke, the Japanese envoy who had walked out of the League of Nations during its debate on Manchuria, was Foreign Minister from July 1940 to July 1941 in one of Premier Konoe's cabinets. At the age of 13, in 1893, he had gone to sea and had been "dumped ashore" in the United States by his uncle, the ship's captain. He fended for himself by selling coffee door to door and in a variety of other menial chores for the next ten years while he worked his way (as Frank Matsuoka) through Portland schools and law studies at the University of Oregon. In the course of his stay in Oregon, he became a convert to Catholicism. In 1904, two years after returning to Japan, he entered the Japanese diplomatic service. His skill at American English was matched by a directness, even bluntness, in manner which was assumed to be a legacy of his decade in the United States. He served as a director of the Japanese-owned South Manchurian Railways during the 1920s and in 1930 won a seat in the Diet, where he was sometimes referred to as the "delegate from Oregon." Americans sometimes assumed that Matsuoka's easy familiarity with their culture would translate into a sympathetic diplomatic stance. They were usually disappointed. After the war ended, Matsuoka was indicted as a war criminal but died in 1946 before his trial was concluded.

The Axis Pact had a powerful impact on public opinion in America. "[It] has done more than anything else could have done to convince Americans that the war in Europe and the war in Asia are the same war," an educator wrote at the time.

Public opinion polls taken before and after the Axis pact was signed measured the dramatic shift in attitudes. In two polls, Americans were asked, "Do you think the United States should let Japan get control of China, or do you think the United States should risk a war with Japan to prevent it from doing so?" In July, only 12 percent of Americans responded that the United States should risk war; after the pact, that figure more than tripled to 39 percent. A persistent isolationist sentiment, however, was registered by 32 percent of the respondents who continued to say "Let Japan control China" even after the Axis Pact was signed (versus 47 percent before).

In Washington, Roosevelt had to worry that the United States might be drawn into conflict in Europe and then be obliged to face Japan in the Pacific. In Tokyo, for the nearly ten years of his tenure as ambassador, Joseph Grew had cautioned his friend in the White House not to put undue pressure on Japan lest it push Japan into a corner and pull the rug out from under pro-American elements. In September 1940, however, Grew seemed totally frustrated by the turn of events. The Japanese, he wrote, were "unashamedly and frankly opportunist," waiting breathlessly for Britain's defeat. Their own position in the world, Grew said, was being influenced more by Hitler's successes than by any

Ambassador Joseph Grew and Foreign Minister Matsuoka Yosuke at Tokyo luncheon, December 12, 1940.

other factor. In this message, now famous as his "green-light telegram," Grew advised his government to apply greater economic pressure as the only means of checking Japan. The green-light message only confirmed Washington's own plans. High-octane aviation fuel had already been placed on the embargo list in July and in September, within a few days of the signing of the Axis pact, scrap iron and scrap steel was added to the list. The scrap iron embargo was a serious blow to Japan. In the month of August alone, Japan had received license to import 300,000 tons of scrap iron—about a one-year supply. To make up for the loss of each ton of scrap iron, about two tons of iron ore and coking coal were needed; in addition, Japan would have to divert badly needed machines, materials, and skilled workers to mine the coal and ore—largely in Manchuria. The embargo list, however damaging, was a measured step to discourage Japan without punishing it with a total economic embargo which would have included petroleum, Japan's most desperately short commodity.

The Berlin–Rome–Tokyo alliance, however, was never as solid as Americans generally believed it to be. In the long run, its main significance was not that it bolstered Japan's strength much but that it cast the Japanese in the American public mind as accomplices to the Nazis. In theory and practice, the alliance fell well short of its backers' goals. Germany had extensive investments and other economic interests in Asia and was never pleased with the Japanese talk of "Asia for the Asians." China had been an important source of raw materials for Germany, and once those raw materials—such as tungsten—came within grasp of Japan, Japan kept them for itself, German officials complained.

About race, as author and Japan expert Ian Buruma has pointed out, there was a close affinity between the Japanese use of the word *minzoku* and the Nazi use of the word *Volk*: Both of them arouse a kind of national mysticism, both of them imply spiritual unity. However, both Japanese and German nationalists had ideas which did not mesh well. The Japanese, for example, rarely elevated themselves to the same level of a super-race as Hitler's Aryan mythology elevated the Germans, and Japanese intellectuals were well aware that in the Nazi scheme of things they were classified as lesser breeds. Israeli historian Ben-Ami Shillony, in a masterful study of wartime Japan, has pointed out that the Japanese translation of Hitler's *Mein Kampf*, completed only in 1942, was classified as "secret" and banned from the general public because of concern that its release would likely have an unfavorable impact on Japan's relations with its German ally. It is not likely that the Japanese ever learned of the aside Hitler made to one of his generals shortly after Pearl Harbor: "It means the loss of a whole continent, and one must regret it for it's the white race which is the loser."

Finally, at the level of strategic planning, the Axis powers failed to achieve most of their common objectives. Germany and Japan each had their own priorities and timetables. Throughout 1940–1941, Germany pressed Japan to move against the British base at Singapore to prove the solidarity of the Axis alliance; Japan demurred. On June 22, 1941, Germany invaded Russia in the largest military campaign the world had ever seen. Again, Hitler pleaded for Japan to help the Axis cause by invading from the Siberian Far East to squeeze Stalin's armies in a giant pincer. Once again, this time after much deliberation, Japan turned down its ally's request.

At issue in the summer of 1941 was whether Japan should move south or north; she did not have the resources to do both. The army leaned toward an attack to the north, against the Soviet Union, but the navy, more conscious of the need for resources such as oil, argued for a push south. The navy's view prevailed. There was no desire to alarm Britain and the United States any more than necessary, so it was decided to move with caution against a French target only—at least for the moment. At a conference in the presence of the emperor on July 2, 1941, the cabinet and the military supreme command approved plans to occupy French Indochina, either with or without the assent of French authorities. The hapless French government at Vichy had little choice but to yield to Japan's demands, and on July 24, Japanese troops landed unopposed in the French colony.

The Imperial Conference of July 2, 1941, represented a momentous step toward war, and yet, there is evidence that it was taken rather lightly. Japanese military leaders insisted that the advance south would not necessarily lead to war with the Allies. Some professed to believe that the odds were that war would *not* result. The fear of war with Germany *and* Japan would deter the United States, many confidently felt. Nonetheless, while it is clear that most military and civilian leaders were anything but *eager* for war with America, they were willing to take the risk. The policy documents approved on July 2 stated flatly that, in carrying out the southern advance, "our Empire will not be deterred by the possibility of being involved in a war with Great Britain and the United States."

MAGIC AND OIL

In 1941, one of the most potent weapons in the American arsenal looked very much like a typewriter. It was a top-secret crypto-computer device that allowed intelligence officers in Washington to read the coded messages exchanged between the Japanese Foreign Ministry and its envoys around the world. (Imperial Army and Navy codes were another matter.) The very few people who knew about it and were authorized to see the intercepted messages spoke of the operation by the code name MAGIC. Radio circuits from Tokyo–Washington, Tokyo–Moscow, Tokyo–Berlin, and so on, were monitored at U.S. military stations which would copy messages sent to or from the Foreign Ministry in Tokyo and relay the encoded text to Washington, where the code-breaking wizardry of MAGIC went to work. Quite often, the result was that a message from Foreign Minister Matsuoka to Ambassador Nomura Kichisaburo in Washington or Ambassador Oshima Hiroshi in Berlin was intercepted, decoded, translated into English, and in the hands of Secretary of State Cordell Hull before it ever reached its intended recipient. Thanks to MAGIC, Hull was in the enviable position for a diplomat of knowing exactly what bargaining latitude Nomura had been given before a negotiation session at the State Department began. In addition, background briefings on decisions made at the highest level of policy-making—such as the July 2 Imperial Conference—were routinely routed to key Japanese ambassadors abroad and, via MAGIC, to the secretary of state and the president.

Armed with the secret intelligence that Japan was about to launch military operations southward—even at the risk of future war with the United States—President Roosevelt had to assess the future strategy of Japan. Was Japan interested in French Indochina for its own sake? It seemed more likely that the occupation of the French colony was only a prelude to further operations in Southeast Asia, including quite likely a strike at the Philippine Islands and the oil-rich Dutch East Indies. To warn Japan away from such moves, on July 27,

MAGIC was the work of a small team of navy code experts working under William Friedman. After a year-long process of trial, error, and mathematical calculation, they produced, in September 1940, a blueprint for a device that duplicated their conception of the original Japanese encoding machinery. This "analog" device, "a rat's nest of wiring and chattering relays housed in a makeshift black wooden box," proved to be even more reliable than the Japanese originals in eliminating garbled code messages. When World War II came to an end, the dissection of a captured Japanese encoding device revealed that of the several hundred connections in the American-produced analog, only two were wired differently from the Japanese machine's. The cost of this early example of high-tech computerized military hardware to the U.S. taxpayer was $684.85.

three days after the Japanese landings in Indochina, Roosevelt ordered the most severe form of economic sanction still available to him: Japanese assets in the United States were frozen, and all trade with Japan, including oil, was halted. The history of U.S.–Japanese relations had turned into a history of reprisals and counter-reprisals, and this latest move was, as the *New York Times* stated, the "most drastic blow short of actual war." Resource-poor Japan, totally dependent on imported oil, had permitted itself to become dangerously over-reliant on a single country, the United States, for over 80 percent of its petroleum needs. Remaining moderates within the Imperial Navy were now converted into advocates of action. Now with the American embargo in place, the clock was ticking.

To turn the screw on Japan even more, the United States secured promises from the Dutch government-in-exile in London that it would ban the sale of oil from the Dutch East Indies to Japan; oil-purchasing missions from Tokyo returned home from the East Indies empty-handed. The ban on DEI oil was seen by Japanese leaders as the "final, major link in a chain of encirclement," wrote Robert J. C. Butow, the culmination of years of effort on the part of the ABCD[1] powers (America, Britain, China, and the Dutch) to "deny Japan her rightful place in the world by destroying her only available means of self-existence and self-defense."

From that point on "the oil gauge and the clock stood side by side," wrote one State Department official. "Each fall in the level brought the hour of decision closer." In spite of a crash program by the Imperial Navy to buy oil in the months before the embargo, the nation still possessed only a limited reserve of petroleum—a two-year supply if the embargo was not lifted, even less if war broke out. Barrel by barrel—at the rate of four hundred tons per hour, an Imperial Navy officer estimated—Japan was emptying its oil tanks. At a certain date in the near future, Japan's ships and planes and armor would be immobilized without a fight. The navy, always more cautious than the army about the risks of a war with America, joined the growing consensus in the belief that Japan had no choice but to fight or accept the status of a third-rate power. The fighting option meant acceleration of the timetable of the southern-advance strategy to bring the oil, rubber, and tin of Southeast Asia into reach. Ambassador Joseph C. Grew in Tokyo registered his gloomy mood in a diary entry written shortly after the embargo was announced. "The vicious circle of reprisals and counter reprisals is on. . . . Unless radical surprises occur in the world, it is difficult to see how the momentum of the down-grade movement can be arrested, or how far it will go. The obvious conclusion is eventual war." Washington, too, was quickly aware of the desperate mood in Tokyo when MAGIC unscrambled this July 31 Tokyo–Berlin intercept: "To save its very life," Ambassador Oshima was told, "Japan must take immediate steps to break asunder this ever strengthening chain of encirclement which is being woven under the guidance and with the participation of England and the United States. . . ."

---

[1] France was not included in the ABCD formula for some reason, perhaps because it was out of alphabetic sequence or perhaps because it had been effectively neutralized in Asia after Japan completed the occupation of French Indochina in the summer of 1941.

ADMIRAL YAMAMOTO, THE "ARCHITECT OF PEARL HARBOR"

In Japan, the military supreme command prepared itself to open hostilities against the United States, Britain, and the Netherlands, and debated the grand plan of war. Various strategies were put forth, but in the end, it was Admiral Yamamoto Isoroku, the leading proponent of carrier-attack warfare, who prevailed. Yamamoto was far from enthusiastic about Japan's prospects in a war with the United States. After graduating from Japan's Naval War College in 1916, Yamamoto spent several tours of duty in the United States, including a year as a language student at Harvard and two years as naval attaché in Washington. He was a voracious reader (Carl Sandburg was a favorite) and had a reputation as a gambler (he favored poker both while he was in the States and after he returned to duty at sea). He had hitchhiked around the United States as a young man and, as an American naval officer who knew him well writes, "He had been mightily impressed with the power manifest in the Pittsburgh steel mills, the Detroit auto factories, the Kansas wheat fields, and above all by the Texas oil fields." This unusually deep exposure to the United States left Yamamoto with a strong conviction that the descriptive name for America, *Beikoku*, "rice country," was an accurate reflection of the country's abundant resources. After returning to Japan, he argued against the Tripartite Pact on the grounds that it would propel Japan toward war with America. He lectured his fellow officers and naval cadets that they should not draw too much comfort from the vaunted "Japanese spirit" (*Yamato damashi*). Americans were not the weak-willed people spoiled by material luxuries that the Japanese military imagined hopefully. There was a "Yankee spirit" embodied in the frontier experience and the exploits of military heroes like Admiral David Glasgow Farragut (of "Damn the torpedoes!" fame), he reminded his listeners. Whereas Japanese spirit was often based on reckless bravado, he cautioned, Yankee spirit was grounded on science and technology—best illustrated by the solo transatlantic flight of Charles Lindbergh.

By 1941, however, as Japanese leaders prepared for war, Yamamoto's caution gave way to necessity. If conflict with America was unavoidable, he felt, Japan must at all cost avoid a drawn-out war of attrition. Japan could not match America's strategic reserves—the Kansas wheat, Pittsburgh steel, and Texas oil. Only in a brief war could Japan hold its advantage, he reasoned. In September 1941, upon being appointed commander-in-chief of Japan's Combined Fleet, he flatly told the prime minister. "If I am told to fight regardless of consequences, I shall run wild for the first six months or a year, but I have utterly no confidence for the second or third years." The initial advantage he needed would require an attack on the U.S. Navy, whose Pacific Fleet headquarters had only recently (July 1941) been moved from San Diego to Pearl Harbor. By immobilizing much of the U.S. Pacific Fleet, Japan would gain the time necessary to consolidate its control over Southeast Asia, including the Philippines and the oil-rich Dutch East Indies. Making Yamamoto's plan all the more appealing to Japanese leaders was the admiral's assurance that the enemy would not be expecting it. In this estimation, Yamamoto was proven by history to be fully accurate.

Admiral Yamamoto Isoroku, taken in Washington, D.C., 1926.

True, for years the U.S. Army and Navy had conducted war games in anticipation of a Japanese attack on the Hawaiian Islands, but the repetition of those training exercises had become almost a cliché. Almost nobody at the very highest level believed in 1941 that the Japanese would be foolish enough to try to launch an attack half-way across the Pacific when so many of their vital interests were located much closer to home in Southeast Asia. American certainty that Pearl Harbor was an unlikely target for an air attack was reinforced by a technical difficulty known to have nettled Japanese engineers: The waters of Pearl Harbor were so shallow that aerial torpedoes would sink to the mud before they harmlessly exploded. Indeed, only after the war was it learned that a "miracle" solution was worked out to the problem less than a month before the attack on December 7.

KONOE AND TOJO

Throughout September 1941, with war clouds gathering, civilian Premier Konoe Fumimaro proposed a personal meeting between himself and President Roosevelt in either Alaska or Hawaii. It was an act of courage on the part of Konoe, and it led to him being marked for death, in the fashion of the early thirties, by an ultranationalist "squad of heavenly punishment," but police quashed the plot shortly before the execution date. Prince Konoe, we now know, intended to use his influence at the palace to have an imperial rescript issued to thwart extremists from opposing any settlement that might be achieved in a meeting with President Roosevelt. We also know, however, that at the time even Konoe was uncertain whether the militarists could be held in check. The proposal was not lightly rejected by Washington. In the end, the chance for the unusual "summit" was dashed when Washington, fearful that Konoe might not be able to deliver on promises made at such a meeting, demanded that "fundamental issues" be resolved *before* the discussions occur. Whether this "last chance" for peace might have been worth the gamble remains an unanswered historical "what if...?" In any case, Washington's rejection of the demarche left Konoe with no option but to resign in October in favor of his War Minister, General Tojo Hideki.

Premier Tojo would lead Japan as the ranking civil and military authority during most of the Pacific War. To his military colleagues, he was *kamisori Tojo* (razor Tojo) known for his decisiveness and his sharp mind. To Americans, he was "Old Razorhead." He was, along with Emperor Hirohito, the only Japanese face widely recognized abroad—and always grotesquely caricatured, the twin counterparts to Hitler, archetypes of a hated enemy.

The end of civilian government in Japan did not signify a radically new course of action. Events had brought both civilian and military leaders in Japan to believe that Japan was slowly being forced to the brink and that war with the ABD powers was nearly inevitable. Konoe, however, was more inclined than Tojo to compromise and to exhaust the possibilities of negotiations with Washington. Tojo could not tolerate Konoe's willingness to talk about troop withdrawal from China. Certainly, that would improve relations with America, the general agreed; but once Japanese troops left China, Tojo scolded Konoe, every sacrifice of blood and treasure there over the past decade would have been in vain. Moreover, the loss of prestige that would accompany withdrawal from China would imperil Manchukuo's existence as well and the empire's hold on Korea might even be jeopardized. It was at this same time, in September, in another talk with Konoe that Tojo said that there comes a point in the lifetime of every man when he finds it necessary to close his eyes, throw caution to the winds, and "take the leap."[2] The comment suggests the mood of the day in the military leadership: neither arrogance nor confidence, as much as desperation. A countdown to hostilities was set in motion. Deadlines and points of no return were established by the new Tojo cabinet. Yet, even General Tojo agreed that diplomatic efforts should continue in Washington.

THE HULL–NOMURA TALKS

Throughout 1941, the Japanese ambassador in Washington was Nomura Kichisaburo, joined in November by a second envoy, Kurusu Saburo.

---

[2] Tojo's phrase sounds more elegant in Japanese for it refers to leaping with one's eyes closed off the verandah of Kiyomizu temple. Kiyomizu, on the outskirts of Kyoto, sits above a spectacularly deep ravine.

Although Nomura met with FDR occasionally, most of his discussions were with Secretary of State Cordell Hull. The Hull–Nomura talks were not, as many Americans later assumed, a sneaky Japanese ploy to buy time for war plotters back home to complete preparations for an attack. Nomura and Kurusu bargained in good faith, fully aware that preparations for war were gaining momentum in their own country and in the United States. Three important concessions were made by Japan during the course of the year. Through Nomura, Washington was given assurances that Japan would not feel bound by the terms of its Axis Pact to side with Germany if the United States was drawn unwillingly into war (through German attacks on its lend-lease shipping to Britain, for example). Secondly, promises were made that Japan would halt its southward drive—and not attack, for example, the Philippines, Malaya, the Dutch East Indies, and so on. Finally, the third concession concerned the greatest question facing Allied leaders in the latter half of 1941: Would Germany's assault on Russia, launched in June, succeed? If Japan participated by attacking from Siberia, as Hitler devoutly wished, the tide of history might have brought German armies into Moscow and Leningrad by the end of the year. Japan, to the relief of FDR (and Stalin), however, gave assurances that Japan would refrain from such a venture, and by year's end, Hitler's grand plan of conquest was stalled within sight of the Soviet capital by Russian armies and by the Russian winter.[3]

Japan asked in return that the United States lift the trade embargo, unfreeze Japanese assets and, above all, resume the flow of oil.

Where, then, was the stumbling block to the resolution of problems? In a word, the answer was China. And here is the reason for emphasizing so emphatically the importance of Japan's position in China in the 1930s and the American response to it. Throughout the decade, America had presented little resistance as Japan defied growing Chinese nationalism to push its advantage on the continent. However, largely as the result of events in Europe, America had begun to aid China, and administer punishing economic sanctions to Japan. China had suddenly become the keystone of American foreign policy in Asia. Now, as the Hull–Nomura talks progressed, Japan was notified of U.S. demands that Japan withdraw from China. Nomura was told the oil pipeline to Japan would be opened only if and when Japan agreed to pull its armies from China.

A complicating matter in the Washington talks grew out of Nomura's inadequacies. Admiral Nomura was "a hale and hearty type of simple sailor," in the words of historian R. J. C. Butow. He was not a professional diplomat, and on at least one occasion, turned over confidential papers to Hull by mistake and was compelled to ask for their return the next day. In spite of a certain ("sometimes uncertain," Hull said) command of English, the admiral often failed to understand the fine points of his conversations with American officials, a problem made worse by the fact that Nomura frequently eschewed the presence of an interpreter.

---

[3] "Assurances," of course, did not add up to certainties. As late as October 15, 1941, FDR was telling Churchill, "I think they [the Japanese] are headed north [into Siberia]."

Rather than send a professional diplomat to Washington, Tokyo had decided on Nomura because of his genial personality and the fact that he had become personally acquainted with FDR (in World War I, when FDR had been assistant secretary of the navy, and Nomura had served as Japan's naval attaché in Washington). The passing friendship with the president, and Nomura's charm, however, did not accomplish their purpose. Throughout 1941, the American position grew more firm on its demands for a Japanese pullout from China. In the more than sixty talks Nomura had with FDR, Hull, and other high-ranking Americans, the negotiators repeatedly circled the issue of a Japanese troop pullout from China, and the American position remained flexible only as to how quickly and how long the process would take.

As an ambassador, Nomura's first and most important duty was accurate reporting. He grievously failed in that responsibility. Through inexperience or wishful thinking, Nomura neglected for many months to adequately apprise his superiors in Tokyo of either the details or the spirit of Washington's position. Whereas Hull's tone and demeanor was uncompromising, even belligerent at times, the Japanese ambassador continually conveyed in his reports to the Foreign Office hints of conciliation on the part of the American secretary of state. In some cases, Nomura failed to transmit to Tokyo entire documents of great significance. The misunderstandings and false complacency generated in Tokyo seriously exacerbated the already tense Japanese–American relations. In November, when the positions of the two countries became clearly and unequivocally understood by both parties, Japanese leaders were shocked by how rigid the American position had apparently become.

NOVEMBER 1941

On November 20, 1941, Tokyo instructed its emissaries in Washington to present Japan's "final proposals" to Hull. Japan preferred to come to an understanding with the United States that would call for Japanese withdrawal of troops from *parts* of China within two years of the signing of a truce. Certain parts of China, however, including the vital north, would remain occupied for twenty-five years. However, since American assent to this proposition, dubbed "Proposal A," was out of the question, Japan advanced a more agreeable set of terms as its "absolute minimum" conditions. "Proposal B" called for the United States to restore trade relations with Japan and help Japan to obtain Dutch petroleum resources. In return, Japan promised to begin withdrawing its army from the southern part of French Indochina immediately and from the rest of the peninsula in due order. She also promised to refrain from any other advances in Southeast Asia. As to China, Proposal B was conciliatory only in that it attempted to put the troop-withdrawal issue aside for the time being. Further, Japan expected the United States to promise not to do anything which might prejudice Japan's endeavors to restore peace with China. In more straightforward terms, Japan sought assurances that the United States would cease its aid to China. To commit itself to Proposal B, Hull replied, the United States would have to virtually surrender.

Was the November 20 proposal in fact a final offer? Or was there still a chance that Japan might negotiate more concessions? If there was any doubt, an unimpeachable source, MAGIC, quickly supplied the answer. A November 22 message from Tokyo to Nomura and Kurusu was intercepted, decoded, and quickly in the hands of Hull as well as its intended recipients. Tokyo sternly addressed the two ambassadors:

> Stick to our fixed policy and do your very best. Spare no efforts and try to bring about the solution we desire. There are reasons beyond your ability to guess why we wanted to settle Japanese–American relations by the 25th, but if within the next three or four days you can finish your conversations with the Americans; *if the signing can be completed by the 29th* (let me write it out for you—twenty-ninth); if the pertinent notes can be exchanged; if we can get an understanding with Great Britain and the Netherlands; and in short if everything can be finished, *we decided to wait until that date.* This time we mean it, that the dead line absolutely cannot be changed. *After that things are automatically going to happen.* Please take this into your careful consideration and work harder than you ever have before. (Emphasis added to original.)

The MAGIC data, along with other confirming evidence, clearly showed that Japan had reached the end of its bargaining patience. *Something* was going to happen in a very short space of time unless a satisfactory reply was given by Washington. Well aware of the importance of their next move, aware that war or peace hinged on the American reply, Roosevelt and his highest civilian and military advisers pondered their course of action in numerous meetings among themselves and with British, Chinese, and Dutch counterparts throughout Thanksgiving week.

A MODUS VIVENDI

At one point, a consensus seemed to emerge that, with diplomacy dead in the water, something had to be done to avoid a military confrontation. From several quarters, including the White House itself, came suggestions that the United States settle for a *modus vivendi*, a workable compromise which, while not achieving long-term goals, would at least defuse the volatile situation with a temporary truce lasting for a specified period of several months. All of the plans had in common two features: they would downplay the China issue and would allow for the resumption of some trade, including oil shipments, to Japan. Even the War Department approved the idea of a *modus vivendi* on the grounds that "It is of grave importance to the success of our war effort in Europe that we reach a *modus vivendi* with Japan." Army Chief of Staff General George Marshall and Chief of Naval Operations Admiral Harold R. Stark signed a joint memo addressed to the president, saying that "The most essential thing now, from the United States viewpoint, is to gain time."

In the end, however, the *modus vivendi* option was scrapped. When Ambassadors Nomura and Kurusu arrived at Secretary of State Hull's office at 5:00 P.M. on November 26, they received not a *modus vivendi* but a "comprehensive basic proposal." The "Hull ultimatum," as the Japanese call it, reaffirmed the principles which Hull had tediously dictated to the Japanese envoys for months.[4] It formally rejected the Japanese Proposal B of November 20 and called on Japan to evacuate not only French Indochina but all of China as well. In addition, both the United States and Japan would be obligated to support the Nationalist government of China—Japan would be required to disown the client state it had established under Wang Ching-wei. Only when Japan assented to these demands would the oil begin to flow again, the Hull note stipulated. The Japanese envoys seemed stunned, genuinely surprised by Hull's brusqueness and the harsh terms they had received. They requested and were given the opportunity for a meeting with the president late the next day, Thanksgiving, but FDR, though "as charming as ever," refused to budge from Hull's positions. The irresistible force had met the immovable object. The uses of diplomacy had been exhausted.

Did Washington realize that no Japanese government could possibly accept the terms of the Hull note? There were a few who believed that a hard-line policy would deter rather than provoke Japanese aggression. State Department Asian expert Stanley Hornbeck, for example, offered the following wagers in a memorandum dated November 27:

> Were it a matter of placing bets, the undersigned would give odds of five to one that the United States and Japan will not be at "war" on or before December 25. . . ; would wager three to one that the United States and Japan will not be at "war" on or before the 15th of January; would wager even money that the United States and Japan will not be at "war" on or before March (a date more than 90 days from now, and after the period during which it has been estimated by our strategists that it would be to our advantage for us to have 'time' for further preparation and disposals).

Hornbeck's optimistic predictions "go down in history," one historian writes, "along with the optimistic business forecasts of 1929, as a tribute to the chastening uncertainty of social affairs." More common, however, was the anticipation

---

[4] The State Department refers to the November 26 message as a "note." Historian R. J. C. Butow argues persuasively that it was, in fact , *not* an ultimatum. An ultimatum implies an uncompromising demand which, if rejected, will lead to a break in relations or the use of force usually within a specified time period. In its form at least, the Hull note was presented as "tentative." It contained no deadline or threat of force or rupture of relations. Butow argues that it was the Japanese Proposal B of November 20 that came closer to an ultimatum. With the advantage of hindsight, we can be certain that Proposal B was an ultimatum: On the day it was issued, the government in Tokyo was approving details for military government in areas soon to be conquered, with the army taking charge in the Philippines and Hong Kong, the navy in the Dutch East Indies, and so on.

MANCHURIA AGAIN

When Hull called for a Japanese evacuation of China, did he include Manchuria within the meaning of China? Hull's note of November 26 did not clarify that question, but it seems that the secretary did not have Manchuria in mind when he called for a Japanese military withdrawal. When Nomura had brought up the question several months earlier, he was assured by the secretary of state that the Japanese puppet state of Manchukuo was, for all practical purposes, a dead issue. Yet, when the November 26 note was received in Tokyo, the Japanese foreign minister was jarred by the apparent *inclusion* of Manchukuo in the American demands. "If we yielded to the present demands of the United States," he said, "Japan's international position would be inferior even to that which it occupied prior to the Manchurian Incident, and its very existence itself would be endangered." Other members of the Tojo government later professed that they also had all assumed that America had Manchuria in mind as well as China. In 1967, Tojo's finance minister Kaya Okinori maintained that "If you [the United States] had excluded Manchukuo, the decision to wage war or not would have been rediscussed at great length." It was, of course, one thing for Hull to tacitly exclude Manchukuo, to diplomatically ignore it. It would have been quite impossible for him to have *explicitly* recognized it as an independent country, *explicitly* permit Japan to maintain its forces there, *and* still hope to preserve amicable ties with Nationalist China.

that negotiations had indeed failed and that it was necessary to accelerate preparations for any contingency. In a Thanksgiving Day phone conversation with Secretary of War Henry L. Stimson, Hull said, "I have washed my hands of it and it is in the hands of you and [Secretary of Navy Frank] Knox." Army Chief of Staff General George Marshall was reported as saying that the "President and Mr. Hull felt the Japanese were dissatisfied with the current conferences and 'will soon cut loose.'"

Why then, with the U.S. Army and Navy desperately anxious to buy more time, did Hull and the president decide to scrap the *modus vivendi* and go with the hard-line demand for a troop withdrawal which seemed so likely to provoke Japan? The answer is twofold.

First, as Hull weighed the merits of the *modus vivendi*, he asked for the views of the Chinese, British, Dutch, and Australians, all of whom would be affected by hostilities. The Chinese vehemently protested. Chiang Kai-shek had never seemed so agitated, his American adviser in Chungking said. The United States is "still inclined to appease Japan at the expense of China," complained the Chinese ambassador in Washington in a meeting with Hull that went on into the evening of November 25. Chiang, himself, cabled an urgent plea that Washington take an "uncompromising" attitude in its negotiations with Japan regarding such matters as troop withdrawal and maintenance of the embargo. Failure to do that, Chiang insisted, would mean a collapse of the Chinese army. "The certain collapse of our resistance will be unparalleled catastrophe in the world, and I do not know how history in the future will record this episode," the Chinese Generalissimo warned. Hull was clearly disturbed by the tenor of the Chinese remarks but apparently not yet convinced that the *modus vivendi* should be dropped. Still later that same night, a cable arrived from British Prime Minister Winston Churchill. It opened with the disclaimer that "of course, it is for you [FDR] to handle this business" but went on: "There is only one point that disquiets us. What about Chiang Kai Shek? Is he not having a very thin diet? Our anxiety is about China. If they collapse our joint dangers would enormously increase."

There is no certainty that it was Churchill's "thin diet" metaphor that turned the tide and caused Hull and FDR to drop the *modus vivendi*. However, it does seem, as State Department historian Herbert Feis has written, that in the course of the crucial night of November 25–26, Hull "added up the sums of pros and cons." It further seems that the China factor was critically important in shaping the terms the United States government would deliver to Nomura and Kurusu on the 26th. The secretary of state later recalled that at some point it had become clear to him that "the slight prospects of Japan's agreeing to the *modus vivendi* did not warrant assuming the risks involved in proceeding with it, especially the serious risk of collapse of Chinese morale and resistance and even of disintegration of China."

A second factor prompted the hard-line option of November 26. On November 25, while he was still weighing the options open to him, Hull received word from the War Department of Japanese troop movements. Five divisions of soldiers had boarded transports in Shanghai, and the convoy was moving slowly down the south China coast. When the president was given word of the expedition on the morning of November 26, he "fairly blew up," according to Stimson. The news changed everything, the president said, "because it was an evidence of bad faith on the part of the Japanese." The president felt alarmed enough by the news to notify American authorities in the Philippines of the danger they might face:

> "I am particularly concerned," the president declared, "by current southward troop movements from Shanghai and Japan to the Formosa area. Preparations are becoming apparent in China, Formosa, and Indo China for an early aggressive movement of some character although as yet there are no clear indications as to its strength or whether it will be directed against the Burma Road, Thailand, Malay Peninsula, Netherlands East Indies, or the Philippines. Advance against Thailand seems the most probable. I consider it possible that this next Japanese aggression might cause an outbreak of hostilities between the U.S. and Japan."

Some indication of how important the south China coast convoy was being regarded is gleaned from a telephone conversation Ambassador Kurusu made to the Foreign Office in Tokyo on Thanksgiving evening (Washington time). U.S. Navy monitors were of course eavesdropping on the trans-Pacific call and had little difficulty in "breaking" the simple voice-code which Kurusu and the Tokyo staff officer employed. Kurusu first reported that "Miss Kimiko" (FDR) had not revised any of the terms presented to them the day before by "Miss Umeko" (Hull). The problem that was complicating their talks, Kurusu sputtered as he tried to disguise his words, was "that southward matter, that south, south, southward matter [the troop convoy]. . . ." It was having a "considerable effect. You know? Southward matter?" At last, the voice in Tokyo caught on: "Ah so! the south matter? It's having an effect?"

> Kurusu's voice again: "Yes, and at one time the matrimonial question [the negotiations] seemed as if it would be settled. But well, of course, there are other matters involved too. However that was it; that was the monkey wrench. . . . How do things look there? Does it look as if a child might be born?"

> The Tokyo voice (in a very definite tone): "Yes, the birth of the child [a decision] seems imminent."

> Kurusu: "Oh it does? It does seems as if the birth is going to take place? (Pause.) In which direction? (Pause, with confusion) I mean, is it to be a boy [war] or a girl [peace]?"

> Tokyo: (after laughter and hesitation): "It seems as if it will be a strong healthy boy."

> Kurusu: "Oh, it's to be a strong healthy boy?"

KIDO BUTAI

Undetected by any of the American or Allied intelligence community, another Japanese convoy had also just set sail. From the desolate, mist-shrouded Kurile Islands to the northeast of Japan, a formidable armada weighed anchor several hours before Hull, on the other side of the world, handed the November 26 offer to Nomura and Kurusu. Composed of six carriers, two fast battleships, two heavy cruisers, a light cruiser, eight destroyers, three hundred fifty fighter aircraft, dive bombers, torpedo planes, and a train of auxiliary vessels, it was quite simply the most modern, highly trained, and deadly naval air armada ever assembled. This was *Kido Butai*, the Pearl Harbor Striking Force. When Tokyo informed its ambassadors in Washington that they had to bend every effort to resolve difficulties with America by the 29th of November, it was *Kido Butai* plowing across the North Pacific that it had in mind. The fleet could be recalled from its track up until the 29th *if* American demands softened by that date. After that, in the ominous words of the MAGIC intercept, "things are automatically going to happen."

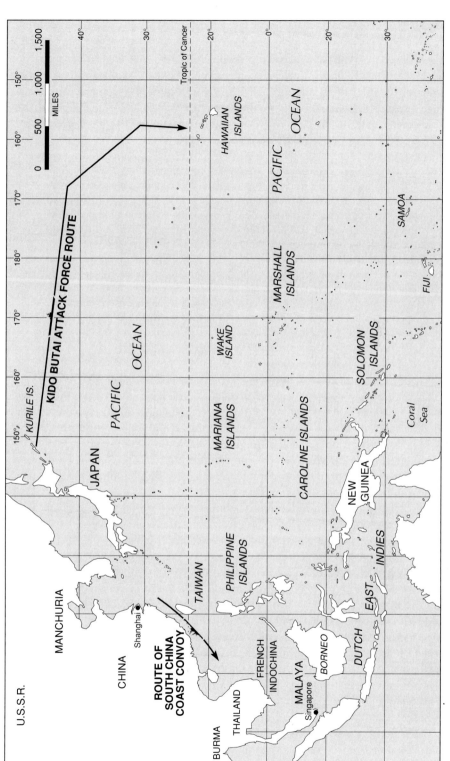

The Week Before Pearl Harbor

In the ten days following Thanksgiving, while Washington awaited a reply to the November 26 note, MAGIC continued to yield its secrets—all of which confirmed suspicions that a grim scenario was unfolding. Here, for example, was what became known as "The Berlin Message," a cable from Tokyo to the Japanese ambassador in Berlin, dispatched on November 30, intercepted, and rushed to the attention of FDR the following day:

> The conversations begun between Tokyo and Washington last April, in spite of the sincere efforts of the Imperial Government, now stand ruptured—broken. . . . In the face of this, our Empire faces a grave situation and must act with determination. Will Your Honor, therefore, immediately interview Chancellor HITLER and Foreign Minister RIBBENTROP and confidentially communicate to them a summary of the developments. Say to them that lately England and the United States have taken a provocative attitude, both of them. Say that they are planning to move military forces into various places in East Asia and that we will inevitably have to counter by also moving troops. *Say very secretly to them that there is extreme danger that war may suddenly break out between the Anglo–Saxon nations and Japan through some clash of arms and add that the time of the breaking out of this war may come quicker than anyone dreams.* (Emphasis added to original.)

With time running out before *something* happened *somewhere*, U.S. authorities strained to pin down specifics. All eyes, however, were riveted on the wrong place, the south China coast, as observers tracked first one convoy and then another one sailing from Taiwan. By December 1, the reports indicated a veritable tide of troop transports and freighters, "including landing boats in considerable numbers," heading south from Chinese ports and Japan itself. The French Indochina port of Haiphong was clogged with equipment, weapons, planes, ships, and troops arriving from the north.

Were the Japanese preparing to launch an attack on neutral Thailand? Japanese diplomatic and espionage activity there had greatly expanded in recent weeks. Did Japan contemplate an attack on Malaya to take out the big British naval base at Singapore? In fact, one of the convoys did land there on December 8 (December 7, U.S. time). Was Japanese strength in French Indochina being augmented in preparation for a strike at southwestern China and the Burma Road? U.S. Army intelligence frequently mentioned this possibility. Or was the Dutch East Indies to be the target? Given Japan's desperate need for oil, that seemed a most likely choice. But American naval and air power in the Philippines lay between Japan and the East Indies. Would not Japan calculate that it must attack the Philippines if it hoped to overrun the East Indies? Decoded messages reporting Japanese ship movements between August 1 and December 6 pointed to an attack on the Philippines: Fifty-nine of the "solved" messages dealt with the Philippines; another twenty-three pointed to the Panama Canal, and only twenty concerned Pearl Harbor. Each possible target had pros and cons, favorable and unfavorable consequences which the Japanese had to weigh—and the ABCD powers tried to fathom.

The point to be noted, however, is that, wisely or unwisely, attention was almost exclusively drawn to Southeast Asia and not to Hawaii. Not surprisingly, then, the most hastily ordered countermeasure taken by America in the period after November 26 was to rush a flight of forty-eight B-17 aircraft from the West Coast to the Philippines to supplement the largest concentration of U.S. air-power outside of the States. Aircraft carriers were ordered from Hawaii to help ferry the pursuit planes needed to escort the bombers to the Philippines before the blow fell. For the United States, this was a fortuitous development that kept the vital carriers out of harm's way on December 7. For Japan, the absence of the carriers from Pearl Harbor was to be a crushing disappointment.

The Sunday, December 7, edition of the *New York Times* reported that the president had dispatched a personal note to Emperor Hirohito. The last-minute appeal was sent, the *Times* said, in response to reports that "125,000 Japanese troops were in Indo-China, on land and along the coast in transports." "A serious warlike move" was about to be made, the *Times* declared, adding its speculation that the troop buildup pointed to an "invasion of Thailand."

Throughout Saturday, December 6, and the early hours of December 7, military intelligence officers were intercepting and decoding a long fourteen-part message from Tokyo to Nomura and Kurusu. The envoys were told to be prepared to present the message, an official reply to the Hull note of November 26, to the Americans "just as soon as you receive instructions." When the MAGIC team had completed processing of the first thirteen parts of the message, the details were deemed so important that they were taken to the White House at 9:00 P.M. for FDR's perusal. After the president read the rambling memorandum, essentially a restatement of the Japanese position written as if to express its case for history, the president turned to his adviser Harry Hopkins and said, "This means war." Hopkins agreed and volunteered his opinion that "since war was undoubtedly going to come at the convenience of the Japanese, it was too bad that we could not strike the first blow and prevent any sort of surprise." Roosevelt nodded and answered, "No, we can't do that. We are a democracy and a peaceful people." Later, much would be made of this Roosevelt–Hopkins exchange by critics anxious to prove that the president failed to properly alert Pearl Harbor even after he, himself, was convinced that war was coming.

By the morning of December 7, the fourteenth part was available. It declared that the Japanese government "regrets to have to notify hereby the American Government that in view of the attitude of the American Government it cannot but consider that it is impossible to reach an agreement through further negotiations." Other cables followed thanking the ambassadors for their efforts and ordering them to present the complete fourteen-part message to the secretary of state at 1:00 P.M. that afternoon, Sunday, December 7. The final instruction advised the Japanese Embassy to destroy its cipher machine and all its codes and secret documents.

Intelligence officers handling MAGIC were especially alarmed by the 1:00 P.M. message, convinced that Tokyo would not have specified that precise hour unless it had a special significance. They were correct, but they had trouble

SURPRISE ATTACK

The attack on Pearl Harbor was scheduled to begin at 7:50 A.M., Hawaii time, on December 7. That corresponded to 1:20 P.M. in Washington, D. C. (In 1941, there was a five-and-one-half-hour time difference between the capital and Hawaii.) By handing their communications over to Secretary of State Cordell Hull at 1:00 P.M., twenty minutes before the attack on Pearl Harbor began, Japan could claim it gave notice, and at the same time, not imperil the strike. The first wave of *Kido Butai* arrived at their target at 7:55 A.M., but the two Japanese ambassadors were delayed while an inexperienced Embassy officer nervously typed and retyped the fourteen-part message. Nomura and Kurusu therefore arrived for their meeting with Hull more than an hour late, at a few minutes past 2:00 P.M., shortly after the secretary of state received the first news of Pearl Harbor. They were unaware that an attack on Pearl Harbor had taken place; nor did they know that one was scheduled to take place; nor did Hull tell them the news that he had just heard. Accordingly they were puzzled by the curt reception they received in the secretary's office. It was not until they returned to the Japanese Embassy that they learned of the news flash from Hawaii.

locating the chief of staff, George Marshall, who could act on their hunch—he was following his usual Sunday morning routine, horseback riding in Rock Creek Park. By 11:40 A.M., however, Marshall had reported to his office and read the MAGIC cables, including the cipher destruction and one-o'clock messages, and agreed that the military theaters, including Hawaii, should be put on alert. There was eighty minutes of warning time remaining. Marshall might have picked up the trans-Pacific telephone on his desk—it had a scrambling device for security purposes. If he had, Pearl Harbor would have had *some* warning, time enough to at least alert battle crews manning anti-aircraft batteries. However, Marshall felt the telephone connection was not dependable enough and opted for the more secure option of a coded radio message. In longhand the general wrote out,

> The Japanese are presenting at 1 P.M. Eastern Standard Time, today, what amounts to an ultimatum. Also they are under orders to destroy their code machine immediately. Just what significance the hour set may have we do not know, but be on alert accordingly.

Atmospheric conditions that Sunday morning were poor. Heavy static blocked the channels to both San Francisco and Honolulu. The warning message was therefore dispatched via Western Union and RCA circuits and arrived in Honolulu while the first Japanese planes from *Kido Butai* were twenty-five miles off the coast of Oahu. There were still a few minutes of alert time, but as fate would have it, the regular teletype link between the downtown RCA office in Honolulu and Army headquarters at Fort Shafter was out of order. So, an RCA clerk, unaware that he was handling a war warning, turned it over to a bicycle messenger boy to deliver. Before the lad could reach Fort Shafter, the war had begun.

PEARL HARBOR DAY

December 7, 1941, began as a relaxed Sunday at military bases in Hawaii. Hawaii was considered good duty, a quiet place in the sun far away from likely trouble spots in the Atlantic. Japanese pilots homed in on radio broadcasts from Honolulu and were relieved to hear that only "soft music" was being played: The attack would be a surprise. A primitive radar system, set up only four months earlier, detected an incoming flight of Japanese planes when they were still 137 miles north of Oahu, but the duty officer who might have acted on the information calculated that the aircraft must be a flight of B-17 bombers due to arrive that morning from the West Coast and decided to ignore the radar report. War warnings had been received from Washington, but they had always indicated that Malaya, Thailand, the Philippines, or some other distant place were the most likely targets. General Walter C. Short had interpreted war alerts which he had received to mean that the most probable menace he faced was from sabotage by local agents of Japan. Accordingly, he had ordered army planes parked wing-to-wing, making them a convenient target for the Japanese fliers from *Kido Butai*. One hundred and eighty-eight of the aircraft were destroyed and almost as many damaged.

For just under two hours, five waves of attacking torpedo planes and dive bombers roared over Battleship Row, Ford Island, Hickham Field, and other military targets which Japanese pilots had been trained to identify during several months of mock attacks. As the last of the planes returned to their carriers shortly before 10:00 A.M., they were able to report that they had reduced the U.S. Pacific Fleet to a smoking ruin. A total of eighteen vessels, densely berthed in landlocked anchorage, including eight battleships, had been sunk or put out of commission. The death toll reached 2433 Americans; another 1178 were wounded. In two of the capsized battleships, survivors tapped out signals to rescuers, but most could not be reached. The signals of the last three men on the *West Virginia* lasted until two days before Christmas. Just below the surface of the water, more than eleven hundred sailors remain entombed in the flooded compartments of the *Arizona*, which rests in place today as a memorial to December 7. The cost to Japan was thirty planes and their pilots. Simply stated, Pearl Harbor was the single worst defeat in American military history.

ASSESSING THE BLAME

The "day of infamy" had barely finished before blame for the disaster began to be assigned. At the beginning, attention was focused on the army and navy commanders in Hawaii. Admiral Husband E. Kimmel, Commander-in-Chief of the U.S. Fleet, was slightly grazed by a spent bullet while standing in his headquarters office. "It would have been merciful if it had killed me," he murmured to an aide, knowing full well that he and General Short would soon be defending themselves against charges that they had been "caught napping." He was correct. The December 7 debacle led to seven administrative investigations and the most extensive congressional inquiry ever undertaken, all of them serving to fuel the debate rather than solving the question of responsibility for the surprise attack. Only the assassination of President Kennedy twenty-two years later stirred as much controversy.

General Short and Admiral Kimmel were charged with "dereliction of duty" for their failure to confer and coordinate adequately after receiving the November 27 "war warning." The result was the disgrace of being removed from their commands and allowed to resign from the service. Short and Kimmel, and many generals and admirals sympathetic to them, have argued that the two commanders in Hawaii were scapegoats and faulted Washington authorities for the failure to share adequately the intelligence gleaned from MAGIC cable traffic which gave the president and others an inside look at Japan's intentions. It is true, of course, that Washington officials removed overseas commanders from its distribution list because of an almost paranoid fear that leaks might breach the security of the MAGIC operation. It is fair to ask whether such extreme secrecy may actually have seriously eroded the intelligence value of the whole MAGIC endeavor. In defense of Washington, however, it is argued that the Hawaiian commanders were repeatedly notified of the possibility of danger, so often that General Marshall and others feared there was risk the islands might slip into a nonchalant frame of mind of one hearing a "cry-wolf" alarm too often.

Moreover, as we have seen, while MAGIC strongly suggested that Japan was moving toward war, it gave no indication that Pearl Harbor had been chosen as a target. The late-November MAGIC intercepts did not even unimpeachably point to war with the United States. The most salient fact in all of the Pearl Harbor controversy, and the one most often ignored or understated, is that, for twelve days prior to December 7, Washington's attention was fastened on the Japanese convoy steaming down the south China coast. Whether through culpable ignorance or excusable ignorance, the president and his chief civilian and military advisers were attempting to fathom the destination of *those* ships. Historian Michael Slackman had that in mind and the widespread press attention to the increasingly tense atmosphere in U.S.–Japanese relations when he wrote with only some exaggeration, "The general drift of Japanese policy could be divined as accurately from the pages of the Honolulu dailies as from the [MAGIC] traffic."

Doubtless both the army and navy were derelict. However, in a more general way, the entire nation, Congress especially, was derelict in permitting the drift into military obsolescence which heightened the dangers of a clash with Japan and Nazi Germany. As one military expert, Rear Admiral Edwin T. Layton, has testified, only round-the-compass, deep ocean reconnaissance could have guaranteed Pearl Harbor adequate advance warning of the approach of an enemy fleet. The aircraft necessary for such an extensive operation were simply not available, however, a legacy to the longtime grip of isolationism on the country. Only six B-17s were flyable in Hawaii. The navy had a larger number of amphibious planes but, allowing for crew and plane fatigue as well as maintenance problems, fewer than thirty were available for daily operations, which meant that the surveillance had to be drastically reduced in scope. Moreover, Kimmel's big dilemma, Layton argues, was that he was supposed to conserve his planes to prepare for *offensive* sorties against the Marshall Islands, far to the west, in the event of hostilities. Years of planning had led Kimmel and most navy officers to be preoccupied with their offensive mission, to strike out against the Japanese-mandated islands in the Pacific. He could not fritter away his patrol-plane resources on countermeasures to a contingency that seemed so improbable. In addition, the number and types of anti-aircraft guns in the Hawaiian Department on December 7 were wholly inadequate to defend the islands.

This brings us back to the point made earlier, that it was accepted wisdom in U.S. military circles that a Japanese attack on Pearl Harbor was somewhere in the realm of fantasy. It was not that Pearl Harbor was impregnable so much that it was thought to be inaccessible. "A Japanese attack on Pearl Harbor is a strategic impossibility," wrote military affairs analyst Major George Fielding Eliot in 1938. When word was brought to U.S. Navy Secretary Knox that Hawaii was under attack on December 7, his response was typical: "My God," he blurted out, "this can't be true, this must mean the Philippines." Ever since the U.S. military chiefs formalized their first contingency plan for war against Japan—the "Orange plan" conceived in 1907 and revised annually—it was assumed that the decisive confrontation would take place far to the west of Hawaii. The Philippines were invariably the chief focus of American concern. Japanese contingency planning closely paralleled the strategic thinking of the admirals in Washington.

In 1907, the year that the first Orange plan was devised in Washington, Japanese military strategists began to consider the United States (along with other countries) as a hypothetical enemy in a future war. Japanese planning centered on the destruction of the American fleet in a showdown battle in the Western Pacific. While the Philippines and Guam were marked for invasion as early as 1923, Hawaii was never mentioned as a target in Japan's annual plans. Indeed, so risky and improbable were operations against Hawaii that Admiral Yamamoto, the architect of the Pearl Harbor plan, was encountering stiff opposition to it from the Naval General Staff until five weeks before the attack. His critics backed off only when Yamamoto threatened to resign. Even Vice-Admiral Nagumo Chuichi, in command of the Pearl Harbor task force, was personally opposed to Yamamoto's plan. Rear Admiral Tomioka Sadatoshi, chief of the operations section on the Naval General Staff, had yielded to Yamamoto's will but remained so apprehensive about his colleague's plan, so fearful that Kimmel's carriers might counterattack, that right up until the morning of December 7 he chided himself for his irresolution and kept a revolver in the drawer of his desk, ready for suicide if the daring attack failed.

The fundamental sense of disbelief U.S. policymakers had concerning a Japanese attack on Hawaii was magnified by the almost unbelievably arrogant assessment of Japanese fighting skills, which caused American planners to consistently underestimate Japanese prowess. Over and over, American and other Western commentators noted how the Buddhist sense of resignation caused Japanese to "fold their hands across their stomachs and die cheerfully for the glory of the Empire" rather than seek solutions, how ships "turned turtle" in the water because of design flaws, how Japanese could not shoot straight because they were slant-eyed, and how "Nipponese" were poor pilots because the whole nation suffered from inner-ear defects and myopia (cartoon Japanese *always* squinted through oversized glasses). John Dower relates the last point to the conviction of many Americans at the time of Pearl Harbor that it could not have been Japanese pilots in the cockpits of those Zeros over Pearl Harbor, it must have been Germans. General Douglas MacArthur in the Philippines thought it must have been white mercenaries at the controls of the planes that wiped out his air force on the ground on December 8 (December 7 in the United States). Even FDR did not categorically dismiss the possibility that the Germans were involved. "There is a rumor that two of the planes . . . had swastikas on them," he told reporters.

THE REVISIONISTS

While partisan attempts to exonerate Short and Kimmel prompted some military men and historians to criticize Washington, a far more sweeping set of historical accusations emerged in the writings of the "revisionists," so called because they have sought and still seek to revise the more or less standard or orthodox interpretations of the beginning of the war. The tenor of the revisionist critique is apparent in the title of one of the early examples of the genre, *Back Door to War: The Roosevelt Foreign Policy 1933–1941*, a 1952 study by Charles C. Tansill, or in the title of a more recent representative, the 1982 work of John Toland, *Infamy: Pearl Harbor and Its Aftermath*.

The revisionist authors are bent on exposing whitewashes and cover-ups and aim to demonstrate that FDR deliberately provoked Japan into an assault on Pearl Harbor. The president and others ignored or even suppressed warnings to the military commanders in Hawaii so as to ensure a successful surprise attack on the American fleet, the revisionists argue. The rationale for this "infamy" was, in the words of Tansill's title, that the president would then have a *casus belli* for entering, via the back door, Britain's struggle against Nazi Germany. It was this war in the Atlantic and in Europe that preoccupied the White House, revisionists maintain. Unless there was some great disaster like Pearl Harbor which would galvanize American public opinion in favor of war, the public and Congress would continue to stay on the sidelines, these authors hold. More than most American presidents, President Roosevelt seemed to arouse extreme responses—of both admiration and contempt for both his foreign and domestic policies. A large segment of the population despised his "New Deal" as socialist. Tansill, who reviled FDR for his alleged lifetime crusade to "save the tottering

Revisionist tales reached the ludicrous when they hit the popular press. Gordon Prange, the most prolific chronicler of the Pearl Harbor story, cites a few examples including the following culled from a Chicago newspaper. In it, the writer alleged that on December 6, sailors were ordered to go into Honolulu and get drunk. "Those who returned to the ships in the night were kept from coming on board by officers with drawn revolvers. . . ." The article went on to assert that planes were defueled "to make absolutely sure that no plane could be gotten into the air." The writer also drew on the almost commonplace canard that the attacking planes were not manned by Japanese. "There seemed to be a few Japs, but the shooting was done by white men," the "eyewitness" recounted, adding that the only Japanese in the attack force were there to take photographs.

British empire," phrased the idea of Roosevelt's responsibility for Pearl Harbor starkly when he wrote: "It seems quite possible that the Far Eastern Military Tribunal brought to trial the wrong persons. It might have been better if the trial had held its sessions in Washington." Claire Booth Luce, celebrity actress and wife of the Time–Life publisher, castigated the president in a much-quoted swipe: "He couldn't lead us into war and so he lied us into war."

The Saturday, December 6, 9:00 P.M. remark of FDR to his aide, "This means war," is often a key link in the revisionist chain of evidence used to indict the president. The president knew after reading MAGIC intercepts that war was imminent and yet failed to alert his commanders in Hawaii? Surely that points to treachery in the White House. A closer look at the presidential remark suggests otherwise. In the first place, the words were attributed to FDR in testimony given four years after the event by an officer who was unsure of the commander-in-chief's precise language. To the best of his recollection, the officer testified, the president "in substance" had said that "This means war." Even if those exact words were uttered by Roosevelt, the more important fact remains that the president did *not* say and did not have any inkling that "This means an attack on Pearl Harbor." President Roosevelt and all of Washington, were, as we have seen, watching the Japanese convoy which was moving toward Malaya.

Much of the argumentation set forth by the revisionists involves highly disputed evidence and reasoning. A few examples drawn from the best-known of the revisionist writers, John Toland, but commonly seen in most revisionist texts, will illustrate their persuasion, although these samples cannot pretend to do justice to the complexity and scope of the debate.

RADIO SILENCE. Toland asserts that ships of the *Kido Butai* were tracked by radio signals to a point about four hundred miles north-northwest of Hawaii in the week prior to December 7. The two Americans who supposedly got the cross bearings on the mysterious signals took steps to pass the information along via intelligence channels to Washington where, according to Toland, they were ignored. Critics of Toland rejoin that nowhere among the surviving piles of intelligence reports which were available to the White House is there a copy of the fleet plottings. This absence of data, of course, is consistent with the massive cover-up which conspiracy-minded revisionists take for granted. In addition to the missing documentation, however, Toland's theory founders on the fact that Japanese authorities have consistently held that the Pearl Harbor strike force maintained absolute radio silence, never sending any messages by radio, even on low-power ship-to-ship channels. Japanese naval planners were well aware of the capability of both British and American intelligence services to trace ship movements through plotted direction-finder bearings and trained rigorously to foil these attempts. The evidence from diaries, testimonials, and other records is overwhelming that all task-force communications were made by flag during the day or blinker at night. Commanders went so far as to remove or seal transmitter keys in order to ensure that some panicky sailor or pilot did not break radio silence.

"WINDS" MESSAGE. Among the most intriguing information imparted by MAGIC was a circular sent to Japanese diplomatic missions on November 19 in which provision was made for an open-code alert. In the event of an "emergency," the Japanese diplomats were advised, regular Japanese-language short-wave news broadcasts would give warnings. (The contingency code presupposed that normal communications between Tokyo and its missions in certain key cities like Washington might be interrupted.) The warnings would come at the middle and the end of a weather forecast, and each sentence would be repeated twice in a precisely worded formula, the diplomats learned. Upon hearing the message, affected embassies would immediately take precautions such as destroying code machines. In the event of a break in British relations, a certain "forecast" would be broadcast; if a break in relations with the Soviet Union was imminent, another coded forecast would be sounded. In case of a rupture in relations with the United States, the listener would hear *"Higashi no kaze, ame"* (East wind, rain). In the days preceding Pearl Harbor, U.S. Army and Navy intelligence services, certain of the importance of a "winds message," made frenzied attempts to pick up the ominous words.

Nearly all the witnesses testifying at the Pearl Harbor investigations insist that no such broadcast was ever heard. Toland, however, cities statements by a naval radioman, Warrant Officer Ralph T. Briggs, who claimed to have heard the "winds" code used several days prior to December 7. He forwarded the intercept to his superior but, again, the crucial document is missing from the Pearl Harbor archives. No "winds" code intercept has ever been found in the files, and Japanese sources insist that none was ever broadcast. Further invalidating the testimony of Briggs was his assertion that he heard the crucial phrase in a navy weather report transmitted by Morse code; the authentic "winds" message was to be broadcast by public radio in voice.

BOMB-PLOT MESSAGES. In October 1941, the U.S. Navy decrypted two messages from Tokyo to the Japanese consulate in Honolulu. These top-secret messages asked the Japanese consulate to provide information not only about when the U.S. fleet was in port but to calculate the precise locations of where U.S. warships were berthed and anchored. These were to be precisely worked out on a map grid, an overlay for Pearl Harbor. At least two high-ranking intelligence officers in Washington who handled the intelligence felt that the gist of it should be transmitted to the Pacific commanders. At the level of Rear Admiral Richmond Kelly Turner, chief of war plans and one of the few privy to MAGIC, it was decided not to forward the bomb-plot message to the chiefs in Hawaii. Nearly everyone agrees that Turner's decision was misguided. "The coordinate grid is the classical method for pinpoint target designation; our battleships had suddenly become 'targets,'" one general later wrote. Denying Kimmel and Stark this vital information must be seen as a serious indictment of the fetish of secrecy that surrounded MAGIC. (By most accounts, it is also an indictment of in-house rivalries and empire-building within the navy bureaucracy.) This, however, constitutes an intelligence failure and not an act of treason and, in any case, was well-removed from the purview of the White House.

SIGNALS AND NOISE

Moreover, even as an intelligence failure, the bomb-plot message is an apt illustration of the complexity of the question of responsibility for Pearl Harbor. Of the literally hundreds of analyses of Pearl Harbor that have been put forth over the past half-century, the single most illuminating is that of Roberta Wohlstetter who argues that the United States failed to anticipate Pearl Harbor "not for want of the relevant materials, but because of a plethora of irrelevant ones." In other words, it is true, she admits, that American military planners had available to them certain "signals" which pointed to an attack on Pearl Harbor—and Wohlstetter's pathbreaking *Pearl Harbor: Warning and Decision* surveys this story with great skill. These signals were deeply embedded, Wohlstetter writes, in an atmosphere of "noise," that is, in the company of all sorts of information that was useless or irrelevant or which pointed to conflicting conclusions. Signals which later seemed to point unequivocally to Pearl Harbor were in the context of November–December 1941 "not merely ambiguous but occasionally inconsistent with such an attack," she writes. In the four months preceding December 7, for example, U.S. intelligence officers deciphered twenty-three Japanese ship-movement messages dealing with the Panama Canal, fifty-nine dealing with the Philippines, and only twenty concerning Pearl Harbor—all of this in addition to the attention riveted to the south China coast convoy and occasional hints of threats to U.S. West Coast facilities from Bellingham to San Diego. Even the possibility of a Japanese attack on Soviet Siberia could not be discounted by Washington policymakers. Admiral Turner argued for the high probability of such an attack up until the last week in November. Wohlstetter draws from all this the following lapidary conclusion:

> They [FDR and everyone] fell victim to the very human tendency to pay attention to the signals that supported their current assumptions about enemy behavior. If no one is listening for signals of an attack against a highly improbable target [Pearl Harbor], then it is difficult for the signals to be heard.

Perhaps it is easier to impute evil intentions than to see incompetence or a complicated series of national policy dilemmas that were often freighted with ambiguity. Naval historians will argue forever whether FDR's transfer of a quarter of the Pacific fleet to the Atlantic in the spring of 1941 to assist in convoy operations there was a wise move. Could the diminished Pacific fleet still discourage Japan from hostility, or did the ship transfers encourage the Japanese to strike? Deterrent or magnet? It is more inviting for some to dismiss the ambiguities, offering instead elaborate White House plots which confirm the pervading distrust Americans have for their political leaders and the fondness they have shown for reducing complex historical process to personal villainy. Surely it makes sense to ask whether it was in character for President Roosevelt, with his special fondness for the navy—he called it "my Navy"—to conceal life-and-death warnings from his commanders. Would he have been willing to doom unknown numbers of sailors and to cripple the Pacific Fleet in order to lure Japan into shooting first? Nations about to launch wars do not usually conspire to inflict massive devastation on their armed forces at the outset. Also, assuming that the president was picking a fight, why was it necessary to leave the fleet in harm's way? As Butow explains:

> "If he [Roosevelt] had known, beforehand, that the Japanese were about to attack Pearl Harbor, it would have been *in character* for him to order the Fleet to sea to investigate and to forestall. One side or the other would then have fired a first shot, and we would have found ourselves at war. If the two naval forces had somehow managed to miss each other, the Japanese would have attacked the Philippines and other American outposts in the Pacific, just as they did on the day they struck at Pearl Harbor, and once again—simply because they had launched hostilities against American territory—we would have found ourselves at war. Roosevelt did not need to resort to a stratagem designed to get the United States into the conflict in Europe by enticing the Japanese into bombing Pearl Harbor. They had already made their own decision to go to war with the Americans, the British, and the Dutch. Early in December 1941 they carried out their plans with deadly effectiveness without any help from the President of the United States. If Roosevelt had known their secrets, if he had received any report at all that they were about to mount a surprise attack against Pearl Harbor, he would have derived enormous pleasure from setting a trap for them.

Perhaps the revisionist persuasion endures and enjoys wide popular appeal because it offers the satisfying illusion that the dire events of 1941 were firmly under American control. In that sense, an analogy might be drawn between the

Pearl Harbor debate and the controversy that erupted a decade later over "Who lost China?" At that time, a popularly held view in America was that the Communist revolution which overran China could be amply explained by the machinations of a misguided or treacherous pro-Communist clique in the U.S. State Department rather than by great historical forces at work in China.

I have tried to suggest that the roots of the Pacific conflict lead us most fruitfully to China, to the long years of struggle with emerging Chinese nationalism, back through the eight-year war, back to the Manchurian affair, back to the war with Russia (fought over Chinese territory, after all), back at least as far as 1894. In that year, Japan, adapting commendably to world pressures and learning well all the West had to teach about survival in the imperialist era, launched its own search for empire—at the expense of China. For America to have shaped events in the Far East in the half-century following 1894, it would have had to commit itself to a China policy far more constructive and forceful than the platitudes of the open-door notes and the Stimson doctrine—"brandishing a wooden pistol," said State Department historian Herbert Feis of the Stimson policy. For all of America's interest in China, for all the myth of the great China market, the reality was that America simply did not see China as an area where American national interests were vitally engaged. It was not until China's fate became tied to the fate of the Allied free world in 1940, a very late moment in history from the point of view of Japan, that the United States earnestly sought to contain Japan's appetite on the mainland and, then, with Hull's demarche of November 26, 1941, to effect Japan's complete withdrawal.

"History is lived forwards but it is written in retrospect. We know the end before we consider the beginning. . . ."

—C. V. Wedgewood.

"Pearl Harbor remains disquieting as one of history's Halloween tricks— or, more respectably, a paradox. It teaches a lesson we cannot learn, for surprise, by definition, is the danger no one thought of."

—Naomi Bliven.

ADDITIONAL READING

The road to Pearl Harbor corpus of literature is so large that some annotated bibliographic essays may be helpful. For example, Waldo Heinrichs, "The Middle Years, 1900–1945, and the Question of a Large U.S. Policy for East Asia," in Warren I. Cohen, ed., *New Frontiers in American–East Asian Relations* (1983); and Louis Morton, "1937–1945," in Ernest R. May and James C. Thomson, Jr., eds., *American–East Asian Relations: A Survey* (1972).

The writings of Robert J. C. Butow constitute a very rich and balanced account of the subject, and I have relied on them extensively. Though written more than thirty years ago, *Tojo and the Coming of the War* (1961) remains a masterpiece of lucid and painstaking scholarship as does Butow's more specialized study of the curious yet pivotally important characters in *The John Doe Associates: Backdoor Diplomacy for Peace* (1981).

Among the most valuable general overviews of the crisis years in U.S.-Japanese relations are Herbert Feis, *The Road to Pearl Harbor: The Coming of the War Between the United States and Japan* (1950); David J. Lu, *From the Marco Polo Bridge to Pearl Harbor: Japan's Entry into World War II* (1961); John Toland, *The Rising Sun: The Decline and the Fall of the Japanese Empire, 1936–1945* (1970); Michael Slackman, *Target: Pearl Harbor* (1990); and Ienaga Saburo, *The Pacific War: World War II and the Japanese Empire, 1931–1945* (1978).

Almost in a class by itself is an 800-page treasurehouse of essays edited by Dorothy Borg and Shumpei Okamoto, *Pearl Harbor as History: Japanese-American Relations, 1931–1941* (1973). In their book, the two editors pair essays written by Americans and Japanese on such topics as the role of the U.S./Japanese navies; the role of the U.S./Japanese armies; the influence of private groups in the United States and Japan; U.S./Japanese press attitudes; and economic and financial considerations in the two countries.

More specialized studies include Michael A. Barnhart, *Japan Prepares for Total War: The Search for Economic Security, 1919–1941* (1987), based on thorough research in archives on both sides of the Pacific; Paul W. Schroeder, *The Axis Alliance and Japanese–Americans Relations, 1941* (1958); John J. Stephan, *Hawaii Under the Rising Sun: Japan's Plans for Conquest after Pearl Harbor* (1984); and Ladislas Farago, *The Broken Seal: The Story of 'Operation Magic' and the Pearl Harbor Disaster* (1967).

Two valuable collections of essays edited by James W. Morley were originally published by Japanese authors in Japanese: *The Fateful Choice: Japan's Advance into Southeast Asia, 1939–1941* (1980) and *Deterrent Diplomacy: Japan, Germany, and the USSR, 1935–1940* (1976). *Japan's Decision for War: Records of the 1941 Policy Conferences* (1967) are translations and annotations by Nobutaka Ike of the records of important high-level meetings of Japanese military and civilian leaders in the year prior to Pearl Harbor.

The most important of the revisionist studies is John Toland, *Infamy: Pearl Harbor and Its Aftermath* (1982). Earlier volumes in the revisionist mold include: Rear Admiral Robert A. Theobald, *The Final Secret of Pearl Harbor* (1954); Charles A. Beard, *President Roosevelt and the Coming of the War, 1941* (1948); and Charles C. Tansill, cited in the text, *Back Door to War* (1952). Recent additions to the school include James Rusbridger and Eric Nave, *Betrayal at Pearl Harbor: How Churchill Lured Roosevelt into World War II* (1991); Robert Smith Thompson, *A Time for War: Franklin D. Roosevelt and the Path to Pearl Harbor* (1991); and William H. Honan, *Visions of Infamy: The Untold Story of How Journalist Hector C. Bywater Devised the Plans That Led to Pearl Harbor* (1991).

Roberta Wohlstetter's salient antirevisionist contribution, *Pearl Harbor: Warning and Decision* (1962) is discussed in the text. Two monumental studies by Gordon Prange constitute the best detailed responses to points raised by revisionist writers. The product of thirty-seven years of research, these two volumes were published after Prange's death in 1980. They are *At Dawn We Slept: The Untold Story of Pearl Harbor* (1981) and *Pearl Harbor: The Verdict of History* (1986). A recent work edited by Hilary Conroy and Harry Wray, *Pearl Harbor Reexamined: Prologue to the Pacific War* (1990), examines many issues raised by the revisionists. Rear Admiral Edwin T. Layton's *And I Was There: Pearl Harbor and Midway: Breaking the Secrets* (1985) does not fit easily into the revisionist or nonrevisionist categories but is a masterful account of the problem of communications within large organizations by an intelligence community insider who was exceptionally familiar with prewar Japan. Two important review articles deserve special mention for their insights: David Kahn, "Did FDR Invite the Pearl Harbor Attack?" *New York Review of Books* (May 27, 1982) and Robert J. C. Butow's review of books by Gordon Prange and John Toland in the *Journal of Japanese Studies* (Summer 1983).

7

WAR IN THE PACIFIC

The attack on Pearl Harbor dealt a stunning blow to American naval power in the Pacific. It was a "disaster, but it could have been a catastrophe," historian John Toland wrote. Catastrophe was avoided because of the fortunate disposition of U.S. aircraft carriers, safely at sea on the morning of December 7, 1941. It would be carriers far more than battleships which would be decisive in naval engagements with Japan in the Pacific. Additionally, the Japanese had blundered in not bombing the oil storage tanks and the submarine pens on that fateful Sunday morning.

More importantly, however, the attack on Pearl Harbor failed to achieve its larger strategic objective. Japanese planners, mindful of how isolationist the United States public and Congress had been and convinced that Americans had little stomach for war, calculated that a dramatic victory at Pearl Harbor, followed by a string of successes throughout the Pacific, would weaken the enemy's resolve. This proved to be a monumental miscalculation. Americans were outraged by the surprise attack and the news of the more than 2400 men killed. For jolting the slumbering American public into a mood of revenge, one Japanese naval officer later observed that "President Roosevelt should have pinned medals on us." When the president appeared before Congress on December 8 to speak of the "date which will live in infamy" and ask for a declaration of war, only one dissenting vote was recorded. Before the week was out, the United States and Germany had exchanged declarations of war. The neutralist mood of the previous decade gave way at once to a spirit of national solidarity and determination without precedent in U.S. history. In decades to come, after American involvement in a costly war in Korea and a costly and unpopular war in Vietnam, most Americans agreed that World War II was the last "good war."

MOBILIZING AMERICA

This unity of purpose helps to explain the immensely successful economic mobilization of the country, which became such an important factor in the eventual Allied victory over Japan. Japanese military strategists were imbued with the traditional samurai warrior's ethic which emphasized "spiritual" virtues, courage and discipline, over material factors such as weapons and industrial capacity. They therefore tended to assume that Japanese armies, though not as well armed and equipped, would in the end prevail over the "soft," comfort-addicted Americans.

Few of these strategists, however, could have foreseen the explosion of productive energies and the massive growth in manufacturing capacity which would occur in the United States. To mention only a few examples, U.S. shipyards were launching formidable navies each year of the war as shipbuilders like the legendary Henry Kaiser used revolutionary prefabrication techniques to trim the time necessary for building 10,000-ton "Liberty ships" to a record seventeen days from keel-laying to launch; smaller merchant ships required less than five days. By 1943, ten million tons of vessels were launched, about forty times the prewar level. On untilled land outside of Detroit, Henry Ford constructed a mile-long factory—the Grand Canyon of the mechanized world, Charles Lindbergh called it—to fabricate bombers. Few believed Ford's promise that he would make one bomber an hour, but by 1943, his Willow Run plant was exceeding that goal. Aircraft production of all types reached a staggering ninety-six thousand planes in 1944. Japanese production in that year was only twenty-eight thousand planes, below the loss rate, and in the following year production slumped drastically. When a special investigatory bureau of the Japanese government was set up to survey national resources in the spring of 1945, it discovered that steel production was less than 100,000 tons per month; U.S. production was more than ten times greater. During the war years, Japan became dependent on imports of rubber from Malaya and the Dutch East Indies; when they were cut back, the largely undeveloped synthetic rubber technology could not fill the breech. In America, a staggering 866,000 tons of synthetic rubber was being produced by the end of the war. Matching this growth in output was an enormous leap in technology—in aeronautics, radar, rocketry, computers, and mass-produced antibiotics, all of which would play an important role in the Allied victory.

Even the movie industry mobilized. Hollywood contributed to the war effort, not simply by selling war bonds but by creating indelible images of the Japanese as fanatic, bestial, and bent on world conquest. The successful director Frank Capra was persuaded by Army Chief of Staff George Marshall to lend his talents to the production of a series of seven propaganda films. Collectively known as

Why We Fight, the documentaries were intended as training films for recruits but on Roosevelt's urging were released to public theaters as well. Capra took miles of both enemy and friendly newsreel footage and edited it into a spirited, unequivocal vision of the free world locked in combat with the forces of darkness. If convincing footage was not available, Capra improvised. Thus, Americans watched contrived scenes of a "conquering Jap army" marching down Pennsylvania Avenue in Washington, D.C. while a narrator recalled similar episodes in Nanking, Hong Kong, and Manila and warned of the "field day" the Imperial Army would have in America.

Similarly, the series portrayed the Japanese as a regimented mass of puppets, totally devoid of individuality. Here, there was ample undoctored footage to document the point. Japan's own newsreels were replete with monotonously repetitive scenes of synchronized obeisance to the emperor and the intonation of patriotic slogans in praise of the monolith: "100 million hearts beating as one." These images, as historian John W. Dower notes in his pathbreaking study of wartime racism, *War Without Mercy*, "did violence to a complex people and society, and diminished and dehumanized the Japanese in Western eyes." Dower, however, draws the following important distinction:

> It was not that the Japanese people were, in actuality, homogeneous and harmonious, devoid of individuality and thoroughly subordinated to the group, but rather that the Japanese ruling groups were constantly exhorting them to become so. Indeed, the government deemed it necessary to draft and propagate a rigid orthodoxy of this sort precisely because the ruling classes were convinced that a great many Japanese did not cherish the more traditional virtues of loyalty and filial piety under the emperor, but instead remained attracted to more democratic values and ideals.

WARTIME DETENTION OF JAPANESE AMERICANS

Americans, as we have seen, were outraged at Japan for their surprise attack on Pearl Harbor. At the same time, they were shocked to learn how unprepared the nation was and determined to "Remember Pearl Harbor"— to make certain that America was not caught off-guard again. From these twin responses flowed an altogether unwarranted conclusion that Japanese Americans, many of them citizens of the United States, were *as a group* a menace to national security and therefore subject to detention in special camps for the duration of the war. President Franklin Roosevelt's Executive Order 9066, signed on February 19, 1942, provided for mass evacuation from their homes and detention of West-Coast Japanese Americans. After hearings lasting less than one hour, both houses of Congress passed legislation the next month to back the president's orders with criminal sanctions. Those affected by the order were the approximately 117,000 persons of Japanese ancestry (defined as anyone with as little as one-eighth Japanese blood) living in the coastal states of California, Oregon, and Washington plus the southwestern corner of Arizona. The vast majority of Nisei living in the continental United States lived in the target areas. Of those affected by the order, approximately two-thirds were native born and, by virtue of that fact, U.S. citizens. The remainder were aliens, "enemy aliens" after December 7, people born in Japan and therefore, under the discriminatory legislation of earlier years, ineligible for American citizenship. No similar wholesale evacuations of other "enemy aliens" such as Germans or Italians were ordered.

PEARL HARBOR PANIC

Contributing to the perception of the Nisei as citizens of doubtful loyalty was the wave of near hysteria that swept the West Coast in the weeks after December 7. The fear was that the Japanese Americans, commonly called Nisei,[1] were "fifth columnists," agents loyal to their ancestral homeland rather than to America. For Americans unsure of the difference between Chinese and Japanese, *Time* and *Life* magazines obliged with pictures and a short course in comparative ethnic anatomy.

Many, it was thought, were planning acts of sabotage or espionage—the image of Nisei as fanatics "who will tie dynamite around their waist and make a human bomb out of themselves" was typical. Nisei could be counted on, it was said, to aid the Japanese military, who were probably planning air or naval bombardment or perhaps even an invasion of the American mainland. At the time, it could not be known for certain what we now know: No operations worthy of the name were planned. With the most minor of exceptions, Japanese military power never touched continental America. The minor exceptions included some hydrogen-filled paper balloons which carried a payload of small incendiary bombs. Most vanished before reaching their destination, but a few rode the eastbound jet stream all the way to Oregon where some minor forest fires resulted. One was eventually carried as far as Iowa, where it startled picknickers. In addition, some shells were lobbed onto some beach-front oil wells near Santa Barbara by an off-shore submarine in February 1942. The famous "Great Los Angeles Air Raid" of February 26, 1942, (later the subject of a movie) never occurred in spite of the *Los Angeles Times* dramatic account of "foreign aircraft flying both in large formation and singly" over the night sky. There *was* a heavy barrage of antiaircraft fire, and the shells raining down on the city did cause some damage and injuries; and there *were* fatalities—several people were killed in auto accidents as drivers careened around in the blacked-out city. However, no Japanese planes were anywhere near the West Coast. Still, wartime confusion and apprehension often adds up to panic.

This would seem to account for the scoop in the *San Francisco Chronicle* that Japanese planes were seen on a reconnaissance mission *inside* the city's Golden Gate on the first night after Pearl Harbor. Lest there be any doubt about the

---

[1] Nisei, literally "second generation," became in common parlance a generic synonym for all Japanese Americans. I will use it in that way here unless there is reason to be more precise in referring to "Issei" (first generation), "Sansei" (third generation), and so on.

HOW TO TELL YOUR FRIENDS FROM THE JAPS
"Virtually all Japanese are short. Japanese are likely to be stockier and broader-hipped than short Chinese. Japanese are seldom fat; they often dry up and grow lean as they age. Although both have the typical epicanthic fold of the upper eyelid, Japanese eyes are usually set closer together. The Chinese expression is likely to be more placid, kindly, open; the Japanese more positive, dogmatic, arrogant. Japanese are hesitant, nervous in conversation, laugh loudly at the wrong time. Japanese walk stiffly erect, hard heeled. Chinese, more relaxed, have an easy gait, sometimes shuffle."

—*Time*, December 22, 1941.

sightings, General John DeWitt, the commanding officer of the Western Defense Command at the San Francisco Presidio, confirmed them. Addressing skeptics, the general said,

> You people do not seem to realize we are at war. So get this: Last night there were planes over this community. They were enemy planes. I mean Japanese planes. And they were tracked out to sea. You think it was a hoax? It is damned nonsense for sensible people to think that the army and navy would practice such a hoax on San Francisco.

In coming weeks, the FBI, local police offices, and military intelligence agencies were swamped with reports from concerned citizens who claimed that they knew of Nisei who were acting suspiciously. Some were said to be spies, some were flashing light signals or making illegal radio transmissions to Japanese ships lurking off the coast. One Nisei in Hawaii was reported to have trained his dog to bark in Morse code from an isolated beach. Americans had been conditioned to believe rumors of Japanese treachery by decades of fast-and-loose racist reporting by the popular press. Those innocent-appearing Japanese American fishermen in Monterey? They weren't really fishermen. At night, they donned their Imperial Navy uniforms and bowed toward the emperor's palace in Tokyo. No convincing evidence of such a scenario was ever put forward but the fact that the *Saturday Evening Post* and other magazines and newspapers printed such stories lent credence.

A few made light of the Army's jittery nerves. *San Francisco Chronicle* columnist Herb Caen dismissed the report of Japanese aircraft flying inside the city's landmark Golden Gate Bridge on the grounds that no one could possibly get across the bridge without paying a toll.

In December 1941, it took only a little random journalistic gossip to convince housewives in some areas that they shouldn't buy tomatoes that had supposedly been dusted with arsenic by murderous Nisei truck farmers. In the vicinity of Los Angeles, Nisei had allegedly planted their crops in such a way that when viewed from the air they would form a giant arrow pointing directly at strategic targets like the Lockheed aircraft plant in Burbank; similar stories surfaced near every major West Coast city. Everyone knew about the Nisei milkmen in Honolulu who allegedly pulled machine guns out of their delivery trucks on the morning of December 7 and opened fire on the defenders, and of the Nisei drivers in Seattle who stalled their cars in order to block vital traffic lanes leading to sensitive dock areas. The Bonneville Dam incident carried especially frightening implications. The power lines there had been "sabotaged." J. Edgar Hoover, director of the FBI, chastised the army for "losing its head" and cited the Bonneville Dam scare as one of the army's "false alarms." The "sabotage" was caused by cattle scratching their backs on the wires, the FBI revealed.

More than a thousand such cases were investigated by the FBI and other agencies who bent the search-and-seizure rules out of shape in their determination to find incriminating evidence. None was found. Not a single conviction for espionage, sabotage, or disloyalty was obtained from this flurry of reports. To be sure, there were security risks among the Japanese community in the United States and hundreds of them, including both citizens of Japan and Japanese Americans, were picked up *on an individual basis* by the FBI immediately after Pearl Harbor. Most were detained for the war. Hoover, never widely celebrated as a civil libertarian, argued that this selective approach was adequate, and the mass evacuation of Japanese could not be justified on security grounds. The claim of military necessity for mass evacuation, he said, was based "primarily upon public and political pressure rather than on factual data." As for the reports of illicit radio transmissions, an official of the Federal Communications Commission allowed that he had "never seen an organization that was so incompetent to cope with radio intelligence requirements" as DeWitt's Military Intelligence Division. "As a matter of fact," the FCC official went on, "the army air stations have been reported by the Signal Corps station as Jap enemy stations."

Nevertheless, public sentiment continued to be inflamed by a wave of racist attacks on the Nisei from a wide range of government and media personalities. All ignored the critical distinction between the Japanese who had attacked the United States and Japanese Americans who were entitled to protection under the Constitution. "A viper is nonetheless a viper wherever the egg is hatched—so the Japanese American, born of Japanese parents, grows up to be a Japanese not an American," the Coast's most influential newspaper, the *Los Angeles Times*, stated. "I am for the immediate removal of every Japanese on the West Coast to a point deep in the interior. Herd 'em up, pack 'em off and give 'em the inside room in the badlands," a well-known Hearst columnist wrote, adding, "Personally, I hate the Japanese. And that goes for all of them." Senator Tom Stewart (Tennessee) rose to the floor of the U.S. Senate to assert that:

> They [the Japanese] are cowardly and immoral. They are different from Americans in every conceivable way, and no Japanese . . . should have the right to claim American citizenship. . . . A Jap is a Jap anywhere you find him, and his taking the oath of allegiance to this country would not help, even if he should be permitted to do so. They do not believe in God and have no respect for an oath.

The views of General DeWitt, in charge of defense preparations on the West Coast, would play a central role in the push for evacuation. DeWitt, a sixty-one-year-old career officer, was due to retire after his tour of duty in San Francisco and was doubtless affected by the prevailing "Pearl Harbor panic." It is understandable that, in the twilight of his career, he did not wish to have his reputation blemished by charges of dereliction of duty of the kind that faced the military commanders in Hawaii who had been dismissed from their posts in disgrace on December 16. It was entirely proper for the general to be on the alert for possible air raids. One has to sympathize with his frustration in persuading unconcerned West-Coast urban residents to drop their business-as-usual mentality and take seriously air raid drills and blackout orders. Even Alcatraz, the federal prison situated in the middle of San Francisco Bay, ignored the blackout and remained a brightly lit beacon on December 8.

"A JAP IS A JAP"

After due allowance is made for hysteria, however, there remained a virulent prejudice at the core of DeWitt's views of Japanese Americans. Testifying in Washington concerning enemy aliens in general, DeWitt said that Germans and Italians could be treated as individuals, but "a Jap is a Jap." Later in the war, when a Congressional committee was looking into the possibility of allowing Nisei to return to their homes, DeWitt explained to them that "The Japanese race is an enemy race." He said, "The racial strains remain undiluted," even among the second- and third-generation Japanese who were born in the United States. He assured the legislators that they need not worry about Germans or Italians ("except in certain cases"), "but the Japs we will be worried about all the time until they are wiped off the face of the map."

Strident appeals for relocation of course were issued by nativist organizations such as the Native Sons and Daughters of the Golden West, which had long sought to "keep California white" by trumpeting the "yellow peril" theme. Calls for mass evacuation also came from "the best people in California," DeWitt claimed, including the state's attorney general (and later the chief justice of the U.S. Supreme Court), Earl Warren. Japanese Americans had been indoctrinated by the idea of Japanese imperialism, Warren told a gathering of sheriffs and district attorneys in early February before the relocation order had been issued by FDR. "They approved of the military conquests of Japan, including the conquest of America," Warren insisted.

When confronted with the unsettling fact that no instances of fifth-column activities or sabotage were being committed by Japanese Americans, Warren explained that "It looks very much to me as though it is a studied effort not to have any until the zero hour arrives." Echoing Warren's concern was the editor of the small-town *Red Bluff Daily News* in northern California He advised his readers to "Refuse to believe any of their [Japanese-American] protestations of loyalty to the American flag. You can't trust a Jap, and the best U.S. flag waver is probably the one with the most dynamite buried in his back yard." The editor concluded, "This is no time to tolerate rattlesnakes in the parlor."

This kind of reasoning, which left the Nisei damned if they did and damned if they did not betray their country, became a staple in the rhetoric of the day. Liberal newspaper columnist Walter Lippmann, perhaps the nation's most prestigious political commentator, lent his credentials to the argument in his syndicated column. Dismissing the fact that no sabotage had been reported, Lippman said, "It is a sign that the blow is well-organized and that it is held back until it can be struck with maximum effect." In a letter to the White House, Attorney General Francis Biddle blasted the media in general, and Lippman in particular, for acting like "Junior G-Men" in predicting a Japanese attack and widespread Nisei sabotage when all indications were to the contrary. "It comes close to shouting FIRE! in the theater; and if race riots occur, these writers will bear a heavy responsibility," the attorney general warned the president.

Behind the panic and the naked racism, however, were the familiar under-currents of the long-standing discrimination against Nisei on economic grounds. Farmers who resented the inroads made in truck gardening by the industrious Japanese and fishing interests who resented Japanese competition were quick to appreciate the opportunity which the relocation program offered them. An official of the influential California Vegetable Grower–Shipper Association was uncommonly forthright in his admission:

> We're charged with wanting to get rid of the Japs for selfish reasons. We might as well be honest. We do want to get rid of them. It's a question of whether the white man lives on the Pacific Coast or the brown man. They came into this valley to work [that is, as paid laborers] and they stayed on here to take over.

"And we don't want them back after the war ends either," echoed another spokesman of the organization.

The silence of national liberal organizations further eroded the chance for fair treatment of the Nisei. The American Civil Liberties Union (ACLU), for example, made little effort to defend the Japanese Americans until after the evacuation order was being implemented. Even the Japanese American Citizens League (JACL), the main organization representing the interests of Nisei, failed to protest the evacuation. While a few of its leaders favored resistance to the government, the official position of the JACL became one of cooperation. Indeed, by the end of the war, the JACL leadership was not merely acquiescing to the reality of internment, some of its leaders found themselves actively collaborating with government intelligence agencies and acting as informers on Japanese Americans suspected of disloyalty. In this way, the internment policy created some long-standing and bitter divisions within the Nisei community.

The decision to go along with the government's policy, JACL leaders hoped, would demonstrate conclusively that Japanese Americans were patriotic, whereas resistance to Washington's orders would only fuel charges that Japanese Americans were disloyal. In addition, as the organization's National Secretary Mike Masaoka testified to Congress, compliance with the relocation policy made sense from the standpoint of the personal welfare of the Nisei "because we may be subject to mob violence and otherwise if we are permitted to remain." This notion, along with the military security rationale, was to become a major justification of the government's decision to round up the Nisei. Decades later, when the issue of compensation for the wartime wrongs to Japanese Americans came up for discussion, critics of the plan frequently argued that the relocation was "for their own good." To most Japanese Americans, the argument was not convincing. To be compelled to spend nine hundred days living behind barbed wire to demonstrate loyalty and gain safety from violent abuse did not seem like the American way. That there were many Nisei who felt that the camps provided safety cannot be doubted. However, as historian Roger Daniels comments, "Surely no sadder comment on wartime democracy in America can be made than that thousands of her own people had been conditioned by mistreatment to prefer a Tule Lake [a detention camp in northern California] to freedom."

HAKKO ICHIU

In the opening months of the war, evidence of Allied might was hard to find. After being mired down for more than four years in the stalemated China war, exhilaration replaced despair in Japan as the Imperial Army and Navy rolled on to one victory after another in an arc of land and sea stretching from the Indian frontier to the bleak Aleutian Islands in the northern Pacific. In 1940, the government of Japan had revived an ancient expression to give voice to its goals. *Hakko ichiu*, attributed to Japan's first emperor, Jimmu, spoke of the world being "under one roof." The phrase could be interpreted to mean a universal brotherhood of peace and harmony. Now *hakko ichiu* took on more strident tones of manifest destiny. "The key to victory lies in a faith in victory. . . . As long as there remains under the policy of *Hakko ichiu* this great spirit of loyalty and patriotism, we have nothing to fear," declared Prime Minister Tojo Hideki. If there were Japanese who doubted the wisdom of a challenge to the Western powers in those days, their voices were muffled. The distinguished novelist Ito Sei reflected the exhilaration of the day when he spoke of the war as a struggle of the "Yamato people . . . to convince themselves from the bottom of their hearts that they are the most excellent people on the face of the globe. We are the 'yellow race' our enemies talk about. We are fighting to determine the superiority or inferiority of the discriminated-against peoples."

It is worth stressing here that the Sino–Japanese War and the Pacific War were both seen not simply as measures to check Western economic and political presence in Asia, but as measures to cleanse the Japanese mind of harmful Western modes of thought as well. In the late thirties, Japanese spokesmen for the "New Order" repeatedly emphasized the need for ending the "long period of dependence on and copying after the West." John W. Dower explains how the Japanese public became comfortable applying "sweeping cultural clichés" (materialistic, hedonistic, exploitative, selfish) to Westerners just as Westerners adjusted easily to their own stereotype adjectives for the Japanese (regimented, treacherous, bestial, fanatic).

Guam and Wake, island outposts in the central Pacific, fell to Japan before the month of December was over. Resistance in the Philippines lasted much longer. Although the Rising Sun flag was hoisted over government buildings in Manila on January 2, 1942, it was not until May 6 that the last American and Filipino defenders on the fortified island of Corregidor in Manila Bay surrendered. On orders from President Roosevelt, General Douglas MacArthur escaped to the safety of Australia, where he began to organize an Allied drive to make good his dramatic pledge, "I shall return." Filipino guerrilla resistance continued from the scattered islands, but MacArthur's large Filipino reserve army had proved to be illusory, untrained, and poorly equipped.

Meanwhile, the British and Dutch Far Eastern empires came under assault. The attack on Hong Kong came simultaneously with the Pearl Harbor attack, and on Christmas Day the crown colony surrendered. On December 10, the pride of the British fleet, the new battleship HMS *Prince of Wales* and the cruiser *Repulse*, patrolling off the coast of Malaya to deter the Japanese, were sent to the bottom by waves of bombing and torpedo attacks from the air. In the space of a little over two hours on that day, Japanese pilots proved that control of the seas no longer rested with capital ships possessing the biggest guns and the thickest armor—the two doomed ships had been the largest Allied vessels in the Western Pacific. "In my whole experience, I do not remember any naval blow so heavy or so painful," Churchill told Parliament.

Japanese jungle troops then marched down the Malayan peninsula, source of most of the world's natural rubber, and by the end of January were poised at the seventy-foot causeway which led to the fortress city of Singapore, home port of the British Far East Fleet, and keystone of the British Empire in Asia. Churchill was stunned to learn—only then—that the main defenses of "impregnable" Singapore, its great coastal batteries, were all pointed seaward and could not be turned around to repel an invasion from the peninsula side of the island. Nevertheless, the British prime minister ordered the city defended to the death. "No surrender can be contemplated," Churchill ordered. Nonetheless, with arms and even water supplies exhausted, Singapore capitulated on February 15. The surrender of the eighty-five thousand-man garrison on that day by General Sir Arthur Percival may have been the single worst military disaster any European nation had ever suffered in Asia. One British soldier quipped that, "A British soldier is equal to ten Japanese, but unfortunately there are eleven Japanese." In fact, however, the Singapore victory was all the sweeter for General Yamashita Tomoyuki because his forces were numerically far inferior to the British.

Three weeks later, the Netherlands lost the island empire it had been building for four hundred years as the Dutch East Indies were overrun. With the capture of the oil-rich islands of Java and Borneo, a major strategic objective of the Japanese military had been achieved. For the first time in its history, the Japanese Empire had its own source of petroleum.

Back on the Asian mainland, all of French Indochina had come under Japanese control. Siam, which had only recently changed its name to Thailand (Land of the Free), the only nation in Southeast Asia to survive the colonial era with its independence, yielded to Japanese pressure. After mere hours of token resistance on Pearl Harbor day, Thailand permitted its territory to be occupied by the Imperial Army. To the west, the British, aided by Chinese troops and a small force of Americans under the command of the redoubtable General Joseph W. ("Vinegar Joe") Stilwell, were compelled to march out of Burma in the spring of 1942. The Burma retreat allowed Japan to cut the Burma Road supply line to China and to threaten India, one of the Allies' "two vital flanks." The other flank, Australia, was also under threat of air attack and perhaps invasion from bases secured by Japan in New Guinea. Both Indians and Australians were being invited by propaganda broadcasts to find their "proper place" in the Greater East Asia Co-Prosperity Sphere.

For the Americans, the trickle of "good news" to come out of the war in these early months was simply erroneous or fabricated by journalists and military censors anxious to brace sagging morale on the home front. Americans took heart in the first week of the war to learn about the daring exploits of Captain Colin Kelly Jr., the first superhero of the war. Kelly had supposedly made an audacious solo bombing run on the battleship *Haruna* and sent it to the bottom in the Philippine Sea—by diving his B-17 into the *Haruna*'s smokestack in the most popular version of the incident. Only later was it confirmed that the *Haruna* was 1500 miles away from Kelly and that no ships had been sunk or even badly damaged by the American pilot who died when his plane was shot down.

From Wake Island came the news of two weeks of gallant resistance by the outnumbered defenders of the important outpost. That much was certainly correct, but what heartened Americans most was word that the beleaguered marines, when asked what they needed, replied "Send us more Japs." It was only after the war was over that the legendary message was shown to be a myth. The true story of the last moments of Wake was stirring enough but full of confusing images. After the island's garrison fought on the beach down to their last bullet, Major James Devereux raised the white flag, a white rag actually, attached to a mop handle and surrendered to a Japanese officer who promptly offered him a cigarette and recalled that he had enjoyed attending the San Francisco World's Fair in 1939.

> CIVILIAN SKEPTICS IN TOKYO
> "The first announcement from the Tokyo army command was that nine planes had been downed. It was . . . a fine, clear spring day, and no one in the city had observed the downing of a single plane. Perhaps, the joke had it, the defenders of the city meant that they had succeded in shooting empty air. The Japanese are great punsters, and the words for 'nine planes' and 'thin air' are homophonous."
>
> —Edward G. Seidensticker, *Tokyo Rising*.

One genuine, if largely symbolic, American triumph in the early stages of the war came with a surprise air raid against the home islands only four months after Pearl Harbor, on April 18,1942. On that day, Colonel James Doolittle led eighty fliers in sixteen medium bombers on a raid over Tokyo and three other cities. As a civilian, Doolittle had a reputation as a stunt pilot (first to land a plane blind-folded) and winner of long-distance trophies. Now in 1942, Doolittle had a mis-sion which would tap his daredevil expertise—getting normally land-based medium bombers airborne within the 750-foot run of the tossing decks of the aircraft carrier *Hornet*. The task was accomplished, and the air raid had an elec-trifying effect on American morale at a time when, as we have seen, the war was not going well for the Allied cause. The Doolittle raid caused only minor phys-ical damage to Japan, but it stunned an overconfident leadership into an aware-ness of Japan's future vulnerability. It was only after the Doolittle attack that the Imperial Army, always more concerned about expanding Japan's power on the mainland, came to support the Imperial Navy's plans for taking bold initia-tives in the Pacific. It was only after the Doolittle attack that the Japanese high command began to think seriously about the need to actually seize the Hawaiian Islands to effectively destroy American power in the Pacific.

CONQUEST OR LIBERATION?

The word *collaboration* had an especially ugly ring to it during the European phase of World War II. French citizens, for example, who collabo-rated with the Germans were treated none too gently when the war ended. The perfidy of the Norwegian collaborator Vidkun Quisling was so widely recog-nized that his name, like Judas, stayed in the language as a generic word for traitor. Collaboration with the Japanese, however, did not always lead to dis-grace. Peoples in the way of Japan's imperial expansion did not in every instance see themselves as victims. Some of those conquered by Japan felt less overrun than liberated—at least in the beginning. The arrival of Japanese armies in the countries of Southeast Asia meant the beginning of the end of Western colonialism, and the spectacle of the yellow race inflicting defeat on

Western colonial powers was psychologically satisfying to many Asian nationalists. "We learned in this way that [our] white masters and the white men in general were not by nature superior, and that Asians could easily remove them," one Indonesian wrote. Arriving in the vast Indonesian archipelago with almost no military government personnel, the Japanese were obliged to turn to native Indonesians to fill the formerly Dutch-staffed bureaucracy. As a student of Indonesian history comments,

> It became apparent to many that the skills of the Dutch colonial official who for so long they had been taught to regard as their superior, were well within the compass of their own abilities. This realization engendered a powerful self-confidence, which increased their belief in their ability to govern themselves.

As a result, in one occupied country after another, collaboration with the Japanese did not constitute a handicap for local nationalists bent upon building a popular power base. A few, like Sukarno in the Dutch East Indies (later named Indonesia) and Aung San in Burma, went on to lead their countries toward independence after the war. Jose P. Laurel, who served as president of the Japanese-sponsored "Republic of the Philippines," continued to play a prominent role in Filipino politics after the war, and his son Salvador (Doy) Laurel was vice president in the 1980s. Benigno Aquino actively collaborated with Japan, saying "We belong to the East." His daughter-in-law, Corazon, later became president. Similarly esteemed, in spite of his collaboration with the Japanese, was the Indian patriot Subhas Chandra Bose, who formed the Indian National Army under the aegis of Japan in 1943 with the intention of leading it into India as part of a great Japanese offensive to drive the British out. His plans were dashed by the reversals suffered by the Japanese in the Burma theater in 1944, and he died in an airplane crash on Taiwan near the end of the war. Nevertheless, both Nehru and Gandhi, political rivals of Bose, saw him as a patriot, and millions of his countrymen still regard him with reverence.

In the end, however, Japan squandered much of the good will it earned as natives of "liberated" territories learned that Japanese overlords could be just as arrogant and cruel as the white man. Girls and women, either because of privation or brute force, were compelled to prostitute themselves in every nation overrun by Japan. "Rape was an accepted prerogative of the Imperial Army," one Japanese historian writes. The grand promise of "Asia for the Asians" was soon seen as concealing an underlying reality of exploitation of weak Asians by strong Japanese. As the war progressed and Japan's industrial needs expanded, the Empire found it necessary to develop the lands of the Greater East Asia Co-Prosperity Sphere as supply bases for vitally needed natural resources. Indonesians, Malays, Burmese, and other peoples suffered grievously as they were torn from their villages as conscript laborers. Extremely harsh methods of requisition of men and materials, plundering of local resources, vile working conditions, and high death rates provoked resistance from the natives. That, in turn, prompted

Japanese military police (the dreaded *Kempeitai*) to adopt cruel measures to intimidate local populations into submission. "The rumor was that if the *Kempeitai* took you away, that was the end. You would not come back alive. They wanted everyone quaking with fear," wrote one Indonesian.

The construction of the 258-mile-long Thai–Burma Railroad as a supply route for Japanese forces was a particularly grim example of the use of forced-labor "sweat armies." This project went on for three years beginning in 1942 in torrid heat and driving monsoons. The disease-ridden jungles took their toll, as did brutal guards, starvation diets, exhaustion, and air raids. The project became well known in the West after the war thanks to the book and 1957 movie *Bridge on the River Kwai* which portrayed the pitiful condition of the Allied prisoners of war who worked on the "railroad of death." Of the approximately sixty thousands POWs, mostly British and Australian, almost one-quarter perished. A far larger number of Indonesian, Burmese, Malayan, and other Asian laborers were recruited to work on the project, and among this group the death toll may have reached into six figures. Resentment of Japan's wartime behavior fuels outbursts of violent anti-Japanese anger even today in Jakarta, Hong Kong, Manila, Bangkok, Singapore, Seoul, and other centers of once-controlled territories.

Yet, almost in spite of themselves, the Japanese did play a positive role in generating change in the occupied territories. In his postwar memoirs, Dr. Ba Maw, who led a Japanese-sponsored regime in Burma from 1942 to 1945, concedes the plundering and the arrogance and yet offers the following counter-observation, which illustrates the danger of judging Japanese imperialism from too sharply defined black and white perspectives:

> Nothing can ever obliterate the role Japan has played in bringing liberation to countless colonial peoples. The phenomenal Japanese victories in the Pacific and in Southeast Asia, which really marked the beginning of the end of all imperialism and colonialism; the national armies Japan helped to create during the war, which in their turn created a new spirit and will in a large part of Asia; the independent states she set up in several Southeast Asian countries as well as her recognition of the provisional government of Free India at a time when not a single other belligerent power permitted even the talk of independence within its own dominions . . . these will outlive all the passing wartime strains and passions and betrayals in the final summing up of history.

THE TIDE TURNS

Midway Island (more correctly, two small islets) stands in a tiny atoll in the Pacific. It received its name from its location, approximately equidistant from Japan and the West Coast of the United States. More important, however, was the fact that Midway stood astride the communications lines in the central Pacific—"Hawaii's sentry" it was called by Vice Admiral Nagumo Chuichi, who would be named as the commander of Midway Task Force. Crucial to the thinking of Japanese strategists was the possibility of luring remnants of the crippled U.S. Pacific Fleet into a showdown engagement where it would be destroyed. Then, control of Midway would permit Japan to interrupt traffic to the island chains of the South Pacific and Australia. In addition, the Japanese Navy would be able to harass and perhaps invade Hawaii only 1100 miles to the east. Japan had not planned to invade the Hawaiian Islands until *after* the raid on Pearl Harbor. The easy success of the December 7 attack led the Navy to calculate that Americans might consider Hawaii expendable, especially if its naval protection was weakened. Plans for an invasion of the Islands as early as the end of 1942 were drafted. If all this could be accomplished, America would be compelled to abandon its effort to dislodge Japan from its newly gained conquests in Southeast Asia, and Japan might be able to force the United States into negotiations to end the war on terms favorable to Japan.

To that end, Yamamoto assembled the largest armada in Japanese naval history—nearly a hundred warships and a fleet train of thirty supply and transport vessels. At his disposal, he was confident, was the element of surprise. By the time an American fleet could respond, the Japanese Navy would have ample time to seize Midway, Yamamoto calculated.

That proved to be wrong. The Americans scored an intelligence coup, the most decisive of the Pacific war, which, though it did not assure U.S. victory at Midway, brought it within grasp. While American planners had good reason to believe that an attack on Midway was a possibility, there were many other plausible targets in the broad Pacific Ocean, including Hawaii itself. It was only when navy cryptanalysts succeeded in breaking the seldom-employed high-level code called the Japanese Flag Officers Code, used for only the most vital command messages, that U.S. strategists could be certain that Midway was the target.

MIDWAY'S FRESH-WATER HOAX

U.S. Navy intelligence analysts were troubled in the spring of 1942 by the frequent mention in Japanese messages of the code designation "AF." It clearly referred to a place name, but which place? A solution to the puzzle became imperative on May 20 when intelligence officers intercepted a message indicating an imminent attack on AF. Navy cryptanalysts devised a plan to trick the enemy into revealing the identification of AF. Everyone knew that Midway relied for fresh water on rainfall and distillation. The plan was to have the Midway garrison send a message reporting that its distilling plant was out of order. The message was sent "in the clear" to ensure that Japanese radio monitors would have no trouble picking it up. They did and, as hoped, took the bait and flashed the word to Tokyo that "AF was short of water." Admiral Chester W. Nimitz, commander-in-chief of the Pacific fleet, had his confirmation of the impending assault on Midway and was able to deploy his forces accordingly.

Accordingly, when the Japanese strike force was deployed against Midway on June 4, it in fact sailed into a trap. Unexpected resistance from waves of dive-bombers from three American aircraft carriers decided the day. In this historic battle, the opposing ships never fired on each other, in fact, they were never within sight of each other. American losses were heavy because many of the successes at Midway were the result of almost suicidal courage (of the kind associated with the Japanese kamikaze pilots later in the war) by American fliers braving murderous antiaircraft fire. Opposition from the redoubtable "Zero" also took its toll. Nevertheless, in the space of fifteen minutes on the morning of June 4, the Japanese advantage was obliterated as three of four carriers were sunk; the fourth was knocked out the next day. Another critical loss was the more than three hundred aircraft and, with them, some of the best and most experienced of Japan's aviators. In the long run, what was even more damaging was the inability of Japanese industry to replace the losses with anything like the speed and efficiency of the Americans.

The role of the U.S. aircraft carrier *Yorktown*, whose dive-bombers played an important part in the victory at Midway, illustrates the point. It was on the scene there only because of near-miraculous renovation it had received at Pearl Harbor. After receiving extensive damage in the Battle of the Coral Sea in May, it had limped back to Hawaii for repairs which the skipper estimated would take ninety days. Admiral Chester W. Nimitz ordered the task completed in seventy-two hours. An army of 1400 welders and shipfitters completed the superhuman

THE ZERO FIGHTER

The Zero fighter aircraft, designed and built by aeronautical engineers of the Mitsubishi Heavy Industries Company, was the mainstay of the Japanese Navy for the entire Pacific war. At the time of Pearl Harbor, and for long after, this carrier-based plane was considered superior to any American fighter aircraft in speed, climb, and maneuverability. Its main weakness, however, was that its light construction and unprotected fuel tanks made it highly vulnerable to gunfire. While many Americans thought that the name came from the red-sun insignia, it actually derived from the year it went operational which in the Japanese calendar being used at the time was Year 2600. The Zero took the last two digits for its model name. (Year 2600 corresponded to 1940.) After the war, the plane's chief designer, Horikoshi Jiro, took some pride in telling how the United States studied carefully a Zero it had captured intact in the 1942 Aleutian Islands campaign before designing the first comparable American fighter, the F6F Hellcat, which began to challenge the Zero in September 1943. In his memoirs, Horikoshi, taking note of the stereotypical American image of the Japanese as "copycats," declared: "Perhaps it is not in good taste for me to say this, but if, as some people believe, Japanese people excel only in imitating and making small gadgets, then the Zero did not exist."

task ahead of schedule. The last of the yard workmen were still on board on May 29th as the ship cleared the dry dock and headed for the Midway engagement.

With the defeat of Admiral Nagumo's fleet at Midway—the first reversal the Japanese Navy had ever suffered—the Empire of Japan was forced to go on the defensive in the Pacific, desperately striving to hang on to the spoils it had already won. There yet remained much fighting—even some local victories by Japan—but the forward momentum of Japan's drive had been blunted, and the invasion plans for Hawaii were cancelled. So great was the calamity that military censors concealed the truth from the Japanese people. On hearing that Japan had at last "secured supreme power in the Pacific," jubilant citizens in Tokyo celebrated with lantern processions. All but a handful of Japanese remained ignorant of the Midway debacle until the end of the war.

ISLAND HOPPING

With the turning of the tide at Midway, the war against Japan moved ahead on three fronts.

On the Asian mainland, especially in China, there would be little commitment of ground troops by the United States, but the 14th Air Force operating from air bases in the deep interior of China would carry the air war to Japanese positions. Any hope that the Japanese military would be seriously weakened by the forces of our ally, the Nationalist Chinese under Chiang Kai-shek, gradually dissolved in the first year or two after Pearl Harbor. Chiang welcomed the American entrance into the war and eagerly sought American financial and matériel support.

However, "Vinegar Joe" Stilwell, in charge of the Allied war effort in China, grew bitterly disillusioned with the "Generalissimo." Stilwell and many of the other "Old China hands" who knew China best were convinced that Chiang counted on an eventual Allied victory against Japan and was therefore content to "coast" out the balance of the war, holding back his best forces and much of the scarce American aid which was funnelled his way. The Generalissimo was keeping these supplies and troops in reserve for an eventual showdown struggle with the Chinese Communists who were regarded by Chiang as more menacing to China than the armies of Japan. As stated earlier, Chiang regarded the Communists as a "disease of the heart" while dismissing the Japanese as a mere "disease of the skin." It was not possible to completely disown Chiang as an ally— too much propaganda effort had gone into making him one of the "Big Four" allies. Additionally, at all costs, Chiang had to be kept in the war against Japan because it was important to keep as many Japanese troops as possible tied down on the Asian mainland rather than risk them being released for duty in the Pacific, where the decisive battles of the war would occur.

It was there, in the Pacific, that the other two battle strategies unfolded. One was assigned to the army under General MacArthur, who had been the U.S.

commander in the Philippines at the time of Pearl Harbor. His evacuation from there to Australia in March 1942, accompanied by his dramatic "I shall return" pledge, made the general one of the best-known figures of World War II. MacArthur argued for a drive through the jungles of New Guinea to the Philippines and from there to the Japanese homeland.

The navy insisted on a parallel offensive through Japanese-controlled island chains in the Pacific. It would not be necessary to capture all of the Japanese-held islands. The stronger bases could be bypassed, because U.S. commanders were certain that Japan would not risk reinforcing threatened positions by any large-scale ocean convoys for fear of attack by American air power. Thus was devised the island-hopping campaign strategy, in full swing by 1943, designed to bring U.S. forces within striking distance of the home islands of Japan by a new long-range bomber being developed by the Boeing Company.

The names of the islands are only unfamiliar dots on the map now, but in the period from 1942 to 1945 they measured the steady drive to close the distance with the Japanese homeland: Guadalcanal in the Solomons, Tarawa in the Gilberts, Kwajalein in the Marshalls, Tinian and Saipan in the Mariana Islands, and many others. The cost for each atoll, white sandy beach and jungle airstrip was measured in hundreds, more often thousands of lives. Air and naval forces would prepare the way for landing forces with weeks of bombardment. In November 1943, Tarawa was "softened up" with about ten tons of explosives per acre, but almost all of the 4500 defenders survived in their sand-covered concrete and steel bunkers. In three days of fighting there, it took an investment of more than three thousand U. S. Marines (a thousand dead and more than two thousand wounded) to capture the tiny coral acreage; only seventeen of the Japanese defenders survived. An old rule of thumb said that military units could not endure casualty rates of more than 30 percent without soon losing combative spirit. Forty percent fell at Tarawa, and the casualty rates climbed higher after that.

In June 1944, as the war against Germany entered its final phase with the Normandy invasion, the island-hopping drive in the Pacific reached the enemy's inner perimeter with the invasion of Saipan. "The rise and fall of Imperial Japan depends on this one battle. Every man shall do his utmost," soldiers and sailors responsible for defending the island were admonished in an order which repeated Admiral Togo Heihachiro's famous words before the Tsushima Straits battle. Here on Saipan—called "impregnable " by Prime Minister Tojo—an especially large garrison of thirty-one thousand troops fought with great ferocity for three weeks.

More than ever before, Americans now encountered the fearsome desperation tactic known as the *banzai* charge. As the front ranks fell, those in the rear climbed or jumped over the dead. Even when it was clear that the Japanese defenses had been overwhelmed and defeat was inevitable, the Japanese disregarded surrender appeals from the Americans. In the last days of the battle, soldiers were reduced to eating tree roots. As ammunition supplies dwindled and organized resistance became impossible, officers relied on their swords, and the rank and file fought on using bayonets or bamboo sticks sharpened into spears. Human tidal waves continued to take a heavy toll in American lives right up until the end. Of the seventy-one thousand Americans who landed on Saipan, more than sixteen thousand were killed or wounded. Almost the entire Japanese garrison—at least thirty thousand—died. Among the last to die were the commanding general and Admiral Nagumo Chuichi who had led the task forces at Pearl Harbor and Midway. Both were assisted by aides to commit ritual suicide.

On nearby Guam, and on some of the larger islands in the Pacific, Japanese diehards pulled back into the jungle to follow the soldier's code of ethics *(senjinkun)* which enjoined all who served the Emperor to remember the heavy debt they owed their country: "I will never suffer the disgrace of being taken alive." Some refused to acknowledge the defeat of Japan even after the Japanese capitulation in 1945. Many lost their resolve and came out of hiding during the 1950s and 1960s but it was not until 1972 that the last of the loyalists surrendered on Guam. It was not until 1974 that Lieutenant Onoda Hiro, the last holdout in the Philippines, emerged—and then only when the lieutenant's former superior was flown to the Islands to relieve Onoda of his wartime obligations. In 1989, forty-four years after the end of the war, two soldiers returned to their homeland from Malaya.

The battle for Saipan introduced a new variation on the fight-to-the-death principle. Saipan was not one of the islands seized by Japan at the beginning of the war. It had belonged to Germany until World War I, after which it was mandated to Japanese administration by the League of Nations. Over the years, it had acquired, in addition to the native Chamorro population, a sizable community of Japanese civilians engaged in fishing and the sugar cane industry. An attempt was made to evacuate some of these civilians, but most remained on the island and, in the end, faced the same destiny as the soldiers. Estimates of the numbers vary widely but at least ten thousand civilians, about two-thirds of the total, perished in the fighting or committed suicide. The last of them, thousands of fathers, mothers, sons, and daughters, gathered on a bluff at the northern tip of the island days after the fighting had subsided. Safety and food were promised by the Americans who used bullhorns to plead with the civilians.

The expression "banzai charge" is an American one. The Japanese never spoke of a banzai attack or banzai charge. Military exercises including attacks, however, were often preceded by a patriotic ritual in which officers would lead their troops in shouting "Long live the Emperor!" (*Tenno heika banzai*). Some confusion concerning the word *banzai* persists because foreigners tend to mispronounce the Japanese horticultural art of bonsai in such a way that it sounds the same as *banzai*. *Bonsai*, correctly pronounced as bone-sigh, refers to dwarf plants grown in a tray. Japanese are sometimes amused, more often baffled, to have foreigners ask them about "*banzai* plants."

Many doubtless believed the propaganda tales of horrible mistreatment that awaited them at the hands of their captors; others preferred any fate to the dishonor of surrender. In any case, almost all of this last grim band threw themselves over the thousand-foot cliffs to death on the jagged rocks below. Historian Ivan Morris calls their deaths "probably the ghastliest in world history since the mass suicide of the Jews in Masada . . . ."

With the capture of Saipan, the Americans now possessed ready-made airfields from which it could launch direct bombing runs on the heart of Japan only 1500 miles to the north. Unlike Midway, the Saipan debacle could not be long concealed from the public. On July 19, almost two weeks after the event, the Japanese people learned that the island had fallen. At the same time, they learned that Prime Minister Tojo had resigned. Tojo, while powerful, did not

---

BESUBORU IV

Americans would feel right at home with the lexicon of Japanese baseball. American terms, modified to conform to Japanese phonetics, are used. A radio announcer calling a game of *besuboru* will describe the *pitcha* throwing the ball to the *kyatcha*. With good pitching, it will be *sutoraiku-wan*, *sutoraiku-tsu* and then *sutoraiku-suree*, sending the batter back to the *dagguoauto*. A hitter will be judged either *seifu* or *autto* by the *umpaiya*. In the event of a *homu-ran*, excited fans might exclaim "*Fure! Fure!* (Hooray! Hooray!)."

The only time indigenous Japanese words for baseball were used was during the Pacific war, when the military outlawed not the game but the "enemy pronunciations." At that time, the military sternly frowned upon the use of English "because it is spoken by Japan's enemy nations"— even "mama" and "papa," long a part of children's vocabulary, was discouraged. For baseball terms, the military provided a list of approved native words. There is a hilarious scene in an old movie spoofing this bit of nationalistic fervor as a flustered umpire, under the stern eye of an Army censor, keeps forgetting to adjust to the newly mandated and strange-sounding terms like "*yoshi hitotsu*" for "strike one."

By 1943, baseball players were playing in unnumbered khaki uniforms and obliged to salute one another. Fans were sometimes treated to army-sponsored grenade-throwing contests before the first inning. Some of the teams had to abandon their Western-sounding names for authentic Japanese names: the Giants became the Kyojin. Incredibly, however, pro baseball continued to be played until mid-way through the 1944 season, when the Osaka team was declared the winner over the Kyojin. It was perhaps a measure of national priorities that ten thousand geisha houses and other amusement centers had been closed a year earlier.

It may only be part of the "folklore of the combat zones," as John Dower suggests, but in addition to usual cries of "Banzai!" and "Marines, you die" which were hurled at Americans, one account has it that "To hell with Babe Ruth" was also included among the insults.

bear comparison to a Hitler or Stalin. It is difficult to imagine either of the European dictators stepping aside at the age of fifty-nine to assume the role of a respected, but largely ignored, elder statesman. Tojo's voluntary resignation was the first peaceful change of government to occur in any of the major belligerent nations in World War II. The accumulation of military disasters had damaged his reputation in both the army and navy. In addition, Tojo had lost the confidence of the civilian leadership which had supported his rise to power in 1941.

Some of this group, including palace intimates, now certain that Japan was doomed, began to quietly discuss among themselves the need for negotiating an end to the war with the Allies. These maneuvers had to be quiet and "behind the scenes," because anyone who overtly championed peace risked assassination by hot-headed young officers and right-wing civilians always on the alert to "destroy traitors around the throne." For the time being, there could be no public and, very little private, contemplation of anything but total resistance. As Tojo said, the fall of Saipan had brought the nation to the most difficult situation in its entire history. "But these developments have also provided us with the opportunity to smash the enemy and win the war." In the meantime, Japan prepared for the war to come home. Work battalions stepped up campaigns to clear away wooden homes and other buildings in Tokyo and other major cities in order to create firebreaks. More than a half million residences would eventually be torn down by neighborhood associations using ropes and hand tools.

THE B-29 AND THE AIR WAR

The war was brought to the Japanese home islands by a new airplane which was designed and built by Boeing in factories in Seattle, Washington, and Wichita, Kansas. Known as the B-29 or Superfortress, it epitomized the enormous technological lead the United States enjoyed over Japan. The four thousand B-29s produced during the war were at the time quite simply the largest and heaviest aircraft ever mass produced. Everything about the plane called for superlatives: the largest propellers, longest wingspan, the most powerful engines. Most importantly for the vast distances of the Pacific theater—the plane was never used in Europe—it had double the flying range of its elder sister, the B-17. It could fly for 3200 miles with a 5000-pound bombload at speeds up to 364 miles per hour. With its pressurized crew compartments, the B-29 could fly six miles high, beyond the reach of fighter planes and anti-aircraft batteries.

Superfortresses flying from bases in China were striking at Japanese cities even before the airfield on Saipan was ready for use, but the available Chinese fields were too distant to reach the cities of northern Japan. Further, furnishing fuel and other matériel to the Chinese bases entailed enormous difficulties. Early in the war, in April 1942, the Japanese had cut the famous "Burma Road," the mountain supply route linking unoccupied China to Allied bases in free India. After the loss of the Burma Road, because of the effective blockade ring

Japan had constructed around China, all supplies had to be flown into China "over the hump," the southern flank of the Himalayas, with peaks higher than the highest of the Rocky Mountains. If the lumbering transport planes were fortunate enough to survive the snowy peaks of the Himalayas, they were then at the mercy of Japanese interceptors. Only a few thousand tons of gasoline and other supplies could be ferried in via this dangerous corridor. It was "like feeding an elephant with an eyedropper," one reporter said. (General Stilwell, given to more earthy metaphors, said that it was like "Trying to manure a ten-acre field with sparrow shit.") With the successes in the island-hopping campaign, however, all B-29 operations could be shifted to Mariana Islands bases like Saipan.

Although B-29s from the Marianas were flying over Japan as early as November 1944, the first few months of raids were relatively small and ineffective. Mechanical defects grounded many of the complex new planes during these early months, and inexperienced crews needed time to sharpen their skills. In addition, an unanticipated technical difficulty plagued the planes on their first runs over Japan. Flying over certain Japanese cities at the high altitudes for which the plane was designed, crews found themselves sucked into raging jet streams with velocities up to two hundred miles per hour. These sub-stratospheric hurricanes—which had not been encountered in the raids over Germany—caused the aircraft to pass the ground at speeds over five hundred miles per hour. This was far too fast for bombardiers to identify targets and fine-tune the equations on their Norden bombsights. On one mission, only slightly more than half of the seventy-two B-29s even found their target—the sprawling Nakajima airplane engine complex at Musashino near Tokyo.

On some missions, only one bomb in fifty hit within a thousand feet of the selected targets. Attempts were made to fly on a reverse run, against the wind, at targets but that was risky because it left the planes almost stationary targets themselves; some crews found themselves literally pushed tailfirst back out to sea. Flying at lower altitudes to get under cloud cover and avoid the high winds was tried. It allowed for more accuracy but left the big planes vulnerable to Japanese fighters and anti-aircraft guns and produced unacceptably steep losses of the B-29s and their highly-trained eleven-man crews. With loss rates creeping up to six percent by early 1945, crews could calculate that they probably would not survive more than sixteen missions.

As a result of the ineffectiveness of the precision raids, a strong head of pressure built to change tactics. Presiding over the new program was Major General Curtis LeMay, who would direct the air war against Japan in the last year of the war. Instead of precision bombing of selected military and industrial targets, the accepted doctrine among strategists since the 1930s, LeMay directed his XXI Bomber Command to begin "area bombing." Instead of daylight raids, night raids were to be favored. Accuracy would be reduced but, with area bombing, less precision was needed, and Japan had very few night fighters to resist the B-29s. Instead of dropping high-explosive bombs, incendiary bombs would be used. High-explosive bombs were effective in blasting the ferro-concrete buildings in German cities, but in Japan where wood was more commonly used in

THE WARTIME MYTH OF TOKYO ROSE

When the war in the Pacific came to an end, the biggest scoop for the more than two hundred journalists who streamed into Japan was to get to Tokyo for an exclusive interview with General Tojo Hideki. The second biggest scoop was to get an "exclusive" with "Tokyo Rose." That was the name given by GIs in the Pacific to a female announcer—to several announcers as it turned out—who broadcast popular American tunes in disc jockey fashion via shortwave radio from Tokyo. It is not easy to say exactly what she meant to captive audiences in foxholes and on board navy ships. To some, the name was equated with treachery. To others, she was seductive. To most, she simply offered fifteen minutes of nostalgia every evening about 6:00 when her "Zero Hour" (the moment before battle) broadcast came on the air.

None of the several women who announced the Zero Hour ever called herself "Tokyo Rose." But a *Cosmopolitan* magazine reporter on the trail of the big scoop persuaded one of the women to accept the label and give his magazine exclusive publication rights to her story in return for a handsome stipend (which was never paid her). In this way, a 27-year-old Nisei from Los Angeles, Ikuko Toguri, became Tokyo Rose. She had been in Tokyo taking care of a sick relative at the outbreak of the war and, like several hundred other Japanese Americans, was trapped in Japan. Like all of them, she was subjected to extreme pressure from Japanese authorities to renounce her American citizenship. Many of them succumbed. Life in wartime Japan was harsh enough what with food shortages, ration cards, travel permits, and the like. To be under suspicion as an enemy alien was to ask for added trouble. But Toguri steadfastly refused. If she had renounced her American citizenship, she could not have been charged with treason—which is what happened after the war was over. In a San Francisco courtroom in 1949, in the last treason trial of the war, she was convicted and received a $10,000 fine and ten-year prison sentence. She was imprisoned until 1956.

To many alive during World War II the name "Tokyo Rose" (like "Axis Sally" in the European theater) can still conjure up the image of a vicious traitor skilled at undermining G.I. morale. However, many of those who have studied the trial transcripts and the available evidence believe that the prosecution suborned Nisei witnesses into giving untruthful evidence against the accused. In addition, many believe that Toguri's broadcasts were anything but malicious or treasonous. One sailor recalled, "She knew what was on our minds. She was lighthearted, and sometimes raunchy about it . . . We didn't take her seriously. There was a tongue-in-cheek quality to the relationship, an understanding between us that is illustrated by the bomber squadron said to have responded to her apology for playing only old records (they were all she had) by addressing her a carton of late releases and parachuting it into the center of Tokyo."

Amid mounting evidence of an unfair trial, President Gerald Ford, in his last full day in office, issued a full and unconditional pardon to Toguri, restoring her rights and her citizenship.

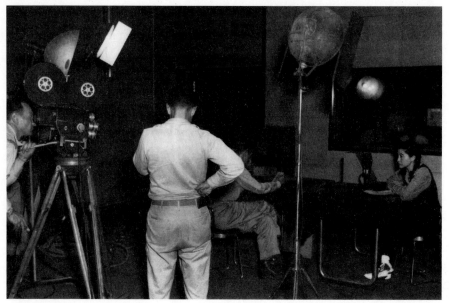

Ikuko Toguri ("Tokyo Rose") reenacts her broadcasts for U.S. Army photographers, 1946.

construction, thousand-pound "blockbuster" bombs tended to simply make large holes in the ground. Only recently, scientists had perfected a deadly new incendiary called napalm. A jellied gasoline, napalm skipped and splashed over everything or everyone in its path and ignited into incandescent tidal waves of flame. Napalm was almost impossible to extinguish and it burned slowly at intense heat until it burned itself out. Used earlier in the war in flame throwers, from February 1945 on napalm became the principal tool in the campaign to incinerate the densely populated cities of Japan.

From this time on, the emphasis of the strategic bombing campaigns was not only to destroy Japan's physical capacity for continued resistance but to destroy Japan's will to fight. By 1945, the mass killing of civilians and destruction of their homes did not seem alien to American purposes or methods. The United States was not the first to engage in the indiscriminate bombing of civilian populations. It had been done in the Spanish Civil War in 1936, Italians had done it in their Ethiopian campaign, and the German Luftwafte had done it on a massive scale against cities like Rotterdam, London, and Coventry in 1940. Then, in turn, German cities like Hamburg and Dresden were torched by the British R.A.F. as well as by Americans. The Japanese, themselves, had shown no qualms about the bombing of Chinese cities.

THE GREAT TOKYO AIR RAID OF MARCH 9–10

Tokyoites knew well how vulnerable to fire their city was. Giant conflagrations were a part of the city's lore from days past, when the great fires were poetically called "flowers of Edo." The earthquake of 1923, the greatest natural calamity in Japan's history, did most of its damage because it struck at exactly mid-day when hibachi stoves, fired up to prepare noon meals, tipped over and started thousands of fires. When Tokyo's air raid sirens wailed on the evening of March 9, 1945, the seven million inhabitants of the greater Tokyo area were not especially alarmed. From earlier raids, residents of Tokyo were familiar with the big silver B-29s and called them, in a mixture of awe and whistling-in-the-dark dread, "*B-san*"—Mister Bs. A few of the B-29s had even been brought down by "ramming." Japanese suicide pilots flew in aircraft stripped of every possible pound of weight, including guns, so that they could ascend to the bombers' altitudes and crash their fighters into the wings of the bombers.

In each of several of the raids during previous weeks, hundreds had died and small districts of the sprawling metropolis had been set ablaze. However, life went on. Trained firemen, equipment, bomb shelters, and other publicly provided civil defense measures were woefully inadequate, but civilians had been instructed to take responsibility for their own households and neighborhoods. Each dozen or so families was organized into a block association (*tonarigumi*), and these 120,000 block associations had a little pump on a cart and a few ladders and shovels to fight fires. Protective hoods were made available to citizens through the block associations which also made certain that each of its households dug holes or trenches for rude shelter. In front of each house was a cistern kept full of water and buckets of sand to douse flames. On March 9, some noted that the stiff winds which were blowing through the Kanto Plains could make it difficult to control the flames if the B-san were in fact headed for the capital as the calm voice on Radio Tokyo warned.

The voice was right. The largest attack force of B-29s ever assembled, 334 planes, began to arrive over the city shortly after 11:00 P.M. The first "pathfinder" squadrons dropped napalm sticks to etch target areas with giant blazing Xs for the main waves. The formations flew at only five thousand feet, and the planes were stripped of all armament in anticipation of little effective resistance from either fighters or anti-aircraft. Both factors allowed each plane to carry an especially heavy bombload—forty clusters of firebombs. Each cluster exploded a half-mile over the ground and spewed forty six-pound napalm incendiaries in a random pattern on the city below. Precision was not an important concern. The object was to saturate all of Tokyo. The fire lanes would be meaningless, for bombs would be dropped on all sides of the breaks.

The tactic worked with deadly effect. Aided by the wind, the fires were so intense that they quickly generated their *own* winds. This was the phenomenon of the "fire-storm," hurricane-velocity winds roaring in from all directions to feed the flames.

Robert Guillain, a journalist and a French national permitted to live in Japan during the war, describes what he saw:

> The inhabitants stayed heroically put as the bombs dropped, faithfully obeying the order that each family defend its own home. But how could they fight the fires with that wind blowing and when a single house might

be hit by ten or even more of the bombs, each weighing up to 6.6 pounds, that were raining down by the thousands? As they fell, cylinders scattered a kind of flaming dew that skittered along the roofs, setting fire to everything it splashed and spreading a wash of dancing flames everywhere . . . .The meager defenses of those thousands of amateur firemen—feeble jets of hand-pumped water, wet mats and sand to be thrown on the bombs when one could get close enough to their terrible heat—were completely inadequate. Roofs collapsed under the bombs' impact and within minutes the frail houses of wood and paper were aflame, lighted from the inside like paper lanterns. The hurricane-force wind puffed up great clots of flame and sent burning planks planing through the air to fell people and set fire to what they touched. Flames from a distant cluster of houses would suddenly spring up close at hand, traveling at the speed of a forest fire. Then screaming families abandoned their homes; sometimes the women had already left, carrying their babies and dragging crates or mattresses. Too late: the circle of fire had closed off their street. Sooner or later, everyone was surrounded by flame . . . .

[P]eople who did not burn from the feet up burned from the head down. Mothers who carried their babies strapped to their backs, Japanese style, would discover too late that the padding that enveloped the infant had caught fire. Refugees clutching their packages crowded into the rare clear spaces—crossroads, gardens, and parks—but the bundles caught fire even faster than clothing and the throng flamed from the inside.

Those who could make it fled in the direction of the wide Sumida River which flows through the center of the city. There are many steel bridges across the river, but they offered no safety for, as Guillain writes, the flames were so fierce that they leaped across the river and its bridges, leaving the bridge clogged with the bodies of those who were trapped there. The river itself was partially evaporated, and even in areas where the flames did not reach, people were choked to death in boats because all of the oxygen over the river was consumed by the heat. In some parts of the city, the 1800°F. heat from the inferno was enough to boil water in canals. At about 3:00 A.M., the last B-29 stragglers left the city, being careful to avoid the thermal updrafts which buffeted some several thousand feet in a matter of seconds. The burning city could be seen from 150 miles out to sea. In three hours' time, sixteen square miles of Tokyo had been burned to the ground, 261,000 houses had disappeared, and a million people had been made homeless in what was still a winter month. There were as many as 200,000 left injured, most of whom found it almost impossible to get any kind of medical attention in the devastated city; even those who were unhurt were left with heat-darkened skin that lasted for weeks or months or lifetimes. Estimates of the death toll vary widely but at least eighty-three thousand perished in the holocaust. It was "the most destructive single bombing raid in history," according to one official history of the war.

At the time of the German air war over England, President Roosevelt had denounced the Luftwaffe tactics as "inhuman barbarism" and said that bombing must be restricted to precision daylight attacks against selected mili-

THE JAPANESE ON GENERAL CURTIS LEMAY
    "More irony: General LeMay's service was great to the United States
in terms of saving American lives by shortening the war, but it scarcely
could be deemed a service to the people of Japan. Yet in 1964 General
LeMay, who had become Chief of Staff of the United States Air Force,
was decorated with the First Class Order of the Grand Cordon of the
Rising Sun, the highest decoration that can be given by the Japanese
government to a foreigner. To be sure, LeMay's decoration was symbolic; all of the American chiefs of staff got automatic decorations from
America's staunch new ally, Japan. But in the case of 'Devil LeMay,' as
the general had come to be known in Japan, many Japanese citizens
believed and still believe an exception might have been made."

Hoito Edoin, *The Night Tokyo Burned.*

tary targets. Five years later, however, carnage and atrocities by all sides in the
war had desensitized everyone to ethical considerations. "Shortening the war"
became the only touchstone of legitimacy. If it could be argued that a measure
would shorten the war and thereby save lives in the long run, that was evidence
enough of the morality of the measure. General LeMay probably spoke for most
when he said that, "The purpose of war is killing the enemy. When you kill
enough of them, they quit." A few months later, the dropping of nuclear bombs
on two Japanese cities was to be questioned in heated debates on both ethical
and practical grounds. It can be argued that if any "moral frontier" was crossed,
it occurred with the Tokyo fire–bomb raid of March 9–10, which was at least as
costly to human life as either of the atomic raids (and, if certain estimates are
accepted, as costly as *both* atomic raids put together). In any case, there was no
high-level soul-searching concerning the morality of fire-bombing Japan's urban
populations.
    Complicating the matter in the case of Japan was the fact that it was not easy
to isolate "urban populations" from "industrial centers." Factories and mills
were frequently surrounded by densely packed and flimsy wooden residences.
In addition, much of Japanese industrial output was decentralized, in the hands
of thousands of small subcontracting "feeder industries." As production shifted
from consumer goods to weapons and ammunition during the war years, small
home or community factories in Tokyo were, for example, turning out parts of
grenades—firing pins, casings, and so on—which were to be stockpiled for the
day when every citizen would be expected to become a front-line soldier. "In
effect," writes a Japanese journalist-historian, "Tokyo had become one huge
arsenal." The use of fire bombs made it impossible to discriminate between
strategic targets and the helpless and innocent.
    In quick succession, other cities were targeted; by early June, over 40 percent
of the nation's most important industrial cities had been gutted, a third of the

buildings in these cities were razed, and the homeless total reached 13 million. Renewed attacks on Tokyo left that city so devastated that it was removed from the bombing list. In one of these raids, on May 25, the prime minister barely escaped with his life when his official residence was destroyed. By accident, apparently, incendiaries had also destroyed buildings on the grounds of the palace, forcing the imperial family to spend the rest of the war living in an underground bunker. By that time, the B-29s were now ranging almost at will over Japan's skies. On a single day, July 10, no less than two thousand Superfortresses and carrier-based planes were in the skies over Japanese cities. Opposition was so light that leaflets would be dropped to warn cities that they were next—both to save lives and increase worker absenteeism. Once the major cities were crippled, LeMay turned his attention to the smaller cities and industrial centers, hitting new ones at the rate of almost one a day. Middle-size provincial cities like Aomori and Toyama were more than 90 percent destroyed. As rapidly as crippled transport facilities would allow, the government ordered evacuation of the cities, and in the spring of 1945 one of the largest mass migrations in human history was under way, as about one out of seven of all those in Japan moved to the relative safety of the countryside. At least 4 million people spilled out from the metropolitan Tokyo area alone. Unfortunately, few of the evacuees had left before the great March 9–10 raid.

An Onion Existence

In the meantime, a blockade ring was being tightened around the home islands. Japan, it will be recalled, had over the previous half-century built a far-flung overseas empire on which it had become dependent. However, the merchant-marine lifeline which transported the tin and rubber from Malaya, rice from Indochina, the iron and coal from Manchuria, and the petroleum from the East Indies were vulnerable to attack from the air and from submarine "wolf packs." Military planners in Japan knew of this vulnerability, and before the war, had calculated that the Empire might stand the loss of as much as 800,000 tons of shipping in each year of the war. Instead, the actual losses grew each year, from 1.2 million tons in the first year of the war to a staggering 3.5 million tons in the third year of the war. By the beginning of 1945, there was little marine transport to be found on the open seas and American hunters had to search for prey among small coastal vessels. Then, in March, the Air Force began the largest aerial mining operation ever undertaken. In the next few months, more than twelve thousand heavy magnetic and acoustic mines were "planted," dropped by parachute into every important port and shipping channel in Japan. They quickly brought chaos and destruction to the coastline, and by the summer of 1945, Japan's coastal shipping had been brought to near paralysis.

The devastating results of the blockade and mine-laying can be seen in every sphere. With petroleum reserves down to only 200,000 barrels (from a high of 12.3 million barrels at the beginning of the war), the government ordered storage tanks torn down for the scrap. Masses of workers, including the very young and old, were mobilized to replenish the reserves with ersatz gasoline made from the roots of pine trees laboriously dug by hand from the ground. By early 1944, the daily lesson time for school children had been cut down to only two hours in many places to allow youngsters to work. The enormous effort and the pitifully small results of this project are a measure of Japan's desperation in 1945. John Toland summarizes the results:

> The pine roots oil project required a work force of millions to grub out the pine roots, as well as more than 37,000 small distillation units, each capable of producing 3 to 4 gallons of crude oil per day. Production eventually reached 70,000 barrels a month, but the process of refining was so difficult that little more than 3,000 barrels of aviation gasoline were produced by the end of the war.

The vital airplane industry was kept alive—assembly lines were still functioning on the last day of the war—but wood replaced aluminum and bamboo substituted for other scarce metals. Inspections and test flights were almost forgotten, and pilot training programs were reduced to under a hundred hours, a tenth of the time given in the U.S. armed forces; newly trained fliers often lacked the skill to fly in formation.

Nearly half the nation's telephone service was out of commission. Electric power transmission, once disrupted by bombing raids, remained dead for weeks or even months. All but two of the ferries linking the main islands of Honshu and Hokkaido were knocked out in a single raid. Transportation was in such short supply that piles of rusting metal adorned sidewalks everywhere: There was no way to move the pots and pans, radiators and heating pipes that were collected in scrap metal drives. The few automobiles still moving were powered by charcoal-fired engines. More commonly, horse-carts and push-carts replaced automotive power. Many families had to do with a single sack of charcoal for heat and cooking through the 1944–45 winter.

Women no longer wore the beautiful kimono. Its flowing silk might encumber machinery and, in any case, it was not somber enough. Instead, the only patriotic ladies' garment was the *monpe*, drab gray pantaloons usually associated with peasants from the northeast of Japan. The clothing ration in Tokyo during the last winter of the war allocated one pair of socks for every four persons; fabrics were so flimsy that they disintegrated after two or three washings. That mattered little, since soap supplies were down 96 percent from prewar years. The government urged citizens to wear wooden clogs rather than shoes, but wood was in such short supply that neighborhood associations had to allocate clogs to families by lottery. One report indicated that wooden coffins could be obtained only on condition that they be returned after use. Sanitation declined, so typhoid, tuberculosis, cholera, dysentery, and other deprivation-related diseases were widespread. As disease rates climbed, doctors, nurses, medicines, and blood plasma almost disappeared from the home front; surgical dressings had to be used over and over. One ironically bright note was that the incidence of beriberi declined, a tribute to the rice husks that had become a part of the diet.

The daily food ration which was only slightly above subsistence level at the beginning of the war fell drastically by 1945. The state's purchasing and distribution system prevented widespread starvation. The 1500 calories per day which was set as a minimum standard by the government in 1945 was not a starvation diet, but it was far below that needed to maintain health and work efficiency; in fact, the actual daily intake for many people was less than the recommended levels. The fish catch was well under half the prewar level by 1945. Annual per-capita sugar consumption in that year was down to three pounds compared to thirty pounds before the war. Conscription of male farmers left farming in the hands of women, children, and old men. Thanks to that and bad weather, the 1945 rice yield was the lowest since 1905. As a result, by the summer of 1945 the sweet potato became the main staple in the Japanese diet. Since even that lowly tuber was in short supply, officials instructed citizens on making do with various weeds, thistles, and leaves. A million youngsters were instructed to collect acorns which could be bleached and ground into a nutritious, albeit odious, flour. When wheat flour was available, it could be blended with rice bran—"add no eggs or sugar" the recipe warned—and fried to make a singularly unappetizing dish called *nukapan*. "It looks just like good custard," one consumer said. "But it tastes bitter, smells like horse dung, and makes you cry when you eat it."

Each Sunday, an enormous tide of people would move from the cities to the countryside in search of food. They would carry with them their possessions for barter with the relatively well-off farmers. Family heirlooms, libraries, furniture, fine kimonos—anything which might be traded for a liter or two of rice or potatoes—were carried off on these bleak Sunday forays. It was like an "onion existence" (*tamanegi seikatsu*), people said, as families peeled away layer after layer of their material possessions in the search for survival.

WAR TO THE DEATH

By 1945, the Japanese people were hearing less of the once-confident notion of the Pacific war as a "decisive war" *(kessen)*. That term was being replaced, not with talk of weakness or surrender, but with the notion of a "war to the death" *(chinamagusai*, more literally, a "bloody war"). As the air raids over Japan gave no sign of producing talk of surrender, it became necessary to continue with the island-hopping campaign in preparation for a possible invasion of the home islands. With less and less resources, Japan's resistance became ever more diehard as Allied forces drew closer to the Japanese home islands.

A striking example of this diehard resistance came in February 1945 with the campaign to seize the island of Iwo Jima, mid-way between Tokyo and Saipan. The eight-square-mile volcanic island was known to be heavily fortified but was seen as an invaluable asset for Americans. Its air base would serve as an emergency landing field for B-29s flying from the Marianas and as a home field for fighters escorting the bombers. The longest and heaviest softening-up bombardment of the Pacific war failed to make a dent in the eleven-mile-long labyrinth of caves, tunnels, and other bombproof emplacements. The twenty-one-man garrison shielded by these thirty-five-foot-deep fortifications was also barely jarred by the seventy-two days of pre-invasion naval and air bombardment. "Like the worm which becomes stronger the more you cut it up, Iwo Jima thrived on our bombardment," one Marine Corps general complained.

The thirty-six days of fighting on Iwo Jima ended with only a few hundred of the garrison taken as prisoners, many of them noncombatant Koreans from a labor battalion. The remainder died in hand-to-hand fighting, by incineration, or by suicide; thousands were entombed in caves that were sealed by Marine demolition units. Even today, shock waves from earthquakes occasionally open fissures, revealing underground installations just as they were in 1945. Among the last to die was the commander, Lt. Gen. Kuribayashi Tadamichi, no stranger to Americans. He had spent several years in the United States as a student of military tactics at Fort Bliss, Texas, and as military attaché in Washington. Before dying while leading the last suicide charge, Kuribayashi wrote to his family in Tokyo, chiding them for complaining about hardships in the capital:

> Our sole source of supply is rain water. I have a cup of water to wash my face, my eyes only, then Lieutenant Fujita [his aide] uses the water. After he is through with it, I keep it for toilet purposes. The soldiers, in general, don't even have that much . . . . I dream in vain of drinking a cup of cool water.

Of the seventy-five thousand Marine invasion force, nearly 30 percent were casualties. The average loss of the assault troops, those who actually fought on the front lines, was 60 percent. Of the casualty toll, 6,821 were killed and more than twenty thousand were wounded; most were in their teens or early twenties. For the first time in an island campaign, Japanese troops inflicted more casualties than they received. Iwo Jima's tactical value, however, was confirmed by the 2251 emergency landings made on its runways by Superforts in the last months of the war. The lives of as many as twenty thousand airmen were thereby saved.

> "Skeletons lie on cots or litters; plasma bottles hang alongside them; splints are in place although mortal flesh has gone; surgical instruments and drugs are neatly arranged on treatment tables with the remains of doctors and attendants close by. To inspect one of these caves is not an excursion, but it would be good medicine for anyone prone to forget the horrors of Iwo Jima."
>
> —Bill Ross, *Iwo Jima*, 1985.

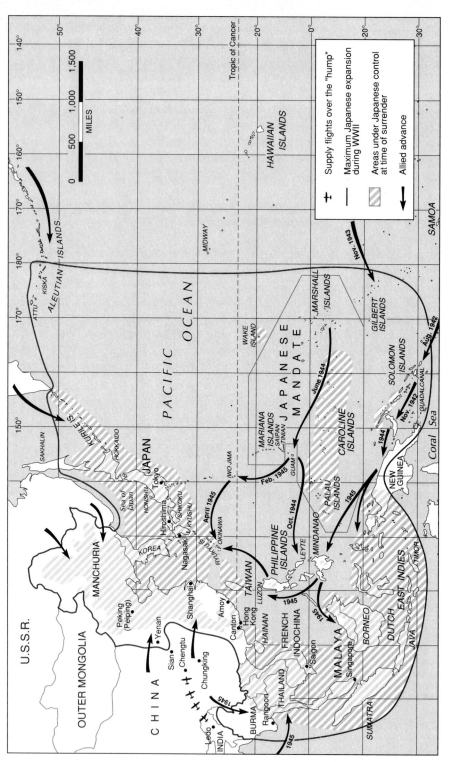

Asia and the Pacific in World War II

Legend:
+ + Supply flights over the "hump"
Maximum Japanese expansion during WWII
Areas under Japanese control at time of surrender
Allied advance

U.S.S.R.

OUTER MONGOLIA

MANCHURIA

C H I N A
Yenan
Sian
Chengtu • Chungking
Peking (Peiping)
Shanghai
Amoy
Canton
Hong Kong
HAINAN

KOREA
Nagasaki
Hiroshima
HONSHU
JAPAN
SHIKOKU
KYUSHU
Tokyo
HOKKAIDO
SAKHALIN
KURILE ISLANDS
Sea of Japan

INDIA
Ledo
BURMA
Rangoon
THAILAND
FRENCH INDOCHINA
Saigon
MALAYA
Singapore
SUMATRA
BORNEO
DUTCH EAST INDIES
JAVA
TIMOR
NEW GUINEA
Coral Sea

TAIWAN
LUZON
PHILIPPINE ISLANDS
Oct. 1944
LEYTE
MINDANAO
PALAU ISLANDS
CAROLINE ISLANDS
JAPANESE MANDATE
MARIANA ISLANDS
SAIPAN TINIAN
GUAM
June 1944
IWO JIMA
Feb. 1945
OKINAWA
April 1945
RYUKYUS

WAKE ISLAND

MARSHALL ISLANDS

GILBERT ISLANDS
Nov. 1943

SOLOMON ISLANDS
GUADALCANAL
Nov. 1942

Aug. 1942

SAMOA

MIDWAY

HAWAIIAN ISLANDS

Tropic of Cancer

PACIFIC OCEAN

ATTU KISKA
ALEUTIAN ISLANDS

1945
1945
1944

MILES
0   500   1,000   1,500

Perhaps the most memorable photograph of the war was Associated Press photographer Joe Rosenthal's instantaneously composed image of six Marines hoisting the American flag over Mount Suribachi, the highest point on the island. The picture, snapped on the fourth day of battle, offers poignant commentary on the brutality of the Iwo Jima campaign: Three of the six men in the photo were killed before learning of the fame that the Pulitizer Prize-winning photograph would shed on them.

While scattered holdouts were still being hunted on Iwo Jima, the last of the island campaigns was launched on April 1, 1945, when 1,200 ships landed the initial wave of 180,000 marines and soldiers on the island of Okinawa. On the very doorstep to Japan, Okinawa was the last barrier to the home islands. In the hands of the Allies, it would serve as site for air and naval bases and as the staging area for the invasion of Japan proper. Accordingly, resistance was greater than anything the United States had encountered in the Pacific. Okinawa would take nearly three months and involve 300,000 Americans. Some of the bloodiest fighting in the war would produce 12,500 U.S. dead and missing and 52,000 wounded. Japanese military losses reached 110,000. In addition, civilians died in even larger numbers than on Saipan; some estimates say that one out of eight Okinawan civilians perished.

Invasion forces gained the beaches with surprisingly little resistance, but on the sixth day of the campaign, the kamikaze appeared. While some kamikaze made an appearance earlier in the war, notably during the American effort to retake the Philippines in late 1944 and early 1945, it was only in the battle for Okinawa that they became a crucial element in the Japanese defense strategy.

KAMIKAZE

Kamikaze means "divine wind." The name recalls events of the thirteenth century, when Japan faced invasion by Mongols who were then riding the crest of a wave of expansion which would result in the establishment of the history's largest empire. In 1281, when Mongols launched the biggest overseas naval expedition the world had ever seen, Japan appeared to be doomed. However, the Mongol invaders had scarcely set foot on Japanese soil when they were repelled by a typhoon which wrecked the Mongol fleet and ended the menace to Japan. Seen as evidence of divine intervention, the kamikaze became part of the Shinto celebration of Japan as a unique country, uniquely protected by the *kami* spirits. Now, six-and-a-half-centuries later, with Japan once again, for only the second time in her history, facing the threat of invasion, the nation looked to the kamikaze for rescue. This time, however, it was not the weather that would save Japan but heroic pilots flying aircraft on one-way suicide missions.

Called *Oka* (cherry blossom, the ancient symbol of purity and samurai courage), the planes used by kamikaze pilots were, in fact, flying bombs. While several models were used, the most common weighed a mere 970 pounds when empty. In the nose of the plane, more than a ton of high explosives were stored.

The suicide pilots of the Pacific War were not called kamikaze by the Japanese. The same written characters which *can* be read as kamikaze can also be read as *shimpu*, meaning exactly the same thing, "divine wind." Because *shimpu* has a more dignified ring to Japanese ears, it was the preferred term. The word kamikaze which has entered English-language dictionaries ("wildly reckless") is often used both in Japan and in the West to refer to a variety of daredevils including hot-dog skiers, break-dancers, and speeding taxi-cab drivers.

When released from its mother plane, the Oka could only glide toward its destination. The function of the kamikaze pilot was to steer the craft until the target was sighted and then throw the switch to the plane's only engines. The power plant was, for the day, a sophisticated collection of three solid-fuel rocket motors which would propel the Oka into a nine-second dive at 570 miles per hour. In the last minute of his life, the pilot was to keep his eyes wide open so that he could adjust the course of his deadly cargo so that it might wreak maximum damage to the enemy's navy. Properly guided, the Oka was supposed to be able to sink or incapacitate any ship afloat.

Americans referred to the kamikaze aircraft as "*baka* bombs," *baka* being Japanese for "idiot." The pilots, while regarded with dread, were occasionally viewed with respect and pity by Americans but more often were seen as maniacs, fanatics. Americans of course had given their lives in battle in suicidal crashes, notably at Midway, just as the kamikaze pilot did. Now in the last stages of the war, however, Japan's kamikaze pilots were not simply acting on spontaneous initiative in the heat of battle. Self-immolation became a part of the general strategy of the armed forces with the mobilization of several thousand young men into the *Shimpu Tokubetsu Kogekitai* (Divine Wind Special Attack Force) under Vice Admiral Onishi Takijiro. This "Special Attack Force" also included human torpedoes known as *Kaiten* (loosely, "to shake the heavens"), tiny one-man submarines which rammed enemy ships.

To Japanese, the men of the Special Attack Force were esteemed as modern-day versions of the samurai who placed honor and service above all considerations including life itself. The most dramatic manifestation of the nation's will to resist, the kamikaze constituted the only morale-building force left to Japan in the dark hours of 1945. Most were in their early twenties and were not professional soldiers or experienced pilots, neither of whom could be spared for suicide missions. The typical kamikaze pilot was a university graduate. According to the fascinating study of Ivan Morris, who analyzed their records, diaries, and letters, "the principal type was quiet, serious, and above average in both culture and sensibility."

Clearly, the contagion of peer pressure, the febrile wartime atmosphere, and years of classroom indoctrination must have exerted powerful psychological influences on the young volunteers. Nevertheless, the men for these suicide missions were not conscripted to the task. It is impossible to generalize with absolute certainty about the entire group—more than five thousand suicide volunteers went to their death—but it seems certain that few if any were coerced by recruitment boards or superior officers. Kamikaze pilots were volunteers, and there was never any shortage of volunteers. Similarly, the stories, widely circulated among Americans, of wild parties at which reluctant volunteers were doped or rendered senseless with *sake*, appear to have little basis in fact, nor were the volunteers motivated by some Buddhist notion of survival after death. This represents a facile Western misreading of both Buddhism and the Japanese. The average, well-educated kamikaze pilot was probably dubious about any popular religious notions that promised rewards after life. If Buddhism worked an influence on him, it was more likely, as Ivan Morris writes, because of its "stress on non-ego and self-denial (*muga*) [which] teaches that we can escape the sufferings inherent in the human condition only by surmounting the illusion of the self and its desires, above all the desire to survive."

Their letters and diary entries, however, reveal little of such Buddhist metaphysics. Still less do they reveal jingoistic bravado. More commonly, what they do reveal are some deep Confucian wellsprings: satisfaction at being able to repay a debt for favors received from family and country. In a last letter, typically dictated from the plane just before takeoff, one lieutenant writes: "Words cannot express my gratitude to the loving parents who reared and tended me to manhood that I might in some small manner reciprocate the grace which His Imperial Majesty has bestowed upon us." This was a perfect expression of the Japanese moral sense grounded in *giri* (duty) and *on* (the debt of gratitude). There was little time for formal indoctrination of the kamikaze pilots, but the warrior primer known as the *Hagakure* instructed the kamikaze pilot, no less than the eighteenth-century samurai for whom it was written, to confront death: "One should expect death daily so that, when the time comes, one can die in peace. Calamity, when it occurs, is not so dreadful as was feared. . . . Die every morning in your mind," the samurai manual concluded.

BATTLESHIP *YAMATO*

Another species of kamikaze which appeared—and disappeared—during the Okinawa campaign was HMS *Yamato*. The word *Yamato*, a venerable synonym for Japan itself, is freighted with emotional significance to Japanese. Used in phrases like *Yamato-damashii* (Yamato spirit), it connoted triumph of the Japanese way. Commissioned shortly after Pearl Harbor, HMS *Yamato* was the largest battleship afloat in the world war. Its specifications were awesome. Its armor was the heaviest installed in any warship. Sixteen-inch steel plate protected the sides of the ship, while the engines and boiler rooms were covered with plate thick enough to withstand a 2500-pound armor-piercing bomb dropped from ten thousand feet. Each of its heavy turrets weighed as much as a heavy destroyer, and each supported three guns, seventy feet in length and capable of hurling 18.1-inch shells which weighed 3,320 pounds—the weight of an automobile—for a distance of almost thirty statute miles.

On April 6, the "unsinkable" *Yamato* and nine escort ships weighed anchor from their home port to Okinawa. The task force had no air cover, and most of the ships had barely enough fuel for a one-way trip. "Returning is simply not in the plans," one of *Yamato's* officers wrote. Instead, it was on a suicide mission, under orders to break through the American fleet off Okinawa, beach itself on the shores of the island, and turn its huge guns against the invading forces. The operation miscarried. Well short of its goal, the *Yamato* was spotted by American reconnaissance planes, and after taking twelve torpedoes, it sank in a vast fireball visible from the coast of Kyushu a hundred miles away. Although crews were authorized to abandon ship at the last minute, 2500 perished including the captain, lashed by his own hand to the ship's compass. There were twelve American casualties. With the sinking of the *Yamato* and five other capital ships on April 7, the Imperial Navy effectively ceased to exist. In the minds of the few who allowed themselves such unpatriotic thoughts, the requiem for battleship *Yamato* was in fact a requiem for the Empire itself.

Military experts disagree on the strictly military significance of the kamikaze. Certainly, the damage they inflicted did not halt the overall U.S. advance in the war. In the Okinawa campaign, the kamikaze corps sank thirty-two ships but failed to destroy a single major target such as an aircraft carrier. Nevertheless, more than three hundred vessels, including several carriers, were put out of commission. Most were able to return to the fray, but sixty-one were so badly damaged as to be out of the war. The toll in human life is beyond dispute. Navy casualties were the heaviest of any campaign in the Pacific, and most of the 5200 sailors killed (and 4800 wounded) were victims of kamikaze attacks. Beyond such statistics, however, it is possible to see the kamikaze as immensely important—in ways which were unintended by Japanese strategists. Far from overawing Americans with their courage, as was expected, the kamikaze generated a wave of revulsion and indignation which, as Ivan Morris notes, "was out of all proportion to their practical importance and had much the same psychological effect as did the German V-1 and V-2 rockets in England, which were similarly despised as 'unfair' weapons." Most importantly, the "fanaticism" of the kamikaze tactics "served to warn the Americans of the immense casualties they could expect if they proceeded with their plans to invade the home islands in the autumn of 1945."

A young radar officer aboard *Yamato* writes of his last hour on the bridge of the ship, with bullets bouncing all around him. It occurs to him that throughout the entire battle "not a single [American] pilot is so rash as to crash his plane into us." He writes: "Coming in again and again on the ideal approach, precisely, calmly, they evoke in us a sense of exhilaration. Virtuosi. Theirs is a strength we cannot divine, a force we cannot fathom."

—Yoshida Mitsuru, *Requiem for Battleship* Yamato.

BAMBOO SPEAR TACTICS

On May 7, while fighting on Okinawa was at its heaviest, the Japanese learned of the capitulation of Nazi Germany to General Dwight Eisenhower. It was clear now that the Allies would soon be able to divert ever more manpower and resources to the Far East. As the battle for Okinawa drew to an end in June 1945, Japan was a totally broken nation. Only in China and in the puppet state of Manchukuo were large formal Japanese armies holding their own. Everywhere else there was defeat and desperation.

A nuclear weapons program had been launched and might have given Japan important leverage had it succeeded. One of Hitler's last acts was to authorize the shipment of a half-ton of uranium oxide to his Axis ally, Japan. In March, one month before the Nazi leader's suicide, the U-234, one of the Reich's largest submarines, left the port of Kiel with provisions for a six- to nine-month trip to Japan. It was in mid-Atlantic when news of German surrender came, and the precious cargo ended up at the U.S. naval base in Portsmouth, New Hampshire. Contrary to some sensationalist postwar accounts, the nuclear fuel would have made little difference even if it had reached Japan. Like everything else in the Japan of 1945, Japan's equivalent of the Americans' "Manhattan Project" was starved for funds, manpower, and equipment and in a state of complete exhaustion. The Japanese scientists worked in a remodeled dining hall and other cramped, out-of-date, ill-equipped labs that could not even count on a steady supply of electricity or water after the spring 1945 air raids began.

No matter how bleak its prospects, there was strong evidence that the leadership was digging in for a fight to the death in the home islands—literally digging in. In the mountains of Nagano prefecture, several thousand Korean laborers were conscripted to excavate an enormous underground tunnel complex which would serve as the Imperial Headquarters operations center when the invasion came. School life virtually came to an end as youngsters down to the age of ten were mobilized to serve in "volunteer labor corps." Males between the ages of fifteen and sixty and females from seventeen to forty were recruited into "voluntary" military service in April 1945. Army soldiers trained them in the use of barbed wire, the construction of pill boxes, the building of traps for armored vehicles, and other guerrilla tactics. "Close-quarter attacks" would make up for the army's lack of effective antitank weapons. Soldiers and volunteers alike were shown how to strap explosives to their waist and throw themselves under the treads of tanks. A graphically illustrated *People's Handbook of Combat Resistance* provided instructions in making Molotov cocktails, karate assaults, attacking from behind with cleavers, and aiming rifles at descending parachutists (allow two-and-a-half lengths).

There were, however, few modern rifles for these hastily organized volunteers. Instead, the army was psychologically conditioning "100 million people" (that is the entire population of the Empire) to die rather than surrender and to take at least one American with them in their death. The "weapons" issued to the home-front militia included pitchforks, bows and arrows, carpenter's awls, knives, ancient muzzle-loading muskets, and, most commonly, sharpened bamboo spears. The bamboo spears recalled the prewar fantasy of General Araki Sadao that "we would be able to conquer Russia easily if we could have three million bamboo spears." These primitive instruments came to symbolize the desperation tactics to which the nation sank in the last months of the war.

By June, the military command was of course no longer under any illusions that it could avoid defeat. It felt, however, that Americans were duly impressed with the increasingly determined resistance they were meeting as they moved closer to the Japanese home islands. They calculated that Americans would not be prepared to accept the awful manpower costs brought on by an invasion of Japan itself. Surely Americans would realize that homeland beaches would be defended in depth by an aroused army and civilian population prepared to die. The resulting carnage would make the Pacific island atolls seem like picnic excursions by comparison. Accordingly, as long as the "bamboo spear psychology" was maintained, there was hope that America might agree to end the war on terms acceptable to Japan.

ESTIMATING CASUALTIES

This too, however, was miscalculation. Consideration had been given to U.S. Navy proposals to make some landings in China and simply intensify the blockade against Japan rather than invade. The army rejected the idea, however, on the grounds that the China operations would be costly and inconclusive, and a blockade of Japan might drag on for years. Undaunted, the Allies went ahead with plans for an assault on the southernmost island of Kyushu near Kagoshima on November 1, 1945. As these plans were being made in the spring of 1945, it should be remembered that the planners had no reason to believe that the United States would possess an atomic bomb before the summer was out. Many of the planners, even those at the very highest levels, did not even know of the existence of the super-secret nuclear weapons project Manhattan.

Code-named Operation "Olympic," the first-stage invasion plan called for an assault force of 650,000. Four months later, Operation "Coronet," an invasion of the main island of Honshu, would take place. A million or more men, this time including British, Australian and Canadians, would take part in the second phase. General MacArthur, designated as the commander of the invasion forces, would have at his disposal a war fleet with a displacement of 15 million tons, an armada which included no less than one hundred aircraft carriers of all sizes. In the grand design for the conquest of Japan, it was estimated that no less than seven million Allied personnel would be directly or indirectly involved.

Nobody knew how many lives an invasion of Japan would take. The various conjectures on casualties are important since those estimates were later used to justify dropping the atomic bombs. It was known that the Japanese Army in Japan numbered almost two million. It was also known that Japan still possessed huge numbers of aircraft, and that over five thousand—mostly light training planes—were being held in reserve and converted for use in kamikaze missions. It had to be assumed that these would take a frightful toll of MacArthur's landing force. After the war was over, the estimate of one million U.S. casualties—dead and wounded—was frequently cited. Several presumably well-informed officials (including Secretary of War Henry L. Stimson and Secretary of State James F. Byrnes) used that figure in postwar memoirs. It is known that Chairman of the Joint Chiefs of Staff Admiral William D. Leahy advised President Truman (Harry Truman became president when Roosevelt died in April 1945) that Operation Olympic might produce 268,000 dead and wounded for the United States. Leahy based his calculations on a repetition of the Okinawa campaign casualty rate.

It is now clear, however, that these decision makers also had substantially lower estimates presented to them. General MacArthur suggested that 50,800 casualties were likely to be incurred in the decisive first thirty days of fighting on Kyushu. Later, however, he reduced his estimates, and in June 1945, when the final authorization to use the bombs was being made, Army Chief of Staff George Marshall put forth a figure of only thirty-one thousand.

While the question of potential casualties remains clouded, a more important concern must be considered: Was an invasion of the home territory of Japan necessary? Or is it possible that a negotiated settlement of the war was possible? Exploring this issue will take us a step further into the controversy concerning the need for exploding the two atomic bombs over Japanese cities in August 1945. Those who argue that the bombs were not necessary to force a Japanese surrender insist that, as early as the fall of Saipan in July 1944 and by no later than the spring of 1945, a peace faction had begun to emerge in Tokyo. Significant members of the Japanese leadership, including the pre-war Prime Minister Konoe Fumimaro, knew that the nation was defeated and were searching for a way to negotiate peace with the Allies. This pro-surrender mood was deepened by the continuing loss of territory in the Pacific and the growing evidence of the destructiveness of American air power.

ADDITIONAL READING

The best single-volume study of the war in the Pacific is Ronald H. Spector, *Eagle Against the Sun: The American War with Japan* (1985). It also contains a fine annotated bibliography. Waldo Heinrichs, "World War II" in *Kodansha Encyclopedia of Japan*, Volume 8 (1983), is a highly condensed and authoritative account. Useful secondary works include: John Toland, *The Rising Sun: The Decline and Fall of the Japanese Empire* (1970); John Costello, *The Pacific War, 1941–1945* (1981); Dan vander Vat, *The Pacific Campaign* (1991); and Edwin P. Hoyt, *Japan's War: The Great Pacific Conflict* (1986).

Two studies by Christopher Thorne masterfully survey the political and cultural dimensions of the war: *Allies of a Kind: The United States, Britain and the War Against Japan* (1978) and *The Issue of War: States, Societies and the Far Eastern Conflict of 1941–1945* (1985). *Power and Culture: The Japanese-American War, 1941–1945* (1981) by Akira Iriye also focuses on the interplay between cultural and international relations during wartime. John W. Dower, *War Without Mercy: Race and Power in the Pacific War* (1986) is a monumentally important exposition of the racist wartime behavior of both the United States and Japan; it also contains a comprehensive bibliography on the literature of the war.

On the China phase of the war, see Chalmers A. Johnson, *Peasant Nationalism and Communist Power: The Emergence of Revolutionary China, 1937–1945* (1962); Michael Lindsay, *The Unknown War: North China, 1937–1945* (1975), with many illustrations; Dick Wilson, *When Tigers Fight: The Story of the Sino–Japanese War, 1937–1945* (1982); Lloyd Eastman, *Seeds of Destruction: Nationalist China in War and Revolution, 1937–1949* (1984); and John Hunter Boyle, *China and Japan at War, 1937–1945: The Politics of Collaboration* (1972).

Many of the leading actors of the war, both Japanese and Americans, have been the subject of biographical studies. See, for example D. Clayton James, *The Years of MacArthur*, 2 vols. (1972–1975); William Manchester, *American Caesar: Douglas MacArthur 1880–1964* (1978); and Barbara Tuchman, *Stilwell and the American Experience in China* (1970). Works on Japanese wartime leaders include Toshiaki Kawahara, *Hirohito and His Times: A Japanese Perspective* (1990); Agawa Hiroyuki, *Yamamoto Isoroku* (1980); and the indispensable *Tojo and the Coming of the War* by Robert J. C. Butow (1961). The fascinating case of "Tokyo Rose" has been discussed in Masayo Duus, *Tokyo Rose: Orphan of the Pacific* (1979); and more recently by Russell Warren Howe, in *The Hunt for "Tokyo Rose"* (1990).

There is scarcely a military battle or a phase of the Pacific War which has not been the subject of a book. Among the notable ones are Bill D. Ross, *Iwo Jima: Legacy of Valor* (1985); Samuel B. Griffith II, *The Battle for Guadalcanal* (1963); William Manchester, *Goodbye Darkness: A Memoir of the Pacific War* (1979); John J. Stephan, *Hawaii Under the Rising Sun: Japan's Plans for Conquest after Pearl Harbor* (1984); Mitsuru Yoshida, *Requiem for Battleship* 'Yamato' (Richard H. Minear, trans., 1985); and Admiral Samuel Eliot Morison's *The Two-Ocean War: A Short History of the United States Navy in the Second World War* (1963) has achieved the status of a classic.

Highly recommended are a number of books which present the war through Japanese eyes: Ben-Ami Shillony, *Politics and Culture in Wartime Japan* (1981); Thomas R. H. Havens, *Valley of Darkness: The Japanese People and World War Two* (1978); Ienaga Saburo, *The Pacific War: World War II and the Japanese, 1931–1945* (1978); Time-Life Books, *Japan at War* (1980); and Donald Keene, "Japanese Writers and the Greater East Asia War," *Journal of Asian Studies*, 23/2 (1964). Translated wartime literature includes Hiroshi Noma, *Zone of Emptiness* (Bernard Frechtman, trans., 1956); Shohei Ooka, *Fires on the Plain* (Ivan Morris, trans., 1957); and Michio Takeyama, *Harp of Burma* (Howard Hibbett, trans., 1966).

There is a vast literature on the subject of the wartime Japanese detention in America. For recently written condensed accounts, see Chapter 6 of *Asian America: Chinese and Japanese in the United States Since 1850* (1988) by Roger Daniels, and Chapter 10 of *Strangers from a Different Shore* (1989) by Ronald Takaki. For more-detailed accounts, see *Justice at War: The Story of the Japanese American Internment Cases* (1983) by Peter Iron; and the official report of the Commission on Wartime Relocation and Internment of Civilians, *Personal Justice Denied* (1982). Masayo Umezawa Duus's *Unlikely Liberators: The Men of the 100th and 442nd* (Peter Duus, trans., 1983) is an account of the the fighting role of Japanese Americans in the European campaigns against Germany.

Many of the entries appended to Chapter 8 may also be useful.

8

HIROSHIMA

The events which brought the Pacific war to an end have become fully as controversial as the events which ushered in the beginning of the war. In order to force the surrender of Japan, nuclear weapons were dropped on two Japanese cities, the only such use in history. From the time the hatch doors of a solitary B-29 were opened to release the first nuclear weapon over Hiroshima on August 6, 1945, the world has never been quite the same.

The colossal cloud which mushroomed into the Japanese skies that morning ushered in the atomic era. For the first time, humankind was forced to confront the possibility of weaponry so awesome as to threaten whole cities or nations with instant annihilation. Indeed, as arsenals of nuclear weapons proliferated in the decades after 1945, notions of Armageddon and the apocalypse, once confined to the dim Biblical past, were updated by some who contemplated the sudden extinction of civilization itself. Thus, to Arthur Koestler, Hiroshima became "the central crisis" of our time. "From the dawn of consciousness until the middle of our century man had to live with the prospect of his death as an individual; since Hiroshima, mankind as a whole has to live with the prospect of its extinction as a biological species." At one extreme, there have been those who responded to this fearsome possibility by advocating nuclear disarmament, unilateral if necessary, to defuse the danger. In response, others have cautioned that nuclear weapons cannot be *dis*invented and, in spite of the fear they provoke, have actually exercised a profoundly stabilizing influence on the international scene since 1945.

More germane to this book, however, is the controversy surrounding the use of the bomb in 1945 to end the war. Indeed, so-called revisionist historians argue that the bomb was *not* used to end the war. They maintain that there was no military necessity for the use of nuclear force against a Japan which was on the verge of total collapse. Rather, they argue, the bomb was used to impress the

Russians. In this sense, it is held that the bomb was not so much the last act of World War II but the first act of the Cold War. To assess this argument, it is necessary to trace the varying responses of the Japanese leadership to the disasters which were overtaking their nation in the spring of 1945.

PEACE AND THE "HONOR OF JAPAN"

The first hints that Japanese officials were contemplating surrender began to reach the Allies shortly after the March 10 Tokyo air raid. At the end of that month, Japanese Foreign Minister Shigemitsu Mamoru approached the ambassador of neutral Sweden to see whether he would be willing to sound out the position of the Allies regarding peace negotiations. Shigemitsu emphasized the gravity of Japan's military situation and "stipulated only that the terms be consonant with the honor of Japan." The Swedish ambassador, en route home after a long tour of duty in Tokyo, agreed to undertake the mission and did manage to brief the American ambassador in Stockholm. At about the same time, in Europe's other major neutral country, Switzerland, two similar probings by Japanese military attachés were under way. The inquiries in Berne reached the man in charge of U.S. covert intelligence operations in Europe, Allen Dulles of the Office of Strategic Services (the OSS, predecessor organization to the Central Intelligence Agency).

In each case, however, the secret contacts accomplished nothing. There was no evidence that the parties involved were authorized by the government, still less by ranking authorities in the army and navy, to conduct negotiations or make commitments. It was well appreciated in Washington that there was a good chance that "peace feelers" were being used for psychological purposes by Tokyo—"to probe vulnerable points in enemy [U.S.] morale without the possibility of official embarrassment." Adding to the confusion was a change of government in Tokyo.

In April 1945, only days after the first peace demarche, a seventy-eight-year-old retired veteran of the navy, Admiral Baron Suzuki Kantaro, became prime minister. Suzuki, in poor health and partially deaf, had no political skills, but he did have close ties with the imperial household, where he had served as head chamberlain for several years. Presently, he would become the highest ranking member of a loose coalition of peace advocates. However, at the time of his taking office, it was not clear that the new prime minister was a dove and, in any case, the slightest public hint that he was would have invited assassination. He headed an unstable cabinet which represented many views. Without the support of army hard-liners, who clearly had doubts about the old man's reliability, he could not have organized a government—and the army demanded, and received, as price for its backing a solemn promise that Suzuki would prosecute the war to the bitter end.

While the peace feelers in Sweden and Switzerland were allowed to wither, the new government did move forward on what it felt was a more promising diplomatic front, with the Soviet Union. Japan had signed a neutrality pact with the U.S.S.R. in 1941, and in the crisis year of 1945, the treaty with the Soviet Union still had one more year to run before it expired. Certain ominous signs of Soviet hostility were appearing. In April, the Russians announced that they would not renew their treaty with Japan once it expired in 1946. As the war in Europe wound down, it was noticed that large numbers of Russian soldiers were being sent from the European war fronts to the Soviet Far East. To counter such moves, it was decided that efforts would be made to "entice" the Kremlin into a more friendly relationship with Japan. At best, it was hoped that Josef Stalin, the Soviet premier, would extend help in the form of oil and other crucial war matériel to Japan. Additionally, the hope was that Stalin would use his influence with the Allies to obtain peace terms favorable to Japan.

THE MOSCOW CONNECTION

In hindsight, the hope for Soviet help seems preposterously naive. Japan's ambassador in Moscow, Sato Naotake, advised his superiors in Tokyo that it would be necessary for Tokyo to first make up its mind. Only if it would admit that it was firmly resolved to surrender could it hope for Soviet intercession. In Tokyo, new Foreign Minister Togo Shigenori knew that he could not offend the army diehards by making such a flat concession. Instead, as Leon V. Sigal writes, "[Togo] was hoping to use the Moscow approach to forge that resolve at home." Togo and those who backed the Moscow approach knew that it was a desperate gamble, but they had few alternatives. They argued that the Soviet Union's wartime alliance with the Western powers was nothing more than a marriage of convenience. The Soviet Union had every reason to believe that America would emerge incredibly strong in the Far East if Japan was totally crushed. Japan *was* still in a position to counter America's strength by granting concessions to Moscow—Togo warned that it might be necessary to offer Stalin control over Manchuria and return to pre-Russo–Japanese War boundaries, for example, in order to appease the Communist leader. Historian Robert J. C. Butow sums up the basis for these admittedly slim hopes on the part of those seeking a negotiated settlement to the war: "Why should the Soviet Union fight in the Far East if she could gain a dominant position there merely by acting as Japan's diplomatic broker?"

Whatever the merits of that argument, it is a fact that entreaties were filed with both the Soviet ambassador in Tokyo and the foreign minister in Moscow. It is also a fact that while these secret entreaties were being made, the army was reaffirming again and again at home its steadfast conviction that "one hundred million" Japanese would crush the Americans on the beaches. By early July, the failure of Moscow to offer its good offices to Japan—indeed, its failure to give any satisfactory responses to Japanese overtures—was causing extreme consternation in Tokyo. On July 12, plans were made to send Prince Konoe Fumimaro on a peace mission to Moscow, with a personal message from the Throne. Still, the Soviets remained cool to the overtures from Tokyo: Soviet Foreign Minister

Vyacheslav Molotov even declined to meet with Ambassador Sato Naotake to discuss a Konoe peace mission. Nevertheless, Foreign Minister Togo continued to press Sato in Moscow to emphasize to Kremlin leaders that Japan was sincere in seeking Soviet help. The appeals from Tokyo grew more urgent, even desperate, in tone. "Convey His Majesty's strong desire to secure a termination of the war," one cable read. Another spoke of the need for Ambassador Sato to exert further efforts "to somehow make the Soviet Union enthusiastic over the special envoy. . . . Since the loss of one day relative to this present matter may result in a thousand years of regret, it is requested that you immediately have a talk with Molotov."

Here, three points need to be stressed. The first is that U.S. intelligence authorities were fully aware of the existence of a peace faction in Tokyo and its determination to bring Moscow into the process as a mediator. As in the critical days of 1941, the United States was still able to read Japan's most secret thoughts via MAGIC. Messages flowing from Tokyo to Moscow, and Moscow back to Tokyo, were intercepted, decoded, translated, and perused in Washington, D.C., almost as quickly as they were by the Japanese principals—who still had no inkling that Americans had broken their top-secret code. As in 1941, the texts of the Japanese cable traffic were guarded very closely in Washington. It is not known exactly which messages were viewed by which policy-maker in Washington, but it is clear that periodic summaries of the Togo–Sato exchanges were read by Secretary of War Henry Stimson and Navy Secretary James Forrestal; it is also known that Secretary of State James F. Byrnes and President Truman were familiar with the gist of these messages.

Second, U.S. authorities were also aware that the peace faction in Tokyo was obliged to act very cautiously lest their moves trigger a violent response from the diehards. Togo, for example, chided Sato for not being careful enough to keep his peace activities sufficiently covert: "If word should ever leak out, the results would be most dire," Sato was warned by the foreign minister.

Third, it is most important to understand that while U.S. authorities knew that there was a responsible peace faction in Tokyo, it also knew that the peace faction was not willing to initiate talks for *unconditional* surrender. Sato repeatedly stated that it was his view that without that willingness the peace faction could not hope to accomplish anything. Repeatedly the response came back from the Japanese capital that unconditional surrender was out of the question. Nobody in Tokyo, neither the peace faction nor certainly the military diehards who would not admit that Japan had lost the war, could accept unconditional surrender. If the Allies were to continue to insist on this point, Togo advised Sato on July 25, "there is no solution other than for us to hold out until complete collapse because of this point alone."

RETAINING THE EMPEROR

Despite the fact that the United States gleaned so much from reading Japan's diplomatic "mail," there was never any serious consideration given to opening up peace talks with Japan. The sticking point was the unconditional surrender issue.

What conditions did Japanese wish to have clarified? Japan wished to know something of the Allies' intentions following surrender. Did the Allies intend to exact war costs and other reparations from the loser? Did the Allies intend to strip Japan of its Empire? All of the Empire? Did the Allies intend to occupy Japan? For how long? Forever? It was possible that some of these concerns could be ignored, but there was one assurance which the Japanese authorities needed to have from the victors: What did the Allies intend to do about the emperor? There was ample evidence from reading American news broadcasts that both popular and Congressional opinion favored a trial of the emperor. Reports from Britain, Australia, and elsewhere were equally vehement in calling for the arrest of the emperor. If the Allies in fact intended to treat Emperor Hirohito as a war criminal and possibly execute him, it is doubtful that even the most ardent supporters of peace would countenance Japan's surrender.

It was not simply a matter of personal reverence for the man Hirohito which prompted this regard for the emperor's fate. Among the leadership of Japan was a profound awareness that Japan was living through the darkest moment of its history. The nation was in ashes, its economic might had been demolished, and the people faced starvation. With surrender, the nation would also be psychologically shattered. For so long, glory and victory had been promised as the eventual reward for courage and suffering; now, this was all coming to be seen as the hollow promises of a bankrupt leadership. Presently, with surrender, the national disillusion would be total. Many feared that there was good reason to think that Japan was facing not merely defeat but national extinction. How could Japan hope to revive itself and rebuild unless there was some central symbol of the nation around which to focus national energies and determination? The army was a logical rallying point for patriotic reconstruction, but the Allies obviously would not permit the Imperial Army to survive in anything like its traditional self. Shinto was also a possible focal point but, it was, after all, impersonal and vague to many and, like the army, was surely destined for radical alteration by the victors.

That left the emperor. Not just the man Hirohito but the imperial institution, as old as the nation itself, the central and unique identifying mark of Japanese polity. If the Allies intended to humiliate the emperor or terminate this institution, it seemed to tradition-minded Japanese men like Prince Konoe that the nation was doomed. If the Allies had no such intentions, why could they not provide Japan with a simple guarantee to that effect?

Konoe also, we now know, was deeply concerned that with each passing day the conditions for a Communist revolution were growing in Japan (as well as in China and elsewhere abroad). Although the Communist movement in Japan had been thoroughly crushed with police roundups beginning in the late 1920s, Konoe feared that the desperate state of people's livelihood would play into the hands of radicals who would promise an overthrow of the old order which was bringing so much grief to the nation. Indeed, by the summer of 1945, there were signs that the much praised unity between people and the army was breaking down as a countrywide war weariness settled on Japan. There were reports, for example, of army discipline eroding, and of riffraff wearing the imperial uniform swarming into towns and villages in search of food. As early as February 1945, Konoe addressed a memorial to the Throne in which he outlined his fears that Communist agitators were recruiting a following within the army itself. "The majority of our professional soldiers come from below middle-class families, and their circumstances make them receptive to Communist doctrine," Konoe declared.

In hindsight, these fears seem preposterous. All but a handful of the radicals remained in prison. The most important exception was Nozaka Sanzo, and he was in Yenan, China, serving with Mao. There were two occasions during 1943–1944 when writers tested the limits of the censors' patience by expressing Marxist sentiments in journals which were widely read by intellectuals. In both cases the culprits were dealt with harshly by the Thought Police, and the journals were shut down for the duration of the war. At the time, however, the fears of a revival of communism were real enough to Prince Konoe and others. It would not have been the first time, after all, that Communists had taken advantage of a nation's disorder and misery and declining military fortunes to usurp power—that was a description of the Bolshevik revolution of 1917. These apprehensions caused Konoe to urge those around him, including the emperor, to seek an end to the war as rapidly as possible. At the same time, though, to insist in any negotiations upon the survival of the imperial institution as *the* stabilizing influence most likely to thwart a Communist revolution.

UNCONDITIONAL SURRENDER

The United States, since early in the war, insisted on unconditional surrender from both Germany and Japan. One reason for this nettlesome policy was grounded in the history of World War I. Adolf Hitler had always claimed that Germany was "betrayed" into capitulation rather than defeated on the battlefield. Using this emotionally charged argument, he had been able to whip up popular support for his program to redress the wrongs of 1918. If the Allies in that year had insisted upon unconditional surrender rather than a mere armistice, Hitler's appeal would have been undercut. Furthermore, in World War II, the Allies—Britain, France, the United States and the Soviet Union—were never without suspicion of each other, each fearing that one or more of the powers would make separate peace arrangements with either Germany or Japan and then bow out of the war.

To allay such fears, Roosevelt and Winston Churchill announced at the January 1943 Casablanca Conference that the war, both in Europe and Asia, would end only with the "unconditional surrender" of the enemy. It was a bold move which fired the resolve of the Allies, but it doubtless made it easier for Hitler and the Japanese leadership to persuade their people to fight to the bitter end.

VIEWS ON KEEPING THE EMPEROR
"I am absolutely convinced that had we said they could keep the emperor, together with the threat of the atomic bomb, they would have accepted, and we would never have had to drop the bomb."

—John J. McCloy, Assistant Secretary of War, to *New York Times*, 1965.

"What do you think we should do with the Japanese emperor after the war?"
"Execute him." (33 %)
"Let the court decide his fate." (17 %)
"Keep him in prison the rest of his life." (11 %)
"Exile." (9 %)
"Nothing." (On grounds that he was figurehead.) (4 %)
"Use him as puppet." (3 %)

—Gallup Poll, June 29, 1945.

Certain basic assurances were given to Japan by President Truman: Surrender would not lead to "the extermination or enslavement of the Japanese people" and it would provide, he said, "for the return of soldiers and sailors to their families, their farms, their jobs." No promises, however, were made regarding the future status of the emperor.[1]

Washington was well aware of the importance of the emperor question, and it was vigorously debated. A so-called "Japan lobby," including the prewar ambassador to Tokyo Joseph C. Grew (after 1944, undersecretary of state) and Henry L. Stimson, pleaded with President Truman to modify the unconditional surrender demands by guaranteeing to the Japanese people that the emperor would not be harmed. They tried to convince the president that the emperor was the only one who *could* surrender, the only one with sufficient authority and prestige to command the military forces of Japan to lay down arms. For a time, they seem to have swayed President Truman to accept their proposals.

PUBLIC OPINION

In the end, however, other advisers to the president, including newly appointed Secretary of State James F. Byrnes, prevailed on the president to retain the unconditional surrender policy and refrain from any concession regarding the emperor. They convinced the president that making a concession to the Japanese would only play into the hands of the military diehards who were saying that America was war-weary after the costly Okinawa campaign. Truman knew that whatever policy he chose involved risks, but in the end he

---

[1] Harry S Truman became president upon the death of Roosevelt on April 12, 1945.

decided that to back away from the policy of unconditional surrender would likely indicate a weakness of will on the part of the Allies and prolong the war.

It would also seem, however, that his decision was influenced by the need to bend to political pressures. His advisers argued that American public opinion would not tolerate an explicit guarantee retaining the emperor. Mail reaching the White House was overwhelmingly in favor of the harshest possible terms for Japan. In a public opinion poll taken at the end of 1944, 13 percent of the respondents voted to "kill all Japanese" after the war was over. Congressional sentiment was equally vengeful: "Let the Japs know unqualifiedly what unconditional surrender means. Let the dirty rats squeal," one congressman demanded. "Probably in all our history," Pulitzer Prize-winner Allan Nevins wrote, "no foe has been so detested as were the Japanese." Lieutenant General Leslie Groves, the military director of the project to develop the atomic bomb, summed up the political ramifications for the White House if the president temporized:

> . . . [I]t would have come out sooner or later in a Congressional hearing, if nowhere else, just when we could have dropped the bomb if we didn't use it. And then, knowing American politics, you know as well as I do that there would have been elections fought on the basis that every mother whose son was killed after such and such a date—the blood was on the President.

WARTIME ATROCITIES

The pursuit of final and total victory by any means was legitimized in the mind of most Americans by the treachery of the attack on Pearl Harbor and the intensity of Japanese resistance in the Pacific campaign. In addition, there was a growing sense of outrage over the reports of Japanese atrocities throughout the war. Americans were also responsible for atrocities, for orders to "take no prisoners," for strafing of seamen in lifeboats, sinking of hospital ships, and the mutilation of the deceased. Also from the point of view of most Japanese, the mass bombings of cities was inhumanity on a colossal scale. Not surprisingly, however, Americans regarded the Japanese as a singularly merciless adversary whose uncivilized conduct of the war nullified any need for humane consideration. Two incidents were particularly important in shaping popular American attitudes concerning the Japanese soldier:

BATAAN DEATH MARCH. To Second World War-era Americans, the name of the Bataan peninsula in the Philippines meant only one thing: death march. In April 1942, when Japanese troops captured this area, they were astounded to find themselves with seventy-six thousand American and Filipino prisoners of war, about three times larger than the number expected. With supplies and a transport system barely capable of sustaining their own forces, the Japanese ordered their dehydrated and starving captors on a sixty-five-mile forced march in the blazing sun. About 7000, including 2300 Americans, did not survive the ordeal. While most died from exhaustion or illness, many were bayoneted, buried alive, or shot. More than any other incident in the war, this grim episode became a focal point of hate and revenge for Americans.

DOOLITTLE RAID EXECUTIONS. After the Doolittle raid on Tokyo, the Japanese government adopted laws making captured airmen involved in indiscriminate bombing raids subject to capital punishment. Scores were executed during the course of the war, but it was the torture and execution of three of the Doolittle flyers which aroused the most ire in the United States and became the subject of a 1944 movie, *Purple Heart*, which depicted the fate of the airmen. (Five others from the Doolittle raid were given life sentences.) Within the small Western community in wartime Tokyo, even among German diplomats, there was shock at the racial condescension in the Japanese press reports on the handling of aviators.

Beyond such specific factors, however, there was a more general dynamic at work. As John Dower has shown in *War Without Mercy*, a masterful study of the Pacific war as a race war, both sides were guilty of depicting the other as bestial, stripped of all human qualities. As these extremist images took hold, Americans became "devils" *(Beiki)* in the mind of Japanese. In America, the cartoon image of the Japanese commonly fixed him as either a grinning, myopic, bucktoothed moron or in the guise of certain subhuman species: vipers, snakes, rats, and monkeys were favored.

Paradoxically, when the Japanese were not depicted as subhuman, they were feared as superhuman. In the minds of some, there developed a new myth of Japanese invincibility, combining their utter ruthlessness, fanaticism, and an unlimited capacity for evil. It entailed, Dower writes, "visions of Japan leading the 'billion' other Asians against the West, and apprehensions of special occult or 'Oriental' powers that were simply beyond the grasp of Europeans and Americans." In either case, however, as Japanese were dehumanized as subhuman or superhuman, it became all the more necessary and all the more justifiable to destroy the enemy once and for all.

More than one out of five American respondents to a *Fortune* magazine poll in December 1945, nearly a half year after the war had ended, expressed the wish that the United States had had the opportunity to use "many more of them [atomic bombs] before Japan had a chance to surrender." A letter to the *Milwaukee Journal* expressed the opinion of many: "When one sets out to destroy vermin, does one try to leave a few alive in the nest? Certainly not."

THE ATOMIC BOMB

In 1939, as war clouds gathered over Europe, Albert Einstein and several other physicists who had sought refuge in America from Axis tyranny,

UNIT 731

Perhaps the most sinister atrocities of the war occurred in a mysterious biological warfare project. Unlike the Doolittle executions and the Bataan savagery, the medical experimentation that occurred at "Unit 731" was not public knowledge until the war was over. Unit 731 was a Japanese Army detachment near Harbin in the puppet state of Manchukuo. Under the command of General Ishii Shiro, the Imperial Army used live human beings as guinea pigs to measure susceptibility to plague, cholera, smallpox, typhus and other diseases. Other experiments included marching poorly clad and poorly fed prisoners to death from exhaustion and freezing victims in "cold rooms"—it was important for Imperial Army planners to know human limits to warfare in extremely cold climates or in high-altitude flying. Most of the victims were Chinese, although it is thought that Allied prisoners of war, including some Americans, also may have been sent to Unit 731.

warned President Franklin Roosevelt that there was a danger that Nazi Germany would obtain a lead in uranium fission which could lead to their development of nuclear weaponry. Full awareness of the import of this news came slowly to the White House, but in 1941 the president became convinced that an atomic bomb could well determine the outcome of the war, a war which at that point was going very well for Germany. In October 1941, two months before Pearl Harbor, Roosevelt authorized an all-out research project, later known by the code name Manhattan (because initial work was done at Columbia University in New York's Manhattan), to ensure that Hitler would not be the first to possess atomic bombs. There is every reason to believe that the bomb, if available, would have been used against Germany if it were needed to bring the war in Europe to an end.

By the time Germany surrendered in May 1945, after four years of joint Anglo-American research and experimentation, the effort to produce a nuclear weapon was nearing climax. The Manhattan Project joined together industry, science, and government, and involved 150,000 persons including hundreds of the world's best physicists, more than a half-million man-years of work, and a blank check which exceeded $2 billion. As scientists worked around the clock to achieve the first successful test explosion of a nuclear device, it is clear that many regarded the bomb, for all its awesome destructive potential, as simply another weapon. When it was ready, it would naturally be used for whatever tactical advantage it might offer in hastening victory. President Truman, artillery captain in World War I, was clearly of this mind. Yet, as work went ahead, many of the key scientists were troubled about using the bomb "without considering the moral responsibilities which are involved"—as the Hungarian-born Jewish refugee Leo Szilard said in a petition to Truman in July 1945.

> **HARRY S TRUMAN ON THE DECISION TO DROP THE BOMB**
> "That was not any decision that you had to worry about. . . . It was just the same as getting a bigger gun than the other fellow had to win the war and that's what it was used for. Nothing else but an artillery weapon."
>
> —Columbia University, April 28, 1959.

The most avidly considered proposal from the scientists—and others in the very select group of government and military officials who were privy to the Manhattan Project—was a demonstration of the bomb. Rather than dropping the bomb unannounced, the United States would invite Japanese officials to witness a harmless, but impressive, explosion of the bomb. Some suggested that it could be dropped on an offshore Japanese island, or perhaps in the mountains. Lewis L. Strauss, then an admiral on the staff of Navy Secretary Forrestal, suggested that he had once visited a large forest of giant cryptomeria trees in Nikko, in the mountains near Tokyo. An atomic blast there, he said, would lay the trees out in windrows from the center of the explosion "as though they were matchsticks and of course set them afire. . . ." It would prove to the Japanese, he was certain, that "we could destroy their cities at will."

The demonstration idea was killed by the military, which found numerous flaws in the scheme. Perhaps most convincingly, the scientists themselves had to concede that in those early days of experimentation, the results of a test explosion could not be accurately predicted. What if the entire Japanese leadership was invited to witness the demonstration of an awesome new weapon, and it turned out to be a dud or nothing more than a "large firecracker" as one said? In addition, there were fears that the Japanese would round up large numbers of

> "If the United States were to be the first to release this new means of indiscriminate destruction upon mankind, she would sacrifice public support throughout the world, precipitate the race for armaments, and prejudice the possibility of reaching an international agreement on the future control of such weapons."
>
> —Atomic scientist James O. Franck.
>
> "But the mind, circling upon itself, may wonder whether, if the exterminating power of the bomb had not been actually displayed, the nations would have been impelled to make even as faltering an effort as they have made to agree on measures to save themselves from mutual extinction by this ultimate weapon."
>
> —State Department Historian Herbert Feis.

Allied prisoners and concentrate them near any known target area. Moreover, the Japanese, armed with advance warning, would take extraordinary measures to bring down any plane carrying such a weapon. Perhaps they would fail, but in a mission already frightfully complex and full of danger, to add more risks was surely foolhardy. If desk admirals and generals at the Pentagon put forth these objections, it seems likely that operational commanders in the field, if they had been asked, would have protested even more vigorously any plan to issue an advance warning of a demonstration.

While the moral issues regarding the use of the weapon were being debated in Washington, work went ahead on the bomb. Final assembly took place at a laboratory built on a lonely mesa at Los Alamos, outside Santa Fe, New Mexico. The work was under the direction of University of California nuclear physicist Robert J. Oppenheimer. Shortly before dawn on the morning of July 16, 1945, the soon to be familiar numbers of the final countdown, "ten–nine–eight. . . ," ushered in the atomic age. The ground trembled, and a blinding flash many times brighter than the sun at noon illuminated the desert. Oppenheimer, who had once studied Sanskrit, recalled a passage from the Hindu scriptures, the Bhagavad-Gita: "I am become Death, the shatterer of worlds."

POTSDAM

Word of the successful detonation was immediately flashed to President Truman. The president had joined Stalin and Churchill for the last of the "Big Three" wartime conferences. Held in the Berlin suburb of Potsdam, Germany, the meeting was intended to discuss issues related to postwar Europe. The agenda did not formally focus on the Far East because the Soviet Union was still not a partner in the war against Japan. Nevertheless, the best method of terminating the war in the Pacific was frequently discussed in informal sessions. On one occasion, Stalin confided to Truman—for the first time—that Japan had been seeking Soviet help to negotiate an end to the war. Because of the MAGIC intercepts, the news came as no surprise to the Americans. On another occasion, Truman casually told Stalin that the United States had developed a new weapon of "unusual destructive force." Again, the news could have come as no surprise to the Soviet leader, who for some time had been well-informed of the progress of the Manhattan Project by Soviet spies planted at Los Alamos.

As the ten-day conference drew to a close on July 26, Truman authorized the broadcast of a last ultimatum to Japan. Approval of this message, known as the Potsdam Declaration, had already been obtained from Britain and China. It made no mention of an atomic bomb, but it called upon the Japanese government to proclaim the "unconditional surrender of all Japanese armed forces." The alternative it threatened was "prompt and utter destruction." It offered no guarantees concerning the safety of Hirohito or the survival of the imperial house. It offered no timetable for an occupation of Japan except to say that occupation armies would be withdrawn after "there has been established in accordance with the freely expressed will of the Japanese people a peacefully inclined and responsible government."

The Japanese word used to reject the Potsdam Declaration, *mokusatsu*, was unfortunate and did not really convey the Cabinet's decision, which was to "table" the Allied demands. The aged Suzuki employed the word, an archaic term which literally means "to kill with silence" but had overtones so ambiguous that it might have been expected to placate both the peace faction and the diehards. Whatever Suzuki's intention, the obscure term was received by both Japanese citizens and the American government as indicating that the Japanese government was "rejecting" the Potsdam demands with contempt. Some have suggested that more moderate and straightforward language ("decline comment," for example) might have bought time for a peace process to emerge and might have changed the course of history. In view of the mood of Washington at the time, that seems unlikely, but the episode does illustrate the delicate nature of peace-making and the language of diplomacy.

Tokyo received the proclamation on July 27 in the course of its regular monitoring of American shortwave transmissions from San Francisco. The proclamation touched off a flurry of discussions among civilian and military leaders in the Japanese capital. Diehards called for flat rejection of the declaration. Moderates hoped that the United States might explain the terms of the Potsdam message. What exactly was meant by a ". . . responsible government"? It did not seem to *preclude* the survival of the emperor but neither did it guarantee survival to this foundation stone of the nation. Without clarification from the United States, the moderates were left with no choice but to agree with the diehards that the Potsdam Declaration could not be accepted. No Japanese statesman was willing to risk signing a death warrant for the imperial institution. Prime Minister Suzuki Kantaro and the other peace advocates feared the Japanese Army diehards just as much as they feared American power. They all feared the verdict of history which would forever soil their names if their actions precipitated Allied disrespect for the emperor.

No official reply was forthcoming from Tokyo, but it was learned on August 28 from reading the Japanese press that the Suzuki government did not regard the Postdam proclamation "as a thing of any great value" and accordingly would "ignore" it.

Once again the Japanese government pressed Moscow for an answer to its appeals for help. As Japan moved toward doom by rejecting the Allies' bid, it continued to hold out hope that Stalin, not a signatory to the Potsdam Declaration, might serve as an honest broker.

HIROSHIMA AND NAGASAKI

On the island of Tinian, in the Marianas, the mysterious 509th Composite Group, a specially trained B-29 squadron, awaited its instructions. For months, it had made practice runs over Japan, but only the commander of the 509th knew precisely what they were training for; most of the crew had never heard the word *atomic*. Now, in early August, a list of target cities was ready and a date was selected. There were only a few Japanese cities which were not in ruins. One prime target, Kyoto, the ancient capital of Japan, was removed from the list on orders from Secretary of War Stimson for reasons both humanitarian and pragmatic. It was (and is) one of the world's great cultural treasurehouses, but in addition, Stimson knew that destruction of Kyoto would only harden Japanese hostility to the United States and perhaps drive them closer to the Soviet Union.

The first choice, therefore, was to be the medium-sized city of Hiroshima. It fulfilled all the requirements for a target city. It had enough concentration of population to deliver the desired shock. After evacuation of about one-third of the city's population to the countryside, approximately 245,000 still remained there in the summer of 1945. Moreover, it had significant military installations, and it had been untouched by conventional bombing. Hiroshima citizens had been puzzled by their good fortune, and rumors circulated to explain the city's fate. According to one, the Americans recognized the beauty of the city and were saving it to use as their own military headquarters. The wildest of the gossip had it that Harry Truman's mother lived there. Only later did the people of Hiroshima learn that their city had been spared conventional raids so that the effects of the atomic bomb could be measured with exactitude. Leaflets had been dropped over the city on August 4 warning the residents that they could expect devastation if the country did not surrender. Similar warnings were routinely dropped over cities. Sometimes the Americans followed up with raids, sometimes they did not.

Early on the morning of August 6, 1945, there had been an air-raid warning alert, but the "all-clear" signal was given at 7:31 A.M. when a single B-29 weather plane flew harmlessly overhead and disappeared. Workers returned to their factories, and children prepared to go to school. Another ordinary day began. Most people were not especially alarmed when a little later three more B-29s appeared thirty-one thousand feet above. Two were observation planes loaded with instruments, and the third was the *Enola Gay*. The inefficient air-warning system did not sound any alert this time, and Japanese had become so accustomed to the nearly daily appearance of the planes trailing their beautiful, long white wakes of vapor that they usually looked up at them until bombs actually fell. The little-known city of Hiroshima was about to acquire a fame as dreadful as any in history.

At 8:15 A.M., the uranium-cored device, floating down from the sky in a parachute, exploded 660 yards above the Aioi bridge near the center of the city. Its force was equivalent to that of twenty thousand tons of TNT. In the measured language of the scientific investigatory commission which later studied the effects of the bomb, "the epicenter instantaneously reached a maximum temperature of several million degrees and an atmospheric pressure of several 100,000 bars; with the formation of the fireball, powerful heat rays and radiation were emitted in all directions within a short interval." Within minutes, a weird "black rain" began to fall, contaminating everyone it touched with radioactive debris. To have even a 50-percent chance of escaping both death and injury,

Recollection of the atomic blast at Hirsoshima in 1970 drawing by survivor Nishioki Kiyoko (age 5 in 1945). Her caption (in part) reads: "My younger brother dies of burns suffered all over his body. (Baby, center left of three persons.) A junior-high school student in the foreground dies with the words, 'Please give this lunch to my mother . . .'"

one had to have been at least 1.3 miles from ground zero. An official U.S. study placed the death toll that day at seventy-one thousand people, nearly a third of the population; subsequently, the death toll was pushed to about eighty thousand. (Several Japanese studies, however, place the death toll much higher.) Thousands more were left suffering from burns and the still unidentified effects of radiation sickness. Among the dead were at least twenty-two American POWs, mostly downed airmen who were being held in prisons, some within a ten-minute walk of the Aioi Bridge epicenter. One American survivor was apparently beaten to death by angry Japanese survivors.

From here it may be easiest to follow events with a day-by-day chronology:

AUGUST 6, 1945. The bombing of Hiroshima.

AUGUST 7, 1945. Tokyo received notice from local authorities of the full dimension of the damage sustained in the atomic attack: "The whole city of Hiroshima was destroyed instantly by a single bomb." Tokyo made no mention of nuclear weapons, but those with access to shortwave radios heard President Truman explain, "It is an atomic bomb. It is a harnessing of the basic power of the universe." If Japan did not now accept the terms of the Potsdam Declaration, the president warned, "they may expect a rain of ruin from the air, the like of which has never been seen on this earth." The top leadership of Japan, however, remained deadlocked. The bomb dropped on Hiroshima did not change the stance of a single member of the high-level, decision-making circles. Those who had been disposed to surrender continued so. The military remained obstinately determined to reject Allied demands. The army undertook a publicity campaign to minimize the significance of the "new-type bomb" to the public. "We have countermeasures," citizens were told. It helped if you turned the other way during the blast, and people wearing white clothing were burned only slightly, said the reassuring army bulletin. For the next several days, in fact, the most striking feature of Japan's newspapers was their "business-as-usual" air. Front-page stories concentrated on upbeat news: a favorable rice harvest was expected, a project to extract fuel oil from birch trees in Manchuria was being implemented, a new tutoring institute for the Crown Prince was being established, and there were warnings of a grim winter—for Europe.

AUGUST 8, 1945. In Moscow, Ambassador Sato was informed that he would be received by Foreign Minister Molotov. Sato allowed himself to be encouraged by this long-anticipated opportunity: At last it was possible that the Kremlin was willing to offer its good offices to help Japan out of the war. As Sato began to speak some Russian words of polite small talk to Molotov, he was interrupted by the foreign minister, who read to him a formal document. It ended by notifying Japan that "from tomorrow, that is from August 9, the Soviet Union will consider herself in a state of war against Japan." Within hours, a million-man Soviet army rolled across the Manchurian frontier and began to overrun the once-vaunted Kwantung Army, now badly depleted due to transfers to the homeland. Other Soviet armies would quickly move into Korea, the Kurile Islands, and southern Sakhalin. This trauma, added to the atomic bombing of Hiroshima, gave the peace faction encouragement to think it might break the stalemate with the diehards and move the nation toward surrender.

AUGUST 9, 1945. The six-member Supreme Council for the Direction of the War met and for the first time the four military members of this panel were forced to withdraw their opposition to surrender proposals—they were prepared to accept Allied terms *in principle*. They still insisted, however, that Japan was not yet defeated, and the safety of the Throne would have to be guaranteed. They also wanted to prevent the Allies from occupying Japan or at least limiting the occupation by excluding certain areas such as Tokyo. They also pointed out that Japanese soldiers and sailors were not permitted to surrender; military penal codes prescribed harsh penalties for anyone who laid down their arms. Accordingly, the Allies would have to permit the Japanese themselves to oversee the demobilization of the Imperial Army and Navy. When Foreign Minister Togo asked the army chief of staff whether he thought that the army

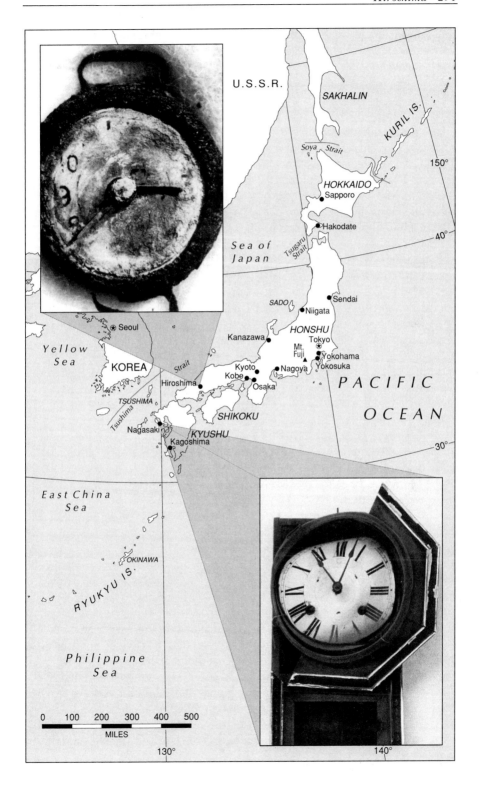

U.S.S.R.

SAKHALIN

KURIL IS.

150°

Soya Strait

HOKKAIDO
● Sapporo

●Hakodate

40°

Sea of
Japan

Tsugaru Strait

SADO
● Niigata
●Sendai

● Seoul

HONSHU
Tokyo
⊛

Yellow
Sea

Kanazawa ●

Mt.
Fuji ▲
●Yokohama
Yokosuka

KOREA

Strait

Kyoto ●
Kobe ●
● Nagoya

PACIFIC

Hiroshima ●

● Osaka

TSUSHIMA

OCEAN

Tsushima

SHIKOKU

Nagasaki ▲

KYUSHU

Kagoshima ●

30°

East China
Sea

Philippine
Sea

OKINAWA

RYUKYU IS.

0   100   200   300   400   500

MILES

130°

140°

could ward off an invasion if the peace talks broke down, General Umezu Yoshikazu argued that it was certain that the "major part" of any invading army would be destroyed. There was still room for negotiations, Umezu insisted, because the Allies would surely make concessions rather than bear the costs of an invasion. In short, the impasse between the peace faction and the diehards still continued.

Before the meeting of the "Big Six" broke up, they received word that the atomic bomb had been dropped again. The target that morning was Kokura. Fortunately for the people of that industrial city, haze obscured the area and the crew of "Bock's Car" proceeded to its secondary target, the port of Nagasaki. At 11:00 A.M., the 200,000 residents of that city saw the *pika,* the distinctive light-ning-blue flash that came just before the double mushroom cloud ascended. Due to a bombardier's error, the bomb dropped on Nagasaki missed the impact zone selected for maximum devastation, and so the death toll—much less than at Hiroshima—was an estimated thirty-eight thousand people. Because of the city's configuration—it is built on hills which acted as firebreaks—no general conflagration ensued. Rumors spread that more cities would be hit by atom bombs in short order. Tokyo—what was left of it—would be next in two or three days, many thought. Army diehards preferred to believe that the United States had exhausted its atomic arsenal. In fact, the diehards were closer to the truth. It would be two weeks before a third atomic bomb would be ready and quite some time after that before a fourth could be assembled. Tokyo was a possible target. Had Tokyo been hit with an atomic bomb it seems quite possible that the war would have been prolonged. As Leon Sigal argues, "It endangered the lives of the very people who alone could authoritatively commit Japan to surrender. It threatened to shatter command-and-control over Japan's widely scattered forces, virtually assuring non-compliance with any order to cease hostilities."

Still, with all of the grim news rushing in from every direction, no minds were changed. In the afternoon, the entire fourteen-man Cabinet met to discuss the next move. The meeting went on until past ten in the evening but ended in deadlock. In the face of this total impasse, members of the peace faction, antic-ipating the Cabinet deadlock, made arrangements for an "Imperial Con-ference," a meeting of the entire government and military leadership in the presence of the emperor.

The Imperial Conference was an infrequently used *ceremony.* It was not employed to thrash out decisions but to ratify decisions *already* reached. By out-lining these decisions in the solemn presence of the emperor, a new govern-ment policy would receive an extraordinary validation it might not otherwise possess. Votes did not need to be taken; such political details would have been completed before coming into the presence of the "August Mind" of His Majesty. The emperor did not say yea or nay; he rarely uttered a word. He *always* approved petitions filed by his government and *never* followed political advice from anyone outside his circle of responsible ministers. On rare occa-sions, very rare occasions, the most that he might do at an Imperial Conference was to hint at displeasure. The merest suggestion of imperial distress would be enough to send his ministers back to study an issue more deliberately. Now, at this perilous moment in the nation's history, his government would come to him without a policy to approve.

TO BEAR THE UNBEARABLE

AUGUST 10, 1945. In the early minutes of this new day, a band of conference-weary officials sat at formal attention at long tables facing the emperor, who had just taken his seat at a small raised dais to their front. The room was a stifling, underground chamber adjoining the emperor's makeshift library, poorly venti-lated on this hot, humid summer night. One by one, Prime Minister Suzuki called upon the assembled members to outline their views for the benefit of the emperor. Foreign Minister Togo presented the opinions of the peace faction and urged acceptance of the Potsdam Declaration—on condition that the impe-rial household would not be violated. However, the days of deliberations and the accumulation of bad news still had not served to modify enough opinions to achieve anything near a consensus. After two hours of inconclusive discussion, Suzuki declared to the assembly that the gravity of the nation's situation left him no recourse but to ask His Imperial Majesty to break the impasse and express his wishes. It was so radical a departure from custom that the war minister was heard to gasp in outrage, "Mr. Prime Minister!"

Hirohito, his mind already made up as a result of recent conferences with peace faction members, arose. After answering the claims of his generals that effective resistance was still possible, the emperor went on:

> I cannot help feeling sad when I think of the people who have served me so faithfully, the soldiers and sailors who have been killed or wounded in far-off battles, the families who have lost all their worldly goods—and often their lives as well—in the air raids at home. It goes without saying that it is unbearable for me to see the brave and loyal fighting men of Japan dis-armed. It is equally unbearable that others who have rendered me devoted service should now be punished as instigators of the war.

"Nevertheless," the emperor concluded, "the time has come when we must bear the unbearable. I swallow my own tears and give my sanction to the proposal to accept the Allied proclamation on the basis outlined by the foreign minister."

With the deadlock at last broken, word was transmitted to the Allies that the Potsdam Declaration was accepted—"with the understanding that the said declaration does not comprise any demand which prejudices the prerogatives of His Majesty as a Sovereign Ruler." The government of Japan was offering to surrender—but *not* unconditionally. Was the Tokyo response an adequate acceptance of the Potsdam terms or not? Now it was Washington's turn to accept or reject.

AUGUST 11, 1945. American authorities remained almost as divided as those in Tokyo. Some, aware that the emperor was not a decision maker and therefore not personally responsible for the war, raised no objection to excusing him from trial as a war criminal. Others stressed the practical importance of the emperor to the Allied cause. Without his support it would be impossible to get the many scattered armies of Japan to lay down their arms and accept a military occupation of the country. However, domestic political considerations remained uppermost in the minds of others, and any concessions to the hated enemy prompted cries of "Appeasement!" Accepting Japan's proposal, Secretary of State Byrnes warned, could lead to the "crucifixion of the President." In the end, a compromise formula was agreed upon. No explicit guarantee of the emperor's future would be made. The message sent to Japan repeated the Potsdam promise that the ultimate form of government of Japan would be established "by the freely expressed will of the Japanese people." In addition, it was added that, "From the moment of surrender the authority of the Emperor and the Japanese Government to rule the state shall be subject to the Supreme Commander of the Allied powers," as it turned out General Douglas MacArthur. Historian Robert J. C. Butow writes that this wording,

> . . . implied that the Supreme Commander would oversee and even limit—but would not eradicate—imperial prerogatives and governmental authority. The Supreme Commander would, in effect, become a generalissimo of the same cut as the shogun of old—the men who had ruled while the Emperors had reigned.

AUGUST 12, 1945. Incredibly, in spite of the emperor's expressed command, military diehards dragged their feet. There were technical problems: Who could be certain that the Foreign Office was accurately translating the demands from Washington? Perhaps the message they were being asked to act on reflected only the Foreign Office's slanted interpretation of Washington's demands. Moreover, the military high command was better aware than civilians of the mood of junior officers. They knew that there were hotheads who would assume that evil men around the emperor had fabricated the call for surrender or had deceived His Majesty into the cowardly move. Many took no comfort from the "freely expressed will" phrasing of the Allies' demand, thinking that the Allies intended to use it in order to encourage subversive elements in Japan to overthrow the monarchy. The day ended without a reply to Washington.

AUGUST 13, 1945. Round-the-clock meetings of the Supreme Council for the Direction of the War and the Cabinet continued—to no avail. Fear of an army coup mounted. Perhaps the only reason a coup attempt had not occurred was that no general announcement of the peace activities going on in the capital had yet been made. As late as August 10, War Minister Anami Korechika had notified servicemen that "we shall fight to the bitter end, ever firm in our faith that we shall find life in death." Late on the 13th, Vice Admiral Onishi Takijiro founder of the kamikaze corps, pleaded for sanction from the emperor for an all-out suicide effort. "If we are prepared to sacrifice 20,000,000 Japanese lives in a special [kamikaze] attack effort, victory shall be ours!" When his plea was rejected, the admiral committed *seppuku*. His followers, however, continued to mount kamikaze attacks, threats of which continued to linger for many days after surrender. Military leaders had stiffened their opposition to peace and after talking to Prime Minister Suzuki had caused him to vacillate. The last meetings of the day adjourned at 11:00 P.M. without a consensus.

AUGUST 14, 1945. American planes drop leaflets over Japanese cities advising the Japanese people of their government's offer to surrender and the American reply. With fear of a military coup by diehard fanatics rapidly escalating, another Imperial Conference is summoned. Again, and this time in an agitated state of mind in which several found it difficult to control their emotions, the most outspoken opponents to peace were given another opportunity to speak. For the second time in four days, the emperor rose to express his wishes. In spite of the possibility of Allied deceit, in spite of the terrible humiliation of surrender, he said, "I cannot endure the thought of letting my people suffer any longer." Again, he used the phrase "bear the unbearable." After directing his ministers to prepare an imperial surrender rescript which he would broadcast to the nation, he concluded, "I am ending this war on my own authority." Radio technicians came to the palace that evening and recordings were made of the imperial surrender decree.

AUGUST 15, 1945. Before dawn, news broadcasts notified the Japanese citizenry to be listening at noon to hear a proclamation from His Majesty. Power from the nation's depleted electricity system was carefully mobilized to ensure that every broadcasting facility in Japan would be able to carry the program. It had never happened before: Ordinary Japanese had never gazed upon the imperial countenance; similarly, they had never heard "the voice of the crane," the "jeweled sound" (*gyoku-on*) of their emperor. No one knew what he would say, but the most common expectation, in keeping with the years of psychological conditioning, was that the he would call for a final, fiery struggle to the death. Some thought that Japan had dropped retaliatory atomic weapons on the United States. Others expected word of an American landing. Almost nobody thought that the war was ending. Indeed, more than a thousand U.S. aircraft were over Japan's skies on this last day of the war in one of the largest bombing missions ever.

Unknown to the people gathering before their radios and loudspeakers was a drama being played out in Tokyo. Throughout the night, the immense park-like grounds of the imperial palace complex in central Tokyo were under siege. Military barracks were in an uproar, radio stations were invaded, and the homes of peace faction dignitaries were attacked. As word spread among army units that the emperor had recorded a surrender announcement, a frantic last-minute race was under way to block the peace moves and expunge the stain on the army's honor. Control of the palace grounds shifted as first one group of guards and then another held sway. Officers who failed to cooperate, including one general, were murdered.

In the early hours, the coup leaders had at least a passive accomplice in the person of War Minister Anami. However, as the hastily organized and bungled maneuverings dissolved into chaos, and larger military units refused to join the coup, Anami committed *seppuku* as a gesture of apology to the emperor and as atonement for his failures. Before the day was over, a wave of hundreds of ceremonial suicides would commence. Nevertheless, at one point the conspirators managed to track down the radio team not long after the recording session had ended. Holding them at bayonet point the furious officers demanded that the technicians hand over the recording. Fortunately for history, Lord Keeper of the Privy Seal Marquess Kido Koichi, had anticipated this possibility and secured the precious discs in a safe in the inner recesses of the palace grounds.

At noon, with order being restored in the capital, the recording, wrapped reverentially in silk brocade, was delivered to the control room of Radio Tokyo. After the playing of *Kimigayo*, the national anthem, a station official gravely introduced the recording of the emperor's voice. People throughout the land stood and bowed their heads in the direction of radios and loudspeakers. The emperor's doleful high-pitched voice was not easy to understand. Only the well-educated could fathom the meaning of the stilted and archaic court expressions used in palace speech. Taboo words like *defeat* and *surrender* never appeared in the proclamation. When the emperor came again to repeat his phrase about bearing the unbearable, many thought that their worst fears were confirmed: The emperor was calling on them to fight on. It was only when an official commentator came on the air to explain the message that the meaning became unambiguous: Japan was accepting Allied demands. The imperial message of August 15, 1945, became for all Japanese alive on that day the common coin of memory. Only those who experienced war first hand could appreciate how vividly Japanese recall that day and the swirl of emotions which accompanied it: the crushing burden of humiliation and defeat, the disillusion and the exhaustion—and the relief. The war was over.

A REVISIONIST INTERPRETATION

The interpretation of the end of the war presented above may be regarded as the standard, orthodox reading. It assumes that military necessity prompted the dropping of the atomic bombs on Japan. It acknowledges that during the last year of the war, Japan was prostrate. It acknowledges that Japanese officials were anxious to end the war on the basis of a negotiated settlement and that American authorities knew of the existence of a peace faction. It insists, however, that there was reason to doubt the ability of the peace faction to prevail in a showdown with military authorities who were in a strong position to impose their *bushido* determination on the nation no matter how high the costs might be. It argues that American decision makers were reasonable in assuming that it would take an invasion of the home islands in order to break the will of the military, and it argues that it was reasonable, in the light of the Pacific island campaigns, to expect that frightfully high casualties—on both sides— would ensue. Accordingly, it was reasonable to think that the use of atomic weapons would shorten the war and save lives—on both sides. It concedes that Washington's continued insistence on unconditional surrender from Japan greatly complicated a settlement with Japan and that assurances regarding the emperor *might* have facilitated a Japanese surrender if not before Hiroshima, at least before Nagasaki. However, it also recognizes that such a concession might have produced exactly the opposite effect and stiffened the will of the diehards.

In disagreement with this line of reasoning has been one proffered by revisionist critics. With the appearance of *Atomic Diplomacy: Hiroshima and Potsdam* by Gar Alperovitz in 1965, the revisionist interpreters began to command attention. Numerous respected scholars added their voices to the revisionist perception of Hiroshima in the late 1960s and 1970s. They often differed among themselves almost as much as they differed with the orthodox school, but they shared in common the belief that the bombs were not so much dictated by the need to bring Japan to surrender but by the onset of the Cold War. Some, indeed, argued that the bombs, rather than Soviet advances into Eastern Europe, were the major factor in initiating the Cold War.

As the wartime alliance that defeated Germany in World War II was breaking up in 1945, the global balance of power was up for grabs. Washington was coming to see the Soviet Union as the principal obstacle to American supremacy in world affairs. Uppermost in the minds of cold warriors like Secretary of State James Byrnes was the vision of the atomic bomb as a counterweight which could be used to gain powerful leverage in bargaining with the Soviet Union. The atomic bomb would "impress" the Soviets, however, only if it was exploded for the world to see, preferably over a large city where the awesome power of the bomb would be manifest. For this reason, Alperovitz argues, the Truman administration orchestrated a "strategy of delayed showdown" with the Soviets: postpone disputes with Stalin until after Japanese cities had been convincingly blown off the map.

The revisionist approach also introduces related questions concerning the Soviet entrance into the war. In February 1945, at the "Big Three" (FDR, Churchill, and Stalin) conference at the Russian port of Yalta, the Allies received from the Soviet leader a secret promise that the USSR would enter the war against Japan within two or three months after the surrender of Germany. At the time, no one yet knew whether or when the atomic bomb would explode or what damage it might do. Accordingly, the assurance of Soviet help against Japan was seen as preventing the loss of countless American lives in the bloody campaigns that seemed to lie ahead. (Appropriate concessions had to be offered. The Yalta agreements provided that the Soviet Union would recover all rights and territory lost at the end of the Russo–Japanese War forty years earlier.)

Japan, of course, continued to hold out hope for Soviet help in the last weeks of the war, totally unmindful that Stalin had already committed himself to a declaration of war against Japan no later than August 8, the ninetieth day after German surrender.

By the time Truman had succeeded to the presidency, certainly by the time the Potsdam Conference approached in the summer of 1945, American strategists no longer looked forward so eagerly to Soviet entrance into the war against Japan. As Manhattan Project scientists in Los Alamos moved closer to the first test explosion in July, there was less and less likelihood that Soviet help would be needed. Japan could probably be brought to her knees by the atomic bombs.

The ideal scenario, as seen from Washington, now envisioned a quick Japanese surrender forced by the atomic bombs. If that could be brought about before Stalin had time to order his troops into action, it would serve two purposes. First, the bomb would intimidate Stalin and permit America to obtain concessions from him in the postwar era. Secondly, it would mean that Soviet troops would not be deployed in advantageous positions all around Asia as the war came to an end. These compelling reasons, some revisionists argue, explain why Truman used the bomb so quickly *rather* than exploring other options such as a modification of surrender terms. This is why atomic bombs were used rather than stepping up conventional bombing. This explains why the bombs had to be dropped on Hiroshima and Nagasaki rather than in a noncombatant demonstration. This is why the president dropped the bombs rather than pursuing the peace feelers which were well-known to Washington. In short, the atomic bomb was dropped because the president did not want Japan to surrender *until* it had been dropped, say the revisionists.

There is an impressive array of evidence, circumstantial evidence at least, which revisionists cite to bolster their view of "atomic diplomacy." For example, nuclear physicist Leo Szilard, commenting on the secretary of state's position on the bomb, said that "Mr. Byrnes did not argue that it was necessary to use the bomb against Japan in order to win the war. . . . Mr. Byrnes's . . . view [was] that our possessing and demonstrating the bomb would make Russia more manageable in Europe." Here is Vannevar Bush, Stimson's chief aide for atomic matters: "That bomb . . . was delivered on time so that there was no necessity for any concessions to Russia at the end of the war." The secretary of state said: "Neither the president nor I were anxious to have them [the Soviet Union] enter the war after we learned of this successful test [of the atomic bomb]." War Secretary Stimson's diary records that in May 1945, he anticipated that it might be necessary to "have it out with Russia" on her demands for concessions in the Far East. "Over any such tangled weave of problems [the atomic bomb] secret would be dominant," he wrote. Like Byrnes, Stimson also advised Truman that the "greatest complication" would occur if the president negotiated with Stalin before the bomb had been "laid on Japan."

What is one to make of the reference by the president to the atomic bomb as his "master card" in dealing with the Soviets, and of his statement that it allowed him to "get a hammer on those boys"? And of Stimson referring to

OPPOSITE VIEWS FROM JAPAN

"The thunderous arrival of the first atomic bomb at Hiroshima was only a coup de grâce for an empire already struggling in particularly agonizing death throes. The world's newest and most devastating of weapons had floated out of the summer sky to destroy a city at a stroke, but its arrival had small effect on the outcome of the war between Japan and the United Nations."

—Kato Masuo, journalist.

"At the time the Army felt that it would be a great shame for them if they were to surrender unconditionally. . . . That's why we asked for the decision of the Emperor. The A-bomb provided an excellent help, because the A-bomb sacrificed many people other than Japanese military men. This provided us with an excuse that America would not refrain from doing such evils, that therefore there would be no other choice but to cease the war to save many innocent Japanese citizens. If the A-bomb had not been dropped we would have had great difficulty to find a good reason to end the war."

—Sakomizu Hisatsune, secretary to the Cabinet in 1945.

OPPOSITE VIEWS FROM THE WEST

". . . it was not one atomic bomb, or two, which brought surrender; it was the experience of what an atomic bomb will actually do to a community, *plus the dread of many more,* that was effective." [Italics in original.]

—Dr. Karl Compton, Manhattan Project scientist.

"It would be a mistake to suppose that the fate of Japan was settled by the atomic bomb. Her defeat was certain before the first bomb fell."

—Winston Churchill, British prime minister.

Byrnes as wearing the bomb "ostentatiously on his hip" in negotiating with the Russians?

The revisionists also point to *ex post facto* evidence that the bomb was not needed. After the war was over, for example, a high-level collection of military and scientific experts were ordered by the president to conduct the United States Strategic Bombing Survey in Japan, with a view to evaluating the importance and potentialities of air power as an instrument of military strategy in the future. The group's 1946 report concluded:

It is the Survey's opinion that certainly prior to December 31, 1945 and in all probability prior to November 1, 1945, Japan would have surrendered even if the atomic bombs had not been dropped, even if Russia had not entered the war, and even if no invasion had been planned or contemplated.

AMERICAN WRITERS REFLECT ON HIROSHIMA AND NAGASAKI
   "There is such a thing as a just war. I fought in one (World War II) and am proud of it. The problem is lack of restraint, and a need for vengeance. The bombing of Dresden was completely unnecessary, and the British knew it. They wanted revenge for the London blitz and the leveling of Coventry and the humiliation at Dunkirk and so on. [At Hiroshima] what Americans had to avenge was Pearl Harbor."

—Kurt Vonnegut, Jr.

   "When the bombs dropped and news began to circulate that 'Operation Olympic' would not, after all, take place, that we would not be obliged to run up the beaches near Tokyo assault-firing while being mortared and shelled, for all the fake manliness of our facades we cried with relief and joy. We were going to live. We were going to grow up to adulthood after all."

—Paul Fussell.

   "The power to blow all things to dust

   Was kept for people God could trust

   And granted unto them alone

   That evil might be overthrown."

—Popular syndicated poet, Edgar Guest.

   "I feel so rotten about the country's response to the bombings at Hirohima and Nagasaki that I wish I could become a naturalized cat or dog."

—Randall Jarrell.

Revisionists also cite high-ranking military leaders who expressed opinions about the lack of a need for the bomb. While there were many who did so after the war was over, at least two vigorously argued against the dropping of atomic weapons before Hiroshima. General Eisenhower recalled in his postwar memoirs his feelings at Potsdam when he learned from Stimson that the weapon would be used against Japan:

   I voiced to him [Stimson] my grave misgivings, first on the basis of my belief that Japan was already defeated and that dropping the bomb was completely unnecessary, and secondly because I thought that our country should avoid shocking world opinion by the use of a weapon whose employment was, I thought, no longer mandatory as a measure to save American lives. It was my belief that Japan was, at that very moment seeking some way to surrender with a minimum loss of "face."

Admiral William D. Leahy, the chief military adviser at the White House, was the only other high-ranking military man to energetically oppose the dropping of the bombs in the summer of 1945. He later summed up his views: "It is my opinion that the use of this barbarous weapon at Hiroshima and Nagasaki was of no material assistance in our war against Japan. The Japanese were already defeated and ready to surrender. . . ."

For every revisionist argument, critics have come forward with counter-arguments. Usually ignored by advocates of both the orthodox and revisionist schools is the possibility of accepting some of the strongest arguments of each. Barton J. Bernstein, for example, stresses that there is ample evidence to show that Truman and those around him felt that the bomb was needed to conclude the war quickly. Those privy to the secrets of the Manhattan Project had long assumed that the bomb would be used in combat. By 1945, "the bureaucratic momentum and the burden of the long-held assumption were great," Bernstein insists. As a result, the administration considered its options on *how* to use the bomb but never carefully faced the question of *whether* to use it. "It was not a carefully weighed decision but the implementation of an assumption," Bernstein writes.

The bomb, then, would have been used even if there was no Soviet Union. All of this, however, in no way invalidates the argument that policymakers found important bargaining leverage in dealing with postwar problems which were emerging in the summer of 1945. The revisionists, Bernstein says, are correct in citing the importance of "atomic diplomacy" and the value of the bomb as a tool of intimidation. However, Bernstein makes an important distinction between the purpose of the bombs and a side effect of their use, however welcome. Neither the decision nor the timing of the bomb was governed by a consideration of the effect it would have on the Soviet Union. That was a *"secondary, confirming* reason," Bernstein writes. "The primary reason was to end the war speedily with the smallest cost in American lives." (Italics added.)

ADDITIONAL READING

A good place to survey the vast interpretive literature on the use of the atomic bomb is Barton J. Bernstein's essay "The Atomic Bomb and American Foreign Policy, 1941–1945: An Historiographical Controversy," in *Peace and Change* (Spring 1974). Various Cold War revisionist interpretations are to be found in Gar Alperovitz, *Atomic Diplomacy: Hiroshima and Potsdam* (1965, 1985); and Gabriel Kolko, *The Politics of War* (1968).

Edited volumes offer a variety of opinions and perspectives on the issue of "atomic diplomacy." These include Paul Baker, ed., *The Atomic Bomb: The Great Decision* (2nd ed. 1976); Edwin Fogelman, ed., *Hiroshima: The Decision to Use the A-Bomb* (1964); and Barton J. Bernstein, ed., *The Atomic Bomb: The Critical Issues* (1976).

On the political aspects of bringing the war to an end, see Leon V. Sigal, *Fighting to a Finish: The Politics of War Termination in the United States and Japan, 1945* (1988); Robert J. C. Butow, *Japan's Decision to Surrender* (1954); Herbert Feis, *The Atomic Bomb and the End of World War II* (2nd rev. ed., 1966); and the first three chapters of McGeorge Bundy, *Danger and Survival: Choices About the Bomb in the First Fifty Years*

(1988). On the military aspects, see Alvin Coox, *Japan: The Final Agony* (1970). Regarding the Tokyo fire-bomb raids, see Robert Guillain, *I Saw Tokyo Burning* (William Byron, trans., 1981) and Hoito Edoin, *The Night Tokyo Burned* (1987).

For books which take the perspective of the victims, see Kyoko and Mark Selden, eds., *Voices from Hiroshima and Nagasaki* (1989); John Dower and John Junkerman, eds., *The Hiroshima Murals: The Art of Iri Maruki and Toshi Maruki* (1985); John Hersey, *Hiroshima* (1946); Machihiko Hachiya, *Hiroshima Diary: The Journal of a Japanese Physician, August 6–September 30, 1945* (1955); and the moving telecast later published in book form as Japan Broadcasting Corporation (NHK), ed., *Unforgettable Fire: Pictures Drawn by Atomic Bomb Survivors* (1977). Among the numerous Japanese novels on the subject, Masuji Ibuse, *Black Rain* (1981) is the best known. See also Kenzaburo Oe, *The Crazy Iris and Other Stories of the Atomic Aftermath* (1985). *Death in Life: Survivors of Hiroshima* (1967) by the psychiatrist Robert Jay Lifton is based upon his interviews of seventy-five victims.

On Japanese biological warfare experimentation, see Peter Williams and David Wallace, *Unit 731: The Japanese Army's Secret of Secrets* (1989).

On the emperor and his role in history, see Norma Field, *In the Realm of a Dying Emperor: A Portrait of Japan at Century's End* (1991); Edward Behr, *Hirohito: Behind the Myth* (1989); Paul Manning, *Hirohito: The War Years* (1986); and a highly controversial book by David Bergamini, *Japan's Imperial Conspiracy* (1971). The Bergamini book, while fascinating to read, needs to be read in conjunction with one or two scholarly reviews, for example, *American Historical Review* (October 1972); *Pacific Affairs* (Summer 1972); and *Journal of Asian Studies* (February 1972).

9

"WHAT WILL BECOME OF US?"

"People do not wear expressions any different from other days. However, in place of a 'good morning' or 'good afternoon,' people are now greeting each other with the phrase 'What will become of us'?" (From the August 16, 1945, entry of the diary of Yoshizawa Hisako.)

On September 2, 1945, history's largest armada of warships assembled in Tokyo Bay to ring down the curtain on World War II. Admirals and generals wearing the uniforms of the victorious nations in the Pacific war gathered on the quarterdeck of the battleship *Missouri* to observe as nervous Japanese delegates signed the instruments of surrender on behalf of the emperor. The victors make the speeches at such moments. Speaking as master of ceremonies, General Douglas MacArthur took the occasion to remark that Matthew Perry had landed nearby almost a century earlier in order to lift the "veil of isolation" from Japan. "But, alas," MacArthur said, "the knowledge thereby gained of Western science was forged into an instrument of oppression and human enslavement." The general went on, "We are committed to see that the Japanese people are liberated from this condition of slavery."

ALLIED OCCUPATION, 1945–1952

When the emperor announced to the Japanese people on August 15 that they must "bear the unbearable," he meant that Japan must not only surrender to the Allies, but for the first time in its history permit foreign soldiers to occupy Japan's sacred soil. Alone among the nations of the Far East, Japan had never been subjected to hostile armies of occupation. How long these armies would remain was unknown. As it turned out, the Occupation lasted for almost seven years, until Japan regained sovereign control over its affairs with the

Signing the instrument of surrender on board the U.S.S. Missouri, *September 2, 1945.*

signing of a peace treaty in San Francisco in 1951 (effective in the spring of 1952). It would be a watershed period during which Japan would emerge from the ashes of a defeat as severe as any nation had ever known and build the foundation for a prosperity that would astonish the world within a few decades.

While military occupations are common enough in history, the Allied occupation of Japan was to have some distinctive qualities. The most striking was that the purpose of the Occupation went far beyond simply demobilizing the Japanese armed forces and destroying its war potential. The occupation forces were to oversee sweeping political, economic, and social changes. They would rewrite the Japanese constitution, restructure Japanese industry, revolutionize land-holding patterns in the countryside, reorganize the military, modify the form and content of the educational system, and introduce a myriad of smaller innovations—from the PTA to man-on-the-street radio broadcasting—which would add up to a grass-roots revolution in attitudinal changes. All of this was more noteworthy because Japan was *not* a technologically or culturally backward nation. The postwar encounter was therefore "not in the classic imperialist mode of cultural confrontation," say the authors of one study of the period. "It was for East Asia a new kind of Western presence."

Unlike Germany, it was not Japan's fate to be divided into separate zones. The occupation of Japan was almost exclusively an American show. China, as the chief victim of the Asian phase of World War II, might have been expected to play a large role in shaping postwar Japan, but it was preoccupied with economic reconstruction and its own civil war.

From the beginning, General MacArthur was designated as Supreme Commander of the Allied Powers (SCAP), and the vast majority of the half-million-man occupation army which took up posts in Japan were Americans; a token British Commonwealth force was under MacArthur's operational control. Similarly, the 5500 bureaucrats who ran the complex SCAP administration were nearly all Americans. Although an Allied Council for Japan was set up to consult with SCAP, the general met only once with its delegates before handing the chair over to his deputy and then ignoring the council's deliberations. A Far Eastern Commission, meeting in Washington, D. C., was similarly little more than a rubber-stamp body. Not only the Soviets but even America's allies in the Pacific, the British and Australians especially, were furious at MacArthur's high-handed decision to allow the Allied Council to "wither into uselessness."

The Soviets, entitled to participate in the Occupation by virtue of their last-minute entrance into the war, were frustrated enough to complain that their representative on the council was being treated like "a piece of furniture," but in the end the Soviet Union settled for no more than a nominal role in shaping Occupation policy in Japan. Like postwar Eastern Europe, where the United States was frozen out by the unilateral actions of the Soviet Union, Japan was thus drawn into the Cold War which was engulfing the world. Japan would serve as the key Asian bastion against the Communist dictatorships in Asia. "Japan is like a floating aircraft carrier off the coast of Vladivostok," a Japanese prime minister would later say. Thus, whatever else the United States sought to do in Japan in the period from 1945 to 1952, it is clear that one of the main legacies of the Occupation was that Japan was brought close to the strategic goals of the United States in the Pacific.

IMAGES AND REALITIES

As the Occupation began, each side thought the worst of each other. Conditioned by generations of racial stereotypes and years of wartime propaganda, both Americans and Japanese expected to encounter barbaric behavior. Japanese people were most often referred to with the contemptuous epithets "Japs" or "Nips" (from Nippon, the Japanese pronunciation of their country's name), often prefaced by racial slurs such as "yellow" (as in "yellow-bellied Japs"). Buttressed by the image-creating magic of Hollywood, Americans invariably viewed Japanese as cruel and treacherous—"sneaky Jap" became a fixed phrase in the arsenal of wartime bigotry. These hostile impressions were reinforced by vivid memories of atrocities such as the Bataan death march which excited a desire for vengeance in many of those posted for duty in Japan. Sailors arriving at the Yokosuka naval base were reminded of the mistreatment of American POWs and cautioned to "Remember this if you ever catch yourself getting soft and being nice to a Jap."

Japanese images of Americans, while less vicious and less racist, were hardly cordial. Drawing on ancient folk tales, Japanese propagandists frequently portrayed Americans as ogres and fiends and supported their claims with news items such as the photograph in a 1944 issue of *Life* showing a young American woman who had just received a souvenir Japanese skull from her G.I. fiancè. Americans were seen as drunken, depraved, and so lewd that the Japanese government took the precaution of notifying fathers to instruct their daughters to dress unbecomingly so they might escape the gaze of the lecherous GIs who were about to arrive. In more chilling cases, female factory workers were provided with cyanide tablets to take if they faced assault by the foreigners. The offensive smell of Americans added still another unpleasant dimension for the Japanese who partook very little of dairy products and thought Americans were *bata kusai* (reeking of butter)—still a pejorative for things Western.

The Japanese home islands bristled with hundreds of fully-armed divisions of on-duty Japanese soldiers, as the first Americans touched down at Atsugi air base near Tokyo on August 28, still fearing, as did the Japanese authorities, the possibility of suicidal attacks by kamikaze pilots. In spite of the potential for violence and the accumulated animosities which were present, the Occupation commenced without incident. "The big story," wrote one American reporter on the scene, "was what did not happen." With few on either side anxious for more violence, the Occupation ran smoothly through its seven-year course. Both sides found that their stereotypical images of the other were largely groundless. As Edwin O. Reischauer, Japan scholar and later President John Kennedy's appointee as American ambassador to Japan, wrote:

> The Americans, for their part, found the Japanese people not the die-hard fanatics they had expected from their experience with the Japanese army in the battlefields of the Pacific, but a well-educated, disciplined, docile people, eager to cooperate in reforming and rebuilding their nation.

Some of the pidgin spoken by GIs in the Occupation era was so commonly used that it entered English-language dictionaries—*Skoshi*, for example, sometimes abbreviated to *skosh*, from the Japanese word *sukoshi* meaning "little." It could be further contaminated by adding the English word *more* to create *morskosh*, "a little more" as in "Give me morskosh beer." *Honcho*, now a part of the English language ("an assertive leader"), derives from a military term *hancho* (squad leader) which occupation GIs picked up from the old Imperial Army. *Taksan*, from Japanese *takusan*, meaning "numerous" became a pidgin generic for "very" as in "taksan cold today." *Dai-jobee* (from *daijobu*, just fine) might be combined with *daijobee* and *watash* (from *watakushi*, first person pronoun) to produce a sentence like, "Taksan dai-jobee with ol' watash" (It's perfectly okay with me). Roy Andrew Miller, who has catalogued these pidgin phrases, writes that it "is at once rather charming and rather pathetic" that "foreign visitors take to them thinking that they are Japanese . . . while the locals also assiduously imitate them, in the devout belief that they are thus mastering English."

Japanese threw themselves with customary energy into the study of the English language. Language schools mushroomed overnight and conversation textbooks became best-sellers. An English conversation course, unidiomatically named "Come, Come English Conversation," was broadcast every weekday evening at 6:00 P.M. and "enjoyed an unrivaled audience rating throughout the Occupation period and long afterwards," writes one historian. There were a few Americans who made a corresponding effort to master the complexities of the Japanese language. Donald Keene and the translator of *Genji Monogatari*, Edward Seidensticker, were among the small coterie of extraordinarily talented critics of Japanese literature to emerge from the war and its aftermath. Most Americans, however, settled for a few crudely mispronounced barroom phrases. A whole generation of Americans stationed in Japan believed that Japanese called their mothers "mama-san" and that the title of the lilting wartime ballad *"Shina no Yoru"* ("China Nights") was "She Ain't Got No Yoyo." For all the difference in the characters of the two people, between sober-minded Japanese who live in a formal world of rules and the more casual Americans who live by informality, a kind of mutual respect, at least a mutual fascination, developed. Journalist Kawai Kazuo, who lived in both the United States and Japan, explains,

> Even while they sought to enlighten the Japanese, most Americans did not take themselves very seriously. Their exuberant good spirits came as a welcome release to the Japanese, who had long been repressed by the humorless authoritarianism of their militarists . . . .The Americans acted as the Japanese would have liked to act but could not because of their social inhibitions, and thus the Americans became the envied models of a desired conduct.

Needless to say, not all Americans were regarded as models of "desired conduct." Drunken, brawling and abusive GIs were not an uncommon fixture of the night and the number of incidents of assault and rape which went unreported by intimidated Japanese, especially in the first years of the Occupation, must have been high. Biracial orphans were to be seen in the environs of American bases. Young lieutenants who summoned old Japanese men with a brash "boy-san" caused daily insult and humiliation to many Japanese. The firing ranges and the stray shells, the plane crashes into school buildings and village homes, the jet training runs at night, the trees cut down near air bases leading to the destruction of rural windbreaks—all these were irritations which had to be endured. American cars careening through the narrow Japanese streets near any of the thousands of occupation facilities produced horrific accidents and summed up all that was repugnant about the *gaijin* (foreigners)—they were big and they did not understand Japanese ways and they had unlimited power at their disposal.

Japanese films depicting the Occupation era—at least those which were produced after American censorship ended in 1952—stereotypically portray Americans as ill-mannered, self-centered, and loudmouthed. Their aggressive presence was seen to be destructive of the virtues most cherished by traditional Japanese—decorum, self-denial, and reticence. If directors like Ozu Yasujiro, Kobayashi Masaki, Imamura Shohei, and Kurosawa Akira, all of whom came to enjoy distinguished international reputations, could render harsh cinematic judgment on the Americans, they could be equally severe on their own countrymen. In many of their best films, the Occupation period is seen as a time of moral and social chaos during which a disoriented Japanese people prostituted themselves (literally and otherwise) to the culture of the Westerners. The brightest message of hope in these often grim films would be transmitted through an occasional hero who would retain his or her determination to resist the Occupation's despoliation of Japanese culture. In Kurosawa's classic *Ikiru*, the film's hero, the terminally ill sixty-year-old Watanabe, is taken out for a night on the town. At a glittering and sleazy cabaret, everything has been Americanized—the music, the dance, and the stripper. At the end of his foray on the town, Watanabe vomits in disgust. "The equation of sickness with Westernization permeates the Nighttown sequence," one critic writes.

Americans came into contact with Japanese cultural niceties in various ways, but perhaps most commonly at the front door of inns and homes, where Japanese invariably remove their shoes before stepping inside and onto the clean woven tatami grass matting which substitutes for carpets and are an essential part of Japanese domestic architecture. At least a few American GIs never mastered the etiquette. Japanese films wishing to portray boorish American behavior find a convincing and—apparently to most Japanese—immediately recognizable example in the soldier who strolls onto the immaculate tatami in his oversized, muddy boots while a polite Japanese family does its best not to notice the unforgivable breach of manners. How, Japanese wonder, can a people pretending to be civilized wear the same footwear in the street, the dining room, and the bathroom?

A Sexual Nexus

It was the "sexual nexus," as anthropologist Sheila K. Johnson calls it, which brought most Americans and Japanese together, commonly in bars and brothels. The largest of the red-light operations, quite possibly the largest in the world, was located in the Tokyo suburb of Funabashi and was run with an assembly-line efficiency that earned it the name "Willow Run" after the giant Ford Motor plant. (By coincidence, "flower and willow world" was a vintage Japanese euphemism for prostitution.) The Japanese were familiar with the sexual exploitation of women by the military—everyone knew about the battalions of Korean "comfort girls" recruited to follow the Imperial Army overseas—but it did not make it any less offensive that Americans could now buy the attentions of Japanese women in return for a pair of nylon stockings or a can of C-rations.

Still, there were other dimensions to the "sexual nexus." By 1955, about twenty thousand GIs had married Japanese women despite a variety of roadblocks erected by military chaplains and SCAP authorities. Japanese men, not accustomed to public displays of deference to women, were stunned to see GIs give up their seats on crowded trolleys to Japanese women. Philosopher Tsurumi Shunsuke comments on how Americans influenced postwar male–female relationships in his country. Japanese, he writes, "daily witnessed the gestures of Americans in the streets, at least in the big cities where U.S. soldiers were stationed. They set models for the exchange of gestures between boys and girls." Before the war, women customarily walked several steps behind men. To do otherwise, Tsurumi remarks, might have suggested a relationship so immoral as to prompt intervention by a policeman. In 1945, he states, a decisive change took place; a new age had arrived.

The sexual nexus brought with it an unfortunate set of stereotypes that do not die easily. As Sheila Johnson writes, "When American GIs reached Japan and found women who brought them their slippers, fixed them tea, and drew them a hot bath, all without being asked, they thought they had arrived in a paradise for men." The Western image of Japanese woman began to take shape as least as far back as 1904 when, in the first act of *Madama Butterfly*, Lieutenant Pinkerton gazed at his new bride, Cho-Cho San, and gushed, "To think that this little toy is my wife! My wife!" In the postwar era, best-sellers like James Michener's novel and film *Sayonara* reinforced the image of docility and servility and doubtless infuriated one-half of his American audience by having "Major Gruver" contrast the appearance of American women ("hard and angular faces") with "Katsumi" ("softer, more human face") and then deliver this peroration: "I concluded that no man could comprehend women until he had known the women of Japan with their unbelievable combination of unremitting work, endless suffering and boundless warmth." As Johnson notes, numerous scholars and writers, including many American women, have devoted themselves in recent years to demonstrating that the range of virtues, talents, and ambitions of contemporary Japanese women go far beyond those suggested in *Sayonara*.

JEEPS AND CHEWING GUM

Even the lowly jeep figured in the Japanese fascination with American style. To Americans, the wartime jeep was simply rugged transportation. To some Japanese, it represented an unfettered life-style that appeared to be an attractive alternative to their own, more rigid social system. A professor of literature at Tokyo University, Kamei Shunsuke, recalls his own youthful reaction upon seeing a jeep roar into his rural hometown soon after the Occupation began. The soldiers—the cruel and vicious Yankees he had been taught about—were soon distributing chocolate and chewing gum to the crowd of curious children that gathered. Then they were off as suddenly as they had come. It was the jeep, however, rather than the gifts which remained in his memory. "This is the boy's first close look at Americans," he recalls.

> He is charmed by their buoyancy and the practical lines of their lightweight jeeps, a contrast to the authoritative black limousines used by the Japanese army echelon during the war years. How lighthearted the Americans seem, he marvels; this must be what democracy is all about . . . .The open, lightweight jeeps that the country boy saw soon after the war symbolized the possibilities of a truly open society.

*The first American jeep in Tokyo draws the attention of crowds,
September 1945.*

In addition, however, Japanese were simply awestruck by the material wealth
and comfortable lives of Americans. In the winter of 1945–1946, even the prime
minister of Japan would obtain penicillen only as a personal gift from
MacArthur. While ordinary trains were so overcrowded with Japanese passengers that many lives were lost in accidents, a lonely corporal might ride for free
in solitary splendor in the white-striped cars marked "*Shinchu-gun*" (Occupation
forces).[1] The four thousand daily caloric ration for American soldiers was four
times the intake of many Japanese. At a time when scavenging in American
garbage dumps was a daily routine for many, and even the most fortunate
Japanese were preoccupied with a primitive struggle for necessities, recruits in
MacArthur's army could afford to buy Japanese art treasures as souvenirs with a
carton of Luckies or a few cans of Spam.

The American movies which began to appear in Ginza theaters only a few
months after the end of the war greatly reinforced the image of American prosperity. In neighborhoods still filled with rubble, customers would begin lining
up at four in the morning to see *The Best Years of Our Lives* and emerge to
wonder, "Could such a life really exist in this world?" Cowboy films had an
especially popular following because the wide open spaces in the "Westerns"
evoked awe, but also because the cowboy represented a rugged individualism
which was both foreign to the group-centered Japanese and yet appealing. An
opposite interpretation holds that Japanese fondness for cowboy movies hinged
on a Japanese misinterpretation of the genre. According to this view, many
Japanese saw cowboys as very familiar and thoroughly Japanese. They saw them

---

[1] Occupation forces were always translated into Japanese as *Shinchu-gun*, literally "military forces stationed in Japan" rather than the harsher *Senryo-gun*, "occupation forces."

GIs bargain with a former Japanese soldier reduced to selling trinkets in Tokyo, September 1945.

as humble men, living simply and working within the group to right the wrongs of the Wild West.

Even the cartoon strip "Blondie," which ran (with Japanese captions) for much of the Occupation period in Japan's leading newspaper and gained a huge audience, contributed to the image of a carefree and affluent America. "The enormous, sumptuous sandwiches" remained in the recollections of one Japanese commentator years later. Serious scholars in Japan found the time to analyze the appeal of Blondie which, above all, conveyed optimism. One writer, noting that though not rich, the Bumsteads were comfortable and secure and quoted Blondie herself on the "nature of happiness": "Dagwood, you have a nice job, good wife, children. And you have the latest fountain pen with a life-time guarantee too." There was hope for cross-cultural understanding if even Blondie's zany logic could translate across the langue barrier and convey a measure of cheer in grim times.

To be sure, all of this culture shock bred different emotions, and for many, the era has left a legacy of painful memories. For some, the confrontation with

American plenty produced, as one Japanese recalls, "a certain servility, a beggarly sense of dependance on the United States." Others recall how their reluctant dependence upon American generosity was like rubbing salt in their wounds. Novelist Nosaka Akiyuki wrote movingly in his memoirs, published thirty years after the end of the war, of his surviving the bombing of his native Kobe and his experience as one of the "burned out black market" generation who lived by their wits and accepted the chewing gum that was handed out so liberally by the GIs. "It was, after all, better than not having any. But the saliva that trickled out of my mouth as I chewed mingled with tears of mortification. I no longer chew gum and I refuse to drink Coca Cola. And I dislike those who do."

Still, if present-day recollections of those dark years are often bitter, the prevailing mood at the time was not one of sullen resentment. Rather, disillusion with their own leadership and the disasters it had brought to the nation left most Japanese eager to accept Americans as guides to a brighter future.

RELIEF

Moreover, direct relief aid was provided to Japanese in the form of food, fuel, and medicine which was vitally necessary to prevent widespread death during at least the first two or three years of the Occupation. Wars often bring starvation and disease in their train, and in the wake of this war there were pleas for relief assistance from China, the Philippines, Burma, and numerous other countries. Notwithstanding the fact that those countries were allies, and Japan was the enemy, Japan's needs received the highest priority.

The single most indisputably successful program of the Occupation period may well have been the work of a public health doctor, Colonel Crawford F. Sams, head of SCAP's Public Health and Welfare Section, who organized eighty thousand Japanese and American public health personnel in eight hundred stations across Japan. Massive epidemics were expected among a Japanese population weakened by malnutrition and ravaged by a wide range of communicable diseases. Complicating the problem was the widespread destruction of medical facilities and water and sewage systems in the air raids. Further complicating the problem was the flow of millions of repatriates back from the Asian mainland and Pacific islands. Virtually the entire population of Japan received some kind of vaccination or public health treatment between 1945 and 1952. In the single immunization campaign against tuberculosis, extremely prevalent in Japan even in the best of times, almost half of the Japanese were vaccinated. As a result of what were possibly the largest anti-epidemic campaigns in history, murderous diseases like typhoid, diphtheria, cholera, and smallpox were either eradicated or brought under control. Life expectancy rose from forty-seven years in 1946 to sixty-three years at the end of the Occupation.

Citing as an example the fact that in 1948, 92 percent of the staples ration for the nonfarming population consisted of U.S. Army surplus, Theodore Cohen, a key civilian official at MacArthur's General Headquarters (GHQ), states flatly that "there was no starvation, and U.S. Army foods saved the day." Cohen's

Description of the life-style of Professor "Nosaka" (ficticious name) living in Tokyo in 1947:

"He has been instrumental in introducing democratic reforms into his university, and he has been active in neighborhood governmental problems in his section of the city. Yet this man, who is playing a significant role in the intellectual changes going on in Japan, lives in a way that would make many Americans seriously consider joining any political movement that offered promises of economic betterment. He and his family live in a tiny house, which provides not more than 50 square feet per person, although it is more than most Japanese city families now have. It has no heat, no running water, and lighting amounts to one 15-watt bulb per room. The house construction is so flimsy that indoor wintertime temperatures are never far above those outside. The family owns no radio and no stove. Cooking is done over a charcoal brazier, the common method in Japan and that only when the family can secure enough charcoal.

"Although the family has enough clothes, Nosaka has only one pair of shoes. The rest of the family has none. They wear geta, or wooden clogs. Their diet is not adequate. Nosaka and his wife may average 2,000 calories a day, and the children less. Fruits and vegetables are decidedly inadequate, particularly in the wintertime. They are able to buy almost no meat, and rationed fish is eaten only infrequently, often in bad condition.

"Nosaka's salary, when supplemented by earnings from part-time jobs, is barely enough to care for this simple existence. It leaves nothing for amusement, savings, recreation, or children's education."

—U.S. Congress, *United States Policy in the Far East.*

claim is exaggerated. There is ample evidence that there was starvation—the British Commonwealth representative on the Allied Council, W. McMahon Ball, recalled people congregating around the Shinagawa railway station in Tokyo and dying. There certainly was widespread suffering and chronic malnutrition, severe enough to stunt the growth of children living through the grim years from 1945 to 1948. In the end, after Japanese recovery, a prosperous Japan was asked to repay the loans. However, Japan was spared the mass starvation everyone predicted.

The decision to rescue Japanese by drawing on the literally millions of tons of supplies stored in army warehouses in preparation for an invasion of Japan was not made in Washington, but in Tokyo by General MacArthur. In Washington, the Joint Chiefs of Staff had ordered that the United States provide to Japanese food relief only to the "extent . . . needed to prevent such widespread disease and unrest as would endanger the occupying forces or interfere with military operations." MacArthur was to go far beyond the letter and spirit of that directive. It is not necessary to presume that humanitarian motives alone motivated the general. Significant relief efforts were not undertaken until the winter of 1945–1946 when distress was intense and public demonstrations were spreading. Political considerations were obviously on the general's mind when he warned that "starvation . . . renders a people an easy prey to any ideology that brings with it life-sustaining food." Throughout the Occupation, it is apparent that MacArthur never lost sight of the fact that a blunder on the part of the U.S. forces or any kind of mass distress among Japanese would play into the hands of the Japan Communist Party (JCP). When Tokuda Kyuichi, the JCP's leader, was released from prison on MacArthur's orders in October 1945, Tokuda told confidants that controlling food was the key to controlling Japan, and the JCP would therefore concentrate on infiltrating the food supply system. "It never entered Tokuda's mind," Theodore Cohen writes, "that the Americans would actually bring in such massive food shipments for the starving Japanese."

Before the general's tenure as occupation chief came to an end in 1951, more than $2 billion in relief and welfare goods and services had been provided to Japan. As with all the programs which emanated from the GHQ, there were blunders which revealed cultural distances too great to be bridged by SCAP lieutenants and home economics experts rushed to Japan from America. One such group arrived to lecture Japanese housewives on the merits and the preparation of corn bread, an item totally missing from the Japanese diet. A Japanese observer commented that the Americans added insult to injury by giving wide publicity to recipes that called for adding to the cornmeal generous quantities of eggs, milk, and butter, all of which were in scarce supply at the time. "So the Japanese simply parboiled the cracked corn and chewed on it three times a day for week after week and continued to grumble."

Still, to thoughtful Japanese who assumed that an occupying army would requisition food rather than provide it, it was this substantive aid rather than the random GI handouts of candy and gum that measured American concern.

MacArthur as Shogun

MacArthur's shadow loomed so large on the Japanese scene for six years (until President Truman dismissed him in 1951 in connection with the general's conduct of the Korean War) that it is easy to see the Occupation as his own private triumph. An overworked SCAP public relations staff attributed all reform programs to the general, censored open criticism of him, and fostered attitudes approaching idolatry around the sixth floor of the old Daiichi Insurance Company. From there, across the moat from the imperial palace in one of the few downtown Tokyo buildings not destroyed in the fire-bomb raids, MacArthur governed Japan. State Department planner George Kennan referred—in private—to the general as a cross between Catherine the Great and Stalin. "Never before in the history of the United States had such enormous and absolute power been placed in the hands of a single individual," wrote U.S. Ambassador William J. Sebald.

At the end of the Pacific war, MacArthur was sixty-five. In spite of numerous critics who despised him for his theatricality and arrogance, he was a military legend. Indeed, as one of the youngest and most decorated generals in U.S. military history, he was something of a legend by the end of the *first* World War. In 1945, he anxiously accepted the challenge posed by Japan: A successful tour of duty there could confirm his place in history not only as a soldier but as a statesman. (It also needs to be mentioned, as a politician. MacArthur was abundantly interested in a nomination to the presidency and his name figured in no less than four campaigns from 1940 to 1952.) He thought of himself as a man of destiny, and in his trademark Olympian rhetoric, did not hesitate to include his own name in the company of Alexander, Caesar, and Napoleon. Though great generals, he said, they failed with conquered countries by being too harsh. "I shall not," he predicted.

Japanese soon learned that one of MacArthur's first acts in Japan was to make even the slapping of a Japanese by an occupation soldier punishable by a five-year jail sentence. While many Allied officers had looked forward to personally disarming Japanese armed forces, MacArthur refused to permit any such humiliating exercise. In his General Order Number One, SCAP assigned the responsibility for demobilizing the 3.5 million soldiers stationed in the home islands to the Japanese themselves, and it was carried out without incident in less than two months' time. The task of repatriating 6.6 million Japanese military and civilian personnel stationed in the areas conquered by Japan proved to be far more complex and required massive American logistical support, but by the end of 1946, this task had been largely completed. The only major exception in the repatriation process stemmed from the Soviet Union's failure to account for or repatriate the more than one million Japanese troops held in that country. As late as 1970, the Japanese government insisted that 300,000 men, many of whom were presumably still alive, had still not been accounted for by Moscow.

For all his theatricality—the corncob pipe and crushed cap became familiar emblems—the general had a flair for making the correct gesture at the right moment. His arrival at Atsugi illustrates his "dramatic touch." This was a time when the handful of American troops then present in the country were "virtually lost in a sea of still armed and excited Japanese," journalist Kawai Kazuo notes. The general carried no weapons and insisted that his bodyguards also carry no weapons as a gesture of trust in the good faith of the Japanese. In open shirt and with pipe in hand, MacArthur alighted from the *Bataan* and "proceeded with uncharacteristic informality to deal with the Japanese as if inaugurating an Occupation were a matter of daily routine." Kawai concludes:

> It was a masterpiece of psychology which completely disarmed Japanese apprehensions. From that moment, whatever danger there might have been of a fanatic attack on the Americans vanished in a wave of Japanese admiration and gratitude.

If MacArthur had a capacity for the dramatic gesture, he lacked the common touch. MacArthur did not mingle. He never saw ordinary Japanese citizens

General Douglas MacArthur meets the press upon his arrival in Japan, August 28, 1945.

except for those who appeared along the daily one-mile procession route from his residence at the American Embassy to the Daiichi building—white lines on the sidewalk advised a sometimes worshipful public where they could see the sleek black Cadillac with the license number "1" proceeding at a slow, stately pace known to old soldiers as "dead-march drag." He never left Tokyo to visit other parts of the nation. Although he made himself available to hosts of important visitors from America, his contacts with Japanese officialdom were limited to a select group from the very highest ranks.

For all his self-proclaimed knowledge of the "Oriental mind," he dismissed or disparaged Buddhism and Shintoism and actively championed Christianity as an antidote to the revolutionary appeal of Communism. "Japan is a spiritual vacuum," he told one of the groups of Christian leaders who were frequent guests at the Daiichi headquarters. "If you do not fill it with Christianity, it will be filled with Communism." MacArthur's staff, occasionally embarrassed by the general's frequent use of Christian rhetoric—he once compared his labors in Tokyo to a symbolic crucifixion—humored him by supplying him with grossly inflated figures on the conversion rate of Japanese to Christianity. Japanese citizens indulged him by welcoming the flood of ten million Bibles which the general arranged; the pages of many ended up as a substitute for cigarette paper which was a costly black-market commodity. By the time of MacArthur's departure from Japan in 1951, the number of Christians in Japan was barely larger than it had been in 1941 and still well under one percent of the population.

SCAP (the acronym refers to the staff apparatus around MacArthur as well as the general himself) did not become a military government of the kind that was established in Germany at the same time. Washington calculated that it was preferable to oversee and work through the existing Japanese government rather than abolish it. Accordingly, a SCAP bureaucratic structure developed in approximate parallel to the formal government of Japan. It was inevitable that MacArthur, operating from behind the scenes in a shadow government, would be compared to a Tokugawa shogun.

MacArthur's General Headquarters (GHQ) was divided into sections, including Government, Public Health and Welfare, Economic and Scientific, Civil Information and Education, and Legal. The sections were staffed by both military officers and civilians, many of the latter having had experience in the Washington bureaucracy of the New Deal era or in now-defunct wartime agencies. Few knew anything about Japan, and almost none could speak Japanese. Many possessed only the most narrow qualifications for the awesome responsibilities they were assigned by SCAP. Major Daniel Imboden, chief of the Press Division of the Civil Information and Education Section, had once owned a newspaper in San Luis Obispo, California, for example. In 1945, he assumed command over the press in a country of a hundred million with a "big three" of newspapers, each of which boasted circulations several times larger than the *New York Times*.

While the existing machinery of the Japanese government continued to function throughout the Occupation, SCAP took direct control over the media through the enforcement of rigid press and radio codes which provided for censorship of manuscripts and radio programs. In the initial stages of the Occupation at least, SCAP officers, assisted by about five thousand native Japanese translators, also scrutinized theatrical scripts, movie scenarios, and even the pamphlets of professional societies and clubs. The Japanese public was scarcely aware of the censorship program, because news of the censorship system was itself strictly censored. The censors targeted yellow journalism and reactionaries in the initial stages and later concentrated increasingly on the radical left.

Years later, after archives were opened to permit historical analysis of the occupation period, critics of the United States were quick to point out the irony of MacArthur pursuing such undemocratic methods in the pursuit of a democratization program. The charge has some merit. Censors were especially on the lookout for any criticisms of U.S. conduct of the war and anything which would incite mistrust or resentment of SCAP policies or personnel. References in reprinted wartime literature to American troops as "enemy troops" were routinely deleted or modified. The Supreme Commander was of course off limits to criticism by either Japanese or Americans—the threat of expulsion or denial of press privileges acted to stifle criticism from the American journalists. In one famous incident, Major General Charles A. Willoughby, MacArthur's chief of intelligence, halted the press run of a Tokyo newspaper whose offensive editorial on his boss had somehow eluded the censors. The editorial writer had admonished the Japanese for viewing the general with an "adoration that verges on idolatry" and urged them to stand on their own two feet. Willoughby, who was at the center of the commander's inner group of confidants, had evidently overlooked the distinctly American sentiments of the editorial in deciding that it "was not in good taste" and in ordering military policemen to board trains to seize already printed copies of the newspaper.

Still, if there were excesses, they were not as pervasive or as typical as some critics have contended. Clever Japanese writers soon learned ways to skirt SCAP rules. A reference to GI black marketeering or rape was sure to receive the scissors, but the problem could probably be resolved by changing "GI" to "blue-eyed nationals" or "men with nine-inch footprints." In any case, censorship policies were relaxed well before the end of the Occupation. The most drastic demands, for prepublication censorship, lasted only until June 1947. Then, after a shift to postpublication censorship for the next two years, all censorship operations ceased in 1949.

In addition, while heavy handed, SCAP censors were more often arbitrary than consistent. True, for example, it took several years for censors to pass a translation of John Hersey's *Hiroshima*, with its gripping portrayal of the first atomic bombing from the perspective of the victims. On the other hand, Japanese accounts of the bombing, with gruesome descriptions and criticisms of America for dropping the bomb on a virtually defeated Japan, were published uncensored. During the first year of the Occupation, theater censors banned 322 plays, most of them *Kabuki* performances which were judged to glorify "feudal ideology or militarism, blind loyalty, a cheap valuation of human life, relegation of women to a subservient status in society, and glorification of revenge." The result was virtually to decimate the repertories of the *Kabuki* stage—but only for a single year. By late 1946, SCAP had given up its effort to reform three centuries of *Kabuki* tradition, and "its old buoyancy was back." In general, Japanese literature was liberated and flourished during this era, especially when compared to the clamped-down atmosphere which prevailed before the war, when even the published word "social" was avoided because it sounded too close to the forbidden "socialism."

TRIALS AND PURGES

While the primary purpose of the Occupation was not punitive, the Allied Powers did create the Far Eastern equivalent of the Nuremberg trials to try twenty-eight so-called "Class-A war criminals," those charged with "the planning, preparation, initiation, or waging" of a war of aggression. This International Military Tribunal for the Far East (commonly known as the Tokyo Trials), presided over by eleven judges from the victor nations, met for more than two-and-a-half years beginning in the spring of 1946. On November 4, 1948, the tribunal's president, Sir William Webb of Australia, read the judgment of the majority, who found all the accused guilty. Seven, including General Tojo Hideki, were sentenced to the gallows. Elsewhere in Japan, and in China, the Philippines and other countries Japan had occupied, another five thousand war criminals were charged with lesser crimes, including mistreatment of prisoners of war.

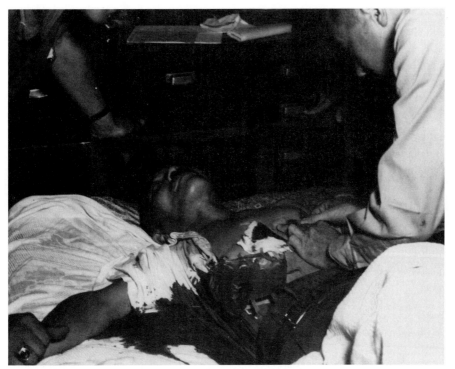

U.S. Army officers arrive to arrest General Tojo Hideki who had just attempted suicide.

While the Tokyo Trials were regarded with uncritical approval by most of the American public, some critical voices insist that the defendants received "victors' justice" and nothing more. They call attention to the fact that the only war crimes which were investigated were those committed by the losers and hold that American actions, including the indiscriminate fire-bomb raids and the dropping of the atomic bombs, should have been investigated. They also point to procedural irregularities such as the fact that there were no judges from neutral nations and that only one judge, Pal of India, who dissented vigorously from the majority opinion, had training in international law.

The standards of fairness are much more questionable in the trials of some of the lesser war criminals such as Generals Homma Masaharu and Yamashita Tomoyuki. Both were found guilty and eventually executed on the grounds that they held "command responsibility"—Homma for the Bataan death march and Yamashita, the "Tiger of Malay," for massacres of civilian inhabitants of Manila near the end of the war. In both cases, the atrocities themselves cannot be contested, though in neither case was there convincing evidence that the generals in question ordered, approved of, or were in any way directly responsible for the crimes. In both trials, procedural flaws such as hearsay evidence abounded.

AMERICANS ON YAMASHITA'S TRIAL

"No one in a position of command in any army, from sergeant to general, can escape these implications. Indeed the fate of some future President of the United States and his Chief of Staff and military advisors may well have been sealed by this decision. That the life of General Yamashita, a leader of enemy forces vanquished in the field of battle, is to be taken without regard to the due processes of law. There will be few to protest. But tomorrow the precedent here established can be turned against others."

—Justice Frank Murphy, in dissenting arguments to the Supreme Court.

"I have reviewed the proceedings in vain search for some mitigating circumstances on his behalf. I can find none . . . . The soldier, be he friend or foe, is charged with the protection of the weak and unarmed. It is the very essence and reason for his being. When he violates this sacred trust, he not only profanes his entire cult but he threatens the very fabric of international society."

—General Douglas MacArthur.

The U.S. Supreme Court reviewed the findings of the military courts and upheld the verdicts. However, Associate Justice Frank Murphy dissented, saying that "the lives of Yamashita and Homma, leaders of enemy forces vanquished on the field of battle, are taken without regard to the due process of law." Even staunch defenders of MacArthur agree that his determination to have his two military opponents executed stemmed more from a spirit of revenge than any commitment to justice. William Manchester, author of the generally laudatory biography, *American Caesar*, writes that MacArthur's role in the case reveals "shadowy places in [his] character."

Far more sweeping than the trials was the "Removal and Exclusion of Undesirable Personnel from Public Office," popularly known as the "purge." SCAP's purge resulted in the removal of about 200,000 Japanese military, government, and business leaders from their wartime positions and their exclusion from public office on grounds that they had been "active exponents of militarism and militant nationalism." The purge, though much smaller than the one imposed on the German leadership, hit the business community especially hard—according to one estimate, one out of every four top business executives in Japan was compelled to retire. The effort had only limited success in that many of those purged retained behind-the-scenes influence, and more than one of those purged or imprisoned by the Occupation rose to the rank of prime minister after the Occupation ended. Still, the purge did clear the way for a partially new generation of business and political leaders to emerge in Japan.

THE EMPEROR

Conspicuously absent from the ranks of those tried or purged was the emperor. In spite of the fact that the terms agreed upon at the end of the war seemed to suggest that the United States would allow the Japanese people to choose whether or not to retain their emperor, there were many in Congress and in the nation's newspapers and among the Allies who called loudly for holding Hirohito responsible for war guilt. Much of this was racist demogoguery and grounded in the political expediency of the moment.

Still, sober-minded scholars, from both sides of the Pacific, could harbor doubts about his complete innocence. A number of these Japan specialists took the occasion of the emperor's death in 1989 to deplore the decision by the United States forty-four years earlier to grant "selective immunity" to Hirohito. In a signed statement circulated to the scholarly community, they argued that the emperor, in spite of his largely figurehead role, *could* have intervened in the political process and in fact had done so on a few well-documented occasions. Nevertheless, he not only failed to speak out to bring the war to an end until the last moment but at certain critical junctures insisted to his closest advisers that the nation must fight on. His failure to call for peace, born in part of his concern to ensure that his own imperial sway remain unchallenged, made him at least as accountable for the death and suffering of his own people as many of those who were brought to trial as Class-A war criminals, it was argued. Seeing him as neither monster nor god, the authors of the 1989 statement found Hirohito to be a "flawed and weak human being who was complicit in the process of causing enormous human destruction and who concentrated through times of cataclysmic change on doing his job and saving his own skin."

THE MOTOSHIMA AFFAIR. At the same time as the scholars' statement, the "Motoshima affair" brought the issue of the emperor's war guilt into a sharp public focus in Japan. Motoshima Hitoshi, mayor of Nagasaki, had responded to a question at a session of the city assembly in December 1988 while Hirohito lay near death. Please comment on the emperor's war responsibility, he was asked. In a brief reply the mayor affirmed that he believed that the emperor did bear some responsibility for the war. Moreover, if the emperor had resolved to end the war earlier, Motoshima declared, there would have been no battle of Okinawa and no nuclear attacks on Hiroshima and Nagasaki. "I myself belonged to the education unit in the western division of the army, and I instructed the troops to die for the emperor. I have friends who died shouting 'banzai' to the emperor," the mayor later told reporters. Nonetheless, the mayor said, it had been the will of the great majority of the Japanese people as well as of the Allied powers that Hirohito was to be released from having to take responsibility for his wartime conduct and that he was to become the symbol of the new constitution. "My interpretation is that we must adhere to that position," Motoshima concluded. The mayor's measured comments triggered a flood of soul-searching responses from housewives, army veterans, students, farmers, peace activists, and members of disadvantaged minorities like the Koreans. The gist of the thousands of letters that poured into the mayor's office was that there was too much concealment of the truth, too much distortion of history. At the same time, however, the mayor's remarks served to provoke right-wing organizations with names like the "Rising Sun Society" to calls for retribution against the mayor and his family. In an assassination attempt all too reminiscent of the 1930s wave of terror, the mayor was shot by a fanatic in January 1990 and seriously, though not fatally, wounded. The shooting had been "inevitable," a "patriotic" group announced, because the mayor's criticism of Hirohito had posed a "grave threat to the state."

MACARTHUR AND THE EMPEROR. In 1945, however, MacArthur and the men in Washington who were responsible for planning for the Occupation were nearly unanimous in the assessment that the emperor had to stay. At that time, there was no way of knowing how long the Occupation might last or how much opposition might be encountered. Given such uncertainties, it seemed foolish to outrage Japanese sensitivities by subjecting the emperor to a humiliating trial. A million reinforcements might be needed, MacArthur estimated, to handle the violent response of the Japanese public to such a move. A discredited god was of much greater use to SCAP than a martyred god.

To that end, MacArthur, with lofty disregard for traditional protocol, had the *emperor* pay *him* a visit soon after the Occupation began. The supreme commander greeted the emperor with courtesy, offered a cigarette to calm his jittery hands, and recalled that as a young lieutenant accompanying his father on an assignment in the Far East, he had been received in audience decades earlier by Hirohito's grandfather, the Meiji Emperor. When Japanese saw a photograph of the pair in the September 28 newspapers, there could be no remaining doubt about who was running Japan. The casually posed general seemed to tower above the nervous-appearing emperor at his side. Hirohito wore a severely formal cutaway, while MacArthur was dressed in a plain suntan uniform without tie. Attempts by shocked Japanese officials to have the photograph suppressed were quickly overridden by SCAP.

While the imperial institution was to be preserved, it would be necessary to define with precision its place in Japanese polity. In the Meiji constitution, sovereignty and all powers of government were assigned to the emperor, who was described as "sacred and inviolable." It was well known, however, to reform-minded Japanese and SCAP officers alike, that in actual practice modern emperors had not sought to assert their own political wills. This ambiguous situation permitted militant nationalists to carry out policies which they claimed represented the imperial will and thereby place themselves and their policies beyond reproach. Since it was SCAP's announced intention to democratize Japan, the precise function of the emperor had to be clarified so as to bring responsibility and accountability to the process of political decision making. This was done with precision and force in a new constitution which came into

*General MacArthur and Emperor
Hirohito meet, September 1945.*

effect in 1947. It expressly states that the emperor "shall not have powers related to government" and that he is simply "the symbol of the State and of the unity of the people, deriving his position from the will of the people with whom resides sovereign power."

To underscore the point further, SCAP insisted that the emperor issue a statement renouncing his divinity. The imperial rescript issued on January 1, 1946, declared that the ties that bind the emperor and his people "do not depend upon mere legends and myths" and "are not predicated upon the false conception that the Emperor is divine and that the Japanese people are superior to other races and fated to rule the world." Overseas military adventures could no longer be justified as reflecting the sacred intent of the emperor.

Next, SCAP decided to humanize the emperor, have him appear in public with a minimum of protocol, so that he might stand as a symbol of the democratization process. Ordinary Japanese who had never been allowed to gaze on the imperial face or utter the name Hirohito were soon startled to find the man descending into mine shafts, throwing out first baseballs in the American manner, and trudging through rubble-strewn streets to visit factories and schools. The emperor, by all accounts a painfully shy man far more interested in marine biology than in public affairs, was obviously ill at ease in carrying out these assignments, and the Japanese public soon began to call him "Mr. Ah, so!" from the single contribution he made to all conversations. Even more irreverently, some who only months before had been his subjects took satisfaction in flexing their newly acquired democratic options by referring to him as "Tenchan" which translates as something like "Emp-baby," a slur which might have

> The real "reason the Emperor came out and said he wasn't God was because he found out that MacArthur was."
>
> —Congressman Maury Maverick, Texas.
>
> "[MacArthur] even had his own pronunciations, which were not to be corrected by any person—or any dictionary. If the dictionary disagreed, it had better change and get down to date. For instance, the word hara-kiri, which was frequently heard in Tokyo in those days. To MacArthur it was ha-RICK-iri. And that was that."
>
> —Hugh Baillie, head of United Press, after visit to Tokyo, 1945.

earned the culprit capital punishment prior to August 1945. If public mockery of those on high is a mark of democracy, the Japanese were learning.

To ensure that Emperor Hirohito's successor, Crown Prince Akihito, learned to speak English, Elizabeth Gray Vining, a widowed author of children's books from Pennsylvania, was assigned to the imperial household in 1946. Vining, a devout Quaker, gave not only English instruction, as it turned out, but for four years engaged the young prince and several other members of the imperial family in morning Bible readings, "Monopoly" lessons, and moral training parables drawn from the experiences of William Penn and the Indians. In subtle ways, she nudged her young charges toward a more democratic and independent-minded outlook than they were accustomed. She once asked the young Akihito what he intended to do after class. When he answered that "It is not decided," she pursued: "Who decides?" "The chamberlains," the crown prince replied. "Why don't *you* decide? This is your afternoon," Vining suggested to the young prince who would succeed his father as emperor in 1989. She recounted her work in *Windows for the Crown Prince*, whose best-seller status in 1952 suggested the prevailing fascination of Americans with Japan.

Japanese, however, were not always charmed by the picture of this foreigner, the first ever permitted inside the living quarters of the imperial palace, taking it upon herself to shape the character and attitudes of the future emperor in an alien way. Nor are Japanese usually pleased when foreigners assign American names to them. In an expression of the democratic impulse, Vining gave all her pupils American names—Akihito was Jimmy. To many Japanese, this was not so much democratic as patronizing.

CONSTITUTIONAL REFORMS

The new constitution, which came into effect on May 3, 1947, following approval by both houses of the Diet, does not read like a Japanese document. It reads like a translated document and indeed it is. It was MacArthur's intention that the Japanese should themselves draw up a new constitution, and a committee of respected jurists was assigned that task. However, SCAP rejected the committee's working draft on the grounds that it would not adequately foster the kind of democratic changes which American reformers intended. The Japanese, for example, could not bring themselves to tamper with the sovereign position the emperor enjoyed in the Meiji Constitution. Accordingly, MacArthur assigned the task of drafting a Japanese Constitution to officer-lawyers in SCAP's Government section. The *democratic* constitution of 1947, ostensibly adopted in accordance with the "will of the Japanese people," was thus paradoxically an American document *imposed* upon Japan. If citizens of Alabama, Colorado, and Montana find some of the language familiar, it is because clauses in the quite lengthy (103 articles) Japanese Constitution were lifted from those states' constitutions. Article 89, for example, prohibiting state grants to private schools, was borrowed from Montana.

Because of its foreign origins, it was widely predicted that the 1947 constitution would not survive the Occupation. Once the authority of the Occupation came to an end in 1952, after all, the government of Japan was fully sovereign and free to discard what was sometimes called the "MacArthur Constitution." It has never done so. The document remains in force. As we will see, a few of its clauses are highly controversial but, although there is provision for amendment, it remains unchanged from 1947.

Whereas the Meiji Constitution emphasized the duties and obligations of the citizenry and restricted liberties (which were provided for only "within the limits" of the law), the new constitution is noted for its extensive enumeration of rights. There are guarantees of religious freedom, assembly, free speech, press, and so on— all of the rights provided for in the American Bill of Rights. In addition, the Japanese Constitution reflects the New Deal liberalism of its drafters by guaranteeing the right to an education and the right of labor to organize and engage in collective bargaining. It further promises that the state will promote social welfare and security and public health.

In order to strengthen the chances for democracy, the prewar power of various unofficial advisory groups such as the *genro* (elder statesmen) was abolished. Similarly, the prewar nobility which dated back to the Meiji era was eliminated. With a stroke of the pen the barons, counts, and viscounts of the old peerage lost their titles, privileges, and the security of a guaranteed livelihood. While some SCAP officials favored restructuring Japan's political system in the image of the American one the Americans knew best, it made more sense to build on the prewar experience of Japan which had led the country toward a British parliamentary form of government. As a consequence, supreme political power was assigned to the Diet, with the prime minister to be elected by members of the House of Representatives. The prime minister was given the authority to select his cabinet which, following British custom, is "responsible" to the Diet, meaning that it and the prime minister are obliged to resign in the event of a resolution of nonconfidence by the Diet.

SCAP's Government section initially favored a unicameral parliament but, in a rather unusual display of compromise, bowed to wishes of Japanese parliamentarians who argued for a bicameral Diet. Accordingly, a House of Councillors, empowered to override the decisions of the House of Representatives when it can muster a two-thirds vote, emerged to replace the discarded House of Peers.

Political parties, though not mentioned in the constitution, as in Britain compete for control of the Diet. Unlike Britain, however, Japanese conservatives, representing the interests of farmers and big business, have dominated the Diet for the entire postwar era with the exception of a ten-month period from 1947 to 1948, when there was a Socialist-led government. The chief conservative party has been known since 1955 as the Liberal Democratic Party (LDP). The "one-party" political system that Japan has enjoyed (or "suffered" for those of the socialist persuasion) throughout the postwar era has made for great stability which permitted the government the luxury of implementing exceptionally long-range plans and vision. The economic growth that flowed from this essentially unified establishment has served to reinforce the conservatives's grip on power: the citizenry has not been inclined to change horses in the middle of the stream of postwar prosperity.

WOMEN'S RIGHTS

MacArthur, though not usually regarded as a radical feminist, is frequently given credit for writing into the Japanese Constitution an Equal Rights Amendment for Japanese women of the kind that American feminists have long labored—without success—to have adopted in the United States. Japanese women gained the vote in 1947, and by 1968 more women than men were turning out at the polls. Women also began to take their seats in the Diet, and in 1986 the Socialists, the nation's largest opposition party, broke new ground by electing a woman, Doi Takako, as its secretary general, thus raising the possibility of a woman prime minister.

The humble Parent–Teacher Association, unknown in Japan before World War II, was encouraged by SCAP and soon became a permanent feature of the school scene, perhaps even more so than in the United States. Most families—and that means mothers from most families—are now actively involved in PTAs. There is disagreement about how much impact the PTAs have had on educational policies, but it is clear that they have brought the average middle-class housewive into much greater contact with the larger outside world than they had known before the war. As a woman member of the Tokyo Metropolitan Board of Social Education wrote in 1975, "The PTA is turning out a new breed of woman that is willing to question authority."

In addition, the postwar constitution and implementing legislation gave women the same rights as men with regard to property ownership and inheritance (brothers had received preferential treatment in the past). In case of disputes in such matters, the Meiji Civil Code asserted that "cripples and disabled persons and wives cannot undertake any legal action."

Until 1947, women were entitled to fewer grounds for divorce than men. Equality provisions in the new constitution changed that. Although the divorce rate in Japan is far lower than in most countries in the Western world, three out of four contemporary divorces in Japan are initiated by women. This is a far cry from the Tokugawa era when only men could obtain a divorce and when the grounds for divorce included infertility, indolence, or excessive chattering. The divorce ensued upon the delivery by the husband to his wife a note signifying his intentions, a note so abrupt that it was known as the "three-and-a half lines" message *(mikudarihan)*. Similarly, old laws subjected only errant wives to punishment for adultery. In 1947, after heated debate in a Diet filled for the first time with dozens of female representatives, it was decided that adultery would no longer be defined as a criminal act but that it would remain as grounds for divorce with both wives and husbands equally liable.

Women were now to enjoy the same parental rights as men. Contract marriage was forbidden as was concubinage. In traditional times, the basic unit of society had been the household, transferring its daughters "out" and brides "in" at marriage. Now, with the passage of the Civil Code of 1947, the names of *both* the new husband and wife are entered as founders of a new family into the important household registries *(jumin torokuhyo)* which establish residence for voting, schooling, and social-security rights. Thus was subverted overnight the centuries of legal and social practice which affirmed that the head of the household was male and the relationship between a man and his parents as more important than the ties between husband and wife.

The removal of legal grounds for discrimination has not of course translated into true equality in practice. The idea of separate spheres for men and women, with women prevailing at home and men outside, is deeply engrained in the Japanese mind and remains accepted by both sexes more than forty years after the constitutional advances of 1947. As Kyoko Inoue, a linguist and constitutional scholar, has written, the Japanese "interpreted the expression 'equality of the sexes' to mean men and women were essentially equal in their ability to fulfill their respective roles in the family." Inoue adds that this was "much different from what the Americans had intended—that women have, or should have, equal rights."

Discrimination and barriers remain, perhaps not surprising for a people whose written symbol for woman shows a person kneeling with hands folded in a posture of deference. The problems are most evident in the workplace, where women rarely rise to even middle levels of management. For all the advances made by Japanese women, and notwithstanding legal guarantees of equal wages for equal work, Japan, as late as the 1970s and early 1980s, remained one of the few nations in the world where the hourly wage gap between men and women in manufacturing was widening.

While some of the credit for the constitutional reforms doubtless belongs to MacArthur himself, a small group of American female staffers of very junior rank played a crucial and almost totally unsung role in bringing about the legal emancipation of Japanese women. Beate Sirota, a Viennese-born expert on Japan, fluent in the language, was probably more responsible for the far-reaching language on women's rights in the constitution than any other single person; she was a twenty-two-year-old civilian in SCAP's Government section at the time. Ethel B. Weed used her civilian-life skills—she had been a public relations specialist in Cleveland before joining the Women's Army Corps—to promote the development of democratically run women's clubs and organizations to replace the old state-led organizations whose function was mainly to enlist women's support for the war effort. Though only a first lieutenant, she "was on the scene and in most cases she was a central participant" in virtually all discussions and debate concerning occupation policy affecting women.

Still more deserving of credit was the corps of Japanese feminists who had labored for decades to reform the status of women and attitudes toward women. As early as 1911, the women's literary magazine *Bluestockings* (*Seito*) was promoting the self-awakening of women with the rallying cry of Hiratsuka Raicho, its founder, "In the beginning, there was the sun, and it was woman." Without the foundations for change built by women like Kato Shizue (a pioneer in the movement for family planning), Ichikawa Fusae (founder of the Women's Suffrage League in 1924), and scores of lesser known iconoclasts who challenged conventional customs and often paid for their defiance with ostracism or worse, it is unlikely that the American-sponsored reforms would have taken hold. To the extent that the SCAP's legal reforms were accepted in practice, they reflect internal changes that were occurring long before August 1945.

Moreover, these internal changes derived not simply from the activities of liberal reformers but also out of pragmatic responses to certain situational demands. Wartime labor shortages prompted significant numbers of women to enter the job market for the first time, as factory workers, street-car conductors, and teachers. Women took over much of the food-rationing and fire-fighting activities during the air raids. The result of all this was to change existing male–female economic and social relationships in ways that were of course totally unintended and unexpected by the conservative leadership which ran

HUSBANDS ON THE DOLE
"Men were away during the war, reinforcing the wife's authority in financial affairs. After 1945, dynamic women took over the running of the household from their demoralized husbands.

"Low postwar wages turned husbands into meek delivery boys who handed the pay envelope over to their wife un-opened. Until recently most Japanese workers were paid in cash, so at least men could feel the outside of the envelope and get a sense of what was inside. But with the spread of electronic banking, the husband never sees his own hard-earned salary until the wife doles out his monthly allowance from their bank account."

—Yoshida Tadao, *Keizai Orai*, 1986.

the country. Carrying this "situational" interpretation forward to the post-occupation period, one writer commented on women's rights as follows:

> If the women are now divorcing tyrannical husbands—as they are doing
> in increasing numbers—it is not because the Occupation-sponsored laws say
> they can, but it is because husbands are no longer their only available meal
> ticket. If the women are now attaining public office—as they are doing
> increasingly—it is not because the new law says that they now have the
> same political rights as men, but it is because there are now more women
> with experience in industry and in business and in labor unions and in civic
> organizations who are capable of holding their own against the men at their
> own game.

EDUCATION

If the political and social reforms engineered by SCAP were to be accepted and sink roots in Japan it would be necessary for Japanese to be educated to appreciate the changes that were occurring about them. The schools, therefore, were targeted for extensive modification.

At the heart of the problem was the fact that in prewar years, but especially in the decade of the 1930s when Japan veered toward militarism, the nation's schools had been used to foster nationalistic and militaristic attitudes among the students. Mythology was turned into authentic history in textbooks which spoke of the "Land of the Gods" with a 2600-year-old imperial past, one which could rival China's, when historians can find no evidence that Japan's imperial line goes back beyond the fifth century. By the time the Greater East Asia Co-Prosperity Sphere was promulgated in 1940 in the midst of the war with China, assumptions of racial and cultural superiority had become linked with expansionism to produce official notions of "Japanism" *(Nipponshugi)* which resembled Nazism.

To question such officially prescribed truths was to invite the sharpest of rebukes or, in the case of a scholar, a ruined career. The emphasis on rote learning, always strong in Japanese schools, became more pronounced as students were encouraged to cultivate the discipline and unquestioning loyalty of soldiers. School sports grew more martial as baseball was phased out and replaced by drilling and traditional martial arts. Army officers were stationed in middle and secondary schools to oversee military training and "to build up the morale of the nation." The daily ritual of bowing to the imperial portrait enshrined in every school took on overtones of cult worship. Religion was brought into the indoctrination system as students were regularly marched off to Shinto shrines for stern lectures from the priests on the importance of duty to the emperor and the glory of the nation's culture and its divine mission.

A measure of the gulf between the prewar ethos and that which SCAP was trying to inculcate is found in the case of the assistant principal of a Tokyo

> "The [occupation] era was like the Meiji restoration. Everybody was trying everything. Then it was modernization, Westernization, now it was democratization, Americanization. It was like the school teacher in Yamanashi prefecture when we asked him what he was teaching now that the war had ended: he replied instantly, 'Democracy.'
>
> "'But,' we asked, 'what do you mean by democracy?'
>
> "'Oh,' he shot back, 'we are waiting to be told by the Ministry of Education.'"
>
> —John K. Emmerson, *The Japanese Thread:*
> *A Life in the U.S. Foreign Service.*

middle school reported in January 1948, long after extensive purges and resignations had cleansed the professional ranks of more than a hundred thousand unsuitable teachers. The administrator was found to be still teaching from a book entitled *Seppuku* (Disembowelment) which he himself had written in 1943 on the virtues of ritual suicide as a means of atoning for the dishonor of defeat. To underscore the superiority of the Japanese way, he contrasted it with the behavior of Americans, British, and Dutch who had become prisoners of war. "With no sense of shame . . . they ask immediately that their families be notified of their capture. After that, they set about making their quarters as comfortable as possible awaiting the day of the return home. Their families, in addition, instead of disowning them for their cowardice, welcome them home with open arms."

As with other occupation programs, successes in educational reform came largely because of an eagerness for change by the Japanese themselves. A small SCAP staff, headed by a Marine Corps lieutenant colonel who in civilian life had been a high-school principal, set guidelines that would affect eighteen million students and a million teachers and administrators. SCAP education officers, sometimes appreciated by Japanese officials for their idealism and dedication, though generally scorned for their limited academic expertise and still more-limited knowledge of Japan, were dispatched, one to each prefecture, to oversee implementation of the policies shaped at the general headquarters in Tokyo. Meeting the expectations of the often overzealous SCAP officers no doubt prompted many Japanese school officials to make superficial changes to curry favor. Years later, middle-school principals were known to joke about how they would order their students to commence square dancing upon hearing the sound of an approaching American jeep.

THE STODDARD MISSION

A United States Education Mission, headed by Dr. George D. Stoddard, later president of the University of Illinois, spent several weeks in Japan in 1946 and issued a report which was to become the basis for the Occupation's reforms in education. The Stoddard Report's recommendation to phase out the use of *kanji*, ideograph-based characters, in favor of phonetic *romaji*, a Romanized alphabet, illustrates the sometimes impractical fervor of American reform efforts. At first glance, the proposal appeared to have great merit as a step in democratizing the education process. It is manifestly quicker to learn twenty-six simple letters rather than the thousands of complex *kanji* which require years of rote memory to master. Such proposals, however, had long been considered—and rejected—by the Japanese themselves. The Japanese language simply does not lend itself to a phonetic spelling system, mainly because of the multitude of homonyms, words with the same pronunciation but different meanings. *Seiko*, for example, means success, but it also means steel manufacture and sexual intercourse and at least a dozen other things. While the use of Roman letters gives no clue as to which meaning the writer intends, the use of different *kanji* pinpoints the various meanings with precision. The American recommendation was therefore soon dropped. A Japanese commission did, however, come up with a more practical suggestion, which was quickly adopted, to limit the number of *kanji* in general use (to 1850) and to simplify the writing of those *kanji* by reducing the number of strokes required. Those widely applauded changes remain in place today.

Other proposals were rigorously implemented. Throughout Japan, coeducation was established in all public schools, a reform welcomed by mothers who appreciated that it meant that their daughters would be exposed to education equal in quality to that enjoyed by boys. For several months, the teaching of history was suspended until authorities were convinced that it could be taught without the jingoist excesses of the past. The prewar courses on moral education (*shushin*)—at the heart of the old curriculum and stressing filial piety, duty, and obedience to authority—were ordered permanently dropped on the grounds that such training had too easily lent itself to an unquestioning loyalty to the state and was out of step with new efforts to instill respect for the rights of the individual. Five years after SCAP's authority came to an end, in 1957, amidst much debate, the courses were restored (under a new name), minus the ultranationalist emphasis of the past and including a survey of religious beliefs of other cultures. Rightist critics, who deplore what they perceive to be a moral drift and insufficient patriotism among Japanese youth, frequently lay the blame at the door of the Occupation and call for a revival of the prewar style of *shushin* classes.

Other suggestions were put into effect but achieved only limited success. In an effort to reduce elitism in higher education—which was dominated by a very few imperial universities and two private universities whose graduates monopolized positions of influence in government, industry, and the professions—the Stoddard mission greatly expanded the system of four-year colleges. It was decreed that each prefecture should have its own national university, and virtually every instititution of higher learning was allowed to call itself a university. Because of these moves and the proliferation of new private universities, university enrollments expanded rapidly. In the end, however, the hierarchical structure of higher education was enhanced rather than diminished. The poor-to-middling quality of the new institutions ensured that the same few universities from the prewar years continued to hold a monopoly on prestige. The prewar system of extremely competitive entrance examinations remained the key to upward mobility for the elite. The name of Tokyo Imperial University (abbreviated as Teidai) was changed to Tokyo University (Todai) after the war, but its place at the apex of the educational hierarchy remains unchallenged. As one writer observed, "a diploma from this school is practically a ticket into the ruling class."

Similarly, the Stoddard mission's attempt to rearrange the political control of education was only partially successful. The highly centralized authority of the Ministry of Education was deemed to be the source of the objectionable prewar trend toward regimentation and nationalistic indoctrination. The Stoddard group was therefore committed to a dispersal of control among autonomous, popularly elected local school boards which would be made responsible for such matters as textbook selection, the hiring of faculty, and the appointment of superintendents. In practice, the Ministry of Education eventually gained a great deal of centralized power. Although local boards select textbooks, for example, their selections must come from a list approved by the ministry in Tokyo. Similarly, the ministry closely supervises the curricula at the lower levels. At the senior high school level, uniformity is assured, because students are preparing for university entrance examinations which are identical nationwide. Edwin O. Reischauer comments on the students produced by this virtually identical national education: "They emerge into society with a uniformity of information and attitudes that is matched only in a small close-knit primitive society or a modern totalitarian state."

Perhaps the most enduring and satisfying change to emerge from the Occupation educational reforms was the production of a freer atmosphere in the classrooms and a more tolerant attitude toward independent thought and initiative. Though, by American standards, Japanese students and teachers still seem governed by conformity to an unhealthy degree, a Japanese could write in 1960 that,

> It may not be too common a sight, but one now does occasionally see school children on their civics "projects" swarming through the city hall in search of officials to interview or sprawling over the desks of a police station while pestering harassed police officers with embarrassingly frank questions. These children may not know as much arithmetic or as many names of ancient emperors as their parents did at their age, but they give the impression that they will eventually become more capable than their parents of understanding the responsibilities of democratic citizenship. They are still not quite as brash as American youngsters, but their comparatively uninhibited curiosity and their relative lack of fear of authority stand in wholesome contrast to the repression of the pupils under the old lock-step system of education.

SCAP AND COED SCHOOLING

"Until 1945, secondary education was strictly segregated; male and female students attended separate schools. Educational reform in the Osaka area where I lived was radical and dramatic.

"An enthusiastic young American army officer, a first lieutenant, traveled from one school district to the next preaching coeducation. Rumor had it that he had begun in Kyushu, Japan's southernmost main island, and made his way northward to Osaka.

"One day our teachers told us we had to choose between attending our school and the local girls' middle school. Stunned, we were summoned to the auditorium and ordered to close our eyes. The principal asked those who wanted to move to the girls' school to raise their hand. When that didn't work, we drew lots.

"Half of the student body and teaching staff transferred to the girls' school, and vice versa. Embarrassed adolescents suddenly found themselves thrown together in a kind of shotgun wedding.

"I was told later that the U.S. officer eventually reached Nagoya, which lies between Osaka and Tokyo, before being reassigned to other duties. This may explain why in Tokyo and elsewhere in eastern Japan, male students still outnumber their female classmates at former boys' schools. In Osaka, the sexes are divided more or less equally.

"Forty years ago, sexual integration was tantamount to heresy. But the idea of changing schools appealed to me. I was tired of being told to emulate our illustrious graduates—military heroes and famous politicians. I was the only one who raised his hand and volunteered for the move . . . .

"My world was turned upside down. Previously, even being seen in the company of the opposite sex was a serious breach of social norms. Now we were sharing textbooks . . . .

"The sudden break with the past was exhilarating. Young men and women looked together toward a future that, for the first time in Japanese history, would be determined by the people themselves."

Oda Makoto, *Mainichi Shimbun* (newspaper), August 1, 1988.

School radio facilities, which in prewar years had been used to coordinate nationwide calisthenics, were brought into use to broadcast programs such as the "What am I?" series which carried the message that adolescent curiosity and rebelliousness were healthy. Beyond the schools, radio, which had been an indispensable tool of wartime propaganda, was now effectively used in a variety of innovative ways as SCAP sometimes recommended and sometimes actually drafted new programming ideas. In 1946, at a time when predictions of imminent mass starvation were being heard, the Japan Broadcasting Corporation (NHK) went on the air with the first "Man on the Street" interviews. People were asked to relate, for the benefit of listeners all over the country, their views on important national issues as well as their private tricks for survival—thinning out already watery rice gruel, cooking potato vines, and so on.

At first, it was not easy to persuade people to speak before the microphones—ordinary citizens had never been asked to publicly express their views on national concerns—but interviewees soon warmed up to the idea, and the program gained a huge national audience. New discussion programs featuring free-wheeling debates by panels representing left, middle-of-the-road, and conservative viewpoints were also little short of sensational to Japanese audiences eager for information but accustomed to hearing what one expert calls an "unmitigated flow of state propaganda." Social issues, such as the question of romantic love versus arranged marriages, were also aired—that particular round-table discussion was so popular that receivers were set up in public parks to accommodate those who didn't own sets.

LAND REFORM

The single most successful undertaking of the occupation era was a three-year-long drive to reform land-holding patterns in the countryside. At the end of the war, Japan was still a predominantly rural country with half of the work force engaged in farming. The problem, long recognized by the Japanese themselves, was that 70 percent of the farmers were tenants—meaning that they had to rent all or some of the land they farmed; about 46 percent of all the cultivated land was tenanted. Landlords could squeeze extortion-like land rents from their tenants. "The farmer is like a sesame seed," went an old saying. "The more you squeeze the more you get." If the tenant complained or failed to pay, he could be summarily expelled by the landlord, who could easily find more properly humble tenants. The peasant had no written contract or security and knew that the power of the state would crush attempts to organize meaningful opposition to the landlord class. The result was that most tenants were poor and oppressed in the best of times. Then, every few years or so when a crop failure occurred or agricultural prices dropped, peasants would be reduced to eating the bark off trees or selling daughters to the agents of urban brothels. City dwellers looked down on rural folk in the prewar years with a combination of pity and scorn. A health worker and aspiring writer recorded in vivid terms his impressions upon encountering these people "who have given up hope;"

> They are as black as their dirt walls and lead grubby, joyless lives that can be compared to those of insects that crawl along the ground and stay alive by licking the dirt. They may walk upright, but most of the time their spirit crawls along the ground. . . .To tell the truth, there are among them, one feels, people who would have been better off had they not been born. In fact, in my opinion, the majority of them fall into this category.

There is no evidence that SCAP was moved by the personal plight of the peasantry. The impulse that gave birth to the Land Reform Law of October

1946 was political and was based upon several considerations. SCAP felt that the economic conditions in the Japanese countryside had been an important factor in fostering aggressive policies in Asia in the 1930s; elimination of those conditions would help ensure that Japan would never again be a menace to the world. Secondly, SCAP was determined to democratize Japan, and it was recognized that political reforms alone would not be sufficient to achieve that goal. There was no hope for true democracy in Japan while the rural half of its population remained economically servile. A third reason for promoting land reform was to stamp out agrarian radicalism. This goal was neatly summed up by Wolf Ladejinsky, a Department of Agriculture expert on loan to SCAP. It was necessary, he wrote, to "multiply the number of freeholders and prevent the Communists from making political capital by posing as advocates of peasant interests."

Ladejinsky, another of the New Deal veterans to serve in the Occupation, was a naturalized Russian immigrant who had put himself through the City College of New York by selling newspapers. His ideas on the need for a radical restructuring of land-holding patterns had reached MacArthur in the form of a memo on the subject read by the general in the early days of the Occupation. Although Ladejinsky held only the modest title of Special Adviser to the Chief of the Natural Resources Section, he had the attention of MacArthur, who was intrigued by his ideas as well as his continental manner and Russian accent. MacArthur, after dazzling the newly arrived adviser with his own knowledge of agricultural reforms since antiquity, from the Greeks of Solon through the more-recent efforts of his father in the Philippines, bestowed his full confidence on Ladejinsky.

The land reform process took three years to complete. While some of the credit for it belongs to SCAP officials like Ladejinsky, land reform had long been on the agenda of Japanese reformers and would doubtless have been proposed by the Japanese side. What was different in 1946 was that the conservative opposition which had bedeviled reformers in the past would dissolve in the face of MacArthur's unchallengable authority and his determination to move ahead with radical change. In early 1947, the reform was launched with a comprehensive program of propaganda, including the distributon of posters bearing slogans like "Landlords Cannot Take Back Land At Will" to every village. Like many of its other reform efforts, SCAP's land program included many trial-by-error campaigns. One SCAP officer's zealous efforts to transplant 4-H clubs died an early death, for example. On the other hand, the use of radio to promote a new class consciousness among the farmers and to broadcast "extension service" advice on everything from the proper time for planting potatoes to silkworm disease countermeasures, was distinctly successful.

It would be wrong, however, to imagine that land reform meant that SCAP colonels ran about the countryside handing out titles to the land. The implementation of the reform program required the massive participation of Japanese at all levels to carry out the tedious business of evaluating the property rights of some six million families, a third of which had good reason for obstructing the process. A myriad of tiny but crucial questions had to be resolved: For example, did a vegetable garden on the former site of a bombed-out building constitute agricultural land? Prodigiuous effort went into just verifying who was the actual cultivator of a given piece of land on that certain day in October 1946 which was decreed to be the reform's benchmark day. To accomplish all this, a Central Agricultural Land Commission was established at the national level; forty-six prefectural commisions served beneath it. These groups, in turn, coordinated the labors of thirteen locally elected land commisions which represented landlords, tenants, and third-party citizens. All together, thirty-six thousand paid officials, 115,000 commission members, and some quarter of a million village volunteers participated.

GRASS-ROOTS DEMOCRACY

Thus, the significance of the program went well beyond its economic accomplishments. Land redistribution involved an exercise in grass-roots democracy and social change as tenants, conditioned by tradition to listen to their landlords' instructions with cringing demeanor, found themselves participating as equals in one of the most sweeping political and economic revolutions seen during this century. The novelist Kumao Tokuhei imagines an old tenant's musings:

> In a man's lifetime, he's apt to experience incredible events. Of course, there are many things that will cause him pain and grief but there are likely to be one or two things that will make him deleriously happy. "Maybe this is just a dream," Yosuke thought, and quietly pinched himself. It hurt. It wasn't a dream after all. "The upland fields and rice paddies will all be mine! I won't have to pay any more rent. I won't have to bow and scrape to the landlord anymore."

And British sociologist Ronald Dore, a leading authority on rural Japan, writes of an acquaintance:

> It is difficult to forget the quiet pride with which a formerly very poor tenant in the Yamanashi village spoke of his election as hamlet chief designate for the following year. He had, he said, long been saving up to buy a power thresher. He would now have to postpone his plans because being hamlet chief is "bound to be a bit expensive." He "belonged" to the hamlet in a way that he had never done in the days when it would have been unthinkable that he could ever become hamlet chief.

The Land Law of 1946, amended by another ten laws as well as scores of ordinances and ministerial regulations issued in the next three years, banned absentee land ownership and permitted tenant farmers to purchase the land that they had been farming under the old system. To ensure that the old patterns were not revived, it was decreed that farmers who cultivated their own land would henceforth be allowed to own a maximum of 7.5 acres for their own use together with about 2.5 acres that could be rented out to others in the village.

(Exact acreages varied in different parts of Japan to allow for differences in terrain and climate; larger landholdings were granted in Hokkaido, for example.)

Financing the land redistribution proved to be less of a problem than anticipated. The land in question was not confiscated. The government of Japan purchased the land from landholders who were compensated with bonds. In turn, the land was sold to the former tenants. The problem of repayment by impoverished tenants was solved in two ways. First, long-term, low-interest loans were made available to ease the burden. More importantly, however, the rapid growth of inflation in the early occupation years meant that the new landholders ended up paying for their plots of land with rapidly depreciated yen. The net result was that, in the end, the land was exchanged at close to confiscatory prices, the value of some parcels being measured in cartons of cigarettes.

While the landowners were allowed to keep their woodlands and grasslands—the reform applied only to arable land—there is no question but that the reform meant financial calamity for landlord families, the majority of which had only been moderately wealthy. It is easy to imagine the plight of a farmer returning home from years of overseas military service to discover that the twenty or thirty acres of land which had provided well-being for generations of ancestors was being distributed to his neighbors. Yet, the whole process was accomplished with a minimum of friction, little violence, and not a single death. Of the 560,000 dispossession cases that were processed, almost one-quarter led to disputes, but only 110 incidents between landlords and tenants involved physical violence. By 1950, nearly five million acres of land had been purchased from 2.34 million landowners and sold to 4.75 million tenants, and MacArthur was able to announce that 89 percent of the nation's farmland was in the hands of those who farmed it. The result was the virtual elimination of the tenant farming class. A few elected to remain in tenant status out of choice—by 1957 they accounted for only 1.1 percent of the farming population.

Wolf Ladejinsky went on to assist the Republic of China (Taiwan) in its successful land-reform program, but while at home he came under fire from right-wing groups during the Macarthy era for his radicalism and was dismissed as a "security risk" by President Dwight Eisenhower's Secretary of Agriculture, Ezra Taft Benson. Ladejinsky's fate underscores the difficulty of assigning a "right" or "left" label to SCAP's land-reform program. On the one hand, the policy of virtual confiscation of land was further left than proposals being made by the Japan Communist Party at the time. The Japanese program indeed deserves comparison with the revolutionary program undertaken by the newly installed People's Republic of China (PRC) from 1950 to 1953. Both endeavors swept away deeply entrenched feudalistic systems of land ownership, though the process under Mao Tse-Tung affected far larger numbers of peasants and was accompanied by extensive violence.

The Chinese effort was clearly less successful because the PRC peasants ended up in highly regimented collectives where they were deprived of any land ownership, a system so unstable and unproductive that it was dismantled after Mao's death. Japanese peasants on the other hand, far from becoming poor and fanning the fires of class unrest as Ladejinsky feared, were transformed into rural capitalists with a tangible stake in the economy and have shared in the general economic prosperity of the nation. By the 1950s most farm houses had conveniences like washing machines and refrigerators, by the 1960s color TVs, and by the 1970s automobiles and vacations in Hawaii were becoming the rule rather than the exception.

THE LDP'S RURAL BASE

The farmers of Japan gained far more than an improved standard of living. They also became a political force, the rock-solid anchor of the conservative political establishment of Japan. It is this development that prompts some revisionist historians to see land reform as a basically rightist ploy by SCAP and conservative allies within the Japanese government. Conservatives have no more loyal constituency than the farm bloc. A principal reason for the monopoly the LDP has enjoyed on power over the past several decades is that it has little opposition at the polls in most agricultural regions. The success of land reform in turning peasants into prosperous farmers seriously undercuts the strength of the Socialist Party in the countryside where it might have been expected to build a strong electoral base. In return for rural support, a powerful farm lobby is rewarded by protectionist legislation and subsidies which keep the cost of rice and other products artificially high—many times higher than the world price in the case of rice. In some years, more than half of the farmers' income is provided by various kinds of government subsidies.

Making this linkage between the farmer and the LDP more odious to critics is that it endures only because the LDP has blocked legislative efforts to fairly redistrict Japan for voting purposes. Japan has become rapidly urbanized since the Occupation era, when voting districts were established. At present, only seven percent of the Japanese people are engaged in agriculture, but because demographic changes have not been reflected in any redrawing of election districts, rural areas have become seriously overrepresented in the parliament. What this means in practice is that there are four or five times as many voters for each parliament seat in some urban districts as there are for a seat in some rural areas. To put it another way, a farmer enjoys four or five times the voting impact of his urban counterpart.

Few of these developments could have been foreseen by SCAP reformers in 1946. While much of the outcome would have been welcome—the LDP is valued as a staunch supporter of the United States in international affairs—other developments would have been quite unwelcome. The Japanese farmer, particularly the rice farmer, for example, has been center stage in the ongoing trade dispute that clouds U.S.–Japan relations. The Japanese farmer has strongly pressured the LDP to deny the United States open access to Japanese consumers interested in buying American rice, citrus products, or beef, and by the 1970s this had become a major source of the "trade friction" that bedevils the two countries.

ZAIBATSU BUSTING

The initial SCAP policy regarding the economy was summarized in the phrase "merchants of death" which was used to designate the big business combines of the prewar era known as the *zaibatsu*. (The four largest and best known of these were Mitsubishi, Mitsui, Sumitomo, and Yasuda.) The phrase was grounded in the notion that the *zaibatsu* had stood behind the military expansion of Japan in the prewar era. The notion was far from correct. While some big business enterprises had profited from exploitation schemes in conquered territories, and all had cooperated in the production of war matériel, the *zaibatsu* had more often resisted Japan's military buildup and reckless overseas adventures because of the tax burden that they implied. Further, the business elite did not wish to antagonize the nations of the industrial West because of the feeling that Japan's future lay with friendly trade relations with the West rather than military expansion.

Nevertheless, key policymakers in both Washington and Tokyo held firmly to the view that the *zaibatsu* were both past and potentially future warmongers. In addition, their enormous size and power were seen as an impediment to democracy. The concentration of so much economic might in so few hands was viewed as inhibiting the growth of a healthy middle class and a spirit of independence among workers; the labor union movement had in fact been smashed before the war. As a result of these judgments, the "Basic Initial Post-Surrender Directive," given to MacArthur as his charter in the opening days of the Occupation, ordered a "program for the dissolution of the large industrial and banking combinations which have exercised control of a great part of Japan's trade and industry."

As the initial directive was elaborated by planners in Tokyo and Washington in the months ahead, it became clear that the "deconcentration" program, as it was being called, would radically alter the prewar structure of Japan's economy. By 1947, the details of the program had been incorporated into a study which was being considered by the rubber-stamp organization known as the Far Eastern Commission. The document known as FEC-230 provided for the dissolution of any "excessive concentration of economic power." Measures would be taken to make certain that these entitites could never be revived. The network of subsidiaries and affiliates which were tied to parent companies by interlocking directorates, mutual shareholding, and other arrangements were to be broken up. The leading families and all other individuals who had exercised controlling power in the *zaibatsu* would be purged and divested of their assets. The assets and other business properties of the giant corporations would be disposed of to "desirable purchasers"—that is smaller enterprises—as rapidly as possible "even if it requires that holdings be disposed of at a fraction of their real value." In addition, from the beginning, it was the Allies' intention to saddle Japan with a staggering reparations burden. Financial restitution to those nations which had suffered under Japanese rule was to be carried out by dismantling Japanese factories and shipping them to China, Burma, the Philippines, and other claimants.

LABOR

Some of these steps were already being taken by 1947—*zaibatsu* families and other business leaders had been purged, and some industrial plants had been distributed as installments on the reparations debt, for example. In addition, SCAP took steps to revitalize the labor union movement. As a result of behind-the-scenes efforts by SCAP officers, including MacArthur himself, the Diet passed a number of laws to provide a clear statutory basis for labor standards such as wages, hours, and safety; the right of labor to organize, bargain collectively, and strike; and machinery for arbitration and conciliation. For all those legislative gains, however, Japanese labor had many grievances, including a conservative government which was disinclined to enforce the new laws with appropriate vigor. Scores of radical labor organizers, including the leadership of the prewar Japan Communist Party (JCP) which had languished in prisons since police roundups of the late 1920s, were set free on MacArthur's orders and began to mobilize support for unions. The JCP's first postwar manifesto began with an expresssion of "our deepest gratitude that the occupation of Japan by the Allied forces, dedicated to liberating the world from fascism and militarism, has opened the way for a democratic revolution." From a pathetically low 707 members in October 1945, union membership rose to 6.3 million members by late 1947. In some sectors, such as mining, membership exceeded 90 percent of the workforce.

Labor militancy escalated sharply as unions in certain key industries, including newspapers and railways, called for "production control" *(seisan kanri)* tactics, aimed at seizing decision-making authority from management. Strikes, walkouts, sit-down protests, angry parades, and food seizures produced more and more confrontations with the police and sporadic violence. Warnings from MacArthur to "undisciplined elements" went unheeded. When a general strike threatened to shut down power plants, utilities, schools, communications, and

---

"MILITANT" LABOR, JAPANESE STYLE

"The techniques used by Japanese unions to enforce their demands were many and varied, often ingenious and imaginative. Outstanding of course was the strike, the classic weapon of labor, and to Japanese workers a cherished symbol of their new freedom. In the early days many workers went on strike out of sheer exuberance; such strikes were of course short-lived. Sometimes they were not properly strikes at all. In the fall of 1945 the telephone operators in Sendai 'struck'; they remained at their switchboards, but persons calling the exchange were greeted with: *'Moshi, moshi!* [Hello!] We are on strike! Long live democracy! Number please?'"

—Miriam Farley, *Aspects of Japan's Labor Problems*, 1950.

railways on February 1, 1947, SCAP intervened. Just hours before the strike was due to begin, a communique from the GHQ flatly forbade the action on the grounds that it would prevent the movement of food, fuel, and other essentials. "The paralysis . . . would produce dreadful consequences upon every Japanese home," the announcement said. The kind of moderate labor union activity envisaged by SCAP at the beginning of the Occupation did not include Communist-led general strikes which threatened chaos.

After February 1, SCAP took an increasingly stern attitude toward radical unionism, and under heavy government and management pressure, union membership declined after the peak year of 1948. While labor–management tensions did not cease, unionists tended more and more to belong to docile "enterprise unions" organized on the basis of individual companies (or even individual factories within a company) rather than horizontally across an entire industry or an entire trade. Critics say that these tend to be similar to the "company unions" scorned by American labor as toothless instruments of paternalistic management, hardly unions at all. Defenders say that the Japanese enterprise union, which includes not just the production workers but administrative staff as well, better suits the group-centered Japanese style of social organization which seeks consensus through compromise. Critics say that by organizing only at the local level, labor loses much of its collective bargaining leverage. Defenders, while admitting that there are abuses of the enterprise union system, hail the gains which accrue to both capital and labor when workers identify their own personal prosperity so closely with the prosperity of their company.

In any case the forces of the radical left which had enthusiastically welcomed SCAP's reforms only a few years earlier now felt betrayed by the United States' role in weakening the trade union movement and talked more of an open, armed struggle. Alarmed by an increase in violent incidents, SCAP ordered the "Red purge" of 1950 to sweep Communists from key private-sector industries as well as from the public sector. The move only confirmed the conviction of those on the left that the United States was turning its back on its earlier reform goals.

REVERSE-COURSE POLICY

Accompanying this reverse course in labor was the decision to abandon the economic deconcentration program which had only begun to be implemented by 1947. Several factors emerged in 1947–1948 to prompt the United States to concentrate on reviving the Japanese economy rather than restructuring it.

Foremost, was the wretched state of the economy. In 1948, three years into the Occupation, industry remained stagnant and output was still far below the levels of 1936, the last prewar year.

The moribund economy, in turn, contributed to labor unrest and runaway inflation. As might be expected from the fact that gasoline cost occupation personnel sixteen cents a gallon while it was virtually unobtainable on the legitimate Japanese market for any price, the black market flourished and brought crime, official corruption, and general demoralization in its wake. In 1947, the death of a prominent Tokyo judge underscored the extent of the black market. The man died, it was reported, from malnutrition because he refused to eat anything purchased on the black market.

In addition, the burdensome relief costs to the United States showed no sign of lessening. Until the Japanese economy regained its health, it seemed that the American taxpayer would be obliged to supply Japan's basic needs.

The most important factor in reversing the course of the Occupation was the onset of the Cold War in Europe and the rising tide of communism in China. For so long, Washington's Far Eastern policy had considered China as the main strategic anchor of the United States in Asia and the Pacific. By 1948 and increasingly in 1949, however, as the Communist armies of Mao swept southward on the China mainland, eventually driving Chiang Kai-shek's Nationalist armies and government to exile on the island of Taiwan, America needed a strong ally to replace the eclipsed Chinese Nationalists. Japan would become that ally, the center of resistance to communism in the East. Accordingly, the initial post-surrender plan to maintain Japan's economy at the cottage-industry level no longer seemed wise.

When George Kennan, the first high-ranking State Department official to go to Japan after the war, visited MacArthur in March 1948, he carried the message that occupation policy must henceforth aim at "the economic rehabilitation of Japan and the restoration of her ability to contribute constructively to the stability and prosperity of the Far Eastern region. . . ." "Old Japan hands," sometimes referred to as the "Japan Crowd," including both government and corporate leaders anxious to resume or establish business ties in Japan, were at the same time putting pressure on the State Department to abandon the *zaibatsu* dissolution program. The American Council for Japan was organized in 1948 to lobby for their goals, and *Newsweek* magazine lent its columns to these interests for frequent and scathing denunciation of the pending FEC-230 reforms and the "doctrinaire New Dealers" who were behind them. SCAP reacted to the uncommonly sharp criticisms from *Newsweek* by denying for a time re-entry rights to its Tokyo correspondent wishing to return there for reporting duties.

Quite incredibly, in view of MacArthur's deserved reputation as a staunch anti-Communist, the general and his staff were coming under public attack from conservative quarters in the United States for adopting socialistic and un-American policies "in order to appease Russia." The economic deconcentration program was denounced by one prominent Wall Street spokesman as nothing less than a "declaration of war on capitalism." Kennan did not at the time publicly engage in such rhetoric, but his *Memoirs* later revealed his belief that the policies pursued by MacArthur's headquarters up to 1948 seemed "to be such that if they had been devised for the specific purpose of rendering Japanese society vulnerable to Communist political pressures and paving the way for a Communist takeover, they could scarcely have been other than what they were." Within days of Kennan's 1948 visit to Tokyo, the United States formally withdrew backing for the radical FEC-230 proposals and, with American blessing and support, the Japanese economy, led by the only somewhat modified survivors of the prewar *zaibatsu*, moved off dead center and began to expand. Kennan was later to reflect that, except for his role in launching the Marshall Plan in Europe, setting the "reverse course" in Japan was "the most significant contribution I was ever able to make in government."

THE KOREAN WAR

The Korean War gave a tremendous shot in the arm for the recovering Japanese economy. It was during the first year of the Korean War that the Japanese economy recovered to prewar levels and then shot ahead rapidly thanks, in large measure, to the "procurement boom" (*tokuju bumu*). During the early 1950s, the Pentagon signed procurement contracts in Japan for $2 billion, an amount equal to almost two-thirds of all Japanese exports during those years. For someone wondering what a military contract can mean to a company struggling to get on its feet, the experience of the Nihon Matai Company is instructive. The company, which made gunny sacks, was invited by the U.S. Army Procurement Office at the port of Yokohama to drop in for contract talks shortly after the Korean War began.

> The officer in charge announced: "We need all the gunny sacks you have, and we need them urgently for making combat sandbags. It doesn't matter if they're used or not. Name your price and we'll pay it." We jumped at the offer, feeling as though we were living through a fantastic dream. Until then we had barely eked out an existence by making sacks for rice at a very small price. We would have made a fine profit by selling the bags for ten cents each, but the U.S. Army paid us twice that much for the first few lots, and then went on to order more than 200 million sacks.

Nihon Matai soon increased its workforce from thirty to 150. With its first sales, it purchased a hundred new sewing machines, and with later profits the firm diversified into textiles and other activities. To imagine the benefits provided by the Korean conflict to Japan's hitherto flat economy the experience of the little Nihon Matai company needs to be multiplied a thousand-fold or more. By 1952, the war accounted for no less than 63 percent of all Japanese exports. Even after the cease-fire in 1953, as historian Thomas R. H. Havens has shown, the payments by the United States in connection with its bases and personnel in Japan averaged nearly $600 million for the rest of the decade.

If the economy of Japan was helped, so was the U.S. war effort. Japan was transformed almost overnight into a huge supply depot to provide logistical assistance to the U.S. forces in Korea. To take one example, U.S. forces in Korea were moved in fleets of Second World War-vintage trucks, most of which came from rebuild and overhaul operations carried on by Japanese mechanics in private industry. The Pentagon estimated that without such skilled workers, an additional quarter-million service troops would have been required.

The Korean War proved to be an unexpected windfall for the Japanese economy—and in the 1960s the Vietnam War triggered an even greater "boom." At the same time, however, Japan's involvement in those wars, however ancillary and indirect, proved to be profoundly disturbing to many Japanese who felt it immoral for their nation to collaborate in America's anti-Communist wars in Asia, and doubly immoral for the nation to profit by its American alliance. Demonstrations outside the National Diet building and American Embassy in Tokyo and in front of the gates of U.S. military bases throughout Japan became commonplace in the 1950s and 1960s. Some of the demonstrators were motivated by antiwar sentiments, others by the conviction that Communist revolutions represented the best hope for the Asian proletariat. Many university professors and students, mindful that Japanese intellectuals had been notoriously docile in acquiescing to Japan's militarism in the 1930s, were outspoken participants in the demonstrations against their nation's involvement in the American wars in Korea and Vietnam.

ARTICLE IX

The most striking provision of the new Japanese Constitution was the so-called "peace clause," Article IX. It stated, in part: "Aspiring sincerely to an international peace based on justice and order, the Japanese people forever renounce war as a sovereign right of the nation and the threat or use of force as means of settling international disputes." Lest there be any doubt about the meaning of this unique statement—no other nation has renounced the right to wage war— Article IX goes on to avow that "land, sea, and air forces, as well as other war potential, will never be maintained."

The origins of Article IX are still debated but it seems clear that Washington was, at best, divided on the question of the military in the future of Japan. While there was general agreement that Japan had to be disarmed, there were few who wished to commit themselves to a perpetually demilitarized Japan. A desire for vengeance was strong in many quarters, but at the same time pragmatic voices were suggesting that a militarily destitute Japan would be a liability should the Cold War intensify. What advantage could there be in burning all the bridges?

MacArthur cut through the indecision and imposed his own private vision on those who were drafting Article IX. It does not square with the usual picture of the general to cast him as a dove, still less as someone unresponsive to the value of Japan as a Cold War partner. If it is difficult to accept fully an argument from idealism, the general's frequent assertion that he hated war "as the scourge of mankind" and was therefore determined to turn Japan into the "Switzerland of Asia," there are other reasons for his adamancy on the wording of Article IX. He felt, correctly, that the Japanese people, disillusioned by their fate under militarism, sincerely favored the principle of unilateral pacifism and that rearmament would open him to ridicule by the Japanese people for his failure to implement vigorous and farsighted reforms. Indeed, it was Shidehara Kijuro, prime minister at the time the constitution was drafted, who suggested to MacArthur that there should be a formal renunciation of war. Further, as we have seen, the general was determined to keep the emperor system intact. He knew, however, that this faced stiff opposition from the Allies, who argued that the emperor would inevitably become a rallying point for future militarists bent on aggression. By unequivocally banning war and arms, MacArthur reasoned that he could negate that argument.

Yet we know that by the time the Occupation came to an end in 1952, Japan had about 110,000 men under arms supplied by the United States and was being pressured to increase its strength. Some of the same factors, especially the onset of the Cold War, that prompted the United States to alter the course of its economic reforms would cause a similar change of course regarding U.S. attitudes concerning a rearmed Japan.

THE COLD WAR AND JAPAN

By 1947, but increasingly in 1948, a mounting tide of fear and distrust replaced the spirit of common cause that had prevailed between the Soviet Union and the Allies during World War II. A Cold War commenced as the Soviet Union sought to protect and expand its frontiers by creating an East European bloc of satellite nations. Discord over such matters as the closing of the borders of Berlin to all traffic with the West in the summer of 1948 broadened into a wider confrontation that threatened a third world war between the United States and the Soviet Union, which had emerged as the "superpowers" of the postwar era. While the main arena of the Cold War was Europe, Asia was not exempt from its tensions. Hostile armies faced each other across the divided Korean peninsula where the Cold War became a real war in 1950. In the countries of Southeast Asia, where the wartime presence of Japanese armies had exposed to native populations for the first time the vulnerability of Western imperial powers, Communist agitators took the lead in organizing anti-colonial insurgency movements. The British were under mounting pressure on the Malayan peninsula. Ho Chi Minh's armies were at war with the French in Vietnam and would drive them from that colony in 1954. In the Philippines, given independence by the United States in 1946, a Communist insurrection threatened the new republic. The Dutch East Indies and Burma were also the scenes of violent Communist uprisings. Most importantly, as discussed earlier, after twenty-one years of struggle in the countryside, Mao's guerrilla bands, by 1948–1949, were marching in triumph down the avenues of China's major cities.

It was this worldwide turn of events which caused the United States to rethink its original policies in Japan. Once it became clear that a Nationalist China under Chiang Kai-shek was not going to be an ally of any consequence in the years ahead, did it still make sense to keep Japan weak and defenseless?

Policymakers in Washington were urging that it did not. State Department planner George Kennan put the case succinctly. "The deterioration of the situation in China heightened greatly the importance of what might now happen in Japan. Japan as we saw it was more important than China [after 1948] as a potential factor in world political developments. It was the sole great potential military industrial arsenal in the Far East." By 1950, MacArthur was ready to agree. A new and more flexible interpretation of Article IX, one by no means evident in its wording, emerged. Renunciation of war did not mean that Japan was giving up "its right to self-defense in case of predatory attack," MacArthur wrote in 1950 shortly before ordering the Japanese government to form an embryonic army called the "National Police Reserve." It is no coincidence that this first step in the gradual rearmament of Japan would come only days after troops of Communist North Korea crossed the 38th parallel into the Republic of Korea.

As early as 1947, MacArthur had announced that the principal objectives of the Occupation had been achieved and it was time to negotiate a peace treaty which would return full sovereignty to Japan. The announcement was clearly premature. Critics at home, as well as among the Allies, delayed meaningful discussion of the issue. However, by 1950, during the involvement of the United States in the Korean War, it became more urgent to end the drain on U.S. resources by terminating the Occupation. The central issue which had to be resolved in any treaty with Japan was the security of Japan in the post-Occupation era and the future of American military bases within Japan. It was obvious that Japan would provide very little of her own defense capability. Prime Minister Yoshida Shigeru had agreed only reluctantly to the formation of the National Police Reserve and steadfastly opposed pressure to increase its size on the grounds that doing so would rouse opposition at home, rekindle anxiety among Japan's wartime victims, and most importantly, would drain funds away from economic development which for Yoshida and the other conservatives in the political mainstream was the nation's highest priority. When those arguments failed to convince, Yoshida simply cited Article IX of the constitution and reminded his American listeners of its authorship.

Since Japan's own military strength would for the forseeable future be minimal, the Japanese conservative leadership argued that after the Occupation came to an end some sort of continued American presence in Japan was nearly inevitable. Socialists, radical labor leaders, and pacifists disagreed. They insisted that America would draw Japan into the Cold War to advance the global aims of the United States, with the risk that Japan might become the first target in the event of an escalation to all-out war between the superpowers. Japanese became all the more anxious about this risk after the Soviet Union exploded its first atomic bomb in 1949. Since the U.S. position was that a peace treaty and an end to the Occupation required Japanese assent to American bases, the conservative position in favor of the American military "umbrella" prevailed.

Accordingly, on September 8, 1951, in San Francisco, two treaties were signed. The first, a treaty of peace signed at the Opera House, declared an end to the war, restoration of sovereignty to Japan, and an end to the Occupation.

The second treaty, the United States–Japan Security Treaty, signed later in the day at the historic army post known as the Presidio, provided for American army, navy, and air bases on the soil of independent Japan under arrangements to be worked out in an administrative agreement. On April 28, 1952, after ratification formalities, the two treaties and the administrative agreement went into force. From that day, American military presence in Japan was based on treaty relationship rather than conquest. That still remains true although certain details of the relationship were modified in a new treaty signed in 1960. In the original treaty, for example, the treaty could not be broken unless both countries agreed; under the 1960 treaty, either nation may terminate it with a one-year notice of intent.

ASSESSING THE OCCUPATION AND THE U.S.–JAPAN SECURITY TREATY

In the 1960s, after the Occupation had ended and there was time to ponder its effects, a school of Japanese authors centering on mystery writer Matsumoto Seicho applied the name "black mist" *(kuroi kiri)* to the Occupation era and raised suspicions about the Americans to a high level. The immensely popular stories in the black mist genre emphasized the sinister nature of various odd real-life crimes and incidents which occurred during the occupation years including a train derailment, an assassination, and a bank robbery in which the robber, posing as a public health officer, persuaded the entire bank staff to drink lethal doses of potassium cyanide. In this latter case, the Teigin Bank incident of 1949, Matsumoto argued that the true culprits behind the robbery were agents of an experimental bacteriological warfare unit of the U.S. Army working in league with ex-Imperial Army officers who had been engaged in the same kind of research as members of the notorious "Unit 731" (discussed in Chapter 8) during the war years. Matsumoto's theory did not change the verdict of the courts but did persuade millions of Japanese that dark conspiracies pervaded the land when the Americans were in power.

While Matsumoto represents a leftist view of the Occupation, critics from the right have argued that the American Occupation deprived Japan of its soul, its spirit, and precipitated a "national identity crisis." How, they ask, can the continuity of Japanese culture be preserved in classrooms where military heroes of the past are discredited, Shinto is studied as just another of the world's religions and nobody ever thinks of paying solemn respect to the emperor? Rightist critics of the Occupation have remained a vocal minority in demanding a revision of the Constitution, including elimination of the war renunciation clauses of Article IX which they regard as an American affront to Japanese national dignity.

At another level of discourse, revisionist scholars have challenged the generally positive assessment of the Occupation era which has been emphasized here. These scholars, many of them writing from a Marxist perspective, have stressed not the changes brought about by SCAP reformers but the aspects of postwar Japan which in their view did *not* change—the renewed suppression of the radical left and a revival of the prewar economic and financial structures. They argue that fundamental conflicts of interest between labor and capital sharply divided Japanese society in 1945 and deplore the way in which SCAP, though intitially disposed to strengthen labor, changed course and threw its weight on the side of management after it became clear that labor was embarked on militant "production control" tactics aimed at worker domination of industry. Behind SCAP's determination to restore Japanese business and industry at the expense of labor (and at the expense of the reparations program), were powerful Wall Street pressures on Washington. These pressures, some argue, were even more important in explaining the "reverse course" than fears of Soviet expansionism.

Revisionists find the individual political and social reforms undertaken by generally well-intentioned Americans of less importance than the larger imperatives of American policy which were dictated by the Cold War and indeed by imperialist urges going back to the William McKinley era when American expansionists first began to speak of converting the Pacific into an "American lake." Conveniently, these Occupation critics find that MacArthur himself came close to announcing the fulfillment of that goal in a speech in 1949 in which he declared that "the Pacific has become an Anglo–Saxon lake," and Okinawa was its "broad main bastion." Because of the overarching importance of this vision and the Cold War as a policy determinant, revisionists argue that Japan was denied the opportunity of playing a neutral role in postwar Asia in spite of the fact that neither the Soviet Union nor China contemplated aggressive action against Japan.

The revisionists have been sympathetic to—and indeed were sometimes active participants in—the mass *demo* (demonstrations) against the U.S. military presence in Japan and other arrangements of the U.S.–Japan Security Treaty. The demonstrations culminated in a month-long wave of protests, the largest in Japanese history, during the spring of 1960. At that time, Prime Minister Kishi Nobusuke rammed a revised version of the treaty through the Diet and prepared to welcome President Dwight Eisenhower to Japan to celebrate the new accord. The "Old Left" (Socialists, Communists, radical labor, ban-the-bomb groups, and like), augmented by enormous snake-dancing echelons of students shouting *Ampo hantai* (Oppose the security treaty), staged the largest protest demonstrations, mass "sitdowns," and general strikes in Japanese history. (These demonstrations and student-led demonstrations in Korea occurring at about the same time were to usher in campus revolts which spread to the rest of the world and became a hallmark feature of the late 1960s.)

With the aid of an extremely supportive press, though far less general citizen backing, the angry demonstrations created such a spectacle of power and disorder that Kishi was forced to cancel the Eisenhower visit and, shortly after that, to resign from office. Indeed, Kishi was himself as much the object of the protesters' wrath as the security treaty. The prime minister had been an economic czar in prewar Manchukuo and a member of the wartime Tojo cabinet. In spite of this unsavory past, he had risen to high office with American blessing. An uncompromising anti-Communist, Kishi was seen by the left as a compliant instrument of American wishes who could be expected to move Japan in the direction of a despotic police state at home and a loyal ally to the American crusade against communism in Asia.

However, while Kishi was out, the security treaty remained law. In the decade of the 1960s, in part because the public deplored the excesses of violence that sometimes accompanied the leftist protests and in part because an ever-expanding prosperity dampened support for the left, the demonstrations tapered off. By 1970, when the security treaty came up for renewal, the opposition was only a shadowy hint of what it had been ten years earlier.

There can be no doubt that the United States injected itself into Japanese life in a massive way, and American values and institutions became ensnared in the processes of Japanese recovery in the years after 1945. There can be no doubt, either, that Japan became locked into the status of a junior partner in its relations with the United States and that this relationship prevailed far beyond the end of the Occupation and left Japan incapable or unwilling to exercise autonomy in its conduct of international affairs. Well into the decade of the 1970s when Japan was becoming an economic superpower in its own right, it still deferred to the United States in matters of vital concern to the United States, in Vietnam and in relations with China, for example. Historian Carol Gluck observes that "Japanese contemporary discourse betrays nearly obsessive concern with the United States, while the fraction of American comment devoted to Japan tends to take the postwar alliance rather casually for granted."

A BREAK WITH THE PAST?

Some historians emphasize that the Occupation did not represent a total break with the past and argue that it simply accelerated changes which were part of an ongoing modernization process that had begun in the Meiji period and even earlier. Others hold that the United States played a more decisive role in shaping the politics, economics, and culture of postwar Japan. Takemae Eiji, an authority on the Occupation era, cites the importance of Occupation policies which kept Japan a united country under the virtually sole jurisdiction of the United States. Compare the fate of Japan, he insists, to the fate of Germany and Korea, where divided jurisdictions led to divided nations. In the absence of orders from the occupation army, he argues, such things as the liberalization of the old constitution, the abolition of the special police, the end of antileftist legislation, and the growth of local self-government would not have occurred. "Today," he concludes, "popular sovereignty, pacifism, respect for fundamental human rights, and local self-government have become the essence of the new constitutional order," and these legacies of the Occupation act as "a bulwark against the revival of the old emperor system, remilitarization, and against a return of the police state."

METAPHORS FOR THE OCCUPATION

"Most of the truly important postwar changes seem to be simply the acceleration of changes that were already taking place in prewar Japan. . . . The war and the occupation between them seem to have swept away barriers to the forward motion of these currents. So, instead of diverting Japan into a new channel, the Occupation cleared the old one of the obstruction of militaristic reaction and changed a slow and meandering stream into a rushing torrent."

—Edwin O. Reischauer.

"The reforms of the occupation did not simply accelerate changes which were predetermined in nature. In significant measures they determined the character and direction of postwar changes. In effect, they were the gas pedal but also the steering wheel. Without the reforms of the occupation, the postwar changes might have led in a very different direction."

—Takemae Eiji.

Americans should be suspicious of self-congratulatory American claims to success, but the following summation of the record of the Occupation by the *Asahi*, Japan's largest and possibly most prestigious newspaper, merits attention—the more so because the paper's editorial stance has often been anti-American.

> The fact that the Occupation proved to be as successful as it did in accomplishing its myriad functions, ranging from writing a new constitution for Japan to censoring public information and feeding hungry people, speaks well for the diligence and good will of most of its members. Working with only the loosest of guidelines, limited experience, and the most superficial understanding of Japanese society, Occupation reformers managed, with Japanese cooperation, to effect a social revolution that has been the foundation of postwar Japan.

ADDITIONAL READING

An interpretive essay would be a good place to start any serious inquiry into occupation-era historiography. See Carol Gluck, "Entangling Illusions—Japanese and American Views of the Occupation," in Warren I. Cohen, ed., *New Frontiers in American–East Asian Relations* (1983). For a brief overview, see Peter Frost, "Occupation," in *Kodansha Encyclopedia of Japan*, Volume 6 (1983).

General surveys of the Occupation era include John Curtis Perry, *Beneath the Eagle's Wings* (1981); Howard Schonberger, *Aftermath of War: Americans and the Remaking of Japan* (1988); Michael Schaller, *The American Occupation of Japan: The Origins of the Cold War in Asia* (1985); and Kawai Kazuo, *Japan's American Interlude* (1960). Robert E. Ward and Sakamoto Yoshikazu, eds., *Democratizing Japan: The Allied Occupation* (1987) contains a rich source of essays by both Japanese and Western writers on topics such as writing the constitution, bureaucratic reform, women's rights, local government, and big business.

Several of MacArthur's aides have written flattering accounts of their chief, including *MacArthur: His Rendezvous with History* (1956) by Courtney Whitney; and *MacArthur 1945–51* (1954) by Charles Willoughby. More-reliable studies include D. Clayton James, *The Years of MacArthur* (Vol. II, 1985); Michael Schaller, *Douglas MacArthur: The Far Eastern General* (1989); and William Manchester, *American Caesar* (1978). *Empire and Aftermath: Yoshida Shigeru and the Japanese Experience, 1878–1954* (1979) by John Dower is a masterful study of the most important Japanese personage in the Occupation era.

There are numerous excellent specialized studies on various undertakings of the Occupation. For example, see Ronald P. Dore, *Land Reform in Japan* (1959); Joe B. Moore, *Japanese Workers and the Struggle for Power, 1945–1947* (1983); Chalmers Johnson, *Conspiracy at Matsukawa* (1972); Nishi Toshio, *Unconditional Democracy: Education and Politics in Occupied Japan, 1945–1952* (1982); and William P. Woodard, *The Allied Occupation of Japan and Japanese Religions* (1972). Kyoko Inoue's cross-linguistic study of the give and take that went on between SCAP and the Japanese government to produce the postwar constitution is unique: *MacArthur's Japanese Constitution: A Linguistic and Cultural Study of Its Making* (1991).

In addition, several participants and observers have written first-hand accounts of various aspects of the occupation. These include Theodore Cohen (Herbert Passin, ed.), *Remaking Japan: The American Occupation as New Deal* (1987); Alfred Oppler, *Legal Reform in Occupied Japan: A Participant Looks Back* (1976); Eleanor Hadley, *Anti-Trust in Japan* (1970); Justin Williams, Sr., *Japan's Political Revolution Under MacArthur: A Participant's Account* (1979); Otis Cary, *War-Wasted Asia: Letters, 1945–46* (1975); Hans Baerwald, *The Purge of Japanese Leaders Under the Occupation* (1959); and Harry Emerson Wildes, *Typhoon in Tokyo* (1954). Journalistic accounts include Mark Gayn, *Japan Diary* (1948) and Richard Hughes, *Foreign Devil* (1972).

The International Military Tribunal for the Far East has not yet been thoroughly explored. The best single-volume study now available is *Victor's Justice: The Tokyo War Crimes Trial* (1971) by Richard Minear. Less satisfactory is Philip R. Piccigallo, *The Japanese on Trial: Allied War Crimes Operations in the East, 1945–1951* (1979). Shiroyama Saburo's *War Criminal: The Life and Death of Hirota Koki* (1974) has been translated from the original Japanese into English by John Bester.

On Article IX, the security treaty, and related matters, see: Meirion and Susie Harries, *Sheathing the Sword: The Demilitarization of Postwar Japan* (1987): Albert Axelbank, *Black Star Over Japan: Rising Forces of Militarism* (1972); Edward A. Olsen, *U.S.–Japan Strategic Reciprocity: A Neo-Internationalist View* (1985); and Thomas R. H. Havens, *Fire Across the Sea: The Vietnam War and Japan, 1965–1975* (1987).

For Japanese views of the occupation era, see *Asahi* Shinbum, ed., *The Pacific Rivals: A Japanese View of Japanese–American Relations* (1972); and Mainichi Daily News ed., *Fifty Years of Light and Dark: The Hirohito Era* (1975).

Richard B. Finn, *MacArthur, Yoshida, and Postwar Japan* (1992) is a recent and comprehensive survey by an officer of the Occupation.

10

ECONOMIC MIRACLE

It was not easy for Americans reading about Japan in the 1980s, when evidence of its economic might was everywhere, to imagine how pessimistically experts in the recent past have regarded Japan's economic promise. In the pre-World War II era, John E. Orchard was one of the small body of experts who, through frequent visits and study, seemed to know the country well. His 1930 study of Japan's economic position, with its largely favorable assessment of past gains, quickened foreign interest in Japan. The future, however, appeared to Orchard "none too brilliant." The country's chief assets were its cheap labor and the nearby markets for its low-cost manufactures in the more backward countries of Asia. Beyond that, however, Orchard went on, "Japan's possibilities for industrialization are limited and there seems to be no prospect that Japan can attain a position of major importance as a manufacturing nation."

UNDERESTIMATING JAPAN

In Washington, as we have seen, Japan was of immense importance to America as a part of the American global alliance against communism in the Cold War years. That view of Japan, however, was not always matched by a parallel appreciation of the future economic significance of Japan. In 1950, State Department key policymaker on Japan, John Foster Dulles, in response to a query from a Japanese official about future trade possibilities with the United States suggested that Japan might consider the possibility of shirts and pajamas. And perhaps cocktail napkins.

While Dulles was quick to see that Japan could become the "workshop of Asia" and make good its contribution to the Cold War by integrating its

> Pete Hamill, an American journalist visiting Tokyo in 1989, thirty-nine years after Dulles' "cocktail napkins" suggestion, writes that he asked his Japanese friends what they would like to buy from the United States if the price was right. After some thought most of them answered "Towels." "The quality of Japanese towels is dreadful," they pointed out. "Nobody should imagine that the streets of Tokyo will soon fill up with Oldsmobiles," Hamill writes.

economy to the poorer countries of non-Communist Southeast Asia by entering into barter agreements with those nations, there was no sign that Dulles or others in Washington imagined that Japan's future economic dominance was a cause for concern. Rather, Dulles was more inclined to lecture Japanese that they would have to "stand on their own feet." In 1954, as Dwight Eisenhower's secretary of state, Dulles presided over a White House cabinet meeting when the topic of Japan's economic future came up. The president allowed that America should have no objection if China—even Communist China—wanted to buy the "cheap straw hats, cheap cotton shirts, sneakers, bicycles and all the rest of that sort of stuff from Japan." Dulles agreed but went on to indicate, according to the official minutes of the meeting, "there was little future for Japanese products in the United States." The secretary told the cabinet that he had just returned from meetings with the Japanese prime minister and that he had told him "frankly, that Japan should not expect to find a big U.S. market because the Japanese don't make the things we want."

In the post-World War II era, Professor Edwin O. Reischauer of Harvard emerged as the most authoritative American voice on Japan. The most substantial of his early works, *The United States and Japan*, published in several editions beginning in 1950, was a natural first source for an informed reader to consult. In 1957, by which time Japan was recovering nicely from the worst effects of the war, Reischauer, though optimistic about Japan's political prospects, sounded a reprise of economist John Orchard's remarks of a generation earlier. "The economic situation in Japan may be so fundamentally unsound that no policies, no matter how wise, can save her from slow economic starvation . . .," Reischauer predicted. As historian Peter Duus writes, Reischauer's observation was "a mainstream view, shared by foreign and Japanese observers alike." The inaccuracy of the experts' forecasts underscores how risky it is to engage in that habit, a fact one American writer noted in modestly claiming that his own political predictions were "90 percent accurate 40 percent of the time." The failure of the experts to foresee Japan's economic leap forward also underscores just how remarkable it has been. In the post-World War II period, especially in the last twenty-five years or so, the story of the Japan–American nexus was dominated, often overwhelmed, by the economic ascendance of Japan and by growing "trade friction" *(boeki masatsu)* as the Japanese call it.

THE MIRACLE YEARS

At the time of Professor Reischauer's 1957 surmise, though nobody knew it, Japan was already in the third year of what would turn out to be a period of sustained economic growth unparalleled in modern history. With the gross national product (GNP, often viewed as the broadest measure of a nation's economic productivity) growing at nine percent each year from 1955 to 1960, the "economic miracle" was under way. When Prime Minister Ikeda Hayato announced in 1960 an "income doubling plan" to be fulfilled during the decade, it was widely regarded as the exaggerated sloganeering of a skilled politician. In fact, Ikeda's plan was easily overachieved. With the GNP growing at 10 percent from 1960 to 1965 and over 13 percent each year from 1965 to 1970, Japan surpassed in total output one European leader after another, England, France, and finally Germany (all with smaller populations, of course). By the end of the 1960s, Japan ranked as number three in the world, behind only the United States and the Soviet Union in output.

In a fully industrialized country—no longer "developing" but developed—such steep growth rates inevitably erode. Several severe crises buffeted Japan in the early 1970s to erode its progress. The *oiru shokku* (oil shock), the Arab embargo in late 1973, hit the entire world in the pocketbook, but Japan, totally dependent on imports for its petroleum supplies, was especially devastated by the soaring prices. In part, because Japan moved swiftly to streamline its industrial base by shifting away from energy-intensive manufacturing, the effects of the oil shock were minimized. After a year of zero growth in 1974, Japan resumed its progress in 1975—not at the double-digit rate of earlier years, but at a very respectable 8.7 percent in the seventies and only a little less in the following decade. By just about any standard, it is fair to speak of an economic miracle between the years 1955 and 1973, and many would say that the term still describes the dynamism of Japan's industrial machine. In terms of GNP, the United States (with double Japan's population) was still far ahead, but measured in dollars on a per-capita basis, Japan's GNP surpassed the United States by the late 1980s.[1]

AFFLUENT JAPAN

In 1957, Japanese spoke of the "three treasures" (washing machines, vacuum cleaners, and refrigerators) as the prize objects of household desire; the

---

[1] The reader needs to be cautioned about statistical comparisons between Japan and the United States. After the sharp devaluation of the dollar in 1985–1986, Japan's wealth was inflated—some would argue "artificially inflated." In its effect, the devaluation approximately doubled the value of each Japanese yen as the American dollar was correspondingly devalued (that is, weakened). The idea behind this policy, initiated by the United States, was that Japanese products in the United States were selling well because they were underpriced, and they were underpriced because the yen was weak in relation to the dollar. With a stronger yen, the cost of Japanese imports to America would go up and discourage American consumers. Conversely, Japanese would be more tempted to buy American goods which now became cheaper. The devaluation scheme did not produce dramatically successful results for the American side, perhaps indicating serious weakness in the Americans' theory.

washing machine was fairly common, but vacuum cleaners and refrigerators were owned by only one in a hundred households at that time. Thirty years later, a "luxury boom" was transforming the consumer market in Japan in ways that could not have been dreamed of in earlier years. Japanese buyers at some New York art auctions were buying half the impressionist paintings selling in the $1 million-plus range. To decorate its office gallery, Yasuda Fire and Marine Insurance Co. paid $40 million for a single van Gogh painting in 1987; three years later a Japanese private collector purchased a pair of French paintings for $160 million at auction. Japanese citizens were buying so much expensive foreign art that those purchases were becoming a significant factor in narrowing their country's enormous trade surplus—incontestable evidence of a national buying binge. Half of luxury luggage maker Louis Vuitton's worldwide revenue came from the French company's outlets in Japan. The press delighted in reporting the splashy tastes of the nouveau riche: mink coats for pets, European sports cars, and $350 cups of coffee. (The formula for the latter includes Evian water heated in a gold kettle and poured through Jamaican Blue Mountain coffee, dusted with real gold, and served in gold-plated Royal Minton china.) Among a people renowned for their work ethic, a fondness for leisure intruded. Since there was no suitable Japanese word for "leisure," the English was borrowed and converted into *rejya* (as in *rejya bumu*, leisure boom). Similarly, a travel boom took nearly one Japanese in ten—described as "laden with cash"—on overseas vacations in 1990.

Foreigners who lived in Japan in earlier times recall that trash collection services were infrequent and minimal—they were little needed by frugal, resourceful Japanese. Now, with affluence and the continued shortage of household space in which to store the fruits of affluence, the era of *sodai gomi* (bulk garbage) has arrived. On ordained dates each month, households pile their old, unwanted TV sets, sofas, desks, sinks, motorcycles, refrigerators, beds—anything too large for regular trash service—on designated street corners to be collected and compacted. *Gomi*-hunting, scavenging, has become a pasttime for some foreigners trying to cope with the high cost of living in Japan.

Younger people, armed with credit cards and cash, one foreign observer wrote, "appeared to be directing their considerable energies wholly toward self-improvement through shopping." The Japanese press responded to what one writer called the "unmitigated 'me-ism' and conspicuous consumption" of the new generation with an ongoing flood of concerned commentary. One Japanese editor wrote of the social consequences of the youthful preoccupation with material possessions:

> Today's young people have been exposed to TV from birth. Their rooms are equipped with personal computers, CD players, TVs, videos, and cordless telephones. But these devices, which shape their view of the world, provide only vicarious experience. They talk to friends by telephone rather than meet in person. Their lifestyles leave little room for affective relationships and quality interaction. Unable to relax even with acquaintances, they stick to polite, stilted language.

Foreign Trade

Foreign trade has been an essential factor in Japan's modern expansion. Japan is by no means as dependent upon foreign trade as many other countries—European nations, for example, export twice the percentage of their GNP that Japan does. Still, Japan's dire need for imported oil, food, and many other resources makes foreign trade a critical necessity. Japan has found the United States to be an open, accessible market—Japan's largest market—for its exports. In the late 1960s, an ominous trend appeared in U.S.–Japan trade relations. Until that time, the United States had enjoyed a favorable balance of trade with Japan (that is, selling more goods and services to Japan than were bought). At first, the trade imbalance was only a billion dollars, but in the 1970s American trade experts watched the figures as if following the temperature chart of a sick patient. In some years, the fever subsided but in general the trend worsened. By the end of the 1970s, the trade imbalance had reached $13 billion in a single year. In 1986, of a staggering worldwide trade deficit of $170, the United States had run up a debt to Japan of $58 billion. In 1985, for the first time since World War I, the United States became a debtor nation. In a very short period of time, the United States had gone from being the world's largest creditor nation to becoming the world's largest debtor nation. By 1990, the U.S. foreign debt was nearing $700 billion, a figure that was almost equivalent to the total debt of all the other debtor nations in the world.

In 1960, not a single Japanese bank ranked among the world's fifty largest. As recently as 1978, a major study of world banking could be written with scarcely a mention of Japanese financial institutions. By 1990, however, nine of the ten largest banks in the world were Japanese and they had accumulated the world's biggest pool of liquid capital available for investment anywhere in the world. The savings deposits of the Japanese by that year accounted for about 30 percent of the entire world's bank deposits. The same breathtaking surge of wealth increased the value of Japanese stocks to the point where they were almost equal to that of the United States and all of Europe together. In 1989, for the first time, Japan overtook the United States to become the world's largest foreign-aid donor, giving Japan, as critics point out, an increasingly effective wedge for entry into foreign markets. Each year, close to a third of the U.S. treasury notes and government securities offered by the Treasury Department were being purchased by Japanese.

The Propensity to Save and Japan's Financial Ascendancy

In the jargon of the economist, the Japanese have a high "propensity to save." Throughout the entire era of the "economic miracle," the average Japanese family saved about 20 percent of its disposable income each year. In recent years the figure has dropped somewhat, but the 16 percent rate of the early 1990s still allowed Japanese to claim that they were the most frugal people in the world with a savings rate more than four times that of Americans. Scholars dispute whether the explanation lies deep in cultural roots—a vestige of the traditional frugality of the samurai, for example—or in more contemporary factors. Ecomonic surveys suggest, for example, that savings decisions reflect the high costs of education and parents' determination to make any sacrifice to provide the best possible education for their children. (The same explanation helps to account for the striking decline in the size of the nuclear family which since the early 1970s has fallen to under 2.0 children per family.) Most importantly, government tax policies encourage savings by leaving interest income largely untaxed. As a further incentive to save, interest expenses (on home mortgages, for example) are generally *not* tax deductible.

Since the equity market (such as the stock market) in Japan is relatively small, household savings typically have been channeled into accounts in banks highly regulated by the government or into the official postal savings system. Because millions of savers bargain with a small number of banks, the government has been able to keep the rate of return very low—bad news for savers but good news for businesses in need of a constant flow of cheap capital infusions with which to expand. Those monies have been available to Japanese industry and that in turn helped to account for one of the most striking features of the modern Japanese economic scene: the willingness of Japanese companies to take a long-range view of business activity. Because Japanese firms do not have to worry about anxious stockholders nearly as much as American firms do, they can afford to take low profits over a fairly extended period—as long, of course, as the company's bank remains confident of the long-term future. An American aluminum manufacturing executive comments admiringly of the Japanese far-sightedness:

> The difference with the Japanese companies is that they do everything in the long run. If they have a market for one million tons, they build a plant for 4 million. Then they lose money until they hit the break-even point, but eventually it pays off.

By the end of the 1980s, Japan had accumulated a half trillion dollars in available capital resources and was buying up the American debt, rescuing the American government from bankruptcy (or hyperinflation) and investing heavily in the American economy. In 1987, California's ailing Bank of America sought and received a rescue infusion of $130 million capital from a consortium of Japanese banks; forty years earlier the same bank was one of the first to extend loans to finance Japan's war-devastated textile industry. American citizens, saving only about four percent of their disposable income, were in effect supported in an ongoing "consumption binge" by Japanese citizens—"buying VCRs and selling IOUs," one commentator said.

Wounded American pride was only a little comforted to learn that in 1991 Japan's largest business organization, Keidanren, announced that as part of a "good citizenship campaign," Japanese corporate philanthropy in the United States would rise to a half-billion dollars in 1991. As with nearly all issues arising between the two countries, Americans were of two minds about Japan's generosity. It could hardly be dismissed as token since it would outpace the total amount of all overseas American corporate giving and amounted to five times the total aggregate charity of Britain, France, and Germany to U.S. non-profit organizations. With $110 million targeted for higher education, $60 million for the arts and culture, another $60 million for community projects (like the United Way), the usefulness of the donations could not be discounted. Still, there was resentment and suspicion. "Now, they are treating us as a charity case!" some complained. They're out to "win the hearts of American people so they won't . . . criticize Japanese trade practices. It's propaganda," one economist wrote.

BUYING INTO AMERICA

Japan's rapid financial ascendancy, taken with the devalued dollar and extraordinarily high cost of land in that country, made purchase of American land and businesses an especially attractive option in the 1980s. It was "as if America were having a fire sale, with every company and building marked 40 to 50 percent off the original price," one economist observed. This issue also sharpened emotions in America, especially as Japanese took control of such high-profile trophies as 7 Eleven, the Pebble Beach Company (of golf course fame), Saks Fifth Avenue, the giant entertainment industry MCA, and Firestone (sold to Japan's Bridgestone Tire Company). Sony's multi-billion-dollar purchase of Columbia Pictures and CBS Records prompted concern about the "soul of America" being bought up by Japanese—musician Bruce Springsteen now works for them, it was noted.

To Americans, perhaps the most chafing transactions involved the sale (in part or whole) of landmark real estate to Japanese firms—the Exxon building in New York City, One Prudential Plaza in Chicago, Crocker Center in San Francisco, and a third of all the office buildings in downtown Los Angeles. In 1989, Mitsubishi Real Estate purchased controlling interest in New York's Rockefeller Center. The Mitsubishi firm, Japan's largest real estate company, owns immense holdings of incredibly expensive land in the business and financial center of Tokyo known as Marunouchi, so valuable that the Rockefeller Center holdings made scarcely a dent in Mitsubishi Estate's finances. In Tokyo's compacted downtown, the average cost of leasing commercial real estate had risen to more than twenty times the price in New York City. Rockefeller Center, a magnificent cluster of buildings in the center of Manhattan, with its famous ice-skating rink and perhaps the most coveted business address in America, *is* something close to the "soul of America" if any real estate can be so described. The Rockefeller Center sale illustrates some of the complexities of the emerging economic relationship between Japan and America. It also demonstrates how volatile public response can become to the issue of Japanese investments in America. The term "Japan bashing" is often applied too loosely to include frank

A political cartoon from 1990 reflects resentment over Japanese investments in the United States.

discussion and legitimate grievances, but the occasions of hate-motivated racist bashing should be repugnant to all Americans.

A public opinion poll taken in 1990, after the Rockefeller Center deal, revealed that 69 percent of Americans felt that Japanese companies were investing "too much" in America. Critics of American reliance on Japanese investments, such as Texas Congressman John Bryant, contend that, "Foreign access to sensitive high technology and research capabilities narrows our strategic and competitive edge. Foreign influence in vital energy and defense industries may endanger our national security." Adds Senator Frank Murkowski of Alaska, "Once they [foreigners] own your assets, they own you." Japan specialist Professor Chalmers Johnson commented, "If you think that ownership doesn't matter, you are not playing the capitalism game anymore." Many fear that in any global recession, the Japanese would quickly shift the burden of unemployment to the United States and away from their own country. Other critics hold that Japanese companies work to keep knowledge-intensive, high-paying jobs in Japan while allocating low-paying, low-skilled jobs to the United States. Referring to the "high-value added"[2] segment of an enterprise, former Governor Richard Lamm of Colorado maintains that "it is *always* added in

---

[2] High-value added refers to processes or products which nurture skills and technologies for more industrial growth. Assembly and distribution, often assigned by Japanese to their overseas enterprises, do *not* add much to the value of a product and therefore do not generate high profits. The greatest value is often found in the design and creation of the tools needed to make the product rather than in the actual manufacture of it.

Japan. We are seeing in many places that they keep seventy-five percent of the value-added in Japan," He said unequivocally, "I do not want Japanese coming in our state. I don't want the Arabs owning our banks or the Japanese owning our means of production. It terrifies me."

The potential for racism to intrude is illustrated by the remarks of popular TV and newspaper commentator Andy Rooney who mockingly referred to "Locke-feller Center." Without any apology, he conceded that he was "vaguely anti-Japanese. Don't ask me why. Just prejudice, I guess. I'm very comfortable with some of my prejudices and have no thought of changing them now." Perhaps the Japanese would also like to buy the "Gland Canyon" or "Mount Lush-more," he added. The use of battlefield imagery (war, attack, counterattack, invasion, and so on), often with less-than-subtle references to Pearl Harbor, to describe Japanese trade and investment practices does little to illuminate com-plex issues and much to inflame the feelings of Japanese. *Newsweek's* cover story on the Sony buyout of Columbia Pictures contained the headline "Japan Invades Hollywood." (The Pacific edition, distributed throughout Japan, was edited to read "Japan Moves Into Hollywood.")

All of this is not far removed in spirit from headlines like "Next Time You Buy a TV, Remember Pearl Harbor," over the column of a popular New York colum-nist who compares Pearl Harbor with their "far more successful economic war against this country." Or from the comments of a prominent statesman in 1985 noting that it was the fortieth anniversary of the end of World War II. "To clarify two facts," he said: "First, we're still at war with Japan. Second, we're losing."

The Japanese public understandably blanched when they read (in 1992) the remarks of Senator Ernest F. Hollings who told a group of American factory workers that they "should draw a mushroom cloud and put underneath it: 'Made in America by lazy and illiterate Americans and tested in Japan.'" The South Carolina senator's comments stunned officials in that state who work dili-gently and successfully to attract Japanese capital to South Carolina. Hollings' allusion to the 1945 nuclear bombing of Japanese cities was made in response to the intemperate use by a prominent Japanese of the adjectives "lazy" and "illit-erate" to describe American workers. The exchange would seem to underscore the importance of civil restrained discourse on both sides of the Pacific.

"THE TOKYO EXPRESSWAY"

Others, including many economists, have come forward to defend the Rock-efeller transaction and Japan's overseas investments in general. They empha-size a lesson from history: that countries which have done the most to keep out foreign investors (Burma and North Korea are notorious contemporary exam-ples) have stagnated while countries most open to foreign investment have prospered. America itself set a striking precedent. It was foreign capital inflows, especially from private British investors, which helped the United States develop its roads, canals, banks, steel industry, and especially its railroads in the nineteenth century. The General Motors–Toyota joint venture in Fremont, California, revived a defunct GM plant entirely along Japanese lines and, in the words of one American auto industry expert, "converted a crew of largely middle-aged, rabble-rousing former GM workers into a crack force that is beating the bumpers off Big Three plants in efficiency and product quality."

In middle America, Japanese presence has been especially strong. Seeking to steer clear of big urban centers and the powerful unions (as well as social problems) that are centered there, Japanese industry has settled in isolated rural areas and sought to cultivate local support. In a vast industrial network stretching north from Tennessee to Illinois, Indiana, and Ohio, Japanese auto, steel, chemical, and tire manufacturers have opened up some 100,000 manufacturing jobs in recent years. A section of Interstate Highway 75 in central Ohio is popularly known as the "Tokyo Expressway" because of its proliferation of Japanese factories—often occupying land that was cornfields until recently. After the Japanese Bridgestone firm acquired Firestone, they agreed to invest $1.5 billion in the American company. At a once-failing Firestone plant in Tennessee, new Japanese managers increased the factory's productivity, saved the jobs of 1400 workers, and spared the region from the harsh effects of a plant closing. "Does this combination give us a new lease on life?" the Firestone board chairman asked rhetorically. "You bet it does."

Most American states now operate offices, mini-embassies, in Japan to solicit Japanese investments. Incentives offer a measure of how eagerly American governors court Japanese businesses. In 1977, Ohio, a pioneer in these endeavors, persuaded Honda to build a plant in that state with a promise of $22 million in subsidies and tax breaks. By the 1980s, the stakes were much higher. In 1986, Kentucky had to offer a $100 million package to induce Toyota to build a plant of comparable size to Honda's Ohio venture. Should we actually pay foreigners to invest here by luring them with tax breaks and other subsidies? The answer is yes, writes one economist, "if what we pay them to come here is less than what would be the cost of building the factories, buying the equipment and training American workers ourselves." Others, however, point out that this state versus state competition in America promotes contempt for the United States among Japanese for whom such a divided national stance would be unthinkable.

The defenders of Japanese investments maintain that in the new global market, "national origins" of products and the nationality of ownership is no longer as important. Sony now exports to Europe audiotapes made in a factory in Alabama. Honda autos manufactured in Ohio are exported to Asia—some even to Japan. Chrysler owns a major interest in Mitsubishi Motors, which in turn owns part of Hyundai, the South Korean company whose cars enjoy a low-price advantage in America. An officer of American-owned National Semiconductor Corporation says that his company remains competitive by "using Russian engineers living in Israel to design chips that are made in America and then assembled in Asia."[3] Harvard economist Robert Reich asks "Is that an American product?" Reich adds

---

[3] These complications make "buying American" a nettlesome task. It means rejecting certain Chevrolet and Pontiac models (made in Canada and Korea respectively), avoiding Burger King (owned by a British company), the A & P grocery chain (German-controlled), and Zenith TVs (manufactured in Mexico). Is it more American to purchase a John Deere tractor (whose engine is produced in Japan) or a Komatsu model (made by the Japanese firm's U.S. plant)?

that, not so long ago, the United States invested massively in Europe—notwithstanding the complaints of some Europeans that their resources were being "parasitically exploited" and that they were being overwhelmed by American culture. Even today, American overseas holdings, several trillions of dollars worth around the globe, are far larger than Japan's. Further, despite the rise in foreign investment in America, foreigners still control only about five percent of America's assets, the Japanese about one percent. In other countries, such as the former West Germany, foreign control runs as high as 20 percent.

Why, many Japanese ask, has Japanese purchase of U.S. assets aroused such an angry response when money invested by Western nations seemed not to disturb the American public? Until recently, both England and the Netherlands had larger investment portfolios in America than Japan, and nobody sounded the alarm as Maryland Congresswoman Helen Bentley did. "The United States is rapidly becoming a colony of Japan," she said. Could it be, the Japanese Ministry of Foreign Affairs asked, that Americans were uncomfortable with the fact that Japan was the first non-Western nation to have a significant economic presence in the United States?

Furthermore, if Americans have any reservations about the merits of the Rockefeller sale, they should recall that, as one attorney familiar with the case stated, "You could probably count the unhappy [American] stockholders on the fingers of one hand." Japanese management specialist Ohmae Kenichi expands on the theme of what he calls the "borderless world":

> Did the trade deficit force the Rockefeller Group to sell Rockefeller Center? Of course not. The people running the trust simply wanted liquidity and higher after-tax returns, on investments that one would hope would create new jobs and build American competitiveness. So, American investment bankers helped them sell it. If the Japanese are buying America, then American capitalists are just as surely selling it.

Critics of Japanese protectionism, however, argue that the "borderless world" where investments move freely across international borders simply does not exist. Japanese are misguided, American critics say, to compare Japanese investments in the United States with Dutch investments. The issue, Americans insist, is *reciprocity*. American firms face few obstacles in opening factories, offices, sales outlets in Amsterdam. In Tokyo, the obstacles can be enormous. Only the largest firms with enormous financial reserves can survive the long and costly process of running the bureaucratic maze, battling with everything from national laws to protective local business councils. As the largest toy retailer in the world, Toys "R" Us was able to persevere in its three-year-long battle to open an outlet in Japan—with the aid of strong pressure from the U.S. government. Many American firms with less resources and less direct help from Washington have been discouraged from even trying.

Other experts insist that Americans concerned about their declining competitiveness are concentrating on the wrong set of Japanese investment figures.

More important than Japan's overseas investments are the scale of its investments at home. By 1990, Japan was investing one-quarter of its annual GNP in new capital projects—new factories, new equipment, new technology, all of which promise benefits far down the road. The United States, because of its own sluggish growth rates, might have been expected to invest a larger percentage to remain competitive. In fact, while Japan's capital investment rates were going up in the late 1980s, America continued to underinvest. By 1990, only about one-tenth of the U.S. GNP was set aside for new capital projects. Similarly, investments in research and development have added up to only two percent of GNP in the United States while they almost reach three percent in Japan. Except in defense and space, federal support for R&D has languished in the United States over the past twenty years. The result is that Japanese scientists and engineers are "ready to embrace the microelectronic and molecular technologies of the future," as economist Robert Reich observes. By contrast, America has sacrificed not just breakthrough discoveries "but the know-how and experience that come from *doing* current research." Professor Chalmers Johnson adds the following pithy warning: " . . . in another decade or so, the two economies are going to divide and the danger is that the U.S. will end up producing ICBMs and soybeans, and Japan will produce everything in between."

Why is it, Johnson goes on, that the Japanese invest so much of their GNP in capital projects when the nation has so much in the way of consumption needs which have not been satisfied? He also asks the corollary question: Why do Americans consume so much when they have such high unmet capital investment needs? Johnson's answer is that government policies (often the *lack* of government policies in the case of the United States) are crucial in both instances. This explanation will be considered in the pages ahead.

STEEL

Japan's "miracle" years may be usefully studied by looking at a few key industries, observing their impact on the Japanese–American nexus, and most importantly making an attempt to explore some causes for Japan's economic ascendancy.

Little was left of the Japanese iron and steel industry as the result of the rain of destruction during the Pacific war. From a grim point of view, this permitted Japan to rebuild its heavy industry, once capital resources could be mobilized, with the latest innovations in furnace-making and energy-saving systems. Ironically, the scarcity of raw materials also came to benefit the steel industry. Japan sought out cheaply priced Australian and Indian iron ores and American coking coal. The end result was that Japan came to produce the world's lowest-cost steel and became the world's leading exporter of steel. It did not happen overnight to be sure. In 1950, five years after the war's end, the production level in Japan had only reached five million tons, still less than Japan's peak wartime levels and only about half of France's output. Even in 1960, productivity (a measure of how much one worker produces in a given period of time) was still only half that of an American steelworker. In a ten-year period beginning in 1964, however, the man-hours required to produce a ton of steel in Japan's modern electric furnaces was reduced from twenty-five to nine. In 1970, after passing France, then West Germany, and then Britain, Japan's output had expanded to 93 million tons, and it was closing in on the United States. That goal had been achieved by 1980, by which time Japan was also the world's leading exporter of steel. Bigness can be important in an industry like steel, where "economies of scale" count and by 1978, of the world's twenty largest modern steel furnaces, none was in the United States and fourteen were in Japan.

After absorbing overseas freighting costs, Japan could still deliver steel at U.S. sites cheaper than plants in Pittsburgh could. The full impact of this began to hit home as Americans read about massive layoffs in the U.S. steel industry and, at the same time, learned that Japanese steel was being used in such mammoth projects as the Alaska pipeline—or, ironically, to build a bridge across the San Joaquin River at Antioch, California, just five miles away from the American Bridge Division of the U.S. Steel Corporation. The U.S. industry asked for and received protection in the form of "voluntary" restrictions on steel exports by the Japanese producers. Eastern steel centers, once the showcase heart of American industrial might, were being turned into a "rustbelt," with half the nation's steel workers jobless by 1980 and scores of plants being sold for scrap.

In addition to a modernized plant structure, availability of cheap resources, and accessibility to open markets, especially American markets, another factor playing a key role in the expansion of Japan's steel industry—as in many other industries—has been the close collaboration between government and business. This tight-working partnership has given rise to the expression "Japan, Inc." popular among American businessmen who found that the cozy links between the business elites *(zaikai)*, and bureaucratic elites *(kankai)* produced a formidable adversary.

On the academic level, Professor Chalmers Johnson coined the phrase "capitalist developmental state" to refer to the Japanese arrangement. (Singapore, Taiwan, Hong Kong, and South Korea also fall under this rubric.) Johnson's term describes a system which, though not the highly centralized command economy on the model of the former Soviet Union, is still far removed from the species of capitalism Americans know. In the capitalist developmental state, the main energizing factor is "industrial policy." There is a strong bias in the United States, shared by government and business leaders alike, against any governmental effort to fine-tune the economy. A former undersecretary of commerce put it succinctly: "We have an industrial policy in this country. The policy is that we don't want an industrial policy." The Japanese do not share this bias. The idea that government should organize, coordinate, and steer the nation's industrial structure enjoys a broad social and political mandate in Japan. As examples from Chapter 3 revealed, the Meiji government, almost from its inception, was an advanced modern bureaucracy strongly inclined toward intervention in the economy. The achieving of rational, forward-looking developmental goals—"prosperous nation, strong army"—was unquestionably the principal orientation of government and business alike. The enduring sense of vulnerability brought on by the nation's have-not condition reinforces the conviction that government *must* interfere. Johnson explains what industrial policy means for Japan:

> It means governmental affirmative action on behalf of domestic industry to foster the orderly retreat of declining industries and to build the high-value-added industries of the future. It works on the supply side and takes as its criterion the number of truly valuable jobs held by a nation's workers. It favors computer chips over potato chips.

THE BUREAUCRACY

Who is it within the Japanese government that shapes the nation's "industrial policy" and provides the "administrative guidance" to business? In large measure, the answer is the state bureaucracy. "State bureaucracy" refers not to the politicians, the elected members of the Diet, but a group commonly referred to in America as the "civil service." Consider for a moment the quite striking difference between the Japanese bureaucracy and its American counterpart. In Japan, the various ministries (finance, foreign affairs, and so on) appear to correspond to American departments (treasury, state, and so on). The fact is, however, that the Japanese ministries have a far greater political voice than their American counterparts. In Japan, as in the United States, the lower-level functionaries of the civil service are not regarded with any special awe and, in fact, are often caricatured, as in America, as petty tyrants mired in red tape.

It is at the higher strata of the two bureaucracies that the systems differ sharply. The higher civil service in the United States, roughly three thousand officials in the top four levels, is *appointed*, the majority of the positions allocated by the president to political favorites. In Japan, the higher bureaucracy is *not* appointed—the prime minister appoints only the minister at the very top (and a parliamentary vice minister). In Japan then, the elite bureaucracy is composed of career professionals who have risen through the ranks in a particular ministry and at a certain stage of their careers manage to defy the odds and pass the higher civil service examinations. The one in forty who moves through this final screening process to the pinnacle of the profession is almost certainly a man and almost certainly a graduate of one of the prestigious universties we have discussed. If he is admitted into the cream of the cream, a powerful ministry like finance or international trade and industry, he is almost certainly a graduate of the law faculty at Todai.

These people command enormous prestige in Japanese society, and in terms of political influence, they overshadow the Diet. The Diet must of course authorize budgets, actually drafted by Ministry of Finance bureaucrats, and give a final stamp of approval to all legislation. In fact, however, the Diet spends much of its time mediating disputes between rival ministries and industries. The most striking difference between the U.S. and Japanese systems is that in Japan it is the bureaucracy which initiates and frames most of the legislation. More than 90 percent of all laws enacted in Japan come up from the ministries (that is, the bureaucracy) where they have been researched and drafted by the bureaucrats whose long "institutional memory" (they do not come and go at each election time) gives them a special expertise.

MITI

While more than one governmental agency has worked to fashion Japan's industrial policy, the "maestro that orchestrated" it was the Ministry of International Trade and Industry (MITI). In the 1950s and 1960s, MITI favored steel over just about everything. Through their control of foreign exchange and the licensing of foreign technology, MITI officials were in a position to set goals for specific industries and allocate the assignment of costly new technology. In a process known as *amakudari* ("descending from heaven"), top bureaucrats from this key ministry filtered into the steel industry after retirement (typically at age fifty) from their ministerial careers. Once there, they did not issue orders— Japanese groups don't work that way—but provided "administrative guidance" *(gyosei shido)* more in keeping with Japanese social dynamics. With their important connections in government, they were able to facilitate a flow of aid and advice to the high-priority steel sector. Consortiums, illegal in the United States, were fostered to facilitate the purchase of coking coal and iron at rock-bottom prices. Cartels, illegal in the United States, were permitted in order to moderate excessive competition in the industry. Nippon Steel Corporation, the world's largest producer, was the product of a 1970 merger. To cut transportation costs, MITI fostered the creation of government-subsidized coastal industrial parks. It encouraged the shutdown of inefficient open-hearth furnaces and their replacement with semi-robotized plants. One of them, the Ohgishima facility, built on an island of reclaimed fill in Tokyo Bay, was probably the most modern in the world when it was completed in 1979. It uses about 40 percent less energy and a third less workers than a conventional mill would.

An important factor in making Japan's steel industry the most efficient in the world was long-term financing. At $4 billion, the Ohgishima facility cost twice as much to build as a conventional mill. MITI saw to it that the steel industry received tax breaks and a steady flow of capital and interest-subsidized loans from the Japan Development Bank (JDB), also staffed by *amakudari* ex-bureaucrats.[4] With this kind of backing, the steel industry was willing to invest far more heavily in costly expansion programs than they would have dared on their own. As *Atlantic* editor and Japan expert James Fallows notes, steel producers were willing to take extraordinary investment risks because they knew that MITI would be there if trouble arose, that MITI, through its administrative guidance

---

[4] The JDB received all *its* initial capital from SCAP's allocation of yen proceeds of U.S. aid products during the occupation years.

channels, "would divide the work fairly whenever the market went slack." Some students of the Japan–U.S. trade crisis believe that the United States can never hope to compete with Japan until it emulates some of Japan's accomplishments in fostering productive government–business relationships. Any serious "competitiveness plan," writes economist Robert Kuttner, must include "a trade policy that acknowledges that government-industry collaboration, both at home and abroad, is an inevitable characteristic of modern industrial society."

If competitiveness in steel was important, it still did not touch the average American in the way other commodities did. Most Americans in the 1950s still thought of Japanese merchandise as shabby dime-store toys and Christmas-tree lights. However, it was in that decade that the pejorative overtone of the "Made in Japan" label was gradually replaced by a superlative one. High-quality cameras edged in on the prewar command of the Germans in optics. The well-deserved reputation of the Swiss as watchmakers was challenged by Japan. Western music had never been heard in Japan until the last century, but Yamaha began to replace Steinway as the piano of choice in American homes and studios. Still, if there was a single Japanese export that captured the fancy of Americans it was probably the automobile.

CHALLENGING DETROIT

In 1957, the struggling Nissan Automobile Company displayed a little car called the Datsun at an auto show in Los Angeles. Nissan had some experience in auto manufacturing prior to World War II, but most of its plant was levelled during the war. Dirt floors were still common at Nissan plants. The quartet of engineers who accompanied the car to its Los Angeles debut were each allowed a parsimonious $15 per day for expenses by company auditors. The car they were exhibiting, one of them recalled, was the ugliest he had ever seen. "Is that a car or a black box that moves?" he wondered. Its brakes were not very good because Japanese drivers never got going fast enough to require truly strong brakes. It vibrated badly at fifty miles per hour, and overheated rapidly once it reached a top speed of fifty-nine miles per hour. Very few Japanese at that time could afford a personal car, so the main customers were taxi companies. Accordingly, Japanese cars in 1957 were designed for short hauls on bad roads, "for function, not pleasure," explains writer David Halberstam, an authority on the auto industry.

> The car was not built for the highway, with acceleration, speed, and comfort; in Japan highways barely existed. It was built for survival in the city, to be driven on some of the worst streets in the world by drivers who drove with such ferocity that their fellow citizens called them kamikazes. . . .

It cannot be said that the little Japanese car with an Austin engine—Nissan had signed a licensing tie-up with the English company—was an instant success, but the Nissan engineers did have at least one moment of exhilaration.

Nissan employees did not see their cars as competition to the big, powerful automobiles turned out by Detroit. However, they did hold Volkswagen in high respect for "doing everything right" so soon after the German defeat in World War II. The Nissan group was test driving their *ponkotsu* (roughly, "junk-heap") one day on a stretch of the San Diego Freeway—there were no test tracks in Japan. On this occasion, two Americans in a Volkswagen pulled alongside the Nissan, the Americans staring in a way that seemed to say that the Datsun was "unworthy." A race ensued and Halberstam relates what happened:

> Back and forth they went, one car taking a little lead and then the other, until they came to the big slope, not a steep hill but steady and punishing for a small car. Tanabe [Kuniyuki, a member of the Datsun engineering team] decided to go to third gear and give it all the power he had. Gradually the Datsun began to pull away from the VW. At first it was a small edge, and then the length of the car, and then the VW began to slip back. Tanabe did not wave out the window, but he did not take his eye off the rearview mirror until the VW disappeared. We can beat the Volkswagen, he kept thinking, we can beat the Volkswagen. What a good engine, what a tough little engine. Then it dawned on him: If we can beat the Volkswagen in a country where people are still lined up to buy it, we will be all right in America, we poor little Japanese.

In 1956, only twelve thousand private cars—tiny and unattractive—were made in Japan. That figure had grown to 165,000 by 1960. In 1967, the industry celebrated its first million-car year, and by 1980, production had ballooned to more than seven million. Exports really only began to take off in about 1965 when 100,000 cars were sold abroad. In 1973, the *Wall Street Journal*, perhaps reflecting Detroit's wishful thinking, found "signs that the party is over" for Japan's car-makers and predicted a downturn. The opposite happened. Japanese car sales in America grew rapidly after the 1973 Arab oil embargo as American taste shifted from Detroit's gas-guzzlers to the smaller, fuel-efficient cars which Japan was ready to supply.

By 1976, worker productivity had grown so impressively that Nissan and Toyota employees were turning out forty-two and forty-seven cars per man-year respectively. None of their major competitors in Europe was able to produce even twenty cars per man-year. In 1970, Volkswagen was still the major foreign car exporter to America. In rapid order, however, Japanese companies—first Toyota, then Nissan, and in 1978, Honda—passed the German leader to become the largest exporters to the world's largest car-consuming market, the United States. In typical years, cars accounted for about sixty percent of the nation's annual trade deficit with Japan. During the years between 1965–1980, Japan's export sales soared forty-fold to reach four million. Well over half of its auto production went to overseas markets by 1980, and in typical years more than a third of those vehicles went to Japan's best customer, the United States. In 1986, eleven Japanese auto and truck manufacturers were producing cars at 153 sites in forty-three countries. A single company, Toyota, collected all by itself 9 percent of the entire world market share.

Detroit was so damaged by the explosive growth of the Japanese auto industry that Washington put pressure on Japan in 1981, the first year in which Japan surpassed the United States in total auto production, to "voluntarily" restrain its auto sales to the United States to a specific number of vehicles per year. The import ceiling agreement, intended for four years, permitted Washington to plead innocent to charges of protectionism because Tokyo had voluntarily committed itself to cut its export market. However, the voluntary restraint on auto exports, regarded as a temporary measure to give American industry some "breathing room" in which it might regain its strength, appears to have been a failure. In 1992, more than a decade after the first restraint agreement, Japan was still being asked to limit its auto export volume to the United States. Also, voluntary restraint agreements were imposed on Japan in other sectors of the economy from time to time.

Most of the Japanese auto companies, like Toyota and Nissan, had modest prewar experience in auto manufacturing, but others, like Honda, entered the car business much later. In 1948 company founder Honda Soichiro was refitting war surplus engines onto bicycles. That led to motorcycles so well engineered and priced that Honda's firm was able to roll over the British motorcycle industry in a decade. Trucks were next; it was only after 1967 that Honda marketed its first passenger car. Fifteen years later, Honda became the first Japanese car-maker to open a plant in America. Then, in 1989, Honda's Accord outsold the Ford Taurus to become the best-selling car model in the United States. No foreign car had been No. 1 before—though that raised the question of what a "foreign car" was, since many of the Accords were by that time made in Marysville, Ohio, rather than Japan.

The American auto industry underwent an almost mirror-image decline compared to Japan's rise. In 1980, Chrysler, hovering near bankruptcy and firing thousands of skilled employees in order to meet payrolls, was revived only after a huge "bailout" from Washington. In the 1980s, unemployment reached 16 percent in the auto industry, while the general rate was less than half that figure. Despite some dramatic increases in investment and productivity, Detroit's Big Three automakers had a number of red-ink years in the 1980s, and entering the early 1990s there were multi-billion-dollar record-breaking quarterly losses. Some industry analysts were prompted to talk of the "very real possibility," as one put it, "that one or even two of the three American giants may fail." While such a view is extremely speculative, few were dismissing it as preposterous,

---

Datsun is not a Japanese word. An experimental car called the DAT was produced in Japan in 1911—the name deriving from the initial letters of the three founders of the company. In 1931 when the company introduced a new model, it was called the "Datson," "son of DAT." When Nissan Motors acquired the company, the "son" was changed to "sun" to avoid inauspicious connotations: *son* (pronounced sone, rhymes with the English *bone*), can mean "damage" or "loss" in Japanese.

and the very fact that such a proposition could be seriously conjectured underscored the gravity of the industry's decline. The auto industry is almost uniquely important in America, accounting for four percent of GNP, a large chunk for a single segment of business. Failures here are especially ominous because the industry directly employs 750,000 Americans plus millions more in related industries such as rubber, glass, and textiles.

RESCUE OPERATION AT MAZDA

Again, as in the case of the steel industry, MITI played an important role in steering the automobile industry to its phenomenal growth. A striking example occurred at the time of the Arab oil embargo in the fall of 1973. The Toyo Kogyo Automobile Corporation had experimented with a powerful but quiet rotary engine in its Mazda passenger car manufactured at its Hiroshima plant. The car was doing well, especially in American sales, but the gamble on the Wankel engine failed because of one important reason: It was notoriously fuel inefficient. That did not matter until soaring gasoline prices collapsed the demand for Mazda cars; by 1975, the company was on the verge of bankruptcy. The Japanese government determined that Mazda was too big to sacrifice, too important to the economy of Japan, especially to the economy of the Hiroshima region. MITI officials "counseled" with the press to play down Mazda's problems, it urged rival auto firms against taking advantage of Mazda's difficulties in the marketplace, and directed the automaker's large suppliers (such as Mitsubishi Steel) to continue normal dealings with the troubled company. The Japanese government did not loan money or even guarantee a loan to Mazda as in the case of Washington's bailout of Chrysler a few years later. However, the Japanese government played a role in encouraging Sumitomo Bank, Toyo Kogho's *keiretsu* partner, to announce that *it* would carry Mazda's much-needed loans. Sumitomo Bank itself was guaranteed against failure by the government of Japan. This is a typical example of the way in which the government exercised power over the direction of economic development. Since the end of the war when credit was scarce, Japan followed a policy of the "socialization of credit risk" by rationing credit to favorite industries via large banks which were given assurances that their loans would not be permitted to fail.

Beyond the government, however, the rescue of Mazda offers a good opportunity to see how Japanese businesses and community work in a crisis situation. The company union cooperated in the rescue operation, throwing no roadblocks in management plans to dispatch to various parts of Japan several thousand of its seasoned industrial workers as "volunteers" for one- to three-year-long tours of duty selling Mazda cars on a neighborhood door-to-door basis. This kind of flexible union–management partnership concerning work rules would be unheard of in most countries, including the United States. Because of the tradition of lifetime employment, layoffs were avoided, but the work force was gradually cut back by a third through attrition and early retirement incentives. All paychecks were temporarily trimmed in a belt-tightening measure with top management taking the largest cuts. Extra hours were worked and, again, top management was not immune. The executive vice president later recalled the four-year crisis period:

> I worked sixteen hour days. . . . I did my thinking and reading at midnight—worrying over the abacus. When you are absorbed in something, you cease eating and sleeping. I lived alone in Hiroshima for the entire time, but my wife came from Osaka to host foreign visitors and join me in serving as go-between in Toyo Kogyo marriages. I saw her perhaps once a week over the four years.

Allies cooperated to expand their purchases of Mazdas. The city and prefectural governments, in an example of Japan, Inc. at work, added Mazdas to their auto fleets. Industry friends like the Sumitomo Bank lobbied to have companies in the huge Sumitomo conglomerate of companies buy more Mazda cars and trucks. The prefectural assembly passed a bill which allowed Mazdas to require lower registration fees because its cars could pass stricter emission standards, a legal maneuver that made Mazda price competitive with the industry giants, Toyota and Nissan. Suppliers agreed to hire scores of Mazda engineers on a temporary basis. The engineers then worked to achieve cost reduction in the suppliers' shops which could then be passed on in the form of lower prices to Mazda. At Mazda itself, "Quality Circles," worker-participation programs commonly found in large enterprises, were expanded and vitalized. The innovations and improvements generated by 1600 of these circles were a major factor in the extraordinary improvement of productivity at Mazda. In the seven years from 1974 to 1981, productivity more than doubled as the output per factory employee ratio leaped from thirty-three vehicles to seventy-five. The upshot of all of this was that, after several years, the company had regained its health and became more of an international competitor than it had been. "The Toyo Kogyo turnaround is a lesson in managing interdependence," writes anthropologist and Japan expert Thomas P. Rohlen.

THE DEMING PRIZE

The American nexus once again needs to be considered. The "Quality Circle" approach to management efficiency was not a Japanese invention. Traditional Japanese artisans were of course past masters at quality control, but individual craftsmanship is vastly different from excellence achieved in mass production in a factory setting where thousands of workers interact.

Something close to a national obsession with quality control in manufacturing may be traced back to two organizations founded before the economic miracle began. The Japanese Union of Scientists and Engineers (JUSE) was established during the Occupation with assistance from SCAP as a marriage between science and industry. JUSE rallied factory enginneers and foremen all over Japan to the cause of production excellence by helping to establish strict industrial standards through training programs, and by innovative radio broadcasts on quality control heard by millions of workers in the 1950s. The Japan Productivity Center (JPC), established three years after the Occupation came to an end, again with financial support from the United States, was another pioneer in the introduction of quality control and efficiency to the Japanese factory. It dispatched hundreds of teams of Japanese businessmen, including groups from the struggling steel and auto industries, to study American industrial style. Noda Nobuo, later a Mitsubishi executive, recalled his JPC-sponsored visit to the United States in the late 1950s:

> We were amazed by everything we saw. . . . American technology was so advanced and our own so backward that we wondered whether our observations and reports would be of any use in Japan. . . . Everywhere we went the Americans briefed us with the kind of generosity of parents teaching children.

The very phrase "Quality Circle" (or more often "QC") was introduced to Japan during the occupation period by W. E. Deming, a Census Bureau statistician whom SCAP brought to Japan to lecture on the subject of product improvement. In a series of lectures to Japanese business managers in the summer of 1950, Deming told them that they could use statistical analysis to build quality into their products and thereby change their image abroad in five years' time. In addition to imparting his technical expertise in such matters as time control, Deming sold the Japanese on the more general principle that quality is not achieved by a few inspectors who spot defects on an assembly line but by involving the entire work force in setting production standards and "getting the job done right the first time."

Deming's ideas caught on, and in 1951 grateful Japanese business leaders memorialized his name with an annual prize, "the Deming award," the highest award for industrial productivity and quality. They are pursued by Japanese-based corporations "with almost the intensity of Sir Gawain pursuing the Holy Grail," one business expert wrote. While Deming is little known in his native country (at age 92 he was still alive in 1992) and his many books little read, to Japanese businessmen Deming is a household name. In steel mills and camera factories, Deming-style "self-supervisory" groups (typically eight to ten workers engaged in the same production activity) meet regularly to improve quality. "The enthusiasm of the quest for quality is contagious," writes an American admirer of Japan's QC groups. Deming is quite possibly the most revered American of the postwar era. It is a tribute to Deming's success and the earnest determination of his Japanese disciples that the flow of advice has shifted in recent years. By the 1980s, the JPC was receiving more study missions from abroad—including the United States—than it was sending.

FORD AND TOYOTA

"There is no secret to how we learned to do what we do, Mr. Caldwell. We learned it at the Rouge." Toyoda Eiji,[5] for more than two decades the driving force in the Toyota Motor Company, was toasting the head of the Ford Motor Company on the latter's 1982 visit to Japan. Earlier in the century, Henry Ford had invented assembly-line mass production so efficient that a Model-T, affordable to "Everyman," could be built on the moving line in only ninety-three minutes. The "Rouge" was Henry Ford's monumental factory complex on the River Rouge near Detroit—27 miles of conveyor belts, 93 miles of railroad tracks, seventy-five thousand employees. In his flattering remarks about learning from Ford, Toyoda may have been engaging in the ordinary courtesy shown by Japanese to guests. However, even before the war, in 1934, the Ford Motor Company had received representatives of the "Toyoda Automatic Loom Company"—the loom company was considering branching out into an auto venture which would become the Toyota Motor Company. Ford, as well as other American firms, allowed the Japanese group to study factory layout, parts manufacturing, and the like. The first Toyota appeared the next year: a hybrid car, with Ford brakes, Chevrolet front axle, and the streamlined body of the 1934 Chrysler Airflow.

Toyoda Eiji, however, also had in mind his own visit to the "Rouge" in the summer of 1950. The daily output of the various Ford plants was about seven thousand units at that time, Toyota turned out a piddling forty. By adding up the entire production since the 1930s, Toyota was still well short of Ford's daily output. Toyoda had gone to Michigan to discuss a possible tie-up with the Ford Motor Company. Complications arose and Toyoda returned home empty handed. If a merger had gone through, Toyota's future independence would surely have been compromised. In any case, Toyota teams stayed in Michigan for a half-year analyzing Ford facilities. Upon returning to Japan, Toyoda Eiji drew up a five-year modernization plan to double production capacity without increasing personnel. The plan was exceeded, and the postwar Toyota enterprise, with a flood of orders from the Korean War "procurement boom," was on its way.

HIGH-TECH INDUSTRIES

It was one thing for America to watch its competitiveness in steel and autos decline. Those sectors both played to Japan's strength in mass production

---

[5] The spelling shift from the family name, Toyoda, to the company name, Toyota, was a decision of the Toyoda family in the 1930s. According to one source, the family consulted a numerologist who advised using the modified English spelling of the family name. When written in Japanese *kana* syllabics, "Toyoda" requires ten strokes of the pen, "Toyota" only eight. The number eight was believed to be auspicious for the Toyoda family, and as the source of this arcana writes, "in retrospect no one is inclined to quibble."

and standardized process technology. However, it was more disturbing to watch Japan "chip" away at America's prestige in high-tech industries such as consumer electronics, semiconductors and computers. As Daniel Okimoto, an authority on the Japanese political economy, observes, those branches of the economy "depended on new product innovation, state-of-the-art design, creative software applications, and complex systems integration—areas in which the Japanese were thought to be weak." Since the nineteenth century and Thomas Edison's invention of the phonograph in 1887, the world had regarded the United States as a leader in consumer electronics manufacturing. In the post-World War II era, the global spread of TV owed its origins to American know-how. As late as 1970, U.S. companies held a 90 percent share of the American market for color television receivers; by 1990, that share had slipped to ten percent.

The pioneer breakthrough that was indispensable to the founding of postwar high-technology industries occurred in 1947 when scientist William Shockley and two colleagues at AT&T's Bell Laboratories invented the transistor. Like vacuum tubes, transistors regulate the flow of electricity, but transistors were only a hundredth of the size and weight of the tubes, used much less power, and did not burn out as tubes did. With a tremendous potential for military, industrial, and consumer use, the transistor launched the postwar electronics revolution and won the inventors a Nobel Prize. The results of Shockley's research were keenly studied in Japan in 1948 by two businessmen-engineers, Morita Akio and Ibuka Masaru. They were founders of the Tokyo Telecommunications Engineering Company (TTEC), a grand name for what was essentially a radio-repair shop recently capitalized with a $500 loan from Morita's father and operating out of the charred, gutted ruins of a Ginza department store.

In 1953, the company's business-savvy vice president Morita traveled to the United States to negotiate the possibility of licensing transistor technology from the Western Electric Company (WEC), which then held the patent rights. The transistor had been developed for use in the telephone industry, and the Pentagon had interest in its application to weapons technology, but, with one exception, no practical use for the device had been found in consumer electronics. WEC did have plans for using it in hearing aids. Morita recalls, "Of course, we were not interested in the hearing aid market, which is very limited. We wanted to make something that could be used by everybody. . . ." Getting WEC to sell the rights presented no problem. United States antitrust laws placed AT&T's patent in the public domain, available to all comers, including the Japanese. There was a price of course, $25,000. MITI, as Japan's custodian of foreign exchange, was skeptical about the drain of such a large cache of dollars from the nation's small treasury, but after a year the Tokyo firm received the necessary permission to purchase the patent rights.

Miniaturization and compactness has always appealed to the Japanese sense of taste. As Morita notes, "Our boxes have been made to nest, our fans fold; our art rolls into neat scrolls. . . . And we set as our goal a radio small enough to fit into a shirt pocket." It took several years of radical modification of Shockley's

Sony is not a Japanese word. Morita explains that he and his partner realized that "Tokyo Telecommunications Engineering Company," either in Japanese or its English translation, was a cumbersome name. Since they had a Western market in mind, they searched for a name with a Western ring. Someone looked up *sound* in a Latin dictionary and for a time *sonus* was considered along with variations like *sunny* and *sonny*. In the end, they settled on *Sony*. "The new name had the advantage of not meaning anything but *Sony* in any language; it was easy to remember, and it carried the connotations we wanted," recalls Morita.

device in Tokyo laboratories before the transistor could be used in a high-frequency radio. One of these modifications, the Esaki diode, the work of TTEC's Esaki Reona (Leo), revolutionized circuit design in the areas of frequency generation and amplification and won Esaki a Nobel Prize in physics.

In 1957, the Tokyo firm, now calling itself Sony, offered to the world the first pocket-sized transistor radio. (Morita concedes that it was a little too large for most pockets but the company designed special shirts for its salesmen.) The radio was an immediate hit in Japan and, for the first time, the firm was able to establish a market in the United States, a major turning point in the fortunes of the company. Morita considered offers from an American firm to market Sony's products in the United States under an American brand name. It was tempting for the still tiny firm to rely on a large American firm with superior marketing and advertising experience, but Morita rejected the offer, calculating that it was time for Sony to establish its own name abroad no matter how great the obstacles might be.

It took a decade for the American operation to become profitable, but by the end of the 1960s, Sony had expanded from radios and tape recorders into television by countering American manufacturers' trend toward bigger screens with five- and seven-inch models. In 1969, after only a decade of experience in international markets, Sony could boast sales of a million micro-television receivers. In the same year, the American Apollo mission carrying the first men to the moon also carried Sony tape recorders. Twenty years later, of the best-known brand names in the world, Sony ranked third (after Coca Cola and IBM).

THE CREATIVITY QUESTION

Leo Esaki's career has raised questions about creativity in the social environment of his native country, and the Japanese Nobel Prize winner has fueled the discussion. In contrast to America's individualist ethos, Esaki writes that "Japanese are brought up to believe that the group is the secret of their country's economic strength and that the success story of Japan is the result of individual self-sacrifice." Noting that Japanese Nobel Prize winners number only one percent of the total,[6] Esaki writes that the lack of scholars of world stature "illustrates the difficulty of producing creative personalities in a society that is strongly group-oriented. We have batters who can hit but few who can hit a home run." While there are large numbers of competent scientists, there are few geniuses due to the cultural pressures for conformity and a stifling seniority system that equates age with wisdom, Esaki says. His own experience seems to verify his assertions. He made a permanent move from Japan to the United States in 1960 to join the Watson Laboratories of IBM. At the time he received his Nobel Prize, a Japanese paper lamented his foreign residence: "We suffer a brain-drain, not for any lack of funds, equipment or high standards in individual fields, but for a system that holds down adventurous spirits."

The "they-can-copy-but-can-they-create?" question surfaced again in 1987 when news came from Sweden that Tonegawa Susumu had won Japan's first Nobel Prize in medicine. The initial pride in the Japanese news coverage quickly gave way to sober reflection when it was realized that Dr. Tonegawa had not done any research in Japan in twenty-four years. In 1963, he left to do research in the United States and Switzerland and, at the time of his award, was pursuing work in molecular biology at the Massachusetts Institute of Technology. "Had I stayed at a Japanese university," he told the press, "I may not have been able to do this kind of work." To do original work in Japan, talented scientists, especially young ones—Tonegawa was twenty-four when he left—"have no choice but to get out of Japan." While that statement exaggerates the problem, many Japanese scholars were quick to express their agreement. An economist just back from a trip to the United States, wrote that, in Japan,

> . . . the social ideal is the hard-working, low-keyed craftsman. To maintain group harmony, we are encouraged to downplay individualism. Society frowns on people who stand out from the crowd. Boat-rockers are shunned for disrupting the status quo. In the United States . . . self-expression is highly valued. For better or for worse, Americans are aggressive. They believe you must make yourself heard to be appreciated. Quiet, self-effacing Japanese researchers cut a poor figure in U.S. research labs.

CHIPPING AWAY

If consumer electronics may be thought of as the less-sophisticated end of the high-technology industrial spectrum, semiconductor memory chips would be at the more-sophisticated end. These fingernail-size wafers which process vast bits of information extremely rapidly are required for modern prod-

---

[6] The Japanese performance in Nobel prizes for science is better—though far from exemplary. Even allowing for the "Stockholm is a long way from Tokyo" defense, Japan's five science awards pale when compared to Britain's 77 or America's 140 (as of 1988).

ucts ranging from washing machines to laser weapons. Here too, is a repetition of some of the themes just explored. The initial impetus of the memory chip came from the invention of the integrated circuit which channels electron flows used to process information. The integrated circuit was invented in 1959 by two Americans working for private companies. Through the 1960s and 1970s, the United States dominated the world market for the design, manufacture, and export of the microchips that were at the heart of the global electronic revolution. However, just as steel and autos yielded to Japanese pressure in earlier decades, the semiconductor industry was giving way.

In the manufacture of the 64K RAM chips, where competition was keenest, the United States controlled the lion's share of the world market. In a thirteen-year period, however, that changed. By 1986, four of the main U.S. makers were out of business, Japan's NEC (Nippon Electric Corporation) had overtaken IBM as the world's largest producer of microchips, and Japan had 65 percent of the world market for all memory products. The U.S. share of the world market had dwindled to under 30 percent. Successive years saw the gap between Japan and the United States widen.

The American lead in technology could no longer be taken for granted. In another industry which American know-how had launched, an American lead had dissolved. Making this trend the more alarming was the close link between semiconductors, computers, and national defense. Already, in the early 1980s the Pentagon's respect for Japanese technology was evident in its reliance on Japan for 40 percent of its microchip requirements. In the 1990–1991 Gulf War, American reliance on other fields of Japanese high-tech endeavor was revealed. Optical elements of precision-guidance systems used in that war and composite materials used to make high-speed aircraft were increasingly being supplied from Japan. Semiconductor chips inside the vaunted Patriot missile, and most other American "smart weapons," were housed in ceramic packaging which was produced almost exclusively by the Kyoto Ceramics Company (known as Kyocera).

How did it all happen? Some give major attention to the role of MITI. Again, as in the case of steel, direct subsidies from MITI or other government agencies were probably not important, though tax incentives were a factor. More importantly, MITI created a "favorable environment." "Private capital cannot undertake investment if there is too much risk. MITI gave us the confidence," one Japanese company executive explained. During the 1960s, and well on into the 1970s, MITI saw to it that potential U.S. competitors such as IBM and Texas Instruments were either denied or restricted in their applications to manufacture and sell products in Japan. MITI's "Very Large Scale Integration" program, launched in 1976, targeted the 64K memory chip as a high priority and organized the industry to master the technology with the results seen above.

The quality factor cannot be discounted. Japan's infant microchip industries were protected but not coddled; they had to perform and they did. The giant American electronics firm Hewlett Packard unnerved the semiconductor industry when it revealed in 1979 that chips it imported from its Japanese suppliers had a defect rate one-tenth that of American-made chips. Similarly, at about the same time, American business was shaken to learn that the rate of defects dropped from an astonishing 150 to 180 per 100 sets (more than one and a half defects per television) to the three to four range after a Motorola plant had been taken over by the Japanese.

The Kyocera story illustrates. The firm has a short history in a country where corporate giants like Mitsui can trace their firm's histories back to the early Tokugawa era: Inamori Kazuo founded Kyocera in 1961. By all odds, he should not have succeeded. He was only twenty-three, had no personal fortune, and had no ties to the "old-boy" network. He attended a "lunch box" college[7] rather than one of the right universities—normally a fatal mistake in Japan. However, he made himself an expert on the properties of industrial ceramics which are resistant to heat, do not corrode, and are excellent insulators. His passion for work earned for him the nickname "Mr. A.M." because it was said that he never left the job before 3:00 A.M. and slept in his office during Kyocera's early years. A trip to Dallas in 1963 gave the fledgling company its first break: Texas Instruments gave him a large trial order.

Inamori knew that his main competition was a German firm with an established reputation, but he recalls that he was certain that the president of the German firm was not in front of his kilns twenty hours a day. Inamori was. "We got the contract," he said, "because we were good at mixing and baking, because the top people in the company were in front of the kilns all the time, and they could control the variances and keep the quality consistent, which is very hard in ceramics," Inamori told author David Halberstam. Kyocera won the competition and became the supplier for semiconductor ceramic packages to Texas Instruments, Fairchild, and other U.S. semiconductor companies. In the space of another twenty-five years, Kyocera came to control 90 percent of the world market for ceramic semiconductor packages. To U.S. Commerce Department trade negotiator Clyde V. Prestowitz, Jr., Inamori later confided that breaking into the U.S. market had been easier than cracking the Japanese market. "It was," he said, "one of the most important factors in the success of his company." Sony's Morita confirmed that his "outsider" company, lacking connections to the mainline giants of the economic establishment, also had the same experience: The U.S. market had been easier to penetrate than Japan's. The plight of Kyocera and Sony, finding it more difficult to compete on their home ground than abroad, adds weight to the allegations of American businessmen who complain of the roadblocks thrown in their path as they sought to market products and services in the affluent Japan of recent decades. The question of reciprocity in trade relations, of the "level playing field," is the subject of the following chapter.

---

[7] The lunch-box college in Japanese is *eki-ben daigaku. Ekiben* are small box lunches sold at train stations—not all stations but only in those where express trains stop for the moment or two passengers need to grab an *ekiben. Ekiben daigaku* refer to the numerous colleges *(daigaku)* which mushroomed throughout Japan in the immediate postwar period. They are so numerous, the saying has it, that you will find them in any town big enough to warrant an express train stop.

BESUBORU V

Japan's postwar pro teams, divided since 1950 into Central and Pacific leagues of six clubs each, are known by English names spelled out in Roman letters on the uniforms. Most of the teams are animalized—as the Tigers, Lions, and Buffaloes, for example, with a few like the Carp and Dragons adding a dash of soy sauce. Teams such as the Seibu Lions from Tokyo are associated with cities but are actually owned by corporations that generally think of their teams as promotional assets rather than profit-making ventures. The Lions belong to the Seibu railroad-and-hotel conglomerate. The Hiroshima Carp are owned by Mazda, which, as we have seen, has its headquarters in that city.

In his book, *You Gotta Have* Wa, a fascinating study that illuminates not only baseball but Japanese spirit and character as well, Robert Whiting discusses some of the features that distinguish Japanese baseball from the American sport. The *wa* in the title refers to the Confucian notion of social harmony or team spirit and it means that grandstanding is out. The slugger who wins the game with a grand-slam home run in the bottom of the ninth still insists that the victory is *okagesama-de*—in other words, thanks to the team and thanks to the paramilitary rooting sections. These highly disciplined support groups chant, not just at crucial moments but for most of the match, in synch. Batters bow to the umpires. Teams bow to each other after the game. Tie games are commonplace, and even welcome, because neither side loses face. The games generally last much longer in Japan than in the United States. This is mainly because of prolonged staring contests during which pitcher and batter face off to take the full measure of each other's psyches—in the manner of sumo wrestlers or samurai engaging in *hara-gei*.

Batters are not supposed to let themselves get hit by inside pitches; those who do are expected to show their cool by jumping up and letting the pitcher know they are okay, with a smile. In recent years, however, a disturbing American influence has crept into *besuboru*—beaned batters are now more likely to charge the mound in search of a brawl. Or, in an Eastern variation, attempt a flying kung-fu leg-kick on the offending pitcher. Unlike American fans who will happily wrestle each other to see who keeps a foul ball hit into the stands, Japanese spectators hand them over to stadium attendants.

A postwar innovation in the Japanese sport has been the addition of foreign, often American, players to the teams—two per team are allowed. Usually chosen for their power at the plate, the Americans have performed well on the field. Far more than their small numbers would suggest, they have won the coveted annual "triple crown," and in November 1989, an American was selected as the most valuable player in each of the leagues.

However, the inter-ethnic tensions in Japanese baseball reprise some of those we have seen in economic relationships. Americans are likely to say that the Japanese work too hard, wear themselves out, and use unfair methods. American expatriate players say, for example, that they are prevented from taking a crack at the most prestigious of national records, the single-season tally of 55 home runs achieved by Oh Sadamaru, "Japan's Babe Ruth." (In a recent poll asking fifteen thousand college students whom they admired most in the world, Oh scored No. 3 after Mom and Dad.) The *gaijin* players grouse that pitchers give intentional walks to American batters when they get close to Oh's almost-sacred record. They object to umpires who condone, as a *gaijin* newsman complained, "a strike zone you could drive a Datsun through."

In turn, Japanese are prone to charge that the Americans are lazy whiners, and that they destroy the *wa* spirit by trying to escape team rules—no long hair, mustaches, or beards in some clubs. Perhaps the most commonly heard grievance is that the *gaijin* are only in the game for the money and that huge salaries (some over $1 million annually) demoralize the rest of the team who get by with much smaller pay. They also say that Americans grumble about having to run ten miles and practice for eight hours on game days and demand to be exempted from such agonizing regimens as the "1000-ground-ball drill."

ADDITIONAL READING

Authors who have stressed cultural factors as the explanation for Japan's economic miracle include: Ezra Vogel, *Japan as Number 1: Lessons for America* (1979); Ezra Vogel, ed., *Modern Japanese Organization and Decision Making* (1975); James C. Abegglen, *Management and Worker: The Japanese Solution* (1973) and his more recent *Kaisha: The Japanese Corporation* (1985); William G. Ouchi, *Theory Z: How American Business Can Meet the Japanese Challenge* (1981); Morishima Michio, *Why Has Japan Succeeded: Western Technology and the Japanese Ethos* (1982); and Frank Gibney, *Japan: The Fragile Super Power* (1975) and his more recent *Miracle By Design* (1982).

W. Mark Fruin, *Kikkoman: Company, Clan, and Community* (1983) is highly regarded as a model of the case-study method in business history. Michael A. Cusumano discusses two Japanese automotive giants in *The Japanese Automobile Industry: Technology and Management at Nissan and Toyota* (1985) and David Halberstam compares Ford and Nissan in *The Reckoning* (1985). Halberstam's *The Next Century* (1991) is also valuable. Any and all of Ronald Dore's many studies are rich in insights, but *Taking Japan Seriously: A Confucian Perspective on Leading Economic Issues* (1987); *Flexible Rigidities: Industrial Policy and Structural Adjustment in the Japanese Economy, 1970–1980* (1986); and *British Factory–Japanese Factory* (1973) are particularly relevant to this chapter.

Other valuable studies of Japanese business methods include: Thomas P. Rohlen, *For Harmony and Strength: Japanese White-Collar Organization in Anthropological Perspective* (1974); Sato Kazuo and Hoshino Yasuo, eds., *The Anatomy of Japanese Business* (1984); and John Bennet and Ishino Iwao, *Paternalism in the Japanese Economy* (1963).

Two massive collections of essays survey nearly every aspect of recent scholarship concerning the Japanese economy and its international economic relations: Kozo Yamamura and Yasukichi Yasuba, eds., *The Political Economy of Japan: The Domestic Transformation* (1987) and Takashi Inoguchi and Daniel I. Okimoto, eds., *The Political Economy of Japan: The Changing International Context* (1988).

Finally, most of the books recommended as additional reading for Chapter 11 may also be consulted.

11

"DRIFTING APART?"

In the years since the end of World War II, the American image of the Japanese, as seen in popular writing and on the Hollywood screen, reversed the unflattering portrayals of earlier times. While sometimes leaning too far in the direction of maudlin sentimentality, best-sellers like James Michener's *Sayonara* (1954), Oliver Statler's *Japanese Inn* (1961), and James Clavell's *Shogun* (1975) presented portrayals of both contemporary and historical Japanese as honorable and appealing personalities. The appearance in 1992 of *Rising Sun*, by the successful thriller writer Michael Crichton, represents a jarring change. Crichton's book was noteworthy for the explosive critical attention it received, most of which was directed not at the subject of the book—a murder mystery with ample sex and violence—but the background against which the book is set: American-Japanese trade tension. "We are definitely at war with Japan," says the fictional Los Angeles detective John Connor who speaks Japanese, knows his way around sushi bars, and, although he is shown to have a grudging admiration for the Japanese, lectures the reader throughout on the difficulty of doing business with them.

In a singular departure from the mystery genre format, Crichton underscores the true-life purpose of his novel after concluding the final pages of his fictional story. The "back matter" of the book is introduced by a quotation from Sony's Morita Akio: "If you don't want Japan to buy it, don't sell it." In Crichton's "Afterword," he writes that the Japanese have "invented a new kind of trade—adversarial trade, trade like war, trade intended to wipe out the competition—which America has failed to understand for decades." Perhaps the most unusual feature of this murder mystery is an appended bibliography presenting several dozen scholarly sources whose opinions Crichton drew upon to form his judgments about Japan's "economic behavior." The list is eminently respectable, a testimony to the author's inquiring mind. Yet, what Crichton extracts is a portrait of a vile people, a one-sided polemic, a lawyer's brief for a "Yellow Peril" reborn.

Rising Sun may represent only a momentary departure from the generally positive Japanese images of recent decades or it may signal a return to the caricatures of treachery and insidious evil of earlier eras. The *Rising Sun*'s fictional "Nakamoto Corporation," we learn, "presents an impenetrable mask to the rest of the world," a 1990s version of the turn-of-the-century Asian cliché "inscrutable." Crichton portrays the Japanese as manipulative businessmen-gangsters who are destroying American industries and infiltrating American political and cultural institutions: "They *own* the government," says a policeman. "Shit! we're *giving* this country away," he adds in a crude expression of frustration which reprises the themes of political economists Pat Choate's 1990 study, *Agents of Influence: How Japan's Lobbyists in the United States Manipulate America's Political and Economic System.* As the subtitle of Choate's book reveals, it is an examination of the way in which well-paid American lawyers and lobbyists peddle influence on behalf of corporate Japan. The names of a flurry of other books appearing in the past few years similarly conjure up a Japan bent upon economic domination of America. A few representatives titles include: *Yen! Japan's New Financial Empire and Its Threat to America; The Coming War With Japan;* and *Zaibatsu America: How Japanese Firms Are Colonizing Vital U.S. Industries.*

FREE TRADE THEORY

To analyze in a systematic fashion the acrimony and the debate surrounding U.S.-Japan "trade friction," it is useful to commence with a look at some theoretical underpinnings of international trade theory.

The place to begin is *The Wealth of Nations*, a book written at the time of the American Revolution by a Scotsman, Adam Smith, sometimes described as the first philosopher of economics. Smith pondered some fundamental questions about freedom and order. As an individualist attracted to freedom, he wondered if individuals following their own self-interests, often motivated by the purest of greed, might produce a desirable social order and human progress. Smith saw all of us as *homo economicus*, economic men, and that if left alone, free from government interference, we would usually make rational cost–benefit decisions, always seeking to maximize gain and reduce loss. "It is not from the benevolence of the butcher, the brewer and the banker, that we expect our dinner, but from their regard to their own interest," Smith wrote. In that way, a system of efficient, constantly self-adjusting production and exchange would evolve, transforming sellers' private greed into social good—as if by an "invisible hand," he said, coining perhaps the most durable metaphor in economic history.

Although the word *capitalism* was introduced some years after Smith's death, he was the first to present a systematic exposition of its most important principles including that of *laissez-faire* ("permit to act," but loosely more like "government hands off"). Citizens should rely on their government for national security, law and order, protection of the weakest, and for providing what is now commonly called "infrastructure" but little else. Smith saw government as incapable of making the same sensible decisions as those made in the free marketplace by *homo economicus*. Government decisions were more likely to represent "special interest groups" (to use the contemporary term). By minimizing government interference and maximizing competition, the invisible hand of free-market forces could work its wonders, could increase the "wealth of nations."

Smith's *laissez-faire* principles, refined by disciples like David Ricardo, applied just as well to the world of international trade. In his discussion of foreign trade, Ricardo spoke of the "comparative advantage" nations had in production of various goods. Trade is expanded and wealth is increased, he said, when nations stick to businesses where they have "natural" advantages. Clearly Scotland possessed a comparative advantage in growing rye, Peru in growing bananas, he noted. It would not make sense for Scottsmen to try to grow their own bananas. Again, the workings of the free marketplace would automatically steer demand to the world's most efficient suppliers. Any effort to restrict or protect a nation's commerce would only produce short-term benefits for inefficient groups at the expense of the general consuming public forced to pay higher prices for imports. The "classical" philosophers like Smith and Ricardo were especially irate at the entrenched power of reactionary landed interests who controlled Britain through Parliament. "Free trade" became their rallying cry. If British agriculture could not swim without protection in the form of tariffs, then it should be allowed to sink, the classicists insisted. True believers in free trade do not even ask whether there is a "level playing field," or whether trading partners act fairly. If Nation A wishes to exploit itself, work for slave wages to sell nicely made jeans to Nation B for $10 when they cost Nation B $30 to make, why should Nation B object? Nation B's consumers will be pleased with the deal. The $20 which is saved can then be invested in industries where Nation B has its best advantage.

To economists in the tradition of Smith and Ricardo, protectionism—trying to preserve the obviously uncompetitive jeans industry—is viewed "as the economic equivalent of steroids—giving a specific local fillip while weakening the nation's economic fiber in the long run by misallocating scarce resources and featherbedding inefficiency," one economist has recently put it. While Smith and Ricardo are now thought of as conservatives, they were latter-day "consumer advocates," radical in their condemnation of the rural gentry who profited at the expense of the general public. Free-trade advocates continue to see themselves as defenders of the consumer. Who suffered, they ask, when Washington, at the behest of the auto industry and unions, pressured Japan to establish its voluntary restraint quotas on auto exports to the United States? Obviously, the consumer. Their statistical assessment goes like this: The quota, by restraining competition, raised the price of a car by about $1000. True, the quota saved 26,200 jobs in the American auto industry. That figures out to a per-consumer cost of $160,000 for each job that was rescued. That was $160,000 those consumers couldn't spend elsewhere or save. "Can anyone doubt that sucking $160,000 out of the rest of the economy destroyed more than one job?" the free-trade economist asks. By one calculation, the cost to consumers of the quota placed on automobiles in 1980 alone was $5 billion.

The United States has not always been a staunch defender of free trade. In the early days of the Republic, Alexander Hamilton championed protectionist measures to launch and nurture "infant" industries in this predominantly rural land where few factories existed. In 1930, as we have seen, the Hoover administration enacted the Smoot–Hawley tariff to ease the effects of the Great Depression. The result was the opposite: Within two years, twenty-five governments around the world, including Japan, had retaliated with their own steep tariffs and quotas. As U.S. exports shrivelled, unemployment expanded. As the fabric of international commerce unraveled, the worldwide depression deepened. Free-trade political economists would argue that all of this in turn caused the decline of democracy throughout the world and sowed the seeds of World War II. The Smoot-Hawley tariff, by shutting out Japanese imports, gave ammunition to Japanese militarists who argued that Japan could prosper only through territorial conquest.

In part at least, just because of the disastrous legacy of the Smoot–Hawley tariff, a belief in free trade became a major foundation stone of America's postwar international posture and a central tenet of the global economic order. Nations wishing to receive aid from the United States through organizations like the World Bank were called upon to open their economies to free competition. In 1948, when the United States controlled about half the economic activity in the world and was capable of swamping the world with its productive and trade surpluses, it launched the Marshall Plan to counterattack the despair and disintegration of Western Europe. With U.S. assistance, Europe would rebuild its factories so that they could produce goods which would be sold to each other and to the United States whose markets were deliberately kept open. The plan worked, Western Europe was revived, and the larger strategic purpose of the Marshall Plan—to preserve democratic institutions in the countries of Western Europe and enable them to become strong enough to hold off aggression and subversion—was accomplished. Far from bankrupting the United States, as critics had predicted, the plan helped to steer America into a period of unparalleled prosperity.

Japan did not receive Marshall Plan aid but did enjoy the benefits of the open American market. Company loyalty, hard work, quality control, frugality, and entrepreneurial talents were essential to the creation of the economic miracle in Japan. Nevertheless, these assets would have meant little if America had built barriers to the introduction of Japan's textiles, then cameras, then steel and automobiles. As journalist Murray Sayle has pointed out, even George Meany, United Auto Workers' president in the 1950s, fought to get Japanese cars into the American market against the opposition of his own union. Meany, like many labor union leaders, was hardly a true-believer in the Adam Smith credo. "Free trade," Meany once said, "is a joke and a myth, and a government policy dedicated to 'free trade' is more than a joke—it is a prescription for disaster." However, Cold War geopolitical considerations weighed heavily in American thinking in those days and Meany knew that only exports, jobs, and improved living standards would save Japan from communism, and so keep that pivotal and unpredictable country loyal to the free world. This was clearly a "one-sided arrangement," Sayle observes, and in time, certainly by the 1970s, the costly Cold War maneuvers to build Japan into a prosperous ally had outlived their purpose. It was time to demand of Japan strict adherence to free trade principles, many were saying. On the other hand, many American observers of Japan are satisfied that Japan, while not a model of free-trade openness, has made satisfactory progress in that direction.

DEFENDING JAPAN

Japan tries to play fair, its supporters say. The tariff rates Japan imposes on imports are among the lowest in the developed world. The tedious inspection and modification requirements that in past years kept U.S. goods sitting on the docks in Yokohama have been at least partially relaxed. If Japan in the past was inhospitable to American business, that no longer remains true, they hold. Japan is host to hundreds of U.S. firms that have captured profitable—even major—shares of its markets. In a recent year, for example, Schick razor blades controlled 70 percent of the safety-blade market and Coca-Cola is perennially No. 1 in the soft-drink market and earns more from its sales in Japan than it does from sales in the United States. Some big-city street intersections support two or three McDonalds, Domino's Pizzas, Kentucky Fried Chickens, Dunkin' Donuts, and Haagen Daaz ice cream stores. Direct marketing companies like Amway and Tupperware do not go door-to-door in Japan but flourish by working through networks of family and friends. Kodak, Ritz crackers, M & Ms, Band Aids, Nike, Levi's, Pampers, and Max Factor are all household names in Japan. Nor is it only consumer products that are marketable in Japan. IBM, the biggest U. S. business in Japan, posted sales of $9.3 billion in one recent year. Other companies with sales of a half-billion dollars or more in the same year included Caltex, Exxon, Motorola, Caterpillar, Texas Instruments, General Electric, and Hewlett-Packard. While the United States has complaints about restrictions on U.S. farm foods, the fact is that Japan is the biggest consumer of U.S. farm products including corn and soybeans.

American firms would achieve an even greater penetration of the Japanese market, some say, if they made greater efforts. It takes a long time for Americans to learn how to overcome cultural barriers and master Japanese ways of doing business. American businesses are frequently criticized for having a too-short profit horizon. How many American businessmen in Japan take the trouble to learn Japanese? Whatever the number, it is miniscule compared to the thousands of Japanese businessmen stationed in this country who have made themselves fluent in English. Why, the most frequently asked question goes, did Detroit never design a right-hand-drive car for the Japanese consumer if it was serious about breaking into that market? Could Japan have made inroads into the U.S. auto market without accommodating American drivers' preferences?

American Shortcomings

If America wishes to understand the loss of its competitive edge, it needs to pay attention to its own shortcomings, argue many Japanese as well as American observers. Polls in Japan reveal that a majority of Japanese believe that Americans grouse about trade problems primarily of their own making. A string of uncomplimentary adjectives comes to the mind of many Japanese when they think of Americans: lazy, irresponsible, hedonistic, besieged by drugs and alcohol addiction, and riven by racial tensions. With the exception of amphetamine stimulants to which many tired Japanese businessmen are addicted, Japan has no serious drug problem. Japanese often resent Americans for losing their edge and then demanding of them that they give up the fruits of their own hard work, frugality, and disciplined approach to life. Americans join in: "We lazy spendthrifts (with a savings rate among the lowest in the developed world, and a trade deficit to prove it) have no business telling the Japanese to consume more, save less, and take some time to smell the cherry blossoms," the *New Republic* recently editorialized. American chief executive officers (CEOs), they say, insist on outrageously high income packages—often during times when their company earnings are dipping and while exhorting employees to make painful concessions in the name of improved competitiveness. *Business Week*, scarcely known as a hostile judge of big business, noted in a 1991 analysis of executive pay the example of an auto manufacturer "awash in red ink and fighting for survival" and yet paying its CEO nearly $5 million during the previous year. The magazine estimated that CEO compensation jumped by 212 percent in the 1980s while the average factory worker saw his pay increase by just 53 percent. The CEO in one well-known firm received in a single day what the company's average employee received for an entire year's work, *Business Week* commented.

Making comparisons between income levels of CEOs in American versus Japanese firms is complicated by varying systems of perks, subsidies, expense accounts, bonuses, and so on. For example, the management staff in Japanese firms are often provided with golf-club memberships which can cost a half million dollars or more. Still, there are striking differences in executive compensation in the two countries. One recent estimate was that the average chief executive of a major corporation in the United States made eighty-five times the pay of a typical American factory worker. (Management expert Peter Drucker states that a ratio of twenty to one is about right.) In Japan, by contrast, the boss receives only seventeen times the pay of an ordinary worker. The gap between CEO pay and upper and middle management in America is so high as to produce alienation at even those levels, turning colleagues into adversaries it has been said. In Japan, annual salary packages of the largest, "world-class" company CEOs rarely rise above the half-million dollar mark and bonuses which can boost pay from 20 to 30 percent of the salary are invariably tied to company performance and typically are given to all of the company's regular employees. Japanese executives are baffled to hear of their American counterparts voting themselves generous compensation packages while workers are dismissed or asked to tighten their belts. In times of trouble, Japanese corporate leaders are liable to take the largest cuts in wages. Japanese businessmen often ask why their American counterparts cannot see that the prevailing level of corporate greed in America is bound to affect morale and reduce productivity in the workplace. It is a fair question.

American workers, detractors say, have lost the pride of workmanship and scarcely know the meaning of corporate devotion. Absenteeism in American factories—especially on Mondays—is almost legendary. Absenteeism is not a significant problem in Japanese factories. American industry loses far more workdays to strikes than Japan. Can there be any doubt that the success of the Japanese auto industry owes something to the fact that it has not experienced a strike since 1955? Furthermore, the "strikes" and work slowdowns which do occur in Japanese factories are often more ritualistic than substantive. Humorist Art Buchwald's description of a visit to a Japanese television plant catches the flavor of a typical factory demonstration:

> "What is the significance of the red headband?" my friend asked the manager who was showing him around.
> "The workers are on strike and that is their way of telling us."
> "But if they are on strike, why are they working?"
> The manager seemed amazed at the question. "If they didn't work they wouldn't get paid, and we would lose production. This would never do."
> "So instead of going out they wear their red headbands?"
> "Yes. That's to let us know they are unhappy. Naturally we are very disturbed that they are unhappy, so we try to negotiate the grievances."
> "Is the red band the only way you know they're unhappy?"
> The manager answered, "No, they show their discontent in many ways. For example, when they're on strike they come to work 15 minutes early and they stand in the courtyard and sing songs telling of their unhappiness with the management."
> "Do they sabotage the TV sets they're assembling?"
> The manager was aghast. "That would not be an honorable thing to do. As a matter of fact, they work even harder and with more proficiency to show how unhappy they are. The better they perform, the more unhappy we in management become and the more eager we are to reach a settlement."

> "Alfred Sloan once boasted that General Motors continued to pay dividends to stockholders right through the depression even though it had to lay off workers. A Japanese business leader would never say such a thing and, if he did anything remotely resembling it, he would try to hide it, for valuing profits above his employees would destroy his relationship with his workers. The primary commitment of a Japanese firm is not to its stockholders but to its employees."
>
> —Ezra Vogel, *Japan as No. 1.*

LIFETIME EMPLOYMENT

Japan's vaunted "lifetime employment" system, an important feature in that country's economic scene, is not always correctly understood in the West. It does not mean that *all* Japanese workers are guaranteed jobs for life. Those outside the system are quite vulnerable to dismissals during economic downturns. However, the one-third of the workforce who *are* career employees tend to be concentrated in the large, cutting-edge export industries that have driven the economy in recent decades. For these employees, lifetime employment means reciprocal obligations: Workers owe loyalty to the company and the company owes the workers a job for "lifetime," or more correctly until retirement at a rather early age.

Young men—and it is mainly men we are talking about here since women are not expected to pursue lifetime business careers—join a company, typically after graduation from college, with the expectation of staying with the firm until retirement in their late fifties or early sixties. Since the company knows that it will have the service of its employees for their entire careers, it thinks nothing of devoting years to extensive worker-training programs. The training programs, in turn, ensure superb quality work in the future. Workers become married to their companies in ways which Americans can only faintly comprehend. Wearing the company lapel pin, singing the company song, participating in company calisthenics before work in the morning, working late without compensation, spending after-work hours on company-related entertainment, joining in company sports rallies, welcoming the boss' mediation in marriage, living in company-subsidized housing, dying with company-subsidized funerals—these are some of the commonplace habits and expectations of lifetime employees.

It might surprise Americans, however, to discover how egalitarian the workplace appears in Japan. Senior managers wear the same uniforms as shop-floor workers. Top corporate officers are *not* usually isolated in plush-carpeted suites insulated by secretaries in outer offices. Factories and offices tend to have single restaurants and coffee shops with very little segregation by rank. The very arrangement of desks within an office (in small infacing clusters) serves to underscore the sense of working in a group—office personnel are never oriented so that members of a section are looking at the backs of others in the same group. Even the reciprocal pouring of drinks, a staple of after-hour, office-group socializing, is an expression of the egalitarian spirit designed to get everyone loosened up and communicating freely. "The gesture of filling another's glass is a convenient bridge across strained relationships. No one is forgotten. No one need pour his own drink," writes anthropologist Thomas Rohlen in a study based on his field work in a Japanese bank.

In contrast, Chrysler's Lee Iacocca, a frequent critic of Japan's trade practices, claimed not long ago that his company's "youth committee" got carried away with programs they practiced at Honda. "They wanted us [executives] to eat in the cafeteria and go through the rain to the parking lot like everybody else. We don't go for that," the Chrysler chief said.

In return for loyalty and the worker's complete identification with his company, the firm assures job security to its workers. Even if the company disbands or is absorbed by another, the worker knows that, barring a catastrophic turn of events, a job will be arranged for him. This kind of career job security, then, gives a kind of solidarity of purpose to the workplace that is not easy to find in America or in any Western country. Workers associate the company's well-being with their own personal security and well-being to a degree uncommon in other countries. It is no exaggeration to say that Japanese workers find their identity in the workplace.

No one need agree that all of this solidarity is transferable to America, or even that it is unqualifiedly healthy. The workaholic phenomenon in Japan sometimes approaches dehumanizing levels. At its extremes, it can be fatal. *Karoshi*— death from overwork—entered the Japanese vocabulary in 1981 to describe the plight of office workers addicted to punishingly long hours. Although the government does not recognize *karoshi* (for purposes of survivor benefit claims for example), worker advocates document a growing incidence of this "sudden-death syndrome." A few years ago, when the Labor Ministry encouraged corporations to eliminate half-day Saturday work, the result was that many employees compensated for the lost time by working extra hours on the Monday–Friday schedule. Whether voluntarily or as a result of group pressure, Japanese *sara-riman* (white-collar workers) take only half of their paid vacations. How many American fathers are willing to be deprived of seeing their children grow up? Japan has nearly become, in the words of psychiatrist Doi Takeo, a "fatherless society." Because of the long workday, or the quite common business custom of *tanshin funin*—a company transfer where the family is left behind—children see little of their fathers. A recent government report concludes that Japanese children "tend to consult with friends when they need advice." All Japanese households risk becoming de facto single-parent families.

Americans may have little interest in transplanting the extreme corporate loyalty of Japan to the American scene, but it is imperative to understand that it has worked for the Japanese. If "workaholism" is dehumanizing, so is unemployment and Japanese unemployment rates in recent decades have stayed in the one to two percent range, far under America's.

EDUCATION

No nation with a twenty-five to thirty percent national high-school dropout rate has a serious chance to compete with Japan where the comparable rate is around three percent. America remains attached to the 180-day school year, while Japanese youngsters spend 243 days in school. A Japanese child has received four more years of schooling by the time he or she leaves high school. The intensity of the educational experience is almost beyond comprehension for most American students. Almost half of Japanese students receive tutoring or attend special after-class academies *(juku)* following a school day which is already longer than the American day. Japanese are the first to concede that their educational system, especially at the college level, leaves much to be desired. Many Japanese educators deplore the emphasis on conformity and rote memory that dominates the Japanese classroom; conversely, they admire the questioning spirit of open inquiry in American schools.

But the Japanese system is magnificent at teaching the basics. "In many respects," writes anthropologist Thomas Rohlen, "the upper half of Japan's graduating high-school students possess a level of knowledge and the analytic skills equivalent to the average American graduating from college." Little wonder that Japanese firms opening factories in the United States are dismayed to find that they have to hire college graduates to find skill levels that would be expected from Japanese high-school graduates. Japanese youngsters routinely place first while U.S. children end up near the bottom in international mathematics and science exams. At least one-half of Japanese high-school students can perform mathematics that a mere five percent of U.S. students can. Science and math are the fuel that drives a nation's competitiveness, and yet very few American states require the three years of math, and even fewer states require the three years of science—or the six years of a foreign language—which are found in the Japanese system. Throughout the entire Japanese school system this sharp focus on basics and high standards is mandated by the *Mombusho* (Ministry of Education) in Tokyo. Americans passionately debate questions concerning uniform national standards in education. In Japan, the subject is a non-issue.

NERDS AND GEEKS VERSUS THE *"GAMBATTE!"*
(HANG IN THERE!) SPIRIT

"[In the United States] children who prefer to read books rather than play football, prefer to build model airplanes rather than get wasted at parties with their classmates, become social outcasts. Ostracized for their intelligence and refusal to conform to society's anti-intellectual values, many are deprived of a chance to learn adequate social skills and acquire good communication tools.

"Enough is enough.

"Nerds and geeks must stop being ashamed of who they are. . . . In most industrialized nations, not least of all our economic rivals in East Asia, a kid who studies hard is lauded and held up as an example to other students. . . . Until the words 'nerd' and 'geek' become terms of approbation and not derision, we do not stand a chance."

—Leonid Fridman, founding member of Harvard University's
"Society of Nerds and Geeks," 1990.

"After visiting Japanese schools, I saw an issue of *Esquire* proclaiming that America's new watchword should be 'cooling out.' My God! After 'laid back' and 'Miller time,' haven't we had enough of this already? I propose a different phrase, a truly vital import from Japan: '*Gambatte!*'"

—James Fallows, *The Atlantic*, March 1987.

The National Science Foundation declared in 1990 that some sixty thousand math and science teachers in America's secondary schools were not fully qualified to do their jobs. All in all, technical literacy is probably more widely diffused throughout Japanese business than anywhere else in the world. For each million of its population, Japan has five thousand technical workers; the United States has but 3,500. Japan graduates twice as many engineers per capita as the United States does.[1] Hundreds of engineering teaching posts at U.S. colleges go begging. Were it not for foreign students studying on American campuses, the situation would be far more critical: They receive 40 percent of U.S. doctorate degrees in mathematics and 55 percent of those in engineering. For a country trying to regain its technological supremacy, these figures are not encouraging.

Much of America's best young talent, for better or worse, graduates with law degrees. There are 307 lawyers for each one hundred thousand of population in America; the comparable figure for Japan is twelve. A 1992 poll by *Business Week* of executives of leading American corporations revealed that 62 percent of the respondents felt the U.S. civil justice system "significantly hampers the ability of U.S. companies to compete with Japanese and European companies."

THE REVISIONISTS

In recent years, a growing body of literature written by a small but persuasive band of Japan experts has taken the trade debate to a new plane by arguing that in dealing with Japan, conventional free-trade practices simply will not work. Not only does Japan remain radically uncommitted to free-trade principles but it has been so historically predisposed to interference in the marketplace as to be nearly incapable of getting into step with Adam Smith. Anthropologist Ronald Dore traces this trait back to Confucian wellsprings: "They [the Japanese] believe—like all good Confucianists—that you cannot get a decent, moral society, not even an efficient society, simply out of the mechanisms of the market powered by the motivational fuel of self-interest." Elsewhere, Dore expands:

> The Japanese, in spite of what their political leaders say at summit conferences about the glories of free enterprise in the Free World, and in spite of the fact that a British publisher with a new book about Adam Smith can expect to sell half the edition in Japan, have never really caught up with

[1] A recent study by business historian Earl H. Kinmonth contests the widely accepted assumption that Japan has many more engineers than the United States. Kinmonth argues that the term *gijutsusha* which is usually considered to be the Japanese word for "engineer" actually embraces a much wider category than the English-language term does. *Gijutsusha*, for example, includes computer specialists, technicians of many kinds and even some blue-collar workers. When figures are adjusted to reconcile these semantic distinctions "the alleged difference between the U.S. and Japan disappears," Kinmonth states. While arguing that the numerical superiority of the Japanese engineering force is a myth, Kinmonth argues that more attention must be paid to the "qualitative differences in engineers and how they are used in industry." His article ("Japanese Engineers and American Myth Makers," *Pacific Affairs*, Fall 1991) is an apt illustration of the perils in cross-cultural statistical analysis.

Adam Smith. They have never managed actually to bring themselves to *believe* in the invisible hand.

What Dore and others do is to elevate to sophisticated heights the assessments of so-called "Japan bashers" like the chairman of Chrysler Corporation, Lee Iacocca: "Japan is a rigged market. If you don't believe that, you're living on another planet." *Atlantic* editor, James Fallows; Japan scholar, Chalmers Johnson; Dutch journalist and a longtime resident of Japan, Karel van Wolferen; and former U.S. trade negotiator, Clyde V. Prestowitz emerged in the 1980s as "revisionists,"[2] challenging conventional notions that Japan is just like any other capitalist country except that it is more successful because Japanese work harder, save more, and rarely change jobs. The revisionists argue that Japan has developed a different, more effective breed of capitalism—one driven as much by national goals as individual profit. Moreover, the revisionists say, the system works well—for Japan—and there is little reason for outsiders to hope that the Japanese system will evolve into an American-style one. Instead, they write, "If having particular industries, such as supercomputers, is as important to the U.S. as having an aircraft industry has been, then American should take steps to ensure their vitality, rather than badger Japan to abandon its own efforts."

The revisionists contend that the Japanese economy is chronically biased in favor of corporate reinvestment and investment abroad at the expense of the Japanese consumer's living standard. Following Johnson's lead, they argue that Japan is a "capitalist development state," run by "an executive committee" of big business and government bureaucracy which uses a variety of strategies to suppress consumption and channel personal investment with the object of gaining global market share.

How else, revisionists ask, can one explain the baffling enigma of a modern nation of 125 million several decades into its "economic miracle" and yet unconnected to sewers? That remains true of approximately two-thirds of Japanese homes which are serviced by large vehicles which look like fuel trucks to Westerners but regularly pump out the cesspools of individual residences. It is not unheard of for cities with populations of fifty thousand or more to have no municipal sewage system. If Japan had a "consumer-driven economy," if the Japanese leaders were more concerned about meeting the material welfare needs of their people rather than gaining global market share, revisionists argue, investment priorities would be shifted and the shabby infrastucture improved. Japanese planners have responded in the early 1990s with government schemes to allot as much as $3 trillion to infrastructure improvements before the year 2000. For the time being, however, the Japanese still joke that their country "has a first-class economy and a third-class standard of living" (some throw in "a second-class political system" to the mix).

---

[2] The "revisionist" label, as applied here in questions relating to international trade, does not imply any kinship with "revisionists" who have addressed other historical issues such as the dropping of atomic bombs on Japan at the end of the Pacific war.

Further evidence that Japan lacks a consumer-driven economy is the "47th Street Photo" paradox. At that New York discount store (and many others), Japanese cameras and other electronic items invariably sell for less, usually far less, than they do in Tokyo. "If Japan's markets were open to new contenders and to price competition, 47th Street Photo itself could make a fortune by shipping Japanese cameras and audio systems back to Tokyo and selling them there," writes Fallows. Is it possible that Japanese consumers are truly given free-market choices when in one recent year the Korean auto manufacturer Hyundai was able to sell only 150 of its inexpensive cars in Japan? That year was 1988 when many of that small number were sold as "souvenirs" of the Seoul Olympics. In the first quarter of 1989, Hyundai sales in Japan plummeted to seven cars. This was at a time when U.S. customers were buying three hundred thousand of the Korean vehicles (and Canadians were buying almost as many). Are Japanese consumer tastes *that* much different from North America? Peter Drucker, widely respected in Japan for his views on their economy, argues that

---

THE REVISIONISTS ON THE "PRODUCER FIRST" POLICIES

"With enough work, almost anything could be sold in Japan, even American rice or Korean cars. The difference is the natural tendency of the system. The United States, putting the consumer's interest first, naturally buys up whatever offers the best value, unless some lobby or cartel stands in the way. Japan, putting the (Japanese) producer's interest first, naturally resists importing anything but raw materials. Selling to America is like rolling a ball downhill. Selling to Japan is like fighting against guerrillas, or bailing against a siphon, or betting against the house. You can win, but the odds are not on your side."

—James Fallows, Washington editor of the *Atlantic*, 1987.

"When confronted with the evidence that Japanese customers' preferences no more dictate what is on the shelves than they do in Moscow, Japanese spokesmen usually retreat to the argument that foreign salesmen do not try hard enough in Japan. This implies that Japanese salesmen did and do work hard in making their products available to American consumers. This is not true. The people who worked hard in postwar American retailing were the American buyers who went abroad to find low-cost suppliers and spent time in places such as Taiwan, Hong Kong, and Singapore instructing local manufacturers in the patterns and standards they required. In Japan, by contrast, wholesalers and manufacturers use their leverage to prevent their customers from changing to cheaper sources, and they are undeterred by the courts or the so-called antitrust authorities."

—Chalmers Johnson, political scientist at the University of California (San Diego), 1990.

this is an example of Japan's "adversarial trade." Japan does not like to import the kinds of products she exports, especially high-value goods, Drucker insists.

Some Japanese corporate leaders, seeking to ease the trade friction, responded to these western complaints with strong self-criticism. Sony's Morita Akio, for example, recently (1992) told his colleagues in the Japanese business world that the "time has come for a fundamental rethinking." Admitting that Japanese corporations had relentlessly pursued market share through "razor-thin profit margins" which no western company could match, Morita urged Japanese firms to cut work hours and pay their workers and shareholders more. Japan, he said, "must reinvent itself to blend in with the prevailing attitudes and practices of international business."

A few examples of the issues raised by the revisionists will bring the trade friction into sharper focus.

RICE

Rice has been at or near the top of the agenda in trade negotiations between Japan and the United States for at least the past two decades. The government of Japan blocks the importation of almost all rice, a particularly distressing policy for California rice farmers who can grow rice much cheaper than Japanese rice farmers. The reason has nothing to do with the skill or diligence of the Japanese farmer. The yield per acre in Japan compares favorably with other rice-producing countries; but the yield per worker does not. A glance at the size of typical rice farms reveals the reason for the difference in production costs. In California's Central Valley, that farm would run to four or five hundred acres and yet it can be operated by only a small number of people. It can be seeded from the air and the crop rushed to market or port via fast, economical highways. Even British farms are fifty-six times larger than their Japanese counterparts which on the average occupy only 2.9 acres, are often terraced on mountainsides, served by narrow roads, and are tended with meticulous care like a prize garden plot. "I have been farming for 35 years," writes one farmer in a Tokyo newspaper recently, "and it has always taken me at least 320 hours a year to cultivate one acre. In 1985, I visited a rice farm in California run by a Japanese American. His fields require only six hours' labor an acre per year. There's no comparison."

As a result of production inefficiency in Japan, home-grown Japanese rice costs five or six times the world-market price. The government pays the farmer at these artificially high levels, in effect paying approximately half of the farmer's wages. History has been turned upside down. The farmer, who in earlier times was overtaxed to support the growth of a modern industrial sector, is now being fed by that industrial sector (and the consuming public who are part of it). To soften the blow of the higher prices to the consumer, the government also regulates the distribution of rice—at subsidized prices—in designated stores. Because of similar, though not so radical, protectionist arrangements for other agricultural crops, including citrus, melons, and beef, the average

Japanese family spends 30 percent of its income on food, about twice the percentage an American family allocates for its food budget.

This "insistence on devoting so much land to farming, especially rice, is insane," writes *Atlantic* editor James Fallows. It is "as if Manhattan were attempting to grow its own wheat and corn." No other major industrialized country treats its principal foodstuff as a controlled commodity, regulating and protecting it at a cost of several billions of dollars each year. In addition to fueling American charges of protectionism, the Japanese rice policy produces some wild distortions in the costs of land. Japanese economist Kenichi Ohmae relates land selling prices to profitability in California and Japan. He estimates that in California a rice farm is sold for about thirty times its annual profit. Japanese rice land, however, may sell for *two thousand* times its annual profit. As a result, of course, it *doesn't* sell. What family hoping to convert paddy into a homesite or a small business could afford such astronomical prices? With flat-land expansion room so costly, urban populations implode and Japanese are condemned to life in tiny "rabbit-hutch" homes.

How can we understand these distortions? A political explanation is imperative. As explained in Chapter 9, the ruling Liberal Democratic Party, in return for its ongoing patronage of rural interests, wins a consistent base of support from grateful farmers who are well-organized in farm cooperatives. The political strength of the farm lobby becomes all the more important to the ruling LDP by virtue of the overrepresentation of rural areas in the Diet; the postwar urbanization of Japan has not yet been reflected in properly redrawn voting districts.

To grasp the rice issue, however, Japanese insist that cultural factors must be considered, and indeed the Japanese position often seems less guided by economic principle than by cultural rhetoric.

To Japanese, rice is almost synonymous with food—the word *gohan* means both rice and a meal. A poetic name for early Japan was *Mizuho-no-kuni* (Land of Abundant Rice). Though consumption of rice has decreased steadily in recent years—in part because of the popularity of Western-style convenience food—only one in twenty Japanese families does *not* prepare rice every day. There can be few homes without a *denkigama*, an automatic cooker which keeps the rice warm, moist and ready for reheating. Beyond its importance as a staple, however, lies an emotional importance and a symbolic value that is not easy for Americans to fathom. When Akihito ascended to the Chrysanthemum Throne as emperor in 1989 he made a ceremonial offering of rice to the Sun Goddess—as his ancestors had. For reasons not easy to explain, Japanese, who were school children 40 years ago, can become singularly wistful when they recall the lunch-pail that they took to school. Unless the family was in dire straits, it always included a reminder of *hi-no-maru*, the national flag, in the form of a sour red plum placed on a field of snowy white rice.

It helps to remember, as all Japanese over a certain age do, that during and immediately after World War II, rice was a luxury for most and malnutrition or worse was a constant menace. These older people remember foraging for food

TWO JAPANESE VIEWS

"If cheap foreign rice were allowed in, Japanese farmers would be forced out of business, their fields abandoned. Once left fallow, wet-rice paddies cannot be brought back into production. In a few years they are covered with wild vegetation. The soil chemistry changes so that the land can never again be used for growing rice. Proponents of foreign rice want to abolish the so-called food control system under which the government guarantees the purchase of domestically produced rice. This would force Japanese agriculture to become internationally competitive, they argue, because the market would weed out inefficient sectors—by which they mean primarily rice farming. But what will Japan do when supplies of foreign rice dries up? The farmers and fields will not be there anymore because without price supports, Japanese rice farmers simply cannot afford to grow our staple food. Rice farming is a way of life, not just a matter of economic efficiency. Farmers know that if we do not till the soil, it rapidly deteriorates. We own our rice fields, but they are more than personal property. They are also part of a national heritage."

—Yamashita Soichi, farmer and writer, 1986.

"Opponents of liberalization argue that self-sufficiency in rice is essential for national security. If Japan freed rice imports, they claim, it would soon be at the mercy of rice-exporting nations which could cut off supplies at any time. This fear is totally groundless. During the oil crisis of 1973–1974, many pundits predicted that Japan's petroleum supply would dry up. I correctly argued that this would not happen. Oil is a commodity, and producers favor customers who buy large quantities. The same is true of rice. As long as we are willing and able to pay for it, we can be sure of an adequate supply."

—Hasegawa Keitaro, economic analyst, *Tokyo Shimbun*, 1986.

and feel keenly how vulnerable Japan was to food-supply interruptions. They recall the "Nixon shock" *(shokku)*, one feature of which was a U.S. soybean embargo to Japan.[3] Americans may wonder how curtailment of a steady flow of lowly soybeans could arouse national anxiety but it did, if only for a brief time.

---

[3] The "Nixon shock" was actually a series of shocks emanating from Washington in the years 1971–1973. On several matters of high importance in which Japan had interests and views, the Richard Nixon White House, without notifying or consulting Tokyo, made unilateral announcements which left pro-Americans in Japan appearing as distinctly unequal partners. Officials in the Ministry of Foreign Affairs, who prided themselves on being the "caretakers of the alliance," were especially wounded by the affronts. The most serious was the decision in 1971 to reverse U.S. policy toward China and move toward "normalization" of relations by scheduling a visit (in 1972) of President Nixon to open talks with the Communist government in Beijing. The soybean embargo, a relatively minor shock, came in 1973 in response to a crisis caused by El Niño's decimation of North American fishing grounds. American poultry producers wanted a more ample supply of soy beans to be used as a cheap protein substitute for fish meal.

An indispensable part of the breakfast menu for most Japanese is *misoshiro*, soybean soup. Tofu and numerous other dietary staples include soybeans. Only a small fraction of Japan's needs are homegrown; 80 percent of its soybean needs are supplied by the United States. Therefore, when Nixon, the president of a friendly power, without consultation, ordered the embargo to protect American domestic economic interests, the Japanese were "shocked" into a realization of their vulnerability.

Even this sense of dependence and peril does not get at the *mystique* that rice holds for Japanese. James Fallows, who frequently has been quoted as a critic of Japanese trade policies, writes sympathetically on this subject:

> When they think of rice, even today's urbanized Japanese think of their devoted uncle or grandmother stooped over in the fields. When they go back to the home village, they want to see the same familiar paddies, green, well tended, bearing the new year's crop. At the busy commuter-railroad station near my house in Tokyo thousands of passengers push and shove each morning but tenderly avoid the boxes of rice seedlings, pale and fresh in the springtime rains, stalks heavy with golden ears during the fall monsoon. When the first Japanese settlers moved to Hokkaido, a hundred years ago, it was a land of wheat and barley but no rice. On their deathbeds, Professor Hemmi Kenzo, of Tokyo University, has said, the lonely pioneers would ask their children to place a few grains of rice in a bamboo tube and shake it, "so the parent could at least hear the sound of rice once before he or she died."

A FREE RIDE?

Proponents of the "free-ride" theory insist that Japan has prospered because, since 1945, the United States has provided most of her defense requirements. Protected for decades by the American nuclear umbrella and conventional forces, Japan has been able to shirk its own costly responsibilities and concentrate its energy and investment in profitable economic ventures, while America hobbled itself with enormous military budgets. The Japan Self Defense Forces (JSDF), they argue, have never yet reached even the low manpower levels authorized in the 1950s. They point to the level of military spending in Japan— for years the government allocated no more than one percent of the GNP to defense budgets. By the late 1980s, that unofficial barrier—a "policy guideline" adopted in 1976—was breached but only barely. In any case, typical NATO costs ran three or four times that percentage, the American expenditures were about six times higher, and at the height of the Cold War, the Soviet Union and China were devoting vastly higher shares of their GNP to military buildup. In the United States, some Congressional critics of Japan have called for Japan to raise its defense allocations as much as threefold.

For nearly every argument there is a counterargument. True, the JSDF is small and untested, but it constitutes one of the best-equipped and best-trained non-nuclear forces in the world, with excellent air and submarine-defense capabilities. With F-1 fighter aircraft, HAWK surface-to-air missiles, destroyers with Aegis fire-control technology, and multiple-launch rocket systems, the Japan Self-Defense Forces *could* bring a powerful military machine into being virtually overnight.

True, the one percent figure pales when compared to other nations, but one percent of *Japan's* constantly surging GNP adds up to an impressive sum. By 1991, depending on the accounting methods used, Japan's defense budgets ranked it somewhere between third and sixth in the world in terms of gross expenditures.

True, the United States spends billions of dollars each year to station upward of fifty thousand troops in scores of large and small installations throughout Japan (especially on Okinawa). Japan, however, pays an increasingly large share of the rent and maintenance costs for those American servicemen, on average more than four times what America's NATO allies have been paying to maintain U.S. facilities on their territories. U.S. Congressional critics who speak of a free-ride and ask why it is that the United States "spends all these dollars to defend a rich country that is an economic competitor" miss the point. Since Japan bears most the of the "in-country" costs, it is cheaper for the U.S. Navy to homeport the aircraft carrier *Independence* in Yokosuka than in the United States.

True, in recent decades, the United States would have preferred that Japan contribute more to the military burden of containing communism. However, Article IX, after all, was imposed on Japan by the United States and resonated perfectly with the pacifist mood of postwar Japan. That mood no longer fills the streets with demonstrations protesting the presence of U.S. bases on Japanese soil—as it did in earlier times. Proposals to disband the JSDF are no longer a significant factor at election times, though the pacifist disposition runs deep among Japanese of all backgrounds and age groups. It is no exaggeration to say that most Japanese think of the defense forces primarily as rescue and clean-up squads, helpful after typhoons, floods, and earthquakes. In 1991, Japan made a sizable "checkbook" contribution to the multinational coalition effort in the Gulf War, but the commitment of even token minesweeping units to the Gulf after the fighting was over was enough to trigger a constitutional crisis. A similarly bitter fight ensued in the Diet over the question of a Japanese commitment of a small force of soldiers to United Nations peacekeeping operations; in the end, the Diet disapproved of that. In 1992, however, as demands for U.N. peace missions in various parts of the world increased, the Diet approved Japanese participation, but only under the strictest provisions designed to ensure that Japanese soldiers would not be sent into combat situations abroad.

Finally, has it ever been in the U.S. interest to encourage a large-scale expansion of Japanese military might? A Pentagon official, responding to a Congressional resolution urging Japan to devote three percent of its GNP to a military budget, asked: "What would the additional funds be used for? A nuclear capability? Offensive projection forces? Japanese carrier task forces and long-range missiles? . . . Is that what Congress wants?"

Will that enhance stability in East Asia? Asian leaders surely do not think so. Any expansion of Japanese military power is wildly unpopular in Asia. Anti-Japanese protests erupt throughout the old Co-Prosperity Sphere from Seoul to Singapore at hints of a projection of Japanese military strength into that area (or beyond, to the Persian Gulf, for example). Singapore's former Prime Minister Lee Kuan Yew spoke for much of Asia a few years ago when he made Japan's continued low-defense posture and its reliance on the U.S.–Japan Security Treaty a condition for his optimism about the region's future. "It could be disastrous if the Japanese decided that their economic-security relationship with the U.S. was no longer valid and that they must build up their own defense," the Southeast Asian leader said.

What many Americans see as a reasonable responsibility for Japan is not that it increases its military expenditures but that it commits itself more to global leadership roles. As we have seen, Japan has already taken steps in that direction, in one recent year passing the United States as a leading source of foreign assistance. Why not increase the one percent of its GNP presently devoted to foreign aid to four or five percent in assistance to poorer countries?

SCIENTIFIC RESEARCH

An extension of the free-ride criticism suggests that Japan has neglected to contribute its share of basic scientific research to the world. Nobel Prize winner Esaki noted that, at a time when Japan controlled eleven percent of the world's GNP, it was not contributing a like percentage to the "world's store of talent in science, the arts, and international organizations. . . ." The level of Japan's industrial technology is not low, but the technical expertise is not buttressed by a broad base of scientific research, Esaki said. Partly in response to pressure from the United States, the situation has begun to change in recent years. *The Economist*, while still ranking Japan in 1990 "as one of the stingiest supporters of basic science in the industrialized world," allows that government and business support of long-range research in such areas as superconductivity, nuclear energy, and bacteriology began to rapidly expand in the late 1980s.

While approximately the same number of people are engaged in scientific research in Japan and the United States (when calculated on a per capita basis), the big difference is that in America about half are engaged in defense and space-related projects; much of that research takes place in universities. In Japan, most of the research takes place in business-sponsored laboratories and naturally enough is geared toward profit-oriented commercial applications. Though the commercial R&D which goes on in Japan also tends to be largely inaccessible to U.S. companies, Americans are poorly trained to track the Japanese science and technology which is available. More strikingly, American scientists often blame U.S. companies for their short-term views, for failing to take advantage of U.S. university research efforts. An M.I.T. labor director, working on high-strength composite metals which may someday replace steel and plastic, states that the Japanese participate with an enthusiasm that outstrips that of Americans. U.S. firms, he says, "aren't even taking advantage of what they can do here." A director of the Sony Corporation Research Center comments on the same phenomenon, the Japanese talent for moving from basic research to practical application:

> The following scenario has occurred more and more often of late. An American researcher presents some abstract concept for a new mechanism or process at a scientific symposium. Within six months or a year he finds a Japanese paper has been published analyzing each facet of his idea in detail using a working model, when neither the American nor his colleagues had made any progress with it.

STRUCTURAL IMPEDIMENTS

In 1989, the ongoing trade negotiations between U.S. and Japanese representatives began to focus on "structural impediments" to healthy economic relations. Each side created an agenda of complaints concerning flaws in the fundamental economic structures of the other, flaws which often had origins in the deepest historical and socio-cultural features of the two nations. The Japanese negotiators concentrated on some American structural problems we have already touched on—such as the large budget deficits, low savings rates, rampant crime, and the poor quality of public education. Japanese comments on the condition of the United States do not make pleasant reading for Americans. One economist said that the United States was becoming a "vegetable nation" suffering from a kind of degenerative disease which makes it unconscious of its problems. "The whole U.S. society seems to be deteriorating," a senior diplomat remarked. "Americans are losing their ability to communicate among themselves. Everyone is either fighting or hiring lawyers, and America's ability to integrate different elements into a melting pot is weakening. So Americans are looking for scapegoats and blaming Japan." Japanese lecturing Americans on the subject of our structural flaws often sounds like American parents scolding prodigal children: stop loafing, quit borrowing so much money, clean up your lives, hit the books, take some pride in your work, and quit blaming others for your own shortcomings.

PAPA–MAMA STORES IN JAPAN

Among the American complaints in the structural impediments talks is that the retail distribution system in Japan is a barrier to foreign imports. Before consumer products reach the buyer, they travel through a labyrinthine network of wholesalers and middlemen and finally end up in tiny neighborhood stores— "mom-and-pop" stores in the United States, but "papa-mama" in Japan. The myriad tiny neighborhood stores account for well over half of retail sales in Japan—versus five percent in Europe and only three percent in the United

States. This multi-layered system is deeply embedded in the fabric of Japanese society. Business relationships spanning many generations are common. They are based on longstanding friendships, family ties, personal introductions, and school links. A complex web of mutual obligations and informal practices keeps the network operating smoothly. Small-lot deliveries are essential, of course. Cash-short retailers are given flexible methods of settling accounts. Informal quasi-consignment agreements permit shopkeepers to return unsold goods. Personal credit and delivery arrangements keep neighborhood customers happy.

Japanese insist the system works well and contributes mightily to the close-knit, village-like quality of the big-city neighborhoods. American anthropologist Theodore C. Bestor, who has studied the social effects of the small stores, agrees that they make Japanese cities "livable." He writes, "The shopkeepers are committed to the local community. They clean the streets in front of their stores; they're on the local fire brigade, they help with local garbage recycling."

Foreign firms are less enamored of the retail complex. They complain that it is all but impossible for them to penetrate the tightly-knit maze. It would be much easier to sell in Japan if there were a few large retail chains to cope with, they argue. With goods changing hands so many times, and with retailers selling at low volume, the prices to Japanese consumers are necessarily very high. Why, then, does Japan, a country which prides itself on efficiency, tolerate such market inefficiencies? Why do not large retail outlets enter the market to sell in high volume at low prices? The reason, point out revisionist critics, is that the government of Japan interferes to prevent market forces from operating freely. In the 1970s, retail store laws were enacted to "protect" smaller retailers from new competition which might take advantage of economies of scale. These laws in effect gave small shopkeepers veto power over the establishment in their neighborhoods of large stores. Large manufacturers, in turn, support the system because it allows them to sell at artificially high prices, unhampered by foreign competition. To American trade negotiators, all this adds up to a classical example of the "structural impediment" at work: government and business in collusion to thwart foreign access to the Japanese market.

KEIRETSU

Another of the main American complaints centers on informal arrangements in the Japanese bureaucratic and corporate world which shield the Japanese market from effective foreign competition. An important focus of American— and European—concern are the *keiretsu*, or industrial groupings. Some see *keiretsu* as modern-day versions of the feudal warrior society: The component companies are autonomous units (like the *daimyo* of old) but linked together as vassals by strong bonds of mutual dependence and loyalty. The *keiretsu* conglomerates are similar to the prewar *zaibatsu* from which some of them are descended—Sumitomo, Mitsui, and Mitsubishi are prominent *keiretsu* and were prominent *zaibatsu*; Sony and Matsushita, on the other hand, are *keiretsu* with no links to the prewar *zaibatsu*. Typically, each *keiretsu* numbers a score or more major companies (Toshiba and Toyota are members of the Mitsui *keiretsu*, for example) plus perhaps a hundred or more sub-subsidiaries under its wing. The groupings are tied together by interlocking directorships and cross-holdings of stocks but even more by the informal social and educational bonds of the executives, the so-called *jinmyaku* (personal network) relationships. *Keiretsu* managers and executives constantly consult each other. The American side argues that the bonds which tie Japanese companies together in *keiretsu* should be relaxed so as to permit foreign companies to break into the Japanese market. Without a relaxation of *keiretsu* links, Japanese firms will invariably buy from each other rather than foreign companies, Americans insist. "Sweetheart" deals will continue to be preferred over the competitive bidding of the free marketplace. It is not hard to see here the potential for an angry Japanese reaction: that they are being asked to change their most basic group-centered habits in order to accommodate whiny American losers.

The construction business is the scene of insider maneuvers at their worst, American industry spokesmen say. *Dango* literally means a "conference," but in business parlance, it carries overtones of "bid-rigging." At these meetings, the "competitors" set prices and decide how they will apportion the work on a given project. No American firm is ever invited into the *dango*—unless it participates in a joint venture with a Japanese firm. This kind of pre-bidding collusion violates Japan's antimonoply law, but it is widespread as ample evidence by both American and Japanese authors confirms. "It flourishes virtually unchecked," writes Chalmers Johnson, "because it is a source of huge payoffs to the ruling party and because innumerable officials of the Ministry of Construction take up lucrative positions in private construction firms when they retire." The government of Japan denies the existence of *dango*, but as former U.S. trade negotiator in the Reagan administration Clyde Prestowitz explains, *dango* is privately regarded by Japanese as a way of avoiding confusion and dividing the pie among all those who play the game properly. Prestowitz says:

> Confusion is the opposite of the harmony the Japanese cherish, and thus is to be avoided at all costs. Were open bidding introduced in Japan's construction industry, it is certain there would be a major shakeout with many tiny operators going bankrupt. From that point of view, the Japanese system is a kind of social-security system. Fundamentally, this is what Japan's keiretsu are all about. They are a kind of dango on a large scale. They impose certain order. Everyone knows who is related to whom, who deals with whom; and in return for certain limitations on freedom, one receives security.

Prestowitz's explanation casts *dango* into a positive rationale most Japanese would find agreeable, but American firms remain outsiders to the process. The construction industry is immensely profitable, and more than one American company has developed a superior international reputation of the kind that should make it a formidable bidder—if bidding is kept open. Osaka's offshore

Kansai International Airport, at $10 billion and rising, Japan's largest public works project ever, generated enormous ill will among the thirty-five American companies who registered to work on the airport when it was announced that none of them had been chosen as a prime contractor and only one would serve in a consulting role. At the time the Osaka project was launched, an industry official in the United States argued that Japanese construction firms were doing about $5 billion worth of business as prime contractors in America, while American firms had managed to get "essentially zero" in Japan. Another spokesman corrected him: American construction in Japan had been limited "to the remodeling of two Wendy's hamburger stands," he noted.

The realities of the day do not permit a happy ending to the story of Japanese–American trade friction—at least none is in sight. Rather, there is an anxious persuasion in the air that differences have become so settled as to be irreconcilable. After years of hostility and warfare, the former enemies bound their destinies together beginning in the occupation years. The marathon of trade talks between the two countries over the years has led to a sense of burnout and a feeling that the best that can be hoped for is an incremental gain here and there while fundamental problems remain unchanged. Now, says Glen Fukushima, a former American trade official and currently an executive with AT&T in Japan, though problems are sometimes "papered over with rhetoric. . . . There's no doubt we are drifting apart."

ADDITIONAL READING

"Revisionism," discussed in the text, is represented by Chalmers Johnson, whose *MITI and the Japanese Miracle* (1982) may be regarded as the pioneer work of the school. Three other writers often identified as revisionists are James Fallows, Karel van Wolferen, and Clyde Prestowitz. Fallows and van Wolferen are discussed in the bibliography appended to Chapter 1. Prestowitz is the author of *Trading Places: How We Are Giving Our Future to Japan and How to Reclaim It* (1988).

Other important works include Daniel I. Okimoto, *Between MITI and the Market* (1989); Daniel Okimoto and Thomas P. Rohlen, eds., *Inside the Japanese System* (1988); William S. Dietrich, *In the Shadow of the Rising Sun* (1991); Ellen L. Frost, *For Richer For Poorer: The New U.S.–Japan Relationship* (1987); and Hugh Patrick, ed., with Larry Meissner, *Japan's High Technology Industries: Lessons and Limitations of Industrial Policy* (1986). Any of the books by Kenichi Ohmae are provacative. For example, *The Borderless World* (1990); *Triad Power* (1985); and *Beyond National Borders* (1989).

Two volumes published by the Society for Japanese Studies may not be easily accessible, but they are especially valuable as rich sources of articles by both Japanese and Western authors surveying many viewpoints and aspects of the U.S.–Japan trade conflict. Both are edited by Kozo Yamamura. They are *Japanese Investment in the United States: Should We Be Concerned?* (1989) and *Japan's Economic Structure: Should It Change?* (1990).

On "papa-mama" stores, I quoted *Neighborhood Tokyo* (1989) by Theodore C. Bestor.

The Japan That Can Say "No" (1991) by Ishihara Shintaro (trans. by Frank Baldwin) is a polemic by Japan's best-known nationalist. It aroused controversy for its outspoken remarks on the U.S.–Japan relationship both here and in Japan where it was originally published as *"No" to ieru Nihon* (1989). Sony's Morita Akio contributed to the original Japanese version of the book, but his chapters were not included in the English version.

Several recent books have taken a very strong stand on Japan: George Friedman and Meredith Lebard, *The Coming War with Japan* (1991); Pat Choate, *Agents of Influence: How Japan's Lobbyists in the United States Manipulate America's Political and Economic System* (1990); William J. Holstein, *The Japanese Power Game: What It Means for America* (1990).

For the detour into classical and international trade theory, the non-specialist may wish to do what I did, which is consult standard textbooks. I found useful: Tom Riddell, et al, *Economics: A Tool for Understanding Society* (4th ed., 1990) and Turley Mings, *The Study of Economics* (4th ed., 1991).

Finally, see the additional reading appended to Chapter 10. Most of it also applies to Chapter 11.

12

LOOKING AHEAD

We began discussing the Japanese economic miracle with a lesson on the danger of economic forecasting. The Japanese people confounded the experts of past generations, and that should be warning enough for us to be cautious about indulging in predictions here. The trends we have highlighted in the previous two chapters may—or may not—continue. In discussing the factors which lay behind Japan's economic miracle and the growing trade friction with the United States, we have been looking at the past, the very recent past, but not the future. Some of the trends of that recent past already show signs of reversal.

NEW TRENDS

Japan's great "cash fountain" of the 1980s started to dry up in the early 1990s, a sign that the era of almost limitless cheap capital may—or may not—be ending. An increasingly vigorous challenge from Asian NICs (newly industrializing countries like Taiwan and Singapore) may—or may not—erode Japan's export-led miracle. Growing protectionist sentiment in both Europe and America may—or may not—slow down Japan's growth rate.

Japanese investors have begun in recent years to place more and more emphasis on investments in other parts of Asia to take advantage of cheap labor and to transfer environmental burdens away from their own shores. At the beginning of the 1990s, the charts showing cumulative Japanese investments in the United States revealed a striking turnaround from the year-by-year increases in the eighties to a sharp decline. In 1991, for the first time in the postwar era, Japan conducted significantly more trade with its Asian neighbors than with the United States. A "re-Asianization of Japan" appears to be a future trend which bears watching. An important byproduct of this new trend may well be that the Japanese will have much less capital with which to invest in or buy up U.S. companies. Americans who deplored the projection of Japanese economic power into America will then face a new crisis as Japanese start up new ventures and create new jobs in Malaysia and Thailand rather than Kentucky and Tennessee.

Most worrisome for long-term economic forecasting is Japan's rapidly maturing population. This phenomenon which is being repeated throughout the world but nowhere has the demographic shift been as dramatic as in Japan. The plunging birth rate and the world's longest life expectancy are combining to produce a "graying" of Japan that seems certain to foreshadow a crisis ahead. Because of the demographic tides, by the year 2010 Japan will have the lowest ratio of working-age people (fifteen to sixty-four years of age) among any of the leading industrial nations in the world. Now (1992), there are a little less than six people in their active years (age twenty to sixty-four) for every person over 65; by 2020, it is expected that the figure will be reduced by half. The resulting decline in the productive population is already forcing Japan to curb its traditional xenophobia and import "guest workers" in large numbers from poor countries of Asia and the Middle East. Many Japanese experts fear that the ever larger need for health and retirement expenditures is certain to whittle away at the nation's enviously high savings rates and may well lead to a decline of overall economic dynamism in the decades ahead.

A NEW SPECIES

Older Japanese wonder if the next generation has the fortitude and will to maintain Japan's driving economy. Seniors shake their heads at the self-indulgent behavior of the young, so different from traditional Japanese that they have been designated *shinjinrui*, a new species of mankind. The *shinjinrui*, mainly urban Japanese in their twenties and thirties, have succumbed, it is said, to the good life as defined by consumerism and the advertising industry. Making sacrifices for future generations has no appeal to the *shinjinrui* nor do they appreciate the sacrifices their parents went through. Less idealistic and more self-centered than their parents, they pride themselves in being "cool," which in Japan as elsewhere often equates with fashionable brand-name shopping. In *Nantonaku, Kurisutaru* (Somehow, Crystal), a 1980s best-selling novel (*mirion sera*, million seller), which captured the listless hedonism of the "new species," an extensive product glossary was required to list the scores of mostly foreign-made "in" products favored by the emerging Japanese equivalent of America's yuppies.

College students applying for jobs, it is said, wish to steer clear of the "three Ks": *kiken* (dangerous), *kitsui* (hard) and *kitanai* (messy). A recent government survey revealed that workers under thirty are two to three times as willing to shift jobs as those over forty. An astonishingly low 15 percent of students said that they planned to follow the traditional pattern of taking a job with a company after college and sticking with it for life. Public opinion polls reveal that the generation born in the 1960s gives far higher priorities to "individual fulfillment" and "a comfortable life" than their elders do. The *shinjinrui* are less apt to spend evenings on the town with office colleagues and less willing to work on Saturdays. "The younger workers do what they are told and not one iota more," a dismayed employer complains.

Some of the older generation look with tolerance, even approval, at the new ethic of the *shinjinrui*. "They might save our country," writes a journalist; adding:

> Some people say that they don't work, but compared with foreigners, they do. We are overworking so much, which causes so much trade friction. This younger generation may tell us we should stop running and walk at a slower pace.

More often, however, the *shinjinrui* draw adverse comments. Older Japanese deplore the aimlessness of a new era, the *musekinin jidai* (age of irresponsibility), and see the *shinjinrui* as in part the product of and in part responsible for contemporary culture that has lost its moorings. "Where did we go wrong?" they ask. Did a suddenly affluent generation become too permissive with its children? Did the pressures of education finally become too much for the young? Should the individualizing force of television and personal computers (*pasokon* in Japanese) be blamed? Many see a sinister, if unintended, American influence displacing the old work and group ethic. "The young people today are getting the wrong information from the U.S.A.: being lazy, having fun, enjoying life—these are good things and that to sweat and work are not trendy," comments one Japanese.

WHO WON THE WAR, ANYWAY?

In December 1991, the fiftieth anniversary of the attack on Pearl Harbor generated much commentary on that defining moment in history. Still discussed was the question of a White House conspiracy—although the hard evidence for such a theory is missing, and most experts remain profoundly skeptical. Still discussed was the issue of guilt—had Japan come to terms with its responsibility for the death and suffering of a half-century earlier? On both sides of the Pacific, historians and the public alike were divided in their responses. Repeatedly over the past decade or so, two emperors and several prime ministers, both at home and speaking on trips abroad, had publicly expressed in various terms Japan's "sincere contrition" for wartime transgressions. Yet, there remained a solid core of opinion which insisted that there was a balance of evils between the imperialism of the West which came first and Japanese imperialism which came later and that there was a moral equivalency between Pearl

Harbor and Hiroshima. If the surprise attack on Pearl Harbor was repugnant, apologists for Japan say, at least the target was military, and the victims were mostly soldiers and sailors—in contrast to Hiroshima.

But those questions aside, the subplot of much of the Pearl Harbor anniversary discussion centered on another matter: Who won the war, anyway? Those fond of irony could savor the reports that the Pearl Harbor Survivors Association would meet in Honolulu's Sheraton Hotel, now owned by Japanese corporate interests. Had not Japan gained by peaceful—albeit sometimes ruthless—means the kind of economic security it had envisioned when it established the New Order in East Asia a little more than a half-century ago? There can be no doubt that it had, although total economic autonomy will remain elusive for crowded, resource-poor Japan which will always be more vulnerable to adverse shifts in the global economy than the United States. The catastrophic plummet of certain business indicators (notably the stock market which lost more than half its value in a period from 1989 to 1992) is a measure of the ever fragile, ever nervous economy of Japan.

But the questions become more difficult. Does it matter that Japan has become, as Ezra Vogel wrote in 1979, Number One? If so, at what price? "The Japanese have been working hard for thousands of years because they needed the money," wrote Amaya Naohiro, chairman of the Dentsu Institute for Human Studies. However, Amaya continues, "They have never had time to stop and ask, 'What is money for?'"

Does it matter that U.S. economic and technological decline has accompanied the Japanese ascent? Many farsighted Japanese argue that disastrous news from Detroit is as unsettling to Japanese business as it is to Americans. An American collapse will weaken the buying power of Japan's best customer. If so, is there any reasonable justification for thinking that the decline is over? If not, and most critical of all, how can the United States hope to reverse its sagging fortunes and regain something of the economic dynamism it once had? By continuing to pressure Japan to make piecemeal concessions—to take more American oranges, baseball bats, perhaps even cars and rice? Is there any valid reason for hoping that Japan will undertake to remove its own "*structural* impediments" to freer trade? Those structural impediments come close to being defining elements of the Japanese economy and of Japanese culture. We cannot very well ask Japanese to quit speaking and writing their uncommonly difficult language so that we can improve our competitive standing with them. Is it any more proper to ask them to quit working on Saturdays? Can we reasonably expect them to dismantle a professional bureaucratic system that has managed their industry and trade with stunning success? Or does the answer to the American decline lie in America—in successfully coping with social calamities such as crime and drugs and in raising educational standards, for example?

Most important is the challenging analysis and proposals put forth by the so-called revisionists. Their critique of Japan–U.S. relations seems likely to become a touchstone for the 1990s in the same way that Ezra Vogel's *Japan as Number 1* did for the 1980s. The most persuasive of these experts on Japan, often mistakenly identified as "bashers," carefully avoid labeling the Japanese system as "bad" or even "unfair." On the contrary, they insist, the way the Japanese handle their problems (with emphasis on personal savings, for example) is "admirable," even "superior." Americans have no reason to hate Japanese, they declare, but they have every reason to investigate where the U.S. and Japanese systems differ and then act accordingly. Above all, say revisionists like political scientist Chalmers Johnson, the United States needs to create a professional bureaucracy of the kind that works so effectively in Japan and then permit it a greater role in shaping U.S. industrial policy.

Japanese often say that they have lost respect for us because we appear unable to solve our domestic problems. Americans are galled with Japan for remaining so bound to their own social and economic system that they fail to support a world system in trade and security from which they benefit. Many Japanese feel that the United States despises them for their hard work and makes unreasonable demands on them to change the very ways that have made them so successful. They feel that Americans, so blessed by nature, fail to appreciate how the Japanese are forced by an ungenerous nature to live on the narrow margin of their own human talent and endurance. Some of these people have been and remain ardent friends of the United States. "Most Japanese," an educator states, "realize that the world needs a strong, healthy and economically dynamic United States." Japanese have not been alarmed by America's global strength, then, as much as they are with the erosion of that strength in the wake of declining work ethics, moral principles, and the quality of American products, many believe. Others, however, do resent American power and say that it is time for Japan to be more assertive in its dealings with the United States. In his book *The Japan That Can Say "No,"* Ishihara Shintaro writes that "No other nation will pay attention to Japan if Japan cannot say 'no' to the United States." Critics of Japan believe that Japan has said "yes" often enough to American requests but drags its feet when it comes to implementing promises.

The trade dispute, as we have seen, has a way of tapping into latent racism. The 1982 Detroit incident involving a young Chinese American by the name of Vincent Chin was an aberration to be sure but it should be easy to appreciate the revulsion a story like this harvests in the Japanese press. Chin, it may be recalled, was bludgeoned to death by two white autoworkers wielding baseball bats. Calling Chin a "Jap," they cursed that "It's because of you [obscenity] that we're out of work." If such savagery is uncommon, any reflective American will have to admit that there is an unfortunate ring of truth to the following comment appearing in a recent *Fortune* magazine:

> Suddenly the Japanese have become the people it is okay to hate. Growl at any other race at a New York or Washington salon, and your dinner partner turns away in embarrassment. Deride the Japanese, and hear your table mates cheer and pile on the abuse of their own. . . .

Yet, as we have seen, there are legitimate grievances. Almost reflexively Japanese seem to regard any criticism from Americans as *Nihon-tataki* (Japan bashing) and assume that it is inspired by racial loathing. Americans, in turn, see the Japanese as indulging themselves in a paranoic sense of victimization and using "Japan bashing" as a ploy to stifle discussion of hard issues in need of hard discussion. The economic relationship between Japan and the United States is too important to neglect—the two countries account for 40 percent of the world's economic output and 40 percent of aid to poor nations. A healthy and balanced partnership must be created.

The demise of the Cold War and the collapse of Soviet and Eastern European Communism came with breathtaking speed in 1990–1991. As the East-West confrontation suddenly lost its power to threaten and define our lives, a sense of exhilaration swept over the world. Could it be, asked then U.S. State Department official Francis Fukuyama, that with the apparent triumph of liberal revolutionary ideas the major problems in world history had been solved? In his sweeping and imaginative book, *The End of History and the Last Man* (1992), Fukuyama explores that question and reminds us how much more tractable Cold War ideological disputes were when compared to such matters as the "apparently unremovable trade surplus" Japan enjoys with the United States and the rest of the world. No overnight collapse of some Berlin Wall can be expected to ease U.S.-Japan tensions. "Persistent cultural differences between ostensibly liberal democratic capitalist states will prove much harder to eradicate" than the old East-West ideological differences, Fukuyama predicts.

However acrimonious the Japan–U.S. nexus becomes, both sides by this time in history possess enormous reservoirs of goodwill and mutual understanding that were all but completely missing in 1941. There is no need for Americans to forget Pearl Harbor. George Santayana's line, "Those who cannot remember the past are condemned to repeat it," remains valid. Perhaps the most important thing Americans could remember is that the United States, when aroused, as it was by the events of December 7, 1941, rose to the occasion of a great challenge. If that same sense of purpose cannot be renewed without being triggered by war, it will be a sad commentary on our national character. While it is imperative to remember the past, it is also necessary to avoid being imprisoned by the past and by chauvinist and isolationist attitudes that were two of the unfortunate hallmarks of the American yesterday.

CREDITS

411

INDEX

The index incorporates a glossary of important Japanese-language terms which appear in the text. In addition, since the names of important authors mentioned in the text and in the Additional Readings have been included, the index may also be used for bibliographic purposes.